2

Science Fiction
Film Directors,
1895–1998

OKANAGAN COLLEGE
LIBRARY
BRITISH COLUMBIA

Science Fiction Film Directors, 1895–1998

DENNIS FISCHER

Volume 2

(Directors: Laughlin–Zemeckis; A Guide to the Directors Covered in Appendix A; Appendix A; Appendix B; Selected Bibliography; Index)

McFarland & Company, Inc., Publishers
Jefferson, North Carolina, and London

Volume 2

LIBRARY OF CONGRESS CATALOGUING-IN-PUBLICATION DATA

Fischer, Dennis.
Science fiction film directors, 1895–1998 / by Dennis Fischer.
p. cm.
"A companion volume to the author's Horror film directors, 1931–1990."
Includes bibliographical references and index.

2 volume set—
ISBN 978-0-7864-6091-5
softcover : 50# alkaline paper ♾

1. Science fiction films—History and criticism.
2. Motion picture producers and directors—Biography—Dictionaries.
PN1995.9.S26F54 2011 791.43'615—dc21 99-29838

BRITISH LIBRARY CATALOGUING DATA ARE AVAILABLE

© 2000 Dennis Fischer. All rights reserved

No part of this book may be reproduced or transmitted in any form or by any means, electronic or mechanical, including photocopying or recording, or by any information storage and retrieval system, without permission in writing from the publisher.

Front cover: *Brazil*, 1984, directed by Terry Gilliam (Universal Pictures/Photofest); cover design by David K. Landis (Shake It Loose Graphics)

Manufactured in the United States of America

McFarland & Company, Inc., Publishers
Box 611, Jefferson, North Carolina 28640
www.mcfarlandpub.com

Table of Contents

Volume 1

The Directors

Volume 2

The Directors

MICHAEL LAUGHLIN (1940–)

Strange Behavior (aka *Dead Kids; Small Town Massacre*) (1981); *Mesmerized* (aka *My Letter to George*; *Shocked*; 1982); *Strange Invaders* (1984)

Born in Bloomington, Illinois, in 1940, Michael Laughlin began his film career as a producer, beginning in 1968 with Michael Sarne's *Joanna.* He also produced such cult features as Floyd Mutrux's *Dusty and Sweets McGee* and Monte Hellman's *Two-Lane Blacktop* before becoming a director.

Strange Behavior was shot in New Zealand under the title *Dead Kids* and was coscripted by Laughlin and Bill Condon (later director of *Candyman 2* and *Gods and Monsters*). The film received some surprisingly kind reviews when it was released, even though it wasn't really very original or clever. The plot has to do with a doctor (Fiona Lewis) working at the psychology lab of the local college conducting some brain experiments on teenagers which are turning them into killers. Michael Murphy plays the concerned father whose son is one of those affected. There are a few tongue-in-cheek touches, but Laughlin would do much better on his next science fiction effort.

Laughlin was also responsible for the unusual drama *Mesmerized,* based on an original treatment by Jerzy Skolimowski, in which an orphan (Jodie Foster) weds a stern old man (John Lithgow) in late 1800s New Zealand and resolves to poison him.

Laughlin's most interesting film thus far has been *Strange Invaders,* which he wrote in connection with William Condon (later writer-director of *Candyman 2: Farewell to the Flesh* and the James Whale character study *Gods and Monsters*). The film opens in 1958 when some aliens invade a small midwestern hamlet, turning the inhabitants into small, glowing, white-specked blue globes and then assuming their identities.

Paul LeMat is charming as Charles Bigelow, a professor who happened to have married Margaret (Diana Scarwid), one of the aliens, who is suddenly recalled to her "home" town and takes their daughter Elizabeth (Lulu Sylbert). Anxious to get his daughter back, Bigelow follows her there and learns the truth. He barely escapes with his life, but when he tries to tell someone, the only person who ends up listening to him is Betty Walker (Nancy Allen), a reporter at a sensationalistic supermarket tabloid.

Complicating matters are the fact that the aliens have sent some agents to keep Bigelow quiet, including a menacing woman (Fiona Lewis) who disguises herself as a waitress and an Avon lady. Laughlin also gets a good shock out of a scene where an alien removes his outer covering and displays his insectoid shape in the mirror. (A good science fiction in-joke is that one of the aliens, Arthur Newman, is played by noted fifties alien fighter Kenneth Tobey.)

Additionally, Mrs. Benjamin (Louise Fletcher), a U.S. government scientist, wants the whole thing hushed up and arranges to have both Bigelow and Walker taken into custody. They evade the dragnet by taking the train and track down one of the aliens' victims, Willie Collins (Michael Lerner) who resides in a sanitarium.

Laughlin keeps viewers off-balance throughout the film's length, varying the tone from light satire to genuine horror (as in the death of the likable maintenance man Earl, played by Wallace Shawn). In the end, however, the aliens transform the globes back into people before leaving the planet and they do not turn out to be so bad, and neither is the film itself. Uneven and uncertain in places, *Strange Invaders* does have a charm all its own.

Since then, Laughlin has only been credited with writing *Shan Hai yi jiu er ling* (aka *Once Upon a Time in Shanghai*, 1991), making it hard to tell what happened to this once promising talent. However, he has unexpectedly reappeared with a new film from New Line called *Town and Country*, with Warren Beatty, Diane Keaton, and Goldie Hawn, only to be rewritten by Buck Henry and direction assumed by Peter Chelsom.

BRETT LEONARD

The Dead Pit (1989); *The Lawnmower Man* (1992); *Hideaway; Virtuosity* (1995)
Other Projects: *Kiss the Frog; T. Rex: Back to the Cretaceous* (1998); *Siegfried & Roy's Magic Box* (1999)

After the horror film *The Dead Pit*, Brett Leonard made his science fiction film debut as the cowriter and director of *The Lawnmower Man*, which was very loosely based on a Stephen King story to which elements of new virtual reality concepts were grafted on. It featured a future Bond, Pierce Brosnan, and actor Jeff Fahey in an awful blond wig.

"I was brought Stephen King's short story 'The Lawnmower Man' and was asked by the executive producers [Allied Vision] who owned the rights if I could make a movie from this short story," Leonard said. "I told them, although I could incorporate some of the action of this ten page short story, namely, a lawnmower chasing a guy through a house, I could not base an entire feature film around that singular concept. So I added the virtual reality components to the story to expand it enough to make it an interesting feature film."

Leonard merged King's story about a gardener who cuts down his employers as well as the grass with Leonard's original screenplay *Cybergod*, exploring the concept of virtual reality, which involves a computer simulation system that, by means of a headset and hand controls, allows the user to experience a technologically created environment that seems virtually real.

To create *The Lawnmower Man's* virtual visuals, several special effects houses were commissioned. Xaos Computer Animation and Design created seven minutes of computer graphics to illustrate this virtual reality.

"Because the theme of *The Lawnmower Man* is virtual reality and the film is not actually seen in virtual reality," explains Xaos' Helene Plotkin, "we were able to use traditional computer animation techniques. The program allows you to design a stage and create believeable three-dimensional models with that framework. We developed whirling primal vortices, beings exploding into thousands of particles and film footage dissolving into abstract, swirling colors. What you see on the screen is a computer-generated image of the actor's hand and how he's affecting things within the virtual reality realm. It's almost like being in a control room with monitors projecting these great images."

Angel Studios of San Diego also contributed seven minutes of virtual reality graphics. They came up with the CyberJobe, a computer version of Jeff Fahey's character. The animators used more than 70 photographs of Fahey's facial and vocal gestures to create accurate lip-synching for their computer creations. Explains Angel's animation director Michael Limber, "Our goal was to create a character powerful enough to sustain the plot of the film, allowing the directorial themes and moods to pass smoothly from the live action into the cyber-action."

Additional virtual reality scenes include a relaxed environment depicting a surreal lava landscape, and a cybersex environment. Traditional 3-D graphics were used to create the virtual reality sexual tryst between Jobe and Marnie Burke (Jenny Wright). To create realistic motion, a program called hierarchical animation was employed to make the anatomically connected body parts move together in rhythm.

Another breakthrough of the film was the Gemini Process, which allows for images shot on film to be edited on video, mixed with special effects, and then transferred back to 35mm film. Joe Gareri of The Post Group explains, "What we did was to take the video and do red, green, and blue color separations. Then we sent it to Pacific Title, where they recomposed the separations onto a color negative before sending it out to be developed. The end result is terrific. The vivid colors produced by the computer graphic companies lose none of their sharpness."

The plot centers on Dr. Lawrence Angelo (Brosnan) who has been giving a chimpanzee injections of an intelligence drug that also increases its aggression and then

An example of CGI cybersex from Brett Leonard's *The Lawnmower Man.*

immersing the animal in a virtual reality war game simulation as part of an experiment for The Shop, a CIA–like organization that Stephen King created for his novel *Firestarter*. Unfortunately, the serum has a side effect of causing uncontrollably violent, paranoiac behavior.

Nevertheless, Dr. Angelo decides to try his serum on a human being and selects the slow-witted gardener Jobe Smith as his guinea pig. Angelo wishes to prove that he can use the drug and virtual reality to teach Jobe and raise his intelligence from that of a six-year-old to normal intelligence. Jobe finds himself learning 30 times faster than normal and becomes aware of when others are making fun of him. He also finds himself attracted to Marnie Burke.

However, Dr. Angelo's facilities are limited, so he decides to continue the experiment back at The Shop, where his education program is substituted with the heightened aggression scenario that the Shop is interested in. Suddenly, Jobe develops extraordinary powers, including the abilities to read minds, affect the thoughts of others, and telekinesis. Wanting to become even more powerful, Jobe injects himself with even more of the drug, which creates in him arrogant, angry, and psychotic delusions, including a belief that he can merge with the world's communication system and become, in effect, God. It's then up to Dr. Angelo to figure out how to pull his plug.

"With producing a film like this," said Leonard, "timing is very important. A lot of these new technologies and special effects are just coming into being where they're able to be utilized cost effectively. We found people and collaborators working with this amazing computer technology who are very motivated to show their stuff in the film.

"It's time in Hollywood when ... you have to put more production dollars on the screen. That sense kind of pervaded this project. We just hit it right as these technologies were able to be utilized. The bridge between computer graphic effects and 35mm film came into being just as we were reaching postproduction of the film.

"*The Lawnmower Man* shows viewers what virtual reality will look like in about five years or so ... as we get to the turn of the century, we are going to see lots of things based on the way our minds and bodies interface with machines. That's the kind of mythology we are playing with in *The Lawnmower Man*. Unlike the industrial revolution, in which the stakes were external, we are now facing the kind of technology that can shift the entire realm of human existence for good or ill."

After the initial R-rated theatrical release, an unrated director's cut was released to video where it enjoyed a fair amount of success. (The theatrical version ran 105 minutes, while the director's cut was a whopping 140 minutes long.) The film proved successful enough to spawn a sequel, which Leonard had no connection to.

The sequel, *Lawnmower Man 2: Beyond Cyberspace*, was written and directed by Farhad Mann (*Max Headroom*) and opens with clips from the first feature, though it immediately breaks chronology with the previous film. In the eight years it has taken for a ten-year-old character to turn 18, the world outside has suddenly turned into the far future for no discernible reason. Matt Frewer replaces Jeff Fahey as the villainous Jobe, with an explanation given that Jobe's face "was so damaged in the explosion we had to do a total reconstruction" to justify the differences in appearance. This time only a disillusioned chip-designer dropout (Patrick Bergin) and a group of teens led by Austin O'Brien (*Last Action Hero*) can stop Jobe. The acting is uniformly abysmal and every computer cliché is trotted out yet again in this embarrassingly bad retread of the original. One can't blame Leonard for not wanting to get involved.

Leonard's second film was *Hideaway*, starring Jeff Goldblum and Christine Lahti, and based on the Dean R. Koontz novel. (Koontz also supplied the novel basis for Donald Cammell's *Demon Seed*, in which a computer impregnates Julie Christie.)

Hideaway begins with a terrible accident involving Hatch and Lindey Harrison (Goldblum and Lahti) and their teenaged daughter Regina (Alicia Silverstone), after which Hatch is clinically dead for two hours. Thanks to the pioneering work of Dr. Jonas Nyebvern (Alfred Molina), Hatch is brought back to life, but is he the same?

Leonard shows death from Hatch's point of view as a series of multicolored tunnels coupled with a morphing identity. Hatch does get to meet the spirit of his dead younger daughter, who was killed a year previously in a hit-and-run accident. She is about to lead him on to the afterlife when he is yanked back to our present reality.

Miraculously, his brain has not become pudding after

being deprived of oxygen for two hours, but Hatch discovers that whenever he experiences pain, say from a cut, it brings on terrible homicidal visions. It turns out that Hatch is psychically linked to a psychotic killer (Jeremy Sisto), who himself is possessed by a demon who calls himself Vassago. The closer Hatch comes to the truth, the more everybody else becomes convinced that he is nuts. Even worse, Vassago learns through him more about his next intended victim — Regina, their surviving teenaged daughter.

Leonard once more shows that he knows how to handle special effects and deals with a potentially interesting premise. He is adept at building both shocks and suspense. However, the biggest drawback is that this film owes a bit too much inspiration to Nicolas Roeg's classic horror thriller *Don't Look Now*, based on the Daphne du Maurier novel. Both films feature a dead daughter, ominous visions, and an inevitable meeting with a mad slasher, but the Roeg film remains far more dazzling in its use of cinema, leaving one disappointed in this reasonably well-made modern update.

Unfortunately and to its detriment, the movie considerably alters the plot of the novel. The character of Regina is not as appealing in the film, and much that made the book work well is absent or altered. Apparently Koontz tried, without success, to get his name removed from the movie.

Leonard conceived and directed for Peter Gabriel and Pepsi Co. the ride film "Kiss The Frog," which was highlighted on Gabriel's 1995 tour and was nominated for two MTV Awards, winning one for Best Special Effects.

Leonard partnered with Michael Lewis to create L3 Communications, a link-up of high technology companies for the purpose of developing film and multimedia projects.

Virtuosity tries to top the serial killer subgenre sweepstakes by artificially creating via virtual reality an ultimate superkiller. The program, called SID 6.7, is a composite of all the worst known serial killers from Charles Manson to John Wayne Gacy, and is created by the 1999 police department as part of a virtual reality training system. Unfortunately, the program develops sentience and finds a way to emerge from virtual reality and into our own, initiating a horrifying killing spree.

Former LAPD cop Parker Barnes (Denzel Washington), who has been serving time in prison for wasting the serial killer who viciously slaughtered his family, is freed and sent to track SID (Australian actor Russell Crowe) down because one of the dominant killers that made up SID's profile was the one Barnes blasted, and SID takes this as an invitation to play some cat-and-mouse games.

Concerning Denzel Washington in *Virtuosity*, Leonard said, "Denzel is one of the best actors of his generation. So working with him as a director was a great, expanding experience for me. His focus and intense desire for [veracity] in every moment, even when it is in such a fantastic context, as is portrayed in this film, is one of the things that I feel make the film most unique. And to see him execute his energy with Russells' [Crowe's] energy as SID 6.7 was the kind of maximum acting chops experience that a filmmaker can have."

He described the film as "a nonstop action film. Every scene was a glorious battle. And I do mean glorious." The film is meant to be an allegory about our media culture's obsessive focus on aberrant human psychology and the nature of violence (SID terrorizes a TV station, creating a program called "Death TV" which, he promises, will be a "killer in the ratings"); however, the thematic material is largely buried under the film's various vivid action scenes.

Eric Bernt's script indulges a bit too much in unlikely conveniences, such as a policeman leaving his car running right where SID can get at it, or a criminal psychologist (Kelly Lynch), who is assisting Barnes, leaving her daughter alone and vulnerable despite one element of SID's history being his desire to torture the pursuing Barnes through his family (and sure enough, for the climax the killer kidnaps the little girl).

Virtuosity has both Leonard's strengths and weaknesses on view. Leonard seems genuinely excited about the possibilities of virtual reality and helps create some clever digital effects. His film's story has a few unusual or offbeat ideas (SID can replenish its real-life form by sucking minerals from any convenient source of glass; he creates an impromptu "symphony of terror" out of the sampled screams of some nightclub victims), but most of the characters and situations seem stock and occasionally lame to boot. Crowe chews the scenery with some diabolical panache, but Washington, usually an excellent actor, occasionally seems swamped in his underwritten role. The film is unusual enough to be interesting, but never convincing enough to be chilling the way its makers intended.

Leonard's most recent SF project was the IMAX 3-D mini-feature *T-Rex: Back to the Cretaceous*. In this 45 minute film, Ally Hayden (Liz Stayber), daughter of the divorced paleontologist father Dr. Donald Hayden (Peter Horton), pouts about being left behind when her father goes off on his bone-hunting expeditions. Wandering around the museum in which Dr. Hayden has his offices, Ally knocks a dinosaur egg off her father's desk and sniffing the dino-dust causes her to start having hallucinations inhabited by hadrosaurs, pterodactyls, and a Tyrannosaurus rex.

Ally wanders in and out of the Cretaceous period, rescuing a T-Rex egg from a predator and seeing the comet-induced nuclear holocaust that wiped out the dinosaurs, and then bumps into both Charles Knight (Tuck Milligan), the celebrated dinosaur illustrator of the 1920s, and Barnum Brown (Laurie Muldoon), described as "the most famous bone hunter in history." Leonard keeps things lively and employs 3-D well, especially in scenes where a hammer-wielding paleontologist sends chips flying toward your face or another where Donald and an assistant rappel down a mountain. However, some IMAX theaters refused to play the film because they considered it more entertainment than informative.

Nonetheless, it is a spectacular and engaging use of the technology, and an opportunity to catch computer-generated dinosaurs in thrilling 3-D. Leonard has shown himself open to exploring science fiction concepts and working with innovations, and it will be interesting to check out what he works on in the future.

RICHARD LESTER (1932–)

The Running, Jumping, and Standing Still Film (short, 1959); *Ring-a-Ding Rhythm* (British title: *It's Trad, Dad*) (1962); *Mouse on the Moon* (1963); *A Hard Day's Night* (1964); *The Knack ... And How to Get It*; *Help!* (1965); *A Funny Thing Happened on the Way to the Forum* (1966); *How I Won the War* (1967); *Petulia* (1968); *The Bed Sitting Room* (1969); *The Three Musketeers* (1973); *Juggernaut* (1974); *The Four Musketeers; Royal Flash* (1975); *The Ritz; Robin and Marian* (1976); *Butch and Sundance: The Early Years; Cuba* (1979); *Superman II* (1980); *Superman III* (1983); *Finders Keepers* (1984); *Return of the Musketeers* (1989); *Get Back* (documentary, 1991)

Television: *Downbeat; The Dick Lester Show* (1955); *Idiot Weekly, Price 2d; A Show Called Fred; Son of Fred* (1956); *After Hours* (with Michael Bentine) (1958); *Have Jazz, Will Travel* (pilot) (1960)

Richard Lester might seem out of place in a work on science fiction directors, but a close examination of his filmography shows that he returned to the genre time and time again, from the prosaic *Mouse on the Moon*, the more surreal hijinks in *Help!*, to the entirely *sui generis* after-the-bomb comedy *The Bed Sitting Room*, as well as shepherding the *Superman* sequels. He brings to his work a lively energy and attention to detail that have paid off handsomely at times while failing him at others.

Lester was born on January 19, 1932, in Philadelphia, Pennsylvania to a school teacher and would-be playwright named Elliott Lester and his eccentric wife, Ella, whom Lester has described as the world's worst cook. Lester soon proved himself precocious and his parents started sending him to a private tutor at the age of three and enrolled him in school early. As a consequence, Lester was several years younger than his compatriots at the William Penn Charter Boys' School and all throughout his education.

The Lesters lived in an isolated area, and Elliott's first and only attempt to drive a car proved a disaster. As Richard's older sister Dorothy was sixteen years older than her half-brother, she left home shortly after the new arrival, leaving Richard to have run of the house. The area was so crime-free that the doors were always left open and the shades were never drawn. Lester never possessed a keyring or a sense of privacy until he finally left the country.

In the forties, Lester decided to teach himself the piano, but discovered that he was a poor sight reader. Nevertheless, he tried his hand at composing music and decided he was a better composer than player.

At the age of 15, Lester entered the University of Pennsylvania where he studied clinical psychology, a field he began to view with suspicion and cynicism after being assigned field work assessing and testing mentally retarded children in a clinic. He resolved to abandon psychology after his degree and began to write music for the University Drama Society and the Mask and Wig Club.

Lester became part of a vocal group (called Vocal Group) which was hired to back singer Ginny Stevens on WCAU, the local CBS station in downtown Philadelphia, but the group was fired after three performances. Nevertheless, Lester decided to apply for a job at CBS in 1951 and was hired as a stagehand. Ambitious, Lester worked his way first to floor manager, then to assistant director, and finally won some opportunities to direct live shows using multiple cameras.

After a couple of years, however, he handed in his resignation and set off for Europe, touring France, Rome, Austria, Munich and Spain. He tried his luck as a roving guitar player without much success, then switched to smuggling. He turned down an opportunity to smuggle marijuana and instead smuggled currency and cigarette lighters (the latter of which were banned by the Spanish government, who had a monopoly on matches).

He hit upon the idea of making his way to London to raise interest in a musical he had written, *Curtains for Harry*, for which he found no takers. However, as good fortune would have it, Associated Rediffusion was beginning commercial television broadcasts that August, and Lester was able to offer his services as an experienced television director. Lester was expected not only to turn out his own programs, but also to tutor the inexperienced trainees that the studio had hired, including Douglas Hearn and Philip Saville.

The woman whom Lester was asked to share an office with, Deirdre Vivian Smith, a classically trained dancer, would soon become his wife. Deirdre had appeared in Gene Kelly's *Invitation to the Dance* and worked with Jack Cole on *Gentlemen Marry Brunettes* as well as appearing in various stage shows. She was initially turned off by Lester's brashness, but was quickly impressed by his ability to quickly pull a production together and his personal charm.

Lester's first assignment was to put together a showcase for American singer Marti Stephen, and then he went on to direct British commercial TV's first jazz show, *Downbeat*, which featured Deirdre dancing to "Slaughter on Tenth Avenue" among other features.

Wanting to showcase his own talents as a singer, piano, bass, and guitar player, Lester created and was the star of *The Dick Lester Show*, a live, supposedly behind-the-scenes look at an under-rehearsed show that was suddenly shoved on the air. Unfortunately, it looked as under-rehearsed as it pretended to be and was an unmitigated disaster that was yanked off the air after the first airing. The show's sole support, apart from the Reg Owen Orchestra, was a young Liverpool actor named Alun Owen, with whom Lester traded weak ad libs. Owen would later write *A Hard Day's Night* for Lester.

Peter Sellers happened to catch the broadcast and called up Lester. "[I]t was either one of the worst shows I've ever seen, or you are on to something. If it was the latter, would you like to meet for lunch?" asked the star. Lester readily agreed and met with the famous Goon Show star who was considering doing a television version of the famous radio show.

Unfortunately, Harry Secombe, who anchored the lunacy of Peter Sellers and Spike Milligan on the radio show, had prior commitments and the BBC owned the copyright to the word "Goon," so the new project was christened *Idiot Weekly, Price 2d.* It went on to rave reviews and spawned two follow-ups, *A Show Called Fred* and *Son of Fred.* Only a few isolated episodes of these series survive, but by all accounts, they were amusing precursors to the type of carte blanche craziness found on *Monty Python's Flying Circus* a decade and a half later.

This association led to *The Running, Jumping and Standing Still Film*, an 11 minute short starring Peter Sellers, Spike Milligan, Mario Fabrizi, and Leo McKern that was shot for £70 using a 16mm camera that had just been purchased by Peter Sellers. The film was done as a lark, shot silently, with Lester composing and adding a musical score later. Sellers showed it to the critic from the *Daily Express*, who encouraged him to submit it to the Edinburgh Film Festival, where it was well received. It later won an award at the San Francisco Festival and garnered an Academy Award nomination as best short, Lester's only Academy Award nomination to date.

The film offered a zany look at how the British spend their Sundays, with Spike Milligan as an outdoor enthusiast, David Lodge as a non-stop athlete, Lester himself as an outdoor painter, and Mario Fabrizi as a photographer who develops his film with the chemicals in a pond. Sellers, who assisted with the cinematography, appears only briefly as a frogman in full gear who encounters a man racing around a gramophone with a needle in his hand to get it to play. The film also offers Graham Stark as a British astronaut with delusions of grandeur who plans to ascend in a kite and who in turn is assaulted by Leo McKern, who then retires to his caravan.

The film depicts each of these individuals as grimly pursuing their hobbies in determined isolation only to run afoul of others who are just as determined to pursue their avocations. The short is a trifle, spiced with absurdity, more interested in minute behavioral quirks than in a plot.

"After the success of *The Running, Jumping and Standing Still Film* and the Academy Award nominations," Lester recalled, "I went roaring around, saying, 'I'm a film director' to a lot of people, and they would look at the short and say: 'It's very funny — if we ever want a full-length version of that, we'll call you.' Well, to this day, nobody's called me for *that*."

Then in mid–1961, expatriate American producer Milton Subotsky, the cohead of Amicus Pictures and producer of *Rock! Rock! Rock!*, sent Lester a 23 page script he had written. Lester assumed it was merely a treatment, but was informed that that was the entire script — the rest of the film was to be filled up with as many musical numbers as would be needed for a seventy-plus minute running time. Would Lester be interested in directing?

The film, *It's Trad, Dad,* had a total budget of £60,000 and a three-week shooting schedule at Shepperton studios. Lester arranged for a line-up of traditional jazz groups interspersed with pop acts such as Gene Vincent, Del Shannon, John Leyton and the Brooks Brothers. Subotsky's script was a trifle about a pair of teens, Craig (Craig Douglas) and Helen (singing star Helen Shapiro) who want to hire some music acts for a dance that they plan to put on over the objections of the staid Town Council. (The same plot popped up decades later as the basis for *Footloose.*)

The town is surrealistically and amusingly meant to represent Anywhere in Great Britain and remains anonymous. Lester includes a shot of a sign saying "You Are Now Entering" with the name of the town blank. The shops are given ultra-plain descriptive names: "News," "Travel," "Discs," "Bank" and "Restaurant." The English township has become interchangeable and faceless.

The film celebrates the cheerful vivacity of the young over the conservative tendencies of the Establishment, who only cave in when it becomes convinced that supporting the dance will be to its own political advantage once the media portrays the Mayor as a liberal supporter of youth. Likewise, the local DJs — played by real British DJs Alan Freeman, David Jacobs, and Pete Murray — are shown as self-absorbed and only participate when they espy an opportunity for self-promotion.

However, the true highlights of the film are the musical numbers. When Chubby Checker's "The Twist" began zooming up the charts, Lester prompted Subotsky to recruit Checker to do a number to be filmed in New York. Subotsky agreed, provided that Lester pay his own fare there, and penned the tune "The Lose-Your-Inhibition Twist" for Checker to sing. While in the U.S., Lester also lined up Gary "U.S." Bonds and Gene McDaniels to each perform a number ("Seven Day Weekend" and Burt Bacharach's "Another Tear Falls" respectively).

The film's primary value is as a showcase for these performers, many of whom have no other cinematic record of their work. The Brooke Brothers sing "Double Trouble," while the late Del Shannon does "She Never Talked About Me," John Leyton performs "Lonely City" and Gene Vincent does "Spaceship to Mars." Helen Shapiro is given two numbers, "Sometime Yesterday" and "Let's Talk About Love."

Even the trad jazz numbers shine with Acker Bilk doing "Frankie and Johnny," accompanied by an inset of stills illustrating the song; Terry Lightfoot performs "Tavern in the Town," the Temperance Seven play "Let's Have a Dream" in English and French (with French subtitles for those who wish to sing along), and the climax has Otillie Patterson belting out "Down By the Riverside" and "When the Saints Go Marching In," about as wholesome a pair of songs ever presented in what was ostensibly an exploitation pop jazz/rock vehicle.

Lester's technique consisted of filming each act performing their song three times in front of three cameras, giving him nine different angles to choose from, which easily allowed him to edit the footage to the beat of the music, or break-up the frame in inventive ways. In these musical stagings, one can clearly see the talent that created *A Hard Day's Night* fully formed.

However, Britain's fondness for trad jazz music died down as quickly as the "skiffle" and "ska" crazes did, and Beatlemania was still just around the corner. The film was retitled in the United States by its distributor, Columbia, as *Ring-a-Ding Rhythm,* but this was one British import that didn't travel well and soon sank without a trace. However, the film took in £300,000 in Britain alone, and the British critics applauded the freshness of Lester's approach. Peculiarly enough, *It's Trad, Dad* became the best reviewed movie of Lester's career.

On the recommendation of Peter Sellers, Lester was offered the job of directing *Mouse on the Moon,* his first science fiction film and the sequel to Jack Arnold's *The Mouse that Roared,* the film which established Sellers with the American cinema-going public. The film was to be an adaptation of original author Leonard Wibberly's own sequel, but Sellers declined appearing in the second film and had to be replaced by three different actors.

The main character this time around is Prime Minister Count Rupert of Mountjoy (Ron Moody), who is desperate for funds to fix the Duchy of Grand Fenwick's plumbing and hits upon the idea of asking America for a loan to do rocket research. The Americans surprisingly agree because they deem such a magnanimous gesture as being a masterstroke of international diplomacy. Not to be outdone, the Russians counter by supplying Grand Fenwick with a rocket.

Meanwhile, the little nation state is experiencing troubled times after its wine crop has failed and its fermented grapes are given to exploding. However, local scientist Kokintz (David Kossoff) realizes that the faulty spirits make an excellent rocket fuel, and it's not long before Grand Fenwick makes a genuine bid to join the space race.

Margaret Rutherford was hired to play ditzy Queen Gloriana XIII, but Lester soon found that his erstwhile star was considered to be uninsurable because of her age and blood pressure. Lester solved the problem by filming the majority of Rutherford's scenes in two days and putting up his and producer Walter Shenson's salary in case the star should fall ill. Rutherford found herself a trifle bewildered when she was sat down in a chair and was asked to recite all her lines looking either to one side or the other while backgrounds were changed behind her.

Strangely enough, the sense of separation from everything around her that this strategy caused works for her character and the film. Queen Gloriana isn't too connected to mundane realities and is given to imbibing too much of the local wine. To her, the rocket simply remains "that nasty great tin thing," she continually forgets that her husband is dead, she delights in the horrendous musical stylings of Fenwick's fetid bandmaster (Clive Dunn), and she never quite seems to know if she is launching a battleship or opening a pig breeders' convention.

While the first *Mouse* film offered more in the way of a satire, the second descends into farce. To save expenses, the film reuses sets left over from Cornel Wilde's *Lancelot and Guinevere*, but the cramped scale of things becomes part of the joke. Grand Fenwick, "the smallest and least progressive country in the world," symbolically represents Great Britain with all her post-imperial pretensions at being a superpower.

Mouse on the Moon is not without some satirical bite, particularly with Mountjoy's character, who justifies extracting money from Americans under false pretenses with, "The American taxpayer has *always* been deceived: it is his birthright." He has tried grooming his son, Vincent of Mountjoy (Bernard Cribbins) for a political career, observing, "He had all the makings of a great politician — as a child he was fantastically sly and dishonest." He even goes on Fenwickian television à la Harold Macmillan, to proclaim to the people that he has "led you into a situation where you have never had it so bad."

Vincent wants to be an astronaut, teams up with Kokintz, and plays the bashful hero to June Ritchie's pert heroine. Comedian Terry-Thomas pops up as Spender, a British Intelligence agent who singularly lacks any of that vital quality (e.g., he mistakes "cistern" for "system"). Mario Fabrizi gets in an amusing turn as Mountjoy's sycophantic servant. George Chisholm has an extended bit as a waiter who continually runs from exploding bottles of Fenwick's finest, a portion added by Lester along with some wine vat jokes when he and Michael Pertwee spent a week polishing the script.

Mouse on the Moon continually pokes fun at British traditions, especially the one about putting everything on hold for a tea break. The idiocies of nationalism are given a few barbs as when a British newscaster comments on the successful American space launch, insisting that the launch would not have been possible without the precision of a British watch worn by one of the astronauts.

The American and Russians are depicted as being almost identical, each with their own team of German scientists and identical dialogue. Composer Ron Grainer provides a lively score, and for a scene where representatives from the superpowers meet in Grand Fenwick, provides each with an associative theme: "Rule Britannia" for Great Britain, "Song of the Volga Boatman" for the Russians, and "Columbia, Gem of the Ocean" as the U.S. American, Russian, and Fenwickian rockets are launched simultaneously, and all land at the same time, depriving each one of the greater glory of being first on the moon.

The idea of "taking their problems with them" occurs once Vincent and the Professor step on the moon, only to be pelted by the garbage that has been pursuing them through space. Their rocketship is full of rustic details, such as hot water bottles on the wall, sausages hanging from the ceiling, and beer pump handles for controls. The space race is depicted as a kind of grand lunacy.

Moon opens amusingly enough with a Maurice Binder title sequence, but while most of Lester's comedies are frantic, this one is slow and amiable, never quite reaching the heights of humor that its premise promises. Lester himself commented to Joseph Gelmis in *The Film Director as Superstar*, "In making *The Mouse on the Moon*, I had to use the sets and characters from *The Mouse That Roared*. All the actors were already cast. All their mannerisms were stereotyped. And since the first film was apparently financially successful, nobody would dream of changing anything in it. That's a desperate way to make a film. But it enabled me to shoot seven weeks in color, so I did it. It was useful experience. But I don't think it was in any way *my* film, looking back on it."

Mouse on the Moon came in on time and on budget, which made a favorable impression on United Artists. Producer Shenson had been approached by UA to make a quick film with the Beatles "before their popularity declined," and the Beatles had seen and liked *The Running, Jumping, and Standing Still Film*, so Lester was offered the job of directing *A Hard Day's Night*.

The phrase "A Hard Day's Night" was coined by a drunken Ringo after a long recording session and was picked up by Shenson as an ideal title for a Beatles film. Shenson picked Lester to direct the first Beatles film and thereby won him everlasting fame and an identification that no amount of other talented work could erase. The Beatles themselves selected Alun Owen as the writer of the film simply because he was talented and from Liverpool like themselves. The Beatles hoped Owen would provide something fresh, something away from the old musical clichés of a singer romantically involved who elects to put on a show for a good cause. The idea became that the resulting film, *A Hard Day's Night*, would be pseudo-*cinéma vérité*, depicting a possible day in the life of the Beatles with the four lads playing themselves.

This idea suited Lester fine, as it would allow for the kind of spontaneity that he was comfortable with, while still leaving room for interesting character bits and comedy. In observing his subject, Owen was surprised at the amount of pushing and jostling endured by the Beatles as the objects of adulation by their fans and the media. When Lester asked John Lennon how he had liked Stockholm, Lennon replied, "It was a plane, a room, a car, and a cheese sandwich." That was all of the local landscape they had been able to experience given their vast celebrity, and that concept became the claustrophobic nexus for the film.

Explained Lester, "They hated getting up in the morning, and they hated the whole principle of filmmaking as an orderly craft. But they were quite willing to do it, because they were intelligent and realized the importance to me of following a schedule....

"What I was trying to do was to capture the feeling they managed to give to the people around them and therefore I had to make them as natural as possible. We decided on the approach by going to Paris and watching them do a radio show. They were revolutionaries in a goldfish bowl," noted Lester in Joseph Gelmis' *The Film Director as Superstar.*

A Hard Day's Night presents the musical group as inoffensive social revolutionaries who overturn the staid values of the oppressive upper classes (beginning with a *Financial Times* reader on a train and continuing through their encounter with the press — displaying upper class accents and a greater interest in the food than the subject at hand — and finally in Victor Spinetti's amusingly paranoid television director). Whatever the realities, the film chooses to depict the Beatles as likable innocents, possessing great power to move the masses, but no genuine freedom, in fact, prisoners of their own career. Power without freedom was to become a major theme in Lester's subsequent career.

Thus, their quiet moment of freedom, when they take to and romp around in a field to the strains of "Can't Buy Me Love," is one of the most joyous in the film, as the quick cutting seems to create a ballet of youthful high spirits in what was then a fresh and startling way, rather than the conventional song-and-dance number of past film musicals. The fresh approach, classic Beatles songs, and depiction of swinging London in the sixties have made *A Hard Day's Night* one of the most acclaimed and popular musicals of all time.

Lester began his association with United Artists with a hit and talked the studio into making his next film, *The Knack and How to Get It. The Knack* shows us young men who speak to each other without communicating. Based on Ann Jellicoe's original play, "The Knack" refers to Tolen's (Ray Brooks) knack for picking up girls to have sex with in contrast to his frustrated Irish landlord Colin (a very young Michael Crawford) who seeks to learn the secret of Tolen's success. Entering into the mix are Tom (Donald Donnelly), an Irish lad obsessed with animals and painting rooms white, and Nancy (Rita Tushingham), a newly arrived girl looking for a room whom Tolen selects as a demonstration of his ability.

Lester and cowriter Charles Wood greatly altered Jellicoe's play, which depicts Tolen as a proto-fascist who has the tables turned on him by Nancy when she shatters his assumption of his own irresistibility by claiming to have been raped. Instead, Tolen is shown as a capitalist who is always peddling something, boasting that he gives the customers what they want so they come back for more, and who is deflated because Nancy in the end chooses the more conventionally romantic Colin over him.

Part of Lester's technique was to secretly film older people watching his actors perform, and then dubbing in amusing or revealing comments for them to make. Once more, there is a contrast between the freewheeling, lively, appealing youngsters and the conservative, grumpy, older generation who prefer to criticize than to live life.

Another part of Lester's technique is having a dialogue continue through various visual discontinuities, so that the characters are quickly shifted from one locale to another while their obsessions seem to remain the same. There is also a touch of surrealism, as when Colin and Tom transport a double bedstead through London traffic. ("I think a bed's place is definitely in the home," one old fogey comments. It is also used for double entendres as when Nancy notes, "I am being picked up, aren't I?" as Tom and Colin lift her while she sits on the bed as it is being lifted down some steps.)

However well it may have captured the *zeitgeist,* though, *The Knack*, like *Billy Liar, Georgy Girl*, or *What's New, Pussycat?* has not dated well, but seems mired in the mores of its time with characters that are basically callow, shallow, and uninteresting. Perhaps its biggest problem is also one of attitude. We are meant to admire the characters' sexual frankness, but not their pursuit of hedonism; like their vitality, but deplore their obsessions; disdain the romantic illusions of the past, but also spurn the disillusionment of the elderly. The film succeeds in capturing a mood, but not a story.

While it is not generally commented on, there is a science fiction subplot to Lester's second Beatles film, *Help!,* which was originally titled "Eight Arms to Hold You." Written by *Knack* collaborator Charles Wood, *Help!*'s plot involves an Indian cult led by Clang (Leo McKern) who seeks to kill whomever wears the sacred sacrificial ring of Kali, which just happens to be Ringo, who was sent the ring by a fan, Ahme (Eleanor Bron). The plot was built around locations that the Beatles actually wished to go to as a sort of working vacation (stardom had thus far precluded their getting any time off), hence a plot that involves treks to the Swiss Alps (Paul wanted to learn to ski) and the Bahamas (which was in the middle of winter at the time), as well as a number of fanciful jokes and gags.

The resulting color film is a total contrast to *A Hard Day's Night*'s more naturalistic, black and white approach. According to Alexander Walker, cameraman Gilbert Taylor found himself so unnerved by Beatlemania that he declined to work on the second film, leading to his being replaced by David Watkin. While the first film worked from the Beatles' actual personalities, the second one caused them, in the words of John Lennon, to feel like "guest stars in [our] own film." The Beatles are no longer shown as working class heroes, but as high-living celebrities living in an ostentatious pop art flat.

In some ways, the film is a compromise, as Lester had already depicted their working life in the first film, and was told by their manager that he did not want any allusions to the Beatles' smoking, drinking, or dating, nor was there to be any romantic interest. Instead, they become bystanders in a James Bond meets Gunga Din type plot, and are each given a distinctive personality trait — Paul is cocky and cute, John is sardonic, George is disdainful, and Ringo plays a lovable lug. George was perhaps the most affected by the experience after being exposed to a sitar in the course of making the movie, and developed a subsequent strong interest in Eastern music.

Apart from the fine musical numbers, the other thing that holds the film together is its various allusions to Britain's checkered past and present: George makes reference to Scott of the Antarctic and Titus Oates, the India and Bahaman influences reflect the glories of the British empire, Scotland Yard and Buckingham Palace are reminders of British tradition, but the most telling is the science fiction subplot involving the scientists Foot (Victor Spinetti) and Algernon (Roy Kinnear).

These scientists invoke the failure of the promised technological miracle to transform Britain. Foot is forever complaining about Britain's inadequate resources and the superiority of German and American technology. They try to shake the ring off Ringo's finger with no success, they accidentally shrink Paul McCartney from six feet to six centimeters (parodying Jack Arnold's *The Incredible Shrinking Man*), they employ a device which alters the time flow, but the power they seek is forever beyond their grasp.

Some of *Help!'s* rapid cutting occurred because an increasingly nervous Ringo Starr developed a twitch every six seconds, which Lester wished to excise. "One only uses a cut because a take doesn't really work," the director noted. "The cut is an after-the-fact attempt to correct your mistakes, to put in something or take out something that should have been done differently."

Lester was to experience similar problems when, on his next film, an adaptation of the Broadway stage success *A Funny Thing Happened on the Way to the Forum*, star Phil Silvers, who was undergoing a painful divorce at the time, suddenly experienced a total inability to remember his lines. His performance had to be pieced together one line at a time, often disrupting the comedic rhythms of the film.

If that weren't enough, Lester was fundamentally at odds with his producer (and former comedy director) Melvin Frank over the approach the film should take. Frank expected Lester to simply transfer the bawdy stage musical to the screen, while Lester felt that the film should reflect and comment on the cruelties and injustice of the Roman society which is its setting.

Explained Lester in an interview in *Movie* magazine No. 16,

> I became very interested in the sordid quality of Rome and started reading Caropino and examining life and behaviour in Rome from a historical point of view, and so built the set, filled it with vegetables and fruit and left them to rot for two weeks so that all the flies and wasps got into it. I brought peasants down from the hills and little villages in the centre of Spain and made them live in the sets. We gave them each a particular job, sharpening knives, making pottery... We just left them to do a specific job for the whole film. I liked all that and was getting involved in it; it had nothing to do with all these Broadway Jewish jokes.

This led to Lester rewriting much of the script as filming went on, perhaps putting too much trust in his previous films' facility for improvising. Lester cut some of the songs from the stage show and reconceptualized the others. The film begins with slave Pseudolus (Zero Mostel) singing Stephen Sondheim's classic "Comedy Tonight," and introducing the principal settings, the houses of Senex (Michael Hordern) whose son Hero (Michael Crawford) owns Pseudolus; of Erronius (an ailing Buster Keaton), who spends most of the film searching for his lost son and daughter; and of Lycus (Silvers) who runs concubines in his brothel.

Pseudolus plans his freedom by uniting his master with Philia (Annette Andre), the woman of his dreams, who resides at Lycus', and who has already been promised to Miles Gloriosus (Leon Greene), the man who raped Thrace thrice. Pseudolus thwarts Gloriosus by having Senex's slave Hysterium (Jack Gilbert) pretend to be the now "dead" intended, only to have the egomaniacal ("Poor little moth. She fluttered too near my flame") Gloriosus order "her" cremated, at which point Hysterium and Pseudolus flee, initiating an extended chase that brings everything happily together.

Composer Ken Thorne won an Oscar for his orchestral arrangements of Stephen Sondheim's score, which uses

Roy Kinnear (left) and John Lennon in Lester's *How I Won the War*.

jazzy arrangements of the tunes to score other sequences in the film.

Lester's canny use of the frame can be seen when viewing the film in its proper 1.85 aspect ratio. The VHS video version tends to cut off a number of gags carefully set up on the edges of the frame. As a comedy, the film proved to be highly uneven, but for the opportunity it offers of seeing Silvers and Mostel try to outhustle each other, the film does have its pleasures.

Having tackled the exploitation of others in *Funny Thing*, Lester turned his attention to the subject of the ignobility of war in *How I Won the War*. The film depicts the rose-colored reminiscences of the inept Lt. Goodbody (Michael Crawford), who recalls his most dangerous mission — to set up a cricket pitch behind enemy lines in the Sahara for "morale" and to impress a visiting military dignitary (who when he sees it, simply comments, "What wotten bowling — dwive on"). As he misleads his men from Africa to France, his tattered platoon is systematically wiped out. His attitude is clear in his line, "War is, without a doubt, the noblest of games."

His "team," whose suffering and death he is seemingly indifferent to, include Clapper (Roy Kinnear), obsessed with his wife's infidelity; Juniper (Jack MacGowran), a music hall comic; Gripweed (John Lennon in a very minor role), a kleptomaniac who can only gripe; and Musketeer Juniper (Jack Hedley) who has retreated into madness as a survival mechanism.

How I Won the War is based on the novel by Patrick Ryan and was scripted by Charles Wood, but its satire of war-time insanity is neither particularly fresh nor especially funny. Contributing to the confusion, when it was released in America, scenes that were supposed to be tinted were printed in black and white, so that it is bewildering when the spirits of the dead trudge along behind Goodbody's platoon in the colors of the areas of their demise as those colors are no longer there. These colorful soldiers indicate that as far as the officers are concerned, the men are interchangeable and there are plenty more around to fill in any gaps. Also, Goodbody continues to address men long dead and admits that "They all looked the same to me," whereas the different unreal colors show them to be quite unalike.

Of course, American audiences will also have a hard time understanding the cricket references as well, so Lester's assertion that war simply is *not* cricket, but a rather bloody business, may not have the resonance intended. Additionally difficult for foreign audiences are allusions to British war films and attitudes towards Montgomery, which are essential in understanding this difficult film.

What the film does most successfully is skewer the concept of war nostalgia and satirize conventional war films. Lester's mixture of black humor and the horrors of war, however, kept audiences off balance and failed to even entertain those that could parse the thick British slang oftentimes employed. *How I Won the War* is tragic without being affecting because no one in the film is truly sympathetic, only absurd (e.g. Clapper saying to the enemy, "Have a heart, eh?" just before being bayoneted in the chest or Grapple [Michael Hordern] saying to Goodbody when Goodbody is being court-martialed, "If it weren't for the British army, you wouldn't be here today"). The film constantly undermines any possibility of audience sympathy for the protagonists or the situation, consequently alienating them and ensuring its commercial as well as artistic failure.

Lester's next film, *Petulia*, on the other hand, was a great critical success, partly because it dealt obliquely with the Vietnam war at a time when the subject seemed almost taboo. For a short time after its release, *Petulia* was hailed as a cinematic masterpiece, though now it seems largely forgotten as its topicality is seen at a further remove. *Petulia* did suffer from expectations that it would be another Lester comedy when in fact there was nothing comic about it. Given his experiences on *A Funny Thing Happened on the Way to the Forum*, Lester insisted on and received final cut and total artistic control, much to Warner Bros. later consternation.

Lester had revisited America as part of research for the film, and what struck him most was the level of "casual violence"; that Americans tended to reach their breaking point much quicker and were more prone to shout at each other than the English. Believing in serendipity, Lester constantly incorporated found experiences into his narrative tapestry.

Part of the impetus for the character of Petulia (Julie Christie) is that she is a person who comes to realize that by demanding so much from her husband David (Richard Chamberlain), she renders him impotent, so she decides that her responsibility is to learn to settle for 60 percent of someone as the only way to go on living, accepting that nobody is capable of living up to his or her full potential.

She comes to realize that by telling her husband, "Your fantastic, you're the most marvelous man I've ever known," on their wedding day, that she has put him on a pedestal and set up expectations that he is uncertain he can fulfill. When she realizes this, she breaks off with Archie (George C. Scott) despite her husband's beating her, warning Archie, "I'd turn those marvelous hands of yours into fists," and telling her husband who tried to kill her, "When I married you, you were the gentlest man I knew, David."

Another key aspect to Petulia is that she is a compulsive liar, telling stories about her mother and grandfather that are patently untrue, and lying about stealing a tuba she has rented. She lies constantly, but cannot seem to help herself. Nor is Archie, the middle-aged surgeon who falls in love with her, very admirable, walking out on his wife (Shirley Knight) and children simply because he is bored and eventually abandoning Petulia as well.

The characters in the film are all in flux, trying to adjust, and subject to many modern pressures and confusions. Even the kind characters are shown as being capable of cruelty and insensitivity. They are afraid of commitment because they have all learned that with commitment comes pain. All of them wallow in guilt and remorse over the hurt they have caused others. They fail to realize their potentials because they are too caught up in meeting the expectations of the people they love.

The Beatles considered making another film with Lester to finish up their contract with United Artists and had hired playwright Joe Orton to fashion a screenplay, which he called *Up Against It: Prick Up Your Ears.* (The subtitle was later used for a biography of the playwright which director Stephen Frears made into a film.) However the group, along with Shenson and their manager Brian Epstein, hated the result and vetoed it. Oscar Lewenstein, who had staged several of Orton's plays, showed the property to Lester, who initially seemed to feel it would be a step backwards, but later saw possibilities as a musical-political frolic for Mick Jagger, while the Beatles went on to do *Let It Be* with director Michael Lindsay-Hogg.

Lester and Lewenstein asked Orton to come by and discuss developing the property with them, but a driver sent to fetch him got no answer and only saw a pair of legs stretched out on the floor. The pair called Peggy Ramsay, who phoned the police. The police discovered that Orton had been beaten to death by his gay lover Kenneth Halliwell, who had then taken his own life. Orton's work proved impossible to adapt, and Lester abandoned it, turning his attention to a play by Spike Milligan and John Antrobus.

The Bed Sitting Room marked an absurdist return to science fiction for Lester, depicting a post-apocalyptic England where 20 survivors of the nuclear holocaust attempt to carry on in the classical English tradition. Of the remaining twenty, it has been decided that Mrs. Ethel Shroake is closest to the throne, and so she is declared the Queen. Mate (Spike Milligan) represents the complete postal system. Frank Thornton is now the BBC, and lacking broadcast equipment, wanders around and appears from behind the burned out shells of hollow television sets to present favorite headlines of the past (there being no news gathering organizations left, hence no news). Marty Feldman plays a Nurse who is responsible for the National Health and wants to wallpaper wombs so fetuses won't want to leave. A man on a bicycle generates all the electricity that is available. The comedy team of Peter Cook and Dudley Moore represent the entire police force, who keep an eye on things from a Volvo tied to a large balloon and demolish standing buildings to give the Enemy fewer targets in the long-awaited second attack. There is even a final pathetic pervert (Roy Kinnear), decked out in rubber goods, who is disappointed that his loutish behavior is met with the purest apathy before stumbling away in shame. These are people who are trying to desperately cling to something from the past, but the bomb has vaporized all meaning from their lives.

Given the film's limited budget, Lester does a marvelous job of suggesting a post apocalyptic world, filling his film with memorable imagery such as a subway escalator that emerges from the earth to dump its riders onto a barren desert, putting the shattered dome of St. Paul's cathedral in a stagnant lake, showing us Regents Park as a muddy swamp, illustrating the missing population with a huge mound of boots and shoes, as well as set after set of false teeth being fished from a polluted stream. With hardly anyone left to produce anything, life has been reduced to a desperate search for food.

Complicating matters is the fact that the survivors are all mutating into other things. The title is a reference to the fact that Lord Fortnum (a Learish Ralph Richardson) is slowly being transformed into a bed sitting room (wallpaper sprouts out of his sleeve; a brick falls from his pocket). He is appalled not so much that he is transforming, but at the lack of social status such a transformation implies, that he will be a "rented accommodation" at 29 Cul-de-Sac Place, Paddington, rather than say "Woburn Abbey." However, some things never change, as Fortnum

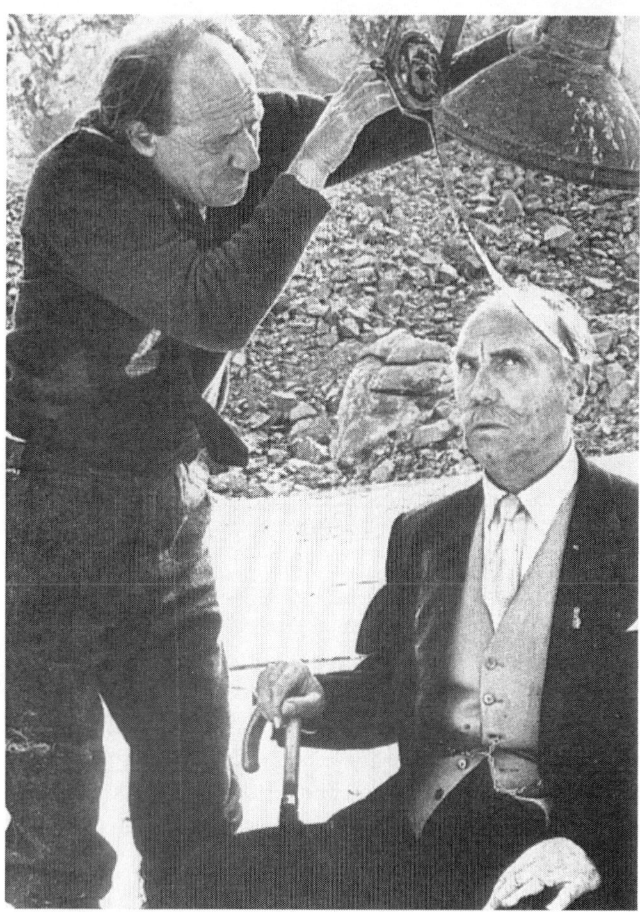

Bules Martin (Michael Hordern, left) attempts to aid Lord Fortnum (Ralph Richardson) from turning into a Bed Sitting Room in Lester's absurdist science fiction comedy.

stipulates, "No coloreds. No children. And especially no colored children."

Meanwhile a housewife (Mona Washbourne) becomes a cupboard (emblematic of her utilitarian role in society), the Prime Minister (Arthur Lowe) turns into a parrot (symbol of a literal talking head), and one of the policemen turns into a sheepdog (symbolic of an obedient servant who keeps things in line).

The war ironically broke out just as a peace accord was signed. Lord Fortnum is proud of his Early Warning Hat, which he explains, "gives you an extra four minutes in bed," and allowed him to sleep through the entire two minute and twenty-eight second war. The devastation is such that the concept of winners and losers becomes meaningless.

Placed amongst these individuals as institutions is a desperate family — Penelope (Rita Tushingham), seventeen months pregnant with God knows what; Mum, who reenacts a fond domestic situation by throwing crockery at the Fallout Shelter Man (Harry Secombe); and father, the Prime Minister, who tries to assure that "It's family life that's important," and ends up being eaten after transforming. Bules Martin (Michael Hordern), who at one point carves a banana as if it were a Sunday roast, pays pathetic court to Penelope and persuades her to marry him, with the help of Mate, who provides an Instant God Kit complete with cash register, and the Vicar, who conducts services not from *the* Good Book, but from *a* good book — *Lady Chatterley's Lover* to be exact.

The Bed Sitting Room has a very Goon Show type of humor, not surprising as it was adapted from a play by Spike Milligan, which varies widely from brilliant to belabored, especially when it comes to puns. (A reference to Britain's nuclear detergent rather than deterrent, with its implications of cleaning out the workings of society, is funny, as is father's comment to Bules after his virility test, "Enough of your cheek and impotence," but when Moore inquires if the architect of St. Paul's was Wren only to have Cook respond, "Looks a bit cloudy, but there's no rain...." one can only wince.)

Unfortunately for the film, it has a tendency, like the characters, to meander, never arriving at any place in particular. Instead, it comes off as a succession of bits in search of a plot or a consistent tone. (Spike Milligan even rips off a famous Ernie Kovaks visual joke as Bules Martin tries pouring something into the Fallout Shelter Man's glass while tilted to one side.) The main point of the film seems to be that bourgeois life's activities and rituals are fundamentally hollow and meaningless, and if we could view them outside of their normal context, we would be aware, as the characters in the film are not, of how meaningless and absurd these traditions are.

Commenting on the film, Lester said, "It's a sad film, a sort of nostalgic view back to the days when we used to be frightened of the bomb. Seriously, it's based on the concern that, because of all our other problems, we have sufficiently pushed the bomb into the background, that's it's become a period piece, a piece of nostalgia from those days when we were all marching and organized and worrying about the fact that there were B-52s overhead.

"It is such an impossible condition for the mind to grasp that we have to use the techniques of absurdity.... So we push man's perversions and foibles to the extreme. And then take those twenty people who have survived and let them carry on exactly as they might do.

"We're trying to reproduce what Hiroshima was like, but stylized. One of the camera operators was at Hiroshima three months after it was bombed and he took a lot of photographs. We're reproducing that, in some ways. We spent the last two days at a reject pottery dump. It was entirely filled with broken plates, bits of fused glass."

Still, *The Bed Sitting Room* is one of the boldest science fiction films ever made, one brimming with social commentary and ideas as it depicts a deformed world whose inhabitants are unsuccessfully trying to will a vision of normalcy back into existence, clinging to the familiar in ways that only reminds us of what was lost. It is a film of ideas rather than characters, and comes off as rather cold and dispassionate, though the wasted landscape is unmistakably despairing in mood and tone. It is not entirely successful black comedy, but it is admirably ambitious and deserves to be better known.

When Lester screened *The Bed Sitting Room* for UA heads Arnold and David Picker, he did not at first tell them that he had not made the Mick Jagger musical he had had tentative approval for. The Pickers hated the picture and soon Lester lost all support from the studio that had produced most of his movies. The film was awarded the Gandhi Peace Prize at the 1969 Berlin Film Festival, but performed very poorly at the box office.

Next Lester tried tackling *Send Him Vicious*, a political thriller about Rhodesia, which was rejected as being uncommercial. Lester then bought the rights to and had Charles Wood adapt George MacDonald Fraser's *Flashman* with John Alderton in the lead when suddenly UA changed its mind. (Half a decade later, he would adapt the book's sequel, *Royal Flash*, as a film starring Malcolm McDowell.)

Lester then planned to join a directors' cooperative with John Boorman, Tony Richardson, Lindsay Anderson, Ken Russell, Joseph Losey and Karel Reisz, but United Artists objected to Tony Richardson and Joseph Losey and so the whole deal fell apart. With no film work to do, Lester found himself concocting commercials for Italy's *Carouseli*, a unique concept wherein a series of two minute shorts were each followed by a twenty second commercial that was unrelated to what had gone before, and each would be destroyed after a single airing. Lester made up ten of the shorts, improvising gags at a French Foreign Legion Fort in the Sahara.

He was then hired to make a $250,000 science fiction-oriented commercial for Braniff airlines. Shot by cameraman Nicolas Roeg, the three-minute commercial presented a future world where people behave as badly on airlines as they do on present-day subways. Lester's commercial won an award for World's Best Commercial.

Finally, in 1972 he received a call from Ilya Salkind. The Salkinds had been brainstorming one day about a film that would reunite the Beatles and hit upon a comedy version of Alexander Dumas' *The Three Musketeers* as a possible candidate. Their previous productions, Abel Gance's *Battle of Austerlitz, Ballad in Blue*, Romain Gary's *Kill! Kill! Kill!*, Orson Welles' *The Trial*, and Edward Dmytryk's *Bluebeard* had all bombed, but this did not discourage the enterprising producers.

Coming back to Earth, they gave up the idea of reuniting the Beatles, but pursued the concept of a comic *Three Musketeers* with their investors, who suggested that the film be a sexy romp and star Leonard Whiting (fresh from Zeffirelli's *Romeo and Juliet*), Ursula Andress, Richard Burton, and Raquel Welch. The project was initially offered to Tony Richardson, who insisted on final cut and was rejected. (Richardson later complained that they mistook D'Artagnan for one of the titular musketeers, overlooking Aramis in the process.) The Beatles connection had brought the name of Richard Lester to mind, and so the Salkinds contacted him.

Initial plans for the feature were that it was to be a three-and-a-half hour roadshow spectacular, and George MacDonald Fraser was fortuitously hired to write the relatively faithful and rollicking adaptation, which was less sensationalistically sexy than high-spirited, adventurous, and romantic. Lester found himself delighted by the script and the possibilities it offered. It was also planned to shoot the film in Hungary, but Lester soon learned that bureaucratic red tape would make that an impossibility, so the entire production was relocated to Spain with a concomitant increase in cost of about 20 percent.

Still, Lester managed to create a very sumptuous looking film for a mere $5 million, or actually two films, as it was decided to split the films in the middle, ending the first film, *The Three Musketeers*, on the upbeat note of D'Artagnan becoming a musketeer, and saving the darker half of the story for an automatic sequel that was shot simultaneously, *The Four Musketeers*. This decision was kept from the actors, who later filed suit for further compensation for having done a second film for the price of one.

Lester originally wanted Charlton Heston for Athos, who in turn wanted to work with the director but asked to have a smaller part, partially due to his limited availability. Lester then offered him Cardinal Richelieu and persuaded Heston to underplay the part straight and menacing with the result that the imperious cleric remains one of Heston's finest performances.

Michael York was cast as the energetic and enthusiastic D'Artagnan after Lester caught his work in Losey's *Accident* and Zeffirelli's *Romeo and Juliet*. Since Dumas had described Athos as "burly," he thought of Oliver Reed, who proved a perfect choice. As Aramis is a foppish priest-killer, Lester went with Richard Chamberlain (who subsequently became cast in other swashbuckling roles, mostly in made-for-TV movies). Finally, he cast the talented Frank Finlay against type as Porthos, whose twitterpated vanity steals several scenes.

To satisfy the Salkinds' requirements for glamour, Faye Dunaway was cast as the villainous Milady de Winter and Raquel Welch proved an able physical comedian as Constance Bonancieux, although initially Welch caused the director headaches when, after insisting she wait until she came on location to discuss any changes in the script, she threatened to walk while much of the financing was based upon her participation. Though Lester had been reluctant to have her on the film in the first place, once they met, the pair actually hit it off very well and Welch turned in one of her finest and funniest performances for the film. (Welch did insist on having her own dress designer, and her costumes were prepared by Ron Talsky, who shared an Academy Award nomination with Yvonne Blake, who designed the clothes for everyone else in the film.)

Nor could Welch get over that Lester cast Spike Milligan as her jealous husband, as the two do make a humorously inappropriate pair. Lester had chosen Christopher Cazenove to play the Duke of Buckingham, but the Salkinds felt Simon Ward would be a bigger name and paid Cazenove off. Lester regular Roy Kinnear became D'Artagnan's servant Planchet, Christopher Lee made a suitably dastardly Rochefort, Jean-Pierre Cassel was airily egotistical and oblivious as Louis XIII, and Geraldine Chaplin looked perfect to play the beautiful but shallow and cruel Anne of Austria. (Lester had planned to dub Chaplin's voice, which he felt was not impressive enough for a royal, but Chaplin pointed out she had the right to redub in her contract.)

Lester was able to bring a new look to the fencing scenes in the film by studying a 17th century text by Thibault on the art of fencing and having fight arranger Bill Hobbs faithfully employ his suggested moves amplified by practicality. Lester learned that 17th century blades were thicker and heavier, causing fighters to put more weight on the front foot and hack with them, using daggers and capes to fend off blows from their rivals.

Among other problems that had to be dealt with, once a drunk Oliver Reed almost got arrested for diving into a restaurant's fish tank and biting carrots, leaving spectators with the impression that he was eating raw fish. Reed was also hospitalized for several days when he took a sword clean through his wrist. Michael York kept getting thrown from his mount and received several cuts on his chin during the dueling scenes.

Still, *The Three Musketeers* remains the finest and most entertaining swashbuckler ever made and one of Lester's lasting legacies. A recent remake has not dimmed its luster in the slightest. By contrast, the clubfooted *Royal Flash*, while continuing to display Lester's eye for period detail, takes a sort of "sword in cheek" approach that rapidly wears out its welcome, despite Reed's amusing turn as Bismarck and Malcolm McDowell's game attempt at portraying George MacDonald Fraser's roguish anti-hero.

More successful is the taut thriller *Juggernaut,* which plays both as a straightforward thriller and as a wry commentary on Britain's fading glory (the ship threatened in the film is the *Britannic*, on which everything is falling apart, the stabilizers are causing the boat to rock, the general facilities are shabby and run down, the passengers stoical despite bombs exploding in their midst, and the captain is seedy and demoralized).

Richard Harris heads a first-rate cast and gives one of his best performances as Fallon, the demolitions expert who has to deal with a wily unknown terrorist named Juggernaut who threatens to set off a bomb unless his ransom is paid and who taunts the demolition experts. The superintendent back on shore (Anthony Hopkins) is especially concerned because his wife (Caroline Mortimer) is onboard. Able support is given by David Hemmings, Shirley Knight, Omar Sharif, Ian Holm, Lester regular Roy Kinnear, and Freddie Jones. Lester keeps this from being a routine disaster film and keeps the crisis riveting throughout, working from Richard DeKoker and Alan Plater's fine script.

Unfortunately, *The Ritz*, based on Terence McNally's off–Broadway play, proved as frantic and desperate as its main character (Jack Weston) who attempts to hide out from his murderous brother-in-law in an all-gay New York bathhouse while avoiding being raped by some of the inhabitants therein. Sadly, Weston is not only kept center stage but proves relentlessly unfunny in his predicament, with Rita Moreno walking away with what acting honors are available by re-creating her role as no-talent entertainer Goodie Gomez.

Lester returned to evoking medieval times in James Goldman's *Robin and Marian*, an elegiac look at the myth of Robin Hood, featuring Sean Connery as the past-his-prime ex-robber who has become disillusioned and depressed after fighting in the Crusades and then discovering that King Richard is a genocidal madman. Returning to Sherwood, his finds his "merry men" to be little more than derelicts and he loses his zest for living until his renewed romance with Maid Marian (Audrey Hepburn) rekindles his spirit and gives meaning to his life once more.

Goldman had hoped to interest David Lean in the project, but was unable to get it to his attention. John Frankenheimer was attached for a time and suggested Audrey Hepburn to play the now mature Marian. The actress fell in love with the part, delighted to be given the opportunity to play a woman her own age. Originally, Goldman sought Connery to play Little John, but Connery thought he would make a better Robin. Goldman then hoped to have Richard Harris play Little John and Nicol Williamson play the ironically evil Richard the Lionheart, only for the two actors to express more interest in playing the other's role. Robert Shaw was brought on board to play the Sheriff of Nottingham.

To keep filmmaking costs down, *Robin and Marian*

was shot in Spain, with the Urbassa Plain standing in for Sherwood Forest. As in Goldman's *The Lion in Winter*, Goldman stands several elements of historical legend on their head. For example, in the film, the Sheriff is actually more intelligent than Robin Hood, who is shown to be a flawed hero. (In fact, all Robin Hood films so far have glossed over the fact that Richard the Lionheart never learned to speak English, was rarely in his kingdom, and never was a good king to his subjects, dying a mere three months after returning from the Crusades himself.)

The film ends ironically with Maid Marian poisoning Robin after he has finally defeated the Sheriff of Nottingham because she realizes that "he'll never have a better day than this" and that Robin's life can only be a series of disappointments thereafter, and then drinks poisoned wine and dies with him, leaving the realm of the living and entering the realm of legend forever.

Lester originally wanted to call the film *The Death of Robin Hood*, but the studio felt that selling the film as a love story was more commercial, advertising it with the legend, "Love is the greatest adventure of them all." Those looking for another romp like *The Three Musketeers* were inevitably disappointed. Though the film is suffused with some gentle humor, it is far from the madcap work that people associated with Lester because of his early films. Still, while *Robin and Marian* flopped financially, many have come to consider it one of Connery's best films.

Connery returned to work with Lester on the ill-fated *Cuba*. The project was unfortunately begun before a script was finalized. According to Lester, his intentions were to create a romantic thriller set in the chaotic final days of Baptista, "to portray an impression of the moment one regime was replaced by the next. I thought it would be fascinating as a piece of film ... I wanted to make a political film within which no one spoke about politics and a love story in which no one spoke about love."

Instead, Lester made a movie in which the audience keeps waiting for something to jell or become exciting, and it never does. Charles Wood's script became a subject of contention and went through several changes until weather forced the production to commence or simply shut down altogether. Connery's character Robert Dapes is a professional soldier hired in hopes of his preventing the rebels from advancing, a hopeless proposition at best and he knows it. Still, his attraction to Alexandra Pulido (last minute replacement Brooke Adams filling in for a departing Diana Rigg) entices him to stay despite being already married to wealthy playboy aristocrat Juan (Chris Sarandon).

The final result never went anywhere, as a story or as a film. *Cuba* opened disastrously with few viewers and scathing reviews. One has a sense that a potentially interesting subject matter was blown simply because the filmmakers never got a handle on what kind of story to make out of it.

Because of Lester's successful handling of the *Three Musketeer* features, the Salkinds and Pierre Spengler offered Lester the opportunity to direct Ilya's latest pet project, *Superman — The Movie*, which like *Musketeers* was planned to be filmed as one four hour epic that would be cut into two self-sufficent features. Lester turned it down, explaining that he did not like fantasy films generally and was not at all familiar with the source material. He suggested to the producers that they make it a period piece and told them they would be better off seeking someone else.

The Salkinds then turned to James Bond director Guy Hamilton, but while they discovered that they could not afford to make the film in Rome as originally planned and so switched to England, Hamilton explained that because of tax reasons he would be unable to work in England, and so the Salkinds had to scramble after somebody else.

That proved to be Richard Donner. However, the producers became increasingly agitated at the spiraling upward costs that were incurred under Donner's direction, but discovered that their American distributor, Warner Bros. opposed any plans to replace him, having been quite pleased with footage of Marlon Brando, who had been signed to the film for a hefty multimillion dollar salary sent to them.

Spengler decided that the solution would be to hire Lester as a producer, and so Lester and his lawyer were summoned to a meeting with Alexander Salkind; however, the negotiations would not go forward until the question of Lester's *Musketeers* percentage was finally satisfactorily settled. Lester stipulated that he would act as a go-between but would not usurp Donner, and that after his past dealings with them, his salary must be paid promptly by the Salkinds every Thursday.

Lester did his best to reassure Donner that he had no ambitions to take over the film, and would only talk to cast or crew with Donner's express permission, that he was there as a way of settling with the Salkinds. While Donner was initially hesitant, he later admitted that Lester was a big help to him.

It was Lester who suggested abandoning the idea of shooting both films simultaneously so that the first one, at least, could be brought under control, because if the first one was not a success, the footage for the second would be rendered worthless. Lester helped to coordinate a second live unit directed by future Bond director John Glen. The effects work was also getting far behind schedule, so a second model unit was proposed and instituted by Lester, who brought together past associate and cameraman Paul Wilson with special effects expert Derek Meddings.

Lester was used to working quickly and under low

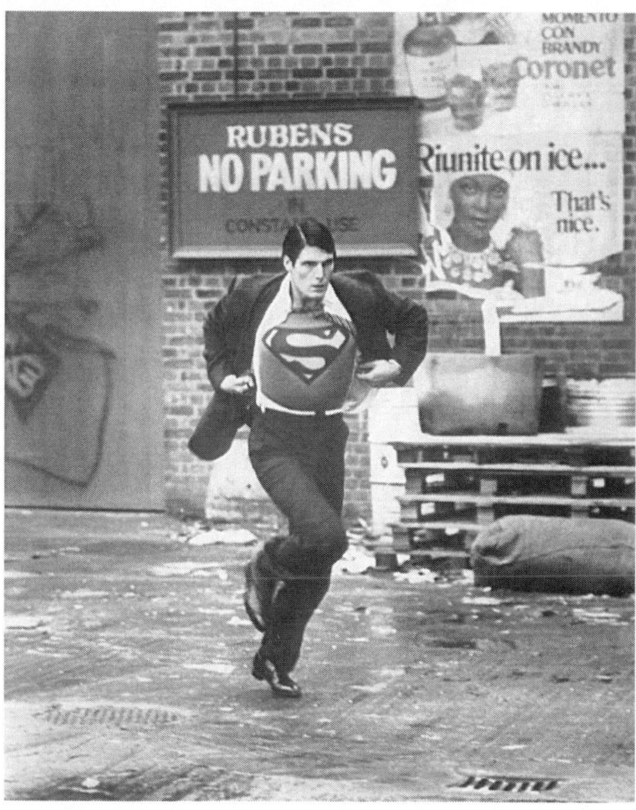

Clark Kent (Christopher Reeve) unveils his true nature in Lester's *Superman II.*

budgets. He became somewhat appalled when Donner would wait around for the light to be right only to have a storm break out and delay all shooting for several days. Meanwhile, as filming progressed, Lester was also wrapped up in preparing for the production of *Bruce and Sundance: The Early Days*, the ill-advised prequel to the highly entertaining *Butch Cassidy and the Sundance Kid.*

After filming was finally completed, Lester noted a flaw in the film. There was no jeopardy for any of the principal players. Then he remembered Puzo's idea of killing Lois Lane, but how would Superman bring her back? By borrowing the planned ending for the second film with Superman going back in time to revive Lois Lane and rescue her, he helped create what Spengler considered the "perfect" climax to the film.

Richard Donner and *Superman*'s producers began another epic battle after the film's completion. The producers maintained that Donner had far exceeded his budget, while he countered that he had never even been given a budget. What was more, he had worked with the understanding that the film would take him nine months to complete, when in fact it had taken 28 months, including pre- and postproduction, and he had not received any additional salary.

Though it contains what was then the longest credit crawl in history, Lester insisted to Spengler that Lester's work as a producer on the film go uncredited so that Spengler could claim the full glory rather than having it taken from him by a "name," plus as Lester was known as a director, a credit might raise questions in people's minds about Donner directing the film, when in fact Donner was the sole director.

The Salkinds found themselves coming up short financially, and because they were under pressure from their creditors, demanded that Warner Bros. pay $15 million, ostensibly to purchase additional foreign rights before they would turn over the negative. As Warners had already spent $7 million promoting the film and sold it to some 750 American theaters for its December openings, they felt they had little choice but to pay up. It proved fortuitous for them, as when the film became a massive, global hit, it brought in additional revenues for those territories that more than compensated Warners on their "investment."

Alex Salkind was threatened with arrest by Los Angeles magnate William Foreman, who claimed that Salkind misappropriated some $20 million from his German concern. Salkind escaped prison by citing diplomatic status in Costa Rica and flying down to Mexico under heavy sedation (Salkind suffers from extreme claustrophobia). He later paid Foreman $23.4 million to buy out his interest and insisted that the first *Superman* film had cost an incredible $130 million, though there was no way to confirm that figure.

In order to make the television premiere of *Superman—The Movie* more of an event, and increase the payment they would receive for selling it to television, the Salkinds agreed to assemble a three-hour with commercials version of Donner's film, allowing viewers to see some of the interesting footage that was cut (e.g., a brief shot of Kirk Alyn, the original film Superman, on a train, as Lois' father; Superman overcoming various booby traps in reaching Luthor's lair).

Following his assistance on Dick Donner's *Superman*, Lester was tapped to helm the sequel, *Superman II*, but originally turned it down. Donner had refused to work with Spengler again after their bitter feuds over funds. The Salkinds suggested Hamilton once again, but Warners preferred Donner, though would agree to Lester, who had already turned it down. Warners, delighted that the first film was raking in money for them hand over fist all over the world, then suggested that the producers double Lester's salary and Warners would be willing to pick up the difference if it would get the film into production.

In Andrew Yule's *Richard Lester and the Beatles*, Lester explains his decision to make the movie:

> Frankly, I liked the idea of what was going on, I sussed out that it was going to be dead easy. It was a different way of

> working from what I was used to, with all the sequences storyboarded and no ad-libbing required. I went on to learn more on *Superman II* technically than on all my previous films combined, and enjoyed working with up to four units at a time; if a major problem developed at one unit it was, "Sorry lads, they're desperate for me elsewhere, let me know when you're at the next stage!"

Lester has described the film as one of the smoothest-running productions he has ever made. In addition to Lester's unit, second units were set up under Peter Duffel, production designer John Barry, and veteran director Andre De Toth. Additionally, Donner's material that had already been shot for the second film was at times re-cut, re-voiced, re-scripted, or simply thrown out. The driving force behind the project was to make a movie of comparable quality at a fraction of the original's cost, something simpler and lighter.

Nevertheless, according to Gene Hackman, Donner shot all the scenes with Lex Luthor, and much of the super-battle sequence in Times Square between Superman and the three escaped criminals from the Phantom Zone was initially done under Donner. Scenes with Brando in the second film all had to be scrapped and were re-shot by Lester because after the success of the first film, Brando began demanding larger sums of money for his work, and the Salkinds and Warners decided it would be simpler to just remove Jor-El from the film. (For some reason, Ned Beatty's Otis is also largely absent from the sequel.)

Originally, the missile that Lex Luthor fired at the end of the first Superman film was to strike the Phantom Zone rectangle and set the prisoners free, but it was decided to create a new opening that would give the feeling that some time had passed between films.

Instead, for *Superman II* , the supercriminals, General Zod (Terence Stamp), Ursa (Sarah Douglas), and Non (Jack O'Halloran) are freed from the Phantom Zone after Superman saves Lois Lane from a gang of terrorists, who have secreted a hydrogen bomb on one of the Eiffel Tower's elevators that Superman sends into space where it explodes, inadvertently releasing Krypton's most fearsome villains, who soon begin terrorizing astronauts on the moon. Lester felt that the film should get into superheroics as quickly as possible, since that is what the audience paid to see and would expect. (For viewers unfamiliar with Superman's origin, a montage of scenes from the first film behind the opening credits supply the necessary background information.)

Gene Hackman's scenes as Lex Luthor were filmed by Richard Donner, partially explaining why, for example, Valerie Perrine's Miss Teschmacher makes such a brief token appearance, arriving in a hot air balloon to retrieve Luthor from prison and then disappearing from the rest of the film.

To fill the void left by Brando, Superman now receives instructions from the image of his mother, Lara (Susannah York). Margot Kidder became increasingly unhappy because she felt the Salkinds had tried to screw her out of $40,000 while she was in the middle of a divorce and badly in debt with a child to look after. Consequently, she hired a lawyer and made a million dollar deal for her participation in the sequel, earning the Salkinds' enmity, and they in turn tried to eliminate her from the next sequel.

Lester concentrates the film around resolving Superman's bizarre love triangle, where he as Clark Kent/Superman is his own rival for the affections of Lois Lane. When Lois and Clark are sent to Niagara Falls to expose a honeymoon racket, and she sees Superman suddenly appear to save a drowning child, Lois foolishly attempts to test her theory that Clark is actually Superman by placing herself equally in danger. The inventive Clark quickly figures out a way to save Lois and save face by rescuing her without changing his costume or revealing his superhuman abilities.

However, when Clark's hand accidentally slips into a roaring fireplace without being burned, the game is given away, and Superman decides to confide to Lois all his secrets, taking her to the Fortress of Solitude, which is secretly tucked away in the Arctic. After Lara advises him that if he is to live life with a mortal, he must live as a mortal and sacrifice his powers by exposing himself to rays from Krypton's red sun, he willingly does so for the woman he loves (and for the first time makes love to) only to discover that it couldn't have happened at a worse time.

The three Kryptonian invaders wreak havoc on an Iowa town and then head off to Washington in search of bigger game. Zod declares himself ruler of Earth and challenges anyone to question his sovereignty. Just then, Kent is beaten by a bully in a roadside diner, driving the point home of the difficulties of living as a normal human being. Incredibly, Kent walks all the way back to his Arctic fortress to reverse the process, which presumably could not be reversed, but all it takes is a dose of a green crystal (apparently not green kryptonite, Superman's most notorious weakness) from home.

Superman II is a movie that revels in its comic book origins. Either you are excited at the prospect of seeing superpowerful beings bash at each other with city buses and the like, or you are seeing the wrong movie. The big confrontation is quickly arranged by Luthor, when in exchange for dominion over Australia, he informs the trio that Superman is the son of Jor-El, who had imprisoned them, and would be bound to turn up at the *Daily Planet* eventually.

After a colorfully destructive battle, the supervillains are lured away from the city to Superman's Fortress of Solitude where he tricks them into exposing themselves to the superpower-robbing ray. Then he magically erases Lois'

Richard Lester (center) poses with his *Superman III* producers, Ilya Salkind and Pierre Spengler.

memories of his identity with a superkiss. After a bit of flag-waving, where he carries the American flag back to the White House and its reinstated President (E.G. Marshall in a bad toupee), the film ends with Superman spitefully settling the score with the man in the diner who had beat his alter ego up, whom Kent pushes through a pinball machine and offers the lame explanation, "I've been working out."

Lester's sequel is sillier and less mythic than Donner's original, and so suffers in comparison. Even so, Donner's *Superman* is a sometimes lumbering leviathan with the early, crystal-laden scenes of Krypton and its destruction resembling an Irwin Allen production, but it manages to get its mythic legs once Superman reaches Earth as a child and is raised by Glenn Ford, who plays his adopted father Jonathan Kent. Nor is the first film without its whimsy, as when a desperate Clark spots an open air telephone booth unsuitable for changing when he first arrives in Metropolis, though Ned Beatty's attempts at comedy relief as the bumbling Otis quickly prove tiresome and Hackman's Luthor, though amusing, seems to have stepped out of an episode of the old *Batman* TV series.

Lester's *Superman II*, by contrast, is more tightly controlled but given fewer opportunities to capture the joy of being a superbeing with the power to fly. Its tastefully done bed scene falls short of the romanticism behind the original's flying sequence despite the handicap of being underscored by the execrable "Can You Read My Mind." Lester's take on the concept is less grandiose and less serious with all the benefits and liabilities that implies.

With the money rolling in again, Lester was contacted about *Superman III*, and once more turned it down despite being offered one of the highest salaries ever paid a director. In this case, he should have stuck to his guns, but his wife Deirdre persuaded him that it would be stupid to reject such a fabulous fortune.

Superman III tries to be an all-out camp comedy and in the process quickly becomes the worst of the *Superman* films. Richard Pryor is a terrifically talented comedian, most adept at stand-up comedy, but apart from his concert films, he never really found his legs as a cinematic actor despite his general likeability, comic talents, and appearances in a few extremely successful films. He almost always seemed to work better working from his own material rather than someone else's, and this time his computer nerd character, Gus Gorman, and the humor itself is rather dire.

Lester wanted Pryor because he felt Pryor's naturalness would give the subject a base of reality and reduce the mythic element that he thought had been overdone thus far. He soon discovered that Pryor was unable to say the same line twice in the same way, inventing fresh possibilities every time. After the film was finished, Lester felt he had overindulged the actor and trimmed each of his scenes a bit, but Warner Bros. begged that they be reinstated, and against his better judgment, Lester complied. (Even worse, the Salkinds made a deal for a three-hour with commercials television version, which meant that 19 more minutes of rejected material was reinstated for its network premiere. Unlike the expanded edition of Donner's *Superman*, these new bits added nothing.)

Instead, David and Leslie Newman's unfunny script, this time absent input from Mario Puzo, led to a movie that is more of an anathema. Margot Kidder now squabbled with the producers and was largely written out, with Lana Lang (Annette O'Toole) brought in to take her place as Superman's love interest. At Reeve's insistence, Kidder was given a brief cameo designed to explain her disappearance for the majority of the movie, but this proves little enough compensation. Instead, Superman's love for her seems insincere as he quickly rekindles an old Smallville flame with Lana Lang after he shows up as Kent to his high school reunion, and then as Superman when he saves her son from a chemical plant fire by extinguishing it.

Superman III only flies during its brief Rube Goldberg opening in which Gorman decides to singlemindedly pursue his newfound goal of becoming a computer technician and is oblivious to the chain reaction of disasters he leaves in his wake. The film then becomes subsumed to the idiocies of the plot, which has perennial loser Gorman discover that he has a natural talent as a computer hacker and is soon embezzling thousands of dollars.

His talents come to the attention of Ross Webster (Robert Vaughn in a contemptibly unengaged performance), a crooked megalomaniac intent on taking over the world economy who exploits Gorman's talents in order to reprogram a satellite to create floods and tornadoes to destroy the coffee crop in Columbia (Ross is a ruthless man after money, and the only thing he can think of to go after in Columbia is coffee?!), thereby allowing Webster to dominate the market. However, Superman foils the plot and manages to undo all the damage, making the superhero a target for Webster's rage.

Webster orders Gus to analyze a Kryptonite sample in order to create a weapon to neutralize his enemy, but lacking a new substance, it instead creates an evil Hyde version of Superman (who does cartoony things like straighten the Leaning Tower of Pisa) before the two halves of Superman split in two.

If one felt that the film was as dumb as it possibly could be, it becomes really asinine from there with the two Supermans reunited into one again and then battling Webster's supercomputer-driven mountain fortress's defenses. Gorman's supercomputer transforms Webster's annoying sister Vera (Annie Ross) into a machine and sends missiles after the Man of Steel via images copped from an arcade game. Gorman comes to regret sincerely the trouble he has caused and helps Superman defeat Webster and the computer.

Superman III grossed far less than its predecessor, garnering only $37 million at the domestic box office compared with $65 million for *Superman II*. Nevertheless, when the Salkinds sold the franchise to the Golan/Globus team at Cannon, they offered *Superman IV* to Lester to direct, who once more refused, leaving the job to Sydney J. Furie. Christopher Reeve agreed to do *Superman IV* under the condition that Cannon make a script he was interested in, *Street Smart*, which featured an interesting premise and a stand-out part for Morgan Freeman as a vicious black pimp. Reeve hoped to make an anti-nuclear weapons statement with this latest installment in the series, and so such elements were incorporated into the storyline, and Reeve received story credit along with screenwriters Lawrence Konner and Mark Rosenthal.

(Two screenwriters, Barry Taff and Kenneth Stoller, sued Reeve, Warner Bros. and the Cannon Group for $45 million for ripping off a treatment that had been submitted to him under the title *Superman: The Confrontation*. Reeve claimed that he had never read it but had merely flipped through the pages of the treatment while talking on the phone in order to make it seem as if he had read it thoroughly when he rejected it.)

Superman IV: The Quest for Peace was directed by Sidney J. Furie, and despite being the most genuinely comic bookish film of the series, featuring an effects-filled battle between two super titans (albeit the low budget effects work here is none too convincing), and bringing back Margot Kidder and Gene Hackman, the film's domestic box office take ended up a pitifully small $8 million.

Sadly, there is even talk of a Superman curse, as Christopher Reeve broke his neck in an equestrian accident shortly after completing John Carpenter's remake of *Village of the Damned*, while Margot Kidder had a hard time finding acting jobs and for a brief time became a homeless person who was committed to a mental institution before her case received national attention and she began to make a recovery with sporadic guest appearances on other people's shows. (Such superstitious foolishness always gets concocted whenever tragedy strikes a group connected to a high-profile project.)

Lester then found himself working on project after project which just never got off the ground. These included one with Robin Williams as a Russian comic (no relation to *Moscow on the Hudson*), an adaptation of Joseph Conrad's *Victory*, Garry Trudeau's *Zoo Plane*, and then ended up turning down *The Three Amigos*. He tried to make *Made in Japan*, a comedy about public baths in Japan, which reunited him with Charles Wood, who tried to persuade him to make Donald Barthelme's *The King*, but Lester did not care for it.

Lester has practically made a career of turning down projects for the past three decades including: *A Clockwork Orange; The Master and the Margarita; Myra Breckenridge; Catch-22; The Seven Percent Solution; Plaza Suite; The Wiz; Dick Tracy; Popeye; A Farewell to Arms; Someone Is Killing the Great Chefs of Europe; Meteor; Play It Again, Sam* (before Woody Allen became attached as its star)*; American Hot Wax; Nomads; Sting II; Dog Day Afternoon; Tommy; Don't Look Now; The Sailor Who Fell from Grace with the Sea; The Rose; The Adventures of Baron Munchausen; Man of La Mancha; Private Benjamin; Out of Africa; The Prince of Tides; An Officer and a Gentleman; Return to Oz; Ladyhawke; Fatal Attraction; Romancing the Stone; Best Friends; Little Dorrit;*

Author! Author!; Scandal; At Play in the Fields of the Lord; Taipan; Desperately Seeking Susan; Into the Night; Leviathan; The Mosquito Coast; Flashdance; Cocoon; Clue; The Princess Bride; Gorky Park; a Dino De Laurentiis remake of *20,000 Leagues Under the Sea; Scaramouche; Good Morning, Vietnam; Something Wicked This Way Comes; Highlander*, and *Evita.*

Dino De Laurentiis had sent several projects to Lester, who politely turned them down as he did not feel he was the right director for the subject. When De Laurentiis, having exhausted the goodwill of most of the major studios who had been stung by his expensive flops, decided to open up his own studios in Wilmington, North Carolina, he contacted Lester for advice about what films to make with the understanding that Lester would be allowed to make one film a year provided it had a budget no higher than $5 million.

Lester found a project that excited him that had just foundered over at MGM, but De Laurentiis and his committees declared it "unfunny" and so the rights to *A Fish Called Wanda*, one of the best comedies of modern times, reverted back to MGM. Lester would propose projects that would be rejected, and he in turn rejected the projects, such as *Dune II* and a low budget version of *Total Recall*, that Dino offered him. Despite the *succès d'estime* of David Lynch's *Blue Velvet*, DEG (for De Laurentiis Entertainment Group) went quickly bankrupt after the release of its disastrous production slate without Lester ever having made a film for them.

Shortly afterwards, daughter Rafaella tried to interest him in directing a film about a reindeer called *Prancer*, while Dino himself offered him *Once Upon a Crime*, both of which Lester turned down.

When Lester finally did get something together, it was the decidedly lackluster *Finders Keepers*, based on Charles Dennis' novel *The Next to Last Train to Ride.* Lester agreed to do the film as a favor to Terence Marsh, his production designer on *Juggernaut* and *Royal Flash.* The picture desperately needed another re-write to prevent it from becoming the pathetic kooky caper comedy it actually became. Sadly, neither Michael O'Keefe nor Beverly D'Angelo seem up to the demands of their roles, despite able support from Louis Gossett, Jr., Ed Lauter, Pamela Stephenson, Brian Dennehy, and David Wayne stealing the show as the world's oldest conductor. The film may be best remembered now as the cinematic debut of comic Jim Carrey. The end result was a frantic but unfunny farce about characters including con artists and a bumbling hitman in search of $5 million hidden in a coffin on a train that heads nowhere fast.

Lester then came down with hepatitis in October 1987, which put him out of action for half a year. Spengler had split from the Salkinds and considered making a sequel to the Musketeer movies, depending on Michael York's participation. Once York agreed, Spengler submitted to Lester who found the idea appealing, and they contacted George MacDonald Fraser to adapt Dumas' own sequel, the never-before-filmed *Twenty Years After*, which would be retitled *The Return of the Musketeers.*

Most of the original cast readily agreed to return, although Richard Chamberlain would only give one week of his time. C. Thomas Howell was cast as the son of Athos with Kim Cattrall cast as Milady's daughter (a son in the Dumas version altered to attract a female lead). As Richilieu would be dead, Philippe Noiret was brought in to play Cardinal Mazzaras. Even Christopher Lee returned as Rochefort, despite his character unquestionably being killed at the end of *The Four Musketeers.* Oliver Reed, Frank Finlay, Geraldine Chaplin, Jean-Pierre Cassel, and Roy Kinnear all play their old roles.

Spengler set the film up as a $10 million British-French-Spanish coproduction. Unfortunately, tragedy clouded the production midway through when Roy Kinnear's horse threw him, fracturing his pelvis, and he died of shock and hemorrhage the next day. Lester was beside himself with grief and wanted to abandon the picture, but Spengler begged him to finish it, and York, Reed, and Finlay all agreed. (York would later accuse Lester of being callous towards Kinnear's widow Carmel because he was initially unable to comfort or console her. Lester, who had worked with Kinnear for years, knew that Roy would not have been on that horse but for him. Still recovering from hepatitis, he kept away from everyone except when he was working on the set.)

Following a couple disastrous previews, Universal declined to release the film theatrically, sending it directly to cable years later in this country. In Britain, the film was savaged by the press. Depressed by the loss of Kinnear, whose death continues to haunt him, Lester lost interest both in the film and in filmmaking that carried any element of risk, which is almost a prerequisite of comedy.

This is sad in that *Return of the Musketeers* is actually one of the better latter-day Lester films, which in its jaunty spirit at times captures the fun of its predecessor. Unfortunately, the plot hinges on a rescue attempt for Charles I of England, and any history buff knows how that mission will turn out. The cast is quite talented and comfortable with their roles, and Lester manages several inventive bits of slapstick comedy. The result puts to shame most recent satirical swashbucklers that have failed to recapture the zesty fun of the genre and seem to prefer to concentrate on costumes and elaborate stunts than capturing the characters and the spirit which made such films endearing and enduring in the first place.

Lester's last film thus far has been his documentary *Get*

Back recording Paul McCartney's 1989–1990 concert tour. McCartney's band includes Chris Whitten on drums, Hamish Stuart and Robbie McIntosh, both formerly of the Average White Band, on guitar; and Paul "Wix" Wickens and Linda McCartney on keyboards, while McCartney himself plays bass, piano, and occasionally both electric and acoustic guitar. The film includes twenty numbers, fourteen of which come from the Beatles' repertoire. Lester's direction is fairly subdued. The camera doesn't whip around the stage, trying to catch Paul's every move, but then, McCartney has never been a particularly physical performer. Instead, the visuals are a combination of shots that capture the experience and evocative newsreel montages of both the Beatles and nonmusical events from the sixties. Lester seems to be combining the best material from several shows, showcasing performances from all over the world.

Lester was also tapped by McCartney to prepare a special fifteen-minute film of images that linger most vividly from the past to the present (from the moon landing to Tiananmen Square), along with footage of Paul and his family, which is projected by three projectors and accompanied by six songs. The short was shown as a warm-up for the concert, but which is not included in *Get Back*.

Mostly, *Get Back* captures McCartney's joy in performing, taking Beatles songs that had heretofore never been performed live by their composer and trotting them out for admiring and enthusiastic fans all over the world. With all of Lester's talent, this is still a performer's film and not a director's one. Lester now seems content to rest on his laurels and his investments. Having had a long-ranging career fashioning some truly memorable and unusual films, Lester is certainly entitled to a dignified retirement, having made notable contributions to the thriller, swashbuckler, and science fiction genres as well as establishing a style in the sixties that was distinctly his own.

EUGÈNE LOURIÉ (1903–1991)

The Beast from 20,000 Fathoms (1953); *Napoleon* (2nd Unit only, 1954); *Si Paris Nous Était Conté* (2nd Unit only, 1955); *The Colossus of New York* (1958); *The Giant Behemoth* (aka *Behemoth the Sea Monster*) (1959); *Gorgo; Back Street* (2nd Unit only) (1961); *That Touch of Mink* (2nd Unit only); *A Crack in the World* (2nd Unit only, 1965)

Television: *Foreign Intrigue* (six episodes) (1955); "Away Borders," *Telephone Hour* (1956); *The Chemical Story* (1958); "Chemical Story," *World of giants* (1959)

Eugène Lourié is better noted as one of the greatest art directors and production designers of the movies than as a film director, but his entire directorial *oeuvre* was in the science fiction genre. He was born in Kharkov, Russia, in 1903, which he described as being "full of turmoil for my family and me: war, revolution, exile, and eventual escape to Turkey, then France."

In 1911, while still in Kharkov, Lourié experienced the cinema for the first time, and recalls loyally following the exploits of Pearl White in *The Perils of Pauline* and those of Eddie Polo in *The King of the Circus* despite the violent happenings of the Russian Revolution in 1917. His first work for a film was two years later in Yalta where he worked as an extra in Volkov's *Black Crows*.

The following year in Istanbul, Lourié arranged to get a job at a cinema arranging its publicity campaign. He would draw and paint new posters for the biweekly changes of program, in exchange for money and a spot atop the theater's grand piano to sleep on at night. He eventually lost the job to a clever competitor who convinced the owner that he would paint posters faster, better, for less money and with Turkish lettering that Lourié relied on a Turkish painter to help him with.

By 1921, Lourié finally made it to Paris, where one of his first jobs was as a scenery painter at France's Albatross studios. There he was initially assigned by art director Loshakov to paint the top of some 40 foot columns for director Ivan Mosjouchine's *Le Brasuer ardent* (aka *The Fiery Furnace*). Eventually, Lourié became Loshakov's assistant, though his primary objective had been to study painting at an art school and had initially taken the studio job as temporary summer work.

Lourié did spend some time painting murals and stage scenery for theaters, but he still received and accepted offers of film work, designing costumes for *Le Joueur d'échecs* (aka *The Chessplayer*) and *Cagliostro*. At last he decided to

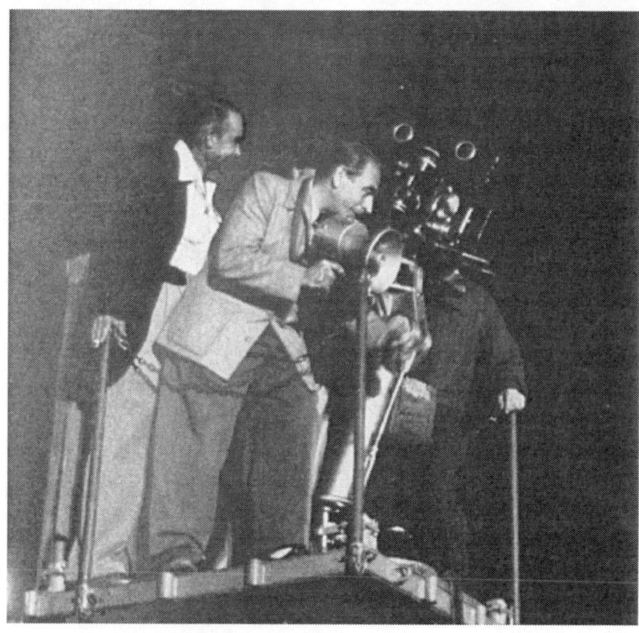

Eugene Lourié (with megaphone) directing a Long Beach night shoot for *The Beast from 20,000 Fathoms.*

become a full-fledged production designer, responsible for choosing the locations where a film will be shot; for supervising the choosing and placing of the furniture, the set dressing, the colors used in the sets; for designing and coordinating the construction of new sets when they are needed; for supervising the making of hundreds of action sketches, the storyboards that illustrate the continuity of the shooting script; for creating the pretty paintings that show what the sets will look like; and for conferring with the director during the preparation of the film and often during the actual shooting, as well as tackling those day-to-day problems that occur during the shooting and preparation of films.

In collaboration with Alexandre Benois and Pierre Schildknecht, Lourié worked on Abel Gance's silent epic *Napoleon.* He collaborated on several of Jean Renoir's greatest films including *Les Bas Fonds* (English title: *The Lower Depths*), *La Grande Illusion, La Bête humaine, La Règle du jeu* (English title: *The Rules of the Game*), *This Land Is Mine, The Southerner, The River,* and *The Diary of a Chambermaid.* Several of these films have been universally declared as all-time masterpieces of cinema. Lourié himself suggested Renoir as the director for *The Lower Depths* to Alexander Kamenka, head of Albatross Pictures, over Kamenka's choice of Tourjansky because Lourié felt that Renoir would bring a more unexpected and fresh approach and be more in tune with a modern French audience. (He and Renoir agreed to make the story more universal and to eliminate anything specifically Russian — no samovars, icons, Russian boots, and Russian beards.)

However, Lourié's strength was the realism of his designs, and this realism is better seen in *La Grande Illusion* and *Rules of the Game,* Renoir's masterpieces, and *La Bête humaine,* the latter freely adapted from Zola. Lourié gave up the elaborateness of his previous designs to concentrate only on the essential. Reality is captured so precisely that both films give the impression of being shot on location whereas all the interiors were shot on sets. (For scenes requiring vistas from windows, Lourié would set up only one false wall on location and have the rest of the scene shot in the studio.) Lourié also did production work for Max Ophuls' *Werther.*

Lourié came to the United States, and arriving in New York, met Julien Duvivier and Anatole Litvak, both of whom tried to dissuade him from going to Hollywood. Ironically, a short time later Lourié designed Duvivier's film *The Imposter* and Litvak's film *The Long Night.* Lourié began his career in Hollywood as a technical adviser on fellow countryman and *emigré* Robert Florey's *The Desert Song.* His first work as a production designer in Hollywood was on Jean Renoir's polemical *This Land Is Mine,* followed by work on Roy Willian Neill's Sherlock Holmes adventure *House of Fear* and Walter Reisch's *Song of Scheherazade.* He was especially proud of the work he did on Zoltan Korda's *Sahara* (where Korda was subjected to contempt from his star Humphrey Bogart, who would have preferred that a friend of his direct the project, except Korda was the one who owned the rights), Robert Siodmak's *The Strange Affair of Uncle Harry* (a film compromised by its censorship-imposed unrealistic Hollywood ending), John Brahms' *The Diamond Queen,* Chaplin's *Limelight,* Richard Quine's *So This Is Paris,* Michael Anderson's *Flight from Ashiya,* Curtis Harrington's *What's the Matter with Helen?,* Sam Fuller's *Shock Corridor* and *The Naked Kiss,* and Clint Eastwood's *Bronco Billy.*

Having worked as an art director, Lourié felt, was excellent preparation to becoming a director, because in designing one has to visualize the action as well as the settings, to work under tight budgets and short schedules, to make thorough preparations including breaking down shooting scripts into individual shots.

In the early spring of 1952, Lourié was called by Hal Chester, one of the producers of Mutual Films (the others being Jack Dietz and editor Bernie Burton). They planned to produce three low-budget films for an independent circuit of regional distributors, and asked Lourié if he would be interested in doing art direction for their three pictures.

One of the outlines they had, *The Monster from Beneath the Sea,* was about a prehistoric dinosaur coming alive after being frozen in the Arctic for millions of years. As Lourié explained to Paul Mandell in *Fantastic Films* #14:

> The scripts for these films didn't exist at that time; I was just given the stories in rough outline form. Of the three, one of them interested me — the one for *The Beast*. It presented a kind of challenge. When I asked Dietz as to who will direct this picture, he said: "On our budget, we don't know!" The budget was $150,000 — who could direct this picture for so little money? I told him that nobody will direct on his money and his schedule, but if he wanted, I would do it. Dietz took it as a joke! Three weeks later he called me and said: "Are you serious?" I said yes, that I was always interested in directing a motion picture but the opportunity had never presented itself until now. Dietz said, "Okay, you have a job, but take care of the script first!" So I began to work with writers and developed it. And strangely enough, the prison escape material fell into the hands of Dave Diamond some years later, the man who produced *The Giant Behemoth* for me. I wrote a script for him (together with my friend Dan Hyatt) entitled *Revolt in the Big House*, and it was produced by Allied Artists in 1958.

Jack Dietz called back and explained that Mutual abandoned the idea of doing three films, but they would like to go ahead with the dinosaur saga. Having only an outline to work from, Lourié needed to get a usable script. He consulted with a writer who wished to remain anonymous because of blacklisting (and whom Lourié refused to name) and began to construct a storyline showing live characters and action. While Lourié claims he and the unnamed writer wrote 80 percent of the script, screen credit went to Fred Freiberger and Lou Morheim, who were hired to polish the script.

Lourié quickly settled on stop motion animation as being the best way to bring their dinosaur to life, though he himself had no previous experience with stop motion. Chester explained that Willis O'Brien was too expensive (final production costs on *Mighty Joe Young* had soared to $2.5 million), but he had contacted a young animator who had assisted O'Brien with *Mighty Joe Young* named Ray Harryhausen. Harryhausen understood that for his technique to be appealing to producers, he must bring the costs down, and that he could do so by utilizing fewer miniatures and glass paintings than O'Brien had, using front and rear projection and split screen techniques instead.

Lourié met with Harryhausen in his garage, which also served as his workshop, where he was filming *Rapunzel*, one of his stop motion "Mother Goose Stories" shorts. Harryhausen showed the erstwhile director some footage, and Lourié was impressed with the smoothness of the movements. Harryhausen suggested that they buy from RKO the special equipment they had built for *King Kong*, a small-scale stop-motion, rear-projection camera. With this camera, Harryhausen could matte out certain portions of live action shots, animate the beast in front of this projection, make contre-mattes, and reproject the formerly matted out action without the footage going to a costly and time-consuming specialized film lab.

Lourié became convinced that Harryhausen would do a good job and would be a valuable partner. Fortunately, Harryhausen had the skills and patience needed — it can often take six to eight hours to animate one minute of film, which requires 1,440 frames to be exposed — and wanted to launch himself on a solo effects career. It would take Harryhausen a full six months to complete all the effects for *The Beast from 20,000 Fathoms*.

The Beast from 20,000 Fathoms begins in the frozen immensities of the Arctic seas, an experimental blast of an atomic device melts huge amounts of ice, freeing and bringing to life a prehistoric dinosaur, which had been in suspended animation for millions of years. Hereditary instinct and sea currents drive the animal south where it meets up with a hostile civilized world. The same basic idea made up the climax of *The Lost World*, which Willis O'Brien created in 1925, which ends with an apotosaurus running rampant through the streets of London much as the dinosaur does in *Beast*. Rather than pay a high price for the rights, Lourié came across a short story by Ray Bradbury called "The Foghorn," which is simply about a dinosaur who is attracted to the wail of a foghorn, mistaking it for a mating call from another of its species. The dinosaur crawls out of the ocean, destroys the lighthouse, and slithers back into the sea.

As Bradbury had a following, especially among science fiction circles, Jack Dietz believed it would be advantageous to add his name to the main titles, acquired the rights to the story, and the lighthouse incident was incorporated into the narrative, an incident that takes up only a couple scant minutes of screentime.

After breaking down the costs of the picture, Lourié estimated they would need a budget of $200,000, which was given the green light. Lourié did rough sketches of what the beast should look like and turned them over to Harryhausen, who made his own modifications. Stages were rented at the Motion Picture Center studios on Cahuenga in Hollywood, while Harryhausen set about constructing the dinosaur and preparing his mini-animation studio.

In July of 1952, Lourié traveled to New York with Burton for a week to shoot process plates and background scenes on the waterfront and streets of lower Manhattan. It was vitally important that the camera remain absolutely steady to avoid jerkiness of motion when the footage would be used as background for the frame-by-frame animation. Lourié worked with a minimal crew: a production manager who also served as assistant and script clerk; one able cameraman and his assistant; and one grip, who carried equipment in his station wagon, which also served as their camera car and platform for high set-ups.

As a guide for Harryhausen, Lourié made sketches as to where the beast would be placed in each shot, keeping in mind the relative sizes of the beast and cars, people, and the surrounding buildings. Harryhausen would look these over and make occasional improvements.

Some Greenwich Village intellectuals were hired to impersonate Fulton pier stevedores, but they proved unsatisfactory, so some regular fish market stevedores were recruited (according to Lourié, they were eager to be photographed so that they could show their wives that they had not been drinking on the job). For the big crowd scenes in downtown Manhattan the next day, the budget only allowed for the hiring of 50 extras and 29 cars, but only 25 extras and 12 cars showed up on site because local rules required that extras working on Sunday had to be paid double and the unit production manager refused to authorize the additional expense.

To overcome this difficulty, Lourié designed his shots so that every scene was very short, while the tempo of running crowds remain undiminished. Quick montages of these short scenes gave the impression of a running multitude, plus additional shooting would occur later in Hollywood on the New York street set at Paramount with some 400 extras on hand. The location shooting simply allowed for the filmmakers to employ recognizable landmarks for greater believability. The entire New York junket cost only $5,000.

For his leads, Lourié selected an actor he had seen in *The Thief of Venice*, Paul Christian (aka Paul Hubschmid), who had an engaging personality, to play Tom Nesbitt, the man who first spots the beast, described as a "rhedosaurus," and the likewise affable Cecil Kellaway to play Prof. Thurgood Elson, the world's greatest paleontologist. Paula Raymond was assigned the role of Lee Hunter, the requisite female scientist and love interest. Kenneth Tobey, star of *The Thing*, has a nothing part as a single-minded military man. To give an interesting dimension to Kellaway's museum office, Lourié was able to retrieve and rent the dinosaur skeleton from Howard Hawks' *Bringing Up Baby* and had it reconstructed on the set.

Tobey recalled, "I suppose they got me for *Beast from 20,000 Fathoms* because of *The Thing*. It starts out the same, up in the arctic. It was a very short shoot, compared to *The Thing* just a couple years earlier. We may have had three or four weeks on *Beast*. The director, a French guy named Gene Lourié, was a nice man, but I didn't think he had a lot of experience with actors. It was his first film. So we've got a lot of dialogue up there in the arctic scenes where it's overlapping. That's my contribution. I think it helps the atmosphere."

Unlike most Hollywood films which use "day for night," Lourié did some night shooting at the Pike Amusement Center in Long Beach for the scenes in the deserted dark streets where, lit by searchlights, army columns advance, following the blood puddles left by the wounded beast in its escape toward the sea. (Because of its exposure to radiation, many of the soldiers following the beast become violently ill.) These and the scenes of crowds panicking were expertly photographed by Jack Russell, whose moody, realistic lighting adds immeasurably to the film.

The total shooting for the film was completed in twelve days: nine days shooting on the three stages of the Motion Picture Center, one day of shooting on the Paramount street, and two nights in Long Beach, where the rollercoaster scenes were filmed. A young Lee van Cleef was hired to play the sharpshooter who stops the beast with an isotope gun.

Lourié felt that some scenes in the final film didn't work particularly well, but neither he nor Harryhausen had the opportunity to reshoot any scene. For the most part, the feature is very effective, adopting a rapid pace, and Lourié captures a true feeling of panic in the streets as well as poignant loneliness on the part of the creature as it becomes trapped in Wall Street or caught in the middle of a flaming rollercoaster (actually an elaborate eight-foot miniature that was coated with rubber cement for rapid burning and precut sections pulled by wires to create the action of the beast tearing it apart).

The harshest criticism Lourié received came from his own daughter, who cried, "You are bad, Daddy, bad. You killed the nice beast."

Once he saw the finished picture, Jack Dietz realized that the picture was too good for his regional distributors and so sought a national distributor. He offered the film to Jack Warner, who was more interested in buying it outright than releasing it. Warner had contacted his production manager, Tony Wright, to ask him how much a picture like *Beast* would cost. Wright replied that Warners wouldn't be able to do it for less than a million, so Warner settled with Dietz for $450,000.

It was Warner who retitled the film *The Beast from 20,000 Fathoms*, which coincided with the title of Bradbury's story when it was originally published, and he ordered a new score written for the film by David Buttolph and inserted a useless ballet sequence to a scene of Nesbitt at a theater, but otherwise left the film unaltered. With some exuberant fanfare and publicity, the picture quickly became a huge success, grossing over $5 million at the box office at the end of the first year of release, making it one of 1953's largest grossers, a profit in which Mutual, Lourié and Harryhausen did not share.

Lourié's direction doesn't completely overcome the

film's dull dialogue and plotting in places, but it is imaginative and does give the film a good, distinctive look. His direction is best in the film's major setpieces which include some highly memorable highlights. He is aided by Harryhausen's animation, which invests the beast with some personality including a furtive, sometimes cat-like quality, especially in the thrilling climax.

According to Lourié in *My Work in Films*, after *Beast* he "was getting scripts and offers to direct some sci-fi pictures, all of them unbelievably bad...." Instead, he returned to production designing, did second unit direction on two films for writer-director Sacha Guitry, *Napoleon* and *Si Paris M'Etait Conté*. He also directed several episodes of the syndicated series *Foreign Intrigue* that were set in Stockholm. However, he retained his interest in science fiction, writing a story called "Green Invasions" about plant samples brought back from outer space which grow alarmingly, causing London to be reduced into a shambles by the seemingly indestructible greens, but he was unable to generate enough interest to transform his concept into a film.

Lourié made a deal with Alexander Korda and bought an option on Jules Verne's *Journey to the Center of the Earth* in hopes of making a film of it at RKO, but the studio foundered before the film could be made, and Lourié found that his services had been sold to Joseph Schenck Enterprises. (A few years later Schenck sold the project to Charles Brackett, who would produce the film with Henry Levin directing Brackett's adaptation over at 20th Century–Fox.)

After several successful films featuring giant insects, producer Jack Dietz had the idea for *The Black Scorpion*, and talked Lourié into directing. Lourie began preparing the film and since Harryhausen was unavailable, contacted Willis O'Brien, who at 70 turned animation chores over to his assistant Pete Peterson, who had delightfully animated the scenes with Joe in the back of the truck for *Mighty Joe Young*. Sadly, Peterson was a victim of multiple sclerosis, making the painstaking work of stop motion animation very difficult for him. Lourié worked on the preliminary design of the scorpion and helped design tests with O'Brien and Peterson, who were working out of a garage in the San Fernando Valley. Lourié also worked with a relative of Dietz's on the script for the film, and began filming when he had a falling out with Frank Melford, Dietz's associate, and so left the film.

Edward Ludwig inherited the job after Lourié dropped out. Though not often cited, *Black Scorpion* is one of the better giant bug movies, lagging behind Douglas' *Them!* but well ahead of Juran's *The Deadly Mantis* or Bert I. Gordon's *Earth vs. the Spider*. It was Lourié who brought in Willis O'Brien and Pete Peterson to do *Black Scorpion*'s effects, the main reason the film is remembered today. Unlike most of their oversized brethren, the giant scorpions are not caused by atomic mutation but are simply prehistoric creatures freed by an erupting volcano. The film stars Richard Denning and Carlos Rivas as colorless geologists who put a stop to the scorpions' sudden rampage. While portions of the film are atmospheric and some of the effects are impressive (though an oversized, drooling and unlikely scorpion head shown frequently is not among them), there is an air of incompleteness about it, giving credence to stories that the producers ran out of funds before they were able to properly finish the film.

Lourié bought the rights to a British SF novel entitled *High Vacuum*, which he hoped to make into a movie called *Moonwreck*. In it, a female stowaway on a lunar expedition throws a spaceship off course, causing it to crash-land in a radioactive lunar crater. The crew face a taut situation because there is not enough oxygen for all of them, but they are fortuitously rescued by a Russian expedition. Despite the advent of Sputnik, Lourié couldn't get the project off the ground.

"Then a producer, Dave Diamond, asked me to direct a modestly budgeted coproduction for Allied Artists and England's Eros Films," recalls Lourié. "It was to deal with another kind of monster; this time not a live creature but a blob of expanding radiation. To complete this deal between AA and the English coproducers, Dave had to present the shooting script. Once again I was caught by the reputation of *Beast*. The English producers insisted that our story had to deal with a visible physical creature, a monster, and they let us understand that it should be a duplication of *The Beast from 20,000 Fathoms*."

While waiting for the go-ahead on *The Giant Behemoth*, Lourié was offered *The Colossus of New York*, which was designed to be a cofeature to Jack Arnold's *The Space Children* and was likewise produced by William Alland. Lourié was intrigued by the premise which involved transplanting a scientist's brain into a robot body resulting in a loss of humanity. Alland told Tom Weaver in *Monsters, Mutants, and Heavenly Creatures*:

> I hired a guy named Gene Lourié to be the art director and he persuaded me to let him direct it, and this was a great mistake. It was a far more poignant story, and had far more meaning, than Lourié put into it.... A lot of stuff with the Colossus was just blown through the nose. Particularly the scenes in which he sees himself— realizes what he is — and the horror of that. The relationship with his *father*, the relationship with his own *son* [Charles Herbert], it was blown through the nose, it was not done with the sense of timing and feeling that it *could* have had. *Details* in that film were lost, key elements that would have made it better.

Whereas Lourié told Paul Mandell in *Fantastic Films* #17, "There was no script yet but the premise appeared challenging. However, a week or so before shooting, the script appears and it was worse than expected! I pleaded with Bill Alland to postpone production and concentrate on writing a better script, but to no avail. So we started on the promised date, around the end of 1957, and shot it in eight days. I remember very little of the actual shooting as I remember very little of the scarlet fever I had when I was eight years old."

In *Fantastic Films* #25, lead actor Ross Martin, who played Dr. Jeremy Spensser in the movie as well as providing the eerie voice of Colossus, recalled, "Mr. Lourié was a little tentative; he didn't jump in with both feet. He was very gentle with the actors, an extremely kind, extremely thoughtful kind of director. He wasn't crisp or aggressive about telling us what he wanted and where he wanted us to go. It was more of a search, more European in style, I would guess, than it was American. And he was under the kind of pressure you get in television. We were on a very short shooting schedule."

The Colossus of New York concerns how a father, Dr. William Spensser (Otto Kruger) cannot accept his son's death. Dr. Jeremy Spensser is killed when he rushes into a street to retrieve his son's toy plane and is struck by a truck. The elder Dr. Spensser is a brilliant surgeon and calls upon his other son Henry (John Baragrey), an expert in automation and robots, to fashion a mechanized body to house Jeremy's brain. The result, Colossus (played by Ed Wolff), resembles an eight-foot robot wearing a cloak, though a true robot would have a mechanical and not a human brain.

Although Jeremy's brain is saved, it takes a long time for it to become aware, and in the process, it develops precognitive abilities (it predicts the collision of the *Andrea Doria* and the *Stockholm*) and loses almost all human compassion, though it retains enough human emotion to be distressed at its appearance. It also develops hypnotic powers.

Going outside, it encounters his son Billy (Herbert) and tells him he is a giant. (The son is scripted as something of a dimbulb who from then on refers to the Colossus as "Mr. Giant" and asks, "Are you a good giant or a bad giant?") Colossus heads back to the lab where he is furious at his father for misleading him (William caused him to believe that Jeremy's wife and son were both dead), smashes the remote control that could shut his power off, and forces his father to gather enough money for him to get away.

Colossus clumps off into the East River (with clump-clump sounds inanely dubbed in), but changes his mind, climbs some steps leading out of the river (via reversed footage), and kills Henry with rays that burst from his eyes. (Why his body is equipped with such rays we never learn.) Back at the lab, he smashes a project intended to help mankind, announcing his intention to rid the world of humanitarians. He carries through on his threat by attacking people in the United Nations building. Espying his son, he picks Billy up and requests that the lad shut him off because he realizes that "without a soul, there's nothing but monstrousness" and he doesn't think he can stop himself. The boy complies, the Colossus dies, a trickle in its eyes.

Cornball stuff to be certain, though it borrows from some potent myths, namely *Frankenstein* and *The Golem* with a bit of *Donovan's Brain* thrown in for good measure. What helps make the film particularly ponderous is Nathan Van Cleave's solo piano score, which is unusual but not appropriate. (*Variety* speculated that a musicians' strike was behind the odd choice.)

Wolff, who played the Colossus, appeared as The Gocko in the 1936 serial *Flash Gordon* and was the fly-headed man in *Return of the Fly*. He does not do much to inject personality in the cyborg apart from walk around stiffly and jerkily. Nor, with the exception of Martin, are the other performances more than perfunctory.

Why Jeremy Spensser loses all compassion or his soul once his brain is transplanted is open to question. Are we to believe that the transplantation of organs is inherently evil? That there are some things with which man is not to meddle? No, it's simply an ill-thought out horror gimmick going back to works such as *Alarune* where a woman conceived out of artificial insemination is "soulless" or *The Hands of Orlac* where the personality of a killer becomes transplanted with his hands.

Eugène Lourié's heart was obviously not in this unusual low budget effort, though he does generate a bit of suspense. Unfortunately, the complicated relationships that might have made this story poignant are never properly explored in Thelma Schnee's hackneyed script, and Alland is right that Lourié left the story's emotional possibilities largely unexplored.

Lourié was approached by producer David Diamond to direct *The Giant Behemoth*, a film based on a story written by Robert Abel and Allen Adler. In *Fantastic Films* #15, Lourié told Paul Mandell that "The only element specific was that there was something electrically charged and dangerous—a kind of strange radioactive substance floating on the water.... I started to work, trying to invent visual means to translate the dangers of radiation. But the basic concept did not sit well with the distributors."

When a decent script was not quickly forthcoming, Lourié collaborated with Daniel Hyatt and rushed through a rough draft in 10 days. The script was largely plagiarized from *Beast* and was intended simply as a *pro forma* document to be used only to sign the producers' contract, and then drastically changed and developed in London where they had to start preparations at once. Unfortunately, there never proved to be enough time to rewrite the script for what became *The Giant Behemoth.*

Diamond hired Jack Rabin and his associates to do the effects for the film for $20,000, and they handled the live action effects, subcontracting the film's stop motion and miniature effects to famed animators Willis O'Brien and Pete Peterson, with help from Phil Kellison, who built some of the miniatures destroyed by the Behemoth. Kellison also created a wire controlled head of the creature for a scene where it sinks a ferry, to which O'Brien added a highly detailed skin covering using a latex casting of a real iguana, but unfortunately another special effects technician broke the controls, so the head remains relatively immobile in those scenes.

Lobby card for *The Colossus of New York* in which Billy (Charles Herbert) points the way for Colossus, his father turned robot (Ed Wolff). The film falls short of its intended pathos.

Unlike the six months O'Brien and Peterson had for *The Black Scorpion,* they had to complete their effects for *The Giant Behemoth* in six to eight weeks, with the result that much of their work is used again and again, either reversed, enlarged, or simply repeated (a shot of the Behemoth's foot crushing a car is repeated three times, and one can even spot a split in the foot model). In order to trim the time and expense costs for building miniatures, carefully lit cut out photographic enlargements were used to provide backgrounds for the special effects scenes. To create miniatures for the ferry scene, Kellison purchased English Dinky toy replicas of the cars on the Ferry and built his ferry to scale (about 30 inches long), which was then filmed in Rabin's 20 foot studio water tank. To create the gas tank that explodes, Irving Block simply stacked up a bunch of film cans and superimposed an explosion over them to save the cost of building another miniature.

While *The Giant Behemoth* is largely a low budget retread, it does benefit from superior performances by its leads, Gene Evans and André Morell, who play American marine biologist Steve Karnes and nuclear physicist Prof. James Bickford respectively. Karnes is concerned with the dangers of radioactive waste (making *The Giant Behemoth* one of the first SF films to tackle this issue) and theorizes that something large in the sea could soon become powerfully radioactive, perhaps even mutated.

Lourié shot the film on location documentary style, which adds a feeling of realism to the proceedings. The careful way Lourié framed his shots demonstrates his ability to produce interesting compositions that balance background and foreground elements to help tell the story. Sequences encourage a fascination with the processes that Karnes uses to uncover the mystery, including testing specimens for radioactive contamination.

When a fisherman dies covered with strange burns, and thousands of dead fish wash up on shore, Karnes becomes even more concerned and heads to Cornwall. Karnes and Bickford discover that the fish were killed by radiation.

Finally, the monster comes ashore, with waves of radiation emanating from it (thereby keeping the creature menacing while minimizing the need for shots of the critter interacting with the human characters — the radiation coming from it is more deadly than the creature itself), killing a farmer and destroying his farm. It leaves behind a footprint, which is photographed and taken to paleontologist Dr. Sampson (Jack MacGowran), who delightedly recognizes it as a "paleosaurus." When Karnes theorizes that the monster is dying of its own radiation, the paleontologist explains that "paleosaurs" will head for fresh water to die in, *ergo* it is probably heading for the Thames.

The Behemoth reaches London and wreaks the usual havok, killing Dr. Sampson in the process. Karnes and Bickford point out that blowing up the Behemoth is out of the question, as that would rain deadly radioactive chunks all over the city, and therefore the best course of action would be to increase its radioactivity by firing a

Gorgo contemplates attacking the Tower Bridge as Lourié wrecks London yet again.

radium-tipped torpedo into it. Eventually the rampaging beast is subdued by the torpedo, but the film ends with a report that thousands of dead fish have turned up in America.

Once more Lourié's direction is both atmospheric and inventive, but the inadequate budget prevents *The Giant Behemoth* from eclipsing *The Beast from 20,000 Fathoms*. However, the stop-motion Behemoth is still more effective than those numerous rampaging monsters-in-rubber-suits films from Japan, and as noted earlier, there are some very credible performances and no tacked-on love interest for a change. Lourié however regretted his lack of involvement in the postproduction process this time around, and felt that the film suffered for it. He resolved to have greater control in the future.

Producer Dave Diamond had Lourié and screenwriter Dan Hyatt write an original prison escape film that would utilize a number of already existing stock shots. The pair came up with the script for the film *Revolt in the Big House*, which was produced by Diamond for Allied Artists. Lourié also worked on *The Minotaur*, based on a number of Greek myths and centering around the story of Theseus, his slaying of the Minotaur, his love of Adriane, and the subjugation of Athens by King Minos. Lourié prepared paintings of the film's elaborate special effects shots and took it to producer Bill Forman, who passed, feeling that it was too childish. Lourié also presented the project to Walt Disney, who likewise decided to turn it down. A short time later, Italian director Silvio Amadio made a very low budget version of *The Minotaur*, and many of Lourié's visual ideas were reproduced in Ray Harryhausen's *Jason and the Argonauts*.

Following *The Giant Behemoth*, the King Brothers, having seen the grosses on Japan's giant monster films such as *Godzilla* and *Rodan*, asked Lourié if he had an idea similar to *Beast*. They wanted another film, this time in color, with a prehistoric monster being put in a circus. Frank and Maurice King had secured some Japanese partners with the intention of shooting the film in and around Japan, and asked Lourié, who had been hoping to adapt the British SF novel *High Vacuum* about four astronauts trapped on the moon as *Moonwreck*, if he would be interested in directing it and had any fresh ideas for it.

Lourié decided to go back to the well once again, and in *Gorgo* offering two monsters instead of one. He wanted them to be strikingly different in size, first with a monster of relatively modest dimensions, say 30 feet tall and twice the size of an elephant, which the heroes catch and imprison in a zoo. In the second part of the film, a gigantic beast appears and it proves to be the mother of the first beast come to rescue her baby. Lourié kept a promise to his daughter in that this time the monsters would not be killed but simply slip peacefully back into the sea.

Together with writing partner Daniel Hyatt, Lourié crafted a story they called *Kuru Island*, which took place on one of the Pacific islands and in Tokyo, Japan. Lourié felt that their story had some very poetic qualities and they specifically wrote it to avoid any military confrontations such as had been typical in the genre. "I wanted the creature to confront human beings, but there were no scenes of the military shooting at it and not being able to destroy it," Lourié said. "That concept is really ridiculous — those big guns would definitely kill anything. The creature was not supposed to destroy the town, and there were no stock shots of military intervention. That is so totally boring."

Typically, when the Japanese financiers pulled out, new writers were brought in to revise the screenplay, changing not only the locale of the story, but also adding some violent action and illogical developments of which Lourié disapproved. (Frank King wanted to reset the film in Paris, ignoring Lourié's point that the French capital was nowhere near the sea. He also insisted on inserting scenes of military action to make use of some supposedly impressive stock footage.) Unfortunately for him, by then he had already committed to direct the film, now called *Gorgo*, and had to do the best he could with the altered screenplay.

This time rather than the time-consuming stop motion method, Lourié opted to put a stunt man wearing a rubber-casted suit for his dinosaur. This suit served for both mother and child, whose actions were staged on different sized sets scaled to their relative size. To show the two monsters making their way to the waterfront past burning buildings at the end, the baby had to be shot separately on blue backing, reduced, and printed onto the master shot by a traveling matte process. To design the suit, Lourié contacted Russian special effects man and miniature builder Nicolai Wilke, and then had English special effects technicians create hydraulic systems to control the movements of the eyes, ears, and tail. The suit was so heavy that it could not be worn for more than three hours at a time.

In addition to the miniature dinosaur, a life-size head, paw, and tail were also built for the baby monster. Thus when the monster is transported on a platform truck, its body is covered by a tarpaulin with only the head and paws exposed. The filmmakers got a permit to shoot the truck transporting the beast on Sunday from seven to eight in the morning. Lourié urged Frank King to hire 300 extras and place them along the route; however, King expected there would be enough curious pedestrians that he could save the cost of hiring extras. This backfired when the route proved almost empty, and so Lourié saved the sequence by showing it as a news report on television sets in bars, shop windows, and public places to achieve the feeling of an impressed crowd.

MGM-London special effects head Tom Howard built breakaway miniatures of the Tower Bridge (a set over 200 feet long), Big Ben, and scores of central London streets were built to be mashed by the mama monster, which involved some impressive model work undercut by the use of a water tank that never really looks like the Thames River. Howard was also in charge of the 80 blue screen shots in the film. Unfortunately, there were some density problems and some of the images become transparent, notably an on-the-spot reporter who is supposedly reporting from the scene. According to Lourié, there was insufficient time to make corrects. The principal photography was completed in a mere 24 days, including four days of location work in Ireland. The film's final cost amounted to $650,000, and another $2 million to distribute.

Gorgo would have been more impressive in stop motion, but still the men-in-suits work was filmed with greater care than most other such productions, and Freddy Young's color cinematography was truly colorful, although that is not always apparent on many of today's faded prints. Despite its short length, the film still feels a little overly drawn out; however, *Gorgo* did touch a nerve with audiences, and Spielberg played tribute to the film in his film *Jurassic Park: The Lost World.*

Lourié decided to resume his art directing career, beginning with *Confessions of an Opium Eater*. He teamed up with Sam Fuller and designed two of the director's more famous cult pictures, *Shock Corridor* and *The Naked Kiss.*

While working on *The Giant Behemoth*, Allied Artists producer Les Sansom approached Lourié about another science fiction project which would be shot in Spain. The film, *A Crack in the World*, was about a scientific team trying to tap thermal energy from the molten core of the Earth. The project goes awry, resulting in a series of earthquakes that threaten the very existence of the Earth. The budget was of necessity very modest, a mere $600,000, and Sansom, now head of Security Pictures, was convinced that Lourié could handle both the art direction and the special effects needed.

Lourié was intrigued by the challenge and headed off for Madrid and discovered that everything had to be started from scratch — there were no reliable assistants and technicians in place, studio space still had to be evaluated, and Lourié was caught up in the complex problem of how to achieve the effects sequences in the film. In conferring with the producers, it was decided that a new script would be necessary, but that the basic physical action of the first draft would remain. Lourié was required to write a technical screenplay of effects that would be incorporated into the final draft, now being written by Julian Halevy.

The main setting of the film was a gigantic scientific center in Africa located deep underground where the molten core of the Earth was closest to the earth's surface. Lourié imagined that this center would be built deep in a natural cave, reinforced by buttresses and vaults of concrete to give the impression of a strong, functional structure. The central hall was made spacious and relatively high. In order to build the set economically and still show the high vaulted ceiling, Lourié decided to use hanging miniatures. The actual set was no more than twenty feet high, with the upper part being added by the miniature. To obtain the effect of the high ceiling without actually building it, Lourié used a foreground miniature because it allowed the filmmakers to actually make the rocks shake and fall during the earthquake sequence and to shoot the scene with flickering, changing lights.

Lourié shot the main miniature sequences ahead of the principal photography with actors. Lourié began by shooting a scene depicting the cracks in the Earth advancing towards the buildings of the scientific center. He used a large miniature showing a view of the center, its satellite buildings, and the surrounding hills. The view encompasses quite an area and showed the cracks as they formed in the hills, revealing incandescent lava flowing between the jagged edges of the cracks.

The miniature occupied the entire floor space of one of the largest stages at Bronston studios. In order to show a large view of the hills, the scale had to be relatively small.

Lourié expanded the scale of *Crack in the World* through the artful use of hanging miniatures. At the climax, a well-placed nuclear bomb splits the planet and creates a second moon.

The jagged parting of the Earth was done in a complex but mechanically simple way, using set pieces mounted and moved on dolly rails and wheels. The lava flows inside were moving plastic belts painted in red and orange transparent colors and lit from below with strong lights, directing their beams towards the camera lens. The plastic belts moved on two drums, giving the impression that the "lava" is moving down the hill. When the cracks reached the center, prearranged explosions shatter the buildings. Smoke, steam, and additional avalanches of crumbling stones completed the effect. (Lourié used the same effect later when completing the special effects for *Krakatoa, East of Java*, which received an Academy Award nomination for best special effects, losing out to the lugubrious work on John Sturges' monotonous space drama *Marooned*.)

Lourié also created the illusion of an island volcano looming on the horizon on a deserted beach location near Valencia on the Mediterranean coast. In *My Work in Films*, he explains:

> To realize the scene I decided to use a relatively simple optical matte, the so-called split screen technique. Placing the camera low, the island would appear almost on the horizon line. This line would become the split line; that is, the lower portion of the frame would be the volcano profiled against the sky, a miniature of the smoking, then erupting, volcano, filmed separately and added to the lower half of the frame optically.
>
> On the top of a hill, close to Madrid, a platform was erected, ten feet by ten feet, four feet above the ground. On this platform we built the miniature volcano. The word "miniature" is misleading: our volcano was about eight feet high above the platform. The height of the platform allowed us to place the camera in line with the bottom line of the volcano and to have an unobstructed view of the sky above. The horizontal line of the base of the volcano formed the line where the volcano meets the sea. Miles distant and months later, we shot a view of the sea. Optically combined (it is called "split screen shot"), it became our *composite shot*. On this composite shot I asked the Technicolor lab processing our film to print over the reverse image of the volcano erupting, thus forming the volcano reflection on the water. This reverse image was printed very lightly, not to obscure the movements of the waves.
>
> For the actual shooting of the miniature volcano, we came very early to the hillside location to be ready for the spectacular morning light. We installed our cameras and prepared explosives among peacefully grazing cows. Little did they suspect that we were preparing a terrific eruption. Shooting seemed jeopardized once when the wind blew volcano smoke into the camera. But as the French saying goes, *"Tout s'arrange."* The wind changed direction, the morning light was still lovely, and we completed the scene with time enough to stop on our way to the next village for a breakfast of crusty bread and sausage and a glass of dark wine.

In the course of the film, a bomb is lowered into the crater of the volcano. Men, dressed in heat-reflecting asbestos suits, guide the bomb down through the crater. One man slips and burns to death in the fiery lava. The live action crater set was combined with a miniature set, about twenty feet by twenty feet, depicting the boiling lava lake that steams and hisses at the bottom of the crater. An articulated puppet was dropped inside, caught fire on contact with the lava, and was instantly consumed in boiling magma. A miniature of a gantry tower and a service tower (with a working elevator and moving puppet technicians) for the missile was built on a plateau. Because exploding the metal miniature could create unwanted shrapnel that might endanger the crew, an identical tower was built out of balsa wood to take the place of the original metal one when it came time for the explosion. Alec Weldon and his crew fixed up high pressure tanks with red colored water, steam conduits, and mortars loaded with explosives and powdered paint to create the effect of dark smoke when the explosion occurs. The "magma" burst forth, seeded with sodium and carbide particles which burst into flames. The action was covered with three cameras, shooting at high speed, to give some choice in editing the sequence together.

In the finale of *A Crack in the World*, a portion of Earth's crust is propelled into outer space, surrounded by flames as it turns into a fiery satellite. Lourié finally solved the problem of how to achieve the effect by spraying an ordinary floor mop with glue, sprinkling it with spangles, and making it rotate in front of a black velvet backing. The camera travels and zooms back, and the shot was double-printed together with a night sky. The result looked like a fast-receding satellite, turning and burning, going towards the moon and the stars.

His work on the film began a career as a miniatures and special effects director, working in that capacity on *Battle of the Bulge, Custer of the West, Krakatoa, East of Java,* and *Royal Hunt of the Sun.* (Years later he returned to this kind of work for the super-expensive TV pilot *Supertrain*, featuring an atomic-powered futuristic train, for director-executive producer Dan Curtis, which was spun-off into a short-lived TV series.)

However, Lourié soon returned to the rigors of production designing. He was essential in helping establish the look of the *Kung Fu* TV series on a limited budget, and stayed with the series throughout its run. He also worked briefly on a couple of other science fiction oriented series, namely *Captain Nemo's Return* and *Lucan*, about a boy who grew up with wolves searching for his own identity and pursued by a bounty hunter. His final credits were as art director on Clint Eastwood's *Bronco Billy* and the TV pilot *Freebie and the Bean* and a credit as visual effects consultant on Richard Heffron's TV film *A Whale for the Killing.* He was happy that his work continued to attract interest and sought out new projects until he died in 1991.

While his directorial legacy primarily consists of having attacked New York and London twice each, Lourié was an artist of taste and talent whose ability to establish mood and atmosphere in these works outstrips the work of his competitors, and his films continue to find fans and be regarded with fondness.

GEORGE LUCAS (1944–)

Look at Life (animated short); *THX-1138: 4 EB (Electronic Labyrinth)* (short, 1965); *Herbie* (codirected with Paul Golding, short); *Freiheit* (short); *1:42:08: A Man and His Car* (short, 1966); *Herbie Anyone Lived in a Pretty Hometown* (short); *The Emperor* (documentary short); *6-18-67* (documentary short, 1967); *Filmmaker* (documentary 1968); *THX-1138* (1970); *American Graffiti* (1973); *Star Wars* (1977); *Star Wars: The Phantom Menace* (1999)

George Lucas is the creator of the phenomenally successful *Star Wars* saga and the *Indiana Jones* series, and is Chairman of the Board of Lucasfilm Ltd., LucasArts Entertainment Company, and Lucas Digital Ltd. He is also the Chairman of the Board of the George Lucas Educational Foundation, has served on the boards of the National Geographic Society Education Foundation, the Artists Rights Foundation, the Joseph Campbell Foundation, and the Film Foundation. In addition, he is a member of the USC School of Cinema-Television Board of Councilors.

Born on May 14, 1944, to Methodist parents in the small town of Modesto, California, George Walton Lucas, Jr., has become a symbol of the American Dream personified, someone who was very poor, made a little movie out of his personal vision and went on to become a multimillionaire.

Lucas' father used to operate a stationery and office furniture store, while his mother tended to be sickly. George Lucas, Sr., raised his son with familiar values such as "Work hard, be frugal, don't waste your money"; "Don't stop until the job is done"; "Be true to yourself." The elder Lucas felt that his son didn't listen to him, that he was his mother's pet and tended to be indulged. A scrawny kid, young George was often taunted by local bullies who threw his shoes into the sprinklers. "He was hard to understand. He was always dreaming up things," Lucas Sr. has said.

George Jr. has three sisters, two older, and one, Wendy, three years younger. George was not a good student, but Wendy would often help him with his homework, getting up early to correct the errors in his English papers. The brother and sister would pool their allowances to purchase the latest comic books and then hurriedly read them in a shed behind their house.

At the age of 10, George Sr. bought the family a TV set, and George Jr. spent hours watching cartoons and reruns of old movie serials, especially the old Flash Gordon serials, which Lucas has described as a "primary influence."

At the age of 15, he got his first car, a two-cylinder Fiat Bianchina, and loved the thrill of speeding down Modesto's back roads. He spent his time rebuilding cars and working with pit crews at races. Every day after school, he would go to the Foreign Car Service and work on his Fiat to beef it up. He would grease his hair up with Vaseline, put taps on his pointed black shoes, wear one grimy pair of jeans, and go cruising or hang out with a gang that wore blue felt car coats. Lucas has described himself as a "hellraiser" when he was young, racing cars and flunking out of school.

A near fatal car crash at the age of 18 shortly before graduation turned his career choices away from being an auto mechanic. He was hit broadside while making an illegal left turn and luckily was thrown free because he had lost the roof in a previous crash and his racing seatbelt unexpectedly broke just before his Fiat wrapped itself around a walnut tree. His teachers gave the hospitalized boy mercy passing grades and he enrolled in Modesto Junior College, where he turned his attention to films. His father paid the tuition and two hundred dollars a month; otherwise George was on his own. He found the liberal arts classes required for graduation rather difficult, never having been a fast reader, a good speller, or even adept at math.

Lucas started working in animation, where he learned some of the basics about special effects and met John Korty for whom he would executive produce an animated film, *Twice Upon a Time*. He found he got a background in all the disciplines of filmmaking.

His first film, *Look at Life*, was a one minute short designed to answer a class assignment to use still photographs to create the illusion of movement and feeling. Lucas clipped photos from *Life* magazine, creating a montage of antiwar images, one every five frames or each eighth of a second, and combined them with a jazzy calypso score.

His second short, made with Paul Golding, was *Herbie*, named after a jazz composition by Herbie Hancock that accompanied images of reflections on the surface of a buffed and polished car. Next came *Freiheit*, German for freedom, which starred future film director and former Lucas roommate Randal Kleiser as a student escaping from East Germany into West Germany, being shot and killed in the process and bearing the message, "Without freedom, we're dead."

As a senior at USC, he wrote, edited, and directed a tribute to his beloved car racing*: 1:42:08: A Man and His Car*. The film was made without sync sound and simply featured a sleek yellow car taking laps around a racetrack while the sounds of an engine revving were superimposed. Lucas broke the rules by shooting it in color and by shooting at Willow Springs Raceway, far from the USC campus.

Lucas completed his bachelor of arts degree in Cinema from USC on August 6, 1966. Vietnam loomed large in the country's consciousness, and while Lucas was opposed to it, he considered enlisting in the Air Force on the advice of some Air Force students who told him that with his skills, he could become an officer in the service's photography unit. However, he discovered that his police record for having accumulated so many speeding tickets were enough to keep him from becoming an officer and Lucas had no wish to serve four years of combat duty.

Nevertheless, Lucas was drafted, only to fail his examination because he had diabetes. In the fall of 1966, he found work as an assistant grip for a crew doing documentaries for the United States Information Agency. He was then hired by editor Verna Fields to help log footage on other documentaries, re-entered USC, and became a teaching assistant to a class of navy film students. He quickly improved his skills as an editor, but bristled at other people being able to tell him how to cut what he was working on, which firmed in him the resolve to become the one who calls the shots.

While working for Fields, Lucas met and worked with fellow editor Marcia Griffin. They soon began dating, usually by going to the movies. George and Marcia married in 1969. Marcia became a well-respected film editor, working on such films as *Taxi Driver, New York New York*, and *Alice Doesn't Live Here Anymore*. It was at her suggestion that the ending of *Raiders of the Lost Ark* was reshot because it didn't have any emotional resolution between the Ford and Allen characters.

When Lucas returned to USC as a graduate student, he again collaborated on the script with Paul Golding of *Herbie Anyone Lived in a Pretty Hometown*, based on the E.E. Cummings poem. It became the first USC student production to be filmed in widescreen. It was made in a rushed five-week schedule and relayed the story of a photographer who takes pictures of a young couple and transforms them into black and white stills.

He then tried his hand at a semi-documentary, *The Emperor*, based on the idea that radio promotes fantasy and on Bob Hudson, a disk jockey for KBLA, whose nickname was the same as the title. (Lucas had originally wanted to do a film about Wolfman Jack, but could not locate him.) Lucas intercuts between a Hudson monologue with women flirting with him, traffic shots, frolicking hippies, comments from street listeners, and commercials extolling smoking bananas and offering a used rhino for sale.

According to director John Milius,

> In film school George would be very quiet for a long time and then talk for a very long time. He was a ringleader. So was I. Our idea was to see how much we could get away with. We had very little money for projects and George's fascination was to see how much this small amount of money could get. He was the first person to make a film in color. He knew somebody who owned a race-car track, and one time he managed to get some extra film and he shot a race car going around the track at a hundred and fifty miles an hour. It looked like the Grand Prix, and everybody else was shooting some little movie on campus. He knew somebody who owned an airplane, a P-51, and he said to me, "Think up a story so we can have a P-51 in our movie. People won't believe the shots we'll get." He did a student film called *The Emperor*, and it was really extraordinary. It was about a real-life disc jockey who called himself Emperor Hudson. George said, "I've never seen the titles in the middle. Let's put them there." He had advertisements in it like a radio show. He played with the concepts. He was free. He said we could do anything.
>
> Our leader was Francis Coppola, who had graduated from film school before us. In those days we really felt we were going to change everything, that we were going to make the greatest art — and we did to a degree. We didn't have much money, but we didn't need much. The root, the highest ideal for all of us, was to do what we wanted. Not what the studio said to do. Our driving force was to get freedom. We called Coppola "Francis the Fuehrer." He was really the reckless one. I'd like to see George be a little more reckless but it's hard to be reckless when you become an institution. When we got out of film school, Francis was our leader. He really gave us our chance. The whole concept of the ideal film community where artists could work free from the tyranny of the studios was Francis's. His philosophy was imbued in everyone. George is carrying that out ... with his Skywalker Ranch.

Lucas took his navy students and put them to work on his latest workshop film, taking advantage of the fact that the navy gave its students unlimited access to color film, plus lab processing for it. When he found the older half of the class antagonistic, he broke the class into two groups, one of which would work on his project, and the other would work on another project, with both groups competing to see who could come up with the best project.

Lucas wanted to make a film about the future using existing materials. He was able to finesse filming at USC's computer science department, the underground parking lot at UCLA, and the Los Angeles International and Van Nuys airports. In the process, he created his famous student short *THX-1138: 4 EB: Electronic Labyrinth*.

Lucas mixed video images accompanied by distorted audio signals with an individual's search for an ideal mate and his eventual escape from his oppressive society. It contained traveling shots, sophisticated graphics (numbers run across the screen ticking off the minutes until THX escapes), and optical process shots unseen in other student films of the period. Like all of Lucas' pioneer film work, the dynamics of the film had to do with the editing of images rather than the story. Lucas' student shorts consistently lacked real stories and characters and concerned themselves more with movement and objects. He seemed to have the potential to be a brilliant experimental filmmaker, with little indication that he would prove to become one of the most commercially successful and popular filmmakers of all time.

The student version of *THX* was good enough for Lucas to be given a scholarship to observe and make a short film on the making of *McKenna's Gold* for Columbia. Writer-producer Carl Foreman loaned Lucas and three other film students all the equipment they would need, and each was to produce a 10 minute 16mm film related in some way to *McKenna's Gold* to be used for promotional purposes. Lucas did not feel like being exploited for such purposes under the auspices of receiving a scholarship and decided to create a desert tone poem instead, which he titled *6-18-67* after the day he completed filming it. The short used time lapse photography and displays the life of the desert before, during, and after the coming of the film company. Foreman was surprised and pleased by *6-18-67* and encouraged Lucas to transform *THX* into a full-fledged feature.

In the same year, Lucas entered and won another scholarship from Warner Bros., hoping to find work in the studio's famed animation department. Instead, he was sent to observe production of Francis Ford Coppola's *Finian's Rainbow*. He soon became friends with Coppola who signed him on as a production associate on his next film *The Rain People*, about which Lucas made his first feature-length film, a documentary called *Filmmaker: A Diary by George Lucas*. For $12,000, Lucas made a half-hour *cinéma vérité* documentary showing Coppola as a maverick film director making his personal film and predicting the fall of the studio system. It documents the stresses and strains of a movie production in constant motion. (*The Rain People* was a road movie actually filmed on the road with numerous locations as it follows Shirley Knight and James Caan [making his film debut] on a cross country road trip.) Lucas worked on the film for free in exchange for Coppola finagling $3,000 for him to develop a story treatment for *THX-1138* for Warner Bros.

Coppola is shown as in charge throughout, though when the production reached the Southwest, crewmembers felt the need to shave their beards, which rendered Coppola unrecognizable and seemed to take away much of his authority on the set. Coppola is also shown as frantically altering the script to make use of sudden inspirations, such as the availability of a patriotic parade in Chattanooga, or adding a scene in the Greyhound station. The film has been shown for years as an example of a fine documentary to USC cinema classes.

Lucas was invited by Coppola to be part of his vision for American Zoetrope, named after the early cinematic device that made projected images move when a cylinder was spun. (It was named after a Greek word meaning "life movement.") Coppola leased a warehouse in San Francisco and began creating something that Lucas had long hoped for, a guild of filmmakers far removed from the influences of Los Angeles. Lucas became the outfit's vice president.

Coppola contacted Warner Bros.' new head Ted Ashley and informed him that Coppola had a film ready to go and demanded that Warners put up the money. The studio agreed to advance $3.5 million to develop five scripts, one of which was *THX-1138*, though Warners was concerned that the film might not be able to be made for its projected under $1 million budget and included a clause that the money would have to be repaid by Coppola and Zoetrope if the screenplays and films did not live up to expectations.

Meanwhile, Lucas was hired to be one of several cameramen on David and Albert Maysle's *Gimme Shelter*, the famous Rolling Stones concert film shot at Altamont in which a member of the audience was stabbed to death by the Hells Angels who provided security for the free concert.

Coppola suggested that *THX-1138* might be filmed in a new 3-D process he discovered, but Lucas rejected the idea. Lucas tried to write a screenplay for the film, but felt it had turned out terribly. Coppola agreed and tried to rewrite the script himself, but it soon became apparent that he and Lucas did not share the same concept of the film. Warners didn't care for the script either, so Coppola broke down and paid writer Oliver Hailey to work with Lucas on it. Lucas did not care much for Hailey's efforts either, and decided to collaborate with sound editor Walter Murch, whom he felt brought a spacey insight to his own visual imagination.

While *THX* was facing its difficulties in getting off the ground, Lucas went to John Milius suggesting they work on a Vietnam project and together they began the story treatment for *Apocalypse Now*. Coppola meanwhile prepared an impressive display for *THX-1138* to show the executives at Warner Bros. along with some footage from the student film version, and proposed a budget of $777,777.77 (seven being Coppola's "lucky" number), plus he offered them *Apocalypse Now* even though he hadn't previously been connected with the project. The studio agreed to both projects.

Under Coppola's deal, Lucas was given $15,000 to write and direct *THX-1138*, with the promise of a raise to $25,000 for similar work on *Apocalypse Now*. Lucas was impressed by Francis' ability to make the deal, but annoyed at his dealing himself in on *Apocalypse*. Still, not too many 23-year-olds are given nearly a million dollars to make a movie, so Lucas was pleased.

Costs were kept down on the movie by shooting much of it in the tunnels of the only partially completed BART system, with the Alameda Tube being used for the high speed finale. Finding that many young actors and actresses were not anxious to shave their heads to appear in the film, Lucas recruited reformed drug abusers from Synanon to play extras in his film. Bay area disk jockeys Terry McGovern and Scott Beach were hired to provide disembodied voiceovers for the film.

THX-1138 begins by paying tribute to Buck Rogers by playing an excerpt of the Buck Rogers chapterplay before the Warner Bros. corporate logo appears, an early indication of Lucas' fascination with serials. In the fragmented opening we are introduced to THX-1138 (Robert Duvall), a dull drone of a worker who labors with atomic energy. He causes an accident which kills several people, but no one is upset or excited by this. The populace is kept in control via regular intake of sedatives.

THX goes to an OMM confession booth and admits to messing up a thermal coupling, telling the Christ-like image that he has a hard time concentrating and is vaguely dissatisfied. "Work hard, increase production, prevent accidents, and be happy," commands the OMM, echoing the sloganeering and call to conformity of the sixties.

THX heads home, neglects to take his pills, and watches three-dimensional hologrammic television which presents images of nudity (either a black woman or a black man), of robotic police beating a protestor repeatedly, or an insipid talk show. In Lucas' world, television is merely another kind of drug to keep the masses passive. There is no information, excitement, or enlightenment here.

The next day, suffering from a chemical imbalance, THX vomits in the confession booth, which drones on about "Buy more, buy more now, buy and be happy," the commands of a consumerist society. His roommate LUH 3417 (Maggie McOmie) takes care of him. She confesses

A young George Lucas on the white-walled limbo set of *THX-1138*.

that she has wanted to touch THX many times and gives in to her impulses.

The future shown here is far from a perfectly functioning utopia, a point Lucas underscores by showing one of the robot officers (played by Johnny Weissmuller, Jr., and Robert Feero) malfunctioning by continually running into the side of a corridor. THX's boss SEN 5421 (Donald Pleasence) sends LUH a shift change because he openly wants to become THX's roommate and moves in. THX simply seeks LUH out and continues cuddling her.

One day at work the people monitoring THX note from his respiration that he has "sedation depletion." A mind-block is ordered, causing him to freeze at a crucial juncture and almost causing another disaster. THX is escorted by police and tried in a court on the charge of drug evasion and sexual perversion. He gets sentenced to be conditioned, is pronounced incurable, and sent to detention.

Detention proves to be a white limbo, where the police prod prisoners with pain sticks. THX is probed by a pair of doctors seeking usable body parts. When LUH is also sentenced to detention, she runs to THX and reveals she's pregnant. The pair make love, which causes the police to show up, stun THX and relocate him.

SEN greets him at his new location and begins to ramble on about freedom and leadership. He represents those who talk endlessly about something but end up doing nothing. NCH (Sid Haid) is a violent patient who attacks others and PTO (Ian Wolfe) debates without really getting involved either. (David Ogden Stiers also appears in the film, though his name is misspelled in the credits.) A dwarf is brought in and described as a "shell dweller," another example of which THX later evades as part of his escape. These mysterious characters are obviously precursors to Lucas' Jawas.

THX resolves to simply search for a way out, followed by the ever anxious SEN. Lucas violates the axis of filming, sometimes filming the characters going right to left, sometimes left to right, which adds to the disorientation of this sequence. A hologram (Don Pedro Colley) wanders towards them and asks for food, offering to show them the way out.

The hologram is an electronically generated reality who now finds himself in the real world but has not figured out how to cope with it yet. He shows them the doorway out into a corridor jammed with people, unlike the all-Caucasian, orderly corridors we were shown earlier. THX and the hologram get separated from SEN who elects to ride a tram to the end of the line, loses his nerve, and eventually gets recaptured after helping a young boy reattach his sedation tube (the young of this society are kept sedated as well).

Lucas' vision of a sterile feature filled with long corridors and people in white coveralls was influenced by Menzies' *Things to Come*, but was nevertheless effective and influential.

acters remain ciphers. Lucas does effectively create an alien futuristic environment, but never bothers providing the exposition needed to fully or even partially understand it. While visually inventive at times, the result proved off-putting to many moviegoers and especially to the studio that bankrolled it.

THX-1138 was shot in Techniscope and needs to be seen widescreen. Warner Bros. laserdisc transfer captures most of the original image, but still has a tendency to lop off the outermost right side of the frame. The film was shot on a ten-week shooting schedule and then carefully edited and sound-mixed over the following year. Lalo Schifrin was instructed to create soporific music designed to reflect the slow-wittedness of these drugged denizens of the future.

Naturally after all this work and careful attention, Lucas was quite distressed when Warner Bros. turned the film over to editor Rudi Fehr who pruned four minutes from it to almost negligible effect. "The cuts didn't make the movie any better; they had absolutely no effect on the movie at all," Lucas said in Dale Pollock's *Skywalking*. "It was a very personal kind of film, and I didn't think they had the right to come in and just arbitrarily chop it up at their own whim. I'm not really good with authority figures anyway, so I was completely outraged." Years later, after the success of *Star Wars*, Warners re-released the film with the missing footage restored, but it was still a challenging and unusual film and still failed to find much of an audience.

Meanwhile, unhappy with *THX-1138*, American Zoetrope's deal with Warners fell through and the company owed the studio $300,000. Coppola was able to turn his career around by directing *The Godfather*, with Lucas assisting him on the montage scenes of the gang wars, but Lucas needed a commercial project to prove his viability to Hollywood and expended his efforts on scripting a rock and roll "musical" in which none of the main characters would sing or dance. Lucas took a chance with his last $2,000 and headed to the Cannes Film Festival where he made a deal with David Picker of United Artists for $10,000 to develop a script for *American Graffiti*.

The information that SEN and THX have escaped is sent out and a budget of 14,000 credits is assigned for their recapture. THX and the hologram avoid the police who are searching for them, at one point posing as corpses and receiving tags on their earlobes, indicating their death-in-life existences. THX using the central computer to track down his lover LUH but discovers that she has been consumed and her identity reassigned to a fetus growing in a test tube. (Ted Moehnke was able to get a mold of a dead embryo to make duplicates for this scene by donating some medical equipment to the University of California.)

Rather than deal with or alter his repressive society, THX simply elects to drop out and run away. Lucas' message seems to be that people do not have to participate in repressive societies, that they can simply walk out on them. THX hops into a police pursuit vehicle and heads off for the end of the road. His hologrammic partner, however, never quite figures out how to operate the controls, and crashes the car as soon as he gets it started. The credits expended in mounting THX's capture soon mount up, though two motorcycle robots are sent in pursuit, almost capturing him when his rocket powered vehicle overheats.

Ultimately, the recapture effort exceeds its budget and the officers are recalled, leaving THX free to leave the underground city. Once outside, he encounters a large orange sunrise and a barren landscape, his future now uncertain but unquestionably his own.

THX-1138 is a cold, uninviting film whose central char-

Lucas planned to use the oldies of the fifties to nostalgically re-create cruising and the lost era of the past, much as Martin Scorsese did in re-creating New York's Little Italy in *Mean Streets*. In coming up with his story and characters, Lucas cannibalized his adolescence in Modesto, creating his most human and heartfelt film in the process. He roughed out his ideas with USC classmates Willard Huyck and Gloria Katz.

Lucas in some ways embodied all the four major characters in *American Graffiti*. Steve is anxious to get away from the small town, but ultimately ends up tied down to it. Curt looks back with nostalgia and fears the big city, but realizes that his future depends on his going to college. Milner hangs on to his reputation as king of the road, yet knows that ultimately he will end in defeat or death. Terry is simply a socially backward nerd who tries desperately to get drunk and get laid now that he has the "boss" car Steve has entrusted to him. During one night from sunset to sunrise, these guys, who previously were only concerned about girls, cars, and music, are now confronted with the reality of their adult futures before them and each undergoes a maturation and a rite of passage.

Lucas' rough draft of *American Graffiti* did not turn out well, but he persuaded David Picker at United Artists that his idea had potential. Picker insisted that the story needed improvement and offered $10,000 towards a full screenplay. Lucas teamed up with Gary Kurtz who would produce the proposed picture, and Kurtz spent the money United Artists gave them by hiring classmate Richard Walters to write out a script. Lucas found himself terribly unhappy with Walters' approach to the story, feeling that his script was too overtly sexual and in bad taste, and was also unhappy to find that Kurtz had paid Walters the entire $10,000 for just a first draft, leaving them with nothing towards coming up with satisfactory script. He called in his friends Willard Huyck and Gloria Katz, who had just finished making *Messiah of Evil*, and had them polish up Lucas' draft of the screenplay, which ended up being turned down by every studio in Hollywood including American International Pictures.

Lucas wanted his film to be composed of a number of two and a half minute scenes, each the length of an average song of that era, a total of forty-eight scenes, or twelve for each of the major characters. All these little subplots aided in giving the story momentum and fleshing out the feeling for the era, the entire story taking place in the span of a single night.

Jeff Berg took the rewritten script of *American Graffiti* to Universal Studios where Ned Tanen was taking chances financing low budget films like *Two Lane Blacktop* and *Diary of a Mad Housewife* from new film directors. He listened to Lucas' infectious enthusiastic pitch and agreed to allot $600,000 for the entire production, an amount eventually raised to $750,000 including Lucas' $50,000 writing and directing fee. Tanen also stipulated that Lucas would get to direct the film only if Francis Ford Coppola, now hot after *The Godfather*, would agree to produce it. Coppola agreed knowing that Kurtz would handle the day-to-day chores of physically producing the film, though he wanted to alter the title to the far less poetic *Rock Around the Block*, a concept Lucas wisely nixed.

Universal had difficulty understanding why so much money needed to be spent licensing golden oldie rock songs, suggesting that Lucas trim the soundtrack down to five or six key songs. Lucas planned to edit his film to the rhythm of these memorable old songs, which would be used to evoke memories of when the audience first heard them as well. He chafed at having to trim some 80 selected songs to 45, but considered the $90,000 paid for them well spent. He was especially fortunate in that Tom Pollock had negotiated a deal with music publishers so that no composer received a higher license fee than any other, and since Kurtz knew Dennis Wilson of the Beach Boys, they were able to get two Beach Boy tunes at nominal rates.

Fred Roos and George Lucas conducted an exhaustive search for talented unknowns and came up with a cast that would soon read like a who's who of Hollywood in the 1970s and 1980s: Richard Dreyfuss, Harrison Ford, Cindy Williams, Ron Howard, Paul LeMat, Candy Clark, Charles Martin Smith, Mackenzie Phillips, Bo Hopkins, Kathleen Quinlan, Kay Lenz, and Suzanne Somers.

The production began filming on June 26, 1972, and fell into trouble almost immediately. A key member of the crew was arrested for growing marijuana. Lucas had problems getting the cameras mounted on the cars and lost half a night's shooting. One hour after shooting began, a restaurant fire created a traffic jam and prevented shooting from anywhere in town except on back roads. Assistant cameraman Barney Coangelo slipped off the trailer and was run over by a car and then rushed to the hospital, but fortunately had no broken bones or serious damage.

American Graffiti was originally set to film in San Rafael until a bar owner threatened to sue the city when his business dropped off after Lucas blocked off the main thoroughfare in order to do his filming. After only a few more nights, the company had to relocate to Petaluma. The two cameramen Lucas initially hired simply weren't experienced enough to handle what was needed, so Coppola asked Haskell Wexler to help out. With no money left in the budget, Wexler agreed to take a percentage of *Graffiti*'s eventual profits, and was able to achieve the garish neon look to the film that Lucas wanted even though it wasn't to his taste.

Jim Bloom, a young production assistant, had to round up 400 classic 1950s and early 1960s cars by offering their

Put in a robot or an alien, and one instantly recognizes a science fiction film. Lucas utilized this classic visual shorthand in *Star Wars*, with Luke Skywalker (Mark Hamill) being given charge of the 'droids C-3PO (Anthony Daniels) and R2D2 (Kenny Baker).

owners $25 a night to bring their automobiles to the production. The final scene of Bob Falfa's (Harrison Ford) car crashing kept failing as the car's axels broke one after the other, and then it almost ran over two camera operators shooting at ground level during another attempt. Lucas had to go back a few days later with four cameras to finally film the stunt.

Universal insisted that Verna Fields, who had just finished cutting *The Sugarland Express* for Spielberg, edit the film, and she did complete the initial two-and-three-quarter hour rough cut, which Marcia Lucas then took over and fine tuned, trimming almost an hour from the assemblage and synching it with appropriate oldies to establish the mood of each scene. Lucas originally planned to follow a strict sequence in which Curt's story segues to Toad, who leads to Milner, to Steve, and then back to Curt, but this proved too restrictive and Lucas abandoned it.

American Graffiti received a notorious preview screening on Sunday, January 28, 1973 at 10:00 a.m. in the Northpoint Theater in San Francisco. The audience loved the movie, but Ned Tanen didn't get what Lucas was after and hated it, considering it unreleaseable. Coppola berated Tanen for his insensitivity towards Lucas, who had practically killed himself to make the film on time and on budget (a mere $700,000 and a 28 day shoot), and seeing how much the audience enjoyed it, offered to buy it from Universal. Kurtz calmed everyone down and suggested a meeting in which Tanen could give his suggestions for editing the movie. Lucas simply had the sense that his film was being taken away from him by an insensitive studio yet again, and was unhappy that five minutes were trimmed from the picture over his objections.

Fortunately, the film proved a runaway success, garnering glowing reviews and returning more than $50 million in rentals on a minuscule investment. (Lucas' own salary on the film was $25,000.) Lucas' narrative technique of intertwining seemingly unrelated stories later became a staple of such television series as *Hill Street Blues* and *L.A. Law*, plus the nostalgia of the film helped to spawn the hit TV series *Happy Days*. It also inspired a raft of similar period pieces, most of which fell far short of the original in terms of quality.

A few years later, Lucas let B. W. L. Norton direct a lame sequel entitled *More American Graffiti*, which purported to continue the story of the characters. Lucas had been impressed with Norton's work on *Cisco Pike*, and felt he would be a good choice to handle the material, agreeing to let Norton direct if he liked the script Norton came up with. He wanted to continue the fragmented narrative technique he had pursued in the original film, but this time tell a broader story about the sixties as a decade.

More American Graffiti separates the characters into four separate narratives, each of which is filmed in a different format and each depicting a different phase of the 1960s. Paul Le Mat stars in a widescreen segment about Milner as a race car driver; Charles Martin Smith stars in a Vietnam segment done in a square 16mm format reminiscent of televised battle footage; Candy Clark stars in a widescreen, multiple image and psychedelic split screen reminiscent of Richard Lester's early work, and the Ron Howard/Cindy Williams segment has the squarish look of a TV sitcom.

More American Graffiti demonstrated that Lucas did not have the golden touch, he could make mistakes. The film shows no insight into the sixties, its ostensible subject. Nothing in the Milner section relates to the concerns of the time; the Terry the Toad section seems to say that if we had competent commanders in Vietnam, the war would have been moral; the hippie scene is merely used as a backdrop for a typical wronged-lover comedy, and the Bolanders' story seems intended to show how much fun a student riot could be. That aside, Charles Martin Smith, Candy Clark, and Cindy Williams keep the film moderately entertaining with their nicely nuanced performances.

It took George Lucas two and a half years to write *Star Wars*, which was done only in longhand on blue- and green-lined paper with number two standard pencils. He started writing it in 1973. "There are four or five scripts for *Star Wars*," he said, "and you can see as you flip through them where certain ideas germinated and how the story developed. There was never a script completed that had the entire story as it exists now. But by the time I finished the first *Star Wars*, the basic ideas and plots for *Empire* and *Jedi* were also done. As the stories unfolded, I would take certain ideas and save them; I'd put them aside in notebooks. As I was writing *Star Wars*, I kept taking out all the good parts, and I just kept telling myself I would make other movies someday. It was a mind trip I laid on myself to get me through the script. I just kept taking out stuff, and finally with *Star Wars* I felt I had one little incident that introduced the characters."

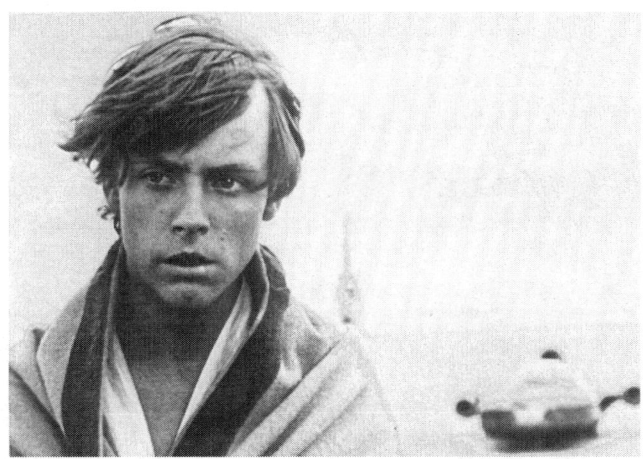

Hamill was surprised that Lucas didn't want him to show more emotion at the sight of his aunt and uncle's death.

Before *American Graffiti*, Marcia Lucas, then George's wife, was working more regularly than he was (George spent much of his time writing) and the couple were making about $12,000 a year. The $15,000 Alan Ladd, Jr. paid Lucas to develop *Star Wars* was a godsend. In Lucas' first treatment for *Star Wars*, the lead character was a girl.

The first draft of *Star Wars* (May 1974) is quite different from the final film. The young Jedi hero in this draft is Anakin Starkiller, son of the great Jedi Kane Starkiller, who is at war with the evil Knights of Sith who wear black, masked Darth Vader outfits. Darth Vader appears as an evil general sans mask. Instead of a Ben Kenobi character, the Starkillers seek out General Luke Skywalker who protects the royal family of Aquilae, including a 14-year-old Princess Leia and her two younger brothers, Biggs and Winder. Anakin's brother Deak is killed by one of the Sith early on, and is then never mentioned again. The emperor lives on the planet Alderaan, which is the imperial planet rather than a desert backwater one. There is a brief cantina scene, Han Solo is a huge, green-skinned monster with no nose and large gills, Chewbacca makes a brief appearance as defender of the Wookees while another pilot is named "Chewie." R2D2 and C-3PO can both speak English and initially escape from the Death Star. Light sabres are called lazerswords. The catchphrase is "May the force of others be with you."

Still, the incident-heavy script is weak in several areas. It takes time for much of anything to happen. The characterization throughout is minimal. The plot splits between two threads, one about Anakin Starkiller and the other about General Skywalker, leaving neither one a clear central character. Skywalker accepts the responsibility of training the young Jedi, but is too occupied by the war to get around to any training.

An underdeveloped Leia falls in love with Luke, though he has done little except irritate her. The one democratic character, a senator, is quickly killed by the General as a possible traitor. There is no central bad guy either on which to focus the audience's attention. Skywalker's attack force seems to consist of only six ships. A number of incidents do suggest material from *Return of the Jedi* in embrionic form, with the Wookees a fierce and primitive people who kill traders and who declare Starkiller a god. The script ends with the destruction of the Death Star, Princess Leia assumes the throne and promotes R2D2 and C3PO to class A-4 and Anakin Starkiller to new Lord Protector of Aquilae as Starkiller and Skywalker salute the new queen. In this form, it is not hard to understand the major studios lack of enthusiasm for the project.

When asked about the genesis of the *Star Wars* project, Lucas said, "When I created the original *Star Wars,* I was very interested in creating a modern myth to take the place that had been occupied by the Western. The Western was sort of the modern American mythology that helped the mores and the values and the way things worked in our society, which mythologies had done through time. I started working on this and realized that it had to be somewhere outside people's known realm of awareness. That is where the Westerns were.

"Greek mythology, or mythology from any country, often takes place in an unknown area but one that is believable to the audience. The only area we have now that is like that is outer space. So I decided outer space was a good idea. Actually I'd been contemplating this for a long time. I also was a big fan of Saturday morning serials, and I'd been playing around with the idea of doing a Saturday morning serial kind of film with an archeologist who was a treasure hunter. And so I was working in that area and put my interest in adventure serials together with my interest in trying to do something that was a modern myth."

The lightsabre duel between Obi-Wan (Alec Guinness) and Darth Vader (David Prowse) is classic good versus evil. The *Millennium Falcon* awaits in the background.

According to *Star Wars* producer Gary Kurtz in an interview with Lawrence French and Paul Mandell in *Cinefantastique*, "The first scripts for *Star Wars* were more or less covering the entire saga. They were long, involved treatments that ultimately wound up becoming all nine stories. The process of writing that George went through with *Star Wars* was to focus the original material down into a workable two-hour piece. But it was out of those initial ideas that the whole saga evolved."

Once he completed the first film, though, Lucas felt little hope of turning the rest of his daydreams into features. Before its release and phenomenal success, he was quoted as believing that he would break even on the film and make money off the merchandising of the various toys, hardly the confidence of someone who expects to make eight more movies of the same material. Only following the enormous success of *Star Wars* did Lucas suddenly refer to planning two additional trilogies.

Lucas claims the first trilogy of *Star Wars* films will deal with social and political issues, how a society evolves, and will depict the breakdown of the galactic Republic and the emergence of the Empire; the second trilogy, the familiar *Star Wars* trilogy, deals with Luke Skywalker's personal growth and self-realization; and the third trilogy is said to deal with moral and philosophical problems.

Back in 1980, Lucas explained his decision to go with the second part of his story by noting that the first trilogy "is more plot-oriented, more soap opera–ish than Luke's story. The problem is like a play, the first act is essentially exposition and you've got to explain everything. That's usually pretty boring so I wanted to avoid that and get into the meat of the matter, get everybody interested."

Lucas is literal and direct in naming his characters, as in Darth Vader (masculine of vadis meaning "Man of no virtue" from Latin), Luke Skywalker (a "skywalker" was a navigator in the old sailing days), Anakin Skywalker (Anakin meaning renewed or the "new"). Additionally, the clothes the characters wear also tell us who they are: Darth Vader wears black, while Luke and Leia wear white. Han Solo wears a white shirt and black vest, suggesting that while he displays outward greed, at heart he is basically a good person. Obi-Wan Kenobi wears brown burlap over white, suggestive of his connection with the Earth and of nature.

R2D2 comes from when Lucas was mixing the soundtrack of *American Graffiti* with Walter Murch. Murch asked for R2D2, that is Reel 2, Dialog 2, and Lucas thought it was a great name for his little robot. The golden figure of C-3PO was based on the Academy Award Oscar. Darth Vader seems inspired by the Jack Kirby created comic book characters of Dr. Doom and Darkseid. Princess Leia seems to derive from Flash Gordon's Princess Freia, who wore a long white gown and wore her hair in two buns, one on each side of her head. The term "Jedi" comes from the Japanese term *jidai-geki*, meaning period drama, usually of the samurai type.

In a *Chicago Sun-Times* (May 18, 1980) interview with Joanne Waterman Williams, Lucas said,

> As a student of anthropology I feel strongly about the role myths and fairy tales play in setting up young people for the way they're supposed to handle themselves in society. It's the kind of thing [psychiatrist] Bruno Bettleheim talks about, the importance of childhood. I realized before I did *Star Wars* that there was no contemporary fairy tale and that the number of parents who sit down and tell their children fairy tales is dwindling.
>
> As families begin to break up, kids are left more to television and they don't hear bedtime stories. As a result, people are learning their mythology from TV, which makes them very confused because it has no point of view, no sense of morality. It's a very amoral thing and as a result, unless a child has a very strong family life or is involved with the church there's no anchor to hold on to. So when I developed *Star Wars* I did it as a contemporary fairy tale. I think that's one of the reasons it has universal appeal.

Lucas admits that he never has really liked writing or directing. "What I enjoy is editing. I started out as an editor. I became a director because I didn't like directors telling me how to edit, and I became a writer because I had to write something in order to be able to direct something." He indicated that he would prefer to work on filmmaking in the pure, abstract sense rather than the giant productions that people have come to expect of him.

"There is more of me in *Star Wars* than I care to admit, for better or worse," Lucas told Denise Worrell in *Icons*. "A lot of it is very unconscious, very personal. You can't get away from that. It comes out of you. It's not something that is done by the numbers, it's very personal. Luke more or less is my alter ego. He can't not be. You can't write a main character and not have him be part of you and not be able to identify with him. I identify with a lot of the characters and you have to in order to write it. Han Solo and Luke are like two brothers, the spiritual brother and the warrior brother with the devil-may-care attitude. A lot of people have said Han Solo is a composite of an old friend I used to race cars with and screenwriter John Milius. Who knows where these characters come from? I didn't base Han Solo on any person.

"The idea of the Force evolved. It has evolved all during my life. I've always had a deep interest in the cosmos — the great mysteries of life. I have always pondered it and been fascinated by it. I've always asked the questions and looked for the answers. I don't know if I am any further along now than when I was five years old. I continue to look. If I know anything, it is that we just don't know what's going on. To deny things that don't fit into our sense of reality, like levitating a chair, to say this doesn't exist, and to close one's reality into a rigid mind-set is not the most productive way of saying that all things are possible. Because you don't understand it, because it doesn't fit into your belief system, you shouldn't reject it."

Director Lawrence Kasdan who collaborated on the scripts for *The Empire Strikes Back* and *Return of the Jedi* commented, "George is very much in tune with his entire history from the time he was very young, and in a way that is useful to him in his work. He is able to draw on those feelings. That kind of openness to your past, and the influences on you, is a very special gift. George has been able to hook into some basic, universal images. He is able to show that someone very small, like a child or Luke, can face someone very big, like a Darth Vader or an Empire or a Death Star. The central image of the whole trilogy I think comes in *Star Wars* when Luke, against all odds, gets through this tiny crack and fires one little rocket into exactly the right spot to bring down this enormous opponent. That is the most powerful feeling: 'Oh, it's not hopeless, I can be like David and kill the giant Goliath with a slingshot.' In *Empire*, when Han Solo is maneuvering the *Millennium Falcon* through the meteoroid field — that's a fantasy every kid has had of avoiding arrows or rocks or an avalanche. In *Jedi*, as the flames chase the *Falcon* out of the Death Star, that is an image everybody has had: 'Oh, if only I could just beat by a few steps the monster or the mugger or the dog that's on my tail.' And whatever feelings you have about Darth Vader, your father, or authority, how reassuring it is to think that there is something good there too. Luke's insistence on his hope that redemption is possible is very inspiring."

There is no question that Lucas carefully analyzed the religious aspects of his story before making the film. Darth Vader and the empire he serves are clearly symbols of evil. The Force represents the power of God or the Holy Spirit. Ben Kenobi is clearly a Christ symbol who instructs Luke in the ways of the Force, is killed by Darth Vader, but then is resurrected in spiritual form and continues to offer guidance in the war against evil.

Via the Force, Luke (Mark Hamill) is taught to place his trust in belief rather than knowledge or technology. Han Solo (Harrison Ford) represents the skeptic who says, "Hocus pocus religions and archaic weapons are no substitute for a good blaster at your side," indicating a general loss of belief. Solo also boasts, "I've been from one end of this galaxy to the other, and I've seen a lot of strange things. Too many ... to think that there could be some such controlling one's actions. I determine my destiny — not some half-mystical energy field." Still, Lucas believes in mystical powers and in the film's climax, Luke trusts the Force rather than his onboard computer to guide his shot to blow up the Death Star. (This anti-technology bent annoyed several science fiction fans.)

Significantly too, Lucas frames the story as having taken place "A long time ago, in a galaxy far, far away," which is often overlooked amid the futuristic trappings of the film. This is a story of good triumphant, of events that already have occurred and been resolved. Whatever battles the Empire might win, because of the simplistic good and evil camps that Lucas divides his universe into, it is easily apparent that it would not win the war.

The religious parallels were extended in the subsequent films. To become a Jedi in *The Empire Strikes Back*, Luke must make a deep, religious commitment. He discovers that the force that might send him into the dark side originates from himself (i.e. original sin, which he must unlearn), and that he must give up his pride and his disbelief and give himself over to the will of the Force, which flows through everything. Yoda makes clear that a true Jedi's relationship with the Force is a passive one ("You will know when you are at peace ... calm, passive. A Jedi uses the Force for knowledge, never for attack," he intones).

Eventually, Luke (Hamill) confronts his evil father Vader (Prowse) in the climax to *Return of the Jedi.* (Lucas originally titled it "Revenge of the Jedi" until reminded that a Jedi is not supposed to crave revenge.)

Luke suffers a crisis of conscience when he discovers that his father is Darth Vader, and in temporarily losing his belief, loses his right hand (à la Christ's admonition, "If your right hand causes you sin, cut it off and throw it away") in the battle with Darth Vader. However, Luke overcomes the twin temptations of joining his father in sin or losing belief all together, and so gains a new hand.

Finally, in *Return of the Jedi*, Luke fights evil but refuses to give into anger. He faces his father with Christian love, depends entirely on faith, lays down his arms and accepts the possibility of martyrdom rather than give in to the Dark Side. This noble willingness to sacrifice himself inspires latent paternal feelings in Vader who steps forward to confront the Emperor rather than see his son killed before his eyes. Anakin Skywalker is thus able to redeem himself before his death, an indication of the Christian belief that God's charity benefits all, that "all men should find salvation and come to know the truth" (1 Tim 2:4). An indication of his redemption occurs at the end of the film when the ghostly figure of Anakin takes his place alongside the spirits Obi-Wan and Yoda at the final victory celebration. The Force or God is depicted as being within everyone, and the ultimate victory belongs to the Force.

Star Wars was a breakthrough film in a number of ways. Its special effects improved upon those of *2001: A Space Odyssey*, which never had spaceships going in front of planets (unless that portion were blacked out by an eclipse). It promoted the idea of a used future, so that equipment would not look like it just emerged from the showroom, but had experienced a bit of wear and tear and was therefore taken for granted. It also started the unfortunate trend of having spaceships appear to bank on non-existent air pockets in space and perpetuated ideas of explosive booms in a vacuum.

The sound design of *Star Wars* was fairly revolutionary for its time, as it became one of the first films to showcase 6-track Dolby Stereo on its 70mm prints. The sound design by Ben Burtt was highly detailed and helped the film achieve a greater sense of realism, giving the film an otherworldly ambiance. Burtt built up a library of thousands of cross-indexed sounds to use that he could mix or process to create the kind of tonalities that Lucas desired. Lucas is a proponent of using technology to make it easier to make movies.

In a promotional interview, Anthony Daniels recalled:

> I was extremely insulted to be asked to audition for the part of a robot. I was a serious actor! Twenty years ago robots were just pieces of tin with occasional rubber bits but no real character. I thought the whole idea was beneath me, but my agent insisted that I make an effort to meet this George Lucas person. It seemed he wanted only two minutes per person, so it wouldn't be a commitment on either side. Oddly, when I walked into the room, I felt some kind of rapport towards this unknown American and we actually managed a halting conversation.
>
> In one of the most embarrassing pauses, I noticed a concept painting of the two robot characters. Bleak, helpless things, I suppose. But they looked so sad and forlorn that I wanted to help them. It was that bleak quality that attracted me to the role.
>
> They sent the script the next day and though I read it several times, it really didn't make much sense to me at all. But I did like See-Threepio. He was childlike in a way that I found quite intriguing — never shy about admitting his terrors or his true feelings, unless they concerned his deep-felt affection for his mechanical chum, Artoo-Deetoo. I thought that relationship was quite charming and had lots of possibilities.
>
> I met George Lucas again and we talked for ages this time, about movement, mime and how the droid might sound. Eventually we ran out of things to talk about so, having really worked up an enthusiasm for the idea, I

> plucked up the courage to ask if I could play the part. "Sure," said George.

The voice for C-3PO was created by Daniels during the first day's filming when he was standing painfully in costume in the middle of the desert.

> Threepio's voice is me speaking in a higher key than my normal voice but with no breath sounds anywhere. Difficult. Plus he has a strangely bleak intonation and emphasis that is faintly dehumanizing, I think. At least that's the way it came out.
>
> I didn't know until months after we'd finished shooting that George didn't like my voice at all. He'd tolerated me all the time but wanted a Bronx car dealer–type character. He'd spent the intervening months trying out other actors in a dubbing studio. Eventually, I understand, he listened to people around him who said my original voice, the inflections and tone, did sort of match the physical character on screen. It was all one. Threepio. So he changed his mind.

Mark Hamill has been criticized for his lowkey performance in *Star Wars*, but he was simply giving the director what he wanted. When he auditioned, he was given no character description, and so played the scene very neutrally, which won him the part. According to an interview Hamill did with James Van Hise, when Luke discovers his home burned out and the bodies of his aunt and uncle, "I wanted to show what my character must be feeling by kneeling down in the sand and screaming and crying, but George wanted it played in a way so that the audience could project their own feelings into my character." This helps give the scene echoes of John Ford's *The Searchers* where Ethan Edwards (John Wayne) sees his adopted family dead and represses his emotions.

Among other difficulties Hamill faced was wearing the uncomfortable Stormtrooper uniforms that were impossible to sit down in. (Actors wearing them had to rest on sawhorses.) The costumes were claustrophobic, the eyeholes had green tints, and wax was placed inside the actors' ears to muffle the sounds of explosions.

For the scene where Luke learns to use the Force by fighting a practice drone with his blast shield down, according to Hamill, "John Stears, the special effects man, was up on a ladder with a fishing pole with this plastic sputnik on the end. But he couldn't make it dart so they had me do it and imagine it was there. It was much like Kerwin Mathews seeing the skeleton that wasn't there in *The Seventh Voyage of Sinbad*. I was real limited. They would say, 'Don't do too much over here or there. Don't look low. Yeah, that looks good through the lens.' You have to believe it yourself or you're going to blow it. Everybody looks at you like, 'Let's see how this guy looks at something that's not there.' It really cracked me up a couple of times while I was shooting. When I gave him a piece that he could use, I thought to myself, 'That looked good,' and then immediately you're out of it and have to get back. It was interesting to say the least."

Star Wars pays numerous homages to other films, and sometimes revamps footage. Shots of Luke and Han firing guns at TIE fighters were lifted from Howard Hawks' *Air Force*. Dog fights during the attack on the Death Star were based on those from *The Bridges of Toko-Ri, The Battle of Britain, The Blue Max, 633 Squadron* and *Tora! Tora! Tora!*

There are a number of mistakes made in *Star Wars* that ended up in the final product, perhaps prompting Lucas to express his qualified happiness with the film: If one looks carefully, one can frequently spot R2D2 heading into a wall rather than a corridor. In the Tattoine desert when C-3PO turns away, R2 is shown with its wheel spinning in the sand unable to get anywhere. When the Jawas sell Luke R2, a red droid moves forward and blows up, and in the next shot is back in place, perfectly OK. When Darth Vader discusses Ben Kenobi, he continues gesturing to underscore a point after he has finished speaking. There is an American astronaut and a man in a werewolf mask in the famous cantina sequence. The alien with the long nose that guides the Stormtroopers to the *Millennium Falcon* keeps hitting his own proboscis. A stormtrooper on the far right of the screen bumps into the huge blast door when it opens on the room in the Death Star where R2D2 and C-3PO are locked in a closet. In Obi-Wan's duel with Darth, you can spot how the light sabres work (they had revolving four-sided blades with reflective material which scintillated a beam of light at the camera).When Han Solo escapes from the Death Star he says, "We're coming up on their century ships" instead of sentry ships. Biggs, Luke's best friend from Tatooine, was largely trimmed from the movie and only makes a brief appearance as the member of the Red 2 wing that gets blown away.

One of the biggest difficulties Lucas faced in making the movie was that his own crew had little faith that he knew what he was doing. His chief cinematographer, Gilbert "Gil" Taylor B.S.C., bristled at Lucas making suggestions regarding the level of light needed and would curse in a Sussex accent that the filmmaker didn't know what the fuck he was doing and blew his top when Lucas took matters in hand and began re-arranging his lighting. Lucas wanted to fire the fiery cameraman, but feared that his British crew might wind up on strike.

Lucas also clashed with designer John Barry, who felt that he should be allowed to make creative contributions to the film rather than simply become the conduit for Lucas' vision. More and more he alienated the crew, demonstrating a pronounced lack of interpersonal skills, and in return many of the crew bad-mouthed him behind his back, making the actual production an extremely unpleasant experience for the sensitive director.

If that weren't enough, once production had wrapped and after a brief break on Maui, Lucas discovered that the initial assembly of shots bore no resemblance to what he had in mind and editing had to restart from scratch, necessitating at least a three-month delay. Worse, when it came time to view the special effects that John Dykstra had completed thus far, he discovered "they had spent a year and $1 million and had only come up with one acceptable shot."

Dykstra, on the other hand, had spent his time creating a new motion control system he dubbed Dysktraflex, while assigning Colin Cantwell and his team of model-makers to manufacture the stunning miniatures used in the film. At that point, there were a number of elements that had been filmed and stored in the effects house library, but very few completed shots. Lucas naturally panicked and ended up in the Marin General Hospital with hypertension (and despite the acclaim awarded Dykstra's effects, never worked with Dykstra again).

Consequently, while Marcia Lucas and others worked on editing the film, Lucas devoted himself to personally supervising the special effects work. A rough assemblage of the film without finished effects, music or sound effects simply left viewers dumb-founded and feeling that the film was a disaster. The cantina scene needed beefing up, and Lucas and Kurtz went to Alan Ladd, Jr., for an extra $100,000 to insert more alien creatures into the sparsely populated sequence with Rick Baker and Rob Bottin filling in for the now absent Stuart Freeborn. Because most of the effects were shot using blue screen instead of back projection, it became possible to revise and improve the background elements later.

Kurtz quickly mastered the technical details he needed to know to get ILM into an efficient operation. By the original Christmas deadline, enough footage had been completed to assemble an exciting teaser trailer which was sent out to theaters accompanied by the "Mars" theme from Holst's Planets suite. The demoralized ILM was revitalized as it started seeing its work come to fruition, and more and more people put in overtime to make the Memorial Day weekend release.

Some of *Star Wars* took shape in the editing. According to editor Paul Hirsch, who was hired to help the film make its deadline as Marcia Lucas was cutting the end battle and Richard Chew worked on the main body of the film:

> *Star Wars* opens up with an initial clash between Darth Vader's troops and Princess Leia's followers — there's a battle going on in space. In the script, and in the original cut, in the middle of the battle we cut down to the surface of the planet and show Luke Skywalker who looks up at the sky with his binoculars and sees the fighting going on — little flashes of light. He gets all excited and jumps into his speeder. Now the rest of this scene, for several reasons, really didn't work. I suggested that we simply axe the whole scene because other parts of the film imparted much of the same information....
>
> Now, with that scene missing, we don't get to the surface of Luke's planet until we're brought there by R2D2 and C-3PO. Now when they're walking around the desert there's an enormous sense of mystery created about where they are. What is this place? When you see the jawas, you think these may be the only inhabitants of the planet. We find rather than cutting to Luke arbitrarily we're taken there through R2D2 and C-3PO landing on the planet, being captured and then delivered to Luke's farm. So we introduce Luke to the story in somewhat of an organic manner.

Regarding the film's climax, Hirsch reports,

> George was having difficulties with Twentieth Century Fox, who had always wanted to cut the end battle from the film. They didn't want to spend the money for the scene, they said, "Look, they go to the Death Star, they rescue the princess, the picture is over." George decided he'd better get this battle done first, so he wouldn't have the plug pulled on him before it could be done. We had to lock this sequence in early so the special effects guys could start working on it. At this point we did tag team editing, Marcia, George and I, for about 5 days.
>
> I suggested, since the effects had not yet been shot, that Vader's ship be made slightly different from the others, in order that his maneuvers stand out. (My inspiration for this has a strange origin. As a New Yorker, it struck me as very interesting how people in California begin to be identified with their cars and vice versa.) Also, by virtue of working with De Palma for so many years, on so many suspense movies, I was very aware of the requirements of suspense. For the end battle to work we needed a sense of time running out. To add this, they went and shot some second unit stuff, shots of the Death Star troopers using a countdown towards the destruction of the rebel planet. All this material gives a counterpoint to Luke's progress in the trench. We then also built up a sequence earlier in the film when Peter Cushing blows up Alderaan, a sequence that duplicates the steps shown later in the film, to give the example of how a planet is blown up. This prepares the audience for the suspenseful effect of the final sequence.

According to Steven Spielberg in 1982, "Lucas was the most surprised kid on the block when *Star Wars* became a megahit. When I was with George a few weeks before the film opened he was predicting $15 million in domestic film rentals. 'Cause he thought he'd made a Walt Disney film that wouldn't have much appeal beyond very young preteens. And he had tapped a nerve that not only went deep but went global.

"George has theories now, about five years later, but at

the time there was no explaining. And I think George realized the meaning of what he had done as much from the critiques he read, and the psychological analysis they pinned to *Star Wars* as from his own introspection."

Star Wars became an international phenomenon, racking up huge grosses all over the world and quickly becoming the top grossing film of all time. (It is still in the top five.) It established the Memorial Day weekend as one of the prime film release dates, starting from a holiday weekend and remaining a hit all summer long. It established science fiction henceforth as potentially the most lucrative film genre of all time, inspiring legions of filmgoers to re-experience this particular trip to other worlds again and again and again. Even the novelization of the film, attributed to Lucas, sold some three million copies.

Suddenly after two huge hits, George founded Industrial Light and Magic, purchased a ranch in Marin County (close to both San Francisco and his old stomping grounds), and hoped to set up a professional creative community fashioned out of his film school experiences where a small group of likeminded people helped each other make films.

In order to keep control, Lucas paid the costs of *Star Wars: The Empire Strikes Back* out of his own pocket, hiring Irvin Kershner to direct. (Lucas thought Kershner's *The Return of a Man Called Horse* was an even better film than the original, and hoped he could do the same for the *Star Wars* saga.) Veteran science fiction writer and screenwriter Leigh Brackett was hired to write the film, but unfortunately died of cancer right after completing her first draft. Lucas liked the work Lawrence Kasdan was doing on the script for *Raiders of the Lost Ark*, and so gave him *The Empire Strikes Back* to revise as well.

As production costs mounted, especially as the dollar was falling against the pound and the budget was heading towards the $30 million range, Lucas worried that Kershner was making the film too well and was concerned that it might not repeat the success of the original. Additional funds had to be borrowed to complete the film.

In a letter, Kirschner himself has written, "*Empire* was budgeted at about $21 million and came in at $26 million. During the shooting the pound sterling inflated, adding greatly to the cost of the film. I followed a schedule that was ever-changing. We began the planning believing that we would have eight sound stages for the 64 sets needed. A week or so before shooting, one of Kubrick's stages from *The Shining* burned to the ground, leaving us with seven stages. This presented us with a severe logistical problem, which haunted us for the entire shoot. The building crews worked 'round the clock, constructing and quickly tearing down the sets. Many times I began shooting on sets not completed. I had to shoot out of sequence within a scene while the builders completed other parts of the set."

Many consider *The Empire Strikes Back* to be the better film, though it is not as well directed as Lucas' *Star Wars*, lacking Lucas' knack for creating wonder matter-of-factly within a scene (e.g. look at the way Lucas handles three-dimensional holograms with the way Kershner handles them).

The film deepens the character's internal conflicts, but suffers from being the least resolved of the *Star Wars* films, ending as it does on a cliffhanger that leaves the fate of Han Solo unresolved.

Following *The Empire Strikes Back*, Lucas decided to lend his name (as presenter and executive producer) and prestige to getting a release for Akira Kurosawa's *Kagemusha: The Shadow Warrior*, persuading 20th Century–Fox to put up half the funds needed for Kurosawa to finish the film, which concerns how a lowly foot soldier is made to impersonate a great warlord he greatly resembles. The film won first prize, the Palme d'Or at the Cannes Film Festival.

Lucas then allowed Steven Spielberg to helm his notion of the exciting adventures of a reckless anthropologist named Indiana after his pet dog in *Raiders of the Lost Ark*. This too took the public by storm (see chapter on Spielberg for details on the Indiana Jones films). *Raiders* became the largest grossing film of 1981, launching a series of sequels and even ending up as a ride at Disneyland, the Indiana Jones Adventure.

Lawrence Kasdan sold his script *Body Heat* to the Ladd Company at Warner Bros., and was told he could direct provided he get a name director as sponsor who could take over should he get into trouble. Lucas became an uncredited executive producer so that Kasdan could get the film made.

Lucas finished up the *Star Wars* trilogy with the disappointing but elaborate *Return of the Jedi*, directed by the late Richard Marquand from a script by Lawrence Kasdan. Compared to the previous Kasdan script, *Return of the Jedi* seems hurriedly written, with plentiful bad dialogue, and is cynically put together. The aliens in the film look like the muppets that they are and seem designed to sell as toys rather than make for convincing alien lifeforms. Even worse, the main aliens in the last third of the film, the Ewoks, seem deliberately designed to corner the teddy bear market (if so, the attempt was unsuccessful).

Lucas also executive produced two telemovie follow-ups, *The Ewok Adventure: Caravan of Courage,* scripted by Bob Carrau and directed by John Korty, and *Ewoks: The Battle of Endor*, written and directed by Jim and Ken Wheat. Both won Emmys for outstanding children's programming and were shown theatrically abroad. There was also an animated spin-off, *Ewoks and Droids Adventure Hour*, later shortened to the half-hour *Ewoks* for its second season, and another special, this one animated and featuring R2D2 and C-3PO called *The Great Heep*, that was directed by Clive Smith and written by soundman Ben Burtt.

His Lucasfilm also sponsored an animated feature using the French technique of *Lumage*, in which images are lit from below and manipulated to move, to create the quaint film *Twice Upon a Time*, directed by John Korty, which failed to capture the public's attention with its very fanciful creations. It told of the Murkworks, which sends out nightmares to people in the real world and which is under the direction of Synonamess Botch, whose plan is thwarted by the film's unlikely protagonists, a shapechanging dog named Ralph and his partner Mumford, who speaks only in sound effects. They are aided by a Bronxian Fairy Godfather and a dimwitted superhero named Rod Rescueman. Marshall Efron, Hamilton Camp, and Paul Frees supplied the main voices.

Lucas assisted Walter Murch on cost and production problems on *Return to Oz* and received a thank you credit in return. He and Coppola teamed as executive producers for Paul Schrader's inventive film *Mishima*, an unusual film biography of the controversial Japanese writer Yukio Mishima. Lucasfilm was also behind Haskell Wexler's politically committed film *Latino*.

The late Jim Henson proposed that Lucasfilm and his Henson Associates work together on an elaborate fantasy titled *Labyrinth*, written by Terry Jones of Monty Python fame. The narrative focuses on a teenage girl (Jennifer Connelly) who, forced to baby-sit her younger brother, wishes he would disappear only for the boy to be kidnapped by the King of the Goblins (David Bowie), forcing her to brave adventures to get him back. The production design was more impressive than the story itself, which proved uninvolving.

Even worse was *Howard the Duck*, which Lucas' friends Hyuck and Katz purchased the rights to. Howard was an off-the-wall comic book character created by Steve Gerber, a duck with human intelligence and a sassy sense of humor who becomes involved in satirical send-ups of superhero adventures. Unfortunately, Kuyck and Katz inflated the project out of proportion and went with an unfortunate duck suit that captured nothing of the personality of the original character. The film went 20 percent overbudget, receiving scathing reviews, and became the biggest bomb of Lucas' career.

In 1985, Lucas wrote and produced the 3-D Francis Ford Coppola directed science fiction short *Captain EO*, starring Michael Jackson as a disco-dancing spaceship captain with a intergalactic crew of puppety creatures with names like Fuzzball, Major Domo, and Hooter. Eo, from the Greek word for "dawn," confronts an evil alien menace (Angelica Huston) whom he transforms with his dancing and goodwill into something good. John Napier designed the sets, Geoffrey Kirkland was the art director, and *A Chorus Line*'s Jeffrey Honaday handled the choreography, and Jackson himself provided two songs for the score. Running 17 minutes and made at a cost of $20 million (making it more expensive than most features of the time), *Captain EO* was designed as a Disneyland theme park attraction which exploited 3-D with some interactive effects. (Laser blasts would seem to leap off the screen and into the audience.)

In 1988, Lucas coproduced the Don Bluth film *The Land Before Time* with kiddie dinosaurs searching for a bountiful land and facing many dangers. (The film has led to at least five made-for-video sequels.) He was executive producer of Coppola's *Tucker: The Man and His Dream*, personally putting up funding for preproduction on the film, and he wrote the story that was the basis for Ron Howard's *Willow*, which tried to rework Campbell's monomyth ingredients one more time, this time with much less success.

Lucas' biggest problem with *Indiana Jones and the Last Crusade* was keeping the budget down to $44 million, given the amount of inflation in Hollywood. The film was originally to have been a haunted house movie, but with Spielberg having already done *Poltergeist*, it was decided to take a different tack. Lucas suggested a story involving the Monkey King in Africa, and Chris Columbus wrote a script, but neither Lucas nor Spielberg was happy with it. A new script centered around the Holy Grail was created by Menno Meyjes, but this did not meet with approval until it was revised by Jeffrey Boam.

Lucas tried to break into television with a pair of series. One, *Maniac Mansion*, was based on a popular computer game and starred Joe Flaherty, Deb Faker, Cathleen Robertson, George Buza, Mary Charlotte Wilcox, and John Hemphill as the oddball Edison family who live in a mansion full of weird gadgets. It debuted on the Family Channel in September of 1990.

More conventional was *The Young Indiana Jones Chronicles*, which premiered in March 1992 on the ABC television network. It showcased the Jones character from the ages of four to his early twenties (Corey Carrier plays Indy at nine; Sean Patrick Flanery at 16), and depicting his encounters with various historical figures. Despite its elaborate production, the series failed to captivate viewers and the stories did little to bring the characters to life. Still, the elaborately produced series won the 1993 Banff Award for Best Continuing Series, a 1993 Golden Globe nomination for Best Dramatic Series, an Angel Award for Quality Programming, and ten Emmy Awards out of 25 nominations.

In 1992, George Lucas was honored with the Irving G. Thalberg Award. The Award was given by the Board of

Governors of the Academy of Motion Picture Arts and Sciences.

Lucas' most recent work was producing the long delayed *The Radioland Murders,* which was based on a story Lucas came up with just after *American Graffiti*. The film, directed by Mel Smith, is an all-star extravaganza about a series of murders at a new radio network, WBN, in 1939 that stem from an attempt to stifle the emerging medium of television which would soon dominate the world's airwaves. The owner, General Whalen (Ned Beatty) has gathered together prospective sponsors, including the flinty Bernie King (Brion James), but as the show starts, one of the band members is murdered, and soon people begin dropping like flies with writer and hero Roger Henderson (Brian Benben) as the main suspect. The cast manages to waste such talents as Mary Stuart Masterson, George Burns, Michael Lerner, Michael McKean, Jeffrey Tambor, Christopher Lloyd, Anita Morris, Corbin Bernsen, Rosemary Clooney, Bobcat Goldthwait, Robert Walden, Billy Barty, Bo Hopkins, Candy Clark, and others.

Lucas takes story credit for the film, though the plot is incredibly similar to the (much funnier) Mitchell Leisen film *Murder at the Vanities* (1934). Smith keeps things going at a fever pitch, but the result is unfortunately more frenzied than funny. Lucas used the film to pioneer successfully a technique of creating elaborate sets digitally in order to keep production costs down, though the modest $10 million product failed to find an audience.

The special effects company established by George Lucas in 1971 has today evolved into three Lucas companies. Lucas Digital Ltd. encompasses Industrial Light & Magic (ILM) and Skywalker Sound, the award-winning visual effects, television commercial production, and audio postproduction businesses. ILM has played a key role in 6 of the top 12 box office hits of all time, winning 14 Academy Awards for Best Visual Effects and 12 Technical Achievement Awards. Skywalker Sound has been a pioneer in breakthrough picture and sound editing technologies and has been honored with 10 Academy Awards.

LucasArts Entertainment Company is a leading international developer and publisher of entertainment software. The company's games have won critical acclaim with more than 100 industry awards for excellence and consistently have been in top ten lists of best-selling software. The company's runaway CD-ROM hit *Rebel Assault* sold more than 1.5 million copies worldwide.

Lucasfilm Ltd. includes all of Lucas' feature film and television productions and the business activities of Licensing and the THX Group. The patented THX Sound System is currently installed in more than 1,400 certified THX theatres worldwide. The THX division also provides presentation enhancement services for theatrical film releases through its Theatre Alignment Program, for laserdisc releases through its THX Laser Disc Program, and for consumer equipment through its Home THX Program.

In 1997, Lucas rereleased the original trilogy in an updated edition that redid many of the old effects shots by using computer graphics imagery. The most significant alteration to *Star Wars* was the insertion of the long-trimmed Jabba the Hut scene where Jabba confronts Han Solo before he enters the *Millennium Falcon*. The original and much differently designed figure of Jabba was replaced by an image that brought it more in line with the look established by *Return of the Jedi*. However, this sequence simply repeats the conversation that Solo had with Greedo back at the bar. Other changes include that Greedo now clearly fires first in his exchange with Han, and backwater Mos Eisley now seems a good deal more populated by computer generated critters.

Additionally, *Empire* had the snow monster revised in its opening, and the Sky City is updated and elaborated on. For *Jedi*, Lucas includes a music video starring several computer-generated creatures that he was unable to pull off with the muppets originally featured. Also, at the end of the film, he added scenes of celebration after the death of the Emperor from several other cultures who will be introduced when Lucas fashions the long-delayed prequel trilogy.

In explaining why he decided to alter these cinematic classics, Lucas reported, "The original inspiration for bringing the films back to the big screen was the twentieth anniversary of the original release of *Star Wars*. Occasionally, we have shown the trilogy as one movie for various fan conventions. So, I said why don't we try to release all three films, as a trilogy, within a few weeks of each other, so that people can see them like the Saturday matinee serials they were originally meant to be. I thought that would be a very appropriate way of celebrating the twentieth anniversary.

"At the same time, I had an ulterior motive that I had been thinking about for a long time — actually ever since the films were finished. There were various things, especially in the original film, that I wasn't satisfied with — special effects shots that never were really finished, scenes that I'd wanted to include that couldn't be included for some reason, mostly money and time. I really wanted to fix the films and have them be complete. A famous filmmaker said, 'Films are never completed; they're only abandoned.' Rather than living with my abandoned movie, I really wanted to go back and complete it. *Empire* and *Jedi* didn't gnaw at me quite the same way as the first one did, because the first one was done under extreme conditions. It was very low-budget, and it was very challenging to get it done in time, considering we had to invent a lot of new technologies and do all kinds of things that had never been done before. The envelope of perfection had to be stretched way beyond what it had been on the other films, and there were a lot more things that I was really anxious to have fixed."

In an interview he gave *Action* in 1974, Lucas admitted that when he directs, he gets "physically sick. I get a very bad cough and a cold when I direct.... It's like climbing mountains, cut and bruised and freezing cold, and you lose your toes and everything and then you get it done and it's all worth it." He has since preferred to become a hands-on creative producer, allowing him to spend more time with his adopted children, but he returned to the director's chair to helm the first of the new *Star Wars* trilogy, initially entitled *The Clone Wars*, then changed to *The Phantom Menace*, which was released in 1999, and expects to direct the sequel.

Preproduction began on the project in London. It was shot at Leavesden Studios, a former Rolls Royce factory that was converted into a large studio facility for the James Bond film *Goldeneye*, which Lucas updated with the latest in technology. *Menace* was produced by Rick McCallum, who oversaw production on Lucas' *Young Indiana Jones Chronicles* television show.

Production on the first *Star Wars* episode began on July 22, 1997, at the Royal Palace in Caserta, Italy, which serves as the site where a young queen (Natalie Portman) is coronated, with additional outdoor scenes being filmed close to the Palace's waterfalls and gardens. The production then moved on to Tunisia in late July and August to film Tatooine scenes, including a lightsabre duel between a Jedi (Liam Neeson) and his dark opponent. There is a temporary setback when a freak thunderstorm destroyed key pieces of one of the sets as well as blowing various costumes across the landscape, though according to Lucas a similar tempest hit the original *Star Wars* production.

Meanwhile, the main sets for the new feature were constructed at England's Leavesden Studio, where filming began in September. Additionally, ILM provided computer-generated sets to increase the epic scope and look of the production. Ewan McGregor portrays the young Obi-Wan Kenobi, a friend and apprentice to Neeson's Jedi. Jake Lloyd plays the 8-year-old Anakin Skywalker, with Pernilla August portraying Shmi, his mother. Kenny Baker returns to the series as R2D2 with Frank Oz returning as the voice of Yoda. Also back is Warwick Davis as an Ewok named Wicket. Terence Stamp was hired to play the president of the Republic, and Ian McDiarmid, who had played the Emperor in *Jedi*, returns as Senator Palpatine. Also involved in this outing is Samuel L. Jackson who asked to be given a small part in the picture.

For his production crew, Lucas retained only visual effects supervisor Dennis Muren and composer John Williams from the previous *Star Wars* films, and assigned major positions to members of his television crew from *Young Indiana Jones Chronicles* including producer Rick McCallum, production designer Gavin Bocquet, and cinematographer David Tattersall.

Star Wars—The Phantom Menace proved an enormous disappointment to fans of the earlier series, as it retained the look of the previous movies but came off as undernourished in terms of plot, character or dialogue, all being distinctly unmemorable. The film makes a hero of 8-year-old Anakin Skywalker (a wooden Jake Lloyd, leading to jokes about him being Mannequin Skywalker), who will grow up to be ruthless mass murderer Darth Vader. He is a chosen one, born of an immaculate conception and sold into slavery to Watto, a greedy, hook-nosed merchant. (The film is rife with insensitive racial stereotypes blatantly attributed to various alien species.)

Two Jedi knights, Qui-Gon (Liam Neeson) and his apprentice Obi Wan (Ewan McGregor) have been sent to settle a trade dispute between lisping, devious fish creatures of the Trade Federation and Queen Amidala of *Dinotopia*-like planet Naboo which is being overrun by scrawny, white battle droids. They are aided by Jamaican-accented underwater creature Jar Jar Binks (voice by Ahmed Best), whose painful comic relief routines subvert the movie. The phantom menace of the title is Senator Palpatine (Ian McDiarmid) who creates the situation so that he can coerce Queen Amidala into leading a voice of no confidence in the Chancellor of the Republic (Terence Stamp), thereby setting up a situation where Palpatine can assume power and eventually become the dread Emperor.

Illogicalities abound in the film. The Force goes from being a spiritual thing to being detectable in the blood. Anakin proves to have the potential to be a great Jedi knight and is a whiz with machinery; however, Yoda, who trained a 20-something Luke, refuses to train 8-year-old Anakin because he's too old, and even worse, because he might turn dangerous, so that somehow it is better not to give Anakin an experienced teacher and train him to be a good guy, but rather leave his mega-force talent ripe for whoever would exploit it. The supposedly good Jedi take no action on slavery on Tatooine, leave mom behind, but take an 8-year-old along with them on a raid into the enemy's heavily defended HQ.

The CGI work is impressive and pervasive, rendering the film more an elaborate cartoon than a live-action feature, and naturally Lucas piles on one action sequence after another, but the only one that really works is the "pod race" which blatantly rips off the chariot race from *Ben Hur*. The climax is an extreme case of *déjà vu*, both *Star Wars* and *Jedi* used it, in which a lone craft penetrates the perimeter defenses to blow up a power source in order to save the day yet again.

Lucas reportedly looks forward to the day when 35mm film will be done away with entirely ("I haven't touched a piece of film for years," he recently announced) in favor of a digital theatrical presentation, and he allowed an all-digital version of *The Phantom Menace* to be screened at four theatres. In 1998, he predicted that computers would change the way motion pictures are made and announced, "The world of special effects and the world of production are merging into one entity. Computers will allow filmmakers to manipulate images the way a painter or sculptor would manipulate his work." Subsequently, he expressed the desire to shoot *Phantom Menace*'s sequels electronically rather than using film. He has also reveled in digital effects' ability to allow him to tinker with scenes almost endlessly, allowing him to add or delete characters, alter textures, movement, or color as suits his whim. He sees himself as living in a transitional era in which digital technology will allow film artists to expand their imaginations greatly.

Despite the passage of the years, *Star Wars* remains an extremely popular item with a wide fan base eager for new adventures. *The Phantom Menace* confirmed audience's hopes by showcasing plenty of action, effects, and the traditional *Star Wars* look while being new material. Lucas has clearly passed the realm of pop ephemera and devised a myth with long-lasting, transgenerational appeal. Its shoot-'em-up thrills are readily accessible to every culture across the world, and the face of science fiction has been indelibly marked by its presence.

WILLIAM MALONE (1947–)

Adventures into the Unknown (shorts, 1961); *The Night Turkey* (1974); *Scared to Death* (1982); *Creature* (1985); *Dead Star* (forthcoming); *The House on Haunted Hill* (1999)
Television: *Holmes and Watson* (pilot, 1975); "Heartbreak Hotel," "Lucky Stiff," *Freddy's Nightmares* (1989); "Easy Come, Easy Go," *Freddy's Nightmares* (1990)

William Malone was born in 1947, in Lansing, Michigan, becoming a science fiction aficionado in the fifties after his mother took him to see *Creature from the Black Lagoon* when he was seven years old. By the age of 14, he had made numerous 8mm films including a series of shorts called *Adventures into the Unknown.* As a teenager, he came out to Los Angeles to start a rock 'n' roll band, but "I couldn't get guys who were not on drugs long enough to show up for rehearsal," he said. At the age of 19, Malone moved to Los Angeles and wrote and produced a number of singles, plus an album for Atlantic Records, but he became disillusioned with the music business.

Malone started making masks and working on special effects, becoming the "head designer" for the Don Post Studios (a mask-making company). Out of his deep love for *Forbidden Planet,* he built a replica of Robby the Robot, which appeared at one of Bob Burns' famous Halloween displays. Word filtered back to the prop guys at the studios, and soon Malone's Robby was invited to appear on an episode of *Columbo* and elsewhere, including appearances in the Joe Dante films *Hollywood Boulevard* and *Gremlins.*

Malone's handiwork also appeared on episodes of *Mork and Mindy, Project UFO,* McDonaldland commercials and others. In 1974, he tackled his first real production, *The Night Turkey,* an elaborate amateur spoof of *The Night Stalker* TV series, which won the best amateur film award at the Westercon science fiction convention. Unfortunately, Malone did not get permission to do his spoof, and the lengthy short was quickly shelved.

In 1975, he directed the pilot for a live-action Saturday morning show starring Jerry Mathers about a robot who thinks he is Sherlock Holmes. For the next several years, Malone directed and produced several short films and documentaries as well as a music video.

"After [the first requests for Robby], I got interested in film again in a very serious way," said Malone. "I worked for a very long time trying to get projects off the ground, which was very frustrating, and then finally about 1979, I concluded that there was no way I was going to get help from anyone, so I wrote a script called *Scared to Death,* and basically sold the cat, the dog, the car, the house, and mortgaged myself [to make it. The film cost a minuscule $78,000].

"We rented a warehouse, I think from the guy who builds Catalina yachts, who had a big warehouse in Northridge, and we used his building to build the sets. I couldn't afford to have anybody build the monster, so I built the monster for it myself. Most of it was built out of sheet foam. There were some sculpted pieces, the head, and hands and feet and the chest piece, but everything else was

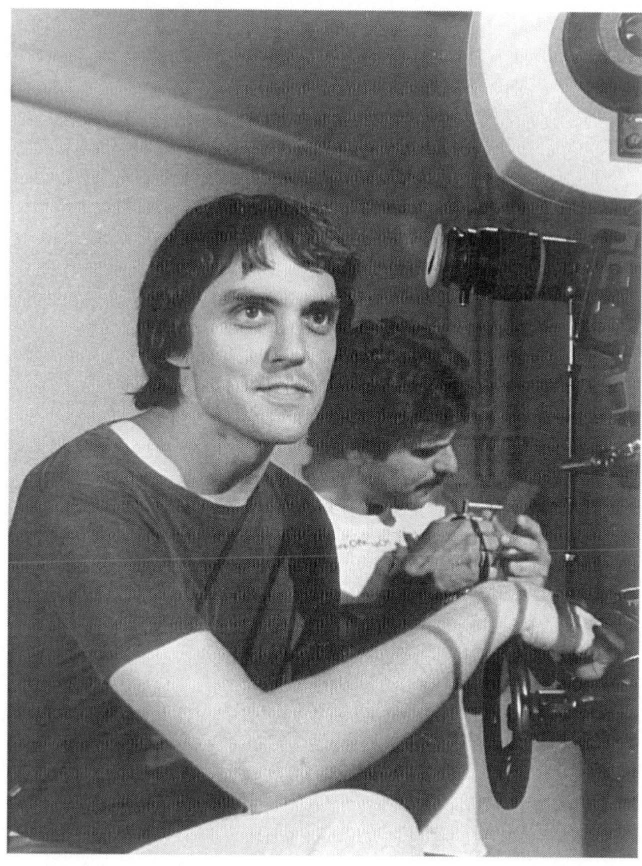

An eager William Malone prepares to direct *Creature*, originally titled *The Titan Find.*

just built out of foam. I didn't have time really to do the kind of work I would have liked to have done 'cause I really wanted to get it going, but I'm fairly happy with it."

Malone and producer Bill Dunn tried to get a science fictional detective project entitled *Murder in the 21st Century* off the ground, but supporters felt the project did not have enough exploitation value and asked Malone to bring them something else the next day. Malone rummaged around and found a two page story synopsis called *The Titan Find,* which he had written six or seven years earlier. The folks at Cardinal Pictures and Trans World Entertainment ended up giving the project the green light and a $3.5 million budget.

Creature was originally filmed under the title *The Titan Find,* which does nothing to disguise its origins as an *Alien* imitator. The Titan referred to is, of course, Saturn's moon where a space expedition has been lost (à la *It's the Terror from Beyond Space*). Mike Davidson (Stan Ivar) heads a team which has gone to investigate, the team consisting of David Perkins (Lyman Ward), an executive from the corporation that has bankrolled the expedition, Dr. Wendy Oliver (Annette McCarthy), security officer Melanie Bryce (Diane Salinger), and several astronauts, Susan Delambra (Marie Laurin), John Pennel (Robert Jaffe), and Beth Sladen (Wendy Schaal).

Their ship has a rough landing on Saturn's moon and the team soon discovers that they were beaten to their objective by a West German team, all of whom are dead except for Hans Rudy Hofner (Klaus Kinski), the captain of the expedition who has somehow managed to survive in this cold and hostile environment. Hofner explains that there is a terrible alien creature on this moon which kills and then re-animates its victims.

Hofner is killed while trying to rig a bomb to destroy the creature. It then murders Delambra and uses her body to lure Pennel to his doom. Pennel's corpse pursues Bryce, who escapes. The alien then invades the ship when only three people are aboard. Davidson, Perkins and Sladen try to rig Hofner's bomb to destroy the creature, but their plan fails and Perkins is killed instead.

The creature becomes trapped, and Bryce returns in time to set off the explosive, eliminating the threat forever. The survivors then rig the German ship so that it can take them safely home.

Creature was produced by Trans World Entertainment for a mere $1.3 million, and proved to be extremely profitable, except to its creator, who fell victim to the creative accounting of Hollywood. The monster costume in *Creature* was a big disappointment to Malone, who enlisted the aid of Doug Beswick to create something workable out of Malone's botched designs.

Regarding Klaus Kinski, Malone said, "Klaus was a maniac actually. What happened when we were making that picture, the executive producers hired him to be in the movie two weeks before we started shooting and there was no part for him, so I had to hurriedly write something for him to do in the picture, and the picture shows it, but these are the sorts of things that happen when you're making a low budget movie.

"Klaus was crazier off camera than the part I wrote for him, and I wrote him as a total looney. The first day of shooting he shows up, and the first thing out of his mouth was, 'I raped my 12-year-old daughter, you know.' I thought, oh *great,* this is going to be fun.

"Halfway through the first day of shooting, the crew came up to me en masse and said, 'Billy, we want you to know we're all going to take Klaus out back and beat the shit out of him.' I said, 'Look guys, you have to wait until the end of the week, and then you can do everything you want.' He was a madman, really, but I will say this, when he's on screen, he just lights up the screen. He's definitely one of the best things in the picture. He really added a lot to it. When we write a script, a lot of times the actors don't give you what you heard in your head. Klaus was one of the few people who gave me exactly what I was writing, the intonation and delivery that I heard for this stuff."

A running gag on the set occurred after Kinski tried to make a pass at the female makeup artist who was applying his makeup by sticking his knee between her legs and telling her, "That is not my knee, that is my cock." From then on, whenever anyone on the set bumped into someone else, it became *de rigueur* to say, "That is not my knee, that is my cock," regardless of the circumstances.

William Malone poses with his re-creations of Gort and Robby the Robot at his home (photo by author).

Malone has also designed the creature for *Syngenor* (1990), a sequel to *Scared to Death*. Malone has also worked for some time trying to launch his space epic *Dead Star* off the ground. *Dead Star* centers around a black hole which could be the gateway for mankind to span the galaxy or a portal through which the legions of hell are unleashed.

The proposed project has already been production designed by H. R. Giger and production designer Michael Novotny. "The premise is once somebody dies, you actually go to an actual physical place," explained Malone. "It's not like passing through another dimension ... your physical being can get there by this machine. Giger, of course, designed everything in the hellish world. Giger's great, though. We asked him to design the demon that's in the picture and a few other elements, and he wound up just sending us reams and reams of drawings and stuff which were great, but he drew everything from the spaceship [the *Bellerophon*, named after a ship referred to in *Forbidden Planet*] that the good guys were using to things we never even dreamed of having him design."

Dead Star is set in the year 2239, where a spaceship commander named Tennison has his wife Rachel murdered by Anton Barlow, a demented archaelogist who was part of the first expedition to take a space jump across the galaxy by using a dimension drive system that mankind has just come up with. "What the expedition finds out is this alien machine which is capable of re-animating the dead and transporting them to hell," said Malone. "Our hero goes out into space to try and track Barlow down, and he basically kidnaps or absconds with this spaceship, kidnaps the crew, and takes them on this journey to find this guy. A lot of it is his internal struggle with what he is doing and the loss of his wife.

"One of the effects of this machine is that the longer you are around it, you begin having these terrible hallucinations of a nightmarish nature, and the hero begins to think he's losing his mind and doesn't realize that this machine is generating all these images."

Malone worked out the original story with Michael Carmody. Malone plans to give the film a new look, getting away from the look of Scott's *Alien* which has become so dominant in SF horror films.

Other projects that he has developed but which have not come to fruition are *The Mirror*, a sort of *Alice Through the Looking Glass* done as a horror film based on Giger's *Necronomicon* in which a woman is transported into a world ruled by machines who are looking to re-create mankind (the project was a go at Orion until it was canceled following the poor box office returns on George Romero's *Monkey Shines*), and *Box*, about the first computer with artificial intelligence

The body of a dead astronaut becomes re-animated by the Creature in *Creature*.

who inadvertently kills someone and so must create a mechanical body and escape before its plug is pulled.

Malone is also listed as one of the scriptwriters for the forthcoming science fiction film *Supernova*, along with Dan Chuba, Thomas Wheeler, and David Campbell Wilson, which is being produced by United Artists/Imperial Entertainment.

Producer Joel Silver (*Predator, Matrix*) and director Robert Zemeckis have set up the Warner Bros.–based film company Dark Castle Entertainment, which will concentrate on medium-budget horror films. The pair hired Malone to direct their first movie, a remake of William Castle's *House on Haunted Hill* starring Geoffrey Rush, Elizabeth Hurley, and Bruce Dern. Dern was hired when Marilyn Manson declined the role of the caretaker of Hill House.

ANTONIO MARGHERITI (1930–)

Vecchia Roma (1953); *Il Planeta Degli Uomini Spenti* (aka *Battle of the Worlds*); *Assignment Outer Space* (aka *Space Men*) (1961); *L'Arciere Degli Uomini Spenti* (aka *La Freccia D'Oro; The Golden Arrow*) (1962); *Il Crollo di Roma* (aka *Fall of Rome*) (1963); *I Giganti di Roma* (aka *Giants of Rome*); *Hercules, Prisoner of Evil; Go! Go! Go! World; La Danza Macabra* (aka *Castle of Terror*; *Castle of Blood*); *Ursus, Il Terror dei Kirghisi* (aka *Hercules, Prisoner of Evil*); *La Vergine di Norumberga* (aka *The Virgin of Nuremberg; Horror Castle; Castle of Terror*); *Il Pelo nel Mondo* (1964); *Anthar L'Invincible* (aka *The Devil of the Desert Against the Son of Hercules*); *I Criminali Delle Galassia* (aka *The Wild Wild Planet*); *I Lunghi Capelli della Morta* (aka *Long Hair of Death); A 007 Sfida ai Killers* (aka *Bob Fleming ... Mission Casablanca*); *Planet on the Prowl* (aka *Il Pianeta Errante; War Between Planets*); *War of the Planets* (aka *I Diafanoidi Vengono da Marte*); *The Killers Are Challenged* (1965); *Snow Devils* (aka *I Diavola della Spazio*; *Snow Demons*) (1966); *Operazione Goldman* (aka *Lightning Bolt*); *Da Uomo a Uomo* (1967); *Joe L'Implaccabile* (aka *Dynamite Joe*); *Io Ti Amo; Nude ... Si Muore* (aka *The Young, the Evil and the Savage; Schoolgirl Killer*) (1968); *Contronatura* (aka *The Unnaturals; The Exterminators*); *Joko, Invoci dio e Mouri* (aka *Vengeance*); *E Dio Disse a Caino ...* (aka *And God Said to Cain*) (1969); *Mr. Superinvisible*; *Nella Stretta Morsa del Ragno* (aka *Web of the Spider*) (1970); *Finalmente ... le mille e una Notte*; *Novelle Galeotte D'Amore del "Decamerone"*; *Seven Deaths in a Cat's Eye* (aka *La Morte negli occhi del Gatto*) (1972); *Ming, Ragazzi!* (aka *Hercules Against Karate*) (1973); *Blood Money*; *Manone il Ladrone*; *Whisky e Fantasmi* (aka *Whisky and Ghosts*) (1974); *Take a Hard Ride*; *The Stranger and the Gunfighter* (aka *La Dove non batte il Sole*) (1975); *Death Rage* (aka *Con la Rabbia Agli Occhi*); *House of 1,000 Pleasures* (1977); *Rip Off* (aka *The Squeeze*) (1978); *Killer Fish* (aka *Treasure of the Piranha; Killer fish-aguato sul fondo*) (1979); *The Last Hunter* (1980); *Car Crash* (1981); *Tiger Joe* (aka *Fuga dal Archipelago Maledetto*); *Hunters of the Golden Cobra* (aka *Cacciatori drel cobra d'oro*); *Invasion of the Flesh Hunters* (aka *Cannibals in the Streets; Apocalisse domani*); *Ark of the Sun God ... Temple of Hell* (aka *I sporavissuti dell città morta*) (1982); *Tornado*; *Yor, the Hunter from the Future* (1983); *Codename: Wildgeese* (aka *Geheimcode Wildgänse*) (1984); *Jungle Raiders* (1984); *Kommando Leopard* (aka *Commando Leopard.*) (1985); *Der Commander*; *Alien from the Deep* (1988); *Indio* (1989); *Indio Part 2: The Revolt* (1991)

Television: *Il Mondi Yor* (1993); *La Isola del Tessoro* (aka *Treasure Island in Outer Space*) (1986);*Genghis Khan* (codirector with Ken Annakin, uncredited) (1992)

Born in Rome, September 19, 1930, Antonio Margheriti has specialized in ultra low budget films including science fiction and action fare, often presented under the pseudonym Anthony M. Dawson. His films are consistently colorful and dull, with comic book storylines. He was the son of a railroad engineer who began his film career as an assistant editor in 1950 working with Mario Serandrei. He also dallied by making short documentaries, beginning with *Vecchia Roma* in 1953. *Vecchia Roma* [Old Rome] tried the unusual tactic of presenting the entire film from a single character's actual point of view, so that we see Rome through his eyes, à la Robert Montgomery's innovative *Lady in the Lake.*

In 1954, Margheriti tried his hand at special effects, working on Pino Mercanti's *I cinque dell'Adamello* and *La notte che la terra tremo* among others. He began writing screenplays in 1955, selling *Classe di ferro* to producer Turi Vasile in 1957. He quickly followed by working on *Promesse di marinalo, Gambe d'oro,* and *Roulotte e roulotte* as well. Margheriti had grown up reading science fiction comic books, and when Vasile offered the opportunity to direct a film called *Space-Men* from a script Margheriti had written with Ennio De Concini for 49 million lire (approximately $30,000), he jumped at the chance. In America, the film was retitled *Assignment Outer Space* and although foreign versions were credited to Anthony Daisies, a translation of Margheriti, the American version credits him as Anthony Dawson.

Assignment Outer Space features a reporter, Ray Peterson (Rik von Nutter, who later played Felix Leiter in *Thunderball*), from Interplanetary News of New York, sent on assignment to a space station, where all inhabitants are addressed by numbers rather than name. (He is assigned IZ41, given military style as India-Zulu-Four-One.)

The commander of the station finds the reporter an unnecessary presence; however, the intrepid newshound does save the life of Y13 (Lucy Farinon), although the commander considers the fuel expended in saving her to be less expendable than Y13 herself and says so in no uncertain terms.

It is then announced that something called *Alpha Two*, a ship returning from Venus, has entered the solar system and is out of control. Some missiles are sent to destroy *Alpha Two*, but they explode before reaching their target, causing scientists to assume that *Alpha Two* has photonic generators that are projecting two spherical shields around the whatever-it-is (this is never made exactly clear). The ship is emitting dangerous levels of heat which will not only kill its crew, but could cause Earth to melt down.

The reporter pilots a two-man workcraft and finds a channel between the protective spheres and so is able to board *Alpha Two*. Not knowing how to shut down the photonic generators, he simply cuts all the wires, shutting down the ship's electronic brain, which seals him inside as well. Luckily, a rescue team is able to cut him out before *Alpha Two* vaporizes in Earth's atmosphere.

Whether as a cost-saving device or an intentional effect, all of Margheriti's space exteriors are shot in black and white, as if space would drain the color from everything. Additionally, the vacuum of space does nothing to eliminate the sound of rockets roaring everywhere they go. Typical of Margheriti's SF work, while the interior sets are colorfully and interestingly designed, the special effects are cheaply and laughably thrown together.

Margheriti's direction here is leaden, and would continue to be throughout his lengthy career. To make his movies in such a short time, Margheriti developed the technique of filming with several cameras simultaneously. Hence, one camera would be recording a master shot, while other cameras would capture needed close-ups, and all would be positioned in such a way that the cameras would remain invisible to one another on film. This demands not only careful attention to lighting, but also severely limits the mobility of the camera and can often cramp camera compositions. However, this economical approach is also what has allowed Margheriti to churn out as many as seven films in a year.

His next SF project and probably his best was *Il Planeta degli Uomini Spenti* (U.S. title: *Battle of the Worlds*) which features Claude Rains in one of his most forgettable films. Rains plays Professor Benson, a scientist who ridicules his fellow scientists' notion that a meteorite is about to collide with Earth, and is surprisingly proven right when the large object stops in space and launches a fleet of flying saucers. The planetoid has a computerized brain system programmed to cause earthlings to battle one another.

Benson learns that this huge mothership was sent out on automatic from a dead alien planet. He becomes obsessed with obtaining the vast amount of knowledge that the aliens' computer must contain. In the film's best sequences, he boards the alien craft and accesses images of the dead alien world with its swirling colors, weird machines, and beautiful but garish designs.

However, once the military learns of the aliens' insidious plan, they launch retaliatory rockets and weapons to prevent Earth's destruction, destroying both Benson and the ship in the process. Like its predecessor, *Battle of the Worlds* pleads for the humanization rather than the militarization of space, but also like its predecessor, the film is largely a triumph of art direction over an often dull story.

The Golden Arrow, made for MGM, was the first film to have Margheriti's actual name on it and the first to have a sizable budget. It starred Tab Hunter in an Arabian Nights style adventure. Next Margheriti tackled some pabulum, including *The Fall of Rome*, where a centurion (Carl Mohner) comes to the aid of some persecuted Christians, and *The Giants of Rome*, which is a gladiator remake of *The Guns of Navarone.*

Margheriti's most inventive movies are his horror films including the Mario Bava–influenced *Horror Castle, Castle*

Lobby card for Antonio Margheriti's *The Wild Wild Planet* gives the title an extra "Wild" for some reason. Tony Russell saves the day when mad scientist Numi shrinks the leaders of the United Democracies and kidnaps them using inflatable ladies.

of Blood, The Long Hair of Death, Web of the Spider (a remake of *Castle of Blood* with Klaus Kinski playing Poe and Anthony Franciosa as Foster), and the Dario Argento inspired *Seven Deaths in the Cat's Eye*. Despite his fondness for science fiction, Margheriti's best work may be found in *La danza macabra* (which shows up under the titles *Castle of Terror* and *Castle of Blood*). The film was written by Gianni Grimaldi and Sergio Corbucci under pseudonyms, and is initially set on and around the Tower Bridge. An English reporter named Alan Foster (Georges Rivière) enters a pub to interview Edgar Allan Poe (Henry Kruger), who claims not to write fiction but only reports what he sees. Poe's claim intrigues Lord Blackwood who bets the doubting reporter that he cannot spend the night in Blackwood Castle. Foster accepts, and so he, Blackwood and Poe journey to the castle, dropping Foster off.

As Foster makes note of an erratic clock, he hears music coming from an adjoining room and sees a couple dancing. He meets Elizabeth (cult favorite Barbara Steele), who explains that her brother Lord Blackwood likes to bet people to stay in the castle in order to give credibility to the stories of its being haunted. The pair are joined by Julia (Margrete Robsahm), who resents the attention Elizabeth pays to Foster.

Lying on a bed, Foster and Elizabeth pledge their love for one another when a well-muscled man bursts in and stabs Elizabeth in the chest. Foster chases him and shoots him with a small pistol, but when he goes to investigate, both bodies have disappeared.

While perusing a volume of metaphysics by him, Foster meets Carmus (Arturo Dominici), a scientist studying a preposterous theory about the senses of a person sometimes surviving after the death of the body. He explains that while Elizabeth's husband was away on a business trip to America, she had an affair with Herbert, the stable boy, and when William returned, Herbert became uncontrollably jealous and strangled William. Herbert was about to strangle Elizabeth as well when Julia clobbered his head with a candlestick and tried to seduce Elizabeth herself until her victim retaliates by stabbing her in the chest with a pair of scissors. (We never learn how Elizabeth died, but what Foster met was her undead senses rather than her real self.)

The film continues its weird and dream-like plot with more visions and murders until all the spirits in the house want to drink Foster's blood in the belief that this will bring them back to life. Foster tries to run away with Elizabeth, who once she is exposed to the sunlight, turns into a skeleton and fades away. Foster ends up wandering through a cemetery containing the graves of the people he met in the house when suddenly the gate swings shut, he falls back, and impales his neck on a spike, joining the other spirits. Blackwood and Poe drive up, with Blackwood callously collecting his wager from the dead man's wallet.

While it is the most atmospheric of the Margheriti films I've seen, thanks to the elegant photography by Riccardo Pallottini, the characters are steadfastly dull and the direction is at best pedestrian except when straining for effect. What motivates Lord Blackwood to lure victims to the castle remains a mystery, but then Margheriti's films were always more about style than sense. Margheriti's later color remake, *Web of the Spider*, failed to be as atmospheric, and except for the participation of Klaus Kinski as Poe, was inferior in every respect.

Fans of Italian horror films also liked *Horror Castle* (aka

The Virgin of Nuremburg; Back to the Killer) with Georges Rivière, Rossana Podestà and Christopher Lee in the tale of a former Nazi officer who indulges in sadism after having had the skin stripped from his skull, and Barbara Steele in *The Long Hair of Death*, where Steele plays a suspected killer who is buried alive and then returns to life to wreak her revenge.

Margheriti returned to science fiction with the memorably titled Gamma I series, which was originally filmed for the Italian TV series *Fantascienza*, but then released theatrically. The first film in the series, *The Wild Wild Planet* (originally titled *I Criminali della Galassia*), was given the largest budget and shooting schedule (four weeks instead of three) because it was coproduced by Joseph Fryd and Walter Manley to be released theatrically in the United States.

Set in A.D. 2015, several important people including some top scientists have disappeared, and we learn that they have been assaulted by bikini-clad alien karate girls who use chemicals to shrink the men small enough that they can be stashed into briefcases. The hero, Mike Halstead (Tony Russell) of the United Democracies in Space, is the commander of Gamma I and he has to solve the problem as well as save his girlfriend Lt. Connie Gomez (Lisa Gastoni) from an operation which will fuse her body with Dr. Nurmi's (Massimo Serato) into a half man/half woman superbeing. Art director Piero Poletto's imaginative work on this film was both extremely colorful and completely unbelievable, a precursor to Pop Art. Riccardo Pallottini's cinematography borders on the pyschedelic.

The subsequent films in the series were *War of the Planets*, *Planet on the Prowl* (aka *War Between the Planets*), and *Snow Devils*. *War of the Planets* featured much of the same cast and crew as *The Wild Wild Planet*. In this one, an alien race made of light called the Diaphanoids, who have settled on Mars, try to take over the bodies of various Earthlings. Mike Halstead and Connie Gomez struggle hard to thwart their plans. The film also featured Lisa Gastoni, credited under the pseudonym Jane Fate, and Franco Nero, who would reach international stardom as Django shortly afterward. Like most of Margheriti's films, the plot and acting are rudimentary and secondary to the cinematography and the production design.

Planet on the Prowl, possibly inspired by *When Worlds Collide*, features Giacomo Rossi-Stuart as the lead, playing Gamma I commander Rod Jackson who investigates a rogue planetoid whose gravity is wreaking havoc on Earth, creating earthquakes, tidal waves, and freak weather conditions. The surprise of the film is that the planetoid is actually an enormous phosphorescent life form which Jackson and his crew must invade in order to destroy it. The film was released in the U.S. in 1971 as *War Between the Planets*, being rescored with Harry Lubin's music for *The Outer Limits* in the process. Unfortunately, it lacks even the visual attractiveness of Margheriti's early films, rendering the weak plot, characterization, and dialogue all the more obvious.

Unfortunately, the last film in the series, *Snow Devils*, is not available for viewing. It is said to be the nadir of this none too thrilling series and featured another errant planet, this one with abominable snowmen aboard.

For a time, Margheriti switched to directing westerns such as *Take a Hard Ride* with Lee van Cleef, Jim Brown, Fred Williamson, and Jim Kelly and *The Stranger and the Gunfighter*, also starring van Cleef in a kung fu western. *Killer Fish* surprises in that it is not yet another *Jaws* rip-off, but rather is a caper film starring Lee Majors, Karen Black and James Franciscus with an offbeat title. *The Squeeze* is a follow up caper film also starring Black, this time teamed with Lee van Cleef.

He also tried a few more horror films, including *The Young, the Evil, and the Savage*, which was originally to have been directed by Mario Bava, who dropped out to make *Danger: Diabolik* and who came up with the film's story of a young heiress at a young girl's school being stalked by a murderer; *The Unnaturals* in which a seance reveals the dark secrets of a group of wayward travelers; and *Seven Deaths in a Cat's Eye*, with another killer stalking another accursed family castle.

In the midst of these, he did try his hand at another science fiction film, this one the Disneyesque comedy *Mr. Superinvisible*, starring Disney regular Dean Jones as a scientist who thinks he has invented a new virus which could be used in biological warfare and mistakenly drinks a potion which renders him invisible.

Because of Margheriti's background, he was hired to film special effects for two films. The first was Eduardo De Filippo's *Shout Loud, Louder ... I Don't Understand*, a spoof of the spy genre with Raquel Welch and Marcello Mastroiani, and Sergio Leone's *Duck, You Sucker* (aka *A Fistful of Dynamite*) for which Margheriti filmed the train crash at the end using miniatures. He also claims to have added special effects shots as well as the opening and closing sequences to Paul Morrissey's *Flesh for Frankenstein* (aka *Andy Warhol's Frankenstein*), and in Italy he received credit for directing the film as well as its sequel, *Blood for Dracula*.

Later Margheriti decided to jump on the *Raiders of the Lost Ark* bandwagon with *The Last Hunter* and *Hunters of the Golden Cobra*, both starring David Warbeck as Margheriti's cut-rate Harrison Ford clone. Warbeck also starred in *Tiger Joe*, on which Margheriti's long-time cinematographer Riccardo Pallottini died in a plane crash when as he was attempting to get the last shot of the film, his plane flew too low and hit some palm trees, killing him, the pilot, and an assistant cameraman in the crash.

Margheriti returned to the science fiction genre with one of his cheesiest efforts yet. A turkey made in Turkey, *Yor, Hunter from the Future* was originally done as a three hour serial for Italian television based on a book by Juan Zanotto and Ray Collins, which incredibly was picked up by Columbia for release stateside in an edited version and then released to 1400 unsuspecting theaters.

The film stars Reb Brown (best known for being Captain America on TV) as Yor the caveman who fights phony-looking dinosaurs and men in hairy ape costumes and is given to licking the blood of his opponents off his hand and saying things like, "The blood of your enemy makes you stronger." What Yor is hunting for turns out to be the way home. *Yor* has almost no plot, but is packed with incidents, none of them interesting. Yor picks up a pair of attractive ladies along the way, saving one from being sacrificed to some gods, kills a giant bat and removes its wings to make a kind of prehistoric hang glider, and kills a bunch of extras in bad costumes and worse makeup, before the medallion he is wearing transports him into a future where an evil Darth Vaderesque menace who calls himself the Overlord threatens to "cultivate" his seed. This is an unforgivably boring, incoherent mess. What Columbia could have been thinking in offering it as a major summer release remains an utter and total mystery.

Even worse was *Invasion of the Flesh Hunters* (aka *Cannibals in the Streets*). Filmed in and around Georgia, *Cannibals* begins in Vietnam and features actual combat footage intercut with actors playing Viet Cong who hear of their approach. John Saxon plays a Green Beret Captain Hopper who leads an attack on the enemy position. In a particularly gross scene, a VC woman who has been set on fire falls into a pit with a pair of American POWs. She no sooner puts the fire out when the POWs grab her, rip open her blouse, and take a bite out of her breast. Hopper gets bitten by one of the POW zombies when he tries to rescue them.

Back home years later, Hopper still has nightmares about what happened. Coincidentally, one of the POWs, Charlie Bukowski (John Morghen), is released from a hospital, heads off to the nearest war movie, and gets incensed when a couple get it on in front of him, causing him to bite the woman's neck. He runs away from the angry audience on the screen (as opposed to the one watching this fetid flick) and begins spreading his cannibal infection throughout the city.

Soon enough, Hopper has turned into a cannibal as well (there is a teasingly sick scene where a teenage girl seduces Hopper, who exposes her underwear and kneels before the shot cuts away, leaving the audience to wonder what happened). This exercise in unpleasantness is barely science fiction as it speculates that cannibalism can become a contagious disease through some sort of biological mutation. Blandly directed with over-the-top violence that is meant to be humorous but just comes off as dull, *Cannibals in the Streets* simply demonstrates Margheriti's willingness to prostitute himself once more in this halfhearted stab at the Italian cannibal zombie genre which had a brief popularity in the early 1980s.

Despite all his years of practice and extensive career, Margheriti has never made a movie that was not at best mediocre.

IB MELCHIOR (1917–)

The Angry Red Planet (1959); *The Time Travelers* (1964)

Ib Melchior was born September 17, 1917, in Denmark, the son of the Metropolitan Opera singer Lauritz Melchior. He attended the University of Copenhagen, majoring in literature and language, graduating with a degree of Candidatus Phiosophiae. When he was five years old, he saw *The Man Who Laughs* and became fascinated by film. At an early age, he resolved to go to Hollywood and become a film director.

In May 1937, he began his career in show business as a prop boy for the English Players based in Paris at the Theatre de L'Oeuvre after auditioning for an acting part for the director of the troupe. Melchior began getting performing parts, as well as doing set and scenic work, eventually becoming the stage manager and codirector of the company.

In December 1939, the troupe came to America to perform a Broadway show, and Melchior was able to land a job as a stage manager at the famous Radio City Music

Hall and Center Theater where he remained until 1942. After arriving in America, he developed an interest in science fiction literature, reading such writers as E. E. Smith, Theodore Sturgeon, and Curt Siodmak.

Melchior wrote the scripts for *Live Fast, Die Young* (1958) and *When Hell Broke Loose* (1958). He was able to get directing work in television in New York, where he supposedly directed some 500 shows, but discovered to his surprise that despite his experience, he could only get a directing job in Hollywood if a producer insisted on hiring him, thereby allowing him to join the Directors Guild.

The following year, Melchior made his feature directorial debut with *The Angry Red Planet,* coscripted with producer Sid Pink. Pink wrote a story titled "The Planet Mars" in five days and Melchior rewrote the initial draft under the condition that he be allowed to direct the subsequent film. This version Pink rewrote again as he felt that Melchior had eliminated most of the action from the film and added too many extraneous explanations of scientific phenomena. He later accused Melchior of demonstrating little expertise behind the camera, complaining Melchior wasted three hours just to set up his first shot, and credits experienced cinematographer Stanley Cortez (whose credits range from his astonishing work on *The Magnificent Ambersons* and *Night of the Hunter* to lensing low budget SF films such as *The Doomsday Machine* and *They Stole Hitler's Brain*) with overseeing Melchior's work so that something ended up in the can.

The Angry Red Planet employed the gimmick of "Cinemagic," which placed performers in white makeup in front of sets that were simply drawings and then tried to disguise the fact by dying the black-and-white film a different color (in this case red for Mars, of course). The result certainly has an odd look, but not a convincing one. The process was pioneered by Norman Maurer who sold producer Sid Pink on the process and they spent 10 months developing it. (The process was only used once more in the awful science fiction epic *The Three Stooges in Orbit* before being wisely put out to pasture.)

The film itself cost a mere $194,000 with a fourth of the budget going into the expensive lab work to process the black-and-white film onto color film and dye it. The entire shooting schedule was 29 days, with many of the same sets being redressed over and over again. While the rat-bat-spider-crab had a suitably memorable design, special effects man Herman Townsley built the marionette on a 5/16th of an inch to the foot scale, which meant that hiding the wires which held it up proved impossible, and the mechanism itself kept failing to work. Even worse were the other alien menaces designed for the film, an amoeba with two ridiculous rotating eyes that rolled instead of pulsing and undulating, and a three-eyed Martian headpiece worn by midget Billy Curtis that looks flat and unconvincing.

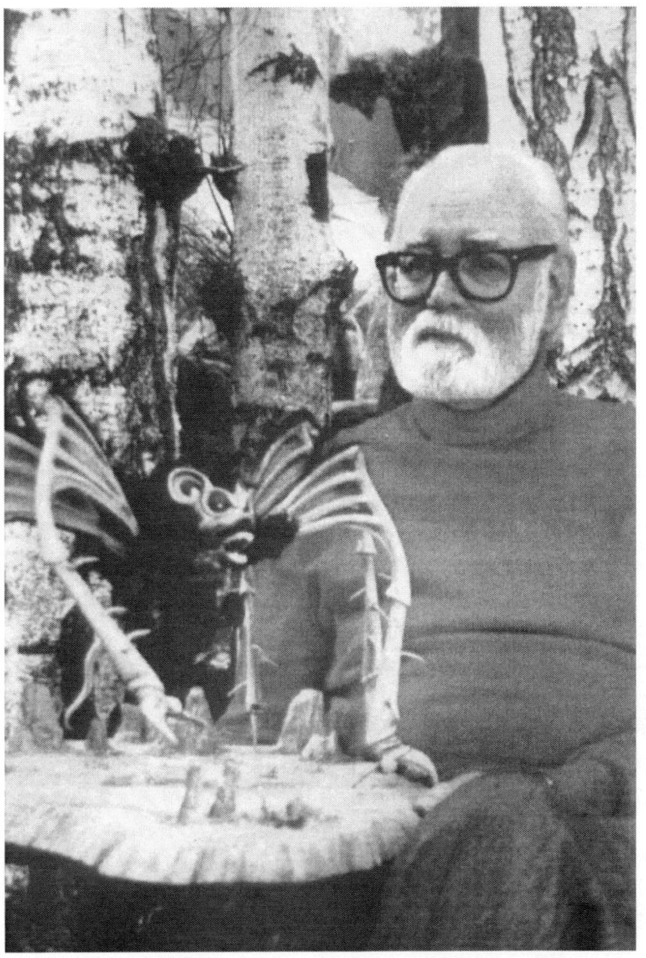

Ib Melchior poses next to his memorable rat-bat-spider-crab from *The Angry Red Planet.*

Melchior's characters are a typically dull lot who display little personality and have trouble expressing themselves interestingly. Melchior's lack of pacing is evident from the very opening of the film, which reeks of stock footage and soporific conversations. There is an attempt to create a sense of mystery about the reappearance of an uncommunicative and apparently dead rocket ship, but it takes some time before Melchior even clues us in on the film's basic plot.

A four-person flight to Mars returns with only two people on board, Dr. Iris Ryan (Nora Hayden) and Colonel Tom O'Bannion (Gerald Mohr) who lies in a coma with slime on his arm. It is quickly discovered that Dr. Ryan is suffering from a mental block about what had happened to O'Bannion, and so is encouraged to tell what she remembers of the expedition in order to jog her memory.

The majority of the film is a flashback of their trip, and we finally get to meet the other two members of the expedition, Prof. Theodore Gettell (science fiction stalwart Les Tremayne), designer of the rocket and the world's foremost authority on space travel, and Sam Jacobs (Jack Kruschen), the "comic relief" chief warrant officer. When they land on the red planet, they discover lush vegetation but initially no signs of higher forms of life. Iris briefly sees a three-eyed Martian outside the viewport, and in fifties convention screams and faints. (Somehow, as a scientist, one would think she would be better prepared for such sights.)

The other men on the trip are condescending and all too quickly ascribe the vision to an overactive imagination. The "big thrills" Melchior comes up with are a carnivorous plant, a forty foot tall rat-bat-spider-crab, which Sam drives off with a sonic gun, a mysterious force field which holds their rocket captive, a gigantic futuristic cityscape, and a giant amoeba that tries to devour them, digesting Sam before it envelops the ship. (Iris tells the others it takes electricity to kill an amoeba, so O'Bannion and Gettell rig up an electrical charge through the ship's metallic hull, driving the amoeba away and fortunately do not fry themselves in the process. Gettell dies of a heart attack from the supposed enormous stresses of taking off, while O'Bannion has become infected by slime from the amoeba.

Now that Iris has told her story, she remembers that the Martians had left a message on their tape recorder. The tape is played and a voice gives the following preachy warning:

> Listen and remember. We have known your planet Earth since the first creature crawled primeval slime on your seas to become man. For centuries we have watched you, listened to your radio signals [for centuries?!], and learned your speech and culture. And now you have invaded our home. Technological adults but spiritual and emotional infants. We kept you here [and] decided your fate. Had the lower life forms on our planet destroyed you, we would have not interfered, but you have survived. Your civilization has not progressed past destruction, war, and violence against yourselves and others. Do as you will to your own planet, but remember the warning. Do not return to Mars. You will be permitted to leave for this sole purpose. Carry the warning to Earth. Do not come here. We can and will destroy you, and all life on your planet if you do not heed us. You have seen us, been permitted to see our world. Go now, and warn mankind not to return.

If the Martians were indeed angry, cinema patrons had every right to be even angrier at the sanctimonious claptrap that Melchior tries to foist upon them here in the name of entertainment. Apart from the memorable designs of the Martian menaces, *Angry Red Planet* really has very little to recommend it, except to render a trip to Mars the cinematic equivalent of a disjointed, hallucinogenic trip on LSD complete with colored perceptions that in no way resemble reality.

In 1960, just after the release of *Angry Red Planet*, Melchior wrote the scenario that was to become Byron Haskin's *Robinson Crusoe on Mars*, which was initially announced as a project by Hertz-Lion Productions. Melchior had been hired by Hertz-Lion to story edit the proposed TV series about action stories from the Bible called *The Sword*. They had also optioned Melchior's *Life* magazine story about the search for a handwritten manuscript of *Hamlet*, but the project that came to fruition was the notorious *13 Demon Street*.

Melchior scripted three half-hour tales, which were to be directed by Curt Siodmak. The first, "A Gift of Murder," has a jealous husband using voodoo to kill a supposed rival, then falling in love with his secretary. His suspicious wife switches photos and ironically causes him to put the whammy on himself. In the second, "Black Nemesis," a phony psychic, desperate for money, kills a rich woman's husband in order to raise money from her by setting up séances, and then draws a gun on a presumed apparition, causing his debtor's bodyguards to eliminate him. Last was "Shadow from Beyond," in which a photographer who kills an old man fakes an accidental death but becomes haunted by a headless shadow. In attempting to destroy the shadow that haunts him, he succeeds only in destroying himself.

Because of financial problems, none of the episodes for the series were ever aired in this country.

Would-be producer Sid Pink made a deal with AIP to film some low budget science fiction films in Denmark, which he felt he could do at substantially less cost than they were done in the U.S. Melchior was commissioned to develop two screenplays from Pink's story ideas. One became the spectacularly inept *Reptilicus* (after *The Giant Claw*, the most ridiculous looking monster in an SF film) and the other was *Journey to the Seventh Planet*.

Journey to the Seventh Planet spun out a variation on Ray Bradbury's story "Mars Is Heaven!," in which astronauts are surprised upon their arrival at an alien planet to be greeted with idyllic scenes from home. In Melchior's version, a giant one-eyed brain creature below the surface of Uranus takes images out of the astronaut's minds and manifests them as material re-constructions; hence, places from their childhood and monsters representing their subconscious fears are encountered. They are also tempted by some bathing beauties in an Edenic setting, which eats away at their morale and self-discipline, but eventually they make their way past the barrier, confront and kill the alien critter that has been tormenting them. The film does include some surrealistic touches, as when one of the astronauts plucks a bush from the ground and there are no roots.

Reptilicus was made for a mere $74,000 at the cramped

Melchior supplied the script for Sid Pink's *Journey to the Seventh Planet* as Earthmen on Uranus defeat an evil space brain that can materialize their fears.

Saga Studios in Denmark. Producer-director Pink tried to give the production a sense of scope by employing a wide lens and keeping some of the photography out of focus to disguise the limitations, but all too often, the limitations were obvious. An ice crystal forest was concocted out of bits of metal decorated with tree branches painted blue. The mole-grub and cyclopean snake monsters made out of papier mâché and chicken wire were so pathetic that AIP actually ponyed up funds to have them replaced. The snake was replaced by a stop motion menace animated by Project Unlimited's stop motion experts Jim Danforth and Wah Chang, while the mole-grub became tinted scenes of the giant tarantula from Bert I. Gordon's *Earth vs. the Spider*. Melchior assisted in recutting the hopeless film and also redubbed several of the characters himself. A shot of the amoeba from *Angry Red Planet* was inserted to replace another menace.

Though largely talky and dull, *Journey to the Seventh Planet* did offer a few interesting ideas and concepts. *Reptilicus*, also directed by Pink, was even more of a disaster. Melchior's key concept was to create a 70-foot monster which could regenerate itself, like a starfish, from any of its pieces, so that any attempts to blow it up would merely cause it to proliferate. Melchior's script described the monster as combining the "characteristics of the giant dinosaurs and a colossal flying Pteradon." Instead, Pink presented a marionette menace that looked somewhat like a dragon having a bad hair day complete with floppy batwings and supported by strings. (Some shots were printed out of focus in an attempt to hide the obvious wires, to little avail.)

In 1962, Melchior was the associate producer on *The Case of Patti Smith*.

Melchior himself was at the helm of his next SF project, *The Time Travelers*, an ultra low budget (less than $250,000) effort shot in 18 days and most notable for its clever ending in which a group of time travelers trap themselves in a never-ending loop by making the mistake of returning to before the time they left. The basic concept for the film originated with a script by David Hewitt called *Journey Into the Unknown*, which Melchior revised and added to.

Scientists Erik von Steiner (Preston Foster), Steve Conners (Philip Carey), and Carol White (Merry Anders) work together on a time portal which can see either into the past or into the future. When some circuits accidentally fuse, they discover that the portal is not a window, but an actual doorway through time, so they and a technician, Danny McKee (Steve Franken), enter the portal and travel 107 years into the future where things are not going very well for humanity.

There they discover the remnants of civilization living in a cave, led by a council headed by Varno (John Hoyt), who explains that Earth was destroyed by a nuclear holocaust. This has caused the planet to be perilously poisoned with the surface being roamed by deadly mutants that continually threaten to invade the remaining underground sanctuary.

However, before this diverting event, Melchior drags us through dull lectures on photons and lasers, has the group take a tour of an android assembly plant, and shows off his low budget art design where a major form of entertainment seems to be tennis balls being dropped behind a colored screen while electronic music plays in the background. Forrest J Ackerman, a friend of Melchior's and his

YOU are in the FUTURE before it happens!
THE TIME TRAVELERS COLOR
ESTON FOSTER · PHILIP CAREY · MERRY ANDERS · JOHN HOYT · DENNIS PATRICK

Lobby card depicting the mutants and androids of Melchior's *The Time Travelers*, whose main characters aim for Alpha Centauri but wind up back in 1964.

science fiction agent, gets to play a bit part in the film as an android technician.

The remaining humans are working on building a rocket which will take them to Alpha Centauri, where they hope to start over. The travelers are invited to come along, but Councilman Willard objects, explaining that the ship was not designed for four extra passengers. Varno assists them in rebuilding their time portal so that they can return to their own time.

Unfortunately, in the climax, the mutants at last enter the cave and cause ruin, destroying the ship and most of the people with it in the process. The travelers make it back to 1964, but discover that they are living at an accelerated rate of one year per minute. If they wait long, they will die, so they run quickly over to the still open original portal and jump 100,000 years into the future, where they encounter a lush green world and the aforementioned time loop paradox and the film repetitively repeats past footage in disjointed fashion, a touch more economy minded than interesting.

He wrote *The Outer Limits* episode "The Premonition," which, like *The Time Travelers*, deals with altering the flow of time, this time with test pilot Jim Darcy (Dewey Martin) returning from a test flight to find the world, except for his wife Linda (Mary Murphy), seemingly frozen in time, but it is actually moving with imperticible slowness. They discover that their daughter Janie was about to be run over by a truck, and must solve the problem both of saving her and returning themselves back to normal time.

Melchior had high hopes for *Robinson Crusoe on Mars* (see chapter on Byron Haskin), but Haskin hated Melchior's approach to the material, finding it too fanciful, and assigned John C. Higgins to rework the material. Melchior was not too pleased with the alterations Higgins made, including Kit's assumption of authority over Friday by announcing in no uncertain terms, "I'm the boss." (Actor Paul Mantee was never comfortable with this part of the screenplay either.) He also found it ridiculous that after establishing that finding oxygen on Mars would be an immense problem that Haskin showed giant flaming fireballs over much of the planet. Still, the film is one of the best with which Melchior is associated.

In 1965, he was assigned with Louis M. Heyward to provide the English language version of Mario Bava's *Planet of the Vampires*, one of the more interestingly designed low budget Italian space opera films, best known for providing the inspiration for the space jockey in Ridley Scott and Dan O'Bannon's *Alien*. Unfortunately, Melchior's approach to dialogue was more talky and dull than sparkling, and the picture sinks from its own pretentions.

Melchior was the writer of *Ambush Bay* (1966), but then pretty much gave up screenwriting. He receives a story credit, however, on one more science fiction film, the highly entertaining *Death Race 2000*, one of the funniest science fiction films ever made, directed by Paul Bartel and written by Charles B. Griffith (*Little Shop of Horrors*) and Robert Thom (*Wild in the Streets*).

Paul Bartel started his film career in animation. A UCLA graduate, he received a Fulbright Scholarship to study film direction in Europe for a year. He then spent a couple of years in the army as an assistant director on documentaries and training films. His first film was the short *Secret Cinema*, which was later remade on Steven Spielberg's *Amazing Stories* show. Bartel made the original short in black and white using trims. He then worked on documentaries and made a second short, *Naughty Nurse*,

David Carradine as the ruthless driver Frankenstein in *Death Race 2000*, a Paul Bartel film loosely based on Melchior's story.

but realizing that this was not bringing him closer to making features, he started writing scripts and working on other people's projects.

One of the scripts, *Blood Relations*, was sold by an enterprising agent to Gene Corman, Roger Corman's brother, who had a deal to make low budget pictures for MGM at the time. (After changing the title to *Private Parts*, MGM did not want their name on it and the title was considered unprintable by many newspapers in the country.)

After directing second unit on Steve Carver's *Big Bad Mama*, mostly handling car stunts, Roger Corman decided he must be good with cars and so offered him *Death Race 2000*. Bartel rewrote the script, was fired, and then rehired. Bartel kept emphasizing the humor while Corman preferred that it be a hard action picture with very little comedy and a lot of violence and blood.

Corman had long wanted to make a film out of Roger Zelazny's *Damnation Alley*, but unfortunately for him, 20th Century–Fox had the rights tied up. He had read a story of Melchior's called "The Driver," which he planned to transform into a movie called *The Race*. United Artists had announced *Rollerball*, an expensive picture with the theme of a cataclysmic national sport, and Corman wanted to make a variation on the idea that could cash in on the attendant publicity.

Robert Thom had the first crack at the script, but in his version, most of the characters were transvestites and none were very sympathetic. After Bartel had an unsuccessful attempt at a draft, Corman hired Charles B. Griffith to rewrite it, and apart from fine-tuning the characters, the final script is mostly his. (Griffith also did the second-unit work on the film involving the hits.)

Bartel had seen David Carradine in the play *The Royal Hunt of the Sun* and was knocked out by him, and so selected him to play the lead of the film, now named Frankenstein, a racer whose body has been torn apart so often that he is an assemblage of replacement parts. (The sinister looking mask for the character was created by Rick Baker.)

During filming, Carradine became very intransient, ripping up his costume when he did not like the fabric, disapproving of things he had approved, and just general surliness until he was threatened with replacement by Lee Majors, after which he became very cooperative.

The cars were created using Volkswagen chassis and could not be driven over 40 miles per hour, so that long shots of the cars were filmed undercranked while closeups were shot with sync sound. Corman at first insisted there be no roll bars put in the cars, but Bartel pointed out that stunt drivers would not work in them without rollbars.

"Roger and I had a major disagreement about how violent the picture should be," Bartell recalled. "I thought the idea was inherently very violent, and so I felt there should be very little blood in it, and I wanted it to be somewhat funnier than it turned out. He felt that people were paying for blood and wanted to see blood, so when I was finished with my cut of the picture, he sent out a second unit to shoot a lot of blood inserts, most of which couldn't be used because the MPAA was threatening to give the picture an X, but in the classic Corman tradition, after they'd given it an R, a few frames were put back into each scene so there was a little more blood in the picture than in fact was originally approved."

Death Race 2000 was brought in for about $480,000. Bartel worked for a year on the film for a $5,000 directing fee. When the film was released in the U.S., the advertising made absolutely no mention that it was a cartoony comedy because Corman felt that a comedy would be hard to sell, as opposed to a typical action film starring a TV star.

The movie begins with the introduction of the 20th annual Transcontinental Road Race, in which the nation's five greatest racers will "risk their lives in the greatest sporting event since the days of Spartacus." The drivers are Calamity Jane (Mary Woronov), Frankenstein (Carradine), Matilda the Hun (Roberta Collins), Nero the Hero (Martin Klove), and Machinegun Joe Viturbo (Sylvester Stallone in his funniest performance), each accompanied by their navigators.

Opposing the race are a group of rebels who object to the President's philosophy of "minority privilege" and "no holds barred" and plan to kidnap Frankenstein in an effort to stop the race, and have planted a rebel, Annie Smith (Simone Griffeth), and leader Thomasina Paine's daughter, as Frankenstein's navigator.

The drivers begin to mow people down, with more points awarded for those under 12 or over 40. Things become more complicated, however, when in trying to score points, Mathilda the Hun and Herman the German are killed using a trick right out of a Chuck Jones cartoon.

The President comes out on TV and tells the people, "There has been a lot of talk about American rebels. We have positive proof that it was none other than the treacherous *French* who have been sabotaging our race, just as they and their stinking European allies have undermined and destroyed our great national economy. Remember that the word sabotogue was French."

Death Race 2000 continues to make satirical jabs and pile up verbal and visual gags (one of the most extreme being Frankenstein's "hand-grenade," a grenade shaped like his hand). The film ends with the death of the President and the exalted Frankenstein being installed in that position, pensioning off the secret police, restoring free elections, ending minority privilege, moving the seat of government back to Los Angeles, and abolishing the race, outraging obnoxious announcer Junior Bruce (radio personality The Real Don Steele) who winds up being run over by the new President. An announcer notes that murder was invented even before man began to think — "Now, of course, man has become known as a thinking man," he intones to bring the film to an appropriately ironic close.

Melchior has since left the filmmaking field to concentrate on writing spy thrillers based on his experiences working for military intelligence in World War II, and has been highly successful in this endeavor.

WILLIAM CAMERON MENZIES (1896–1957)

The Spider (codirector with Kenneth McKenna) (1931); *Always Goodbye* (codirector with Kenneth McKenna) (1931); *Chandu the Magician* (codirector with Marcel Varnel); *Almost Married* (1932); *I Loved You Wednesday* (codirector with Henry King) (1933); *The Wharf Angel* (codirector with George Somnes) (1934); *Things to Come* (1936); *The Green Cockatoo* (aka *Four Dark Hours; Race Gang*) (1937); *Conquest of the Air* (codirected with Alexander Korda, Zoltan Korda, Alexander Esway, Donald Taylor, Alexander Shaw, and John Monk Saunders) (1938); *Address Unknown* (1944); *Drums in the Deep South*; *The Whip Hand* (1951); *Invaders from Mars; The Maze* (1953)

Television: *The Tell-Tale Heart; The Terribly Strange Bed* (1949)

William Cameron Menzies was a man of myriad talents, most notably as one of Hollywood's greatest production designers as well as one of the most influential. He was born in New Haven, Connecticut, on July 29, 1896 to poor Scottish immigrant parents. He grew up loving drawing, fantastic stories, and reading. A Yale graduate, he studied under the great draftsman Edwin Taylor. Menzies attended New York's Art Student League.

Menzies gained his entry into films through a chance meeting with New Jersey–based director George Fitsmaurice, who queried the 19-year-old artist on how he could quickly establish a desert locale, which Menzies was able to achieve by casting shadows from a couple of palm leaves over the principle actors. Menzies began working in Hollywood as an assistant to famed art director Anton Grot (née Antocz Franziszek Groszewski), who later invented and patented a "ripple machine" to create weather and light effects on water scenes for his long-time collaborator director Michael Curtiz on *The Sea Hawk*. Grot and Menzies began to work together on *The Naulahka* (1918), which was set in India and which established them as experts in creating exotic settings.

He then worked on *The Innocent*, and married Toby Mignon before shipping out to the service during World War I, where he served for 22 months in Cuba and Europe. Menzies then joined the Famous Players as an art director and worked as a sketch artist and designer for the Mayflower Company. With the collapse of the eastern studios, Menzies chose to move out to California.

Menzies came to prominence for his fabulous work with Grot on the Douglas Fairbanks/Raoul Walsh silent version of *The Thief of Bagdad*, still considered by many to be one of the most consummately designed Hollywood films ever, though the look of the film was clearly influenced by the

Fritz Lang silent *Destiny* (aka *Der Müde Tod*), designed by Walther Röhrig, Robert Herlth, and Hermann Salfrank. Menzies met Fairbanks through Mary Pickford, for whom he did design drawings for *Rosita*. Fairbanks retained Menzies to work on other spectaculars, including *The Three Musketeers* and *Robin Hood.* Menzies also worked on the Valentino pictures *The Eagle* and *Cobra.*

Menzies worked with the idiosyncratic director Roland West, one of the few independent producer-directors of the time known for his experimental camerawork, for whom Menzies designed three films: *The Bat* (1926), later remade by West in 70mm in 1930 (!) as *The Bat Whispers* (in which form it inspired Bob Kane to create the comic book character The Batman); *The Dove* (1927) for which Menzies won the first assistant director Academy Award ever, and *Alibi* (1929) which features Menzies' fascinating art deco–cum–Expressionistic set designs obviously inspired by *The Cabinet of Dr. Caligari.* Menzies' eye-popping Art Deco sets for the latter film were nominated for an Academy Award, and the movie itself was nominated for Best Film. In it, Chester Morris plays the murderous Chick Williams, a prohibition–era gangster who rejoins his powerful mob after he gets out of prison. When a policeman is murdered during a robbery, Williams falls under suspicion, and a crack detective squad uses every technique in the book to bring him to justice. The film costars Harry Stubbs and Mae Busch.

Menzies helped create the wonderful costumes and worked on the script for the elegantly elaborate 1933 version of *Alice in Wonderland,* was assistant director and created the special effects for the war scenes for *Cavalcade,* and designed the cave sequence climax for Selznick's colorful *The Adventures of Tom Sawyer* (1938).

Selznick was so pleased with Menzies' work that he created a new post for him, that of production designer, for Selznick's masterpiece, *Gone with the Wind,* for which Menzies won a well-deserved Academy Award. In essence, Menzies ghost-directed the entire film by re-creating the entire script in sketch form, showing the actual camera set-ups, lighting, and all other pictorial elements which were used, thereby saving an immense amount of time and money as well as establishing the look of the entire film. Selznick also placed on his production designer the task of all montage sequences, which Menzies not only designed and laid out but also directed, including the famous burning of Atlanta sequence, which for the record marked the last appearance of the huge gate from *King Kong*'s Skull Island, redecorated as a row of households before being burned.

Menzies also designed with Vincent Korda the magnificent spectacle of Korda's *Thief of Bagdad* (1940), one of the most opulent and beloved fantasies of all time. He worked with Hitchcock, creating the memorable windmills in *Foreign Correspondent* (1940) and was brought in to assist in filming the Salvador Dalí–designed dream sequences in *Spellbound.* He began a collaboration with director Sam Wood and together they did *Our Town* (1940), *The Devil and Miss Jones* (1941), *Kings Row* (1942), *The Pride of the Yankees* (1942), *For Whom the Bell Tolls* (1943), and *Ivy* (1947).

Menzies' design work was marked for a "predilection for broken diagonal barriers which cross the frame like jagged slashes and usually turn up during scenes of tension, grief, and separation in the form of fences, walls, palisades, railings," according to Léon Barsacq in *Caligari's Cabinet and Other Grand Illusions: A History of Film Design.* Gillett's *International Encyclopedia of Film* acclaimed him "the most influential designer in Anglo-American cinema...."

Menzies' first two films as a director were both codirected by Kenneth McKenna and were both concerned with magicians doing tricks which showcased Menzies' knowledge of special effects techniques. The first, *The Spider,* features Edmund Lowe performing a series of tricks to unveil a murderer in the audience, and the second, *Always Goodbye* (not to be confused with the Barbara Stanwyck film with the same title made seven years later), was much the same.

Menzies was enamored with special effects, and in Scot Holton and Robert Skotak's retrospective on his career in *Fantascene #4,* they quote Menzies as saying, "The camera is the real heavy because it sees what we don't want it to see.... When I directed *The Spider,* I wanted to use that gag about the magician cutting off the woman's head. Well, I wanted to do it without cutting, shooting it in a single sequence and keeping the camera moving for the entire scene. Of course, we could have cut it together, but it was more fun to do it the other way, just for our own satisfaction."

Not too surprisingly, Menzies' directorial career specialized in special effects films, though mostly he was in such demand as an art director and later as a production designer, he became the highest paid and most in demand designer in films, that his directorial assignments were few and far between. However, his next, though often overlooked, was one of his best.

The "Chandu the Magician" series began life as a West Coast radio program starring Gayne Whitman in 1931. William Fox's Fox studio, which later merged with 20th Century to form 20th Century–Fox, bought the rights and selected Edmund Lowe, who had played a magician in the Fox film *The Spider,* to assay the role of Chandu. The codirector of *The Spider* and codirector of *Chandu the Magician* was the legendary William Cameron Menzies, noted for such SF film classics as *Things to Come, The Whip Hand,* and, of course, *Invaders from Mars.*

Menzies was a genius in film design, and his selection seems obvious in lieu of the many ingenious special effects that the film incorporates. For an early sound film, it has very fluid camera movement and the marvelous effects work stands up well in comparison to today's cinematic magicians.

Chandu's humor is probably attributable to French-born codirector Marcel Varnel, a former actor turned director, who was later noted for handling the comedy stylings of bumbling British comic Will Hay and the Crazy Gang. Varnel's best films are reputed to be *Oh Mr. Porter, Alf's Button Afloat, Old Bones of the River, Ask a Policeman, The Frozen Limits*, and *The Ghost of St. Michael's*, the latter a borderline genre entry starring Will Hay (and not Peter Ustinov who doesn't even appear in this Ealing comedy despite often being attributed as such) with a ghost supposedly piping before deaths occur. (Ustinov actually appeared in the Will Hay comedy *The Goose Steps Out.*)

Both films as well as *Chandu* were made for Fox films, the outfit started by Hungarian immigrant William Fox in 1915 out of his Box Office Attraction Company. Fox developed such stars as Theda Bara and Tom Mix, financed the Murnau classic *Sunrise*, provided a home for such directors as John Ford, Raoul Walsh, and Frank Borzage, and after the sound challenge of Warner Bros., his company countered with Movietone, the first sound-on-film process, which was developed in association with General Electric.

At the end of the 1920s Fox made a bid to dominate Hollywood by trying to buy a controlling interest in Loew's Inc., the parent company of MGM, as well as a 45 percent interest in British Gaumont. Unfortunately for Fox, his timing proved disastrous as he had to deal with an automobile crash which immobilized him for two months while the famous stock market crash of 1929 and a government antitrust action took place.

Fox was saved by the success of Shirley Temple's films; however continuing litigation forced Fox to sell his shares in 1930 to a group of bankers for $18 million for a studio that had been valued at $200 million mere months before. In 1935, Fox merged with Joseph M. Schenk and Darryl Zanuck's two-year-old Twentieth Century, forming the now familiar 20th Century–Fox.

Chandu's cinematographer was the great James Wong Howe (*Mark of the Vampire; Seconds*) who later worked with Menzies again on *Kings' Row*. In *The Art of Hollywood*, Howe is quoted as saying, "William Cameron Menzies designed the sets and sketches for the shots; he'd tell you how high the camera should be, he'd even specify the kind of lens he wanted for a particular shot. The set was designed for one specific shot only; if you varied your angle by an inch you'd shoot over the top.... Menzies created the whole look of the film."

Chandu begins inventively with a waving hand seemingly conjuring up the titles, with the name Chandu looking as if it were fashioned out of sparkling sequins. Unlike many early sound films, *Chandu* has a very fluid look thanks to the many dollies through miniatures that break up the more static shots typical of productions of the period. Miniatures are also used to extend sets and at times were shot and backprojected behind actors to create the impression of immense antiquities on the film's frugal budget.

Indeed, the film is almost an encyclopedia of early special effects techniques, featuring one inventive effect after another throughout its fast paced running time. The opening sets up that Frank Chandler (Lowe) has learned all the secrets of the Yogi and is now christened Chandu. To demonstrate his powers, Chandu does the famous Indian rope trick, disappearing a boy at its apex; performs an example of astral projection, and walks across hot coals, all tricks he will need to use later in the film.

Edmund Lowe was considered a dependable leading man who could play both two-fisted heroes and drawing room Romeos in the 1920s and 1930s, and while his Chandu lacks the mystery and other worldly quality that marked Lugosi's interpretation, his down-to-earth style makes for a clean-cut hero with a wry sense of humor. Lowe's most notable works were his appearance as Sergeant Quirk in 1926's *What Price Glory*, 1929's *In Old Arizona*, 1933's classic *Dinner at Eight*, and he carried the plot with cameos from Karloff and Lugosi in Karl Freund's otherwise unnoteworthy *The Gift of Gab* (1934). Lowe eventually descended uninterestingly into character parts, popping up in such films as *Dillinger, Around the World in Eighty Days* and *The Last Hurrah*.

Chandu's teacher shows the magician a crystal with the image of Roxor (Lugosi), warning of "death and destruction rising from the brain of a madman." He is told that Roxor lives in the cliffs above the third cataract of the Nile and that this great danger will threaten him personally through his family.

Chandu's sister is Dorothy (Virginia Hammond), who has married scientist Robert Regent (Henry B. Walthall). Ralph Morgan (*The Power and the Glory; The Life of Emil Zola; The Monster Maker*) was originally cast as Regent, the inventor of a death ray, but was replaced by Henry B. Walthall, who is best remembered as the Little Colonel in D. W. Griffith's *Birth of a Nation*, as Dr. Manette in the 1935 *A Tale of Two Cities*, and as Edgar Allan Poe in the 1915 film *The Raven*.

Regent has invented a secret death ray capable of destroying whole cities, though his motivation for doing so is never explained. He demonstrates the ray's destructive power by blasting a large block of stone into non-existence. Such rays were commonplace staples in the mainstream pulp magazines of the 1920s and 1930s, inspired by the discovery of X-rays by Wilhelm Konrad Roentgen in 1895 and perhaps the heat ray of H. G. Wells' *The War of the Worlds* (1898).

The machinery in Regent's laboratory is clearly manufactured by famed electrical wizard Kenneth Strickfaden, who provided similar services for *Frankenstein, The Mask of Fu Manchu, Bride of Frankenstein,* and *Young Frankenstein* for that matter.

Roxor arrives at Regent's laboratory and arranges his kidnapping on the spot with the help of some stealthy henchmen who abduct the scientist and lower him into a boat waiting below. Nor does Roxor forget to take Regent's equipment with him as well. We divine his purpose when he promises, "An end to all that is noble, all that is sane."

Lugosi, fresh from his turn as Murder Legendre in *White Zombie,* is in fine form as the wild-eyed madman Roxor, though for the most part his performance harkens back to his turn as Dr. Mirakle in *Murders in the Rue Morgue.* He gives his lines a very similar, exuberant reading with his larger than life delivery and expressive voice making for a commanding presence.

Unlike Mirakle, Roxor has no "advancement of science" justification for his actions. Here he is simply a vindictive albeit clever fiend with an unslaked thirst for destruction. He is a megalomaniac who wants to bring down civilization in order that it regard him in awe and acclaim him as ruler. Like the later Dr. No, he has no real understanding of the technology he wishes to control, it is simply enough that he can ruthlessly extort others into doing his will.

A sandstorm rages outside the building where Regent's family, Dorothy and her daughter Betty Lou (June Viasek) and son Bobby (Nestor Aber), await word from Robert. Sinister figures peer through the windows and the family grows anxious. To the accompaniment of mysterioso music, they see the shadow of Chandu at the end of the hallway. (We later learn that this music is an "astral bell" which alerts Chandu to the presence of great danger, though, of course, it sounds nothing like a bell.)

Clearly, the family is in danger, but Chandu makes for a reassuring protector. He uncovers a letter that Regent wrote to Roxor in response to Roxor's demands for the death ray warning him that Regent will expose Roxor's nefarious plans to the government if he persists. Chandu has thus far been unable to contact Regent with his mental powers, suggesting that Regent is drugged or otherwise has been rendered mentally insensible.

In a clever ploy, Roxor's henchman leaves a kitten at the doorway, causing Betty Lou to open it to rescue the mewling furball; however, the astral bell warns Chandu to check his crystal ball where he espies the henchman grabbing the young teen. Dashing to the door, Chandu stops the henchman with a gesture, putting him under an instant hypnotic spell which causes the henchman to reveal Roxor's whereabouts.

Princess Nadji (Irene Ware, who also appeared with Lugosi in *The Raven*) arrives at a wine seller's seeking Roxor. There Roxor is conferring with Abdulah (Weldon Herburn) who becomes excited at news of the princess' arrival. "I don't know if she is to be a friend or an enemy," Roxor admits, but if she opposes him and Abdulah serves him, she will join Abdulah's harem, promises Roxor.

Nor is Roxor himself immune from Nadji's charms when the princess arrives at his office. He tries to take her cloak so he can feast his eyes on her figure, but she demurs. Frustrated, he simply offers her a chair to sit upon. Lugosi performs these actions with gentlemanly flourish.

Meanwhile, Chandu infiltrates the wine seller's by hypnotizing the doorman and seeks Roxor disguised as an Arab. Roxor reveals his intentions to destroy the great dams that have brought prosperity to Princess Nadji's people unless they make him a modern pharaoh.

"I shall be greater than any pharaoh," Lugosi exults. "Civilization and all its works shall be destroyed. Man shall return to savagery, leaving only one supreme intelligence — me!"

This in a nutshell is Roxor's mad plan, achieving greatness by undermining the advances of the present. It is true that many people today are skeptical about the advantages of modern civilization, but just try to imagine a time when there were no supermarkets and most of a man's day was spent eking out a bare existence by working all day to gather some food and where the average life expectancy was about 40 years of age. That time was as little as a hundred years ago, even in Industrial Age England.

Roxor gloats, and finding that she won't cooperate, takes Nadji prisoner and informs her that she is to be sent to a friend of his as a present. However, he finds that the servant he has handed her to turns out to be Chandu, who has taken the servant's place. Chandu escapes from Roxor's lair by overturning a flaming brazier and carrying Nadji through the flames.

We discover that Chandu and Nadji are old flames who are still in love with each other. We are also introduced to Albert Miggles (Herbert Mundin), a former soldier who used to be an orderly in Captain Chandler's outfit, who is now reduced to wearing a fez and holding camels. He begs Chandu to hire him, which Chandler does after putting a hypnotic spell on Miggles that causes him to see and hear a miniature version of himself every time he tries to take a drink, in order to cure Miggles of his alcoholism. Miggles, of course, supplies the comic relief in the film, and does so far more effectively than most others of his ilk.

This is largely because the part is played by Herbert Mundin. Mundin's most famous role was as Barkis in George Cukor's adaptation of Dickens' *David Copperfield*, but he proved a delightful diversion in many Hollywood films of the 1930s, especially *Adventures of Robin Hood* as Much the Miller, as well as in *Tarzan Escapes, Mutiny on the Bounty, Cavalcade*, and *Love Me Tonight*. His career was cut short by his death in a fatal car crash in 1939.

Roxor's spies learn that the expedition plans to seek Roxor at the ruins of Madune above the third cataract. Meanwhile, Abdulah makes an appearance, but when Nadji orders wine for them, the astral bell sounds. Sure enough, one of Nadji's servants who is actually in Roxor's employ poisons one of the drinks hoping to kill Chandu. Just as he is about to take the glass, the astral bell sounds again, so Chandu tries to force the hapless spy to drink while Miggles drops the glass he swiped upon hearing that the wine has been poisoned. The spy leaps into the Nile to escape with his life. Roxor is indeed a treacherous foe.

Menzies establishes the ruins with a long pan through the corridors of a miniature and then a tilt down to a large set where Roxor has assembled Regent's death ray, which he is still unable to work. Roxor's ruthlessness is further established by his arranging to blind the servant who failed in the poisoning attempt with a red-hot two-pronged poker. He threatens to do the same to Regent if he will not reveal the secret of the death ray, but Regent steadfastly refuses.

Nadji guides the heroes to the base of the tremendous ruins. Miggles pulls on a large ring which causes the wall to pivot open, allowing Chandu, Nadji and Miggles to enter. Miggles is left behind to keep watch while Chandu and Nadji explore. Behind him, one of the statues of pharaohs proves to be a sentinel, and the frightened Miggles seeks out Chandu. The sentinel shuts the trio in a room. Sarcophagi tip forward to reveal armed Arabs behind them, but Chandu is able to hypnotize the men into believing that their rifles have turned into snakes and they flee, though he manages to keep one of them under his control and from him discovers the whereabouts of Regent.

Meanwhile, Abdulah has sent two men aboard Nadji's boat who kidnap the unprotected Betty Lou. Roxor summons Regent and reveals that he will sell Robert's daughter on the slave auction block if he does not cooperate. Regent begs Roxor to kill him instead and let her go, an offer which Roxor refuses.

Outside the slave market, Chandu disguised as an old bearded Arab beggar makes a duplicate of his image to distract the guard away from the door. Once inside, he turns invisible (via mass hypnosis), reappearing to bid on Betty Lou and buy her. He hands the auctioneer what appears to be a bag of coins and whispers in her ear, "Courage, Betty Lou."

Still viewing the proceedings from up above, Roxor tells Regent, "It's not too late to save her." But Regent still refuses. The auctioneer rushes up to split the proceeds, but dumping the contents of the bag reveals a collection of crawling bugs rather than coins. Roxor spots Chandu drawing Betty to the door and alerts the crowd.

Chandu pulls a pistol to keep the crowd at bay and gets Betty astride a horse. Then using his hypnotic powers, his hand and then his body disappears, leaving his empty clothes hanging in the air until they fall to the ground and disappear before the amazed crowd. Roxor realizes that Chandu's powers are a form of extraordinary hypnosis emanating from his eyes and formulates new plans against him.

After more fun with the desperate-for-a-drink Miggles involving scoldings from a miniature version of himself and his seeing a goldfish in his drink, Chandu and Nadji ride off into an ambush led by Abdulah, who taking his cue from Roxor, arranges to have henchmen throw teargas, blinding Chandu and incapacitating the source of his power. While Nadji escapes, Chandu is quickly bound and blindfolded.

Roxor reveals that he will threaten Regent's entire family, which encourages Robert to send a message to them. Regent bribes a guard to send the message: "There is no chance of saving my life. Give the man who brings this a reward. My prayers be with you tonight. Father." The guard brings this message to Roxor who quickly eliminates four words and alters the message to read: "There is a chance of saving my life. Go with the man who brings this and reward my prayers. Be with you tonight. Father." Roxor then sends the altered message to Dorothy.

Roxor then gloats over the helpless Chandu, who tries to taunt him into removing the blindfold. "Your eyes would have no effect on me. If I were alone I would. These silly natives, they believe your tricks," thereby assuming his superiority to his underlings in all matters. However, the more cautious Abdulah prevents Roxor from removing the bandage to prove that his is the superior will.

Instead, a sarcophagus is brought in and the bound Chandu is deposited therein. "A favorite punishment of the priests of Isis who built this temple," Roxor explains. Roxor is aware that yogi can remain buried underground for a long period of time, but he hasn't heard of them surviving underwater, so he arranges for Chandu to be deposited in the nearby Nile.

Regent's family now in Roxor's jail, Regent promises Roxor to show him how to use his machine in exchange for Roxor letting his family go. "There is a way out of that cell and I'll show it to them, but not with you in there," offers the doublecrossing Roxor. Once Regent is removed from the cell, Roxor has a trap door tripped showing a pit that descends to the Nile beneath. The floors start tilting downward as Regent's family cling to handholds and the furniture slides into the pit and splashes into the river.

"Will you serve me now?" demands Roxor. Regent, faced with the destruction of his family before his very eyes, acquiesces.

Underwater in his casket, Chandu breaks his bonds and escapes the watery prison prepared for him.

Regent's beam can go halfway around the world, and Roxor now fires up its dreadful power. "At last, I am king of all," he intones in a series of closeups. "That lever is my sceptre. London, New York, Imperial Rome! I can blast them all into a heap of smoking ruins. Cities of the world shall perish." The directors then show us Roxor's dreams of destruction while he continues his soliloquy:

"All that lives shall know me as master. They'll tremble at my words. Paris. City of fools. Proud of their Napoleon. What will they think when they feel the power of Roxor?!

"Even England. The sacred tradition. Its king, its triumph, its navy will be helpless. They shall bow before me in worship. Me, Roxor!

"I will destroy the dams of the Nile and its roaring floods shall speed down upon hundreds of thousands, drowning them like rats. Roxor the God whose hand deals death."

The miraculously dry Chandu appears and stops Roxor with a hypnotic command. Roxor resists and reaims the ray at Chandu, but Chandu's will proves stronger than Roxor's, whose hand releases the ray's control lever.

Chandu frees Regent's family while Robert reveals that he set the machine to explode. Roxor is left frozen in place in front of the now-glowing death ray machine. Chandu searches for Nadji, as Abdulah tries to ambush him and gouge his eyes out, but Chandu flips him and the pair fight while Nadji hits Abdulah with a chain and Chandu knocks the wily Arab out with a right cross.

The heroes escape the ruins in the nick of time when the raygun explodes, killing Roxor and bringing the ruins down around everyone's ears. Chandu pulls the unharmed Nadji from the wreckage and they embrace beneath a romantic moon. Miggles is followed by his miniature conscience, who asks where they can get a drink. "You ought to be ashamed," the now reformed Miggles tells him. The film ends with the same gong logo that opened it.

Chandu the Magician has no great themes or thoughts buried in it, but was simply cannily crafted as entertainment. While it does present stereotyped Arabs as villains, it doesn't come across as racist, with Roxor's ethnicity left open to question. In fact, one of the most admirable characters is the Arab Princess Nadji, who loves Chandu but who has chosen to devote her life to the well-being of her people. Unlike many movie heroines who stand by the sidelines and scream, she takes an active part when the hero is threatened. In all, she is presented as an admirable woman of true heroic stature, someone who is brave and dedicated, but is also human and feeling.

Chandu the Magician presents a simplistic moral universe conceived entirely in blacks and whites with no greys. That Chandu is a superhero who traffics in deception presents no moral dilemmas because he is on the side of the good and the righteous. Roxor's insane plan and utter ruthlessness comes from the fact that he wears the black hat of the piece. He has suffered no wrongs which serve as a whetstone to his appetite for destruction, he simply craves power and feels that the most effective way of achieving it is to wipe out everybody else until there are no challenges to his ultimate authority.

Of course, Lugosi excels at this kind of portrait. Both as an actor and as a person, he had a ravenous appetite for life, sinking his teeth into it and savoring its juices. No other actor could deliver ripe dialogue with the same memorable relish that Lugosi would bring to it.

Chandu the Magician is a fast moving kids' film with a story typical of the later movie serials but with better design and special effects courtesy of some of the most talented men in Hollywood. It is designed to present wonder after wonder with the result that no particular effect stands out above the rest (although the combining of Miggles with his miniature counterpart seems particularly seamless to these eyes).

The film itself, therefore, becomes a tribute to movies' ability to become a magic carpet that can take the viewer to new and wondrous realms where evil villains disintegrate whole cities with destructive death rays and courageous conjurers pass through foes and flames, making marvels and rescuing pretty princesses. Of such delicate delights are childhood memories made, and such is the enchanting entertainment that *Chandu the Magician* provides.

Things to Come came about when Baroness Moura Budberg, who served as secretary to H. G. Wells, introduced Wells to Alexander Korda, who was fascinated by the writer and was determined to make a film with him. Together they selected one of Wells' most difficult books, *The Shape of Things to Come*, an essay in futurism, looking from the perspective of A.D. 2016 and which predicted the Second World War and space travel as occurring in the next 100 years. (The film narrows the time scheme from A.D. 1936 to A.D. 2036, with Wells predicting the Second World War beginning in 1940.)

Wells, who had once celebrated the "little man," now pinned his hopes on scientific elitism. His major theme was

The image of Theotocupulos (Cedric Hardwicke) decries technology while his image is broadcast above the László Moholy-Nagy–designed futuristic city in Menzies' *Things to Come.*

that Man the Scientist, with his rationality and objectivity, would triumph over Man the Artist, who is caught up in the fears, doubts, and ignorance of "little people." Therefore, scientists would make the cities of the future perfect, eliminating waste, need, greed, inefficiency, and political stupidity.

Korda agreed to let Wells write the script, but as Wells kept continually pontificating, the project began to bog down. Wells wrote three screen treatments and many months had to be spent explaining to him why they could not be made into a film. Korda reluctantly agreed to make the film according to Wells' fourth and final draft, exactly as he had "dictated." Like much of Wells' fiction, authorial mouthpieces rather than characters predominated, and the successes and failings of the film closely match those of Wells himself. Hungarian writer Lajos Biro was dispatched to assist him.

Wells had thrown himself into every aspect of production, giving notes as to the moods the film's music should convey (he was highly pleased with Arthur Bliss' score), and sent memos to the cast that the populace of the future would not live like mindless automatons, but would be freed by machines to pursue their own pleasures. He even insisted on Japanese-style futuristic costumes.

Korda hired Menzies to helm the project after Lewis Milestone declined in favor of directing two less complicated features. Korda's brother Vincent was given the difficult task of designing Wells' future. His greatest accomplishment was the design of "Everytown," the City of the Future, which foreshadowed the look of Aéroport Charles-de-Gaulle with its people-movers conveying crowds through glass tunnels, its indoor terraces, and its chilling inhumanity. László Moholy-Nagy, a Hungarian futurist, was hired as a consultant and designed several back projections depicting huge machines that help rebuild the world. The designs incorporated such London sights as Oxford Circus and the dome of St. Paul's cathedral.

Wells was delighted with the designs, though he made many minute changes so that they reflected his vision of the future accurately. His intention was to depict the Modern State Society that would establish and impose a new "pattern of living upon our race." He felt it was imperative to unify and pacify the human race, which otherwise would fall back into conflict and decay ("Adapt or perish"). Wells complained that "Democracy means the subordination of the state to the ends and welfare of the common individual," and felt that a truly responsible state would subordinate the individual to the long-term welfare of the species, so he advocated a dictatorship that would stamp out personal initiatives and individual motives.

A socialist, influenced by the writings of Claude Henri de Rouvroy, comte de Saint-Simon (author of *Le Monde tel qu'il sera* [*The World to Come*]), Wells proposed a Communist Revision, one that discards Marx and in which the new aristocracy would not be untrained workers or the wealthy privileged, but the makers, an aristocracy of talent, who would use industrialism as the basis of their new world order. One important aspect of Wells' idea is that all men be forced to work to their capacity, and none have the right to be lazy.

According to Wells, the film was to dramatize the Indian vision of life, by which he meant the trio of Hindu gods — Brahma the Creator, Siva the Destroyer, and Vishnu the Possessor. Wells divides his society into three categories, the Poietic (the collective intellect), the Kinetic (the coercive power of military might), and the Dull & Base (proletariats and their passions). Poietics would formulate an idea, the Kinetics would enforce its implementation among the (intellectually) Dull & (morally) Base, whose "natural tendencies will have to be overridden."

An aspect of *Things to Come* which impressed many was its depiction of what London would look like after heavy bombardment. Both Winston Churchill and Adolf Hitler were reputedly impressed with its depiction of what heavy bombing by the Luftwaffe might achieve. Wells predicts how terrorized and demoralized civilian populations might be after heavy bombing. He shows in the future a world linked by global television and the ability of such a device to create special problems. However, his Vernesque Space Gun which fires a projectile at the moon remains scientifically specious.

The cast was selected by Korda from actors who had a solid background in the British stage, and included Raymond Massey and Ralph Richardson. (Massey complained about Wells' overearnest monologues and complained, rightly, that his part was "fantastically difficult to act. A benign big brother was bound to be a bore.") Ernest

Thesiger had originally been cast to play the role of Theotocupulos, but left to play Dr. Praetorius in *The Bride of Frankenstein*, and so the part went to Cedric Hardwicke. Wells rarely created three-dimensional characters, tending to make them mouthpieces of ideas he wanted espoused or refuted, and his work is truly difficult to perform; however, the talented cast does a terrific job of making the ofttimes stilted speeches sound somewhat natural.

Ned Mann, a friend of Menzies who worked on Korda's *Thief of Bagdad*, was hired to handle the film's special effects. Mann brought along several Hollywood professionals including rear projection expert Harry Zech, optical effects man Jack Thomas, model builder Ross Jacklin, traveling matte expert Paul Morell, effects cameraman Eddie Cohen, and mechanical effects expert Lawrence Butler. For their time, the effects work is quite impressive in both design and detail. The aspect of the film that most delighted Wells, however, was its majestical musical score, composed by Sir Arthur Bliss. Rather than compose the music to match the images, Wells insisted that Bliss compose his music and then have images matched to it.

According to Lyle Wheeler, "When Menzies worked as a director, I used to tell him, 'You're no damn good as a director.' The first thing he would ask for when he came on the set is, 'Dig me a hole here,' and that's where he would put his camera. He wanted to photograph ceilings and didn't give a damn what the actors were saying." Nevertheless, Menzies made the movie visually stunning and saw in Wells not a creative usurper but a fellow artist as concerned with the film's substance as he was with its artistic design. Eventually Wells became bored with the lengthy process of filmmaking, stopped visiting the sets, and left Menzies alone to work his magic with Wells' scripted words and images.

Things to Come was the last film Korda made at his old London Studios before moving into his new facility of Denham. Wells enjoyed visiting the sets daily and often complained that the film limited his vision, was taking too long, and was inefficient. Korda continually had to explain why many of Wells' ideas were impractical while Wells would lecture on in his high, squeaky voice.

Menzies conveys a grand sense of scope right from the beginning as a searchlight shines across the letters of the title, standing stark against the horizon. It is 1940 and Christmas in Everytown, while the newspaper headlines are warning of war in Europe. Aviator and inventor John Cabal (Massey) sees for certain what his friends do not—war is coming. (Wells thought it would be an appropriate irony to destroy the old Christian order on the date for celebrating Christ's birthday. Another irony is that John Cabal is meant to recall John Calvin, who was likewise stern and priggish.)

Director-production designer William Cameron Menzies on the set of *Things to Come*.

Despite the signs, the ordinary public (as represented by Passworthy [Edward Chapman]) is indifferent, wrapped up in what Wells called "everydayism," his term for the "false securities and fatuous satisfactions of the everyday life," which he found contrary to the spirit of the "Human Adventure," which sees human life as one continuous drama. The coming war will serve to shake the masses out of their self-serving ignorance and into cognizance of their responsibility to the collective fate of Man. Cabal pokes fun by referring to Passworthy as "Pippa," a reference to Robert Browning's "Pippa's Song," which ends "God's in His heaven—All's right with the world." Cabal knows that human affairs will not take care of themselves for Man's benefit. "If we don't end war, war will end us," he warns.

Menzies associates the toy cannons and soldiers given to the children at Christmas with the sounds of the real thing in the distance. War has come at last, and the first target hit is a movie theater (Wells felt that the cinema, potentially a powerful educational tool in the hands of state-run schools and universities, was wastefully developed merely to provide amusements. He felt film was the art of the future, and later in the year 2036, we see film being used to teach a lesson in school.) Wells accurately predicts the use of radio-controlled missile torpedoes leveling cities (though he is not so accurate about the use of gas).

Once more Menzies creates a memorable contrast by showing us Passworthy's son beating a toy drum before a desolate landscape as the shadows of real soldiers pass him by, and both are obliterated by a bomb. Wells firmly believed that militarism and warfare were childish things, though horrible, and must become things of the past, of mankind's childhood. Therefore, the way to peace was to take the game away from its infantile players and turn it over to the technical intelligentsia, who would regard war as a tiresome distraction rather than as a great and glorious opportunity.

Menzies creates the impression of war with a montage of old-model tanks rolling in one direction being assaulted by technologically advanced tanks (designed by Frank Wells in Streamlined Moderne style, which throughout the film is synonymous with the future) rolling in the other. It is clear that technical prowess will win the day over the reactionary, anti-scientific British forces. Advanced planes fly in formation and drop poison gas. However, in his determination, Cabal's primitive biplane is able to overcome one of the enemy fighters and he follows it to the ground, pulls the dying airman from the wreckage and establishes his kinship with him.

"Why has it come to this? God, why do you have to murder each other!" exclaims Cabal, while the enemy airman responds, "What fools we airmen have been! We've let them make us fight for them like dogs." Both men recognize not only a commonality, but also a common enemy, the criminal patriots who set them against each other. The concern for future generations is underscored by having a young girl trying to escape the oncoming gas by dashing up to them be helped when Cabal takes the enemy's gas mask, straps it to her face, and takes her with him.

This inspires Cabal to form the United Airmen with other technical revolutionaries such as himself, and following the war, the Airmen complete the task of eliminating all separate nation-states and their bellicose nationalisms in order to reconstruct the world along rational lines. Their watchwords are "Research, Invention, World Planning — and Scientific Control." They fight until all weapons are on their side and they have peace on their terms.

An example of their enemy is Rudolf the Victorious (Ralph Richardson), the Boss of Everytown, which in 1970 lies in medieval shambles. Rudolf is the feudalistic military chief of a peasant-like populace who has a vainglorious lust for territorial possession and is shown to be basically motivated by sex. (He is in effect a caricature of big-time political bosses.) He makes war to impress Roxana (Margaretta Scott), his mistress. Together, they want only love and glory, and represent the problem of possessiveness and animal appetites that Wells warns against.

By contrast, the Airmen are the New Puritans. They have no passions or beastly lusts, but are cool-headed intellectuals motivated only by their ideological conviction to govern well by governing scientifically. They do not make war for glory, they make war for peace, a war to end war and nationalism in order to create a unified world state.

One of the aftermaths of the war is the "Wandering Sickness," a peculiar fever that causes men to leave their sickbeds and wander in a hypnotic daze, which wipes out half the world's remaining population and shakes the survivors loose from their old interpersonal ties. Harding (Maurice Braddell), now a doctor, struggles to fight the pestilence with inadequate supplies and no prospect of trade providing more. Rudolf's way of dealing with the wandering sickness is to have all wanderers shot, which Harding sees as a barbaric return to the Dark Ages.

Menzies shows us laborers at work in this ruined town, and demonstrates that the medievalism of Everytown was always present beneath its modern veneer. (One of the film's wittiest images has a peasant steering a tireless, horse-drawn Rolls Royce to bring vegetables into town, who then reminisces about how in the old days he thought nothing of going a hundred miles in it.) Each man continues working for himself with no common understanding and no collective plan, using small craft specialization rather than large-scale mass production. Airplanes, which require a coordinated effort and community of design, are beyond them. Richard Gordon (Derek MeMarney) struggles to repair a dilapidated biplane, but there is not rubber tape or fuel to be had, and he pronounces civilization dead.

However, the arrival of a plane proves Gordon wrong. It is John Cabal's monoplane, designated WT-34 (for World Transport) to emphasize Wells' concepts that civilization is transport, which makes trade possible, and that the world state will supplant and abolish national sovereignty. Cabal emerges dressed in black Airmen tights, his head encased in a giant gas helmet that emphasizes his being an embodiment of Wells' World Brain, the head of a worldwide organization. (The helmet also suggests a halo around Cabal's head, indicating his benevolent intentions.)

Cabal arrives as both savior and judge. The guards Rudolf sends to arrest him are cowed by this imposing figure who seeks out the local warlord. The populace are awed by Cabal and come to worship him. Harding admires his maturity and vigor, and after leading him to Harding's laboratory, tells him about the kind of Boss they have. Cabal promises "No more bosses," and gets Gordon to pledge himself to World Communications, the servant-masters of the world whom he describes as "the Brotherhood of efficiency, the freemasonry of Science. We're the last trustees of civilization when everything else has failed."

Rudolf, by contrast, is a petty gangster. Menzies makes certain that on his desk we see a broken down telephone, indicative of the breakdown in postwar communications and a contrast to Cabal being a representative of World Communications. When Rudolf hears that WC deals in commerce he is excited, though he becomes disappointed to learn that munitions selling is not part of their line of business. He then asks after fuel and spare parts for his plane, but Cabal explains that his new order objects to private airplanes, a pronouncement which mystifies Rudolf until Cabal spells it out for him: "We don't approve of independent sovereign states. We mean to stop them."

Rudolf orders Cabal to the detention room, while Roxana goads him into asserting his prowess and makes false claims about the stranger's arrival fitting in with his plans and expedites his intentions to attack Floss Valley to acquire fuel for his plane. However, when he returns, he finds that Gordon will not work on his planes and Harding will not manufacture poison gas, and both fail to salute him and affirm their duty to all of civilization. Roxana, sensing a shift in power, switches allegiance to Cabal, and conspires to get Gordon into the air so he can alert WC headquarters at Basra. Roxana comes on to Cabal who spurns her advances. She cannot imagine the new world order in which the code of jealousy is abolished and women work as comrades rather than as love objects that men fight over in order to possess.

Rudolf is soon shown fondling another woman and quoting Dryden: "None but the brave deserve the fair" while giving idiotic patriotic speeches and denigrating the technical help, noting who the hell needs chemists anyway, and who wants books, which only muddle the mind. "Why was this science ever allowed?" he complains. "Why was it ever let begun? Science! It's the enemy of everything that's natural in life." He musters the few planes he has been able to fix and foolishly sends them off to fight the arriving force from World Communications, who quickly down their competitors and drop peace gas, which knocks out the populace and kills Rudolf, whose death symbolizes the death of the old "natural" order.

With the brigands out of the way, the new world order asserts itself. Menzies shows the distant ruins of Everytown as huge digging machines excavate an underground city that is to be the center of the Modern World-State. While Cabal's voice drones on about the giant possibilities of science, Menzies shows us these possibilities in an elaborate montage that shows Cabal's industrial idea begin to take shape in the form of this futuristic city (depicted as gleaming white, cold, and somewhat sterile).

The narrative then advances to the year A.D. 2036 as Theotocupulos, a reactionary sculptor, pleads for a return to the sentimental and aesthetic values of the old order. (Theotocupulos' speeches are reminiscent of comments made by Aldous Huxley, whom Wells abhorred, and his name is derived from El Greco's own — Domenikos Theotocopulos.) Theotocupulos is a rebel who represents the return of everydayism. Agitated by news of a Space Gun that will shoot men at the stars, he demands a halt to progress and arranges a broadcast while concealing his purpose.

Meanwhile, Cabal's great-grandson Oswald (also Massey) is ruler of the World Council of Direction and wears Brahma white in the manner of *kata-ginu*, the garb of the samurai class. Theotocupulos feels that the object of life should be happy living, but he is made the object of contempt. Cabal sees that he is encouraging the masses to animalistic individuality, lacking the fuller perspective of human existence as a continuous tissue and succession of births of which his life is only a momentary fragment.

Theotocupulos represents the Humanities, tradition and the wisdom of the past, while Oswald is the representative of science, the "truth" of the future, and Wells portrays these dialectical modes as being perpetually in conflict, never really dialoging with each other. For Oswald, science represents the universal and the unifying, and his religion is the religion of progress, the spirit of eternal creation.

The conflict over the Space Gun represents the idea that new frontiers are opened or closed by force. Theotocupulos ends his talk against the progressive Modern State with a call to "Make the Space Gun the symbol of all that drives us ... and destroy it now." His talk inspires the masses ("A man has a right to do what he likes with himself," observes one) and they turn into a mob that marches on the gun.

Oswald is stunned. The Modern State has eliminated downtrodden classes (basically by making it illegal for anyone to be unemployed), everyone works and shares in the abundance (wealth is collective wealth by definition). Why should they rebel? It is decided to fire the gun before the mob gets there, so Cabal takes off in a helicopter with the two youths who are to pilot it (Cabal's daughter and the son of Ramond Passworthy). The mob gets there at the same time, Cabal makes a speech that life must either move forward or fall back, and the rebellion is literally crushed by the concussion of its being fired. Cabal warns the rebels three times to beware the concussion, but never considers not firing the gun to save their lives, becoming in effect a mass murderer. (Menzies makes the assault on the Space Gun an epic spectacle.)

Things to Come ends with one of the greatest and most impassioned speeches in science fiction cinema, a call for the greatness of man's striving to ever exceed his grasp, to conquer new worlds and new horizons, to face the immensity of the galaxies and not flinch but issue a challenge of achievement. Passworthy asks if there is never to be any rest. Oswald responds:

> Rest enough for the individual man. Too much and too soon, and we call it death. But for Man no rest and no ending. He must go on. Conquest beyond conquest. First this little planet with its winds and waves. And all the laws of mind and matter that restrain him. Then the planets about him. And at last out across the immensity of stars. And when he has conquered all the deeps of space and all the mysteries of time — still he will be beginning.... If we are no more than animals, we must snatch our little scraps of happiness and live and suffer and pass, mattering no more than all the animals do or have done. Is it that — or this? All of the universe — or nothingness? Which shall it be, Passworthy? Which shall it be?

The two men fade out against the stellar background so that only the stars remain as an angelic choir echoes Oswald's question. Common sense reality is left behind in contemplation of mankind's achieving impossible goals under the auspices of a clearly totalitarian state. It is at once inspirational and frightening to contemplate. Not surprisingly, this heavyhanded film has had admirers for its scope and vision and detractors for its preachy anti-selfhood, anti-individualistic liberalistic concepts ever since.

Despite critical huzzahs given to it on its release in 1936, *Things to Come* was a box office bomb of the first magnitude. It took many years for it to recoup its $1 million investment, which made it the most expensive British film produced up to that time. It was certainly one of the most didactic. All told, the production had taken 18 months to complete. (After Arthur Clarke had recommended the film to Stanley Kubrick when they were working on *2001*, Kubrick told Clarke that he would never listen to another of Clarke's film recommendations.) Few science fiction films that followed are as high-minded and few possess the same power to inspire us to believe that mankind can shape its future into something awe-inspiring and glorious.

In 1979, a truly terrible Canadian SF film appeared titled *The Shape of Things to Come*, which whatever its pretensions, had nothing really to do with the original film or even Wells' story.

Menzies' close friend Charles Laughton agreed to star in a production of Robert Graves' *I, Claudius*, provided that Menzies was the director. However, Korda ran into a financial difficulty in paying the last $100,000 he owed to Marlene Dietrich for her $350,000 salary on *Knight Without Amour*. Dietrich told Korda that if he would hire her discoverer, director Joseph von Sternberg, she would forget about the last payment. Korda agreed, Sternberg was in, and Menzies was off the project, but the film was never completed as Laughton had continual difficulty in "finding" his character and then Merle Oberon was involved in a car crash. Korda shelved the project and Lloyds of London was forced to pay the £40,000 spent thus far.

Next Menzies tackled *The Green Cockatoo* with the help of codirector William K. Howard, who was hired to do retakes of dialogue scenes that the studio thought Menzies had handled too artily. The screenplay is credited to Edward O. Berkman and Graham Greene, though Greene's talent is not much in evidence (Greene would refer to the whole experience as "deplorable"). The film starred John Mills as song-and-dance man Jim Connor who becomes involved in a crime melodrama. Made for a low budget, the film was frequently reissued because of the participation of Mills as well as future star Robert Newton. Menzies' action footage is not bad, with one shadowy fight on a landing recalling some of the early imagery in *Things to Come*.

Another obscure Menzies project was *Conquest of the Air*, an elaborate semi-documentary from producer Alexander Korda based on stories by John Monk Saunders, screenwriter of *Wings* and *Dawn Patrol*, and St. Exupery. Menzies was simply one of a series of directors, each assigned his own segment for this film, which relates man's attempts to fly, from Icarus and his wings of wax to the stunt flyers of the 20th century. The film starred Laurence Olivier (giving a terrible performance as Vicent Lunardi with a horrible French accent that recalls the one he used in *49th Parallel*), Franklyn Dyall (as Jerome de Ascoli), Hay Petrie (as Tiberius Cavallo), Henry Victor (as Otto Lilienthal), John Turnball (as Von Zeppelin), Alan Wheatley (as Borelli), John Abbot (as De Rozier), Michael Rennie, and Bryan Powley (as Sir George Cayley).

Many of the early achievements of flight are meticulously re-created, giving viewers a window onto history, supplemented at the end with contemporary newsreel footage. Such air pioneers as Lindbergh, Udet, Amy Johnson, and Amelia Earhart are depicted. Strangely enough, despite the many directors involved, the film lacks any directorial credits whatsoever. Menzies filmed his material in 1936, but it was not assembled until years later. It received a press release showing in January 1938, but was then withdrawn and altered with new narration and documentary footage of early wartime aviation and Churchhill being added for its final release in 1940. (Later, Key Films would cut the material down to 46 minutes and re-release it again in 1944.)

Menzies was to return to the science fiction genre in 1951 with *The Whip Hand* for RKO, which he both production designed and directed. The picture began life as a script by Stanley Rubin called *The Man He Found*, based on a story by Roy Hamilton, which was then revised into a new script by George Bricker and Frank Moss, which they called *The Enemy Within*. It was shot as a post-war anti–Nazi paranoid thriller with Bobby Watson appearing as Hitler, who is ready to start a new campaign to take over the world.

It was then decided, supposedly by RKO head Howard

Hughes, to alter the secretive villains so that they are covert communists seeking to take over the United States using germ warfare instead. The character of Hitler became Dr. Wilhelm Bucholtz (Otto Waldis), a Nazi scientist now in the employ of the communists (and fanatically adherent to their philosophy). The entire film had already been shot when the decision was made to make the film an anti-communist drama, so the Hitler footage was removed, the guards redubbed, and new footage was inserted. Whether Menzies had a hand in these changes is uncertain, but for the most part they do not appear too extensive as either way the villains are mostly guarded and secretive, not wishing to reveal anything to an interloping outsider.

The protagonist of *The Whip Hand* is writer Matt Corbin (Elliot Reid) who is taking a fishing vacation in the little town of Winnoga near the Canadian border. He falls and hurts his head, is surprised when a nearby guard at a gate refuses to let him in, makes it to the town's doctor, Dr. Keller (Edgar Barrier), and discovers that there are no longer fish in the lake, due to some virus. Initially, Corbin plans to take up fishing elsewhere at the suggestion of Loomis (Raymond Burr), who runs the local inn, but everything he observes in the town makes him more and more suspicious that there is an interesting story in this seemingly placid setting. He also develops an interest in Janet Keller (Carla Balenda), Dr. Keller's sister.

It seems the communists killed off the fish to drive away tourists and drive down land prices, buying the land and their privacy cheaply in the process and leaving them free to conduct germ warfare experiments on human guinea pigs (Russian traitors) on a remote island. Corbin conveys a code message to his editor through an old storekeeper (who is murdered), and his editor in turn alerts the authorities, who arrive in time to hold Bucholtz at bay with their tommyguns.

Bucholtz had planned to use a thousand agents to spread the germ cultures—"influenza, parrot fever, Q-fever, tularemia, and bubonic plague"—throughout the U.S., ridding Russia of America's impediment to world communism by eliminating its population; however, he is content to sacrifice himself by detonating an explosive device that will scatter the germs for hundreds of miles.

Bucholtz, kept at bay by the feds in the room with his experimental patients, who are swathed in bandages, does not notice Corbin coming up from behind and knocking him down. The long-suffering, enraged patients attack Bucholtz, making short work of him. In the finale, Corbin shows no ill effects from his exposure to the deadly diseases and his marriage to Janet is announced on the same page as the story exposing the foiled communist plot.

Bill Warren's *Keep Watching the Skies!* describes an opening of the film involving stock footage and narration which was in the script but did not end up in the film itself. The cinematography is by the great chiascuro expert Nicholas Musuraca, who shot some of Val Lewton's greatest films. Menzies' visual design has the film getting increasingly darker and more noirish as it goes along, with shadowy night scenes just before Matt and Janet's betrayal and capture. As per the script, the film is filled with significant looks of suspicion on the part of the Winnoga townspeople, constantly reminding the audience that they are in league with one another against the friendly but inquisitive Corbin and intimidating the few free-thinking souls who are left.

A similar atmosphere of suspicion and paranoia pervades Menzies' next SF project, the classic *Invaders from Mars*, which subtly uses Menzies' designs to suggest a dream reality as seen from the child protagonist's point of view. While places the boy has been are presented realistically, locations such as an observatory, a police station, and a physicist's lab are not. (The police station is famed for being constructed out of a simple corridor backed with oversized doors, a sergeant's extremely high desk with two lamps at the end, and a clock on the wall that never moves. Menzies shoots over the sergeant's shoulder to emphasize his imposing height. The physicist's lab once again features the same corridor and has a few school chemistry supplies to suggest a child's idea of a laboratory.)

The initial story was concocted by John Tucker Battle, based on an experience his wife Rosemary had had as a child where she ran into a woman whom she thought was her mother, but turned out not to be. Battle created a story about Martians landing in a sandpit and turning people into cold, unfeeling slaves as part of a global invasion.

Producers Arthur Gardner and Jules Levy optioned the screenplay, but their rights expired before they could find the funding to get the film into production. The project was taken over by producer Edward L. Alperson, who was Levy's boss, and who hoped to cash in on a Mars invasion film before the release of Byron Haskin's *War of the Worlds*. Screenwriter Richard Blake was assigned to rewrite the screenplay and reduce the budget needed to film it. It was Blake who created the idea of the "dream" ending, which Battle hated so much that he dropped his name from the credits.

Menzies became intrigued by the project, and was excited by its design possibilities. He made a notebook of design sketches based on Blake's script to figure out how the film could be shot strikingly and economically. The designs were made to be simple and uncluttered, emphasizing a few striking elements. Blake took some of Menzies' ideas and incorporated them into his screenplay.

The idea of shooting the film in 3-D was toyed with, and Menzies carefully emphasized depth in his designs.

However, Alperson could not afford it, though the film's title lettering retains the block design used for 3-D films and Menzies stayed true to his designs.

The independent production was set up at Republic Studios, which was notoriously ill-equipped. Production manager Ben Chapman managed to scrounge some pieces of military equipment from the naval station in Long Beach and some stock military footage was purchased to help pad out the film, which ran short of the expected running time once completed.

Art director Boris Leven told Robert Skotak and Scot Holton in *Fantascene* #4, "Menzies was overseeing the entire production. All his thinking and training was along the lines of art direction. I tried to carry out his ideas as much as I could. It was really tough to make this film because it was done on such a shoestring budget ($290,000). Occasionally we had to give up ideas because of the cost. Yet it's effective due to the clever design."

The film is one of the first to use fiberglass and plexiglass in creating the sets. The bubble-marked walls which dissolve under the Martian heat ray were actually constructed out of condoms. The Martian Intelligence, a gold, tentacled head in a globe (played by midget actress Luce Potter) was crafted by the effects department to hide the box in which the actress had to lay. (The special mechanical effects were handled by Theodore Lydecker, Republic's long-time effects expert who provided the effects on *Adventures of Captain Marvel* and other serials.)

Tragically, the notebook with Menzies drawings was lost right before the start of production and was never recovered. Menzies was heartbroken, but soldiered on, working closely with script supervisor Mary Yerke and cinematographer John F. Seitz (*The Lost Weekend; Sunset Boulevard*). The cinecolor used had a tendency to create truly garish greens, which became an important design element.

Two giants, eight foot, six-inch-tall Max Palmer and Lock Martin, were hired to play the main Martian mutants, while midgets were hired as stand-ins for soldiers to emphasize the mutants' height (and be light enough for the men to lift). Norma Koch created the mutant costumes, originally designed to be hirsute, using green velour with noticeable zippers running up the back and stylized masks covering their faces. Some folks have noted that cheap looking monsters such as these would be what Jimmy would likely have seen in watching science fiction matinees, or that such a touch adds to the overall "it's a dream" feeling of the film. Nevertheless, some scenes, such as the mutants carrying the Martian intelligence, are awkwardly staged to have the mutants walk backwards to keep the zippers away from the camera.

One of Menzies' important contributions to the film was to drop the idea of trapdoors being used by the Martians to capture their victims. Instead, he decided to show a mysterious sand whirlpool, which he created by pulling on a slit in the canvas covering the hill and siphoning the sand into an industrial strength vacuum. (The film would then be reversed to show the sand returning to normal.) The result was a simple, arresting image that gave the feel of alien manipulation and is one of the things people most remember about the film.

Invaders from Mars' story centers around David (Jimmy Hunt), the young son of a rocket engineer George Maclean (Leif Erickson), who awakens one night to see a flying saucer descending in the field behind his family's house. His father goes to investigate and disappears for some time, and when he returns, his demeanor is cold and unemotional. David espies an X-shaped scar on his neck and realizes that aliens have taken possession of him.

For its British theatrical release in 1954, Alperson ordered the ending reshot to remove the dream concept. Additional footage at the observatory was also added and cut in, with Jimmy Hunt now taller, having a shorter haircut, and wearing a vest. The new observatory footage is talky and dull, but expands on the idea of flying saucers and alien visitors by pointing to pictures, newspaper clippings, and models. At one point, Dr. Kelston brings out a model of a green saucer similar to, but different from the one seen in the film's opening, which David identified as exactly like the one he saw. (Clearly, it is not.) At the end, there is no replay of the events of the film, the saucer is shown as taking off (the opening done in reverse), and then suddenly blowing up. At the end, Blake and Kelston assure David his parents will be all right and see that he is tucked into bed. This new footage was done under the direction of Wesley Barry, who would later direct *Creation of the Humanoids*.

If that weren't enough, *Invaders from Mars* was further reedited for theatrical reissue in 1976 by producer Wade Williams, excising David's comments of "Gee whiz" and other small moments. Williams wrangled North American rights to the film in return for striking new negatives and prints. He created a third version of the film by eliminating some of the repetitive scenes of mutants rushing through the tunnels and some of the mismatched military footage, while adding the additional observatory material and the saucer exploding, but still retaining the it's-all-a-dream ending.

The most faithful copy of *Invaders from Mars* exists on the Image laserdisc, but this is marred by some bad sound and the image quality is extremely variable at times, though it was transferred from the finest elements available. (The disc also includes the alternate ending and observatory footage as a bonus at the end.)

Menzies directed one last science fiction project, the outrageously oddball *The Maze*, concerning a Scottish laird who has the misfortune to be born an amphibian. Naturally, this is not revealed until quite a ways into this strange and seldom seen little film, which was filmed in 3-D.

Written by Dan Ullman from a novel by Maurice Sandoz (that originally featured illustrations by Salvador Dalí), the story tells of how Gerald McTeam (science fiction stalwart Richard Carlson) is summoned back to Craven Castle, and then fails to return to his fiancée, Kitty (Veronica Hurst). Kitty is naturally worried and so heads off to the castle accompanied by her aunt, Mrs. Murray (Katherine Emery) only to find that Gerald refuses to see them.

They then spent quite a bit of time exploring the cobwebby, bat-infested castle in hopes of eventually bringing Gerald back to his senses, going so far as to invite over a carload of his jolly friends to cheer him up. A grim Gerald sends them away lest they learn the terrible secret that the true laird of the castle, Sir Roger Philip McTeam, is, in a Lovecraftian twist, a two-hundred-year-old toad who swims like a frog (toads do not typically like to swim). Mrs. Murray and Kitty make their way through the castle's elaborate maze (seen from above as an impressive miniature), split up, and Murray finally meets face-to-face with the feckless, unfortunate frog, who in a despondent fit decides to commit suicide by leaping from the tower window onto the camera in the film's most gimmicky shot.

Naturally, Menzies' effectiveness is undermined by an unconvincing frog costume, sodden if unusual (to say the least) story, and pathetic explanation for this strange condition from young McTeam, who claims that the old gentleman had grown up as an amphibian ever since being one in embryonic form. Still, Menzies is able to muster up some sympathy over this peculiar plight, though most of his genius seems to have been devoted to creating an interesting look to the castle and maze on a minuscule budget.

Menzies was hired as associate producer and designer on Michael Anderson's *Around the World in 80 Days*, for which he was assigned to assemble a comic bullfight sequence with Cantinflas. During production, Menzies had an operation for cancer, during which he almost died and which left him speechless for the last year of his life. He finally died of a heart attack a year after the operation.

NICHOLAS MEYER (1945–)

Time After Time (1979); *Star Trek: The Wrath of Khan* (1982); *Volunteers* (1985); *The Deceivers* (1988); *Company Business; Star Trek VI: The Undiscovered Country* (1991); *Vendetta* (1999)

Television: "Pied Piper of Hamelin" *Faerie Tale Theatre* (1982); *The Day After* (1983)

Nicholas Meyer is the son of psychoanalyst and author Dr. Bernard C. Meyer, and was born on December 24, 1945 in New York City. He was only 13 when he made his first attempt at filmmaking by acting in and writing a 70 minute, 8mm opus inspired by Michael Anderson's *Around the World in 80 Days*. He studied literature and film at the University of Iowa where he participated in the writers' workshop before graduating in 1968.

He tried to break into filmmaking in New York, but ended up a pipe salesman at Bloomingdale's department store. Finally, he joined the publicity department at Paramount Pictures in New York as an associate publicist. "My job was primarily to translate press releases into English from, you know, Hollywoodese, so they could be read by civilians," Meyer told me.

Meyer first came to Hollywood to be the unit publicist for the film *Love Story*, writing the book *The Love Story Story* in the process. (It took him six weeks and he sold it for $3,000, which he used as a grubstake once he made his way to Hollywood.) After helping to promote Paramount's late 1960s product, he moved on to become a story editor at Warner Bros., where his job was to sit around and read things for people who did not have the time nor inclination to read them for themselves.

Meyer also launched a successful novel writing career, particularly with *The Seven Percent Solution*, an ingenious Sherlock Holmes pastiche which deals with the fictional character's cocaine addiction and psychoanalyzes him in the process, and which became a best-seller and was adapted by Meyer into an entertaining film for Herbert Ross. His other novels include *Target Practice, The West End Horror* (another Holmes pastiche), *The Black Orchid* (with Barry

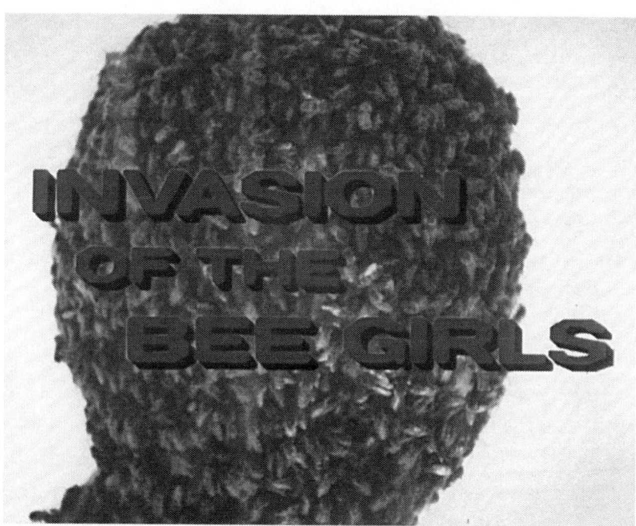

The title shot for the Meyer-scripted *Invasion of the Bee Girls.*

Kay Kaplan), and the autobiographical *Confessions of a Homing Pigeon.*

In 1971, Meyer picked up a paperback entitled *Fifth Business* by Robertson Davies, one of Canada's finest writers. Enraptured by Davies' novel (which Meyer described as life changing), Meyer struggled for the next 14 years to turn the novel into a film he called *Conjuring*, which he wanted to star Christopher Walken and Christopher Reeve. Meyer was fascinated, for example, with how one thrown snowball changes the lives of several characters, helping turn one into a Houdini–like magician and another into a Charles Foster Kane–like millionaire while a third, a pregnant woman, goes simple as a result and becomes a saint complete with miracles and stigmata, about the son she gives premature birth to as a result of being struck by the snowball, and with unexpected miracles (such as a resurrection) that Davies casually inserted into his narrative. The central character is the little boy who ducked the snowball as an instinctive reflex action, and it's also about the day of reckoning for all these people.

Meyer interested producer Herb Jaffe in optioning the book and wrote what he felt was a really fine script which much to his dismay was turned down by every studio in town. (Eventually, Meyer purchased the rights to the book himself outright, but still had no success until he finally relinquished them to someone else.)

Meyer's first screenwriting credit was on *Invasion of the Bee Girls,* which was purchased by producers Fred Weintraub and Paul Heller at Warner Bros. to be made into an exploitation movie directed by Denis Sanders in 1973, although Meyer complains that his script was heavily rewritten. His original title for the project was *The Honey Factor.*

"It was an interesting experience," Meyer said. "I had written this script and it was a really good script. It was a script that could have played at an art house or a drive-in. It had something to say to everybody, and it really worked on a number of levels, which is the kind of thing I usually look for. Right before I started production, I went to visit my parents on Christmas vacation. Let this be a lesson to you — do not visit your parents during preproduction.

"When I got back, Paul Heller said, 'Well, you know we had to make a few adjustments. A script is like a blueprint, isn't it? There are a few changes that we had to make for the director and so forth.' And I said, 'Oh yeah, I understand. Could I see the script?' He said, 'Sure,' and I looked inside and it said screenplay by Nicholas Meyer and Sylvia Snebley. I thought, who the fuck is Sylvia Snebley?

"It was really an absurd piece of material, and I called up my agent and said, 'Get my name off this piece of ridiculousness.' He said, 'No, no, we have to get *her* name off.' I said, "You don't understand ... it's terrible,' and he said, 'No, you don't understand — you need the credit, any credit will do.'

"So it went to the Writers Guild for arbitration and as she hadn't done anything except make it dumb, which was probably on orders from the producers who were faced with the prospect of playing either the drive-ins or art houses in Westwood, decided it better be one than the other, and you can guess which they aimed for, so my name is still on it."

In *Invasion of the Bee Girls*, Special State Investigator Neil Agar (William Smith) jets in from Washington to investigate the mysterious death of a physicist at Brandt Research in Pelham, California. Agar comes into contact with many of the physicists' colleagues including his beautiful research assistant, Julie Zorn (Victoria Vetri).

More deaths occur, eight in all. It soon appears that the victims, all male, are dying from excessive sexual activity resulting in a massive coronary. In a town meeting, it is suggested that all citizens practice complete sexual abstinence, to which much grumbling is heard. A scientist, Henry Murger (Wright King) reveals he knows the secret of the Bee Girls, but he is killed by a female "hit-and-run" driver before he can say anything.

The wives of the victims eventually undergo the transformation to Bee Girls, and we follow Nora Klein (whose husband was a Brandt scientist) to the ominous lab of Dr. Susan Harris (Anitra Ford). There she is grabbed by two women, stripped, and shot with a radiation gun. She is placed in a hexagon-shaped chamber into which millions of bees swarm to cover her body. The bees retreat and her entire body is now encased in a cocoon from which a new Nora emerges, transformed into a Bee Girl.

Julie and Neil figure out the secret of the Bee Girls, but Julie is abducted by Susan Harris. Neil rushes to the lab where Julie is about to undergo the transformation. Firing a shot into the master control board, Neil aborts the Bee Girl plot and destroys the lab. The Bee Girls go down in flames, and Julie is reunited with Neil.

Meyer would go on to write two unusual and superior TV movies. The first is *Judge Dee and the Monastery Murder*, an interesting if unsuccessful pilot directed by Jeremy Paul Kagan and based on *Judge Dee and the Haunted Monastery*, one of a series of offbeat mystery novels by Robert van Gulick, starring Khigh Dhiegh as the 7th century crime-solving Chinese judge who rights wrongs, solves crimes, and deals with domestic problems as well (costars included Mako, James Hong, and Keye Luke). The second is *The Night That Panicked America*, an entertaining and imaginative recounting of the actual production and the aftereffects of Orson Welles' infamous "War of the Worlds" radio broadcast.

According to Meyer, *Judge Dee* "was a very unusual film because everybody in it was Chinese, and it was about the first detective who ever lived, who was a Chinese magistrate from the Teng Empire named Dee Jen Jay. A sinologist named Robert van Gulik, a Dutch diplomat to China, had discovered this man and the stories which had been told about him, and had translated some of his writing. They are all very intricate mysteries — Chinese detective literature. ABC, thinking it would be like *Kung Fu*, decided to do one."

It was during a Writers Guild strike that Meyer wrote the best-selling novel *The 7% Solution*. He loved Conan Doyle's stories, but hated the movies that had been made from them. "I have hated all the movies, almost without exception," Meyer said. "I could not watch them, and although Basil Rathbone could have been a good Sherlock Holmes, he never really got to play him because there is something very silly about all those movies. Plus Nigel Bruce was silly as Watson — very funny, but you can't believe for a minute that this is the man who wrote down all the cases. By the same token, he also plays him as such an idiot that you can't imagine why such a genius chooses such a fool to be his friend. Surely the intelligence of Holmes as well as the vanity is too sophisticated ... plus, they took them out of period....

"I just thought they were all dumb and corny, and Sherlock was never corny to me. He was very *real.* I suppose one of the things I wanted to do by the time I wrote *The 7% Solution* was to depict him as a real three-dimensional person with his own past and his own psychology."

The 7% Solution differs from most Sherlock Holmes stories in that it is actually about exploring the character of Holmes himself rather than simply a recounting of one of his adventures. Several Holmes fans were upset with Meyer for depicting his drug addiction, but said Meyer, "It seems to me that Holmes' drug addiction, instead of diminishing his heroism, rather served to throw it into sharper relief since it was another obstacle he had to overcome in order to be a successful and functioning human being.... [A] lot of people who are addicts are not wicked or bad, they are merely unfortunate, and in the book I tried to show that Holmes' arrival at his addiction was the result of certain traumas in his background which could account for it."

In researching Doyle's life, Meyer discovered that as an ophthalmologist, Doyle had gone to Vienna for six months to study ophthalmology during a time when Sigmund Freud and Doctors Konigsten and Kurler wrote a paper about the use of cocaine as an anesthetic drug during eye surgery. Freud had promoted cocaine as a wonder drug until his good friend Harris von Fleischel tried using it to kick a morphine habit and died. Meyer always thought that Holmes reminded him of his father, a psychoanalyst, and decided it would be interesting to explore what would happen if Holmes tried to kick his cocaine habit, given him by Doyle as a Bohemian, Victorian eccentricity, psychoanalyzing the great detective in the process while solving a mystery.

The film version directed by Herbert Ross is faithful to Meyer's book, and Meyer was involved throughout. Meyer recalls:

> I cast Alan Arkin and Robert Duvall as Freud and Watson. Herb Ross cast Nicol Williamson, but we both chose Oswald Morris to be the cinematographer and Ken Adam to design the movie. I really like the film a lot. My major complaint is with the editing, which I had the least to do with, which I think we had some strong points and some weak points. The strong point, I think, from the psychological point of view, is that the film is edited beautifully. You are always where you want to be. But from the point of view of pace, it isn't very musical. It proceeds along always at the same kind of stately way, whereas I think a drama should go like this (motions his arm in an upward arch). By the time you reach the climax, you should be spinning off the deep end or something should get wilder.
>
> In visualizing the train chase, I anticipated that pieces of the film would get shorter and shorter as the thing sped up. It never did that. And there was stuff I kept begging Herb Ross to cut out. I said, "You don't need this, you don't need that. The audience already understands." And Herb, who's a very wonderful man, has a passion for clarity and was very loyal to the script. It was an absolutely perverse situation. The writer was saying, "Please cut the dialogue," and the director was refusing.
>
> At the end of the movie after Holmes has been hypnotized and you learn all these shocking things about his background, Freud has a speech in which he says, "Now we understand why he doesn't like women, why he became a detective," and all these things. It's the climax of the movie. The audience feels it's the climax of the movie, we ought to get on with it, and I said, "We don't need that speech. We already heard this." It's about 25 seconds long, and he does something so wonderful at the beginning of

> it. I mean who could have anticipated that Alan Arkin would go like this (starts to interlock hands) when he says, "becomes clear," and then Watson's line follows, "You're the greatest detective of them all," and that's all you need. But Herb Ross said to me, "Ohmigod! You're deballing your own script!" That's the word he used — deballing. I'm very proud of the movie … but I wish I could get in there with scissors because I feel there are four minutes total which could be brought out of the film in various places that would improve it.

Meyer read the opening of an unfinished novel by Karl Alexander that postulated H. G. Wells pursuing Jack the Ripper using a time machine into the modern day, and decided to complete the story and transform it into a screenplay, making his directorial debut with the tale. (He later offered his plot to Alexander to incorporate or reject in the novel version, published as *Time After Time.*)

"*Time After Time* is a story of good and evil," said Meyer. "Wells in the movie is not so much based, except in a very superficial sense, on H. G. Wells, but is really much more representative of a civilized human being who rationally expects to approach problems and solve them, who represents the constructive side of the human race. The Ripper — who's interested in the Ripper anyway? Small potatoes. It's just representative of something for me in the movie, which is evil — the destructive, flip side of that thing. It may be true that the actors and the writing make them somehow become three dimensional, but at least originally, as conceived by me, that was the way I was thinking of them as characters."

In order to get a shot at directing the film, Meyer optioned the material with his own money, wrote the screenplay, and brought in his own producer, insisting to Warner Bros. that if they wanted to make the movie, he would have to direct. The studio accepted and later tried to get him to cast Mick Jagger as the Ripper and Malcolm McDowell as Wells. Meyer met with and rejected Jagger, but changed his mind about McDowell, who had primarily been cast as bully boy thugs (*If…*, *A Clockwork Orange*). "Then I thought about it, and I became really intrigued by the idea since I like to let actors act, which is to pretend to be different things, of giving him an opportunity to be cute, which he was. In that case, the more I thought about it, the more I liked it. It's not that [the studio people] never make good suggestions, it's that they mainly don't make good suggestions."

Meyer begins the film with a point of view shot as the Ripper accosts a drunken prostitute who prepares to boff him in an alleyway, asking him what his name is. A hand opens a musical watch as David Warner's voice replies, "My name is John. But my friends call me Jack!" before attacking the woman with a knife.

Unlike many other Ripper films, where the identity of the Ripper is made a mystery, Meyer lets us know right away that Dr. John Stevenson (Warner), a late arrival to H. G. Wells' (Malcolm McDowell, cast against type) dinner party, is the man. He demonstrates his cleverness by handily beating Wells at chess, and telling him that Wells will never beat him until he learns how Stevenson thinks.

Wells shows an experimental time craft to his guests, but thus far has lacked the nerve to try it out. The police come looking for the Ripper and search Wells' abode, but cannot find him, as Stevenson has secreted himself elsewhere in time. (Meyer credits an electrician for suggesting that Wells echo Stevenson's line about "You will win when you learn how I think" and in editing the film laid it in over a shot of Wells checking his basement and discovering that his machine is indeed missing.) When the time machine returns, Wells resolves that he must protect the future, which he expects to be a utopia, from the depredations of the Ripper and tries the machine himself.

Meyer includes a number of delightful touches in the film, from Wells studying his future, fat image at the museum exhibit (and shuddering in horror), to watching this Victorian gentleman come to grips with modern times, learning to deal with automobiles, traffic lights, Hari Krishnas, McDonald's, molded plastic tables ("I never saw wood like this before!"), French fries ("French fries are pomme frites!"), escalators, and horror movies.

One of the themes that Meyer hammers over and over again is that modern times are more violent. This is made evident in everything from the headline "Colts Maul Rams!" to the Ripper flipping the channels from one violent image to another on the television set in his motel room. The Ripper is more at home in this violent era. "I am the future," he declares. "Here, I am but an amateur." And indeed, he blends in and adapts far more readily than the fussy Wells who retains his Victorian garb rather than exchange it, as the Ripper does, for more modern duds such as turtleneck sweaters and sunglasses.

Naturally, any history buff who recalls that Amy Catherine Robbins was Wells' second wife can easily guess the outcome of the ending. Still, there is a lot of emotional feeling in Wells' passionate plea to the Ripper to spare Amy's life because he loves her, that "All ages are the same. Only love makes any of them bearable." Even the Ripper is given a human moment when he hesitates long enough for Wells to remove the key and send him to oblivion, as if he accepts and acknowledges the rough justice of his fate.

Before becoming a film director, Meyer had experience being an actor and had directed stage plays and radio drama, so guiding actors' performances proved no problem for him. "Editing I took to like a duck to water because editing is like writing. Dailies are sentences in a book which hasn't been written yet. You potchkey around with them and learn how to be ruthless and learn how to throw things out if it doesn't work, and to experiment and be loose. Very hard if you have no experience that relates to it at all, but I spent ten years as a writer.

"The hardest thing I learned to do is to rewrite. It's the most boring. It isn't boring now, but it was always the part I used to dread. You put paper in the typewriter, or under your pen if you write by hand as I usually do, and you think it's going to come out perfect. There's going to be a little change. Then there's such a feeling of Oh God, you know, and you have to take out the scissors and the Scotch Tape and go to work. But what you have to learn is that the scissors and the Scotch Tape is the most fun. That every time I could ball up a hunk of paper and throw it in the wastepaper basket and the thing got tighter and tighter, the more I got off on it. I got to love it, and so I loved editing.

Malcolm McDowell plays a time-traveling H. G. Wells, shown here aboard his craft the *Argo* in Nicholas Meyer's charming *Time After Time.*

"The thing I found the most difficult was the camera. I have no background with it at all, and the camerawork in *Time After Time* was extremely simple and crude, and lots of times just plain wrong because you know I haven't even directed a television show.... I was at my best when I was really bold and innovative, and at my most inane and absurd when I just plunked it down and didn't really ... lots of shots I did from hunger. How do I shoot this? Well, I'll put it over there and then it will all be in the picture, and things like that. Sometimes it's a matter of angles [sometimes of moves].

"[For example] when Amy walks into the empty living room after she wakes up and says, 'Herbert? Herbert?' and knocks over the vase of flowers. If I had that to do over again, I'd have the camera way up high when she walked out so that she would look little and defenseless, and then make a very abrupt cut from the floor looking up with the flowers falling into the camera. There'd be that sort of thing.

"And lots of examples. Sometimes there'd be scenes that don't work at all. For example, at the end of the movie when Amy escapes from the Ripper, this is totally inept because in the script it was really beautifully set up why she escaped and none of it worked. The only thing that works is that the audience is so involved with the movie at that point that they don't care why she escaped as long as she gets away, and the next moment when the Ripper jumps into the machine and Wells runs up, that's all very clear.

"But actually, what it was was that it was set up way at the beginning of the movie. There was a little hook that came off the machine, like a projection, something that you could use to lift it up and move it across the room or something, and when Wells first gets out in San Francisco, his watch fob catches on the hook. That was intended to be clear. I don't think it is. At the end of the movie, what was also supposed to happen, and what was supposed to be ironic, is that the Ripper in climbing in catches his watch fob on the same damn hook, and the watch happens to be his little fetish. He instinctively reaches for it, and in instinctively reaching for it, he loses the girl, so you might say he was undone by time. It was a little touch of irony, and I felt so clever when I put it into the script, but I fouled up so badly in the shooting that no one can tell what I intended.

"Another example of wrong camerawork. It's very clear when Wells walks past the 'don't walk' sign and gets into a car accident, but it is much less clear when the Ripper gets hit by a car what I wanted it to be. I was shooting like crazy and going crazy, and I didn't get the shot of a 'don't walk' sign, right? Right before he runs out into the street, so that when he runs out and gets hit, you understand that he's been undone by 20th century technology, by a little thing he didn't master which Wells had learned about. I don't apologize for the performances or the editing or for most of the things in the movie, but the camerawork is not the best. It could have been better; it should have been better."

Warner Bros. hated *Time After Time* until it started going through the roof. *Time After Time* won a Golden Scroll Award from Donald Reed's Academy of Science Fiction, Horror, and Fantasy Films for screenwriting, and also won the Grand Prix du Festival of Avoriaz in France. It remains one of the more delightful filmed time travel tales

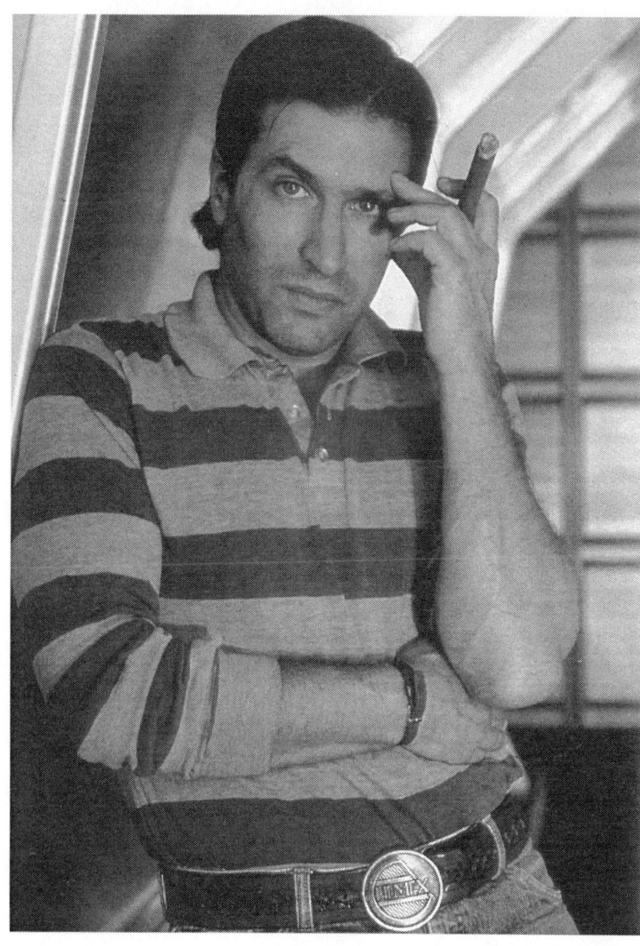

Nicholas Meyer with characteristic cigar aboard the *Enterprise* set contemplating how to inject old allusions and fresh meaning into the *Star Trek* universe.

with engaging characters and its social criticism implicit in the story of a man out of time rather than slathered on in the form of an obvious author's message. Meyer enjoys retaining some ambiguity, and so we never learn the reason for the Ripper's fascination with his pocketwatch, for example, but are free to speculate. In retrospect, Meyer admits that while it remains one of his favorite scripts, he feels that he had not yet learned where to put the camera and expressed a desire to remake the film himself and use what he has learned about directing since then.

Following the gigantic success of *Star Trek: The Motion Picture* despite its spiraling cost overruns, Paramount wanted to make a sequel which could be made on a far more limited budget. They decided they needed someone with expertise in television production and so approached Harve Bennett, who had written for *The Six Million Dollar Man, The Bionic Woman*, and *The Powers of Matthew Star*. Bennett was nervous about taking over a legend but agreed, hiring producer and friend Robert Sallin to produce the film. To find a suitable subject for the story, Bennett screened several of the original TV episodes and felt that "Space Seed," concerning a genetic superman called Khan from Earth's past who is abandoned by Captain Kirk on an alien planet to make his way, provided a good basis for a sequel to find out what might have happened to the character. Working with writer Jack Sowards, Bennett began to put together an elaborate tale of revenge.

Several parties were considered to direct the film and eventually the script was sent to Meyer. "Well," Meyer told me, "I never was anybody's first choice. On *Star Trek*, I don't know how far down the line I was. I accepted it because I wanted to make *Conjuring*, and somebody said, 'Make a big hit movie, and you can do what you want.' Then I saw the first *Star Trek* film, they showed it to me, and I thought I think I could make a better movie than this. That was a good reason to do the sequel in that the first one had not fulfilled its promise. It had not been what it ought to be or what it could have been." Meyer had known William Shatner, but was unfamiliar with the original television show. Looking at a few episodes, he decided *Star Trek* was basically Captain Horatio Hornblower in outer space.

Recalled Meyer in *Starlog*'s Official Movie Magazine, "There was something about this script that intrigued me. It was about the *Enterprise* out on a training mission with a bunch of cadets. Suddenly, they became involved in a life and death situation. The cadets have to grow up fast. At the same time, though, Kirk has to confront a lot of personal things in his own life having to do with his past, his present, and his future.

"Reading the script, it dawned on me what was missing from the first *Trek* movie. The people," Meyer said. What Meyer liked about the old show was that it was about people faced with certain ethical and moral dilemmas, facing problems involving questions of life, death, meaning, honor, and friendship. "The wonderful thing about the old show," said Meyer, "was that no matter how awful or awesome the problem was facing the crew, you always had people to root for. You always had this dizzy feeling of hope. The old show was very optimistic about humanity. There was comradeship, good fellowship and loyalty."

Meyer himself did a quick polish on the script and completed the film during a 43 day shooting schedule. One day, despite being the one directing the picture, Meyer was not allowed on the set because his ID badge had been stolen. The mood on the set was jovial. Whenever Meyer would ask for lights called honeycombs, someone would play the old "Honeycomb" song full blast over the P.A. system to Meyer's frustration and the cast's amusement.

Initially, the screenplay for *The Wrath of Khan* had Spock dying much sooner, but Meyer argued that Spock had to die at the end because the movie would be anticlimactic if he dies in the middle. Then he suggested that Spock suffer a mock death in the first scene, establishing the death theme from the very beginning. Naturally, the studio was concerned about the decision to kill the series' most popular character.

"There was a lot of pressure to back off," recalls Meyer. "They always go for the jugular when they want you to change things. They go for the one thing that makes it distinguished or distinctive. I said, 'Let's be real,' and everybody said, 'Oh yes, let's be real.' Then we got onto how real is real. Then there was a flurry of backpedaling about this and that, and 'you're going to kill the series.' My interest was not in the series; my interest was this movie, to make it the best because it has my name on it.

Director meets ego as Meyer confers with William Shatner in *Star Trek: The Wrath of Khan.* Meyer's "less is more" approach resulted in one of Shatner's better performances.

"And for me there was the task of making the people real. These people had played these parts so much, and had, in a sense, got such a lock on them, such a fix. What they were really fixed on, to some extent, was the television sensibility in which everything always ends up at the end of the hour back where it was at the beginning of the hour. The sensibility that I was trying to bring to it was completely separate. I said, 'Big things are going to happen here, and everything is not going to be the same at the end as it was in the beginning.' It's got everybody aging. That's antithetical to the notion of coming back to where you were. Aging and death."

Regarding his approach to working with actors, Meyer said that if an actor wanted to do another take, he would usually let him. "I do this for a number of reasons," he said. "One, the shot is set up, it usually isn't too hard to go around again. It is always possible the actor will be better, and even if he's not better, I don't want this actor going through the movie feeling that his best work is getting away from him. If he says, 'Will you print take 8?' I'll say sure. Maybe he's right.

"If an actor wants to try something in a scene, I'll always say go try it. There are three possibilities here. One is that he'll get it out of his system. Two is it may be better than what I had; that's the collaboration aspect. Three, it may not be better, but it may suggest a third possibility that may be better than what I have. So I tend not to have too many complaints from actors while working because there is enormous latitude. Occasionally, I'll say I need it to be this way, so we'll do it once my way and once your way, and you'll have to trust me that if your way is better, I will in fact use it."

The film did undergo some changes in the editing process. At one time, there were to be hints of a romance between Saavik and David, as Saavik was halfway in love with Kirk, and once she discovers that he has a son, she transfers her feelings to him. However, while editing the film, she ends up learning that David is Kirk's son much later in the film, and so several short Kirstie Alley bits had to be removed as her reactions no longer made sense. Additionally, details such as the engineering casualty that Scotty brings to the bridge being his own nephew and Khan having lost his wife were trimmed from the film.

While William Shatner resented Ricardo Montalban, who played Khan, Meyer really enjoyed working with him, though noting that the answer to the question he was most often asked was yes, that is Montalban's real chest. Meyer was able to get some unofficial rehearsal time with some of the actors, but not Montalban and recalls:

"When we first started working ... we started with the scene in the cargo bay. It was six minutes of monologue with twenty-three camera moves back and forth. He knew his lines cold, and I showed him the moves, and he got it perfectly the first time we walked through it. But the performance was very different than what you see; it was on the ceiling. I thought, oh my God.

"I said, 'Now that we got the whole thing lined up perfectly, let's talk about interpretation. You know, I think you

Meyer directs Ike Eisenmann as Midshipman Peter Preston, Scott's nephew, whose death scene in *Wrath of Khan* was edited out of the theatrical version but restored by Meyer for the network showing.

It's a matter of choice, of taste. I would rather underplay and let the audience's imaginations rise to meet something halfway.... When I was watching this death scene and I realized that *I* was choked up, I thought, well, we have now transcended the subject matter. This is no longer about a man with pointy ears, which is how I felt because I didn't know it that well."

Because Paramount made a commitment for the film to be in theaters on June 4th, Meyer was forced to begin editing the film while it was still shooting. This required extra long days where for a period of six weeks he was never able to see the light of day. He would direct during the day, eat his lunch while watching dailies, and head to the editing room at night and all day on weekends, putting in 18 hour days on a regular basis seven days a week.

Compounding the problem was that it took time for ILM to deliver all the necessary effects, so early assemblages were filled with cards for missing scenes or inserts, making it difficult to tell whether the film was working or not. The special effects for the film were coordinated by producer Robert Sallin, who saw that all the required elements came together.

are much more powerful and much more dangerous if you're very quiet, if the audience doesn't know what you are capable of. Laurence Olivier once said, 'Never show an audience your top, because if you do, they'll know you have no place to go. It's better to keep it locked down. The thing about Olivier and Brando is that you can't relax watching them because you never know what the hell they're going to do.' I didn't even have to finish this sentence because the man is really smart. And he said, 'Oh yes, I see. Much better, ahhh.'"

According to Meyer, "The scenes that were the most difficult, or at least the most wrenching to do, were the death of Spock. Everybody stood around on the stage in tears, which was very surprising to me because I'm not that experienced as a movie director, and I was amazed at how moved they were. The next day at the dailies, the same thing. Everybody cried.

"I come from the 'less is more' school of thinking. You can have somebody point to something and say, 'Look at that' and you don't have to cut to what he is pointing to. In fact, you can raise considerable tension by not showing the audience what the character sees. For example, once Spock went into the reactor room, I deliberately didn't cut back to him for a long time. After hearing, 'You can't go in there, you can't go ...' you gotta be wondering, 'What's happening to him?' You want to see what's going on there.

One of the difficulties in cutting the film is the problem of sound effects. Each sound effect is placed on its own reel of film, and for one reel of images, there might be as many as 50 different reels of soundtrack material. Any alteration in the images means that each of the soundtrack reels has to be adjusted accordingly. The pressure is on to receive "locked reels" with no further alterations on them, so if the director has an idea to improve a scene by cutting a few frames and speeding up the action, it becomes hell to do and costly besides.

Following his fine work in *Star Trek: Wrath of Khan*, Meyer found time to make a brief on-camera appearance in the television movie *Mae West* (1982) before devoting himself to what would become one of the most famous public service messages of all time, *The Day After*. "I was interested in *The Day After* because of my commitment to trying to stop the arms race, my supporting the nuclear freeze, or my trying to stop us from installing the Pershing IIs in Europe. They don't work. The Pershing doesn't even fly. You launch them and they blow up," said Meyer.

As a drama, this made-for-TV movie is rather clunky, but for hammering home the sober realities of what a nuclear holocaust would be like, it is undeniably effective, and attracted massive attention (and ratings) when it first aired. The project received twelve Emmy nominations including Outstanding Drama Special, Best Direction, Best

Teleplay, Best Cinematography, Best Art Direction/Set Decoration, and Best Supporting Actor for John Lithgow, but only won an Emmy for Best Special Visual Effects.

The story of *The Day After,* written by Edward Hume, centers around a few families in Lawrence, Kansas, the site of our nuclear arsenal, at a time when relations between the United States and the Soviet Union are particularly strained. Berlin is blockaded and problems escalate from there into a nuclear engagement. The families are all fairly normal. Dr. Russell Oakes (Jason Robards) has to adjust to his daughter Marilyn (Kyle Aletter) moving away to Boston, while Jim Dahlberg (John McCullum) is a simple farmer with a family: Eve (Bibi Besch), Denise (Lori Lethin), who is just about to marry her motorbike-riding boyfriend Bruce, Danny (Doug Scott), and Jolene (Ellen Anthony). Both families survive the initial blast and must make do the best they can.

There is also the McCoys, whose husband Billy is in the military, Steve Klein (Steve Guttenberg), a medical student from Kansas University who hooks up with the Dahlbergs, a pregnant woman (Amy Madigan), who is at first impatient and then dispairing, and Joe Huxley (John Lithgow) who monitors radio frequencies for other survivors and reports on the level of radiation.

In an unusual move for the network, once the missiles are launched and the devastation begins, there were no further commercial interruptions (and indeed the project had difficulty in finding sponsors of any kind). There follows the grim prospects of the survivors encountering radiation poisoning and a collapsed society. The film emphasizes how hospitals would be overworked, how the electro-magnetic pulse would disrupt most power sources except for direct current batteries and kerosene, how radiation is an invisible killer, the symptoms of which include hair loss and open sores, leading to a total social breakdown.

The characterizations are all minimal to non-existent, with the emphasis more on the extent of the overall tragedy and the impact upon the survivors, captured in all its harrowing imagery. The film ends with a sobering crawl that declares, "The catastrophic events you have just witnessed are, in all likelihood, less severe than the destruction that would actually occur in the event of a full nuclear strike against the United States. It is hoped that the images of this film will inspire the nations of this earth, their peoples and leaders, to find the means to avert the fateful day."

Meyer took work as a director for hire in *Volunteers,* a misfired comedy written by Ken Levine and David Isaacs which at least has some interesting subtexts. Meyer reported to the *New York Times,* "When I first read the screenplay, it seemed to be addressing the same things that I had been going through over *The Day After.* I was coming to realize what my selfishness was all about. The Peace Corps fascinates me. I've always thought of it as being the one useful thing the federal government has done since the New Deal. But I have always wondered, 'Is it altruistic?' No. It's not altruistic if you accept my fundamental principle, which is 'Everything is connected.' By helping people to make a better life, you ultimately help to preserve your own skin. That's as selfish as you can get."

The classic *Trek* directors, Nicholas Meyer and Leonard Nimoy, hold each other in high esteem.

The idea for the film came when producer Walter F. Parkes and writer Keith Critchlow flew to attend the Tehran Film Festival and passed the time formulating a story about the least altruistic person possible joining the Peace Corps. They turned the idea over to scriptwriters Ken Levine and David Isaacs, who wrote for the *M*A*S*H* TV series, and gave the script to Meyer on his honeymoon.

Not surprisingly, the Peace Corps objected vehemently to every aspect of the script and asked Meyer to change the setting from Thailand to Burma because the Peace Corps does not operate there, and that the organization not be mentioned in the same breath as the CIA. Meyer ignored their requests, figuring that if one can be critical of the army, one should be allowed to tweak the nose of the Peace Corps. The filming itself was all done in Mexico at various locations, which often kept Meyer from being able to view his dailies.

Producer Richard Shepherd wanted Tom Hanks to star at the outset, and Meyer encouraged Hanks to play the part with a New England accent to emphasize the class differences. Hanks stars as Lawrence Bourne III, a blasé, snide, to-the-manor-born snob and Yale graduate whose compulsive gambling creates a situation where he feels it best to get out of town quickly (he foolishly doubles a

$14,000 debt he owes by gambling on the Lakers), and so takes his friend's place in the Peace Corps to evade a pack of determined creditors who are prepared to break his hips.

Off he goes to Thailand with nothing more than his white dinner jacket, boarding a plane full of volunteers who ceaselessly sing Peter, Paul and Mary tunes, and encounters the enthused, boisterous and well-meaning Tom Tuttle (John Candy) "from Tacoma," who immediately alienates the local populace by suggesting they cut down their sacred teakwood trees to build a bridge. Bourne's millionaire father wishes to teach him a lesson and refuses to arrange for his return passage.

Larry could care less about the Peace Corps' plans to build a bridge until a drug smuggler offers him a ticket home and enough money to more than pay off the gambling debt provided he gets the bridge built in six weeks. Properly motivated, Larry devotes himself to the project with a passion.

Volunteers is one of the few films that gleefully attacks naïve liberalism and criticizes the idealistic Peace Corps organization, showing that such government projects are often manipulated to serve the ends of others. (The drug runner wants the bridge to increase his profits; the Communists want it to spread propaganda; and the CIA wants it to infiltrate Communist China. The only people opposed to the project are the locals it pretends to benefit.)

Still, *Volunteers* wears thin as Hanks' character remains rather one-note (the essential joke being that this snooty and initially unlikeable fellow proves to be right, though he does go from despising his surroundings to risking his neck for them) while his love interest, Beth Wexler (Rita Wilson), who despises him after he tries to seduce her on the plane, is under-realized and does not give him much to play off of. (She envies the ease with which he is able to get cooperation from the natives, acquire the small amenities of life, such as a bottle of Coca-Cola, and learns to speak Thai.) Also wasted is John Candy, who is captured and brainwashed by the Communists, disappearing from the story for a long stretch and then given little to do once he returns. There are also a few feeble attempts to parody *Bridge on the River Kwai*. The whole thing winds up happily with Bourne learning compassion, marrying the girl, and using his innate talents to set up his own gambling casino in the middle of nowhere.

In 1987, Meyer received a reputed $1 million to do a script doctoring job on *Fatal Attraction*, coming up with the crowd-pleasing finale to Adrienne Lynne's tepid thriller which premiered at the proper time to capture the fear of AIDS *zeitgeist* of the period. (AIDS was very much in the news, and critics quickly seized on the film's story as being a metaphor for the unexpected consequences of promiscuous, uninhibited sex.)

Ismail Merchant of the renowned Merchant-Ivory team became interested in filming an adaptation of John Masters' book *The Deceivers* (which had already had an uncredited adaptation as Terence Fisher's *Stranglers of Bombay*). The book is loosely based on the true-life adventures of Major-General Sir William Sleeman, who discovered, exposed and destroyed the infamous Thuggee cult of India, whose followers strangled and robbed people in the name of the goddess Kali.

The Rank Organization had purchased the rights many years back, and finally Merchant acquired them and approached producer Michael White, asking if he would be interested in putting up the money for the development of the script. White agreed and they approached Charles Wood to do the adaptation, but ended up not liking his script. Director Marek Kanievska (*Another Country*) expressed interest in the project but not Woods' script, and he initially came on board and took a fact-gathering trip to India. Merchant cast Christopher Reeve for the main role of William Savage, the British officer, and Ernst Goldschmidt at Orion offered $750,000 against distribution rights for the proposed $4 million film.

Suddenly the project started coming apart as Kanievska was committed to another project and became unavailable. Saeed Jaffrey suggested director Stephen Frears, who did not care for the script either, but was willing to work on it with Michael Hirst. Merchant did not care for Hirst's rewrite, which he felt made the film into a pseudo-western and Reeve positively hated it and immediately dropped out of the project. Frears in the meantime became anxious over the idea of filming in India and wanted British amenities flown in. Cinecom committed to the film, but insisted that an American actor play the lead role to make it more "accessible" to an American audience. Merchant contacted Treat Williams about playing the part.

Frears dropped out to make *Prick Up Your Ears*, and Merchant hoped that Indian director Satyajit Ray might make the film, but he felt the material was too violent and lacked the interplay between characters that was his particular interest and strength. Cinecom suggested Meyer, who had read the novel when he was very young, and who proved to be very enthusiastic about the project.

Meyer liked the script and had some ideas about how to improve it. He did not care for the film tests of either Reeve or Williams in the lead, however. Merchant and Meyer ended up agreeing on Pierce Brosnan to play Savage, though Meyer had misgivings about Brosnan's blue eyes, which would hinder his ability to disguise himself as a Hindu, and Brosnan refused to wear contacts. Meyer also thought that having an American play a British officer pretending to be an Indian was a bit too much; fortunately, because of the television series *Remington Steele*, Brosnan was familiar to American audiences and so proved an apt choice.

It was Meyer who suggested Ken Adam be the production designer, who took the film as a challenge to see if it could be done on such a preposterously low budget. While on location, Merchant hired a man named Bonnie Singh on the recommendation of Deepak Nayar, the film's production manager, but hearing some unsettling stories about Singh, soon let him go.

Unfortunately, a short time later it was reported that Basant Byas, the general secretary of the Council for Social, Political, and Economic Studies, had written to the Chief Minister of Rajasthan to demand that the shooting of *The Deceivers* cease because it presented a distorted picture of Indian mythology and culture. This was odd as the government of India had already approved the script and granted permission to shoot the film, but soon another pressure group appeared demanding the same thing. The first day of shooting was disrupted (including stoning by local demonstrators) because the local Collector, the head of police, insisted that local authorities had not granted permission. (Shooting was quickly transferred for the moment to private property over which the authorities had no jurisdiction.)

A controversy grew over the fact that the film would depict a sati or suttee, in which the living widow of a dead man is burned alive on his funeral pyre. (A real-life sati had recently taken place in Deorala and created an uproar there between those who objected to its barbarity and those who defended the ancient tradition. Despite being outlawed under the British raj and under Indian law as a criminal act, the custom had continued in remote or poor areas where an unsupported widow becomes an additional and unwelcome burden on her husband's family.)

Distorted reports were printed in the paper that suggested that the production had filmed an actual sati, when in fact it had no intention of doing so and the company's cameras had yet to arrive from England. Merchant suspected that Bonnie Singh was behind the attacks, as the two people spearheading the attacks were associates of Singh's. Sunauna Mishra filed a lawsuit against the film, charging that it demonized Hindu culture and did not show Indian men and women as being of good character. (The lawsuit was ultimately thrown out as being without merit.)

Despite the various difficulties, the production finally wrapped and was presented to a public that proved largely indifferent. Despite its potentially exciting story, many talented performers (including Saeed Jaffrey, Shashi Kapoor and Keith Mitchell), and unusual period setting, *The Deceivers* failed to engage audiences in its undercover story. There is plentiful depictions of the traditions of the past, including a tiger hunt, a dance sequence, a regimental wedding, and some of the details of the Thuggee cult are interesting, but the film itself became a sad, inert thing, lacking the rousing sense of adventure evoked by *Gunga Din* or even *Indiana Jones and the Temple of Doom.*

Following *The Deceivers,* Meyer hoped to have Paramount produce a script he wrote for *Don Quixote,* but the studio's fortunes had taken a turn for the worse and the project was tabled. Instead, he worked on the script for Walter Hill's *Johnny Handsome* in which a disfigured Mickey Rourke, imprisoned after being abandoned by fellow lowlifes after a heist, is given a new face by a thoughtful plastic surgeon (Forest Whitaker) in hopes that it will decrease his chances of returning to a life of crime. But while Johnny falls in love with a good woman (Ellen Barkin) and tries to go straight, his deep-seated distrust and suspicion of other people lead him to indulge the dark side of his nature. Meyer once again worked as a script doctor, with final credit for the script going to Ken Friedman. It proved yet another disappointing effort from the once quite talented Hill with a pseudo-noir story set in atmospheric New Orleans that is lacking in both credibility and interest. (Compared to a semi-classic such as *Dark Passage* which has a similar plot, it looks quite feeble indeed.)

Meyer did not have better luck with his next directorial project either, the disappointing *Company Business,* which had the misfortune to come out just as the Cold War had ended and according to Meyer suffered from butchering at the hands of the studio as well. Its attempts to be a comedy mostly misfire in its tale of two agents from opposing sides, Gene Hackman from the CIA and Mikhail Baryshnikov from the KGB, who become unlikely allies.

Written and directed by Meyer, *Company Business* was a disappointing foray into the old spy thriller genre. Gene Hackman starred as Sam Boyd, a former CIA agent who is now involved in industrial espionage for a cosmetics company. However, he soon discovers that his cloak and dagger techniques (employed where he secretly films information at a rival firm) are outdated as a bright young lad steals the information required via computer (with Boyd quickly duping him out of it to pass it off as his own findings when his photos fail to turn out clearly enough).

He then gets a call from his old employer and is given a new assignment. He is asked to accompany Grushenko (Mikhail Baryshnikov), a Russian spy for the State Department, and a suitcase packed with a cool $2 million to Berlin where they will be exchanged for a captured pilot. The pair, despite being old hands at this game, find themselves surprised to be nearly wiped out at the exchange (Boyd recognizes the prisoner as someone who was at liberty already back home at an airport).

With nothing to sustain them but the two million in the suitcase, the pair play cat-and-mouse with both the

CIA and the KGB and grudgingly give each other a measure of respect. Unfortunately, Meyer's relatively simple plot (for a spy thriller), while not confusing, does not fascinate or excite in the manner of the best spy thrillers either. The film benefits from supporting performances by Terry O'Quinn and Kurtwood Smith, but given that the Berlin Wall came down, *Company Business* seems to be pretending that the Cold War continued, business as usual, when we know that there are fascinating new developments in the emerging Russian democracy that could have been utilized to fashion a far more interesting thriller.

Meyer was tapped by Leonard Nimoy to return to the *Star Trek* fold and cowrite and direct *Star Trek VI: The Undiscovered Country*. Meyer was intrigued by the story that Nimoy had come up with and immediately set to work on a script with aid from his writing partner Denny Martin Flynn. However, due to studio politics, two other writers, Mark Rosenthal and Lawrence Konner, had been commissioned to write a draft as well, and though it was never used, they were provided with story credit. Meyer's script, like *Company Business*, had been inspired by Gorbachev's glasnost.

Noted Meyer to Mark Altman, Ron Magid, and Ed Gross, "At its best, *Star Trek* appears to function as pop allegory — pop metaphors taking current events and issues — ecology, war and racism, for example — and objectifying them for us to contemplate in a science fiction setting. The world it presents may make no sense as either science or fiction, but it is well and truly sufficient for laying out human questions. Removed from our immediate neighborhoods, it is refreshing and even intriguing to consider Earth matters from the distance of a few light years."

Because Meyer was involved with *Company Business* in London, in order to get the film done on time he collaborated via computer with Dennis Martin Flinn, an experienced thriller writer, to transform the story into a science fictional political thriller. Gene Roddenberry expressed his discomfort with the underpinnings of racism in the story, feeling that it was wrong to have Federation people, even those who later turn out to be assassins and villains, spouting racially derogatory comments, though he was intrigued by the idea of establishing détente with the Klingons, something that was achieved in his *Next Generation* series.

Roddenberry also objected to Meyer and Flinn's plan to turn Saavik into a traitor. Meyer figured that she would be a character unlikely to be suspected and he hoped to work again with Kirstie Alley; however, once more Alley was unavailable and when Kim Cantrall was hired, it was decided to make the character a disciple of Spock's named Valeris.

The starship *Excelsior*, captained by Sulu, witnesses the explosion of an important Klingon moon (while the explosion effect is impressive, the aftermath looks like a bad, preliminary matte painting). Spock decides it would be a good time to negotiate a peace treaty because the Klingon planet will die out in 50 years. Because of possible peace, the *Enterprise* is picked (by Spock) to transport the Klingon ambassador Gorkon's ship to a peace conference.

The *Enterprise* takes off to its destination, with a new helm officer, an outstanding Vulcan named Valeris. Then the *Enterprise* appears to have fired two torpedoes at Gorkon's ship, destroying the gravity. Two assassins beam aboard to murder Gorkon. To the surprise of all, Kirk signals the *Enterprise*'s surrender and beams aboard with McCoy and the pair are quickly arrested, taken to the Klingon home world, and put on trial. (Their defense attorney proves to be an ancestor of Worf, played by Michael Dorn of *The Next Generation* and *Deep Space Nine*.)

Spock realizes the only explanation is that the assassins came from the *Enterprise* and the torpedoes came from a cloaked vessel. Spock's guilt over forcing Kirk into the situation heightens when Kirk and McCoy are sentenced to a lifetime of work in the dilithium mines of frozen prison planet Rura Penthe (location scenes of Alaska mixed with footage shot at Bronson Canyon). Kirk meets a shapeshifter (Iman) who gets them out of prison, where Kirk must get them to a ship. Kirk learns that the shapeshifter was simply setting them up to be killed by the Klingons while trying to escape (a more convenient excuse for two dying than an "accident" would have been), but Kirk convinces the warden to kill the shapeshifter impersonating him just as the *Enterprise* rescues the pair.

The case continues, and a clever plan by Kirk reveals that Lt. Valeris is the one who led the conspiracy on the *Enterprise*. Spock finds out that Admiral Cartwright, General Chang and the Romulan Ambassador are involved. Valeris does not know the location of where the peace conference has been rescheduled, and neither does the *Enterprise* crew. In a last ditch effort, the crew asks Sulu for the location and it is revealed to be Camp Khitomer. Kirk knows that another assassination attempt will be made, this time on the head of the Federation, so the *Enterprise* heads for Khitomer.

The *Enterprise* arrives (with *Excelsior* on her way) at Khitomer, where they are pelted by phaser fire from General Chang and his cloaked Bird of Prey. Uhura recalls that they have gas detection equipment on board, and Spock quickly whips up a way for one of the photon torpedoes to home in on the Bird of Prey's emissions. Once the Klingon ship is hit, both ships fire at the target to destroy the Klingon vessel. Captains Kirk and Sulu beam down, reveal the conspirators (one of whom is an Earthling disguised as a Klingon in a set-up out of *The Manchurian Candidate*), and complete the conference. The wrap-up of the original theatrical cut was a bit too rapid to tell what was going on, so Meyer recut and added three minutes to the home video version.

Upon returning to the *Enterprise*, the crew is informed the ship is to report back to spacedock to be decommissioned. Kirk knows the inevitable and makes his last log:

> This is the final cruise of the Starship *Enterprise* under my command. This ship, and her history, will shortly become the care of another crew, to them and their posterity will we commit our future. They will continue the voyages we have begun, and journey to all the undiscovered countries and boldly go where no man, where no ONE, has gone before....

Once more Meyer emphasizes the military nature of Starfleet, and the ship is given plate metal floor, stacked crewman bunks, and is more military than before, much against Roddenberry's intentions or wishes. However, the story does bring up such concepts as the difficulty of Cold Warriors such as Kirk and Chang in adjusting to a new order of things, of accepting the peace. Kirk must learn to forego his racist and untrusting feelings inspired by the death of his son, David. Spock volunteers him for the mission, likening it to Nixon (a notorious anti–Communist) being the one who opened the door for diplomatic relations with China.

Star Trek: The Undiscovered Country also revels in Meyer's love of mysteries and his fondness for literary allusions, though Chang's non-stop stream of well-known Shakespearean quotations does get to be a bit much, despite the excellence of Plummer's performance. Yet again, the idealized Starfleet is shown to have elements who are uncomfortable with the concept of a new era of rapprochement with their age-old enemies, the Klingons (as well as some Klingons who are clearly unhappy with the idea).

The Klingons are made metaphors for the Soviet Union. Their society is dying because the effort of keeping up with the Federation has exhausted their economy, and they have been careless in environmental matters (with Praxis standing in for Chernobyl). They fear that their culture will be assimilated and destroyed by the Federation, except for the visionary Gorkon, whose accepting nature winds up inspiring Kirk to forego his hatred and bring his peaceful plans to fruition. Topical, entertaining, and interesting, *Star Trek: The Undiscovered Country* once again demonstrated that the *Trek* films were better off with Meyer's involvement than without it.

In April 1993, Meyer directed the debut of his play *Loco Motives*, which is about the night in 1910 when at the age of 82 Leo Tolstoy sneaked out of his bedroom in the middle of the night and boarded a locomotive for God knows where. Part way into the journey, he collapsed and lay comatose for seven days in a rural Russian train station. Meyer's play is set in that station and features flashbacks to Tolstoy's (William Atherton) randy youth in the Crimean War, to literary salons, and to his own study, confronting a gallery of characters from Ivan Turgenev (pompously played by Ron King) to Madame Dostoyevsky.

Meyer depicts Tolstoy as a man of intense contradictions who dismisses Shakespeare as a phrasemonger while seeing himself as King Lear. He shows him as a vegetarian pacifist who puts his feet on the furniture, spits on the floor, and continually rationalizes according to his shifting philosophies. He rails against property and lust while indulging himself sexually. While preaching against violence, he smashes an annoying fly. Attending to his needs are his secretary-wife Sonia (Laurie Waters), who recognizes the power of his fiction and also rightly accuses him of hypocrisy for advocating celibacy while practicing the opposite, and whom he castigates, and his smug "disciple" Alexei Chertkov (Gary Bullock), a religious fanatic who encouraged Tolstoy's indulgence in fervent religious polemics and has no patience for fiction at all. Tolstoy constantly shifts his allegiance between the two, representing art and doctrine. Meyer maintains careful allegiance to the historical facts, but also successfully brings out many fascinating facets of this complex artist.

The same year also saw the production of his screenplay *Sommersby*, a romantic but tepid remake of the French film *The Return of Martin Guerre* about a man who comes to a village claiming that he is a long departed member of the town with Richard Gere in the Gerard Depardieu role. Though he is eventually revealed to be a con-man, the stranger does truly help the townspeople, getting them to pull together and have faith in their future. Unfortunately, for Meyer, the film proved a frustrating experience that bittersweetly became a minor hit. Further adding to his depression and frustration in December of 1993 was the death of his wife Lauren from cancer, following which he seemed to have become inactive.

Meyer's most recent work was as co–executive producer of 1997's *The Odyssey* miniseries, co-written and directed by Andrei Konchalovsky (*Siberiade; Runaway Train*). This $40 million superproduction starred Armand Assante as the wily Odysseus, with Greta Scacchi as Penelope, Isabella Rossellini as Pallas Athena, Vanessa Williams as Calypso, Eric Roberts as Eurymachus, Irene Papas as Odysseus' mother Anticlea, Bernadette Peters as Circe, Christopher Lee as the blind prophet Tiersias, and Michael J. Pollard as Arelous. This adaptation of Homer's great epic places the narrative in chronological order, slights the story of Telemachus' search for his father, and summarizes Odysseus' involvement in the Trojan War in the opening ten minutes.

Konchalovsky, who cowrote the script with Christopher Solimine, commented, "When Homer wrote the story *The Odyssey*, everyone knew about Troy. But for the modern audience to understand that Odysseus himself was a trigger for the Trojan horse, that his intelligence and his wit brought Troy down, we had to add a little piece of *The Iliad* to explore who he was. I can tell you it's not an easy task to make a brief history of *The Iliad* in seven minutes."

This classic narrative seems an obvious choice to have attracted Meyer, who co–executive produced with Francis Ford Coppola, Fred Fuchs, and Robert Halmi, Sr., who had previously adapted *Gulliver's Travels* as a miniseries before. The production was shot in London, Malta, and Turkey over a period of four months, and employs CGI effects as well as creatures created by Jim Henson's Creature Shop (who place an animatronic head atop a Sumo wrestler to create the cyclops Polythemus). The production veers from being lush to looking low budget, and as they do in Homer's original poem, some characters are little more than cameos of belonged figures from mythology, but overall it seems a fairly faithful retelling of one master storyteller's masterpiece by some accomplished movie magicians.

Meyer has also written the screenplays for *Voices* (1995) and *The Informant* (1997). Neither film made a significant impact nor has garnered much attention. He was also brought in to supply additional writing on DreamWorks' elaborate *The Prince of Egypt* animated film, relating the story of Moses.

Meyer has throughout his career paid tribute to the great literary works of the past, while adding fresh and original spins that keep them alive and interesting to modern-day audiences. Though his storytelling knack has sometimes failed him, his was the guiding hand behind one of the most ingenious and heartfelt time travel stories as well as the intelligence that resurrected the *Star Trek* mythos on the big screen.

GEORGE MILLER, M.D. (1945–)

Violence in the Cinema, Part I (1972, short); *Devil in an Evening Dress* (documentary, 1973); *Mad Max* (1979); *Mad Max II* (aka *The Road Warrior*) (1981); *Twilight Zone—The Movie* ("Nightmare at 20,000 Feet" episode) (1983); *Mad Max Beyond Thunderdome* (codirected with George Ogilvie) (1985); *The Witches of Eastwick* (1987); *Dead Calm* (second unit only; 1989); *Lorenzo's Oil* (1992); *40,000 Years of Dreams* (documentary, 1996); *Babe: Pig in the City* (1998)

Television: *The Dismissal* (1983); "Brides of Lizard Gulch," *Badlands* (1988); *In the Nick of Time* (1991)

George Miller was born one of a pair of twins in Chinchilla, Queensland, near Brisbane, Australia, on March 3, 1945. It was a rural town with a population of only 400 in Australia's deep north. In his youth, the Saturday matinees were his only window on the outside world, and much of his childhood was spent playing games with other children that were influenced by the movies they had seen.

Eventually, his family moved to Sydney, and Miller graduated in 1970 from the University of New South Wales as a medical doctor and practiced medicine for a year-and-a-half in Sydney, including a harrowing half-year stint in St. Vincent's Hospital's emergency ward, but his life-long passion for cinema soon interfered with his medical plans. He explains his twin brother John would attend lectures while he spent morning sessions at the movies.

During his final year of study at the University of South Wales, his younger brother involved him in a student film competition. The brothers' one-minute entry won first prize — a course at a film workshop in Melbourne, and thus Miller began to turn his attention to the anatomy of filmmaking. It was at the workshop in 1971 that he met his future creative partner and producer Byron Kennedy, who was likewise attending a film course offered by the Australian Union of Students at Melbourne University.

Kennedy and Miller discovered that they shared a common attitude towards filmmaking and they cocreated two short films before completing the course. Miller worked for two years at a hospital while making short films on weekends. On Easter weekend when he had four days off from his typical 90 hour work week, he called Kennedy and they collaborated and shot a gory, humorous 14 minute short, *Violence in the Cinema, Part I*, a spoof of both cinematic violence and the alarmists who speak out against it, on a budget of $1,500. In it, a cinematic pundit sternly lectures on his theories of cinema violence while all different samples of cinema violence happen to him, often in very stylized fashion, including slow-motion gunshot wounds, getting blown up, thrown out of buildings, being mutilated; however, nothing stops him from giving his lecture. This short was shown at the Sydney Film Festival, the Moscow Film Festival, won two Australian Film Institute Awards, and went to the Cannes film festival where it received some attention. The film was picked up from distribution by Greater Union, was distributed to commercial cinemas in Australia, and eventually earned a small profit.

Encouraged, the pair turned their attention to lengthier projects and put out a docudrama, *Devil in an Evening Dress,* narrated by Frank Thring, before turning their attentions to developing and raising money for a feature about a future, desolate society. Meanwhile, Miller continued earning money as a doctor and assisted on editing some films while Kennedy worked as a cameraman on experimental films and shot a couple of low budget features. They had a hard time finding a charismatic actor to play their lead, turning down numerous casting agents' suggestions, when they found Mel Gibson in a play put on by the students of the National Institute for the Dramatic Arts, and pushed back production two weeks until Gibson was finished with the play and would be available.

The resulting film, *Mad Max,* took a year for the pair to write, working on it on and off, and then another year to raise financing for. The budget was a mere $350,000. Most of the crew were inexperienced, having only shot low budget television on 16mm previously, there were no stunt teams available as Australian filmmakers had not been making action pictures, and Miller found the entire experience amazingly difficult. While many had assumed it was shot in the Australian Outback, the locations were all on the outskirts of Melbourne, never more than 20 miles west from the heart of the city. Students who wanted to watch the filming were recruited to block off the roads for the production. Actual shooting took 12 weeks with another two weeks of second unit. The weather proved extreme — first extreme heat, then extreme cold (it was shot in the Australian winter), and then extremely wet. Miller describes the shoot as "bitter."

In *Projections 2,* Miller told script supervisor Daphne Paris:

> By the time we finished shooting we were told that the film couldn't be edited, that it was a mess. But I knew there was a film there. We had only enough money to spend a month in the cutting room and it looked like a badly cut TV show — arrhythmic, odd. So Byron and I took on the cutting ourselves. I set up the cutting room in the kitchen with very primitive equipment and Byron was in the lounge doing the sound. That's when I got to know the film backwards, literally, every frame of film, I'd seen it a thousand times. I cut it silent, no sound, no music. If it played as a silent movie, then I knew it had a chance of playing as a sound movie. You know your first feature is difficult to watch. All you see is terrible mistakes. You know I honestly thought the film was unreleaseable. That wasn't the case, but I was able to confront the failure of the film before it was ever released, so I suppose that led me to being objective about it. And it turned us from film paupers to being very well off. At that point we'd never considered the possibility it would be a major commercial success.

Mad Max was finally finished in 1978 and went on to become a worldwide success, grossing over $100 million, everywhere except the United States where because of its low budget, Warner Bros. turned it down and it was picked up for distribution by Sam Arkoff's American International Pictures. Concerned that American audiences wouldn't understand the actors' Australian accents, Arkoff had the film dubbed, destroying much of the flavor and thrust of the performances.

In the late 1970s, American critics were noticing a flowering of Australian cinema thanks to such films as Peter Weir's *Picnic at Hanging Rock* and *The Last Wave*; Bruce Beresford's *Breaker Morant*; Gillian Armstrong's *My Brilliant Career*; and Fred Schepisi's *The Chant of Jimmie Blacksmith,* excellent films one and all. Into such an esteemed and serious group of films, an action-oriented semi-exploitation spectacle like *Mad Max* simply didn't fit, and so consequently it was largely ignored upon release by most critics except for a few that noted an urgency to Miller's direction and a sharpness to Tom Paterson and Cliff Hayes' brilliant editing. (Miller and Kennedy worked with Paterson and Hayes for nine months to achieve the film's highly tuned editing style.)

To them, the film was little more than a standard shoot-'em-up with plenty of admittedly well staged car crashes and a simple revenge plot. The cinematography by David Eggby was competent but uneven, and Brian May's score was not especially riveting.

What was missed was that *Mad Max* was a truly cinematic movie, a highly kinetic story told with moving pictures and a minimum of dialogue. The story is largely told through action which is made to be as visually exciting as possible. The "Mad Max" films share the same qualities that made the Sergio Leone spaghetti westerns or Bruce Lee kung fu films so popular worldwide. The plots are simple, even simplistic, and the action is hyperbolic and exaggerated. These are larger-than-life archetypes who express themselves in the international language of cinema. Whatever the language spoken by the viewer, the conflicts of the story clearly came through and the hyperkinetic visuals guaranteed excitement.

From the start, like all good films of this type, *Mad Max* both meets and subverts expectations. The film opens with a shot of the bombed-out or possibly just desolate and decaying "Halls of Justice," and then cuts to two figures on the side of the road. One of them is obviously dressed as a cop, but the other one is peering through a high-powered rifle scope at a pair of kids copulating in a nearby field, raising questions in the audiences mind if these are killers or simply voyeurs out for a thrill.

With his leather jacket and leering grin, one would expect that the figure with the rifle to be a psychopath about to pull the trigger. Instead, he is simply the first cop's superior getting his jollies. Right from the start, Miller has established a feeling that law and order have broken down, showing the supposed keepers of law and order bicker between themselves about who is to drive and by dressing them in similar accouterments to those of the motorcycle psychos that they are supposed to be protecting society against.

The action gets off to a roaring start with the entrance of the Nightrider, leader of a Hell's Angels–type gang who has escaped from prison in one of the souped up police vehicles. The cops give chase, causing an orgy of destruction on the roadways.

Miller makes the spectacular stunt work even more exciting by his striking visual style. He places the camera at fender level to capture the feeling of speeding along the road — we stay on the road involved instead of off the road and on the side as is more often done in these kinds of scenes. He is also adept at sweeping pans, breakneck tracking shots, and shock editing.

"I'm a fuel-injected suicide machine!" the Nightrider screams triumphantly. However, up ahead is Max (Mel Gibson), the top cop on the force, waiting in his ominously idling Interceptor. Miller gives Max's entrance a mythic build-up, keeping his face off camera as he puts on his mirror shades and best determined look, demonstrating that here is a heroic force to be reckoned with. With the other cops having crashed or spun out, he is the court of last resort, and more than equal to the challenge.

Max comes roaring down directly at the Nightrider's car in a parody of the teenaged "chicken" run, and the heretofore overconfident Nightrider finds someone with even more steely nerves than himself. His nerves badly shaken, Nightrider's wild ride ends in a fiery death, completing his prophecy of being a suicide machine and taking his accompanying girlfriend with him.

Still, when the news reports the death of the Nightrider that evening, Max's wife Jessie (Joanne Samuel) questions the morality of it all, asking if he was another of Max's "victims." She compares Max to a monster, and completing the metaphor visually, Max dons a Tor Johnson mask as he plays with his son. This sets up the major thematic question of the film: Has Max become as bad as what he is fighting? The cops get the same kind of thrills from high speed pursuits that the motorpsychos do — are they simply two sides of the same coin?

The psychos refer to the cops as "Bronze," equating the metal of the policemen's badges with the men themselves, suggesting something machinelike and inhuman about them. However, we also see from Jessie's obvious affection for her husband, communicated visually by having her indicate in sign language "I'm crazy about you," that there is a genuine human source under all the leather and metal that are designed to protect these road warriors from the dangers of the road.

Max returns the same message in sign language, establishing a pattern of visual parallels that are drawn throughout the film. A baby who is almost run over at the beginning of the film is echoed by Max's child who *is* run over near the end. Miller makes a shock cut to the bulging eyes of Nightrider right before he dies at the film's beginning, and then does the same thing to Toecutter near the end. We get a shock appearance of a hand when Goose is carted into the hospital midway through the film and a shock appearance of a hand when Max discovers a severed one attached to a chain on his bumper when he reaches May's farm.

The death of the Nightrider triggers his gang, now led by Toecutter (Hugh Keays-Byrne) to ride into the town where Nightrider's casket is waiting at the train depot. There they terrorize the inhabitants, finally chasing after a boy and girl in a fancy car who decide to make a hasty exit from the town. The cyclists catch up to them, wreck their car by attacking it, and then rape them both, a sign of their utter depravity.

Max and his good friend Goose (Steve Bisley) are dispatched to investigate and discover the awful aftermath. The traumatized boy runs away butt naked through a field, while the girl is discovered as a cringing shell of her former self in what was once their car. However, one of the gangmembers, hophead Johnny (Tim Burns), is so wacked out of his skull that he has remained behind high as a kite, ejaculating exhortations about the "Nightrider."

Given the extremity of the offense, we are appalled when the police are forced to let Johnny go because none of the terrified townspeople would show up to testify against him. Frustrated and angry, Goose lashes out at Johnny, breaking his nose, while Johnny in turn swears his revenge.

First Johnny sabotages Goose's motorcycle, and then causes the truck Goose borrows to crash. Toecutter decides that the punishment isn't enough and instructs Johnny to set the car on fire while Goose is still trapped inside as a test of Johnny's manhood. Easily influenced scumbag that he is, Johnny complies.

Hearing of Goose's injury, Max rushes to the hospital where he sees the charred, inhuman looking hand of his former friend fall out from under the hospital shroud. The hand expresses both the friendship between the two men and in its present state is indicative of the monster that lies locked within these high-powered demons of the highway. When he pulls back the shroud to see the rest of his former friend, Miller simply shows Max's horrified reaction, and does a shock cut to a wash of a closeup, as if waves of revulsion are coursing through Max. It is extremely effective, both eloquent and powerful.

In this future, both automobiles and humans can be pronounced "salvageable," again blurring the distinction between men and machines, making them seem almost interchangeable. Throughout the film there are references to scavenging. Miller even counterpoints mechanics piecing cars together from auto wrecks ("a piece here, a piece there") with surgeons discussing which organs from a dying human being are salvageable.

Max goes into denial, stating that the remains he sees are not Goose. No one else seems to evince any emotion over Goose's tragic demise and Max is left in a quandary. A sensitive human being, he is scared by what he is feeling.

He goes to Fifi (Roger Ward, whose voice is particularly badly dubbed in the American version), his station commander, and informs him that he is opting out of the rat race by resigning. "I'm scared," he tells his commander. "It's a rat circus out there, and I'm beginning to enjoy it." Max worries about losing his humanity, that the viciousness of the police will end up matching the viciousness of those they are fighting against.

Fifi suggests the problem is that people don't believe in heroes anymore, and so no one will stand up against the vermin who terrorize society. He tells Max that they can give society back their heroes by being heroes. Rather than accepting Max's resignation, he allows Max to take an extended vacation and as a perk gives him a fuel-injected car with a V-8 engine.

We again get a look at Max's vulnerable and human side as he takes Jessie and the baby on an initially idyllic vacation. Humanity still exists in couples such as Jessie and Max, who are shown to be warm and compassionate — indeed, this is the last time in the series where Max is shown as fully human. However, humanity is threatened by amoral, soulless machine-men such as the chaotic cycle gang.

The cyclists are depicted as being almost inseparable from their machines. Most of them always wear their helmets, which in addition to shielding their faces takes away their individual identity and makes them seem more like automatons. A few of the cyclists are characterized, for example, a pair of gay men who dance with each other, but mostly they are shown as a group that congregates like wasps to come together and attack the helpless and vulnerable.

The second film in the series makes it clear that this is a post-apocalyptic future, where the bomb has dropped, resources are scarce, but Australia has largely been spared. Amidst the devastation are those who feed off the misery of others, deciding that it is easier to take from those who are weaker than having to fend for themselves.

The other survivors are the last bastions of civilization. Miller engages our sympathy for these characters so that when they die, they are not just statistics but real people. The violence in Miller's films is stylized, but it is not depersonalized as it is in many contemporary films where audiences were encouraged to root for indiscriminate killers. While Miller knows that high speed action is thrilling, he also dares to make his audience uncomfortable by confronting them with the reality of the dangers and pain that the parasites of society can inflict.

While Max is away from their car, Toecutter makes a move on Jessie, who quickly sizes him up and knees him in the groin. Another gang member flings a chain at the van in which Jessie and the baby escape, but he loses his hand when the chain catches on the van's railing as Jessie drives it hastily away. The gang pursues to avenge this injury to one of their own.

Miller takes an idyllic scene and economically introduces the threat by showing us a panoramic shot of a beach with Jessie sunbathing below which is disrupted by the unexpected appearance of a motorcycle wheel which rolls into the frame. Miller emphasizes the threat's impersonality by never showing us who is riding that cycle.

When she notices that her dog is missing, Jessie heads for safety, glimpsing menacing figures behind distant trees. She finds her mutilated mutt hanging from one of the tree limbs, an indication of both the gang's presence and their malevolence. She runs to Max who seeks out the marauders, but we know she is not out of danger yet.

The baby is missing, and Jessie discovers the babe behind the garage in the arms of the gang who threaten to cut off one of its hands in a parody of Old Testament justice to even the score for the unfortunate gang member who lost his hand.

Fortunately, May arrives with a shotgun, and together she and Jessie are able to recover the child from the nonplussed gang members, who quickly pursue the fleeing women in their fleeing van. Unfortunately, Max hadn't had time to repair the van's radiator hose and soon the vehicle stalls with the cycle gang close behind.

Humungus (Kjell Nilsson) sports a scavenger punk aesthetic in Miller's *The Road Warrior* and maintains an Achilles/Patroclus relationship with Wez.

The power and economy of the subsequent scene is stunning. Jessie grabs the baby and starts running down the highway. May aims her shotgun at the onrushing gang and fires, missing everybody, and the cyclists roar past in a wave. Jessie continues running for her and her baby's life. Instead of slowing down as we expect, the bikers speed up. Miller cuts from a rear view of Jessie running to a closeup of a motorcycle throttle revved to the maximum, then back to the same point-of-view as before, only instead of Jessie being there, all we see are her shoe and the baby's ball bouncing along the pavement, then the cyclists speeding away.

Max arrives but he is too late. He runs to Jessie's crumpled body and holds it in his arms. Later, in the hospital, he hears that his baby has died and Jessie's condition is critical and uncertain. The scene closes with a shot of Max's face filled with unspoken rage and an obsession for vengeance. His world shattered by vicious thugs, he has chosen madness.

Max redons his police uniform as a gladiator set to do battle and walks into the darkened police garage. In a brilliant dissolve, his "last of the V-8s" souped-up patrol car comes roaring out of the garage, the man having become a machine, indicating that with the loss of his wife and child Max has lost all vestiges of his humanity and will now be a relentless, mechanical force for vengeance, pursuing the perpetrators of this vile act to their extinction.

In short order, Max starts running the bikers over or off the road, forcing Toecutter into the path of an oncoming truck. He is shot in the knee by Toecutter's blond-haired confederate, accounting for the limp he has throughout the sequel, before blowing him away. Finally, to extract revenge for Goose, he handcuffs Johnny's foot to a car and sets up a booby trap whereby gasoline spilling from the car will reach a lighter in ten minutes but out of a perverse sense of fairplay, he leaves Johnny a hacksaw with which Johnny could either amputate his own foot in time to get away or try to saw through the handcuff, which would take too long. Johnny can't believe that Max would violate the rules of his profession in such a blatant manner, underscoring that there is a real difference between the cops and the hooligans, and thus ensures his demise as Max drives away. Max, having completed his purpose, is left a mere shell of a man, an appropriately grim resolution to the film which demonstrates how violence taints all who resort to it.

Miller achieved great success with *Mad Max*, so the demand for a sequel wasn't too surprising. But *Mad Max*, as the above description should make clear, wasn't simplistic exploitation fare, and Miller was an artist of talent with real ambition. Still, he was surprised by how well the film had played in vastly varying cultures, which made him feel that he had had a concrete experience with Jung's "collective unconscious." Like George Lucas before him, he discovered and was intrigued by the ideas in Joseph Campbell's *Hero with a Thousand Faces*, from which he gleaned the essence of mythic story structure.

He decided to make *Mad Max II* (better known in America as *The Road Warrior* as most American audiences weren't familiar with the first *Mad Max*) as a mythic recounting of the refounding of civilization. In contrast to the first film, the second had a decent budget, a terrific cinematographer in Dean Semler, and in Mel Gibson, who had achieved a kind of international stardom with the first film, a star who was increasingly comfortable with the process of acting. While the film was a physically demanding one, Miller felt he had gotten closer to what he had conceived, and relates that when they started shooting, they had almost no screenplay at all, so the film was written very quickly.

The Road Warrior begins with a series of images suggestive of the breakdown of the world and an eventual apocalypse. Miller indicates at the outset that we are hearing a mythic tale, a heroic saga by overlaying these carefully selected images with the following important and poetic narration:

> "My life fades, the vision dims. All that remains are memories. They take me back.... I remember a time of chaos ... ruined dreams ... this wasted land. But most of all, I remember the Road Warrior, the man we called Max. To understand who he was, you have to go back to another time ... when the world was powered by the black fuel and the deserts sprouted great cities of pipe and steel.
>
> "Gone now, swept away. For reasons long forgotten, two mighty warrior tribes went to war and touched off a blaze that engulfed them all. Without fuel, they were nothing. They'd built a house of straw. The thundering machines sputtered and stopped. Their leaders talked ...

> and talked ... and talked, but nothing could stem the avalanche. Their world crumbled ... the cities exploded ... a whirling of looting ... a firestorm of fear. Men began to feed on men.
>
> "On the roads it was a white-line nightmare. Only those mobile enough to scavenge, brutal enough to pillage, would survive. The gangs took over the highways, ready to wage war for a tank of juice. And in the maelstrom of decay, ordinary men were battered and smashed.
>
> "Men like Max ... the warrior Max. In the roar of an engine, he lost everything and became a shell of a man ... a burnt out, desolate man, a man haunted by the demons of his past. A man who wandered out ... into the wasteland. And it was here, in this blighted place, that he learned to live again."

While the original *Mad Max* was set in a crumbling, broken down future, the sequel is clearly set in a post-apocalyptic world. The above narration is recited over scenes from the first film interspersed with newsreel footage that documents the breakdown of society and the rise of chaos. The narrow frame then suddenly widens to accommodate Miller's explosion of high-octane imagery that propels the narrative in an almost relentless frenzy from beginning to end.

Having lost his humanity with the loss of his wife and child, Max is a bitter survivor accompanied only by his dog and the memories of the world he has lost. He avoids human contact and has left what little civilization that remains on Australia's shores for the vast wastelands of its interior. Like his dog, he lives like an animal, often sharing a can of dog food with him as they roam the land searching for "juice" to power his vehicle. He rips off what petrol he can from other wrecked vehicles he finds, but must always be wary of marauders.

Unlike most sequels which are not crafted as well as the original films that inspired them, *The Road Warrior* features superior production values. Miller's direction is highly kinetic and well thought out. Dean Semler's cinematography is crisper, more colorful, and uses the desert's natural scenery quite well. The budget for *The Road Warrior* was $4 million, ten times the amount spent on *Mad Max*, and the additional budget allows for quite a bit of extra gloss to the film as well as more grandiose action setpieces.

When the first *Mad Max* proved to be such an incredible hit around the world, Miller realized that he had tapped into something mythic and so applied the lessons he learned from Joseph Campbell's monomythic hero. Max is cast as a classical hero in the same mode as Shane, the societal outcast who in this case duels with cars instead of guns. Because he protects society by the socially unacceptable method of murder, the hero is a savior of society, but can never become part of it. While neither side is wholly good nor wholly evil, we see in the beleaguered drillers community something worth protecting from the ruthless looting of the marauders who would destroy them, and while Max himself is a grey figure, it is understandable why he sides with order over chaos.

Initially he enters the community in order to return a fallen comrade in exchange for some gas for his vehicle. Unfortunately, the man dies and his bargain with him. The appearance of Lord Humungus (Kjell Nilsson) — a large leader who hides his undoubtedly scarred visage behind a hockey mask and who is proclaimed by one of his followers as the Ayatollah of Rock 'n' rollah — and his gang of motorcycle leather and punk outfitted cutthroats, Max finds himself trapped behind enemy lines and the community finds they need Max as much as he needs their fuel.

Max can no longer remain a loner but must make a choice as to whether or not he should aid this primitive community. At first it's a choice he's reluctant to make knowing the risks involved, but it is a role he comes to savor as he helps participate in the community's survival by loading up with diesel and leaving the compound to bring back a truck rig big enough to carry the load of fuel the group wishes to take with them on their trek to the coast.

From the start, we see a bond forming between the taciturn Max (the sum total of his lines in the film would barely cover a page) and the ever-silent Feral Kid (Emil Minty) who plays Brandon de Wilde to Gibson's Shane. The "feral" epithet is supplied by the credits rather than any characters in the film, and it is meant in its purest sense, that of "savage, primitive, untamed, or wild." The community is so caught up in its own survival that no one has taken the time to raise this child, and so it has grown up like an animal (hence his sense of Max as a kindred spirit), but one that knows how to survive in this harshest of environments. He snarls instead of talks, and uses his razor-edged boomerang with deadly accuracy.

At the opening of the film, Max has encountered a trucker dead in his rig. Clutched in the trucker's hand is the remains of a music box, which neatly symbolizes art, memory, music, the past, and other elusive qualities. Upon meeting the Kid, Max passes on the music box as a kind of legacy, just as the narrator is passing on this tale of his tribal beginnings to us. Miller captures the Kid eyeing Max and carefully trying to imitate his limping lope (Max still suffers from the knee injury sustained in the first film). One of the things that Miller does that provides *The Road Warrior* with its sense of wonder is that he frequently films scenes from the Kid's eye level, as if we were looking at this crazy and cruel world through his dispassionate yet wondering eyes.

The subtle engine powering this tale, more important than the frantic and exciting action sequences, are the subtle interrelationships of the characters which are cinematically expressed sans dialogue. One important character is the Gyro Captain (Bruce Spence), who is the proverbial joker in the deck. He is an irreconcilable oddball who with his very (weird) existence betrays the believability of the movie, and yet becomes the most believable thing in it. Life is full of unpredictable strangeness, a fact that the movies sometimes forget. The Gyro captain is introduced as a comic antagonist who sets out his rattlesnake guarded gyrocopter as bait for Max who desires the fuel it might contain, but the wily desert rat instead is taken prisoner by Max (who has likewise booby trapped his own car). The grounded pilot at first looks out only for himself, but gradually, he comes to respect and even like Max, appreciating his mercy, his strength and his survival skills. He too has been a loner, but he warms to human contact and it eventually redeems him, bringing forth his latent humanity.

He is strongly contrasted by Wez (Vernon Wells), a punk rock homosexual warrior/athlete who is a nightmare made flesh. During an attack which opens the film, Max killed Wez's lover and now his frantic fury knows no bounds. He is what the Feral Kid could turn into if not for the appearance of Max. Wez's intensity grabs the screen with both hands and does not let go. He is an imposing figure with his mohawk, do-it-yourself armor (scavenged out of football pads, hockey shin guards, and a mini-crossbow strapped on his arm for firing while riding a motorcycle), and lithesome grace. He wears bright and fierce plumage that along with his gymnastic ability dazzles his opponents, providing an edge in often fatal encounters.

The Road Warrior is so crammed with breathless, nonstop action that there is little in the way of a plot, but the characterization is quickly and neatly built up, and there are several superb moments and sure touches. In addition to the kinetic action, the film is suffused in awe, wonder, and mythology. (Examples are scenes such as one where the Feral Kid compares the sharpness of his boomerang with the steel blades of the gyrocopter, and the rescue of Max by the Gyro captain who flies the wounded warrior over a smoldering battlefield that seems almost a hallucination as time and sound are distorted in the wounded Max's mind. When the Gyro captain speaks to him, what he hears is the voice of Lord Humungus saying, "Climb aboard, chum." This subtly underscores Max's choice between the chaos and death below and the friendship and life above.)

Despite their despicable excesses, the barbaric marauders are also given a human side. They have known love and honor. Lord Humungus comforts Wez on the loss of his lover by saying, "We've all lost someone we love." These marauders are evil, possessed of a cruel streak of humor (they laugh when Humungus' announcer loses his fingers to the Feral Kid's boomerang), but despite their savagery, they still register as human.

Miller continues to demonstrate his mastery of editing and framing. He uses his widescreen compositions well to give his characters a context, a bleak background that helps us understand why these people are driven to such desperate actions, so we know that the savagery of the men is matched by the savagery of the background. He also fills his screen with important but unstated, unemphasized details, trusting that he does not need to belabor the obvious for his audience.

Miller borrows heavily from the techniques used by Steven Spielberg in *Duel*, which opened with a subjective shot from inside Dennis Weaver's car as he drives from his home to the highway. Miller's camera becomes an active participant in the action, with the roadway duels taking place along the narrow confines of the road itself. In *Duel*, it was only when Weaver left his car that we saw the action from the side or from angles other than the front or back of the car or truck as they moved down their highway to hell. Miller uses this same technique for his action sequences. The camera is either inside the cars or traveling down the road with them to catch all the constantly moving action. The feeling of the backgrounds is wide (because of the wasteland) and claustrophobic (because of the narrow limitations of the blacktop the cars travel along).

In the grand finale, the characters and possibilities meet head-on. Both Wez and the Feral Kid have focused on Max and crawled onto his truck, and when they confront each other, they scream down each other's throats. The impact is felt through the visuals. The Kid confronts in Wez his counterpart, his inner demon, and rejects it. (It is revealed at the end that he grew up to become the narrator of the film, and hence one of the founders of this incipient civilization.)

The Gyro captain affirms his commitment to the new civilization by risking life and limb to aid what ultimately turns out to be an elaborate diversion. In the sardonic conclusion, probably inspired by *Treasure of the Sierra Madre*, Max discovers that the truck of "fuel" he was driving was filled with sand and was used to draw off Humungus' main forces. (The fuel is actually hid in cans aboard a school bus that the raiders consider beneath their notice as they prepare to ransack the encampment, only for it to explode in their faces.) Lacking Max, the Gyro captain takes over as the group's leader, completing his transition back to humanity and society.

Max undergoes no profound changes, except to discover that he can still feel, that he can make commitments to others and to himself. In the words of the narrator, "He learned to live again."

Miller's vision is "apocalyptic" not only in the modern

sense of a cataclysm, but also in the original sense of a prophetic revelation or disclosure. In the first film, Max discovered that in his dedication to the rat race on the highways, he was losing his humanity, with fate conspiring to prevent a reprieve. In *The Road Warrior*, he regains that lost humanity, and it effects a catharsis for both himself and ourselves in the audience. But he remains a tough, lone wolf survivalist until *Mad Max Beyond Thunderdome*, where he discovers that there are circumstances under which he cannot bring himself to kill, and at the end willingly sacrifices himself for the sake of another community so that it may soar to safety and establish itself.

At the beginning of *The Road Warrior*, he extolls his own importance ("If you want to get out of here, you're going to have to talk to me."). However, by the end of the film, he loses that cocky sense of self-sufficiency. Max comes to need others. He is driven partially by his affection for a boy who looks up to him, and by a renewed sense of commitment. He receives the aid of not only the Gyro captain (who carried him from certain death and who drops bombs on marauders during the high-speed chase at the finale), but also other key members of the key community who give their lives keeping marauders away from the truck. However, when he discovers that he himself was used by the community as a ruse and that the last laugh is on him, he can accept it. He is returned to his solitude and does not join the community he was so vital to in its pilgrimage to the coast. Our last view of him is, like so many shots in the film, from the perspective of the Feral Kid, looking out the bus window as it rolls slowly away from the solitary figure in dirty black who stands almost silhouetted against a vibrant orange sky. Despite the reaffirmation of Max's humanity, he remains a man apart from others, understanding their need of him but by nature unable to become a part of the community they prize so much. He truly is a hero of monomythic proportions, a ronin who sets right wrongs and then must wander on to wherever he's needed next.

Where Miller was needed next was television. Though he had previously disdained the medium, when Rupert Murdoch offered to allow him to do a miniseries on whatever subject he wanted so long as it was bold, Miller could not refuse. Instead, he set right to work making *The Dismissal*, a six hour miniseries on Australian's constitutional crisis of 1975. It was on the series that he first worked with Philip Noyce and George Ogilvie, whose previously directorial work had been in the theater and who led workshops that allowed all the creative people to inter-relate and learn from one another.

While in postproduction on *The Dismissal*, Miller was contacted by and met with Steven Spielberg and Frank Marshall, who were preparing *Twilight Zone — The Movie*.

Doctor turned director George Miller framing a shot for *Twilight Zone — The Movie*.

Three episodes had been planned, but they were prepared to add a fourth for Miller to do, and Miller happily accepted the assignment of creating a 25 minute episode based on Matheson's "Nightmare at 20,000 Feet."

"The wonderful thing about doing this film is that it's the same challenge Rod Serling had with each *Twilight Zone*," related Miller. "You have to tell a story and establish a number of characters in just a short period of time, so everything you do has to be very concentrated.

"Everything is heightened — every sound is louder and more significant; he watches the stewardesses' eyes, waiting for any sign that something is wrong. He is simply a rational man afraid of flying. It could be you or I," Miller said. John Lithgow gives a *tour de force* as the protagonist.

After completing his *Twilight Zone* segment, Miller returned to Australia to resume his ventures there. In July, 1983, his friend and partner Byron Kennedy was killed in a helicopter crash in New South Wales. Despite the personal and professional loss, Miller went on to coproduce two 10-hour miniseries for Australian television — *Bodyline* and *The Cowra Breakout* — before beginning production on *Mad Max Beyond Thunderdome*.

Following the worldwide success of *Mad Max II*, Miller didn't give any serious thought to a third film in the series until one day in Los Angeles over a casual conversation about storytelling with Terry Hayes. "Terry mentioned an idea he had — a story which centered on a tribe of feral children, in a remote corner of the world, waiting for a legendary lost leader. It was then that I realize we were talking about the next chapter in the *Mad Max* saga," reported Miller.

Miller took the unusual step of sharing directing chores with George Ogilvie. "But now that we've done it and enjoyed it thoroughly," he reported at the time, "I don't understand why it isn't done more often. Storytelling is by

Aunty Entity (Tina Turner, center), her Imperial Guards, and their scrounged together vehicles fueled by pigshit in *Mad Max Beyond Thunderdome.*

its nature a collaborative process. And though it's not an easy notion to come to terms with, most times the collective process brings about better work than the individual effort."

Another change in Miller's approach was the use of video monitors, so that he can see what is happening through the camera all the time. The ability to have instant playback allowed Miller instantly to see whether he got it right or not, but he had to guard against letting his concentration down during a take simply because the machine was simultaneously videoing it as well.

Beyond Thunderdome relies more on broad, physical humor than the previous installments. Max finds himself in a bizarre world of pratfalls in pigshit, the self-amused Aunty Entity (an energetic Tina Turner), the over-the-top comic frustration of Ironbar (Angry Andersson), the conniving sneakiness of the Collector (Frank Thring), and the sweet, sincere expectation of several wayward waifs to seek in Max a savior.

From the instant Mel Gibson's unnamed Max rides into the first scene of *Mad Max Beyond Thunderdome,* we're as far from *The Road Warrior* as it was from *Mad Max.* It's 15 years later, Max is still a wanderer, but the juice is all gone, and the roads seem to have disappeared with it. The revving engine that was the heartbeat of the first two films is now but a memory. Max's hair is now graying and long, echoing the look of the Feral Kid and Christ at the same time. Whereas the earlier, grimmer films were about conquering and dying, this one turns out to be about creating and giving birth to.

Beyond Thunderdome's greatest action setpiece is the bungie battle inside Thunderdome midway through the movie where Max realizes that if he wishes to live with himself, there are simply some things he cannot bring himself to do and so resists Aunty's insistent call to kill the mongoloid Blaster (Paul Larsson). Aunty is the ruler of BarterTown, but cannot control Master (Angelo Rossitto), the dwarf whose know-how keeps BarterTown running and who, because of his alliance with the incredibly muscular Blaster, scorns Entity's attempts to control him. Entity simply exploits the raggedy man Max in a bid to undercut Master's power base, but when the fierce Blaster is revealed to be no more than an innocent idiot, he reclaims his humanity and rejects the role of executioner.

One of Miller's points in the film is that Max's simple act of compassion, of not killing a man for profit, ends up shattering this world. The consequence of Max's act is that he must undergo some dark trials, but the result is also the regeneration of another society. This simple act marks the death of the old way and the regeneration of the new.

Max is forced to face the Wheel of Fortune, his fate determined game show style by a spin of the wheel, and he is sentenced to banishment in the desert wilderness. Set backwards on a donkey which chases after a vial of water at the end of a stick and with an oversized mask over Max's head to hide his identity, he appears to be a holy fool sent to confront the swirling sandstorms and sandpits of the barren wasteland.

Collapsing of thirst, Max looks dead when he's found by a young girl (Helen Buday) in aboriginal garb who bravely pulls the body on an improvised sled to Crack in the Earth, an oasis inhabited by a tribe of lost children. Flat on his back, dead to the world in an apparent coma, his face, body and robes covered with light-colored sand, Max has the appearance of a knight laid out on his shield.

Mad Max (Mel Gibson) turns savior, leading these marooned children out of the wilderness while establishing a legend in *Mad Max Beyond Thunderdome*.

The children have been seeking a savior and mistake Max for the same, a man dubbed Captain Walker, the airline pilot who abandoned them in this paradise years before and promised to return and rescue them, a promise they have awaited with mystical fervor.

Max and his sense of self and of purpose are brought back to life by hearing these children's story, but he is especially shocked when the kids draw back a bamboo curtain and reveal a painting resembling Max on their cave wall, the arms and shoulders covered by representations of dozens of minuscule children being carried to freedom (Gibson's wince of horror and wonder when confronted with this image of himself is beautiful to behold, as he is forced to confront how others see him). He is too honest, too authentic to accept the role of messiah seemingly thrust on him and does his best to prevent the more fervent of the others from leaving the comparative paradise they have now for the dangers of the desert and the depravities of BarterTown beyond.

Perhaps it is appropriate for a film crafted by two directors, but the story constantly reinforces images of two people working in combination. Jediah and his son work as a pair to steal Max's goods. MasterBlaster is a two-person combination that obviously works better than either one would alone. The woman who saves Max is able to rescue someone twice her size thanks to her ingenuity. Max in returning to BarterTown carries the smallest of the children piggyback, much as Blaster carried Master. Max sacrifices himself by driving a truck to clear the way for the plane to take off and save the others. The film almost ends with Aunty, sensing their interconnection, sparing Max's life yet again and musing, "Ain't we a pair? Ain't we a pair?"

Mel Gibson's Mad Max seems even more burnt out in *Mad Max Beyond Thunderdome*.

The final chase in the film clearly echoes the exciting chase that climaxed *The Road Warrior*, but with the heroes aboard a train with a limited amount of track, there's no room for unexpected turns. The editing once more is accomplished and exciting. Miller's technique is to edit action sequences silently, feeling that if the film plays well silently, it will play even better once sound effects and music are added. Miller watches for the style of the movement and tries to establish a visual beat. The fact that his films maintain their clarity across diverse cultures with minimal dialogue is a tribute to his visual communication skills.

Beyond Thunderdome actually ends with the revelation that all that we have seen is a mythic story being told in a reinhabited city. The lost children have found their roots and re-established civilization, but they tell the story to remember who they are, where they came from, and why in hopes of staving off any future apocalypse.

Miller considers *Beyond Thunderdome* to be his favorite of the Mad Max films and also the most ambitious. In retrospect, he feels that perhaps he tried to do too much, as an entire film could have been done about BarterTown or a whole movie on the world of the Lost Children, which he felt were skipped through too quickly, but he was attracted to the story because it was completely different than the earlier two entries, except for Mel Gibson's Max character. He feels people were disappointed because it shifted its genre away from the lone action hero triumphing over his adversaries.

He told Michael Stein in *Fantastic Films* #45, "It's funny. The only time I get angry or aggressive is when I'm making a film. Somehow I'm always less satisfied. Maybe because I'm always rushing against time and budget. You always need a bit more time and a bit more money. So I find myself being more of a perfectionist. But I'm not sure why, because I'm not that way in my normal life. Actually, I'm a bit of a slob!"

Miller's next project, *The Witches of Eastwick*, however, was a mixed blessing for him. Miller was terribly stimulated by working with powerful and talented actors such Jack Nicholson, Susan Sarandon, and Michelle Pfeiffer (Cher, less the ensemble player, proved more problematic); however, he was unprepared for dealing with producers like Peter Guber and Jon Peters who were more dealmakers than hands-on producers. He wishes he had been warned about them ahead of time, but acknowledged that he simply failed to research the people he was working with sufficiently, that every member of a crew should be as carefully cast as the cast. He was attracted to the project by the screenplay he was sent, which he found "absolutely delightful, lovely, full of irony. A potent metaphor for the war between men and women, and to that extent it was mythological. And, most of all, it was to be light in tone."

However, John Updike's novel *The Witches of Eastwick* is barely recognizeable in playwright Michael Cristofer's script for the film. Cristofer and Miller transform the material into cosmic farce, a screwball comedy with truly wild visual effects. There remains Updike's premise of a trio of New England women, divorced and/or widowed and dabbling in witchcraft, who conjure the ideal man and end up with the devil instead. Are women witches and men devils? the film seems to ask. But while Updike's devil could just as easily be interpreted as a New York musician who likes to fleece money and self-esteem from the women he seduces, in Miller's film, he is indeed the Devil incarnate.

In Douglas Brode's *The Films of Jack Nicholson*, Miller explains, "My Devil had to be Pan. He's the mythological figure with a cloven hoof whose antisocial act was moving from community to community, causing all women to abandon themselves sexually to him and so enraging the menfolk, this despite the fact that he is not conventionally handsome. The men can't understand why the women do it, and neither for that matter can the women. But his total self-confidence is what allows him to enjoy their favors, impregnate all the women, then move on. To a degree, Christian concepts of chastity for women were created by a male dominated society to protect themselves from such a presence."

Miller told Daphne Paris in *Projections 2* that "The devil has to be as charming as all hell. It's what the great male seducers are like." However, Miller considered Nicholson such an obvious choice for the role that he began by rejecting him out of hand, until at Carol Kane's insistence, he met with the star. "I think what gives him the charisma is that he's both masculine and very feminine, both profane and extremely sublime, all at the same moment and that's what the devil has to be. If the devil comes on malevolent, he's not going to convince anybody. But ultimately the devil is foolish, he's flawed because he's blind to the alternative point of view and that's why he's evil. I really thought about evil a lot during the process of making that film. It's almost impossible to define good and evil, but the closest I got to it is that the root of all evil is ignorance. In particular, if you're ignorant of the Other's place in the universe, then you are capable of evil. In order to kill somebody you must be blind to their humanity, in order to destroy someone you must be incapable of seeing them as human beings. Jack's devil was ultimately blind as to what it was to be a woman and what it was to be in love. It's a problem that men seem to have."

The women Alexandra Medford (Cher), Sukie Ridgemont (Michelle Pfeiffer), and Jane Spofford (Susan Sarandon) are extreme sufferers of "the three D's — Death, Divorce, and Desertion." All three are artists — Alexandra makes odd sculptures; Sukie writes for the local paper; Jane teaches music at the local grammar school — and find they have a peculiar psychic power when they are together (they accidentally disrupt a boring and hypocritical graduation speech when they unexpectedly conjure a fierce thunderstorm). Unlike Updike's experienced witches, these women are dabblers until the man of their dreams (a mysterious foreign prince, someone they can talk to) seemingly materializes.

The Devil (Jack Nicholson) is given no name at first; he simply blows into town along with the storm sporting a limousine and a manservant, setting up shop in a local mansion that centuries before had been the site of witch trials. (All anyone seems to be able to recall about him is that his name begins with a "D." He is eventually named Daryl Van Horne.) All the women throughout the town find him devastatingly attractive. Alexandra's boss becomes misty-eyed at the mere memory of meeting him. Felicia Gabriel (Veronica Cartwright) experiences an orgasm of terror and becomes paralyzed partially out of fear as a pearl necklace bursts at the mere mention of his name, the tiny iridescent globes spilling all over the floor and causing her to trip down a flight of stairs and break her leg.

Gabriel is a closet witch, a Christian who is outraged at the idea of the devil taking up residence with some of the local ladies, fueling the townspeople's outrage at his presence by denouncing his lovers as sluts and whores, resisting his siren call, who ends up experiencing a kind of martyrdom at the hands of the devil who causes her body to rise up against her and causes her to become an outcast even among her fellow churchgoers. Failing to come to terms with her own culpability, she simply considers herself married to a failure and so continually prods her husband to better himself and to fire Sukie with ultimately disastrous results.

Jack Nicholson devours the role of devil incarnate with relish, and it remains one of his finest farcical comic performances. Nicholson is costumed (by Aggie Guerard Rodgers) in a feudal Japanese scalp-lock and baggy Oriental pantaloons, reflecting perhaps Miller's interest in heroic models. He rants beautifully ("When we make a mistake, it's called Evil; when God makes a mistake, it's called Nature!"), and sets free every device in his considerable actor's arsenal. Despite his pot-bellied satyr appearance, Van Horne is so certain of his appeal to women that he makes the most brazen overtures to them, caring not a whit for the opinions of others.

Miller was initially against casting Nicholson. He explained to Brode, "My first instinct was, in getting someone for the devil, you need an actor totally unlike the devil, and Jack clearly has an impish quality. Fortunately, I had a friend who pointed out to me what a gracious person Jack is. Then I realized that he is like a 200-year-old child: very wise in many ways, even beyond his years, but with a certain innocence and naïveté we expect from someone younger. The moment I saw that, I knew he was the only actor to bring a humanity to the role, to pull the devil out of stereotype."

Miller matches Nicholson's freeform explosion of energy by having the camera soar, swoop, swirl in circles, and basically jump through hoops in a series of arresting sequences where no single shot calls attention to itself but rather entire segments grandly fly seemingly beyond previous expectations.

And yet, the film remains grounded appropriately by the witches who seem to have conjured up not the ideal man they expected, but the figure of Eternal Opposition, who will test them and teach them in the process. For gauche, rude and pigheaded as he is, Van Horne is still on some level attractive and appealing. He demonstrates an enlightened understanding of the history of the oppression of women and of female needs.

Alexandra resists the devil's seductive wiles by telling him the truth — that he stinks, that he should go to hell, etc. — and yet her giving in to him seems no less honest and total because he has managed to touch some unhealed wound within her. She succumbs not to his blandishments, but to his understanding of her fear that if she does not take chances, she will not find the fulfillment she seeks.

While Sukie the fecund Earth mother seems to maintain her aura of perfection (though herself surrounded by the chaos of her six female offspring) and only wants someone who is not afraid of possibly impregnating her once again, Jane undergoes an extreme transformation from a buttoned down, brushed back conventional spinster into a raving sex maniac. In the scene most accurately copied from Updike's novel, the devil comes by ostensibly to observe her cello playing and seduces her with the statement, "Passion is precision," transforming her from a spinster to a sensualist with a swoop of her head and her abandonment to her muse of music.

The women feel themselves terribly tricked when they all turn up pregnant (including the heretofore physiologically infertile Jane) and realize that Van Horne has effectively eliminated Felicia. Despite his friendly overtures, they shut him out of their lives and refuse to see their Stud from Hell anymore, until he invokes a curse which exposes each one to her greatest fear sending them not only back into his arms, but also plotting how they can extricate themselves from his clutches permanently and regain their former freedom.

The devil, however, does not see himself as a sinner. The three impregnated women coveted his lustful advances in the first place and now they abandon him. He turns into a tantrum-throwing slob who wants his women to take care of him, give him affection, clean his clothes, and give him a "little respect," all typical husbandly expectations. As he becomes victimized by the women's magic, he starts making comically overblown misogynistic pronouncements such as "Did God make women by mistake or on purpose? Because if it's a mistake, maybe we can do something about it!" Van Horne wants to pin the downfall of men on women.

While women are the keepers of order, who raise families, preserve art, and celebrate their femininity in quiet ways, they can also become completely destructive when aroused, fully the equal of men, who are left impotently cursing the vagaries of fate when they have found that they have lost favor. While the film celebrates the women in it, it ultimately expresses sympathy for the devil who is comically caught in the throes of male sexual panic.

Miller lost interest in direction for a time and instead concentrated on producing. He played a key role in launching both Nicole Kidman and Philip Noyce's international careers by producing and providing second unit direction for Noyce's troubled but ultimately taut 1989 thriller *Dead Calm,* which became an international hit. He was also the producer of two films by director John Duigan, *The Year My Voice Broke* and the delightful comedy *Flirting* (1990), which brought about a return to personal, smaller films in Australia. Additionally, he was brought in to take over production of a 10-hour miniseries, *Dirtwater Dynasty,* that was going over schedule. He enjoyed being able to guide and nurture several projects simultaneously instead of being entirely obsessed with one, and vowed that he would not return to directing until he came across a project that truly aroused his curiosity.

He was to find just such a project in the true tale of the Odones, who fight the medical establishment to save the life of their six-year-old son, which is threatened by an obscure disease. With Miller's medical background, he was an ideal choice to make *Lorenzo's Oil,* which he hoped would aid in making people aware of the need for funding medical research.

Miller's greatest difficulty was in fighting the temptation to become flamboyant because that would diminish the truth of this real life story. He does see the Odones as a heroic couple who are agents of evolution and have shattered settled beliefs in the medical world. In a way, Lorenzo is their magical figure who calls them on to an adventure of discovery, seeking a solution for their son's illness. They would never have chosen themselves to become scientists but for that cruel trick of fate.

He wrings incredible performances out of his lead actors, Nick Nolte and Susan Sarandon as Augusto and Michaela Odone, though Nolte's Italian accent never does quite come across as convincing, the emotional truthfulness of his performance is. Together, the actors show us the lengths of courage and imagination concerned parents can summon up for the sake of their child's life. They become increasingly intolerant of others who do not share their vision. (Michaela fires one attendant after another for not sharing her inflexible resolve.) The film even leaves open the possibility that in her unbending drive Michaela may be an inadvertent monster perpetuating her child's suffering in hopes of an eventual cure, and there is uplift for others in the images of other children who have benefited from the balm the parents develop tempered with the knowledge of others who continue to suffer from adrenoleukodystrophy, which destroys young children's nervous systems, forcing them to remain prisoners unable to hear, see or feel inside their own bodies.

The result is the most emotionally, heartwrenchingly powerful film Miller has ever been associated with. The movie fixates on the images of two parents, their bedridden small son, and their house, but maintains visual interest throughout because Miller avoids making it a "talking heads" movie. He constantly cuts from one set-up to another, exploring the dimensionality of the Odones' living space, as well as prowling with his camera to catch the nuances of the actors' superb performances.

Miller executive produced and cowrote what has been described as the *Citizen Kane* of talking pig movies, the extraordinarily charming *Babe*, which surprised many skeptics by being nominated for Best Picture by the Academy of Motion Picture Arts and Sciences while James Cromwell was nominated for Best Supporting Actor for his role as Farmer Hoggett, though not too many were surprised by its taking home a statuette for Best Special Effects (animation and visual effects by Rhythm & Hues, with animatronic characters by Jim Henson's Creature Shop).

Babe is directed by Chris Noonan and based on the book *The Sheep-Pig* by Dick King-Smith. Beautifully narrated by Roscoe Lee Browne, it recounts the story of Babe (voice by Christine Cavanaugh), an orphaned piglet destined for the slaughterhouse, who has his weight correctly guessed by Farmer Arthur Hoggett (James Cromwell) and ends up the sole pig at Hoggett's farm. There Babe makes friends with the other animals of the barnyard: Fly (voice by Miriam Margolyes), the sheepdog; Ferdinand, the panicky duck; Maa, the elderly ewe, and an amusing trio of singing mice. Babe is an innocent who sometimes wreaks havoc inadvertently, knocking over material in Mrs. Esme Hoggett's (Magda Szubanski) house, but he has a good heart.

Looking up to Fly, he tries his hand at being a sheepdog, which annoys Fly and amuses farmer Hoggett. Babe comes to the rescue when some bad men try to rustle Hoggett's sheep, and when Fly becomes injured, Hoggett has the inspiration to train Babe as a Sheep Pig and enters him in the National Sheepdog Finals. The film becomes a parable about breaking out of molds and taking chances. Hoggett decides to risk looking ridiculous, while if Babe cannot justify his existence, the slaughterhouse could still await.

Fortunately for Babe, Maa teaches him the secret code to get sheep to listen to him, that is chanting, "Baa Ram Ewe, Sheep be true," so that the entire project ends on an appropriately upbeat note. The special effects used to create the talking animals are, for the most part, very convincing and ingeniously done, and no doubt required enormous patience on the part of director Noonan.

Miller went on to direct the sequel, *Babe: A Pig in the City,* himself. Its scheduled premiere party in America on November 15, 1998, however, was abruptly canceled due to some last minute problems with the soundtrack (which had been mixed too loud). To garner a G rating, Miller was required to replace the word "damn" with "darn," and took out a shot of a goldfish flopping around and breathing heavily after its bowl was broken. Nonetheless, the movie was able to make is scheduled premiere, considered essential because there were so many product tie-ins keyed to its opening date.

Said Miller, "We had to remix the entire film. It was so loud, it was a complete assault on the ears." Racing against the clock, Universal assigned its six top dubbers to work 20 hours a day to get it ready on time. Its cancellation did start rumors of a disaster.

Unfortunately, *Babe: A Pig in the City* cost four times what the original *Babe* did and achieved only a fraction of the business. Picking up the story immediately after where its predecessor left off, *Pig in the City* makes too many missteps early on. To begin with, the innocent and eager pig accidentally, but seriously, injures Farmer Hoggett (Cromwell again) right at the start of the movie, thereby threatening the livelihood of the entire farm. Due to Babe's celebrity after winning the Sheep Dog Finals, he and his owner have been offered a substantial sum for appearing at a large fair far away, and Mrs. Hoggett (Szubanki again) heads off for the airport with pig in tow (with the singing mice covertly along for the ride) and the frantic Ferdinand trying to keep up with his lucky pig.

But things keep going from bad to worse, as Babe befriending a dog who sniffs out drugs results in Mrs. Hoggett being detained on suspicion of smuggling, thereby causing her to miss her connection to the farm and stranding them in the big city (which resembles Sydney, Australia, with a few foreign landmarks thrown in for good measure). A pig-faced person at the airport guides them to one of the few hotels in town that clandestinely accepts pets such as young porker Babe.

The pitbull urges the other animals to listen to the Pig, in Miller's *Babe: Pig in the City* (photo by Rhythm and Hues). Miller raises concerns for all homeless animals.

Still, things continue to go dismally as a monkey steals Mrs. Hoggett's luggage, and in attempting to get it back, Babe is dragooned into the ape circus of vaudevillian Fugly Floom (Mickey Rooney) who speaks only in monkey talk. Frantically searching for the missing Babe, Mrs. Hoggett manages to get herself arrested.

Hoping to set things right, Babe participates in a performance for children at a hospital only to back out from under his table at the wrong moment, tripping Floom, who upsets a candle that causes the set to burn down while Floom is taken to the hospital. Floom's niece, who runs the animal hotel, heads off to see after her uncle, leaving her starving animals to fend for themselves.

The best moment in the film comes when Babe has been chased by a pitbull still attached to a chain, and when the dog inadvertently plunges headfirst into the river, the other animals are content to stand by and watch him drown. Kind-hearted Babe bravely jumps in and risks his own life to bring the dog's head out of the water and onto a boat, with the result that the rescued pitbull puts Babe in charge of the menagerie.

However, the animal-hating across-the-way neighbors alert the local animal shelter of critters overrunning the hotel, and most of the hotel's inhabitants are captured and taken to the pound. The bizarre climax has Miller reprising his bungee-cord bit from *Beyond Thunderdome* with Mrs. Hoggett battling those who would separate her from her husband's beloved pig. It is fanciful and silly, and once again there is a happy ending; however, in losing the old cast of characters and introducing a slew of new ones, the sequel lacks the charm and grace of the original.

It also failed to attract audiences the way the first one had, and helped Universal finish up the year with a dismal final quarter. Miller displays ample talent still, and there are wilder designs and stunts than in the original film, but despite calling attention to the plight of urban animals, the effort seems misapplied. There still exist rumors for yet another addition to the Mad Max series, but Miller has amply demonstrated that he is quite capable of delivering other kinds of cinematic clockwork masterpieces and delights. Perhaps the best expression to describe the sensation of his own pell-mell pictures is that at their best, they are totally exhilarating. Miller is a crafty conjurer who is amply capable of whipping up movie magic.

KURT NEUMANN (1908–1958)

Fast Companions; Information Kid; My Pal the King (1932); *The Big Cage; The Secret of the Blue Room; King for a Night* (1933); *Let's Talk It Over; Half a Sinner; Wake Up and Dream* (1934); *Alias Mary Dow; The Affair of Susan* (1935); *Let's Sing Again; Rainbow on the River* (1936); *Espionage; Make a Wish; Hold 'Em Navy* (1937); *Ambush; Unmarried; Island of Lost Men; All Women Have Secrets* (1939); *Ellery Queen—Master Detective; A Night at Earl Carroll's* (1940); *Brooklyn Orchid; About Face; The McGuerins from Brooklyn* (1942); *Fall In; Taxi Mister; Yanks Ahoy!; The Unknown Guest; The Return of the Vampire* (possibly codirected with Lew Landers, uncredited); *Tarzan's Desert Mystery* (codirector with William Thiele, uncredited) (1943); *Tarzan and the Amazons* (1945); *Tarzan and the Leopard Woman* (1946); *Tarzan and the Huntress* (1947); *The Dude Goes West* (1948); *Bad Men of Tombstone; Bad Boy* (1949); *The Kid from Texas; Rocketship X-M* (1950); *Cattle Drive; Reunion in Reno* (1951); *Son of Ali Baba; The Ring; Hiawatha* (1952); *Tarzan and the She-Devil* (1953); *Carnival Story* (1954); *Mohawk; The Desperadoes Are in Town* (1956); *Kronos; The She-Devil; The Deerslayer* (1957); *The Fly; Circus of Love; Machete* (1958); *Counterplot; Watusi* (1959)

Kurt Neumann died at the age of 50 on August 21, 1958, under somewhat mysterious circumstances. Despite having the biggest hit of his career in recently released *The Fly*, he was reportedly grieving over the death of his wife, Irma, who died July 12 that same year, having just completed his final film (*Return to King Solomon's Mines*, released as *Watusi*) ten days earlier, when he was rushed to the hospital which discovered carbon tetrachloride, a deadly poison usually found in cleaning fluid, in his stomach. He was survived by his son, Kurt, Jr., then 24, and his daughter Mary Ann.

Neumann was born on April 5, 1908 in Nuremberg, Germany, and was brought to Hollywood by Carl Laemmle, Jr. At first he was assigned to make Spanish and German versions of Universal pictures and music shorts—his educational background had been in music—which he broke out of by agreeing to direct Slim Summerville comedies.

In 1932, the year he began directing features, he married Irma Ely on August 1. The bride was attended by screen star Lupita Tovar.

Perhaps because of his German background, Neumann was selected to helm *Secret of the Blue Room*, an Americanized version of a German mystery. The film is set in a castle where Robert von Helldorf (Lionel Atwill sans mustache in his first Universal horror film) tells the tale of a haunted blue room from which his sister fell to her death. Other deaths have occurred there: a man found shot inside the locked room, and a detective found dead of fright after staying in the room to solve the mystery.

Tommy Brandt (William Janney) wants to impress von Helldorf's daughter Irene (Gloria Stuart) and volunteers to spend the night in the blue room. His fellow suitors Capt. Walter Brink (Paul Lukas) and Frank Faber (Onslow Stevens) agree to do the same on subsequent nights, but the next morning the room is found empty.

Faber remains true to his word and is found dead the following morning, causing Police Commander Forster (Edward Arnold) to arrive on the scene and begin an inquiry. To break the case, he spends the night in the Blue room and eventually unmasks Tommy as the culprit.

Neumann builds atmosphere with howling winds and roaring thunder. He relies on the very able cast of players and keeps things moving at a good steady pace. Incorporated into the film appears to be some silent footage from a European production which makes the film seem more authentic in its exotic atmosphere than most Universal horror pictures. With its mix of mystery, melodrama, red herrings, and suspicious characters, *The Secret of the Blue Room* enjoys a reputation as a better than average B picture.

In a newspaper article for the *Daily News* (June 17, 1950), Neumann complained of being typecast as a director. After directing *King for a Night* and *My Pal, the King*, he refused to do any more King pictures. When a football film, *Hold 'Em, Navy* proved a success, he was assigned *Touchdown Army* and walked away from one called *One Second to Play*. He was then locked into doing westerns for a while before moving onto more fantastic productions.

First in 1943, he went to Columbia where he provided the idea for Lew Landers' *The Return of the Vampire*, one of Bela Lugosi's more interesting forties productions in which he essayed a vampire that looked like Dracula but was given the name Armand Tesla when Universal refused to allow Columbia to use the name. (Universal sued over the film but settled out of court in exchange for the services of Columbia contractee Larry Parks. While the character of Dracula is in the public domain, the look of the character as it appeared in Universal's 1931 film was protected, creating a situation whereby competing vampires could either assume the name or the look of the character, but not both.)

The film begins in a graveyard in 1918 and introduces the concept of a werewolf (husky Matt Willis) that can talk, who summons Count Tesla to come feast on a fetching female (the often interesting Nina Foch) at a nearby sanitarium. The girl's grandfather (Roland Varno) knows about vampires and discovers Tesla's secret with the aid of a mirror, and impales him with an iron stake.

Twenty-five years later, German assaults wreck the old cemetery and two Civil Defense guards come upon Tesla's impaled body and make the mistake of removing the spike in order to rebury the body, thus reviving the undead vampire, who claws his way out of his grave. Andreas Obry, who had been cured of lycanthropy at Tesla's death, resumes his lycanthropic form and returns to do Tesla's bidding.

The film contains a number of good atmospheric touches, but its relative lack of availability compared to the Universal classics has prevented it from obtaining the reputation and recognition that it deserves. There's a good bit where Frieda Inescort, playing a kind of distaff Van Helsing, brandishes a crucifix and Tesla disappears in an explosion of smoke, and the climax proves fairly exciting with the werewolf turning on his master and dragging him into the sunlight where he is impaled and finally melts away.

The film is one of the few gothic vampire films of the period to be clearly set in what was then a contemporary setting. Apart from supplying the story idea, it is hard to know how involved Neumann was in the production, but some sources give him codirecting credit with Landers, who had previously directed Lugosi in *The Raven*.

Neumann went on to Sol Lesser Productions to pilot and associate produce several Tarzan films beginning with the troubled Tarzan film, originally begun as *Tarzan Against the Sahara* by director William Thiele and then reshot as *Tarzan and the Sheik* before being released as *Tarzan's Desert Mystery*.

The film is an odd hodge-podge in which Tarzan (Johnny Weissmuller) searches the desert for plants from which a serum for malaria can be extracted and encounters a Nazi agent (Otto Kruger), a stranded lady magician (Nancy Kelly), and a sinister sheik (Lloyd Corrigan). The standard issue RKO Tarzan film suddenly goes wildly science fictional in the final reels with Tarzan battling prehistoric monsters (actually stock footage from *One Million B.C.* over which Weissmuller is superimposed), man-eating plants, and throwing bad guys to a giant spider.

Lesser must have liked Neumann's additions, as Neumann replaced Theiele entirely as the director of the next installment, *Tarzan and the Amazons*. This film brought in a new, blond Jane, Brenda Joyce (about which Weissmuller wrily mused, "Kind of looks like Tarzan's been playing the jungle a bit."). In this one, Maria Ouspenskaya (the gypsy woman of *Wolf Man* fame) plays the queen of a lost civilization of women. Some archaeologists seek these Amazons, but Tarzan refuses to show them the way, so they trick Boy (Johnny Sheffield) into doing it.

Weissmuller tried to get away from his Tarzan image through a deal with Pine-Thomas, but a suitable project could not be found before it was time for him and Neumann to begin *Tarzan and the Leopard Woman*, which starred Acquanetta (of the *Captive Wild Woman* series at Universal) as the high priestess of a leopard cult, whose members don the skins and claws of leopards and fanatically attack the encroachment of civilization onto their territory. When they kidnap Jane and Boy, Tarzan goes to rescue them and is rescued in turn by Cheetah rather than throwing back his head and summoning a herd of elephants as he did in the MGM installments.

Weissmuller finally got the chance to do a non–Tarzan film, but the resulting project, *Swamp Fire*, died a quick death at the box office and soon he was back working with Neumann on *Tarzan and the Huntress*. In this a pretty animal trainer (Patricia Morrison) has some unscrupulous companions who trap more than their quota of wild animals. The Apeman saves his animal friends with the aid of the now familiar elephant stampede.

Neumann dropped out of the series to work on some westerns. Weissmuller was increasingly discontented that he was not given a cut of the overall receipts on the series and

Hugh O'Brien, Osa Massen, Lloyd Bridges, John Emery, and Noah Beery, Jr., viewed their trip to Mars from inside this rocketship, as did we in Neumann's original version of *Rocketship X-M.*

would make only one more Tarzan film, *Tarzan and the Mermaids*.

Neumann liked to tell the story of his friend Andrew Morton, who had directed *S.O.S. Iceberg*. Based on that credit, MGM hired Morton to direct "snow scenes for every MGM picture that had snow scenes. You see, he was an established authority on things that were cold," said Neumann.

Neumann was a long-time reader of science fiction stories and in 1949, he decided to write a script about an expedition going to Mars and finding living dinosaurs, but he could not get anyone interested in the project. Subsequently, one of the low budget producers he had approached, Robert L. Lippert, was also approached by special effects technician Jack Rabin, who with Steven Longstreet had devised a project he called *Destination Moon* (not to be confused with the contemporaneous George Pal production). Rabin convinced Lippert that the resulting film could be done inexpensively, and Lippert in turn contacted Neumann and had him prepare new drafts of the script which were briefly called *Rocket to the Moon* and *None Came Back* before going into production as *Rocketship Expedition Moon*. (George Pal's film registered the title *Destination Moon* first and had already gone into production; however, Lippert's film was finished and released first, piggybacking on the publicity for the Pal project.)

While he is rarely given the credit, Neumann launched the science fiction boom of the fifties by creating in *Rocketship X-M*, as it was eventually called, the first significant science fiction film of that era. The film introduces a number of notions which would quickly go on to become science fiction film clichés: trite onboard "comic relief," a rocketship plowing through a meteor shower, a civilization destroyed by an atomic war, and threatening atomic mutations.

The film, while occasionally lumbering, has several interesting ideas. It unfortunately suffers from the fact that the characters are mostly bland and undetailed, so that their interaction remains fairly uninteresting. A last minute change added a sort of love story romance to the film in hopes of giving it a more human touch, but the effort proves futile. The love story remains something grafted on rather than integral to the overall story.

The film was made on a budget of $95,000 and stars a dependable but unexciting cast: Lloyd Bridges, Osa Massen, Hugh O'Brian, John Emery, Noah Beery, Jr., and Morris Ankrum. Its greatest assets are its cinematography, courtesy of the great Karl Struss (*Sunrise, Dr. Jekyll and Mr. Hyde, Limelight*) who went on to become a frequent Neumann collaborator, and its majestic and atmospheric score by Frede Grofé, famed composer of the "Grand Canyon Suite" whose other film credits are as orchestrator for *King of Jazz* (1930) and composer on *Knute Rockne, All American* (1940), *Thousands Cheer* (1943), *Time Out of Mind* (1947), and *Return of Jesse James*. Grofé received only $3,000 for his themes, which were orchestrated and conducted by Albert Glasser, who came up with the idea of using a theremin for the first time on a science fiction score and who would himself go on to score numerous low budget science fiction films.

"Forever, Man has dreamed of visiting the nearest of heavenly bodies — some, for adventurous fantastic reasons; others, like ourselves, because they visualize the successful lunar expedition as a first step toward practical interplanetary travel," explains Professor Fleming (Ankrum) at the news conference which opens the film and sets its serious tone. While the film opens with the first rocket expedition to the moon, due to complaints from Eagle-Lion, who were distributing *Destination Moon*, the members of the expedition pass out during the trip up and incredibly end up near Mars instead.

The crew of ***Rocketship X-M*** view the nuclear-devastated landscape of Mars, actually Red Rock Canyon in the Mojave Desert.

This gimmick is highly improbable given the time and distances involved, but as Bill Warren points out in *Keep Watching the Skies!,* it would have been hard for the filmmakers to create a believable lunar excursion given the look and realities of the lunar terrain. Instead, the exteriors were shot at nearby Red Rock Canyon, which, with Struss' atmospheric lensing and an added red tinting, looked appropriately desolate and otherworldly.

Throughout production, Lippert apparently kept insisting on changes in the screenplay. Originally, a quite different concept of Mars was considered, including putting dinosaurs on Mars using stock footage of lizards from *One Million B.C.,* but the screenplay was revised to make it the site of atomic devastation, which in retrospect proves to be the more interesting choice and gives the film a still timely theme.

The surface proves to be inhabited by feral Martian survivors of an atomic war who keep eerily out of sight until they attack the expedition and kill its leader, Dr. Karl Ekstrom (John Emery), and Bill Corrigan (Noah Beery, Jr.), the unfunny comic relief, and wounding Harry Chamberlain (Hugh O'Brian). They capture one of the Martian mutants (Sherry Moreland) and discover that the atomic war has left her sightless (her eyes are disturbingly blank). In an interesting touch, she proves to be as afraid of them as they are of her.

Harry alerts Floyd Graham (Lloyd Bridges) and Lisa Van Horne (Osa Massen) who manage to take him back to the ship to take off, but en route Harry dies and Floyd and Lisa discover that they have insufficient fuel to splash down safely on Earth, declare their love for each other, and surprisingly end up dying upon re-entry, an unusually bleak ending for a film of this period. *Rocketship X-M,* however, ends on a positive note with the undaunted and determined Prof. Fleming announcing that work will begin on RXM II.

In an interview with Tom Weaver, Lloyd Bridges recalled, "I begged [Neumann] *not* to shoot that love scene, when we're plummeting to the Earth and we pour our hearts to one another. I told him, 'You know, at a time like that, it just doesn't make sense!' It seemed so *wrong* to me to destroy the illusion; I was sure people would laugh at it. But he insisted and who knows whether he was right or not."

Bridges remembers Neumann as "a man who believed we had to do it fast! We had a very short schedule, maybe 10 days or something like that. When we went out on location to shoot the scenes of Mars, we went out to Death Valley. We had to put on our wardrobe and makeup en route, in the plane, so that as soon as the *plane* landed, we were ready to go to work!"

According to Bridges, if a scene did not go smoothly and quickly, Neumann would be forced to skip it because of his time constraints. John Emery loved to spout Shakespeare quotations on the set and patterned himself after John Barrymore. Both Bridges and Hugh O'Brian were quite taken with Osa Massen.

According to fellow actor Hugh O'Brian in *American Classic Screen,* the Martian scenes were:

> [D]one in two days. Everything in two days — no sound, no dialogue, because we were wearing masks. We knew what we were supposed to say, but we just mumbled, 'cause nobody could hear us anyway. When we went back to the studio, we all sat around in chairs and they put a mike over our heads and we did the two days work in about an hour. You know, I remember a funny thing about our director, Kurt Neumann. We were in the Mojave Desert and it was so hot, especially with our heavy costumes, that by the end of the day you were quite dehydrated. So we'd take breaks sitting around these big pails of ice, and Kurt had an icepick. While he was laughing and telling a story, he emphasized a point by jamming the pick right into his leg. And everybody started back in horror. We all knew he limped, but none of us had known about his wooden leg.

Immediately following his experiences with Robert Lippert on *Rocketship X-M,* Neumann told the press,

"Producers work with you all the way through the writing of the script. They're on the set every day while you're shooting, and they make decisions for you. Then they sit in on the cutting and the scoring. If a picture falls on its face when it is released, the director is the dog. It's all his fault. The producer had nothing to do with it."

Rocketship X-M was one of the first fifties SF films to be sold to television, and was one of the first science fiction films I ever saw. Years later, a film entrepreneur named Wade Williams claimed he rescued the movie from oblivion by buying the rights to the film and altering it with special effects footage. The special effects created in 1949 were fairly primitive, with footage of a V-2 rocket standing in for the rocket in a few shots (though one shot of the ship roaring past the camera would later turn up in Lippert's subsequent science fiction films *Spaceways* and *Lost Continent*).

Williams hired Dennis Muren, Tom Scherman, Mike Minor, Robert Skotak, David Stipes, Harry Walters, and Bob and Cathy Burns to create eleven new effects shots (mostly of the rocket, which wasn't shown from the exterior while the expedition was out in space) which were inserted into the film or replaced outmoded footage, giving recent audiences a deceptive feel for what the original was like. It was this version that was released to videotape. Copies of the film as it was originally put together still exist, but have become exceedingly rare. While the new effects footage is of decent quality and certainly doesn't hurt the film, it seems disturbing that Williams would have so little respect for a film he claims to love as to permanently alter from the filmmakers' original intentions, thereby rendering the original version of the film he fell in love with inaccessible. (Of course, his ability to newly copyright his altered version probably played a significant role. Nor is he the only filmmaker to take this tack. Columbia Pictures withdrew Spielberg's original version of *Close Encounters of the Third Kind* once he put out the *Special Edition*, and George Lucas redid some of the special effects sequences in the *Star Wars* trilogy while withdrawing the originals.)

While Fritz Lang's silent *Frau im Mond* (U.S. title: *Girl in the Moon*) (1929) predates *Rocketship X-M* by many years and deserves credit as the first feasible interplanetary expedition film (unlike Georges Méliès' fanciful *Trip to the Moon*), it was the success of *Rocketship X-M* that launched a vogue for many subsequent films which defined science fiction for the mass audience.

That Neumann hoped to make other science fiction projects was evident when he bought the rights to Jules Verne's *20,000 Leagues Under the Sea* from Alexander Korda. He had, according to George Pal, a good script for it, but couldn't find anyone who wanted to make the film, and so was willing to sell it for $15,000. He eventually sold the rights to Al Rogell, a producer at 20th Century–Fox, who found he couldn't sell it either until at last Walt Disney bought the rights and put Richard Fleischer to work on it.

Neumann's next science fiction film was *Kronos*, which again starred John Emery. It has a fairly episodic plot that is nonetheless filled with interesting touches. The story for the film originated with Jack Rabin's matte painting partner Irving Block, who also helped conceive the SF classic *Forbidden Planet* with Allen Adler as well as the stories for *The Atomic Submarine* and *War of the Satellites*. The story was apparently designed as a showcase for Rabin's low budget effects. According to Rabin in *Fantascene* #2, many larger budgeted films with special effects "did not have the ingenuity that went into *Kronos*. The total cost of it was about $160,000." Not bad for a widescreen effort that is filled with effects throughout much of the film's running time.

The technological title terror in *Kronos* is named after Chronos, the titan of Greek myth, who ate his jealous rivals. In the film, a massive robot comes to Earth and eats up everything in sight. Block reported that he wanted the robot "to be anthropomorphic, to look like a robot, but at the same time I wanted it to look like a piece of machinery. I spent a lot of time on it.... At one point it looked more like a construction by Picasso, but I reduced it down by a whole series of steps until it ultimately became just a black box."

Evidence of this change in design occurs when a highly inaccurate newspaper drawings of the menace appear in the film, which show a less blocky, more rounded concept of the automaton. However, as newspaper reporting can be notoriously inaccurate, this works in the film as a sort of subtle satire. (A later photo shown during a radio broadcast is much more accurate.)

The film opens with the idea of a giant asteroid headed for Earth, which when viewed looks obviously artificial. A portion of the asteroid veers off and seems to glow after landing. It attracts the attention of a nearby truck driver and seems to take over his body. The man then drives to Labcentral, a governmental experimental science station, where the driver knocks out the guard and enters the office of Dr. Elliot (Emery), one of the scientists there, before suddenly dying.

Meanwhile, Les (Jeff Morrow) and fellow scientist Arnie (George O'Hanlon) are using the telescope when Les spots what he thinks might be an asteroid, takes some photos, and has them developed by his fiancée Vera (Barbara Lawrence). The results are then fed into SUSIE, a computer whose initials stand for Synchro Unifying Sinometric Integrating Equitensor, which happens to go out of whack when Elliot puts in an appearance. Vera hopes to get Les out to see a movie, but he can't bear to pull himself away from the lab. The "asteroid" is dubbed M47 and according to the computer will strike Earth in 16 hours. Given its mass, it must be intercepted.

Missiles are launched against it, hitting it and exploding. Elliot collapses at the moment of impact, but the "asteroid" survives and plunges "safely" into the Pacific off the coast of Mexico.

Les and Arnie decide to investigate the crash site in their helicopter but find nothing except Vera waiting for them when they return. Back at home, Elliot is very sick and is attended to by Dr. Albert R. Stern (Morris Ankrum), who administers shock treatments from time to time. From Elliot's mumblings, the audience makes out that some aliens have depleted their supply of electrical and atomic energy and have sent a combination accumulator and storehouse to Earth to garner fresh supplies.

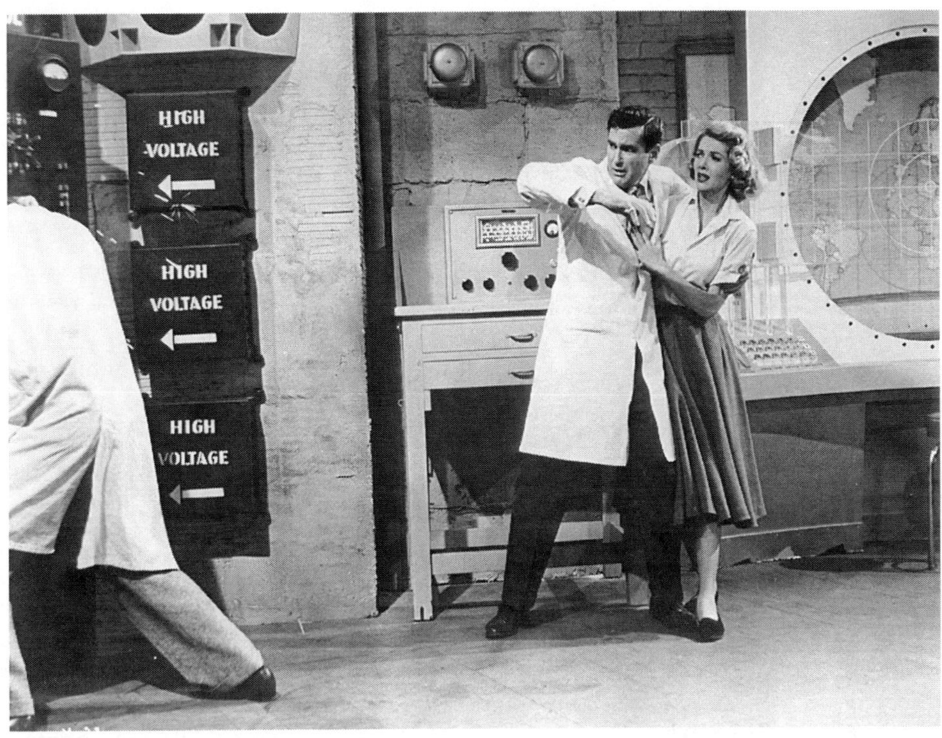

Jeff Morrow and Barbara Lawrence flinch as an alien-possessed John Emery commits suicide by throwing himself into the high voltage circuits in Neumann's *Kronos*.

This accumulator, later dubbed Kronos by Les, appears just as Les and Vera take a swim in the ocean. It is a huge, bulky machine composed of two large black cubes supported by pylons with a large semi-sphere dome on top and two antennae, one with a cube on the end, the other with a sphere. There are four black pylons on the bottom that surround a central white one and stomp up and down when it moves. The scientists land on the machine, where its energy sucking pull removes Arnie's glasses.

Dr. Stern becomes convinced that Elliot's fantasies are in actuality the truth, that he is being controlled by an alien intelligence, which arranges for Stern to be electrocuted on a nearby electrical panel. Elliot researches sources of nuclear and thermonuclear energy, mentally relaying the information to Kronos.

The giant invader then attacks the nearest electrical plant, sucking up its energy and defeating the planes of the Mexican air force which are sent against it. The machine heads north towards the nearest supply of America's nuclear arsenal.

Dr. Elliot recommends that the H-bomb be dropped on it right away, but Les realizes from his observations that that would be the worst possible choice as the machine would simply suck up all the released energy. Elliot argues they cannot wait.

Vera goes to tell Les about something disturbing she has learned from the hospital, but encounters Elliot in his room instead. Sensing that she knows the truth, he attacks her and her calls bring Les to the rescue. Throwing Elliot against an electrical panel causes his original personality to regain consciousness, and he argues that while we can transform matter into energy, the aliens know how to transform energy into matter. Unfortunately, they got so good at it that they transformed all the energy on their planet so that it is almost entirely depleted (with a little warning about how we should be more careful of our own limited resources, an aspect which keeps this film still timely). Before Elliot dies, he tells them that they must reverse the process. In a particularly gruesome touch, at his death a stream of liquid spills from Elliot's head and crackles when it comes in contact with the nearby electrical panel.

Les calls and warns the Pentagon that they must not drop the intended bomb. (Neumann shows two pilots in a cockpit that does not at all match that of the bombing plane used in the stock footage.) At the last moment, the plane is recalled, but Kronos draws the plane back onto itself, causing its payload to explode. The energy released causes it to turn white and grow larger.

Reviewing what Elliot told them, Les suggests they apply Attenberg's theorem, that they destroy the monster with its own energy. If they can change the polarity of the energy, it would create an internal chain reaction and

The poster's come-on for Kurt Neumann's *The Fly*.

Kronos would feed on itself until there was nothing left.

Kronos reaches the outskirts of Los Angeles, sucking up energy and creating black-outs. A pilot comes with the bomb intended to change polarity, but a wind shift prevents him from completing his first attempt. Neumann builds suspense as the bomb run is recalculated (on a slide rule no less) and the pilot releases the bomb on the second attempt. It's a smashing success as Kronos' black exterior begins to break up and melt away. The film ends with Les' firm pronouncement that if they send any more, we'll be ready.

She Devil was based on a story "The Adaptive Ultimate," by short-lived science fiction writer Stanley Weinbaum, written under the pseudonym "John Jessel," which had previously been adapted twice for television. The first time was as "Experiment Perilous" on *Summer Theater* in 1954, and the second time was as the *Science Fiction Theater* episode "Beyond Return" with Zachary Scott and Peter Hanson.

Neumann wrote the screenplay for the film with Carroll Young as well as directing. His version of the story is an unfortunately dull and surprisingly unimaginative one intended as a showcase for star Mari Blanchard, who plays a poverty-stricken tubercular victim Kyra Zelas, who is given an experimental serum by two chemical researchers, Dr. Bach and Dr. Scott (Albert Dekker and Jack Kelly).

The serum, derived from fruit flies, "nature's more adaptive insect," not only cures Kyra, but causes her to develop criminal tendencies and change her hair color from brunette to blond as well as lightening and darkening her skin (an apparent corollary to the way cinematographer Karl Struss achieved the effect using colored filters).

Fascinated, Dr. Scott keeps tabs on Kyra, never interfering even when she resorts to murder by doing away with the wife (Fay Baker) of a wealthy man (John Archer) she has plans for. She marries him and then a few months later kills him off in a car wreck that the serum allows her to survive.

Finally Scott and Bach decide to take steps and create a counter-serum. While she tries to get Scott to murder Bach, she gets injected and immediately contracts tuberculosis again and instantly expires.

The performances, with the exceptions of Dekker and Archer, are uniformly dull. Look for Blossom Rock, later Granny on the *Addams Family*, in a supporting role as Dekker's housekeeper.

Before tackling what was to become Neumann's most famous (and most overrated) science fiction project, he directed *The Deerslayer*, loosely based on the James Fenimore Cooper novel. In it, Natty Bumpo (Lex Barker), who has been reared by the Mohican Indian tribe, gets involved with an old trader (Jay C. Flippen) and his two daughters (Rita Moreno and Cathy O'Donnell) when he saves them from a Heron attack. It turns out the trader had been secretly Indian–hunting to collect bounties on Indian scalps. The Hurons capture him and threaten his life unless he returns those scalps. The Deerslayer saves the man and returns the scalps to the Indians.

Neumann's last science fiction film is one of the most famous, though overrated efforts, *The Fly*. (David Cronenberg's bigger budgeted remake proves to be a far more creative and interesting film, using the situation of a man slowly transforming into a fly as a metaphor about illness, aging, and the ways our bodies can betray us.) *The Fly* sometimes is given credit as the first SF film to deal with matter transmission, although that concept appeared earlier in Corman's *Not of This Earth* among other films. It is true that it was the first film to deal with the problems of matter transmission, although its visually appealing fly monster is still fairly ludicrous as both the half-man, half-fly creatures that as a result of the transmission are given human intelligence.

Neumann both produced and directed from James Clavell's script (Clavell later becoming a best-selling author) which adapted George Langelaan's much reprinted short story which originally had appeared in *Playboy* in the June 1957 issue. The leading role was offered to Michael Rennie, who turned it down, and David Hedison, still going under the name of Al Hedison, became scientific researcher André Delambre. Neumann insisted on Vincent Price to play François, the brother, over the objections of Fox executive producer Buddy Adler. (The Delambre family is apparently made Canadian and the film set in Montreal to stay true to the French names of the original without actually setting the film in France.) The Delambres are extremely rich as a result of their family-run electronics manufacturing firm, and so André devotes himself to the betterment of mankind.

Delambre is working obsessively on matter transmission for a humanitarian ideal, that of transporting food over vast distances to prevent famine, but his wife Helene is concerned that his experiments are "like playing God." However, unlike most science fiction films which would focus on his efforts in the lab, *The Fly* centers its attention on the effects of his work on his family.

Helene is meant to embody the anxieties of her era, explaining, "I get so scared sometimes. The suddenness of our age. Electronics, robots, earth satellites, supersonic flight, and now this. Oh, it's not so much who invents them. It's the fact they exist." (Strangely, atomic energy is significantly absent from her list, and Delambre's machine, which breaks down atomics and transports them, is thus rendered a substitute for atomic energy in both its mysteriousness and its mutating effect on André.)

Despite André's loving relationship with his wife, he secludes himself more and more in his basement laboratory, neglecting such duties as accompanying his wife to social functions, disciplining his son, and attending family meals. He can suddenly appear, whisk his wife away for a night on the town, and just as abruptly stop talking to her and concentrate on his work instead.

After a night at the ballet, he brings her back not to the bedroom but to his basement, where he has a bottle of champagne prepared to celebrate his hoped for success. When Helene gives him an openly sexual gaze, he responds, "You're in an unscientific mood," indicating his lack of attention to her sexual drives. Moreover, after transporting a guinea pig with his device, his response to her is simply, "Now don't kill it with overfeeding," clearly indicating his condescending attitude towards her.

It is an attitude shared by their son, who when his mother changes her mind about catching a fly, responds, "You know how women are." Helene is never given credit for having any strength, passion, or decision-making ability. Accused of killing her husband at the outset, a doctor insists, "Helene Delambre could never kill her husband. It is impossible, unless she is and was insane." From the male point of view in the film, female involvement is unthinkable.

Neumann uses André's misfortune as a kind of metaphor for an inappropriate joining or marriage and for masculinity gone wrong. Once Andre is linked to the fly rather than his wife, he quickly becomes socially dysfunctional. He loses the power of speech, he cannot eat with any grace or manners (demonstrated as he grunts and tears at a steak dinner laid out on fine china), and he has difficulty in restraining himself from attacking his wife. (Neumann's widescreen, multi-faceted fly's point of view shot of Helene screaming is one of the most inventive and memorable images in the film.)

André's once unquestioned authority as head of the household is now completely undermined. His rigidly stratified world has its order threatened just as the fly's black limbs threaten to overcome André's white one. (This dichotomy of black and white is presaged in the film when a black tomcat invades the Delambre's manufacturing plant in search of the fluffy white female cat owned by the family.)

Instead of exchanging vows that tie him to another, André, by his matter transmission experiments, has exchanged his head and arm for that of a fly. While Helene can forgive André's neglect of her, André cannot live without the mutated fly that has his head and arm, and its loss leads to his inevitable demise at the hands of his understanding spouse who crushes the signifiers of his unfitness (his symbolically phallic appendages) in a hydraulic press.

The disorder this feminine force causes is restored when Inspector Charas (Herbert Marshall) crushes the mutated fly (pitifully screaming, "Help me!" in a high voice) and the spider who is about to devour it while François (Price), André's brother who secretly loves Helene, shows no remorse at André's death and will now assume his place in business and in the household, stands idly by. François points out that Charas' actions make him as much a murderer as Helene, and fearing accusations of murder and insanity, the two men calmly converse as though nothing out of the ordinary has taken place, agreeing that André must have committed suicide with the hydraulic press, an assertion that cannot stand up under scrutiny (as Helene lowered the press twice). However, such a posture of denial does seem appropriate for the fifties when denial was a part of American life as the racial and economic inequality that were routinely ignored.

Ben Nye's makeup for the enlarged fly head is impressive and greatly aids the shock of the unveiling scene. Nye made plaster casts of Hedison's face and sculpted a mask from latex sponge. To create the multifaceted eyes, Nye applied 14mm pearl beads to convex wire sockets. For the fly's proboscis, Nye used a rubber tube held tightly in Hedison's mouth with a sucker tip applied to the end. Turkey feathers and green, blue, and black metallic paint were added to give a multicolored, prismatic sheen to the final result. Cinematographer Karl Struss' use of a prism lens to create multiple images representing the fly's point of view helped to complete the film's most memorable moment.

The Fly was made for approximately $450,000. To save expenses, much of the equipment used in the film was purchased at a fraction of its actual cost from postwar army and air force surplus. Neumann was concerned that the production have the appearance of authenticity and justified the expense. He felt that "the things we do must *seem* possible. Thus it is possible to give reality to the most unscientific idea, if your setting and machinery has the texture, if not the actuality, of scientific equipment...."

In Lucy Chase Williams' *The Films of Vincent Price*, she quotes Price's amusing comments on one of the film's most notorious scenes:

> I turned to the detective and said, "There, there you see, I told you." So we go out into the garden and sure enough, there's a great big spider web, And in one corner is a great big spider going chompety chompety chomp. And down here is my nephew [sic] who is a fly with a human head, and the little fly is saying, "Help me...help me..." Now Herbert Marshall, the detective, one of the great actors, and I had to play a very serious scene in front of this little tableau. Well, we'd start the scene and Marshall would say, "Ah, monsieur, I see what you mean, I have doubted you all along..." and he'd start to giggle. And the little voice would say, "Help meee, help meeee." I'd say, "Don't worry, Bart [Marshall's nickname], I've been chasing that damn fly all through the picture." I'd say, "There, Inspector, you see — I've been telling you that my nephew is..." and I'd start to giggle. Little voice says, "Help meee, help meeee." Finally, Herbert Marshall says, "Help you! To hell with you! Help us!"

The Fly shocked 20th Century–Fox by becoming a huge hit, and went on to gross over $3 million, becoming one of the studio's most successful films of that year. Buddy Adler, 20th Century–Fox production chief, quickly demanded a follow-up. The picture spawned two sequels, Ed Bernds' *The Return of the Fly*, also with Vincent Price, and *Curse of the Fly*. It was also the final film that Neumann made in association with 20th Century–Fox.

Neumann soon left the studio to work on his last few films, the German–made *Circus of Love*, a pair of films shot in Puerto Rico —*Machete* (Puerto Rican plantation owner begins to suspect that his wife is being unfaithful), and *Counterplot* (with Forrest Tucker hiding from the police in Puerto Rico until he discovers that the man he slugged in New York was actually murdered by his business partner), and *Watusi*, which was basically fabricated by MGM to make use of leftover footage from *King Solomon's Mines*. Future best-seller James Clavell scripted from H. Rider Haggard's sequel which has George Montgomery and Taina Elg going from hatred to love in the time-honored Hollywood tradition. (The studio practically remade the film a few years later as *Drums of Africa*.)

Sadly, Neumann's last few efforts were simply cobbled together after his demise. However, there was no diminishing his impact on visual science fiction nor his importance as a seminal science fiction film director. His adventurous movies showed us that there was always the possibility of danger and excitement on the frontiers of science.

LEONARD NIMOY (1931–)

Star Trek III: The Search for Spock (1984); *Star Trek IV: The Voyage Home* (1986); *Three Men and a Baby* (1987); *The Good Mother* (1988); *Body Wars* (1989); *Funny About Love* (1990); *Holy Matrimony* (1995)

Television: "Death on a Barge," *Night Gallery* (1972); "The Triangle," *The Powers of Matthew Star* (1982); *T. J. Hooker* (1982); *Deadly Games* pilot (1995)

Actor–*Star Trek* icon turned director Leonard Nimoy was born in the tenements of Boston, Massachusetts on March 26, 1931. He was a quiet eight year old who liked to play ball and participate in science projects at the Elizabeth Peabody House, a youth community center founded in the late 1890s by a wealthy woman who wanted to help immigrant children in the Jewish, Italian, and Irish neighborhoods of Boston.

"I was walking down the hallway one day and one of the women told me to go into a classroom," Nimoy recalled. "There was a woman sitting there and she asked me, 'Can you sing?' I hadn't really thought about singing before, but she asked me to sing something like 'God Bless America,' so I did. That's how I became Hansel in the Peabody House's production of *Hansel and Gretel*. That was how I first made it to the stage."

When he grew up, Nimoy attended Boston and Antioch Colleges, all the while honing his craft in local community theater. While serving in the Army, where he was in the special services unit in charge of developing talent for the shows to entertain the troops, he acted in Atlanta's community theaters, and after he got out of the service, he further honed his acting craft working at the Pasadena Playhouse for six months.

When he was 17, Nimoy was cast as Ralphie in Clifford Odets' play *Awake and Sing*, which deals with the struggles of a matriarchal Jewish family during the Depression, a background the Jewish Nimoy knew well, and as a consequence the experience decided him on an acting career. "I realized that I had to do this work. It lit a passion in me that exists to this day. I never wanted to do anything else," he admitted. He became a devotee of Stanislavski, particularly the concepts expressed in *Building a Character*.

"The stage is an exploration of the psychological, emotional, and physical territories of life that can't be done anywhere else," the actor said. "That's why people go to plays. And that's why I got involved with acting in the first place."

To make ends meet when he first came to Hollywood, Nimoy worked in an ice cream parlor on the Sunset Strip. He took Brando for a model and gadded about in jeans and a T-shirt.

In 1951, Nimoy was cast in his first major role, the title role of *Kid Monk Baroni*, after being in Hollywood for only a year. The film told the story of a deformed Italian boy from New York's East Side who grew up to become a boxer. It was to be the first of a long line of alienated characters that Nimoy was to play. The same year he appeared in *Rhubarb*, starring Ray Milland and Jan Sterling.

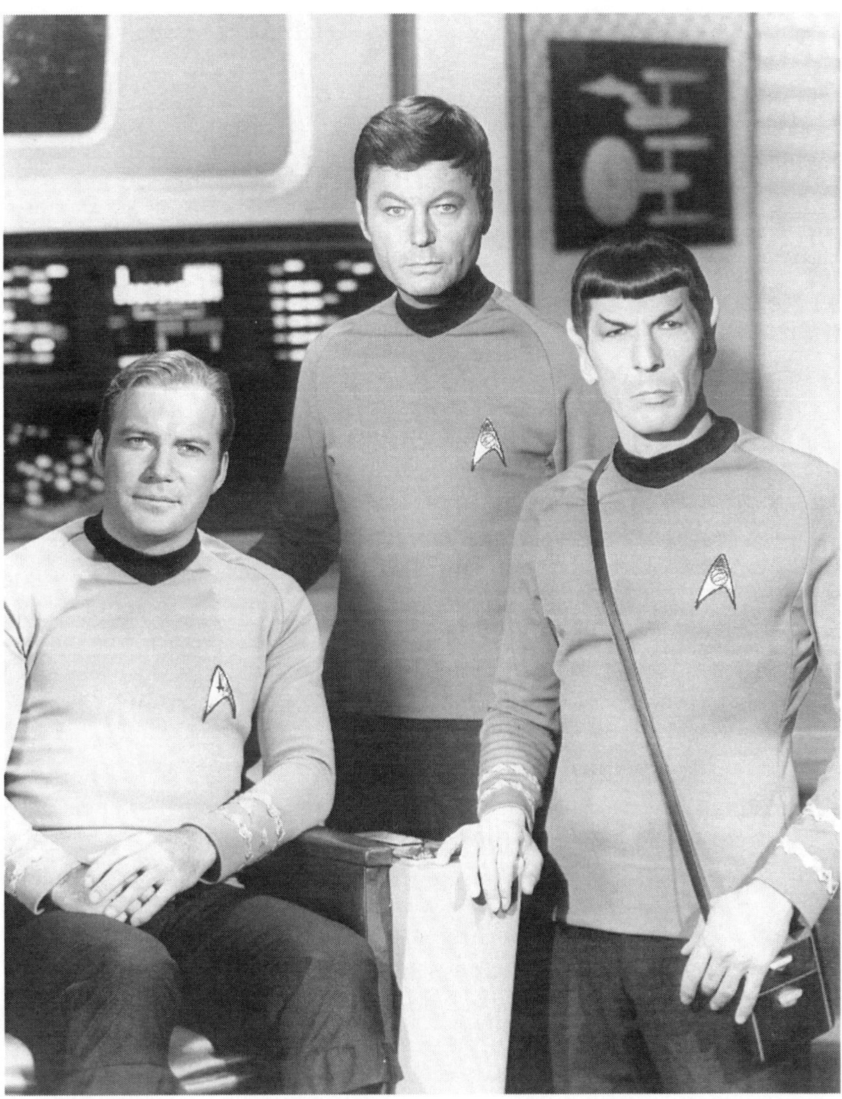

Leonard Nimoy (right) while portraying Spock on the original *Star Trek* series with his costars William Shatner and DeForest Kelley as Captain Kirk and Dr. McCoy.

His next role marked his first foray into science fiction, playing one of the aliens in the serial *Zombies of the Stratosphere*, which was re-released in a feature version in 1958 as *Satan's Satellites*. His only other significant science fiction film role prior to *Star Trek* was playing the lead alien intelligence in Bruno V. DeSota's *The Brain Eaters*, an ultra low budget rip-off of Robert Heinlein's novel *The Puppet Masters* which actually manages to misspell Nimoy's name in the credits. He also appeared briefly as a soldier who disbelieves reports of giant ants in Gordon Douglas' classic *Them!*

Nimoy married actress Sandi Zober in 1954 shortly before beginning a tour of Army duty at Fort McPherson, Georgia, with the Special Services Detachment where he put together shows for G.I.s, which he emceed, wrote, and narrated. He also worked with the Atlanta Theater Guild, directing and starring in *A Streetcar Named Desire*.

Following his army tour, he began to make inroads into becoming a regular television actor, appearing in such series as *West Point, The Roughriders*, and *M Squad*. He also opened his own drama studio, taught acting at Synanon, and raised a family. His daughter, Julie, was born on March 21, 1955, with his son, Adam, now a director, born the following year on August 9, 1956.

By the early sixties, Nimoy was a well known stage actor on the West Coast and was instrumental in bringing the work of Genet to America. He had few movie assignments, such as *The Balcony* and *Deathwatch*, but worked regularly on television, and eventually joined the cast of *Star Trek*.

Nimoy was to have appeared in John Frankenheimer's science fiction classic *Seconds*, but his part was trimmed before the film's release. Originally, he was to have played the husband of the Rock Hudson character's daughter in one of the scenes that was to have emphasized the character's loss of connection with his family. Frankenheimer subsequently regretted the cut and requested that if it can be found, the scene be restored to the laserdisc release. Unfortunately, no one was able to find the lost footage.

Nimoy's most important role was that of Mr. Spock, the half–Vulcan, half-human alien hybrid on *Star Trek*, that has proven to be one of the most popular alien characters of all time. Vulcans are portrayed as a race once ravaged by wars who decided to repress their emotions and devote themselves totally to logic. (Some people make the mistake of assuming that Vulcans have no emotions, but nothing is further from the truth. They are simply stoics who refused to be ruled by their emotions and consider emotional displays to be bad form or bad manners.) Because of his contact with humans and his human half, Spock continually must confront his emotional side, sometimes accepting or rejecting it.

Viewers in the sixties admired Spock's coolness, his intelligence, and his ability to be supremely capable at whatever task he undertook. Gene Roddenberry, the creator of *Star Trek*, insisted on Spock's presence over the network's objections (they were concerned about his "satanic" appearance) because Spock as an alien is a continual visual reminder that this is a science fiction show. The character took the public by storm, almost overshadowing William Shatner's Captain Kirk, the ostensible star of the show.

Recalls Nimoy,

> The first time I heard about *Star Trek* was in 1964. Gene Roddenberry was producing a television series called *The Lieutenant*. It starred Gary Lockwood as a marine corps officer and I was hired to do a guest-starring role. I was playing a flamboyant Hollywood actor who wanted to do a movie about the marine corps. When the job was finished, Gene called my agent, my agent called me, and they asked for a meeting. I went in to see Gene at what was then Desilu Studios, and he told me that he was preparing a pilot for a science fiction series to be called *Star Trek*, that he had in mind for me to play an alien character. As the talk continued, Gene showed me around the studio, he showed me the sets that were being developed and the wardrobe that had been designed, the prop department, and so forth. I began to realize that he was selling me on the idea of being in this series, unusual for an actor. I figured all I had to do was keep my mouth shut and I might end up with a good job here.
>
> Gene told me that he was determined to have at least one extra-terrestrial prominent on his starship. He'd like to have more, but making human actors into other life forms was too expensive for television in those days. Pointed ears, skin color, plus some changes in eyebrows and hair style were all he felt he could afford, but he was certain that his Mr. Spock idea, properly handled and properly acted, could establish that we were in the 23rd century and that interplanetary travel was an established fact.

Nimoy appeared as the character, still in rough form, in the first pilot which starred Jeffrey Hunter as Captain Christopher Pike. NBC rejected the pilot as "too cerebral," and asked to see something more action/adventure oriented, so a second pilot was ordered. When Hunter's girlfriend began making too many demands, Hunter was replaced with Canadian actor William Shatner, who had a broader acting style and took over as Captain James Kirk. The network insisted that Roddenberry dump his mistress, Majel Barrett, from the show, so Spock was promoted to second-in-command and given her character's unemotional qualities.

The show developed a chemistry around the three main characters of Kirk, Spock, and Dr. McCoy (DeForest Kelley). Kirk is the man of action who must make the right decision. Spock argues the thinking side of a problem, what would be the rational approach. Dr. McCoy argues the emotional side of the same problem, how should he feel about it. Because of their opposite natures, Spock and McCoy would indulge in affectionate verbal sparring.

Nimoy himself came up with the concept of the Vulcan Nerve Pinch when Richard Matheson's script for "The Enemy Within" called for him to knock out an evil doppelgänger of Kirk with the butt of his phaser. Nimoy felt that there ought to be a more sophisticated way of rendering a person unconscious, and told the director so.

"He said, 'Well, what do you have in mind?'" Nimoy recalled. "I said, 'Well, Mr. Spock had gone to the Vulcan Institute of Technology and he's studied the human anatomy very carefully; also, Vulcans have the ability to project a certain kind of special energy from their fingertips, which, if it is properly applied to certain pressure points on the human neck and shoulder, the human will be rendered unconscious.'

"He said, 'Let's try it.' I discussed it with Bill Shatner, and he knew exactly what I had in mind, and when I came up behind Bill and put my hand on his neck and shoulder, he really sold it. It was his reaction that really makes you believe that it really works."

Nimoy also created the Vulcan hand salute from covertly watching the kohanim during a Jewish religious ceremony, where the priests bow their heads and their hands form *shin*, the first Hebrew letter of *Shaddai*, which means the Almighty.

However, once Gene Roddenberry left in all but name during the show's third season, Nimoy became increasingly frustrated with the new producers who, he felt, did not really understand the show or its character dynamics. Moved to a late night Friday slot when much of the youthful audience for the show was out on dates, the already low ratings slipped even further and by the end of the year *Star Trek* was canceled.

Following *Star Trek's* cancellation, Nimoy took on the role of Paris, master of disguise, for two years for the old *Mission: Impossible* series, replacing Martin Landau's Roland Hand. (Ironically, Landau was one of the few actors considered for the role of Mr. Spock prior to Nimoy's commitment.) He also appeared in *Stranded*, playing Spence Atherton, a Miami lawyer who survives a plane crash in the Andes Mountains along with several others in an unsuccessful pilot that was later expanded and released theatrically as *Valley of Mystery*.

While Nimoy made a few more motion picture appearances (e.g. *Catlow*, an offbeat western with Yul Brynner) and television appearances (e.g. the semi-science-fictional pilot *Baffled*, in which he played Tom Kovack, a race car driver who develops psychic abilities after a crash who is called upon to assist police and government investigations), he concentrated his time and energy on the theater. He appeared in productions of *Fiddler on the Roof*, *The Man in the Glass Booth* at the Old Globe Theater in San Diego, *Oliver!* at the Melody Top Theater in Milwaukee, *Six Rms Riv Vu* with Sandy Dennis in Florida, *Full Circle* with Bibi Anderson in Washington, D.C., and later on Broadway in both *Full Circle* and *Equus*. He also created a one man show, *Vincent*, based on the life of Vincent Van Gogh in which he played Van Gogh's brother Theo, which he toured with, and played the title role in the Royal Shakespeare Company's *Sherlock Holmes*.

Nimoy published several collections of bad poetry and amateur photography in the 1970s including *You and I*, *Will I Think of You*, *These Words Are for You*, and *We Are All Children Searching for Love*, all of which sold respectably well despite their vapid content. He also made some rather embarrassingly bad recordings as a vocal artist for Coral Records, tying in with his Mr. Spock celebrity.

From 1976 to 1982, Nimoy hosted the pseudo-documentary series *In Search Of*... which gave credence to various examples of pseudo-science. Rational explanations for various mysterious phenomena were often rejected or overlooked in favor of more outrageous or sensational explanations. Whatever Spock's reputation for logic was, Nimoy's hosting duties never evoked Spock's logical spirit but instead pandered to audience's expectations. His finest hour on television came playing opposite Ingrid Bergman in *A Woman Called Golda*, a part which he initially turned down but then accepted at Harve Bennett's insistence and won an Emmy nomination in the process.

Finally, Nimoy settled his long-time dispute with Paramount over the studio's profiting from his likeness as Spock without compensating Nimoy, and Nimoy agreed to appear in *Star Trek — The Motion Picture*, directed by Robert Wise. The plot had to do with one of the *Voyager* probes encountering an alien device designed to gather data and becoming altered into V'Ger, a giant cloud-like device that gathers data and destroys everything in its path which is on an intercept course with Earth. The *Enterprise* crew is recalled to meet the threat.

Nimoy's Spock role was conceived to show a marked change in the character. Having striven for a Vulcan concept of purification in which Spock would give himself totally over to logical thought and banish his emotions and feelings (known on Vulcan as the test of *Kolinahr*), Spock remains stoically distant from his family of friends aboard the *Enterprise* throughout the film. This was meant to create an atmosphere of tension, formality, and uneasiness, but it has no meaning to those unfamiliar with the character chemistry on the TV series while it was merely frustrating for those who were.

Star Trek fans were glad to see any new adventures after so many years of the series being off the screen and the $40 million production did manage to make money despite not pleasing too many people. Much of the budget went to costly overtime needed to prepare the film's effects by its preordained release date. After spending $5 million, the original effects providers had spent most of the money updating their equipment rather than creating viable footage, causing them to be replaced with Douglas Trumbull and John Dykstra, then the two biggest names in the effects business, who worked around the clock to provide the spectacle expected. Sadly, this delay did not leave much time for editing the film properly, and portions of this cinematic behemoth became rather lumbering and unwieldy, though composer Jerry Goldsmith came through with a first-rate score, with his title theme later becoming the theme for *Star Trek — The Next Generation*.

One time when I spoke to Nimoy, he reported:

> There were many days when we [the cast] felt frustrated with what we were being given to do as actors and how the characters were being handled. Most of the time, we stood around on the bridge of the *Enterprise* saying, "What is it?" Then somebody would say, "I'm not sure." Then ten minutes later, we would say, "What's it gonna do next?" "I don't know. We'll have to wait and see." You know what I'm talking about.
>
> So I came in a number of times with suggestions of little pieces of material that I gave to Bob Wise, and he said, "OK, let's shoot it." And these were character touches that I felt would help audiences to have some empathy with this feature story. Thus Spock would be experiencing something as a result of V'Ger that the audience could relate

> to, and by understanding true Spock, maybe get some emotional feelings about V'Ger.
>
> We shot a lot of stuff that was cut out of the movie that was later put back in when we needed a longer version for television. I have seen in print and have gotten a lot of letters that tell me that people felt they could relate to the picture better as a result of that material.

Although not all the effects were completed on the newly incorporated footage, it proved popular with the core *Star Trek* audience and the expanded edition was later released on videotape and laserdisc. The main difference is that Spock experiences an emotional moment in the film, crying because he feels empathy for V'Ger, realizing that the entity has made the same mistake that he did in rejecting emotions in favor of pure logic. Spock comes to understand the emptiness that accompanies a complete lack of feelings or emotional attachments.

Because of this concept, Nimoy had to remain stoic through most of the film, never losing his aloofness until the end, which alienated fans from the character. The additional scenes helped to leaven this problem, but nevertheless, when it came time to remaster widescreen copies of *Star Trek—The Motion Picture*, director Wise asked that the additional material not be incorporated, preferring to keep the movie as it had been presented theatrically.

The huge additional expenditures reduced the profitability of the first *Star Trek* feature significantly. It was decided to make the sequel as economically as possible, with the reins in the hands of Paramount's television division rather than its feature division. Nimoy expressed to me the opinion that the filmmakers Bennett and Meyer "went a long way towards putting *Star Trek* back to its natural track." (For the full story on the sequel, *Star Trek: The Wrath of Khan*, see the chapter on Nicholas Meyer.)

With *Star Trek: The Wrath of Khan* pulling in the biggest opening weekend gross of any movie up to that time, Paramount was intensely interested in beginning work on a sequel. Nimoy met with studio executive Gary Nardino. Nimoy, having a longer and more intimate experience with *Star Trek* than the previous two directors and having wanted to direct an episode as far back as the original TV series, proposed that he be allowed to direct the next film. Nardino was receptive to the idea.

Nardino arranged for a meeting with studio head Michael Eisner, who proved terribly enthusiastic about the idea initially and even suggested that Nimoy write it. Nimoy demurred, preferring to leave the writing chores in the hands of producer Harve Bennett, who had already expressed interest to Nimoy in doing that job, despite Bennett's not having scripted an original in many years. However, Eisner began to have doubts when reminded of rumors that Nimoy hated *Star Trek*, or at least the character of Spock. Nimoy denied the allegations, including rumors that he had insisted that Spock be killed and had that incorporated into his contract (Nimoy offered to let Eisner check the contract himself), and Nimoy was accepted as director after another meeting.

Nimoy told the author, "My feeling was that Nick Meyer was still essentially an outsider who was trying to find out how to use all of these elements that have been laying there cooking for 18 years, and I said, 'I think I can do the job. I think I can do as well if not better.' I have some inside information on the characters that neither of them [Wise nor Meyer] had, so I went for the brass ring and finally they said, 'OK, let's do it.'"

He and Bennett began to collaborate on ideas for the script. At the last moment during *The Wrath of Khan*, Bennett had added a sequence where Spock melds with McCoy and mutters, "Remember," which was intended to leave an opening, though Bennett had no idea how he would employ that device at the time. (It is remarkably similar to the ending of Spielberg's *E.T.*) It was decided that the climax of the new film should be the full resurrection of Spock, though Bennett did script an earlier treatment where a feral Spock harrasses some Romulans who have secretly landed on the Genesis planet.

In one early draft of Bennett's the *Enterprise* crew would land on Vulcan and be attacked by the Vulcans there, angry at being in the hands of "the intellectually inferior Federation," a display of emotion that would be highly out of character with the rest of the series. Other races seem to be fully informed about the "secret" Genesis project and begin demanding parity. Meanwhile, Romulans are busily mining the Genesis planet for the dilithium crystals, needed to power spaceships through the stars, that they find there in abundance. Something or someone is mysteriously killing off the Romulan sentries one by one, and it turns out to be a bearded, amnesiac Spock, who gets captured along with the rest of the *Enterprise* party once they arrive and eventually he regains his memory.

While some elements of this early draft remained in the final script, including the destruction of the *Enterprise*, Nimoy felt that Klingons would make better heavies, and the story was extensively revised. Along the way, the rampaging Vulcan idea was thrown out as Spock goes through a literal re-birth including re-experiencing adolescence in a drastically sped up manner, thereby reducing Nimoy's participation as an actor still further.

It was also decided to bring back the characters of Kirk's son, David (Merritt Buttrick) and Lt. Saavik; however, Kirstie Alley's agent insisted on a salary as large as that being paid to DeForest Kelley. *Star Trek III: The Search for Spock* was to be made on a limited budget of about $16 million, and neither Nimoy nor Bennett would agree to the increased salary demands, so Nimoy recast the role with Robin Curtis. Carol Marcus was eliminated early on because she would interfere with the storyline about David cheating by using protomatter.

To play the villain, Klingon Commander Kruge, Nimoy wanted Jurgen Prochnow or Edward James Olmos, but Prochnow wanted too much money and Bennett felt that Olmos' height was not imposing enough. They settled on Christopher Lloyd, who plays the role with a silly, lip-smacking villainy that is more comic than threatening. (The problem was exacerbated by giving him a puppety, vicious Klingon dog which accompanies him on his ship's bridge.) Future TV star and comic John Larroquette was given the smaller Klingon role of Maltz.

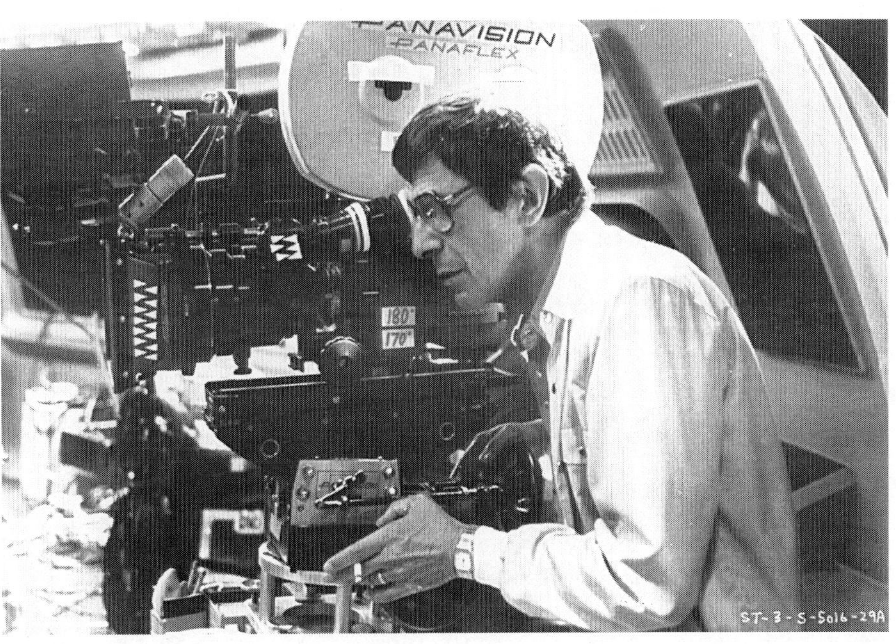

Nimoy spent most of *Star Trek III: The Search for Spock* behind the camera (photo by John Shannon).

To play the Vulcan matriarch T'Lar, Nimoy wanted to go with someone with real stature and regal bearing. He quickly settled on Dame Judith Anderson, whose *Star Trek* fan nephew threatened to disown her if she turned down the role.

Nimoy has commented about making a science fiction film, saying, "It's a very complicated artform, probably the most complex there is. The more difficult it gets, the more challenging it gets, I come to realize there is only one way to do it, and that is to surround yourself with some extremely talented people. If you get the right people, it all comes out just fine."

In his *I Am Spock* book, Nimoy notes, "[T]he director is the one responsible for seeing that the actor's performance hits the mark. I had to keep my eyes open for an enormous number of details — and, for that reason, I was (and still am) grateful when people brought my attention to problems. For the same reason, I also tried to maintain an atmosphere of collaboration on the set, so that people weren't afraid to speak openly about problems or ideas."

Nimoy was very careful that each member of the cast be given his or her own special moment in which to shine. He wanted the story to focus in on the themes of sacrifice and rebirth. As Spock was a character who had risked his life to save his crewmates dozens of times, the crew are made to risk their careers in order to restore Spock back to life, so asserting the converse of the previous picture, that sometimes the needs of the one outweigh the needs of the many.

While Bennett was the principal writer, Nimoy had quite a bit of input. He found Nimoy very contained, indicating when something was promising. "He challenged me," recalled Bennett, "and when I couldn't get what he was trying to say, he'd say, 'Let me write a draft.' And he's a good writer. There are pounds of stuff in the screenplay that are pure Leonard. Great relationship. Very beneficial."

Principal photography began on August 15, 1983, and the film was designed to be shot entirely on Paramount's sound stages, with the sets designed by Jack Chilberg. Nimoy handpicked an experienced production crew that included cinematographer Charles Corell and sound mixer Gene Canamesa. The production was developed through the television division at Paramount under the supervision of executive producer Gary Nardino and producer Harve Bennett in order to keep costs down. It finished exactly on time at the end of its 49 day shooting schedule.

Bennett devised the notion that Spock implanted his soul, or *katra*, into McCoy's consciousness just before dying, and Spock's father Sarek (Mark Lenard) is upset that Spock's body and *katra* have not been taken back to Vulcan for a mysterious religious rite. (Nimoy does make one misstep in this scene by using an extreme closeup of Sarek's lips that on the widescreen in the cinema is overwhelming and distracting, unlike a similar shot in Orson Welles' *Citizen Kane*.)

Kirk's commitment to his Vulcan friend is evident when he reports to Sulu, "The word is no. I am therefore going anyway!" McCoy, who becomes highly agitated with Spock's *katra* implanted in him, when learning the cause, responds in character, "That green-blooded son of a bitch! It's his revenge for all those arguments he lost!"

At an early meeting Shatner called a meeting with

Nimoy directs Christopher Lloyd as the Klingon Kruge in *Star Trek III.*

Bennett and Nimoy and complained that there was not enough of him in the material. He was concerned that it might be seen that he was standing by instead of leading the others. Sensitive to his status as the star of *Star Trek*, and wanting his character to come off as important and likable, the filmmakers agreed to many of Shatner's suggestions. However, Shatner wanted to be in on everything, including McCoy's moment alone with Spock and when Bones meets the Vulcan priestess, and his ego had to be reined in. (It is notable that at the end of the film when the other cast members are gathered around revived Spock, Shatner is off by himself standing in his key light, more intent on looking good than being part of the moment.)

George Takei objected to having his character Sulu called Tiny by a large and officious guard, feeling it would demean the character, so Nimoy agreed to film his scene both with and without the "Tiny" reference, and Takei trusted Nimoy to use the best version. Takei later saw that audiences cheered when Sulu overcomes the obnoxious and insulting stooge and asserts himself by declaring, "Don't call me Tiny!"

Nimoy's direction of *The Search for Spock* is good, but not inspired. He gets good, restrained performances throughout, but sometimes his camera sense fails him. In one scene with Kirk and Sarek, Nimoy starts cutting between extreme close-ups of their eyes and noses. These shots undermine the actors' performances and do not utilize the widescreen well. However, in other scenes, Nimoy is able to give dramatic impetus by using subtle camera movements, and he proves himself apt at suspense techniques and keeps the story moving at a good clip.

One thing that Nimoy's direction can't hide is some of the budget limitations that must have been imposed on this film. While some of ILM's visual effects are spectacular, many of the film's practical effects (fire, explosions, things falling, etc.) have a very unconvincing look to them. Even worse, the sets on the Genesis Planet consistently look like sets—with phony backdrops and foliage quite in evidence.

One of the story points of the film is that the hastily made Genesis Planet, which the film hints was constructed out of a dead moon, is unstable. To demonstrate this fact, the science ship *Grissom*'s sensors detect that widely differing ecological climates are within short distances of each other. For example, a rainforest is located next to a sandy, cactus-filled desert, which is next to a snowy arctic plain. One would expect that such climates would affect each other and reach some kind of equilibrium, and besides, the scenes of snow-covered cacti are simply unconvincing.

Additionally, the scenes where the Genesis Planet is undergoing geological upheavals are also marred by a sense of unreality. The trees fall over neatly with every root still intact, as if they were made out of concrete. Boulders seem to pop up out of the ground for very little reason, except that the Genesis Planet is rapidly aging due to a flaw in the process. (Do aging planets erupt with boulders the way teenagers erupt with acne?) Huge land masses fall away to reveal running lava flows far below, which would be quite spectacular if only the whole thing did not look like a low-budget TV show set.

Tom Burman's makeup is equally slipshod. His lizard-dog pet for Captain Kruge is ill-conceived from the get-go. It looks just like what it is, a puppet, and there is no excuse for it to be running loose on a Klingon bridge. Another embarrassment is the large-eared barroom alien (Alan Miller) that McCoy tries to hire a ship from. His stretched out ears look silly, especially with bits of feather spirit-gummed to them, and his dark lipstick comes to an obvious halt whenever the character opens his lips, revealing that the coloring is not natural.

The film was restructured in the editing, so that the "gathering of the samurai" to steal the *Enterprise* was no longer spread throughout the first third of the film. Nimoy discovered that the fun dissipated whenever he cut away from one of these sequences, so he arranged to place most of them together, allowing the film to build for momentum.

Producer Harve Bennett's script takes religious turns at odd moments, as when McCoy introduces himself to the Vulcan matriarch as "Leonard, son of David." There are already Christ parallels with Spock being resurrected and Kruge being hurled into a fiery pit. Nevertheless, the main values it espouses, of honor, friendship, and decency, are core *Star Trek* beliefs that reflect the idealism of the popu-

Nimoy (behind camera) lines up the scene where Sulu (George Takei) teaches an obnoxious guard not to call him "Tiny."

lar series. It poses, in Nimoy's words, the questions: "What should a person do to help a friend? How deeply should a friendship commitment go? What price should people be willing to pay? And what sacrifices, what obstacles will these people endure?"

Nimoy made regular host appearances on the Nickelodeon show *Lights! Cameras! Action!* which was an hourly program showcasing various aspects of movie-making. It allowed Nimoy to get away from the austere, reserved, severe personality that people associated with him and to do interviews with the movie people who were brought on the show.

In 1985, Nimoy received a star on the Hollywood Walk of Fame. He was feted for taking time out of his busy schedule and for supporting many charities, including the March of Dimes, the Variety Club, United Cerebral Palsy, and the Boston's Children's Hospital. His philanthropic efforts also included the Venic Family Clinic where he and his wife Sandi have received humanitarian awards from various religious organizations for their commitments, and Nimoy went to Vancouver several times to host an annual telethon for retarded children, as well as founding the Adam Nimoy Foundation in Boston for cystic fybrosis.

"*Star Trek III* was sizable in its passion," commented Nimoy. "It was operatic, and I was pleased by that, because I really thought about it in terms of being grand in passion, grand in size, smoke and fire, with a planet disintegrating. Big stuff.

"[For] *Star Trek IV*, we decided it was time to really lighten up and have a good time, kick up our heels and do a caper, get down literally with our feet on the ground of the streets of San Francisco, playing scenes where these guys from another world, another time are literally having a tough time figuring how to get across the street."

Even before *Star Trek III* was released, Jeffrey Katzenberg offered Nimoy the opportunity to direct *Star Trek IV*, telling him, "We want you to make another one for us. This time, the training wheels are off! Give us your vision of *Star Trek*!"

After Khan and Kruge, Nimoy wanted to get away from having a villain in the next adventure. He wanted a *Star Trek* where no one was hurt or killed. Katzenberg also informed Nimoy that Paramount star Eddie Murphy, then at the pinnacle of his career, indicated that he would kill to get into a *Star Trek* movie. Nimoy felt that his part would either have to be terrific or non-existent, otherwise both franchises might be hurt. Murphy agreed to wait and judge the quality of the script.

For *Star Trek IV: The Voyage Home*, Nimoy assumed a more relaxed approach as Spock and Kirk (Shatner, left) search modern-day San Francisco for the answer to a future predicament. The film's gentle humor won it a large cross-over mainstream audience as well.

Meanwhile, Harve Bennett noticed that the most popular episode of the original series, "City on the Edge of Forever," involved time travel and suggested they do a time travel story, taking the *Star Trek* characters into contemporary San Francisco. Nimoy had read *Bophilia* by Harvard biologist Edmund Wilson which is concerned with the vast number of species on Earth that are becoming extinct, warning that a key species could become extinct and the ecology could collapse like a house of cards.

Nimoy toyed with the idea that an epidemic struck in the 23rd century that could only be cured through an extinct species that died along with the rainforests, but rejected the notion as too grim and not too thrilling. Later his friend Ray Danchik brought up the humpback whale, whose whalesong remains something of a mystery. Nimoy decided that the crew would need humpback whales to solve the film's problem.

He approached Bennett with the idea, and the practical-minded producer noted that humpbacks would not be trainable. It was soon learned that the production would have to create most of the whale footage it needed using special effects. Visual effects supervisor Ken Ralston and art director Nilo Rodis brought in robotics expert Walt Conti to create the whale puppets needed, most of which look very convincing. (Only 10% of the footage of the whales was of actual humpbacks — the rest were all effects of one kind or another.)

Two screenplay writers, Steve Meerson and Peter Krikes, were hired to come up with a storyline that would incorporate Eddie Murphy's talents as one of the characters. They pondered having Murphy be a college professor or a con man, and then settled on him being a "psychic investigator" who hosts a late night radio talk show and who becomes convinced that aliens are walking around on this planet, causing him to chase after Spock and company. After several rewrites, it became apparent that the idea was not going to work out and that a fresh approach was needed.

Nimoy and Bennett then contacted Nicholas Meyer to help them out. While Bennett would write the paramilitary bits centered around Starfleet, Meyer would add humor to the modern, Earthbound scenes. As Meyer told me:

> I got involved in number IV because they had another script they were not happy with. Dawn Steele, who [was] the head of Paramount and has been a friend of mine for many years, called me and said, "Would you do us an enormous favor?" And I said, "For Harve and Leonard? Yeah, absolutely." They had a script written. The script, I guess, was for Eddie Murphy as a guest star. I never read it, so I don't know. But they weren't happy with it. They wanted to go back to their original story and write another script. Harve said, "This is what I want to do. I write the first 20 to 25 percent of it, and when they get to Earth or when they're about to get to Earth, then you take it, finish the Earth stuff, and I'll do the ending." We went over each other's stuff. My contribution begins with Spock's crack about, "Judging by the pollution content of the atmosphere, I believe we have arrived at the late 20th century," and goes from there to someplace after they get the whales and leave. I didn't read the other script because I just thought it would confuse me and since they didn't like it, why bother?

Nevertheless, Meerson and Krikes, who had worked some seven months on various outlines and screenplays, contended that much of the structure of the film came from them, and they later accused Harve Bennett of taking credit for many of their ideas. When they learned that Bennett and Meyer were to be given lead writing credits, they requested a Writers' Guild arbitration, and were given lead, cocredit status.

Production was delayed somewhat due to William Shatner's salary demands. Nimoy had a favored nations clause that would give him a salary equal to Shatner's, so he was content to sit back and let Shatner be the "bad guy" for a change. Consequently, both stars ended up being paid a $2 million salary.

Nimoy wanted to bring back as many members of the

Star Trek family as possible, and so incorporated cameos for Robin Curtis as Saavik, Grace Lee Whitney as Janice Rand, Majel Barrett as Christine Chapel, Jane Wyatt as Spock's mother Amanda, and Mark Lenard as Sarek. (Originally, it was intended that Saavik reveal to Kirk that she was pregnant with Spock's child, but all such references were ultimately cut from the script.)

Nimoy picked Catherine Hicks to play Kirk's new love interest, Gillian Taylor, a cetacean biologist, because he felt she had the right combination of wide-eyed innocence mixed with street smart cynicism to pull the role off. He introduced Hicks to Shatner to ensure that the pair hit it off on screen.

During an amusing sequence where Uhura and Chekov accost passers-by, seeking a naval base and "nuclear wessels," a long-haired, female pedestrian came up and offered the advice, "I think they're across the Bay, in Alameda." She had to be quickly tracked down and offered a contract so that the production could use her spontaneous reaction.

Bennett and Nimoy got into an argument over whether the dialogue between the alien probe and the humpback whales should be translated and subtitled. Nimoy felt it would be stronger if their conversation remained a mystery, noting how *2010* failed because it tried to explain the mystery of *2001*. Bennett strongly disagreed, but Nimoy won out. Tensions grew so much between the director and the producer that it was reported that Bennett was ordered off the set by an increasingly irritated Nimoy.

Once more Nimoy holds up the idea that the good of the one can outweigh the needs of the many as Spock and the crew decided to risk rescuing the critically injured Chekov, held captive in a local hospital.

Meyer disliked the idea of Gillian accompanying the crew back into the future. "In my version of the script," he said, "originally, when they all leave to go back, she didn't leave. She said if anyone's going to make sure this kind of disaster doesn't happen, somebody's going to have to stay behind, which I still think is the 'righter' ending. The end in the movie detracts from the importance of people in the present taking responsibility for the ecology and preventing problems of the future by doing something about them today, rather than catering to the fantasy desires of being able to be transported ahead in time to the near-utopian future society of the *Star Trek* era."

Meyer also felt that the film had too many "endings"; however, Bennett was insistent that not only would the whales save the Earth, but also that the *Enterprise* crew be exonerated and be given a new starship to travel in, to carry on their adventures in further installments.

The first non–*Star Trek* movie Nimoy directed was *Three Men and a Baby*, a remake of Coline Serreau's Cesar–award-winning French comedy *Trois Hommes et un Couffin* (aka *Three Men and a Cradle*). It became an incredible hit, grossing some $165 million in domestic release alone. The original version of the script, Nimoy felt, was far too gallic, with the characters expressing what he felt were French attitudes toward life, work, love, and children. (The film was originally to have been directed by Serreau, who left abruptly. Three other directors, Colin Higgins, Mark Rydell, and Arthur Hiller had already been approached and had passed on the project.)

Nimoy met with the writers Jim Cruickshank and James Orr, who complained that Serreau had been very insistent that they produce an exactly translated copy of her original script. Nimoy agreed to give them the chance to rewrite it along their preferred lines.

However, *Three Men and a Baby* is a comic mess. Peter (Tom Selleck), Jack (Ted Danson), and Michael (Steve Guttenberg) are three swinging Manhattan bachelors who inherit Mary, a little baby girl abandoned on their doorstep by her fly-by-night mother. They are men who have never had to grow up. Peter is an architect, erecting toys, Jack is an actor who indulges in make-believe, and Michael is a comic strip artist, creator of Johnny Cool, the tiger who is "the coolest cat in town." They play at life, are dedicated to a lifestyle of "wine, women, and song," and have never learned responsibility.

Mary's mother is one of Jack's former lovers and leading ladies, about whom he comments, "I was doing *Taming of the Shrew*. She was the shrew." Unfortunately, such mysognistic comments are not uncommon as the movie mires itself in sentimentality while these bachelors learn to love Mary, preferring her company to cocaine and even to romantic relations with grown-up women. When the real mother (Nancy Travis) comes to reclaim Mary, they are devastated.

Fortunately for them, the mother returns shortly complaining in a familiar litany that she can't afford the baby because all her money is going to sitters, and she can't live, work, and take care of the baby all at once. Thus she moves in with the men, forming an extended family of five. (The film creates a fantasy solution to a real life problem, though it might have been more interesting if it had taken this polyandrous solution more seriously.) However, this arrangement relegates the mom to a minor role with the focus remaining on the men who find themselves redeemed by parenthood.

Three Men and a Baby achieved a brief resurgence of notoriety on video when it was claimed that a ghost could be seen in one shot (actually, it was nothing more than a life-sized cut-out of one of the characters that appears in the background of one shot). The insipid film inspired an even worse sequel, *Three Men and a Little Lady*, directed by Emile Adrolino, which was quickly buried at the box office.

Better but nowhere near as successful was Nimoy's next movie, *The Good Mother*, based on the acclaimed book by Sue Miller. For Nimoy, the story was about society's difficulty in accepting sexuality and motherhood in the same person, the old Madonna–whore question, where mothers are madonnas and cannot be perceived as being sexual, so that when a woman who is a great mother is revealed to have had a sexual life, she is punished by society.

Several actresses that Nimoy discussed the main part with could not accept that the story did not end with Anna winning and audiences cheering her on, that the story was more about integrity than success. Diane Keaton saw the integrity of the character and was willing to do it as written. Additionally, several males turned down the role of Cutter because he was perceived as abusing a child by simply allowing her to see him naked in the shower.

Diane Keaton stars as Anna, an uptight New England divorceé who grew up repressed, yearning to be a passionate person. She lives a nun's life, occasionally sipping wine, and devoting herself wholly to her daughter. Anna finally gets her chance when she meets Irish sculptor Leo Cutter (Liam Neeson) in a laundromat, and he seduces her first with his sculpture and then with his kisses.

Anna discovers the joys of sex and is visibly looser, less uptight. Leo is a kind man who makes toys for Molly (Asia Viera) and openly spends the night with Anna. However, her joy is dashed when her ex-husband Brian sees an opportunity to sue for custody of their little girl Molly, forcing Anna to have to prove to the law that she is a "good mother." The case hinges on the fact that Anna allowed Molly to see Leo naked in the shower, and despite the fact that the encounter was innocent, she is forced to sacrifice her happiness, give up her lover and assume the guise of a sexual puritan in order to retain custody.

Nimoy's treatment of the material is sensitive, adult, and not sensationalized. Molly admits that sex with her husband was far from thrilling and that she has doubts about her own ability to enjoy lovemaking. Anna's grandmother actually admits that she woke up every day for ten years hating her own existence. Michael Bortman's script tackles some serious issues not often spoken of, but ultimately lacks the courage to be anything more than a maternal melodrama, the story of a woman deemed unfit for motherhood.

Anna becomes convinced that her quest for selfhood was unworthy, that she somehow failed in her obligations as a mother, even though the film indicates otherwise. She has to convince a judge that she regrets her wanton liaison with Leo, yet as important as Molly is, it seems totally wrong for her to do so. (Neeson is especially sensual and appealing in the part, combining aggressiveness with sensitivity, and is by turns a stranger, a lover, a father, a teacher, a penitent, a spurned companion, and a caring human being. In the process, he comes across as more genuine than Keaton's character.)

As a consequence, the film feels compromised, adopting a conservative agenda that it does not sincerely believe in. What starts out as thrilling ends up in tedium offering little else than blandishments about the sanctity of motherhood.

After the disaster of the Shatner–directed *Star Trek V: The Final Frontier*, Frank Mancuso called Nimoy into his office to discuss reviving the floundering film series. Nimoy concocted a storyline along with Dennis Martin Flinn, Lawrence Konner, and Mark Rosenthal. Rosenthal initially wanted a story that would combine the classic Trek with *Star Trek — The Next Generation*, but the television department at Paramount was totally against the idea. It was then decided to do a Klingon story that would reflect the current state of the Cold War.

As Nimoy told Mark Altman, Ron Magid, and Edward Gross, "The Berlin Wall had come down. The Russian government was in severe distress. Communism was falling apart. These changes were creating a new order in our world. I thought there would be a new kind of dialogue, a new thinking of these relationships.... Realizing that over the 25 year history of *Star Trek*, the Klingons have been the constant foe of the Federation, much like the Russians and Communists were to Democracy, I wondered how we could translate these contemporary world affairs into an adventure with Klingons. I thought it was an ideal way for us to have our closure too, because the Klingons for us have always been the Communist Block, the Evil Empire. It just made sense to do that story."

Nimoy was originally going to be the producer, writer, director and star of the film, but that proved too much. Instead, he simply provided the story and served both as actor and executive producer on *Star Trek VI: The Undiscovered Country*. He recruited Meyer to cowrite and direct the film. For further details, see chapter on Nicholas Meyer.

Nimoy admits that his next directorial effort, *Funny About Love*, suffered from an ambitious but bad script by Norman Steinberg (*My Favorite Year*) and David Frankel (*Miami Rhapsody*) and was a project he was unable to salvage. Inspired by a speech columnist Bob Greene gave to some conventioneers, it follows the joys and travails of an emotionally repressed cartoonist (Gene Wilder) who desperately wants to conceive with his wife (Christine Lahti), and in failing, takes up temporarily with a college sorority sister (Mary Stuart Masterson) who brings him joy but lacks the kind of maturity that causes him to return to his wife.

Unfortunately, his next feature, *Holy Matrimony*, starring Patricia Arquette, is even worse. Arquette stars as

Havana, a woman on the run who hides out in a Hutterite community in Alberta, Canada, where local law forces her to marry her 12-year-old brother-in-law. David Weisberg and Douglas S. Cook's script plays the situation for laughs that simply are not there. Nimoy was attracted to the concept by the idea that the story was about an immature woman who needed to revise her thinking about who she was and what her place in the world was. She has a childish fantasy view about how the world would work for her, and then becomes transformed by her marriage to a wise 12-year-old child, who plays the adult in order for her to learn from him. Nimoy was also fascinated by the Hutterite culture, which forbids their participation in motion pictures.

Nimoy provided voices for such diverse projects as *Transformers—The Movie, The Halloween Tree, The Pagemaster,* and *Invasion Earth.*

Deadly Games was a short-lived television series for which Nimoy directed the pilot, "Killshot." The series starred James Calvert as Gus, who creates a video "virtual reality" game which stars himself as the hero, the Cold Steel Kid, and his ex-wife Lauren (Cynthia Gibb) as the damsel in distress he seeks to rescue. His foe is the sinister Sebastian Jackal (Christopher Lloyd in a white suit) who is aided and abetted by Killshot (Tom Rathman), a jock henchman in a football uniform armed with exploding footballs, who is based on a bully Gus knew while in high school.

An anti-matter experiment causes Sebastian Jackal and Killshot to leave the confines of the video game and come to life, complicating the lives of Gus and Lauren. Since he was programmed to be nasty, Jackal is programmed to "destroy life as we know it, step by step, until every pleasure we hold dear, from going to a ball game to falling in love, is just a memory."

The show's attempts at humor and satire prove feeble, and what little appeal the concept might have quickly wore thin.

Then in 1996, television writer Trish Vradenburg sent Nimoy a copy of her first play, *The Apple Doesn't Fall....* "I laughed and cried when I first read it," Nimoy recalled. "I thought it was very funny and very touching." The sitcomy, semi-autobiographical play had a six week run at the Tiffany Theater in West Hollywood with Nimoy as director before it moved to New York. The production starred Florence Stanley and Margaret Whitton as Selma, a mother and her daughter Kate Griswold whose lives are torn apart when Selma suffers the rapid onset of Alzheimer's disease, but has her mental faculties revived by a magical wonder drug.

The cure proves a mixed blessing. After Selma is brought back, she is confronted by how much her life has changed in the months that she was "away"—finding that her family has fallen apart and her husband has left her for a younger woman. She decides to show up at their wedding and to pursue a writing career that she abandoned in favor of being a wife and mother. There are echoes of *Flowers for Algernon* as she frantically tries to get her words on paper before her former condition overtakes her again.

Nimoy previously directed stage productions in the Los Angeles area of *Camino Real* and *Skylark. The Apple Doesn't Fall...* represents his Broadway premiere as a director. "It's been an interesting process trying to direct this play," Nimoy explained, "because every time an intimate moment arrives, a joke steps in. What we've had to decide is whether a laugh helps us to tell the story or does it injure us. I can't recall that I've ever directed a play that stretches the envelope in both directions this much—where you're on the edge of farce and involved with an intimate study of people's lives at the same time."

Nimoy used improvisation to break down traditional patterns of how a scene might be played. He discussed the backgrounds of the characters with the actors portraying them, striving to give them a deeper sense of reality. He claims to enjoy simply getting back to basics. "When you strip something down to its essence is when you find the magic," he said.

Nimoy has used his association with science fiction to help launch the *Alien Voices* series for National Public Radio. Each episode lasts two hours and adapts a science fiction classic, with the scripts written and produced by Nat Segaloff and costarring John De Lancie (best remembered for his work as Q on *Star Trek—The Next Generation*). Among the stories adapted are H. G. Wells' *The Time Machine,* Wells' *First Men in the Moon,* Wells' *The Invisible Man,* Jules Verne's *Journey to the Center of the Earth,* and A. Conan Doyle's *The Lost World.*

At the end of 1998, New Line Television has signed a development deal with Alien Voices, the production company of Leonard Nimoy and John de Lancie. Voices will develop SF-based TV movies for New Line Television, based on the works of such authors as H. G. Wells and Jules Verne, as well as potential on-going science fiction and fantasy series.

As a film director, Nimoy has eschewed fancy camera tricks and prefers working with the thematic content of his films. To him, subtext is really important, and he works with his performers to get them to think about what each scene is about, what they are trying to accomplish, what do they want and what are they trying to avoid, what the audience can discover. As an actor turned director, he most enjoys working with actors, looking for inspiration in the rehearsal process to help bring a scene to creative life.

However, despite his early cinematic successes, that

Nimoy's last few films flopped at the box office seems to have curtailed further exploration of this aspect of his career. Nevertheless, there is no questioning the lasting legacy spawned from the cool, alien intelligence of his Spock character, nor his capable handling of the *Trek* film series' third and particularly the fourth segments which have entertained and kept alive Roddenberry's vision of a hopeful, successfully integrated future where mankind has left behind old problems and prejudices in order to face new frontiers and new challenges.

ARCH OBOLER (1909–1987)

Strange Holiday; Bewitched (1945); *Arnelo Affair* (1947); *Five* (1951); *Bwana Devil; The Twonky* (1953); *One Plus One* (1961); *The Bubble* (aka *Fantastic Invasion of Planet Earth*) (1967); *The Stewardesses* (1969); *Domo Arigato* (1972)

Arch Oboler will forever be best remembered as the writer-producer and voice of the infamous radio program *Lights Out*, perhaps the scariest thing on the radio in the 1930s and 1940s next to Hitler. Oboler was born in Chicago, Illinois, on December 7, 1909 and began selling his first radio scripts in the 1920s while he was still in high school. As a student at the University of Chicago, he sold for $50 a play called "Futuristics" to NBC, which satirized the mores of 1930s American culture from the perspective of the future. It was broadcast from coast-to-coast in November 1933 to help celebrate the opening of Radio City.

Oboler approached NBC about doing a continuing series focusing on the decline and fall of civilizations and the nature of human conflict, but NBC had no interest in such highbrow stuff. In 1934, Wyllis Cooper, a staff writer at NBC affiliate WENR, created a horror anthology program he called *Lights Out*, which announced, "This is the witching hour. It is the hour when dogs howl, and evil is let loose on a sleeping world. Want to hear about it? Then turn out your lights!" NBC committed themselves to a 15-minute program, which premiered countrywide on NBC's Red Network on April 17, 1935, garnering 50,000 letters of protest in the bargain.

A year later, Cooper left the program and went to Hollywood, and Arch Oboler was selected to replace him. Oboler created the series' more memorable signature opening warning, "It is later than you think" as a gong emphasized each word. (Oboler is often mistakenly credited as the creator of the series, but he was only its most memorable writer-producer.) He began writing for the show with the episode "Burial Service," and most of the show's best remembered episodes were written by him, including "State Executioner," "Visitor from Hades," and "Special to Hollywood." He also dabbled in science fiction on the show, including the anti-war stories "Revolt of the Worms" (a scientist, trying to escape from the horrors of war, tries to create the perfect rose, but his growth hormone creates giant earthworms that destroy him and his lab) and "Rocket from Manhattan," (XR-1, the first rocketship to reach the moon, is returning when an atomic war wipes out the Earth) and the infamous "Chicken Heart" episode (a living chicken heart in a laboratory grows to enormous size and swallows up the world) that Bill Cosby imitated brilliantly on his *Wonderfulness* album. In another well-remembered episode, Oboler played the sound of a man being turned inside out like a glove. Oboler used *Lights Out* to experiment with sound design, creating some of the most chilling sound effects in history. He coined the phrase "Theater of the mind" to explain how listeners' imaginations would make his effects seem real.

After two years, Oboler left the series, which continued on without him. In 1939, CBS hired Oboler to oversee a wide-ranging radio anthology, *Arch Oboler's Plays*, which gave Oboler an opportunity to tackle any kind of theme or device that tickled his fancy. This program was distinguished by its near-poetic prose, politically charged themes, and stream-of-consciousness narratives. Beginning in the 1940s, Oboler began writing screenplays, including those for *Escape* (1940), *Gangway for Tomorrow* (1943), and *On Our Merry Way* (1948). He also penned a blank verse Broadway play, *Night of the Auk*, in 1956. He also revived the *Lights Out* series for the 1942–1943 season, and ran a summer series in 1945 and in 1946 as well.

Oboler's first film, *Strange Holiday*, was borderline science fiction. Made in 1942, it was only intended to boost the morale of employees of General Motors, but was released publicly three years later. An adaptation of one of

Oboler's radio plays, the plot has John Stevenson (Claude Rains), a complacent businessman uninterested in world affairs returning from a lengthy fishing trip only to discover that facists had taken over the United States. He is shocked to find that the Constitution has been overthrown and the population remains apathetic. The film ends with Stephenson behind bars exhorting that America must fight to regain its freedom, followed by a heavyhanded montage of American landscapes while a recording of President Roosevelt reciting the "Four Freedoms" is played.

Rains carries most of the film, though Martin Kosleck is fine as the fascist leader. Gloria Holden plays Stevenson's wife, with Bobbie Stebbens and Paul Hilton playing his children. Oboler sold the talky, preachy film to Metro, who did not know what to do with it. Oboler and Rains bought it back and the film, also known as *The Day After Tomorrow,* was released by Elite Productions in 1945, and then by PRC in 1946 in a shortened version.

Oboler's second film, for MGM, *Bewitched,* based on his radio play "Alter Ego," was a forerunner of subsequent multiple personality films such as *Three Faces of Eve.* It is often considered his best directorial work. Phyllis Thaxter plays the schizophrenic killer, with an uncredited Audrey Totter voicing her alter ego. He followed this with *The Arnelo Affair,* based on a story by Jane Burr, which has Lowell Gilmore, Eve Arden, and Frances Gifford caught up in a murder plot. John Hodiak, George Murphy, Dean Stockwell, Warner Anderson, Rudy Dandridge and Joan Woodbury round out the cast of this little seen and less remembered MGM programmer.

Lights Out meanwhile became one of the earliest television shows in 1949, where it was produced by Fred Coe for NBC until 1950, and then by Herbert Swope, Jr., until its demise in 1952 when it was destroyed in the ratings by the new *I Love Lucy* show. Only a few kinescopes exist of this crudely made television series, and the disembodied head opening appears to have been borrowed from Universal's Inner Sanctum series. The episodes were filmed live using minimal sets, and I have been unable to ascertain whether Oboler tried his hand directing any episodes of the show.

He established himself as a heavy-handed science fiction director with *Five,* one of the earliest 1950s science fiction melodramas, as well as the first in a series of "after the bomb" movies. As *Five* opens, the bomb has exploded and somehow the last few human survivors all seem to flock together at one location, which it turns out is Oboler's Frank Lloyd Wright–designed house. Michael (William Phipps) survived because he was alone in an elevator at the top of the Empire State Building, which somehow must have survived Oboler's atomic armageddon, although no other New Yorkers can be counted to be among the survivors.

The other survivors are Rosanne (Susan Douglas), a pregnant woman from California; Eric (James Anderson), a fascist adventurer who survives because he was on the top of Mount Everest; Charles (Charles Lampkin), a black doorman, and Barnstaple (Earl Lee), a bank clerk. Barnstaple becomes somewhat delirious from radiation poisoning, begins to believe he's simply on vacation, and dies shortly afterwards.

The men develop an interest in the last woman, naturally, but Rosanne is convinced that her husband is still alive until Eric takes her and her newborn baby to a nearby city where she finds hubby's remains. In the meantime, the racist adventurer has also secretly disposed of Charles. However, Eric gets his comeuppance as he prepares to rape Rosanne when he discovers radiation scars on his chest, causing him to run off into oblivion.

Rosanne's newborn dies on the trip back, and the film ends with Michael and Rosanne as a new Adam and Eve whose destiny is to repopulate the planet. *Five* was the forerunner of such future atomic annihilation movies as *On the Beach, The World, Flesh and the Devil* and *The Last Woman on Earth.* It did not do well on initial release until Sid Pink (then head of booking for UA and later producer of several of Ib Melchior's SF movies — see chapter on Melchior) revamped the ad campaign, which initially featured four men, one noticeably black, chasing an attractive woman against a background of ruined buildings and offered no clue as to what the story was actually about. It was turned into a big success by emphasizing the nuclear angle by including a mushroom cloud and a tagline, "The story of the last five people left on earth after an atom bomb," to the poster coupled with the broadcast of its Hollywood premiere with Bette Davis in attendance on television. This led to a brief partnership with Oboler and the production of *Bwana Devil.*

In recalling the writer-director, producer Sid Pink wrote in Filmfax #26:

> Who was Arch Oboler? To be truthful, I must say I don't know.... He must have had some talent to write the great shows that were credited to him. I worked very closely with him, for the better part of two years, but never did I see the touch of genius in his writing that I expected. Everything he did while I was his associate was of such mediocre quality that I was at a loss to understand it. He was eccentric enough to be a genius, if eccentricity is the criterion. Physically, he was not a joy to behold. He was short and very stocky, giving him a gnome-like appearance that was further enhanced by the very thick glasses he wore. His extreme vanity showed up in his attempts to cover up his baldness by combing the hair from the back of his head (which he allowed to grow extremely long) to the front to give the semblance of hirsuteness.

Future SF director Arch Oboler during his *Lights Out* days on the NBC radio network.

In 1950, Oboler tried another science fiction feature, *The Twonky*, based on a delightful story by Henry Kuttner, the rights to which Oboler had purchased for his radio show. In it, a creature from the far future ends up in a forties radio manufacturing factory and alters a radio console into a twonky. Twonkies are robots whose only purpose is to help people, whether they want such aid or not. Eventually, the twonky eliminates its master and prepares for a new couple to move in.

Oboler was able to persuade erstwhile invester Buddy Nast that science fiction was the new vogue, and Nast agreed to invest $250,000 for the production of *The Twonky*. In making the movie, Oboler altered the appearance of the twonky to look like a television set. He also altered the Kuttner's humor in typically heavyhanded fashion. *The Twonky* stars Hans Conreid as philosophy professor Kerry West whose wife (Janet Warren) leaves town to attend the birth of her niece and leaves behind a brand new television set. The set startles West by igniting his cigarette and proceeds to make his life miserable. When a delivery man (Ed Max) comes demanding payment, the set duplicates a five dollar bill nineteen times (each, it is later discovered, with identical serial numbers).

The frantic professor contacts his friend Coach Trout (Billy Lynn), who describes the machine as a "twonky," and speculates that it comes from the future. The twonky proves unpredictable. It approves of West smoking, but will not allow him to listen to Mozart or allow him to remain drunk. When he attempts to write a lecture on individualism and art, it zaps him and causes him to alter his notes into a lecture about passion. When Coach Trout tries to attack it, it incapacitates his leg, and later the members of the football team who come to try to help the coach out.

Adding to the looneyness are an attractive bill collector (Gloria Blondell) who invades West's home and refuses to leave until he settles one of his wife's overdue bills, going so far as to take a shower in his bathroom while he has barricaded the bedroom, and after an unsuccessful attempt to rid himself of the twonky by pushing his car over a cliff with the twonky in it, he abandons his car and twonky to take a ride with an elderly English lady who insists on the right to be wrong by driving on the wrong side of the road.

The Twonky is certainly better than its lack of reputation would suggest, with the humor being a bit forced though not painfully so, and the whimsical special effects (mostly of electrical discharges and the twonky, actually an Admiral TV set, moving about on puppety legs) are plentiful. The film conveys a distrust of the new television medium that was entering the home, but apart from a few sarcastic comments from Kerry ("By the end of the day I shall know all the new wrestling moves"), does little to satirize the medium. However, the psychological anxiety of losing one's liberty and freedom and the fear of dealing with an unpredictable device that is seemingly capable of anything is never really communicated visually.

The Twonky had a spectacularly disastrous preview and was eventually foisted on United Artists as part of a package deal with the more popular *Bwana Devil*. It received few playdates and mostly scathing reviews when it was released, and is rarely seen today, even on television. Oboler's direction is amateurish, and he seems to have left the actors floundering on their own. The film became regarded as unreleaseable, but it remains interestingly unusual and sometimes even amusing.

Given the difficulties of getting *The Twonky* to the box office, his production company was almost bankrupt. He needed something sensational that would attract investors. *Bwana Devil*, Oboler's next project, is famous as the first 3-D feature film (it wasn't, but it did launch the 3-D craze of the fifties). Oboler was excited by Milt Gunzberg's Natural Vision process, which used polarized lenses and could project color 3-D, unlike the old Red-Green tinted 3-D used on a successful series of Pete Smith shorts called Audioscopics several years before.

Oboler owned the rights to a book called *The Lions of Gulu*, based upon the true story of two man-eating lions who terrorized laborers and held up the construction of the Trans-African Railroad, and adapted it into a script. With the advent of television, movie attendance was plummeting, and a number of actors expressed interest in becoming involved in the independent production. Robert Stack was signed to play the lead, Jock Hayward, with Barnara Britton as his wife Alice and Nigel Bruce as Dr. Angus Ross. Cameramen were less inclined to risk their reputations on an untried process, so newcomer Joseph Biroc, who demonstrated his ability by shooting a test reel, was signed.

Though the film, now called *Bwana Devil*, was set in East Africa, it was actually filmed at the Paramount Ranch in Malibu over a period of 20 days. During that entire time, the Ansco lab that was developing the film's negative was unable to produce dual matching prints that would allow the filmmakers to check their work. The plot has Hayward and Dr. Ross dealing with the numerous difficulties of guiding thousands of native workers in building the railroad, but a pair of man-eating lions prove to be more than they can effectively cope with.

Britain sends them three big-game hunters to kill the lions, with Hayward's wife coming along with them. However, all three hunters are killed by their prey, leaving it to Hayward to prove his manliness by eliminating the threat of the man-eaters once and for all. Mediocre and cliché, people did not come to *Bwana Devil* for the plot, but the gimmick was impressive enough to draw large crowds (the film grossed $154,000 its first week in two theaters), and was quickly picked up by United Artists for $500,000, who distributed 30 prints to critical lambasting and tremendous box office.

Oboler's *Bwana Devil* would spawn many imitators (15 features were announced in 1953 following its success), both in the shortlived craze in the fifties and the later, equally shortlived revival in 1982–1983 when an awful 3-D Italian western spoof called *Comin' at Ya* did similar business and kicked off the process once again for a whole new generation who were curious to check it out. However, even Oboler himself predicted that the fad would be shortlived, warning that there "is a great temptation in making a three dimensional picture, having objects, from bosoms to zombies, sticking out of the screen into space.

"But gentleman of production," he wrote in *The Film Daily Yearbook of Motion Pictures* (1953), "this is a false path. False because if audiences begin to look upon three dimensional pictures simply as a circus, the law of diminishing returns can quickly catch up with the entire advance. For circuses are not a weekly habit; the trick once seen suffices for a year!" In addition, there were the problems of sloppy projection, faulty prints, and inappropriate screens which contributed to audience dissatisfaction with three-dimensional pictures.

One Plus One, sometimes subtitled *Exploring the Kinsey Reports*, exploited the then controversial Kinsey Report on Human Sexuality to present five mini-dramas that hammer home moralistic points. Leo G. Carroll opens the film as a professor lecturing on sex in modern society, quoting facts and statistics from the report, while members of the audience reflect on their own problems.

In "The Honeymoon," a newlywed bride regrets having premarital sex because her husband is more interested in watching the TV than consummating their marriage. In "Homecoming," a woman who has had a fling must find the courage to confess to her returning husband. "The Divorcee" features a divorcee who tries to interest a rich boyfriend who dumps her once he beds her. In "The Baby," a wife agonizes about having an abortion because her husband doesn't like kids. Finally, in "The Average Man," a 50-year-old married man decides after decades of marital fidelity to have a fling, calls up his old high school flame, and is shocked to discover she's old enough to be a grandmother.

The film is earnest rather than sleazy, but it is also unfortunately dull. It was apparently filmed around Toronto using local talent whose thespic abilities match those of the old educational featurettes one used to endure in high school.

Oboler tried to revive 3-D in 1967 when he made *The Bubble* in a process known as Space-Vision, which required only one projector, but it was withdrawn after limited showings, resurfacing in 1976 in a shorter version under the title *Fantastic Invasion of Planet Earth*. Unfortunately, the overly long and underwritten film only tries the patience of viewers as Catherine (Deborah Walley) and Mark (Michael Cole) have their mountain vacation interrupted when the wife goes into labor. Korean vet Tony (Johnny Desmond) flies them home when they are caught in a storm and land in a strange, unidentified town that soon has a huge transparent dome that alien invaders have set up over it. They find the townsfolk constantly repeating the same dull lines over and over like spaced out zombies and ignore the arrivals' entreaties (except for a doctor who helps deliver the baby).

The pilot's plane is mysteriously dismantled, and the trio discovers that they are some kind of guinea pigs for an unseen alien race who once a week cart off specimens for study. Apparently, the aliens find this group's pathetic escape attempts (largely Tony trying to dig his way under the bubble) as dull as the audience does, and so they finally pack up their saucer and leave. The whole thing plays like an extended, inferior *Twilight Zone* episode that never figured out an ending. (It was later released in edited form as *The Fantastic Invasion of Planet Earth* and has appeared on video under the title *The Zoo*.)

Oboler directed the 3-D softcore porn epic *The Stewardesses* under the pseudonym of Allan Silliphant. The film featured such starlets as Christina Hart, Monica Gayle, and Donna Stanley. It depicts a blonde stewardess experimenting with LSD and trying to have sex with a stone head with a lamp attached. At another point, a woman kills an advertising executive who beat her during sex before jumping out a window herself. The most effective 3-D segment comes during a carnival thrill ride. What's best about the film is its capturing of sixties style kitsch. It may not have been very good, but in those early days of relaxing the Production Code's prohibition against nudity, it didn't have to be, and so managed to rake in a tidy sum (nearly $7 million) at the box office.

Years later, a shorter hardcore version was assembled by inserting new footage by new performers into the film itself. The film was successful enough to inspire many imitators and variants from *Swinging Stewardesses* to *Night Call Nurses*.

Oboler tried to launch 3-D yet again in 1972 with the Japanese made *Domo Arigato*, which Michael Weldon describes as a "G-rated boy-meets-girl movie ... shot in 3-D Spacevision." The film only played once in Los Angeles in the summer of 1990, and I have never caught up with it.

Oboler passed away on March 19, 1987 in California. His numerous plays are largely forgotten and unperformed, his mostly mediocre movies rarely revived, but his influence as a generator of horror and suspense continues unabated, thanks to the many who learned from the *Lights Out* program the suggestive potential of sound and the imagination. He loved to challenge audiences and offer up unsettling speculations about the future, and firmly believed there was no limit to the human imagination.

MAMORU OSHII (1951–)

Urusei Yatsura—Only You (1983); *Urusei Yatsura 2—Beautiful Dreamer* (1984); *Akai Megane* (aka *Red Spectacles*, 1986); *In the Aftermath* (contains material from *Angel's Egg*, 1987); *Kido Keisatsu Patlabor 1999 Tokyo War* (aka *Patlabor The Movie*) (1989); *Kido Keisatsu Patlabor 2 The Movie* (aka *Patlabor 2*; 1993); *Kokaku Kidoutai* (aka *Ghost in the Shell*) (1995)

Television: *Urusei Yatsura* (1981–1986)

Original Animated Videos: *Moon Station Dallos* (4 episodes, 1983–1984); *Angel's Egg* (1985); *Kurenai Megane* (1986); *Kido Keisatus Patlabor* Vol. 1–6 (1988–1993)

The theme that runs through Mamoru Oshii's work is how humanity changes with new technology. He is an unusual Asian filmmaker who sprinkles his films with quotes from the Bible, and his work shows a growing concern with social and spiritual values. Oshii has worked in both live action and animation, and has a rich visual style that shows a remarkable attention to light, color, texture and detail, and he brings a lyrical delicacy to his camera movements.

Mamoru Oshii was born in Tokyo Prefecture, Japan, on August 8, 1951. He came to the industry's attention in 1983 with his self-directed and dramatized movie *Urusei Yatsura—Only You* in which a young Princess's boyfriend, Ataru Moroboshi, is about to marry a beautiful alien Princess, but Lum, the Princess of the Oni, is reluctant to lose her man and rounds up her superpowered girlfriends, Princess Oyuki, the Goddess Benten, and Ran-chan, to help her get him back. *Urusei Yatsura* is derived from the manga by Rumiko Takahashi, and is full of silliness, slapstick, and visual sophistication, as well as bountiful babes who amusingly keep their studs on ice, thawing them for late night "snacking" sessions.

This was quickly followed up by *Urusei Yatsura—Beautiful Dreamer*, written and directed by Oshii. Ataru Moroboshi has a dream which keeps on repeating itself and everybody he knows is involved in it. The plot is an updating of a classic Japanese folk tale.

Oshii then attempted his most daring work, *Angel's Egg*, featuring the delicate designs of Yoshitaka Amano (*Vampire Hunter D*), which follows the meanderings of a frail young woman and her egg, which she believes contains an angel. During her travels, she meets a soldier who carries a crucifix-like weapon, and together they travel the blasted landscape (Oshii has a fondness for ruins in his work) until the impatient soldier breaks open the woman's egg, which is shown to be empty. With its minimal dialogue and abundant symbolism, the film left most viewers puzzled and confused, eager to pierce a mystery without understanding that to do so is to destroy the magic.

Oshii carefully crafts the settings of his films, both theatrical and OAV (Original Animated Videos). He is also marked by a fondness for basset hounds and claims to be very influenced by his dreams which feature images of ruins, fish, water, museums, birds, and young girls. There are reports that he prowls around Tokyo and Hong Kong with a video camera in hand searching for haunting, simple images to place in his films and help set the mood.

Oshii then embarked on a series of six original animated

videos about the Mobile Police Force aka *Patlabor*, set in Tokyo 1998, when ozone depletion has led to rising sea levels and worldwide panic. The series is based on a story and manga by Masami Yuuki. Most of the stories concern defending the Babylon Project, a massive land reclamation project in Tokyo Bay, which is instituted to protect Tokyo, a low-lying city, from being inundated by the sea. To assist in this project, the labors — large powered suits — were designed, but criminals have taken to abusing the labors to commit crimes.

The new police force who use patrol labors, the Patlabors, is created to combat these criminals. The first of the series follows the progress of new recruit Noa Izumi as she learns her way around and gives chase to the bad guys. Subsequent episodes tell stories of terrorists, mad scientists, weird apparitions, and nuclear threats.

Oshii handled the first *Patlabor* movie, which was much darker than the OAV series. The plot details a mad scientist who commits suicide and leaves behind a note indicating that he has designed a time bomb into the operating systems of hundreds of Shinohara labors, and so the mobile police force must mobilize to meet the potential threat which involves an unlikely combination of a computer virus and a typhoon.

More interesting still was *Patlabor 2*, which depicts a Japan under political pressure from those who would have the nation return to its militaristic traditions. Police chief Nagumo finds herself in conflict with her former lover who leads the militarists and is secretly supported by members of the U.S. military. Scenes of a blimp coming down and gassing the streets of Tokyo seem prescient in view of the later gas attack in Japan.

In an interview in *Aniamerica* with Carl Gustav Horn, Oshii noted, "The story is based on political programs that exist in Japan, so it has quite a few deep meanings in it. In *Patlabor 2*, I wanted to describe the Cold War for Japan. It was a war, but a silent war. When the Cold War existed between the U.S. and Russia, the 'stance' of Japan was not to be directly involved. Even though Japan *was* involved with the war, it kept insisting for fifty years that it wasn't. I wanted to describe that fake peace of Japan."

Oshii tried his hand at a live action drama in *Talking Head*, a mystery set in an animé studio where a director disappears and a new director is hired to complete the production while finding the initial director. Oshii filled the film with caricatures of people he knew in the industry. The film came about when an animated project that Oshii hoped to make for Bandai fell through and Bandai offered to allow him to do whatever he wanted.

Oshii had previously filmed two live action films, *Akai Megane*, a combat story set in a socially collapsed Tokyo, and its prequel *Kereberos* (aka *Panzer Corps*). Unfortunately, none of his live action works have been available for viewing here in the United States.

Six months after *Patlabor 2*, Bandai Visual contacted him about making a film adaptation of Masamune Shirow's *Ghost in the Shell*, which the manga writer allowed him free rein on. The original work ran in Kodansha's *Youth Magazine* in 1989, and like all of Masamune's work, featured a female protagonist. Masamune is a cyberpunk manga artist, one of whose favorite themes is what he calls "ghost-hacking," that is the possibility of "hacking" directly into a human brain as humanity and technology become ever more intertwined.

Oshii elaborated on the differences between the manga and the film for *Empire*:

> We changed a few minor things. I really liked the story, but the main problem was the complexity of the manga. The film had to appeal to a wider audience than just those people interested in computer networks. For example, as well as the story elements like cyborgs and computers, we've introduced a basic male/female drama. It's a kind of metaphor; the Puppet Master is a program without a real body... our image is of "him" as being male. In the original manga there's talk of "fusion," but I prefer the term "marriage" because it allows me to exploit the male/female imagery alongside the technical.

Oshii's biggest film to date, *Ghost in the Shell*, was written by Kazunori Ito, who writes under the name Masamune Shirow. The story seems partially inspired by Mary Shelley's *Frankenstein*, as it ponders the question what does it mean to be human and to be able to create a new form of life which will also question its humanity. This film marked a quantum leap for combining computer and cell animation in animé, employing Digital Generated Animation, which combined both CG and cel animation. Digital cel work involves compositing computer generated backgrounds with cel animation. Distortion can be added to backgrounds, focus can be altered and filters can be used to give the impression of depth and dimension. The visual displays in the film were all done with computer graphics, which was also sometimes used to depict how the mind's eye would see certain images.

Animation director for the film, Toshibo Nishikabo, explained, "One major difference is motion, especially the exaggerated action you commonly see in traditional animation. In our film we strive for realism in movement and reaction down to the smallest detail. For instance, in the scene where Kusanagi battles with the tank notice the bullet hits. Normally, when a bullet strikes a target, sparks are added." Nishikabo is proud that sparks are only given off when the bullet hits a metal target and not a stone one.

The crew behind *Ghost in the Shell* (front, left to right) Kumiko Yusa, color setter; Mamoru Oshii, director; Hiromasa Ogura, art director; (back row) Hiroyuki Okiura, character designer; Toshihiko Nishikubo, animation director; Atsushi Takeuchi, mechanical designer; Mitsuhisa Ishikawa, producer.

When asked why he chose to direct *Ghost in the Shell,* Oshii responded:

> My intuition told me that this story about a futuristic world carried an immediate message for our present world. I am also interested in computers through my own personal experience with them. I had the same feeling about *Patlabor,* and I thought it would be interesting to make a film that took place in the near future. There are only a few movies even out of Hollywood which clearly portray the influence and power of computers. I thought this theme would be more effectively conveyed through animation. After giving the subject a lot of consideration, I felt it was the right time to make the movie.
>
> Everyone who worked on this project had a sense of the time being right for animé like this about the future. But because the story is mainly about computers, network access, an "electric brain space," what I was most concerned with was how to bring this world successfully to the screen.

Oshii's concerns were part of the reason he decided to set the movie in Hong Kong. "Since the information network isn't visible, I tried to think of how I could visually represent it. It would be pointless to show the monitor of a personal computer. However, if you think about Hong Kong, you imagine a city teaming with information. For example, there are countless signs and a cacophony of voices and sounds which flow through the city. When I went to Hong Kong, I felt it would provide the perfect setting for the subject and period of the story."

In addition to its complex visual design, the film offers a sophisticated sound design as well. To convey the otherworldliness of the electronic brain conversations, a spatializer was employed to alter the sounds and give them a distant, metallic quality. While the American version suffers from some bad dubbing, uneven pacing, and unclear plotting, there is still much to impress in Oshii's creation of a new future world and its concerns. Because of its potentially confusing form, here is a somewhat detailed description of what transpires:

Ghost in the Shell opens on a cluster of skyscrapers. In the distance, more skyscrapers are under construction. Lights from the high-rise building gleam against the clouds hanging low in the night sky. A young woman is perched precariously on a rooftop, taut with concentration: one false move and she falls to her death. The woman wears goggles enabling thermo-optical camouflage, and sticking from her neck and back are cables connected to circuits inside the building. She is busy bugging.

The woman is Major Motoko Kusanagi, cybernetic operative and leader of secret service unit Shell Squad, formed by the government in order to combat a wave of crime it cannot deal with alone. In a society dominated by the Net, crimes have become both more sophisticated and more brutal. With her hacking devices, Motoko is able to hear the conversation between a corrupt diplomat and a man who appears to be a programmer, as well as to spy on the sunny room where it is taking place.

Meanwhile, the fully-armed storm troopers of the Ministry of Foreign Affair's Section 6 Security Corps rush up the stairs to take position outside the room. Sensing something odd, the body guards inside the room whip out their hidden submachine guns and open fire. Attacked by a hail of bullets, the storm troopers lay low before striking. Inside, they quickly seize the diplomat, who tries to get out of a sticky situation by claiming diplomatic immunity. The Ministry at least wanted to stop the programmer, suspected of contravening arms export laws, from fleeing abroad. However, the wily diplomat insists that the programmer has already signed the necessary papers and wishes to defect.

Just as the Ministry is about to give in and let the suspects slip through the net, the window shatters, and there is the sound of gunfire. The diplomat's head is shot to pieces. In a panic, the storm troopers point their weapons outside. All they see in the glittering night is Motoko, dropping effortlessly down the side of the building with her hands protecting her head and a bewitching smile on her face.

Motoko and the rest of the Shell quad have been informed that an internationally notorious computer criminal has surfaced in Japan. This unique and mysterious super-hacker is suspected of a host of offenses including manipulation of the stock market, illegal data gathering, political maneuvering, terrorist acts and infringement of cybernetic ethics. This unidentified criminal is code named the "Puppet Master" for his habit of taking over human beings in order to manipulate information from them and others.

The Puppet Master made his first unsettling appearance when he infiltrated a hot line to the Foreign Minister. Hoping to put an end to further devious plans, the Shell Squad sets out to capture the Puppet Master. But he falls into the hands of Motoko and friends a little too readily. It seems he allowed himself to be caught — but why?

In the course of investigation, the Shell Squad discovers that the super-hacker started out as a computer virus manufactured by the Foreign Ministry as part of some international racket, before going wild and getting out of control. Knowing that this information could be their undoing, the Foreign Ministry attacks the Shell Squad in the hope of retrieving the Puppet Master. Just then the Puppet Master utters some puzzling words: "I am a new life born in a sea of information. I am driven to seek political asylum..."

This commences the grim struggle between the Shell Squad and the corrupt Security Section 6. All the while the unseen Puppet Master is after something.

James Cameron praised the film, saying, "*Ghost in the Shell* is a stunning work of speculative fiction, the first truly adult animation film to reach a level of literacy and visual excellence. It's [sic] design, the poetry of its visuals, and the depth of its theme set it apart among science fiction films. My compliments to Oshii-san — an important visionary work."

Ghost in the Shell is a smart, stylish animated thriller from Japan decked with all manner of high-tech cunning and more than a little existential angst. Set in the year 2029, the film follows an elite division of cyborg cops who are tracking a superhacker known as Puppet Master, an agent violating not only the security of the world's corporate data but plundering the psyches of its citizenry. The cops, when not tangled in a worldwide web of artificial intelligence and industrial espionage, machinate on the nature of their own essence or existence.

What makes this pop Heidegger riff new is that director Mamora Oshii shrewdly imitates the conventions of live action filmmaking with characters, backgrounds, and camera moves that could be real, this animé has all the multi-hued brilliance of a Japanese woodblock print and the soul of a movie (even if the voice characterizations, dubbed in English, vacillate between the flat and the *Speed Racer* emphatic). It's a clever conceit — and one that pays off—that just as the characters in *Ghost* straddle the worlds of humanity and hardware, the real and artificial, the cartoon is doing the same. It shows Oshii to be a director of great promise.

Motoko Kusanagi, nicknamed "Major," is a female cyborg who leads the Shell Squad. Being an artificial life form with an electric brain, she wonders about her ghost (i.e. soul) in Oshii's *Ghost in the Shell.*

The message of his films is that as technology becomes more complicated, so do our lives. For example, the telephone suddenly allowed people to have relationships with others who were miles away, and new technological differences can bring about equally profound changes, though the exact effects of a globally internetted, digital world have yet to be fully understood, but will undoubtedly bring both bliss and torment into our existences.

KATSUHIRO OTOMO (1954–)

Neo-Tokyo (codirected with Rin Taro and Yoshiaki Kawajiri) (1986); *Robot Carnival* (codirector with Atsuko Fukushima, Kouki Morimoto, Hidetoshi Ohmori, Yasuomi Umetsu, Hiroyuji Kitazume, Mao Lamdo, Hiroyuki Kitakubo, Takashi Nakamura); *Akira* (1987); *Give Me a Gun, Give Me Freedom* (1988); *World Apartment Horror* (1990); *Memories* (co-director, 1996); *Ash* (2000)

Katsuhiro Otomo has closer ties to manga (Japanese comics) than cinema. Nevertheless, his outstanding work on his magnum opus, *Akira*, which features a complex but somewhat realistic view of a futuristic "neo–Tokyo" that is comparable to Ridley Scott's design work on *Blade Runner*, has caused Otomo to be proclaimed the greatest of the animé directors.

Otomo's first manga work was *Jusei* aka *Gun Report* (1973), an adaptation of Prosper Mérimée's novella *Mateo Falcone*. Since then, he has been busy in both the manga and animé industries, producing such work as *Kibun Wa Moh Senso* ("Almost Enjoying the War"), *Highway Star*, the award-winning *Domu* ("A Dream of Childhood") (published in an English–language edition by Dark Horse Comics), *Rohjin Z* (Old Man Z), *Fire Ball*, and storyboarding the opening and closing segments of *Robot Carnival*, Japan's cybernetic successor to *Fantasia*. He has also done commercial work in Japan for such clients as Honda and Canon.

Japan's manga industry is immense, regularly selling millions of weekly black-and-white volumes the size of small telephone books for decades. The diversity of the medium is staggering, with topics ranging from adventure to cooking to badminton. The artistic range is similarly wide, from the child-like simplicity of *Tanaka-kun* to the excessively detailed *Cyber Blue*.

Otomo did character designs for the animated Japanese feature *Harmagedon* (aka *The Great Battle with Genma*), directed by Takamura Mukuo. The film involves a group of psychics drawn together when an evil force approaches the Earth with the intention of destroying it. It starts out by building up the characterizations, and then indulging in elaborate battle scenes on a grand scale (in one, most of Manhattan is destroyed). There are philosophical underpinnings to the story as well, as this elaborate fantasy incorporates elements of Gaian theory, psycho-analytic healing, and preaches on racial tolerance.

Neo-Tokyo, Otomo's first feature film, is an animated anthology film. Rin Taro handled the first segment, "Labyrinth," which is a kind of demonic retelling of Lewis Carroll's *Alice Through the Looking Glass*. A girl and a cat get sucked through a mirror into a twisted maze of a world while pursuing a dancing clown. It is the least interesting segment of the film.

Second up is Yoshiaki Kawajiri's "Running Man," which is brilliantly directed and graphically detailed, but overall has a story that lacks any real substance or meaning. It depicts a futuristic auto race where drivers are cybernetically connected to their vehicles, and we watch as one of the competitive drivers pushes himself past the limits with disastrous consequences.

The best segment of the film, and the only one with a sense of humor, is Otomo's. "The Order to Stop Construction" is an amusing black comedy about a lowly supervisor sent to a third world country to check on the progress of construction there, which is all performed by robots. He is met by a robotic foreman who has gone as mad as Kurtz out in the jungle and insists that the project be completed at all costs. The supervisor's attempts to order a halt to construction prove futile, while the machines themselves keep breaking down and wreaking greater havoc; however, programmed with a surfeit of enthusiasm for its mission, the robotic foreman remains cheerfully unperturbed.

The opening and closing segments of *Robot Carnival*, a collection of animated shorts featuring robots, were codirected by Otomo and Atsuko Fukushima, and are among the better segments in the film. In the opening, a small child in a desert community warns of a coming juggernaut, which advertises the Robot Carnival, but leaves only destruction in its wake. It is a stylish, blackly comic segment. The other segments are a grab-bag of the artistic, the uninteresting, and the entertaining. The shorts include "Dr. Franken's Gears," in which a scientist joyfully powers up a large robot that imitates his actions with disastrous results; "Deprive," where a teenage girl is kidnapped by invading alien robots and is saved by her android protector; "Star Light Angel" is set in the Tokyo Disneyland where entertainment is provided by robots, one of which tries to return a lost pendant of a teenage girl who discovers that the boyfriend who gave her the star-shaped pendant is trying to make time with her female friend; "Cloud" is an arty piece about a walking robot who ignores the images in clouds which are disrupted by atomic bombs that bring about the end of civilization; "Presence" has a man who creates and builds a perfect female companion but lacks the courage to keep her company, rendering her lonely existence meaningless until very late in his life; "Nightmare" features a man on a Vespa motorscooter being chased by a robotic chicken man; "Battle of the Robots" is set in 19th century Japan where a mad American inventor bent on destruction has created a wooden, battery-powered giant robot that destroys a city only to come into conflict with a coal-burning Japanese giant robot that defends the city; and in Otomo and Kukushima's closing, a family finds a silver promotional egg advertising the robot carnival with again catastrophic results.

When Katsuhiro Otomo's *Akira* hit the pages of Japan's *Weekly Young Magazine* in 1982, he created a multilayered tapestry that has not only won him acclaim in Japan, but in Europe and North America as well. Even amid Japan's multitude of manga, *Akira* stood out. Set in "Neo-Tokyo" thirty years after World War III, the story revolves around the title character, a mysterious figure who is almost never seen throughout the series but is worshipped as a messiah by the repressed underclass of Neo-Tokyo.

The main characters are caught up in the struggle they cannot begin to understand. They are Kaneda, fifteen-year-old leader of the Capsules, a biker gang; Tetsuo, his childhood buddy who grew up in an orphanage with him, and whose psychic powers are awakened after he has been kidnapped by the Colonel's police force; Kei and Ryu, members of a group trying to find the other psychic kids and overthrow the government; the Colonel, the military leader who is perfectly willing to sacrifice hundreds of lives to keep Akira's power from being unleashed; and Kiyoko, Takashi, and Masaru — numbers 25, 26, and 27 — three children with the faces of old people who were part of a secret government program that developed and exploited psychic powers in children.

Otomo's ambition with *Akira* was to create an 1,800-page story, to be compiled into five books upon completion. In the actual work, the page count came to 2,200, in six volumes, five of which have been published in English by Marvel Comics. Unsatisfied with the ending, Otomo refused to allow the final section of his saga to be published in the U.S. until a rewrite was done, greatly delaying its publication.

Akira made the transition from the printed page to the large screen in grand fashion. Otomo insisted that it be filmed in 70mm, and eight of Japan's major media and entertainment corporations combined forces to create the Akira Production Committee, who in turn assembled no less than thirty-one animation studios to create the 124 minute movie. Otomo himself had a rare amount of involvement in the project, cowriting the screenplay, directing, storyboarding, and acting as character designer. At times confusing, *Akira* features richly textured backgrounds, spectacular special effects, and some of the most intense and sometimes ultra-violent visuals to grace an animated film.

Kaneda's investigation of Tetsuo uncovers the mystery of Otomo's *Akira*. The film's dazzling future city background was inspired by Ridley Scott's *Blade Runner*.

Equally compelling is the film's soundtrack, composed by Shoji Yamashiro and performed by the Geinoh Yamashirogumi. The Geinoh Yamashirogumi can best be described as an orchestral chorus — a group of over 200 singers using their voices as instruments. Using a combination of traditional music and sounds, modern synthesizers, ritualistic chants and a little digital wizardry, the soundtrack lends even the most hi-tech scenes a certain primal intensity. Hearing Buddhist chanting during the opening clash between the Capsules and their rivals the Clowns, one gets the feeling of watching a ritual battle as old as humanity.

Akira was released in Japan on July 16, 1988 — the same date as the destruction of Tokyo, according to the film's opening. A little over a year later, Streamline Pictures, founded by animation historian Jerry Beck (coauthor of *Looney Tunes and Merrie Melodies*) and television animation producer Carl Macek (script editor on *Robotech*), acquired the rights to distribute the English-language version of *Akira* in the United States. In opening playdates in

New York and Los Angeles, the film fared extremely well and almost immediately developed a cult.

Streamline's first two titles were *Laputa*, Hayao Miyazaki's tale of the quest for Jonathan Swift's flying city, and *Twilight of the Cockroaches*, a live-action/animation feature about a bachelor who peacefully coexists with the roaches in his apartment, until he gets a girlfriend. Both films toured the country's art and repertory cinemas, enjoying favorable but scant media attention. *Akira*, Streamline's third acquisition, blew open the doors, quickly attaining cult movie status.

The movie became Streamline's first and, thus far, most popular video release, and two years later, Criterion released a deluxe CAV laserdisc edition, giving *Akira* the sort of deluxe treatment generally reserved for such revered cinema works as *Blade Runner*. Unfortunately, the English language soundtrack alters the feeling and intent of the Japanese soundtrack a little bit. The main characters voices sound more cartoony than natural, while the test subject voices lose some of their innocence. When members of the motorcycle gang are arrested by the police, the police are not looking for "perpetrators," but rather anti-government elements and activists. Likewise, during a news report that in the English version only mentions that scores of men and women have lost their jobs, the Japanese version fills us in on the failures of the government, its corrupt politicians and their unsuccessful policies. (Anti-government graffiti seen in the film has not been translated either.)

Akira the film shows Otomo's mastery of cinematic techniques. The film opens strikingly in 1988 as the city of Tokyo vanishes under a mushroom cloud, and the story resumes in A.D. 2019 (same year as *Blade Runner*, one of many homages) in Neo-Tokyo. Teenage motorcycle gangs run recklessly in the streets, having nothing better to do than take swipes at one another with whatever industrial flotsam and jetsam is handy. As Tetsuo is chasing a member of the Clowns down an abandoned highway, he suddenly sees a child with a man's face in the glare of his headlight, causing him to crash. Army helicopters suddenly land and take both the child and Tetsuo away. Otomo excels at employing dramatic angles and rapid-paced editing, letting his soundtrack build up tension. We are hurled from one narrative point to the next so quickly that it can take time to catch one's breath and put the pieces of the emerging puzzle together.

The main character is his best friend and gang leader Kaneda, who gets released from police custody and tries to flirt with and assist Kei, a member of the resistance. The chief researcher sees great potential in Tetsuo and boosts his latent psionic powers, which Tetsuo then uses to escape. When Kaneda finds him, Tetsuo is unexpectedly hostile despite Kaneda's assistance in dealing with some rival Clowns. With his new feelings of power, their relationship has changed. More and more he is haunted by images and the name Akira, and the procedure has left him in great pain.

Once more the Colonel takes him into custody, and the other experimental subjects, fearful of his growing connection with Akira, project disturbing images into his mind, but Tetsuo is already more powerful than they are. Meanwhile, a religious cult is active in the streets, busily prophesying the return of Akira while the Colonel faces difficulty in getting his projects funded by an increasingly apathetic ruling council.

Kaneda teams up with Kei in an attempt to infiltrate the secret laboratory and attempt a daring rescue of Tetsuo; however, Tetsuo quickly demonstrates that he does not need their assistance and can teleport out at will and heads to the gang's non-alcoholic bar hangout to score some illegal drugs. Meanwhile, Tetsuo heads for the new Olympic Stadium where Akira's remains have been buried while the Colonel calls out his forces in a futile attempt to stop him.

Tetsuo's power grows beyond his control, and by reuniting the pieces of Akira, he becomes even more powerful yet. Both Kaneda and the Colonel bravely try to stop this emerging threat, but it is the other experimental subjects who appear and help channel Tetsuo's enormous power into less destructive ends in the apocalyptic showdown. While the animation is limited at times, Otomo's striking direction and imagery give it power, and it has the feel of a completely realized universe, filled with fascinating details both familiar and unfamiliar. There is enough ambiguity that fans can debate the meaning of many elements of the film and story, and enough vision that *Akira* has been regarded by many as a modern-day science fiction classic.

Otomo also wrote the interesting 1991 animé piece *Roujin-Z*. Sometime in the near future, Japan's State Medical Emergency Laboratories (SMELS) debuts the Z-001, a new automated care system for the elderly. Rather than pay expensive doctors and nurses, for-profit hospitals have built highly technological beds that are designed to cater to an elderly patient's every need, except the need for companionship. The mechanical bed monitors bodily functions and has an artificial intelligence brain with the ability to mutate the bed's structure to deal with emergencies. Test patient Kijyuro Takazawa discovers that the situation is not to his liking, while the bed tries desperately to cater to his whims. The heroine is a young nurse who protests this state of affairs, believing that patients need tenderness and emotional attention. In a bizarre plot twist, Takazawa's late wife's ghost merges with the machine and the whole thing climaxes in a battle between the bed and a RoboCop-like superweapon. Otomo includes a Buddhist theme about maintaining a fidelity with nature in the face of corporate oppression.

Otomo has turned to live action, and has created a genuinely funny horror film in *World Apartment Horror*, starring Hiroki Tanaka. A flunky for the Yazuka, Tanaka is assigned the task of "cleaning" a house the mob owns and wants to knock down to build a high-rise. He finds, however, that the house is filled with foreigners who do not want to move, and Japanese law forbids companies from tearing down houses that have people living in them. Tanaka must get the foreigners to vacate without killing anyone, because that would attract undue attention. The film slowly develops supernatural overtones as some Filipinos practice magic and unleash a blood curse. It is highly unusual to say the least, but shows that Otomo has a keen eye for imagery.

Unfortunately, Otomo seems to have abandoned the field of animé, and his live action work remains unavailable on these shores. Nevertheless, with his work on *Akira* alone, he has become a name to be reckoned with.

Otomo has worked on Kouji Mortimoto and Tensai Okamuro's film *Memories*. *Memories* is made up of three separate stories. In the first, "Magnetic Rose," two space travelers are drawn into an asteroid world created by one woman's memories. Otomo worked on the second and third segments. In "Stink Bomb," a young lab assistant accidentally transforms himself into a human biological weapon set on a direct course to Tokyo. The final episode, "Cannon Fodder," depicts a day in the life of a city whose entire purpose is the firing of cannons at the enemy.

NICK PARK (1958–)

Archie's Concrete Nightmare (1975); *Creature Comforts; A Grand Day Out* (shorts, 1989); *Sledgehammer* (coanimated music video for Peter Gabriel, 1986); *The Wrong Trousers* (short, 1993); *A Close Shave* (short, 1995); *Chicken Run* (codirected with Peter Lord, forthcoming)

Television: "Penny" *Pee-wee Herman Show; Spitting Image; Friday Night Live* (LWT) (1986)

Commercials: Electricity Board (1990–1993); London Zoo (1990); Chevron (1996–1967); Burger King (1997)

If one judged success by the amount of Academy Awards attained divided by the number of films made, then Nick Park is the most successful filmmaker of all time. Park has specialized in three-dimensional animated shorts, each with a touch of science fiction, that are absolute delights. All of his four major films were nominated for Academy Awards, and one only lost to another Park featurette.

Park was born in Preston, Lancashire, in 1958. He loved cinema from an early age, going each Saturday morning with his two brothers for a matinee. His favorites were films of science fiction, which he enjoyed reading as well as watching. When he was 13, he started making films with an 8mm Bell & Howell camera his parents had bought him, creating his first attempts at animation (despite the fact that his first cartoon was lost while being processed). His early short, *Archie's Concrete Nightmare*, was shown on the BBC in 1975.

Park received a B.A. in Communication Arts from Sheffield Art School in 1980. He later attended the National Film School in Beaconsfield for three years officially (and another year-and-a-half unofficially), initially expecting to become a wildlife photographer, but eventually giving that up. He became exposed to and interested in the works of European animators such as Ladislaw Starewicz, Jiří Trnka, and Jan Svankmajer. Park then went to work for Aardman Animation in Bristol, which was founded in the early 1970s by Peter Lord and David Sproxton.

Park actually started his first Wallace and Gromit film, *A Grand Day Out*, in 1982, as his graduation project, but he was not able to complete it until 1989. (It took him one year just to film the first page of his script.) Park created the figures for his story out of ordinary modeling clay called Harbutts Plasticine and an American clay from Van Aken. Wallace is in reality about nine inches tall, and Gromit is half that.

The film follows the adventures of an amiable inventor with a cheese fixation named Wallace (voice by Peter Sallis), who with his highly intelligent dog Gromit, gets into his homemade rocketship and blasts off for the moon to sample its cheese. Park describes Wallace as "a very self-contained figure. A very homely sort who doesn't mind the odd adventure." On the way to the moon, Gromit tries to build a house of cards, and his exasperated expression as Wallace roughly lands the ship just as Gromit is capping his card pyramid is a masterful comic moment.

In Park's skewed world, the moon is indeed made of cheese, but a strange, mechanical being patrols there and objects to the visitors eating the environment. Wallace merely mistakes it for some kind of coin operated machine and becomes disappointed when it does not perform to his expectations (admittedly, the robot does look like a coin-operated oven). The angered creature then starts tearing metallic pieces off their rocketship until the pair blast off, leaving the creature to fulfill his dreams by using the metal pieces to ski across the moon. Whimsical and delightful, the film is reminiscent of the work of animator Art Clokey, best known for Gumby.

Aardman Animations were cocreators with David Anderson and the Brothers Quay of Peter Gabriel's acclaimed music video for his song "Sledgehammer." Park remembers that director Steve Johnson wanted it to look like a 14-year-old had made it in his attic, and Aardman was only given six days to complete their portion of the video.

Creature Comforts, which was five minutes long, cost between £20,000 and £30,000 to create. It featured pseudo interviews with zoo animals on what it is like living at the London zoo, and features some delightful characterizations. Especially memorable is a puma with a South American accent who can't take the English cold. The film became Park's first Academy Award winner for Best Animated Short.

The Wrong Trousers cost £600,000 to make. The animation was primarily split between Park and another animator named Steve Box, who animated the pernicious penguin. A few other animators were brought in to do bits and pieces, but for most of its length, *The Wrong Trousers* featured only a very small crew.

Wallace and his beloved dog Gromit work as window cleaners in *A Close Shave*.

The Wrong Trousers once more ventures into science fiction as Wallace, as a birthday present, invents a pair of robotic trousers which he calls Techno-Trousers to take Gromit out on walks. (Gromit also receives a dog collar and lead, which he refuses to wear for long in a show of independence.) Unfortunately, the cost of this project forced Wallace to take in a boarder, a penguin who is really the notorious criminal Feathers McGraw but who disguises himself as a chicken, and soon displaces Gromit out of his room, further driving him away by playing ballpark-style organ music at loud volumes during the night. Gromit leaves carrying a bindlestiff and wearing a sou'wester (yellow slicker cape and seaman's hat).

Park fills the film with little Hitchcock touches as Gromit becomes increasingly suspicious of the penguin's actions. Sure enough, when Wallace is asleep, the penguin takes control of the trousers with Wallace in them and uses him to help steal a diamond from a local museum. However, the brave and resourceful Gromit is able to foil his plans and expose the true culprit. It won an Oscar for Best Animated Short.

The delightful pair were featured in one more film, *A Close Shave*, which also combined science fiction and Hitchcockian themes. Park worked with animators Steve Box, Gary Cureton, Peter Peake, and Loyd Price to animate this science fictional sheep saga.

Director Nick Park (left) with Aardman Animation founders Peter Lord and David Sproxton posing with Park's three Oscars.

In *A Close Shave*, somebody has been rustling sheep, but that comes as no great concern to Wallace and Gromit, who run the Wash 'n' Go Window Cleaning Service. They are summoned to the Wool shop run by Wendolene Ramsbottom (voice by Anne Reid), whom Wallace quickly falls for. (A shot of them touching hands while cleaning up wool balls parodies a similar action in the 1945 movie *Brief Encounter*.) Meanwhile, Gromit cleans the windows that Wallace has sprayed with a soap gun filled with Sud-U-Like soap flakes and water.

Wallace's new invention is the Knit-O-Matic, a shaving and/or washing machine, and when a stray sheep named Shaun falls into it, much of his wool is removed and transformed into a knitted sweater for Wallace.

One day while following Shaun, Gromit uncovers some of the rustled sheep outside of Wendolene's shop. Wendolene's dog, Preston, quickly frames Gromit for the rustling and poor Gromit is sent to jail. However, Shaun knows the truth and persuades some of his sheep friends to help break Gromit out of the pokey.

Wendolene and Wallace becoming attracted while picking up balls of wool parodies a similar moment in David Lean's *Brief Encounter*.

It turns out that Preston is a robot dog, built by Wendolene's father, who has been rustling sheep in order to turn them into dog food. Wallace and Gromit try to get away on their motorcycle with the sheep; however, Preston captures everyone except Gromit in the sidecar. Gromit pilots his sidecar/plane through the town, only to fly face to face with the base of a clock tower. Eventually, he makes it into the dog food factory where he attacks with his porridge gun.

Preston the cyberdog winds up getting caught in Wallace's Knit-O-Matic machine, and his metallic nature is revealed in a scene meant to recall Cameron's *Terminator* films. At the end of the film, Wallace is horrified to learn that Wendolene does not care for cheese and realizes that their romance was not to be.

Park has now embarked on his first feature film, *Chicken Run*, which he is codirecting with fellow Aardman animator Peter Lord. The plot involves Rocky the Rooster (Mel Gibson) and Ginger the Chicken (Julia Sqwahla) who lead the other chickens on Mr. and Mrs. Tweedy's farm into a rebellion against their farm of doom. All of Park's animated shorts are filled with delightful touches and unemphasized jokes that reward careful or repeat viewing. Frame for frame, they are some of the most delightful science fiction efforts of the last several years.

ALBERT PYUN (1955–)

The Sword and the Sorcerer (1982); *Radioactive Dreams* (1984); *Dangerously Close* (aka *Choice Kill*) (1986); *Vicious Lips; Down Twisted* (1987); *Alien from L.A.; Odeon* (1988); *Deceit; The Treasure of San Lucas; Lunar Madness; Cyborg* (1989); *Captain America* (1990); *Kickboxer 2: The Road Back; Bloodmatch; Dollman* (1991); *Arcade; Nemesis* (1992); *Knights; Brain Smasher ... A Love Story* (1993); *Kickboxer 4: The Aggressor; Spitfire; Hong Kong '97; Nemesis 2: Nebula; Spitfire* (1994); *Heatseeker; Nemesis 3: Time Lapse*; *Prey Harder; Nemesis 4: Death Angel* (1995); *Blast; Omega Boom; Adrenalin: Fear the Rush* (1996); *Mean Guns* (1997); *Crazy Six; Postmortem* (1998); *Corrupt*; *Ticker*; *Urban Menace*; *Urban Renewal*; *The Wrecking Crew* (1999)

Television: "Ava" *The Fifth Corner* (1992); *Raven Hawk* (1996)

Born in San Diego to a father who was in the marines, Albert Pyun soon moved to Kalua, Hawaii. He began making movies with an 8mm camera when he was eight years old. While he was in high school, he worked as a cameraman on commercials, documentaries, and industrial films. Pyun won a second place award in the Hawaii International Film Festival for one of two short films he created (one was a horror film; the other a western spoof).

Following his graduation, he journeyed to Japan after receiving a fan letter from Toshiro Mifune, who praised some shorts that Pyun had shot. Pyun persuaded Mifune to introduce him to Akira Kurosawa, whom he assisted on several films including *Derzu Usala*. Pyun worked with Kurosawa's cameraman Takao Saira. Pyun also did some work on a couple of TV series and another feature project.

At the age of 20, Pyun returned to Hawaii to become a trailer editor, as well as directing or editing some 60 commercials and documentaries. While there he attended the University of Hawaii. Then in 1976, he moved to Los Angeles to form ITM Productions.

His directorial debut, *The Sword and the Sorcerer*, independently produced for $3.5 million, was shopped around to various independents, all of whom turned it down until John Boorman's *Excalibur* grossed $3 million on its opening weekend and producer Brandon Chase agreed to fund the project for his Group I Films.

Among other frustrations, Pyun was not part of the casting process, and the people who showed up to play certain roles were not always what he wanted or expected, including people who were two feet shorter or 100 pounds lighter than what the script called for. Filming was limited to Laird Studios, Bronson Canyon, and a sweltering location in Riverside, California (the extreme heat caused several actors to pass out, while others got sick from performing inside the Bronson Cave with the entrances sealed off while 20 torches blazed and a fog machine thickened the atmosphere). Stuntman Jack Tyreen died in a stunt which required him to jump off a cliff and land on an airbag 90 feet below, only he missed the bag. The film is dedicated to him. Several other stuntmen were injured as well, usually by props they fell on.

Pyun wanted the film to run two and a half hours, but it was trimmed to 100 minutes and, opening before the larger budgeted and much anticipated *Conan the Barbarian*, it became one of the most successful independent productions ever and helped launch a series of subsequent low budget "sword and sorcery" films.

The film's hero Talon (Lee Horsley) manages to out "Conan" Schwarzenegger's Conan, evincing a bit of personality and by being a muscular barbarian who manages to get crucified (as a centerpiece for the villain's wedding banquet yet) but can rip himself loose by sheer willpower. The villains of the piece are a usurper king named Cromwell (Richard Lynch), leader of the evil Aragons, and an evil wizard named Xusia (Richard Moll, who suffered scratched corneas from his special contact lenses), who in the climax turns into an inhuman, serpent-eyed demon with four-jointed fingers who rips the heart out of the one who resurrects him and then proceeds to waste an entire army with a rotting disease.

Princess Alana (Kathleen Beller), the film's heroine, proves vulnerable but spirited, a far cry from the wimpy scream queens that usually adorn these stories. Her kingdom of Eh-Dan may have been usurped, but she is still game to tackle the threat head-on. There is a triple-bladed magic sword that is improbable and looks unwieldy more than anything else. (During fight scenes, it shattered other swords, and one of the slivers caught Horsley in the forehead and knocked him out for the day.) If that were not enough, Pyun wanted the clashing swords to strike sparks when they hit each other, so when Talan and Cromwell clash in the climactic duel, each sword (one having a positive terminal; the other negative) had enough volts to create a shower of sparks. One stuntman wearing metal was knocked out cold despite protective gloves.

The Sword and the Sorceror largely entertains because the spirit and tone are right, the plot is incident heavy, filled with one damned thing after another, and the whole thing seems frolicsome, even a rape scene where the heroine observes that her attacker seems inadequately armed. For years Pyun hoped to make a sequel, *Tales of the Ancient Empire*, but Group I, who owns the rights, has thus far not allowed one to be made. It remains Pyun's most enjoyable feature despite his prolific output since.

Next Pyun toiled on cowriting and directing *Radioactive Dreams*, an unfortunately witless and very dull apocalyptic sci-fi comedy. He worked with Thomas Karnowski, a friend from his Hawaiian high school with whom he has shot 8mm home movies. Together, they wanted to make a sci-fi comedy about head trips, showing people's capacities to escape from their harsh reality.

The evil King Cromwell of Pyun's *Sword and the Sorcerer* wishes to rule the world.

Radioactive Dreams begins in 1986 as two four-year-old boys are taken to a bomb shelter in the mountains by two men, the villainous Spade Chandler (George Kennedy) and Dash Hammer (Don Murray), and are left there for the next 14 years. Finally in the year 2000, the now grown boys, Marlowe (Michael Dudikoff) and Young Philip (John Stockwell), both heavily influenced by Raymond Chandler's writing, emerge from their mine shaft fall-out shelter to make their way in this brave, new world. The gag is that these men's view of life is entirely shaped by the detective magazines and books that were the only reading matter they had available. Thinking of themselves as "dicks" (as in detectives), they set out to find whoever controls the last unlaunched nuclear missile.

To create his post-apocalyptic world, Pyun chose to shoot the film largely on the volcanic lava beds of Hawaii. The heroes make their way to a place called Video City, which is populated by various stereotypes from the past, from hippies to disco dancers. Pyun wanted the film to recreate a chronological journey through popular culture (1950s greasers, 1960s surfers and hippies, disco freaks from the 1970s, punks and new wavers of the 1980s), and he tries to give each era evoked its own camera style, from *cinéma vérité* to rock video. Once there, the randy pair meet some femme fatales in the form of Rusty Mars (Michele Little) and Niles (Lisa Blount). They end up needing to prevent some bad guys — right-wing, paramilitary weirdos with survivalist training — from getting hold of the two keys which will launch the remaining atomic missiles. Eventually, their adventures strip the two heroes of their makeshift identities, leaving them lost and confused. The whole thing is audacious, silly, and unfortunately dull beyond belief.

Explained Pyun, "We saw the post-nuclear world as one populated by people most of us consider to be 'freaks,' those not in touch with reality. They've taken over and have remade the world into their own vision of what the world should be. Most of the survivors would be people locked into dream-worlds, like hippies or hare krishnas or moonies." Not surprisingly, the film failed to receive much of a release or attention, the first of Pyun's many movie misfires.

Alien from L.A. was seemingly created by Cannon Films as a way to manufacture a movie out of footage from their 1986 *Journey to the Center of the Earth* fiasco, directed by Rusty Lemonade, which had also starred squeaky-voiced *Sports Illustrated* model Kathy Ireland. In *Alien* she appears as Wanda, a cocktail waitress seeking her missing father in Africa when she falls down the proverbial rabbit hole and winds up in the subterranean civilization of Atlantis, where everyone strangely speaks with an Australian accent and is said to have come from outer space.

Wanda locates daddy, rescuing him from the oppressive

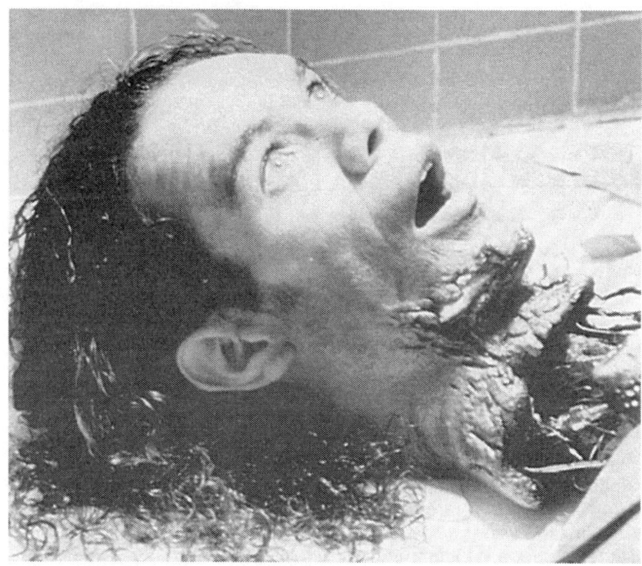

In Pyun's *Nemesis*, cyborg Michelle loses her head after an encounter with Rains.

Atlantean government, and succeeds in bringing him back home, where she finds bliss back at the beach with an Atlantean she met named Charmin', who somehow managed to follow her home. It was not long before this mess found its proper home as fodder for *Mystery Science Theater 3000.*

Cyborg is a kung fu martial arts action film with Sergio Leone's hommages. Kitty Chalmer's script is deliberately vague about the details of this post-apocalyptic future, except that there is currently a period of mass genocide, starvation, and death due to a persistent plague. The story follows cyborg Pearl Prophet (model Dayle Haddon) who attempts to get from New York City to Atlanta to acquire vital information for scientists who are working on a cure for the deadly disease. Unfortunately, her companion in this endeavor is the evil Fender Tremolo (skateboard and surfing champion Vincent Klyn) who wishes to get his hands on the antidote to increase his wealth and power.

Following the pair is Gibson Rickenbocker (Jean-Claude Van Damme in a typically wooden performance), a traveling kickboxer who wants to avenge the death of his family at the hands of Fender and his gang of Flesh Pirates. (At one point, this unlikely savior of mankind finds himself crucified to a tree, but has the strength to pull himself free.)

Pyun does little with the religious subtext of his film, concentrating more on setting up and executing fight scenes between the well-buffed adversaries. Naming the characters after the makers of guitars seems a dumb idea, but then the film's real failing is that it does not explore any potentially interesting concepts but tries to satisfy the audience with a series of action sequences that contribute nothing to our understanding of the characters or their situation. Nevertheless, the film did well enough to spawn a sequel, *Cyborg 2,* written and directed by Michael Schroeder.

According to Pyun, *Captain America* suffered from financial problems, such that many scenes were truncated or entirely omitted during shooting due to the lack of production funds. In *World of Fandom* magazine, Pyun is quoted as saying, "I love my cut of the film, which is 40 minutes longer than any other version. It contains a dozen additional scenes. The beginning of the film is totally different, as is the ending. This version is more of a drama fantasy and contains the crucial elements of a fine screenplay. Most of this was an 'action' picture. Steve Tolkien had written a moving, bittersweet fantasy and it's sad no one ever saw the film version of his screenplay."

Whatever the reasons, *Captain America* proves a very unsatisfactory jaunt down memory lane, although there are clearly attempts to remain true to the original comic book myth. Matt Salinger portrays serviceman Steve Rogers who is transformed into Captain America by the requisite mad scientist and is then pitted against his grand Nazi nemesis the Red Skull (Scott Paulin), who manages to put the hero into suspended animation in the Arctic while he connives in more modern times to assassinate the Kennedys and Martin Luther King.

Captain America is revived from his icy prison and discovers that his old arch enemy has kidnapped the U.S. President (Ronny Cox), and so he sets out to save the day in a flurry of action and a paucity of narrative logic or interest. The excellent supporting cast includes Ned Beatty, Darren McGavin, Michael Nouri, Melinda Dillon, and Bill Mumy.

Dollman was done for Charles Band's Full Moon and is typical of Full Moon's lower grade product. Tim Thomerson stars as crime-fighter Brick Bardo, a wise-ass lecherous cop from the planet Arturos. When Sprug (Frank Collision), an evil floating head, flees towards Earth, Bardo bravely gives chase. Unfortunately for Bardo, Arturosians are only one-sixth the size of this planet's inhabitants. While Sprug allies himself with Braxton Red (Jackie Earle Haley), a South Bronx drug lord, Bardo assists single mother and anti-drug activist Debi Alejandro (Kamala Lopez) as the opposing sides come head to head, so to speak.

Thomerson seems to be doing a bad Clint Eastwood impression while Lopez insufferably lectures the audience about what it already knows. Pyun saves on his effects budget by doing constant POV shots from Bardo's point of view, padding his film with shots of mean streets or pointless gunfire. If there were a truth in advertising law for film titles, it would more accurately be rendered as Dull, man. That still did not prevent Charles Band from filming a sequel, *Dollman vs. Demonic Toys*, which incorporates footage from *Dollman* as well as *Demonic Toys* and *Bad Channels*.

Nemesis borrows heavily from *Escape from New York, Total Recall, Terminator* and *RoboCop* without reaching anywhere near the quality of any of those films. It takes place in the year 2020. Humans are engaged in battle with cyborgs, artificial humans who plan to take over the planet. Martial arts star Olivier Gruner plays Alex Rain, a Los Angeles police officer whose specialty is terminating cyborg terrorists, even though he is part cyborg himself after having a few body parts replaced with cybernetic parts. (While the issue of whether he is really human or machine is raised, it is neither dealt with nor settled.)

Alex's ex-lover Jared (Marjorie Monaghan) absconds with the security plans for an international conference. Police Chief Farnsworth (Tim Thomerson) sends Alex out to stop Jared and her terrorist organization, and to ensure compliance, implants a bomb in Alex's heart which will explode in three days unless the mission has been accomplished.

Rebecca Charles' screenplay is as numbingly unoriginal as Pyun's pedestrian direction remains unexciting. Production designer Colleen Saro and costumer Lizza Wolf work wonders on a very limited budget, but this world of uplinks, downlinks, and corporate group-thinks remains beyond repair. With the exception of a sequence where Alex uses a machine gun to shoot the floor out from underneath him to escape his adversaries, there is a complete absence of cleverness which can't be disguised by the armory of explosives set off throughout the pathetic plot. The dialogue and acting both remain steadfastly subpar.

Gruner lacks even the ability of a Jean-Claude Van Damme in his acting talents. (According to Pyun, Gruner's inability to emote forced him to trim much of the character's dialogue, leaving him an ill-defined central character.) Even at Gruner's specialty, martial arts, he proves uninspiring here due to the lack of impressively choreographed fights. One can take old ideas and turn them into something new and interesting, but *Nemesis* fails to be either.

In fact, the film is unable to avoid some howling continuity errors, such as Gruner in the first scene blasting a cyborg on the right side of her head, but in the next shot, the hole is on the left side. For a shower scene, Gruner wears nothing when seen from the rear, but on the reverse angle he is suddenly shown in a jockstrap.

This did not prevent Pyun, however, from completing three direct-to-video sequels to the film. The first, *Nemesis 2: Nebula* simply dispenses with Gruner in the opening narration while telling the story of an infant sent back in time to an African veldt where she grows up (into bodybuilder Sue Price) and trains to become a freedom fighter against the cyborg onslaught. To make its theft of concepts from *Terminator* even more complete, the film also includes Nebula, a mechanical killer who pursues her in the past.

Knights is a medieval film set in the distant future and stars Kris Kristofferson as a cyborg warrior-savior named Gabriel with a scenery-chewing Lance Henriksen playing an evil cyborg antagonist who searches for human blood to satiate his appetites. Kick-boxing champ Kathy Long, Scott Paulin, Gary Daniels, and Nicholas Guest costar.

Pyun also recently worked on writing and directing a pulpy romantic comedy called *Brain Smasher: A Love Story* starring a somewhat toned down version of foul-mouthed comedian Andrew Dice Clay, as well as Tim Thomerson, Teri Hatcher, the ubiquitous Brion James, and Yuji Okamoto. The plot had something to do with Clay helping a model (Hatcher) battle "Red Lotus Monk" kung fu villains to thwart her sister (Deborah Van Valkenburg) from using a rare flower to achieve world domination.

Keith Cooke stars as a kickboxing martial artist who must fight cyborgs to save his kidnapped trainer in *Heatseeker*, set in a brutal, corporate run America of 2019.

Pyun's last theatrical release, which he both wrote and directed, is *Adrenalin: Fear the Rush. Adrenalin* stars Christophe Lambert (*Subway*), Natasha Henstridge (*Species*), Norbert Weisser, Elizabeth Barondes, Craig Davis and Xavier Decue in a tale about four cops who have to stop a psychopath about to release a deadly virus. The film is set in a post-apocalyptic world of 2007, where much of the population has been wiped out by a deadly microphage. The setting is supposedly a Boston ghetto, where immigrants are quarantined to prevent the spread of the infection, which just happens to look like an Eastern European ghetto. (The film was actually lensed in Bratislava.) Unfortunately, the potentials of the premise are never really explored as Pyun elects to make a short, but snail-paced chase film where the heroes seem to be going in senseless circles, much like Pyun's own career.

STEWART RAFFILL

The Tender Warrior (1971); *Holding* (documentary, 197?); *When the North Wind Blows* (1974); *The Adventures of the Wilderness Family* (1975); *Across the Great Divide* (1976); *The Sea Gypsies* (1978); *High Risk* (1981); *The Ice Pirates* (1983); *The Philadelphia Experiment* (1984); *Mac and Me* (1988); *Mannequin Two: On the Move* (1991); *Tammy and the T. Rex; Lost in Africa* (1994); *The New Swiss Family Robinson* (1998)

Born in Kettering, Northants, England, Stewart Raffill studied agriculture and animal husbandry at the University of Coventry, and holds a degree from Warwickshire Agricultural College. This 6 foot 8 inch, soft-spoken Englishman came to be a director in a round-about way. He moved to the United States in 1961, where his animal background led to work in films such as *The Lion* starring William Holden, Trevor Howard, Pamela Franklin and Capucine. Unable to find any lions they could use in Africa, this 1962 production imported lions from the U.S. which were under Raffill's control.

These stints led to other animal handling chores in such projects as *Big Red, A Tiger Walks, Monkeys Go Home!, Lt. Robin Crusoe U.S.N.* and "The Wacky Zoo of Morgan City" for the *Wonderful World of Disney* TV series. Raffill became an experienced animal wrangler and was head trainer on the *Daktari!, Cowboy in Africa*, and the *Tarzan* TV series. He partnered with his father Joseph, operating Safari Animal Rentals outside Los Angeles.

"I started in the business training wild animals and in Tarzan movies," Raffill recalled. "I made a lot of films in exotic places — South America, Africa, Asia, and places like that. I've always been interested in Africa. I still go there about every two years. A friend of mine has land over there and we just take off for four or five weeks."

Raffill broke into the more creative side of the film business first by producing and directing with his father a children's feature, *The Tender Warrior*, which was shot in the Okefenokee Swamp area of Georgia, and then by scripting the Disney film *Napoleon and Samantha* for director Bernard McEveety. This 1972 family film was about a pair of kids who run away with a pet lion. It marked future Oscar-winner Jody Foster's film debut and was also an early appearance by fellow Oscar-winner Michael Douglas.

His second film as a director, *Holding*, was also made with his father. It was a documentary about what happens to drug dealers imprisoned in a South American jail. The pair prepared a film called *The Snow Tigers* for Sun International, a small independent who had gained big grosses on a pseudo-documentary based on Erich Von Däniken's *Chariots of the Gods?*, narrated by William Shatner, but the plans fell through.

Nevertheless, Sun International set up *The Adventures of the Wilderness Family* for Raffill, about a modern urban family who forsake the big city for fun and adventure in the Rocky Mountain region, which proved another big family film hit. This was followed by a few other rarely seen, independently made films.

Raffill finally hit the big time by cowriting (with Stanford Sherman) and directing *The Ice Pirates* for MGM Pictures. Completed in five months and two weeks, the film sat on the shelf for a while because MGM did not know what to do with it, and who could blame them? *The Ice Pirates* is an incredibly wonky movie, a goofy spoof of sci-fi action sagas. Unfortunately, much of its oddball humor is ill-timed and misguided. It features a campy band of space pirates led by Jason (Robert Urich in a curly wig) who joins forces with the Princess Karina (Mary Crosby) to help her find her explorer father and a long thought mythical water supply in the next galaxy on the Seventh Planet.

Instead of fuel, as in *Mad Max*, the most precious commodity in this galaxy is water, which is in crucially short supply despite all the advanced technology available. The water supply is controlled by the Knights Templar, who run around in spaceships in medieval armor. (John Carradine has a cameo scene as their horribly arthritic supreme commander who clings to life.)

Jason's band of space brigands are futuristic Robin Hoods who steal water from the rich to sell at the space pirate depot, as water is the most readily exchangeable commodity in the galaxy. He is assisted in this enterprise by his black sidekick, Roscoe (Michael D. Roberts), who fixes their often malfunctioning fighter robots, with Maida (Anjelica Huston), an ace pilot and swordswoman and Zeno (Ron Perlman), crewman and cook, being the main ones. Of course, even with the shortage of water, the pirates find no shortage of drinks available to them.

Jason and Roscoe are captured after boarding a ship belonging to the Princess Karina, whom Jason briefly kidnaps. As a consequence, they are caged up with Killjoy

(John Matuszak), another prisoner, who explains that they are about to be made into eunuchs. Fortunately for the pair, the princess secretly elects to spare them their privates if they will take her to the pirate world to track down her father.

On the pirate world is a bar scene in yet another hommage to that in Lucas' *Star Wars*. Shots of the domed city from *Logan's Run* are used to depict two different sites, while Norman Jewison's *Rollerball* is frequently playing on TV screens. There is also an *Alien*–based joke in that the heroes are embarrassed to discover that their ship is infested with a space herpe.

The look of the film, photographed by Matthew F. Leonetti, is consistently grainy and dismal. The acting aspires to a breezy, comical, tongue-in-cheek style that it never quite attains, which may be partly attributed to the awfulness of the supremely stupid (and proud of it) script. The level of humor may be gauged by the idea of one robot attacking another robot by kicking it in the nuts, so to speak, or a frightened robot wetting oil all over itself.

The ending is totally nonsensical as the heroes fly into a time warp which speeds up their lives, aging them incredibly in a short time, and then returning them to normal at the end of it while the villains, whose ship was one degree off course, are suddenly vanquished and disappear. While the rest of the galaxy continues to deteriorate, the heroes finally made it to a water-filled world that looks suspiciously like Earth. It was not surprising that this hokey, hoary collection of clichés did a belly flop at the box office. However, by that time Raffill had already embarked on another science fiction effort.

The Philadelphia Experiment is a science fiction "what if" story based on a supposed "real life" incident that the Navy refuses to acknowledge as ever taking place. According to the story, back in 1943, the Office of Naval Research was reportedly conducting a series of tests to develop a "radar proof" screen that could prevent ships using this device from being detected by enemy radar. The whole thing was covered up when, in testing the machinery, some serious side effects ensued.

A pair of books about this likely apocryphal incident were published, a thriller titled *Thin Air* and a supposedly factual account titled *The Philadelphia Experiment*, which brought the story to the public's attention. Screenwriter Wallace Bennett thought the story would make good raw material for a screenplay, and interested film director John Carpenter in the project.

Carpenter was unable to come up with a satisfactory script and the project was put on the back burner for a time. Finally, Carpenter, coproducer Doug Curtis, and coscreenwriter Michael Janover spent some time mulling over what the story really needed. It was decided to open the story in the past with the experiment going awry, creating a vortex that sends the heroes into the present. By doing this, they felt they could keep modern audiences interested in the characters' reactions to the present while making wry and humorous commentaries on mankind's present state of affairs.

Robert Symonds (left), Mary Crosby, and Robert Urich on the run from raiders in Stewart Raffill's wonky sci-fi comedy *Ice Pirates.*

According to this new story, the secret project begun in 1943 has recently been revived. The two heroes wind up being imperiled by those who would wish for the project to remain a secret. They befriend a young woman who must guide them and orient them to the present day. New World Pictures picked up this project under its new management (after Roger Corman had sold the company to former Avco-Embassy executives) as their major summer release. William Gray was brought in for some additional rewriting. After Carpenter, who retains an executive producer credit, gave up the idea of directing it, the project was offered to Joe Dante, Jonathan Kaplan, and Harley Cokliss before Raffill was finally signed on as director.

Michael Paré, fresh from his work on Walter Hill's *Streets of Fire* and *Eddie and the Cruisers*, was quickly selected to play the lead, David Herdeg. Bobby Di Cicco was chosen to play Jim Parker, David's friend and fellow time-traveler, while Nancy Allen was pegged to play Allison, the young woman who befriends them.

From a creative standpoint, there were several things which attracted Raffill to the project: "First, I think that it lends itself to doing a science fiction film where you care about the people, where you can make the characters believable and you put them through some spectacular series of special effects. You care about the people, and therefore, the special effects have more significance ... I think that the story itself is fascinating, unpredictable, and entertaining in its essence. It has a mystery as well as a love story, but I think that all of the implicitly interesting things about a

Michael Paré and Nancy Allen are time-crossed lovers in Raffill's *The Philadelphia Experiment.*

bed and back into the vortex. The men from the Navy's secret project are aware of the two men's presence and devote their resources to taking Herdeg down as he and Allison continue to flee and fall in love. Unfortunately, the later portions of the story tend to bog down as Herdeg has to confront the reality that he has lost the world he has known. Once he confronts the head scientist of the secret project, he learns that it was he who went back into the vortex to turn off the shipboard power supplying it before the otherwise uncloseable vortex would destroy the world. He resigns himself to his fate and saves the day, but at the last moment returns to 1984 and the woman he loves.

When I talked to Raffill, he was very enthusiastic about the project. "It's very dramatic and realistic," he said, "and it has some humor in it. I can't avoid that. Life is best faced with a sense of humor, I think.

"It has a lot of effects, and I'm working with Max Anderson who did the effects for me on *Ice Pirates*. We've set up our own optical house this time so that the effects can be done in-house. We're creating a lot of new opticals for *The Philadelphia Experiment*. We're using a lot of solarization, and we have to create a vortex on the surface of the planet which we're using new technologies for. It's been fun creating that and coming up with new things.

"The film is an interesting combination of elements. What happens in a lot of sci-fi films is that the hardware can take precedent over the character development. You can have people going through incredible circumstances, but if you don't care about them, it diminishes the effects. In *The Philadelphia Experiment*, I tried to paint very real characters and give them dimensions that made them very interesting. I wanted to make them characters you can relate to on a human level so that you care when they go into all these science fictional effects and things."

One of the difficulties the production faced was that locations that could stand in for 1943 had to be found. The Navy naturally was not too happy with the whole idea of the film and so refused to cooperate. To represent the destroyer the *Eldridge*, Raffill had to find a 1943 destroyer which he finally located in Charleston, South Carolina, at the Patriots Point Maritime Museum. The former destroyer, the *Laffey*, was once part of the Normandy invasion fleet and later operated in the Pacific, taking part in the battles of Iwo Jima and Okinawa as well as participating in the Bikini atomic bomb tests. This distinguished 376-foot ship was transformed into a set.

In addition, the streets of Charleston were filled with vintage 1940s cars, buses, and military vehicles to provide

man from the past are there as well, although we don't indulge in them excessively."

World War II sailors Herdeg and Parker are aboard ship in the generator room when the radar proof device is turned on. Their ship is sucked up into a vortex, and in trying to escape they are deposited where another vortex has been opened in 1984 as the Navy tries the device on an entire town, which disappears. The confused sailors find themselves stranded in a desert and attacked by a helicopter, which is blown up when electricity shoots from an electrified fence through Parker's body.

The sailors find an empty bottle of Löwenbrau, which makes them fear that the Germans have invaded, but are relieved when they also see a Coca-Cola can. They come to an isolated bar and grill where a color television is showing *Humanoids from the Deep* and there are video games in the background, but somehow this does not strike them as odd. The unclosed vortex is causing a massive windstorm, and Parker's body shorts out the arcade games, much to the anger of the bar owner.

Herdeg goes outside to use the phone to call his base, which is being used by Allison. When Parker and the angered owner come out demanding payment for the broken equipment, Herdeg pulls his service revolver and gets Allison to drive them away from there. Herdeg hopes to get in touch with his father from California, but Allison's car crashes when they are confronted by a police blockade.

Allison refuses to press kidnapping charges, sensing the pair need help, and soon Parker is taken to a hospital where after some seizures he suddenly disappears off his hospital an excellent backdrop for the early portions of the story. From this nostalgically cozy location, Raffill wanted the shift in the time vortex to be quite dramatic. He decided to select one of the most barren and alien locations in the U.S.— the salt flats outside of Wendover, Utah. Additionally, the location proved ideal because it had been the site of an Army Air Force base that was now abandoned.

The visual effects for the vortex rely heavily on motion control and visual distortions. It was created by Max W. Anderson via a new technique involving a complex series of animated dots that shape together to form images. Practical, on-set effects were handled by Larry Cavanaugh, who has worked on such films as *The Long Riders*, *Apocalypse Now*, and *Dogs of War*. To create the 100 mile per hour winds needed, Cavanaugh used seven huge aircraft engines to generate the forceful gale. His most impressive effect in the film is a lightning bolt that hits a massive transformer and causes a tremendous fire. Over 1000 gallons of fuel were used to create the "out-of-control" blaze that sweeps the site.

The film proved popular enough to spawn a video sequel nine years later which Raffill had nothing to do with, *The Philadelphia Experiment II*, directed by Stephen Cornwell. Brad Johnson assumes the Paré role, who becomes involved in a plot in which a Nazi scientist (Gerrit Graham) sends a Stealth bomber back in time in order to allow Germany to win World War II, thereby creating a fascistic modern America. Marjean Holden appears as a futuristic freedom fighter and potential love interest.

Raffill's next film, which he cowrote (with Steve Feke) and directed, *Mac and Me*, was one of the most notorious *E.T.* rip-offs. Produced for a floundering Orion Pictures, the film gives whole new meaning to the concept of product placement, as there are a surfeit of Coca-Cola, Skittles (rather than Reece's Pieces), and McDonald's references shamelessly plugged throughout.

The film begins with a family of aliens (father, mother, older daughter and baby brother) on the moon of a ringed, heavy planet in our solar system encountering a landing probe from Earth that has been sent to take samples. The probe employs a vacuum which unexpectedly sucks the aliens inside the probe. Once the probe returns to Earth, the aliens break free and run away.

Unfortunately, the baby, MAC (for Mysterious Alien Creature), runs in a different direction and hides in the van of a family relocating to a new home. Lone mother Janet (Christine Ebersole) is raising two boys, an older teenager Michael (Jonathan Ward) and young Eric (Jade Calegory), a 10-year-old bound to a wheelchair. MAC has the ability to make unpowered electrical objects (such as remote control toy cars and television sets) switch on suddenly, a fact noted by Eric. He finally espies MAC as he cheerfully drills holes in the wall and uses an electric saw to slice a triangle out of the front door; however, no one seems to believe him.

The cute creature means well, but causes disaster. He decorates the home's interior according to a nature painting that the mom intended to hang. (After a look at a newspaper ad showing what home interiors should look like, he fixes everything.) Eric and his kooky next-door neighbor pal Courtney (Katrina Caspary) capture MAC with the aid of the family vacuum cleaner, and soon learn that he likes to drink Coca-Cola, eat Skittles, and an entire dance sequence takes place later at McDonald's with the Ronald McDonald clown present. Meanwhile, the rest of MAC's family are dying of thirst out in the desert and send him psychic messages about how to find them, which MAC tries to relay to his Earth friends, and the government scientists slowly track the wayward aliens down.

The aliens are obvious puppets with very limited expression, their mouths in a permanent "O" which is perfect for sucking sodas or Skittles with. The parallels with *E.T.* are so obvious as to be embarrassing. Not only are government agents after the critter and a lone mother who does not have a clue as to what is going on in her own house, but the composition of the main kids: a teenage brother, a younger brother, and a young girl is the same. The family lives in a hilly, suburban area of California with an undeveloped backyard area.

Instead of disguising the E.T. as a ghost, he is disguised as a rather large teddy bear. Instead of the alien being in a basket on a bicycle, we get a similar image of it in the lap of a boy in a wheelchair. There is an elaborate chase down the streets of the track homes, and the kids band together to keep the creature out of the hands of the governmental agent.

The biggest twist on *E.T.* is that there is a poorly motivated shoot out that triggers an enormous explosion which kills the boy rather than his alien friends, and it is they who bring the child back to life. Raffill ends the film with the aliens being sworn in in Los Angeles City Hall as American citizens with a promise that they will return. Given the dismal results of this film, it is a relief that they did not keep that promise, although I must say in all fairness the film did delight my undemanding three-year-old son the first time he saw it.

This was followed by *Mannequin Two: On the Move*, a sequel to the surprise hit *Mannequin*, a variation of the 1940s fantasy *One Touch of Venus* written and directed by Michael Gottlieb, in which Andrew McCarthy plays a department store window designer who conjures up the spirit of a long dead Egyptian princess who winds up inhabiting the body of one of the mannequins he has made. Raffill's sequel has William Ragsdale as a Philadelphia department store assistant falling in love with another mannequin/lost spirit (Kristy Swanson), this one of an enchanted Bavarian peasant girl who is kept in a state of rigidity until she finds a lover. While professionally mounted, the sequel lacked the characters (except for Meshach Taylor's offensively stereotypical gay character who is brought out for some lame humor) and even the minimal charm of the original, and not surprisingly failed to repeat its success.

Raffill then attempted to cash in on *Jurassic Park* with *Tammy and the T. Rex*, in which a mad scientist (Terry Kiser) transplants the brain of a dying teen (Joe Franklin) into the body of a mechanical dinosaur. The transplant is a success, but the dinosaur now heads out to revenge itself, accompanied by his girlfriend Tammy (Denise Richards).

Overall, Raffill's career has been neither auspicious nor accomplished, though he did for a time find a niche for himself making family oriented fare. His films try hard to excite and please, but he just keeps missing the mark.

HAROLD RAMIS (1944–)

Caddyshack (1980); *National Lampoon's Christmas Vacation* (1983); *Club Paradise* (1986); *Groundhog Day* (1993); *Stuart Saves His Family* (1995); *Multiplicity* (1996); *Analyze This* (1999)

Harold Ramis is best known as a comedy writer and performer, having served with the National Lampoon Radio Hour and written *Animal House* and *National Lampoon's Vacation*. He also scripted Rodney Dangerfield's two funniest films, *Caddyshack* and *Back to School*, as well as directing the former, and then going on to cowriting, cocreating, and playing one of the pseudo-scientific *Ghostbusters*. Given his background, it is not surprising that he makes an apt comedy director, but what is surprising is how interesting conceptually his comedies are.

Ramis was born on November 21, 1944, in Chicago, Illinois. He received his education at Washington University and St. Louis University. He held a job as a mental ward orderly before becoming a jokes editor for *Playboy*, and then moving on to cofounding with Brian Doyle-Murray the Second City comedy troupe, for which he became a writer-performer, and which supplied *National Lampoon*, *Saturday Night Live*, and *SCTV* with their talented performers and writers.

Groundhog Day takes a terrific premise by Danny Rubin, possibly based on Richard Lupoff's story "12:01" (which in turn was adapted into a made-for-cable movie by Jack Sholder), about a man (Bill Murray) forced to relive the same day over and over again, and slowly becoming a better person in the process. The protagonist's plight comes to resemble what Kübler-Ross described as people's reaction to the news of their impending death. At first, there is disbelief, followed by anger, bargaining, resignation, and finally acceptance.

The man in question is Phil Connors, a jaded, obnoxious Pittsburgh TV weatherman who is hoping to move on and become a network weatherman. His least favorite assignment of the year is his obligatory broadcast of the Groundhog Day festivities in Punxsutawney, Pennsylvania, where his skills are upstaged by an oversized rodent, the famous groundhog Punxsutawney Phil. Predictably, he is also peeved when a sudden blizzard strands him, his producer Rita (Andie MacDowell), and cameraman Larry (Chris Elliott) in the town for another night.

Bill Murray and groundhog from Harold Ramis' time-bending comedy *Groundhog Day*.

Before filming, Ramis observed the actual Groundhog Day festivities in the town of Punxsutawney; however, he discovered that the town did not have an actual town's square, and so filming was actually conducted in the village of Woodstock, Illinois. There production designer David Nichols changed storefronts, erected signs, hung awnings, and constructed "Gobbler's Knob," which was further decorated by local school children, in the middle of Woodstock's town square.

When Phil awakens again at 6 o'clock to the strains of Sonny and Cher's "I Got You Babe," he discovers to his horror that he is reliving the exact same day over again, confronting the same chatterbox bed and breakfast owner, the same annoying former classmate who wants to sell him insurance, the same Groundhog Festival accompanied by the strains of Frank Yankowic's "Pennsylvania Polka." It seems that he is caught in a time loop, that no matter what he does, he always returns to his bed on the morning of Feburary 2.

Consequently, he at first becomes convinced that there are no consequences. His metaphoric fate of being caught in a meaningless existence, reliving the same day over and over again, knowing that his life will make no difference echoes the real life fate of some drinking companions, who convince him that he will suffer no consequences after he deliberately provokes police who throw him in jail only for him to wind up once more back in his bed.

Phil then tries to bed some of the local ladies with less than satisfying results. He finds he becomes increasingly attracted to Rita, learning through trial and error what she likes and what not to say. He provides her with an enchanting day, but she still refuses to go to bed with him on such short notice.

Despairing, Phil tries self-destruction, including kidnapping the town's groundhog and driving a stolen truck over a precipice. The attempts do not alter his fate, so he begins making attempts at self-improvement, beginning with learning to create ice sculptures and taking piano lessons, advancing a little more each day. When an old man he previously spurned dies after Phil has compassionately taken him to the hospital, Phil demands to see his chart to learn the cause of death and attempts to save him by giving him a good meal. Slowly, through sheer repetition and questioning, Phil comes to know everyone in town, what their problems are, and what help they need on the day in question. He becomes the guardian angel of Punxsutawney and is suddenly one of the most beloved figures in town.

Rita cannot help but be impressed when townsperson after townsperson comes up to thank Phil for his assistance, and she ends up purchasing a date with him at the annual Groundhog Day Dinner. Rather than trying to take advantage of her, Phil instead spends his time creating an ice sculpture of her, and having achieved the twin goals of becoming a better person and winning the heart of Rita, is able to break the loop and live the rest of his life a better person than he would have without this unusual experience.

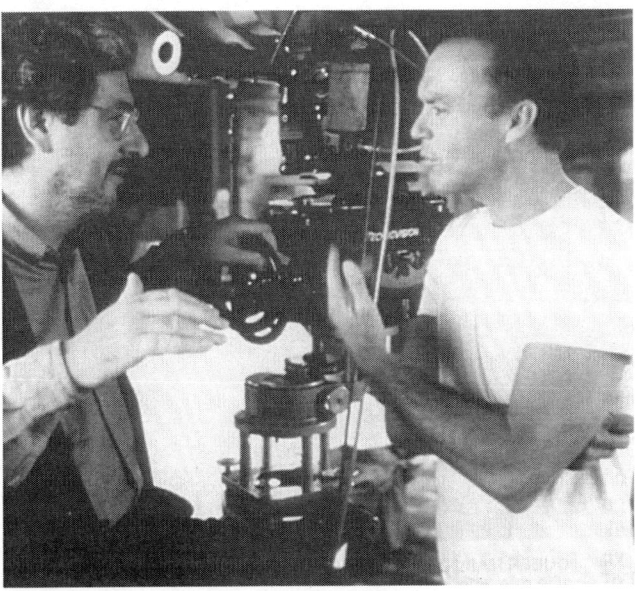

Harold Ramis confers with star Michael Keaton on the set of *Multiplicity*.

Inventive, thoughtful, and funny, *Groundhog Day* is a remarkable film, and one of Bill Murray's best comedies. Ramis considers it the most gratifying film he's done as a director, saying, "[I]t really touched people very deeply about how we live and why we live, and how to make the most of it."

Unfortunately for Ramis, *Stuart Saves His Family* was not similarly clever. Based upon a recurring character created and portrayed by *Saturday Night Live* writer Al Franken, Stuart would regularly mumble New Age–y positive platitudes to cover up his dysfunctional lifestyle and low self-esteem. The wittiest thing in the film is a moment when considering all the things he should have done, Stuart remarks that he "should all over myself." The plot concerns how after the death of a relative, when it is discovered that part of the relative's house stands on the neighbor's property, Stuart was told to open negotiations by his family in order to get the price down. The neighbor suddenly dies and his family wants to greatly increase the price of their property, which they are legally entitled to do after Stuart attempts to renegotiate. Unable to lie about the matter, as his family wishes him to do, Stuart inadvertently alienates the people closest to him.

Ramis' work on the film is certainly amiable enough to maintain a small degree of interest; however, it lacks the big laughs his best work engenders.

Ramis returned to science fiction with *Multiplicity*, a

cloning comedy starring Michael Keaton, more notable for its high price tag than its ability to attract audiences. This is unfortunate as the film expertly touches on some genuine concerns today (having enough time for family as well as career) and Keaton is able to bring off a comic, *tour de force* performance (which suffers on cropped, non-letterboxed copies of the film).

Multiplicity is based on a short story by Ramis' occasional collaborator Chris Miller, which was about an advertising executive with a wife and two kids who does not have time for anything. He sees an ad for a cloning service and decides to get himself cloned, and because things start to work out so well, gets himself cloned again, until he has so many clones that they take over his life and wind up sending him to South America.

Ramis liked the set-up of the story, but not the ending. Then, as Ramis told Kim "Howard" Johnson in *Starlog*, "[I]t dawned on me that the theme should *not* be about being busy. It was really about the divided self, how we're all different people with conflicting desires and interests who are pulled in different directions. It's not just a phenomenon of modern life, but the nature of human experience." Ramis brought in *Splash* scriptwriters Lowell Ganz and Babaloo Mandel to rework the story, centering it around different aspects of Doug Kinney (named after Ramis' friend and *Animal House* collaborator Doug Kenney and played by Michael Keaton).

In the film, Kinney is an overworked and overscheduled contractor who never has time enough for his wife Laura (Andie MacDowell) and his family. He takes up a geneticist's offer to "Xerox" him. When Kinney gets cloned, at first it seems to solve his problem, but then his clone decides that he needs a clone to help out, and soon Kinney must deal with three replicas of himself, each depicting a different aspect of his personality: his Deep Masculine side, his Inner Feminine side, and his Inner Child. Kinney goes frantic trying to keep his copies a secret and comes to realize that it's no good trying to be three or four different people, that instead he needs to integrate himself in a happy and healthy way.

Richard Edlund and Boss Films helped Ramis duplicate multiple images of Keaton within the frame and allowed them to interact with one another. Keaton does a great job of keeping each clone's behavior separate and distinct. Particularly impressive is the physical interaction between the Dougs, which were created by having a stand-in hand an object to Keaton, and then the stand-in's body was matted out and Keaton, placed in the identical position, would have to match the stand-in's body movement in the second pass.

In addition to the numerous optical effects, Ramis also relied on doubles for Keaton for over-the-shoulders shots and the like. Because of the special effects complexities, Ramis took 100 days to shoot the film, 40 percent longer than he would normally take for a film of this size.

"*Multiplicity* is about understanding who you are, and what your real priorities are, and that's what Michael's character does," said Ramis. "He stops being pulled in four different directions and really clarifies his life." *Multiplicity* is the rare science fiction film that does not lose sight of the human element at its core, and despite the cold shoulder it received at the box office, is likely to attract new admirers as it gets discovered over the next several years. It certainly marks Ramis as a science fiction comedy director to watch.

Ramis combined Billy Crystal and Robert De Niro together in *Analyze This*, a comedy about a mobster who comes to a psychiatrist for therapy, which was overshadowed by a similar HBO series that managed to make the same premise into something richer. Ramis' continued evidence of interest in science fiction is apparent by his signing to direct *Galaxy Quest* for DreamWorks. However, he left the film over a dispute with the star Tim Allen who plays a washed-up TV actor of a *Star Trek*–like show who is recruited by aliens to save their world.

Instead, Ramis talked a lot about making a third *Ghostbusters* movie, and commented that the film would involve the original cast (Murray, Ramis, and Dan Aykroyd) coming out of retirement to train a new group of rookie Ghostbusters to fight off poltergeists after Hell is declared full (echoing the production of the animated series *Ghostbusters Extreme*).

BILL REBANE (1937–)

Monster a-Go-Go (aka *Terror at Halfday*) (codirected with Hershell Gordon Lewis) (1965); *Invasion from Inner Earth* (1972); *The Roar of Snowmobiles* (1974); *The Giant Spider Invasion* (1975); *The Alpha Incident* (1976); *The Capture of Bigfoot* (1979); *Rana: The Legend of Shadow Lake* (1981); *The Game* (1982); *Demons of Ludlow* (1983); *Blood Harvest* (aka *The Marvelous Mervo*) (1986); *Twist Race* (short); *Dance Craze* (short); *The Love of Stella* (short); *All Fall Down* (short) (mid-sixties, precise dates unknown)

Though born in Europe, Bill Rebane has resided for most of his life in Gleason, Wisconsin. Rebane began his career in filmmaking by working on industrial films and assisting infamous gore filmmaker Herschel Gordon Lewis with *Lucky Pierre* and *Blood Feast*. He also had experience working for local television. Rebane decided to take the bull by the horns and direct, edit, shoot, and produce his own movie, *Terror at Halfday*. He started with $20,000 but fell short of the funds he needed to complete the film. He also lost Pete Thompson, the actor who plays the scientist in the film, who had other commitments, so Rebane brought in Doc Stamford, who rewrote the script with Rebane and assumed the part of the scientist's brother.

Enter Herschell Gordon Lewis, who purchased the unfinished film from Rebane and by shooting a minimum of transitional scenes and insert shots of notes and letters being looked at by the characters, brought the pieces together into a completed motion picture, though a portion of Rebane's material was simply excised. Lewis then added a satirically absurd narration and released the film as *Monster a Go-Go*.

Comprising seemingly randomly assembled footage, a narrator assures us that the story is about the search for an astronaut lost when his capsule crashed. It is believed that he had transformed into a ten-foot-high monster (portrayed by tall man Henry "Horace" Hite). We see the tall man wander around a field and there is also a lengthy night scene in Chicago that does not appear to have anything to do with anything. The film then comes to an abrupt end when Lewis decided he had used up enough footage to make it feature length, as the narrator astoundingly announces, "Suddenly there was no trail. There was no giant, no monster, no thing called Douglas to be followed. There was nothing in the tunnel but the puzzled men of courage who suddenly found themselves alone with shadows and darkness.... Frank Douglas was rescued alive and well, and of normal size some 8,000 miles away." Few films have been as audacious or stunning in their cynicism.

Lewis wrote an ad campaign for *Monster* that actually sold the film by emphasizing its laughable shortcomings, parodying one of Stan Freberg's commercials. "How did a 10-foot-tall monster get into that little bitty space capsule?" one ad read. And "You've never seen a picture like this—thank goodness!" said another. Despite its stupefying awfulness, the film, released on a double bill with *Moonshine Mountain*, made back its cost.

Meanwhile, Rebane got into making short subject musicals, including *Twist Race, Dance Craze, The Love of Stella*, and *All Fall Down*. He then left for Europe where he had a nine-year stint at Studio Bendesdorf, where he ended up in charge of production. Such films as Richard Lester's *How I Won the War*; *Chitty, Chitty, Bang, Bang*; *$*, and *The Final Guns* were shot there.

Rebane returned to America and began directing his second feature, *Invasion from Inner Earth*, about four people (including Paul Bentzen, Debbi Pick, and Nick Holt) lost in the wilderness who are haunted by an alien creature from under the ground.

Rebane then attempted his most famous, or notorious effort, *Giant Spider Invasion*, which was shot for $350,000 and returned some $13 million at the box office. Unfortunately for Rebane, most of the money ended up in the pocket of the distributor, Group One. Apart from having a few professionals in the cast (Barbara Hale, Alan Hale, and Bill Williams) and attempting to disguise a Volkswagen as a giant spider, the film has little to recommend it. The basic plot is that giant spiders have been falling out of a black hole onto a small farming community. Its single effective moment comes when a woman prepares her morning hi-potency vitamin cocktail, unaware that a tarantula has just fallen into her blender. She drinks her concoction, totally unaware of the presence of pureed arachnid. The superimposed spiders in the film are not frightening or even interesting.

Rebane returned to the big screen with *The Alpha Incident*, made for $220,000, in which the government tries to cover up the spread of an infection from Mars. This truly pathetic trifle, filmed in Gleason, Wisconsin, featured only four people (three of them are Ralph Meeker, John Alderman, and George "Buck" Flower) and only two rooms. Rebane set up his own production complex in Gleason, the Shooting Ranch Studio.

The deficient director went on to make a Bigfoot movie and a movie, *Rana: The Legend of Shadow Lake*, about a monster that is part man, part frog, neither of which I have seen. He served as associate producer on Ulli Lommel's *The Devonsville Terror*, and used much of the same crew to complete his own directorial effort, *The Demons of Ludlow* in which people are murdered because of harmonium haunted by the spirit of a warlock. The town's handless founder turns out to be behind the killings.

Rebane has continued to churn out low-budget efforts which get a small amount of local distribution, such as

Blood Harvest, which starred former 1960s icon Tiny Tim, but his shortcomings as a filmmaker are all too apparent on those films which have received a wider release. He depends on local talent when not using SAG actors and does not prove to have a sure hand in guiding amateur performances or creating even remotely interesting stories. Despite his apparent fondness for science fiction, he ranks with the worst directors in the genre.

CHUCK RUSSELL

A Nightmare on Elm Street 3: Dream Warriors (1987); *The Blob* (1988); *The Mask* (1995); *Eraser* (1996); *Bless the Child* (2000)

"If you had told me when I was 12 years old that one day I'd grow up to make 'monster movies,' I would never have believed that fantasy could come true," said Chuck Russell, who grew up loving 1950s science fiction films. Russell began working in films for Roger Corman and Sunn Classics, often serving as an assistant director and line producer. One of his favorite productions was Paul Bartel's satiric classic *Death Race 2000* (see chapter on Ib Melchior).

Russell served as the executive producer of *Hell Night*, one of the better Halloween imitators starring Linda Blair as one of a group of teens terrorized by some frat boys in a supposedly haunted house who unwittingly release a real maniac. Later Russell cowrote and line produced Joseph Ruben's wonderful science fiction film *Dreamscape*, and also produced *Girls Just Want to Have Fun* and Orion's *Back to School*, one of Rodney Dangerfield's funniest films.

Chuck Russell (center) directing his elaborate, effects-filled remake of *The Blob*.

A Nightmare on Elm Street 3: Dream Warriors is the best of the non–Craven directed sequels, with an interesting premise (supplied by originator Wes Craven himself) and leavened with the outrageous humor that became typical for the rest of the series. Russell coauthored the final screenplay along with Frank Durabont (*Shawshank Redemption*), Craven and Bruce Wagner.

Russell backs the film with disturbing, nightmarish imagery. In one dream, troubled teen Kristen (Patricia Arquette) is plagued by horrible nightmares, including one in which she is led inside Freddy Krueger's (Robert Englund) house by a young towheaded girl. Trying to save the girl from Freddy, Kristen's feet sink into goo, she enters a room full of hanged teens, and the girl she is carrying suddenly becomes a corpse.

Kristen is referred to a psychiatric hospital run by Dr. Gordon (Craig Wasson), whose new intern Dr. Nancy Thompson (Heather Langencamp) was the original *Nightmare* girl and is able to understand and relate to Kristen's problem. Nancy is now a therapist who specializes in what she calls "pattern dreaming." (Lawrence Fishburne [*Event Horizon; The Matrix*] also shows up in an early part as Max, the orderly.) When Kristen has a dream where Freddy as a giant snake tries to eat her, she calls on Nancy who is suddenly able to enter her dream and help repel the macabre menace.

Freddy is trying to kill the last of the Elm Street teens, whose parents were responsible for burning him to death many years before. He transforms Phillip into a ghoulish marionette controlled by arteries from his arms and legs before walking him off the top of the building. As Jennifer watches Zsa Zsa on Dick Cavett, Cavett transforms into Freddy, then so does the television set itself, which grabs Jennifer and electrocutes her body with its internal workings. Joey has his sex fantasy transform into Freddy who binds him to his bed with extra-long tongues that shoot out of his mouth.

Kristen dreams that she returns to her mother, only for Freddy to decapitate mom. She calls for Nancy, but Taryn (Jennifer Rubin) appears instead. Freddy attacks Taryn, turning his hand into hypodermics before overdosing her. Meanwhile, Gordon and Sheriff Thompson (John Saxon) try to put Freddy's spirit to rest by burying his bones and sprinkling holy water on them. Freddy's skeleton reanimates itself to kill Thompson and wound Gordon with a shovel.

Meanwhile, the teens all combine their forces in Kristen's dream to try and turn the tables on Freddy. However, Nancy is fooled by what appears to be the shade of her father, which proves another trick of Freddy as he transforms and kills her. Outraged, the others keep Freddy at bay until Gordon can finally bury him and bring him to his final rest. Or has he?

A Nightmare on Elm Street 3: Dream Warriors connected with horror audiences and established that the franchise was here to stay. Russell proved himself very resourceful on a limited budget, and also though the image sometimes has a faded look, is able to integrate the various imaginative effects scenes very well. Freddy accompanies most demises with a snide quip, but he remains a threatening presence, unlike the jokester of later entries.

It was Russell's idea to remake Irwin Yeaworth's *The Blob*, while taking advantage of the advances in special effects since the late fifties when Yeaworth made his film. "It's something I've always wanted to do," he said. "To take modern effects technology and apply it to a situation where a group of characters in a small town are confronted with an ultimate evil ... we've let our imaginations run wild." He cowrote the script with Frank Darabont, who had helped rewrite *Nightmare on Elm Street 3*, and would later write *The Shawshank Redemption* and *Mary Shelley's Frankenstein*.

"I felt that the creature in the original fell into a category along with Frankenstein and the Mummy where you'd really have to be slow not to be able to get away from it," continued Russell. "So we wanted something that was much more of an efficient predator. In fact, Jack Harris has told me 'you guys have the Blob doing everything we've always wanted to do when we first made it.'"

Russell and Darabont's final script is a contemporary rendition of the classic. The protagonist of the original film was clean-cut Steve McQueen, who in the remake is replaced with local motorcycle riding townee Brian Flagg (Kevin Dillon), who teams up with wholesome cheerleader Meg Penney (Shawnee Smith) and football heartthrob Paul Taylor (Donovan Leitch) to battle the Blob, which is no longer from outer space but has been given a terrestrial origin.

In updating the film, Russell found that there were a couple of images people had from the original film, like the theater scene, that would be a challenge to reinvent for a modern, more sophisticated audience. "Just the idea of showing our movie theatre audience themselves and saying, 'What would you do if you turned around and looked at the back of the projection booth and saw a ton and a half of enraged slime coming at you...'" posed Russell. "There are one or two moments from the original that we refer to but the film is not an homage. I think we're true to the spirit of the original, but we have our own characters. Characters that must rise to heroic proportions when they face a relentless, unstoppable creature that threatens their entire town."

Hoyt Yeatman's Dream Quest effects company handled all the optical effects in the film; Lyle Conway, Stuart Ziff, and Mike Fink along with their creature effects crew were responsible for the basic blob effects, both full-sized and miniature; and make-up effects coordinator Tony Gardner designed and constructed the Blob's victims, including the half-melted cheerleader from Arborville High.

Abbeville, Louisiana, was chosen as the location for the film for its well-preserved downtown and small town charm. Cameras rolled for production at dawn on January 12, 1988. Russell shot the film's night exteriors for three straight weeks, using dozens of locals as extras. After three-and-a-half more weeks on location in Los Angeles, *The Blob* moved indoors to Valencia sound stages where principal photography wrapped on April 6.

Despite its impressive effects, influenced by Rob Bottin's marvelous work on Carpenter's *The Thing*, audiences failed to flock to *The Blob*. The film's main innovation is the incorporation of a subplot in which a biological containment team seal off the town in order to cover up the monster's origin as a man-made weapon and are more concerned with recovering their project than with the safety of the townspeople. Though it sincerely tries, the remake cannot match the ineffable charm of the original.

The character of *The Mask* originated in an obscure comic book from Dark Horse Comics. The original comic was extremely violent and featured much black humor, which has been leavened in Mike Werb's script for Russell's feature version. Rubber-faced comic Jim Carrey is perfect for the part of Stanley Ipkiss, and delivers his finest performance to date in the role.

The premise of *The Mask* is extremely simple: a diver opens a treasure chest containing the mask of Loki, the Norse god of mischief, which when donned in the evening transforms the wearer into his heart's desire and provides him with unlimited power. (Russell shot a Viking funeral opening to help establish the backstory, but decided it wasn't necessary and trimmed the footage from the film.)

The main character, Stanley Ipkiss, is a stereotypical milquetoast banker who is at heart a hopeless romantic, and wearing the mask transforms him into a wild and crazy lover in snazzy duds. Later when evil night club owner of the Coco Bongo Club and crime mastermind Dorian Tyrell dons the mask, it transforms him into an omnipotent monster.

Chuck Russell (left) guides Jim Carrey in his performance as Stanley Ipkiss in *The Mask*.

Thanks to computer graphics imagery, *The Mask* succeeds better than any other film (even *Death Race 2000*) at becoming a live action cartoon. Ipkiss is a Tex Avery fan, and Avery's cartoons inspire many of his antics in the movie. Carrey's acting is cartoony to begin with, and Greg Cannom's inspired makeup helped accentuate the transition between the live action material and the computer graphic exaggerations that are part of the film's overall appeal.

Another star performer in the film is Ipkiss' dog Milo (played by Max), who is the only performer to come anywhere near to upstaging Carrey's antics. Milo fetches keys and Frisbees for his master and shows himself to be a well-trained movie mutt. Cameron Diaz as chanteuse Tina Carlyle also shines as the sexy singer who falls for Ipkiss because he treats her like a person rather than as a party favor. (The film also features Amy Yasbeck in the role of an erstwhile, Lois Lane–type newspaper reporter looking for a really nice guy, the type of role that would normally become Stanley's love interest, and then plays around with those movie convention expectations. Her death scene, in which she is thrown into a printing press, was considered out of tone with the surrounding scenes and her character simply disappears from the movie after she betrays Stanley to the bad guys.)

Here Russell deftly mixes comedy and special effects, keeping the pace snappy. Russell plays around with forties noir references in the look of the film, adding another layer to its cleverness. Carrey is able to make The Mask's self-referential comments "Smokin'!" and "Somebody stop me!" into memorable catchphrases. It is easy to see why the character became popular in a wish fulfillment way (at one point, he jams mufflers up the butts of two mechanics who are overcharging Ipkiss for repair work on his Honda), the semi-superhero also has a mendacious streak. (He gets into trouble with the law by robbing the bank just before the crooks can, although by saving the Mayor and other lives at the end, Ipkiss is let off the hook and Tyrell takes all of the blame.) The best and most innovative and inventive of three Carrey hits in 1994, *The Mask* soon cleaned up at the box office, becoming the biggest hit of Russell's career thus far.

To promote the film, Russell made two personal appearances on the unusual *Space Ghost Coast to Coast* TV show in 1994.

Eraser is almost a generic Arnold Schwarzenegger film, this time with Arnold as a top U.S. Marshal working for the Witness Protection Program in order to "erase" the past of potential, high-profile witnesses. Most of the people he protects are scum, but one day he is assigned to protect Lee (Vanessa Williams), a functionary at a weapons concern who has stumbled onto an illegal arms deal involving electronic-pulse superweapons that puts her life at risk. With the FBI's help, she breaks into her own company's high security computer, loading the incriminating information onto a zip drive, and making a back-up copy for herself. This drives her dismayed boss (James Cromwell) to commit suicide rather than face the consequences of her actions, which soon make her a target for some traitorous Washington insiders who hope to collect big by selling these high-tech weapons.

The Eraser trusts no one, not even his superiors Deguerin (James Caan) and Beller (James Coburn), and for good reason. Deguerin has become corrupt and tries to pin the blame on the Eraser. Russell comes up with a number of noisy action sequences, most memorably in a zoo complete with CGI alligators that take their own "bite" out of crime. Writers Tony Puryear and Walon Green keep things moving speedily along. Despite the high pricetag that comes with any Schwarzenegger film, *Eraser* failed to emerge as a major blockbuster, but still managed to do respectable business throughout the summer.

WILLIAM SACHS

Breakfast (short, date unknown); *South of Hell Mountain* (1971); *There Is No Thirteen* (1973); *Secrets of the Gods* (aka *The Force Beyond*, documentary) (1976); *The Incredible Melting Man* (1977); *Van Nuys Boulevard* (1979); *Galaxina* (1980); *Hot Chili* (1985); *Judgment* (aka *Hitz*) (1989); *The Last Hour* (1991); *Spooky House* (1999)

William Sachs attended school at the University of Maryland before deciding to become a film director and going to England to study at the London Film School. While there, he made a short film, *Breakfast*, which he claims won several prizes in Europe. He then went to Italy where he edited various TV spots and trailers for a time.

He then flew back to New York and began persuading people to invest in his film. He gave Ralph Boda his first job as cinematographer, and made his first film, *There Is No Thirteen*, which he describes as a surrealistic fantasy about a Vietnam veteran and what goes through his mind in a veteran's hospital. Actor-turned-producer Mark Damon starred as the Vietnam veteran who is experiencing flashbacks. The title refers to the number of affairs he has had. It was a thoroughly unpromising start for a relatively uninspired and uninspiring filmmaker.

Inspired, if that's the right word, by Sachs' mother sticking her hand in a bucket of glue and watching it drip, Sachs borrows the basic plot of Robert Day's *First Man Into Space* (1958) to come up with *The Incredible Melting Man*, which goes the Day film one better by adding disgusting makeup effects by future makeup wizard Rick Baker. *Melting Man* spends much of its time showing the character oozing from every orifice and leaving a puddle of sticky ichor around his ankles.

Made for a budget of $250,000, the most expensive item was Baker's effects, which took a couple of months to complete. Sachs worked together with Baker charting the process of decomposition in the movie and had Baker create four different masks. (Sachs hired Baker because he liked a gruesome effect of worms crawling out of someone's face that Baker had done for Jeff Lieberman's *Squirm*.) The entire film was shot in seventeen days.

Astronaut Steve West (Alex Rebar) is on his way to Saturn when something goes wrong. His ship returns to Earth, but mysteriously the rest of his crew is not aboard and West is in bad shape. In the hospital, he rips off his bandages to reveal that he is, in fact, melting (at least the title is not a cheat). He then kills and eats a nurse before escaping.

Dr. Ted Nelson (Burr DeBenning) and General Mike Parry (Myron Healey) are called in to deal with the situation, but the government only wants to cover up the mishap. West makes this difficult as he continues to ingest human flesh after ripping appendages off of innocent bystanders. At one point, Dr. Nelson, hot on West's radioactive trail, stops to examine some slime in a bush only to exclaim, "Oh God, it's his ear."

There is a mysterious connection between West and Nelson and his family. West is drawn to Nelson's family, scoping out his pregnant wife Judy (Ann Sweeny) which results in her losing her baby. Nelson is the only human West responds to, and when he is gone, West loses the last of his vestigal humanity.

Sachs delights in ghoulish touches. One of the best occurs when General Perry is found dead with something clutched in his hand. It's assumed to be a portion of West until it is revealed that it simply is a turkey leg the general had been snacking on when he was killed. Later a couple of security guards end up shooting Nelson rather than West. The film has a hokey ending with West finally melting into a non-ambulatory puddle which is swept away by a custodian at the refinery while we hear that a new Saturn launch will take place next morning.

Sachs followed this up with *Van Nuys Boulevard* in which Bill Adler plays a small town boy who comes to California and checks out the Van Nuys cruising scene, with people going off to the disco, to drag race, and grab something at the hamburger stand. The film received some attention for being just a little bit better than it needed to be, but *American Graffiti* this isn't.

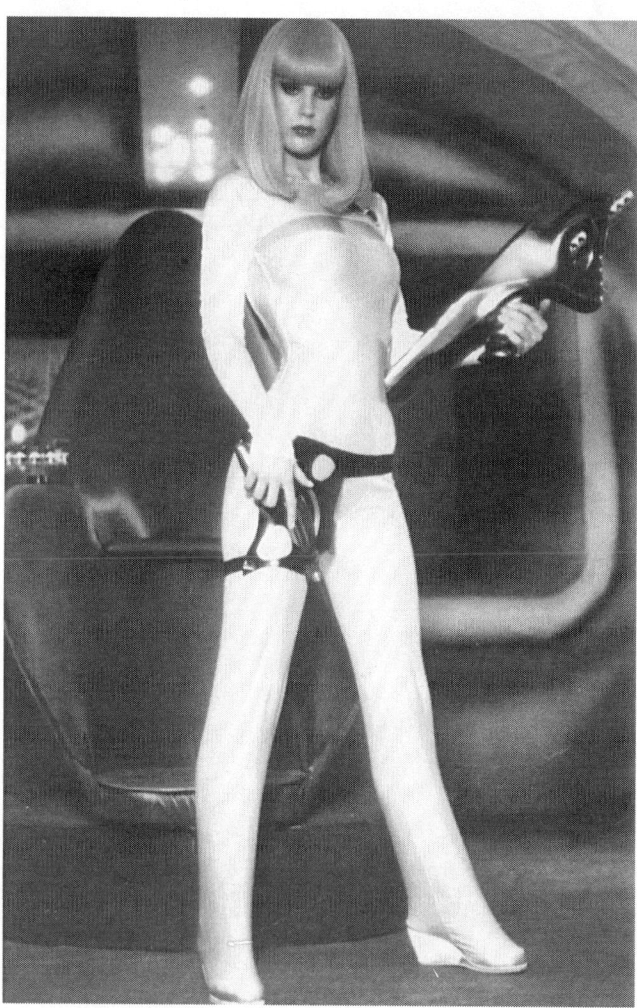

The late Dorothy Stratten as the perfect android (who still needs lifts in her shoes), Galaxina, in William Sachs' often overlooked SF comedy *Galaxina*.

Sachs returned to the SF genre by writing and directing *Galaxina*, best known as one of only three films starring the late model Dorothy Stratten, whose body was discovered the day the film opened, a victim of her estranged husband and whose life story became the subject of Bob Fosse's *Star 80*. What's not often noted about this Crown International release is that it is an occasionally amusing spoof of the sci-fi genre with a few clever touches among the nonsense, as well as one of the early films shot by Dean Cundey.

One of Sachs' oddest touches is that he attempted to create an alien environment on the planet Altair 1 by using infrared Ectachrome film, which causes the sky to turn green, the ground to appear yellow, and the vegetation various shades of red. Some actors had to be specially made up to appear to have somewhat normal skin color while others were left untreated to give them an alien appearance. Unfortunately for Sachs, he quickly learned that even slight variations in temperature or the amount of clouds would alter the look of the footage from shot to shot.

Galaxina (Stratten) is a beautiful but mute humanoid robot whose touch guides the spaceship *Infinity* in the year 3008 which is captained by Captain Cornelius Butt (Avery Schreiber). The ship's job is to chase down unidentified craft, check on galactic beer halls and brothels, and catch speeders. The other crewmembers are a drawling space cowboy named Private Robert "Buzz" McHenry (James David Hinton), gung-ho police type Sgt. Thor (Steven Macht), who shorts out Galaxina's no-touch system by attempting to kiss her; Maurice, a black engineer with useless wings (Lionel Smith), Sam Wo, a Charlie Chan style Asian (Tad Horino) who spouts nonsensical aphorisms, and locked up in the brig is a rock-munching alien called Kitty (Herb Kaplowitz), which looks like a leftover costume from the old *Star Trek* series. Even Angelo Rossitto gets into the act as the monster from the egg.

The film began with a budget under $100,000, though the producers realized that more money needed to be spent on the special effects if it was to attract an audience in the post–*Star Wars* age. One of the film's better gags relates how dull an actual spaceship fight would be with the two combatants firing at each other until one of them blows up when its force field finally gives out. (For once the ships are not buffeted by non-existent winds.)

The crew of the *Infinity* is sent to find the "Blue Star," a large gem that can harness the power of the Universe (and receives an angelic musical cue every time it is mentioned), which was stolen by an evil cyberlizard named Ordric (Ronald Knight) from the planet Mordric who has taken it to the planet Altair 1. To make the journey, the crew place themselves in suspended animation, but not before setting up a weak *Alien* parody when Captain Butt eats an egg inhabited by an alien creature. The creature later cuddles up to the suspended captain and calls him mama.

The ship reaches Altair, and the Captain upon reviving from suspended animation discovers he has grown an enormous beard. Galaxina has reprogrammed herself so that she can speak, now has a normal body temperature, acquires a set of human sex organs from a catalogue, and can now feel love. In a typical science fiction film, when a spaceship crashes, everyone gets up none-the-worse for wear, but in this one, the crew all has whiplash and so must send Galaxina out to complete the mission.

She is sent to seek out Ordric in a western-style ghost town where rumor has it that an Earthman by the name of Frank Future knows the whereabouts of the fabled Blue Star. There is the requisite send-up of the cantina scene from *Star Wars*, as she visits a restaurant owned by Mr. Spot (David Cox) who spouts the worst pointed ears since those of Nadir in *Frankenstein Meets the Space Monster*. (En route, she passed the television version of the Batmobile which adds another level of anachronism to the whole affair.)

Galaxina discovers the gemstone is in the hands of religious bikers who worship the god "Harley Davidson," a classic motorcyle which a recovered Thor and Buzz steal. ("Don't shoot," one cult member warns, "you'll hit god!") Unfortunately, once they get the Blue Star aboard, it winds up being eaten by Kitty.

Since then, Sachs seems to have dropped out of sight except for tackling the occasional low budget project like *The Last Hour*, a sort of low-rent *Die Hard* in which Michael Paré stars as a cop whose ex-wife is kidnapped and taken hostage by a gangster. Neither of his SF movies could be called a great science fiction film, but both show some potential to create something interesting should he ever get an adequate budget and decent script.

STEVEN SAYADIAN

Nightdreams (1981); *Café Flesh* (1982); *Dr. Caligari* (1989)

Steve Sayadian directs under the name "Rinse Dream," and is best known for the science fiction porno movie *Café Flesh*. *Café Flesh* attempts to be "the thinking man's porno," in that it intends to excite on a conceptual rather than a physical level. It depicts a post-nuclear holocaust world where 99% of the population are Sex Negatives, who become ill if they attempt to have sex. Nevertheless, these frustrated voyeurs remember how wonderful sex was and demand to see it performed by those who are still Positive, which they can through a nightclub circuit of live sex acts, one of which is the Café Flesh, presided over by Max Melodramatic (Andrew Nichols), a *Cabaret*-type emcee.

One of the film's bizarre touches is that its heroine, Lana (Pia Snow, better known for her non-porn career as Michelle Bauer), a secret Positive, must feign a disinterest to keep her relationship with Nick (Paul McGibboney). Sayadian and journalist Jerry Stahl, who wrote the script, conceived it not as a porno project, but as *Cabaret* goes New Wave, an irradiated *Ship of Fools*.

According to Stahl in Danny Peary's *Omni's Screen Flights/Screen Fantasies*:

> Sex, clearly, is not the issue here. Apocalypse itself is what titillates. For the jaded throng who view their own future as the function of a World Gone Rotten, Café Flesh is a logical destination.... There are a million dirtier movies in the cosmos. But for an alarmingly large segment of our little world, obliteration seems the sexiest ticket around.
>
> *Café*'s concerns are terminal: the mechanics of lust après mega-death; the impotent salacity of the living doomed; the fetish for fiery climax that gives some folks a secret frisson at the prospect of the Holocaust to come, so that survival itself hinges on continued repression.

Max continually insults and heckles his audience for having nothing better to do than watch the on-stage performers have sex, and by implication attacks the audience that comes to watch films such as this one instead of doing something more constructive. Nevertheless, this same audience remains mesmerized, addicts looking to score a vicarious experience that is missing in their own lives.

The sexual vignettes in the film are "artistically" presented in a fashion that is actually anti-erotic, but full of surreal touches (such as finger-snapping arms that rise from the bottom of the stage during one number). The participants, especially male ones, are decked out in weird masks and outfits. The major turning point in the plot comes when Lana is aroused and gives herself away to Max by masturbating in her seat.

Meanwhile, a government agent exposes the fact that the virginal visitor Angel (Marie Sharp) is a Positive, and so she is forced to perform, but she quickly discovers that she enjoys it. Max harasses Nick and winds up humiliated, revealing that he lost his penis in the war.

Sex star Johnny Rico (Kevin Jay) arrives at the club and performs with Angel. Lana cannot control herself at the sight, and so she too joins the action up on stage as the audience goes wild. The film ends with Lana finding fulfillment while Nick loses the only thing he's ever cared about and is dragged unconscious from the club. It is a bleak and depressing film, hardly what one would expect from a porno movie, and certainly far ahead in artistic quality of other porn science fiction films, which have ranged from *Nude on the Moon* to *Sex Trek: The Next Penetration*.

Sayadian and Stahl reteamed for *Dr. Caligari*, which was aimed directly at the art house market and features more offbeat imagery, including a giant tongue, a woman masturbating in front of a television set, and very strange outfits. The title is meant to be tribute to the Expressionistic classic *The Cabinet of Dr. Caligari*, and in its own way, this film could be interpreted as New Wave expressionism. Madeline Reynal plays Dr. Caligari who runs Caligari's Insane Asylum that is somehow using its patients for hormone experiments, and *Repo Man's* Fox Harris (to whom the film is dedicated) chews the scenery, but heaven help me if I can figure out what it all means. This becomes so plotless and obscure that it simply puzzles rather than delights, confuses rather than illuminates.

JOEL SCHUMACHER (1939–)

The Incredible Shrinking Woman (1981); *D.C. Cab* (aka *Street Fleet*) (1983); *St. Elmo's Fire* (1985); *The Lost Boys* (1987); *Flatliners* (1990); *Dying Young* (1991); *Falling Down* (1993); *The Client* (1994); *Forever* (aka *Batman Forever*) (1995); *A Time to Kill* (1996); *Batman & Robin* (1997); *The Runaway Jury*; *8MM; Flawless* (1999)

Television: *The Virginia Hill Story* (1974); *Amateur Night at the Dixie Bar & Grill* (1979); *2000 Malibu Road* (1992)

Joel Schumacher, a New York native, was born on August 29, 1939, and grew up in Queens, Long Island City in a poor, working class neighborhood. At the age of four, his father died and his mother was often at work six days and three nights a week selling dresses in order to survive. Schumacher fell in love with movies, but at the age of nine, he began working in the fashion industry in order to aid his mother's finances.

He initially launched himself on a career as a designer and display artist for the Henri Bendel department store while he was attending Parson's School of Design. He went on to operate his own boutique, Paraphernalia, before joining Revlon, which bought his store and gave him a job as a clothing designer and packager at $65,000 a year.

He describes himself as an obsessive-compulsive personality who became obsessed with the sex, drugs, and rock 'n' roll culture of the 1960s, becoming a hard-core drug addict in the process, but has since conquered alcohol and drugs, though he later became so addicted to the Nintendo Gameboy game Tetris that he started seeing Tetris pieces falling in his sleep.

In 1970, he was down to 130 pounds, had lost five teeth, and owed $50,000, when he woke up and realized that he was not happy and was not doing what he wanted to do in life. He resolved to go to Hollywood to become a film director even though the odds were against him.

Schumacher started his film career as an art director for television commercials and then as a costume designer, working on such films as *Play It As It Lays, The Last of Sheila, Blume in Love, The Prisoner of Second Avenue, Interiors* and Woody Allen's wonderful science fiction comedy *Sleeper*.

Schumacher designed the garish, early 1970s style costumes for *Sleeper*'s future folk to wear in Allen's brilliant slapstick sci-fi comedy, as well as tuxedoed, silver-domed, mime-faced robotic servants and the supremely silly survival suit which inflates to resemble an overripe fig.

Allen has long harbored a semi-secret love for science fiction, writing a couple of comic SF stories, and incorporating a couple of science fictional segments in his previous film, *Everything You've Always Wanted to Know About Sex**, which features a parody of mad scientist movies and Jack Arnold's *Tarantula*, specifically as John Carradine unleashes a giant female breast to terrorize the countryside, and another segment that showed the physiological workings of an orgasm in a science fictional manner (where Tony Randall and Burt Reynolds operate the brain's command center, pictured like a mini version of Houston's Space Command Center, alerting the stomach to prepare for food and the penis to prepare for action. Allen plays one of the sperm who hopes his creator is preparing for copulation and not just playing with himself).

Allen in *Sleeper* was attempting to find a new comic vocabulary, fusing slapstick from the past with verbal comedy that was more cerebral and psychological in orientation. Allen chafed at the difficulty of presenting what he felt was funniest about the contemporary era, which he felt was the psychological relationships between people, which is neither very visual nor interesting on the screen. He hoped to overcome this problem in *Sleeper* by taking the

Joel Schumacher created the costumes for Woody Allen's beloved SF comedy *Sleeper*. Here director and star Allen takes Diane Keaton for a ride in a futuristic car.

contemporary situations out of the present and projecting them into the future.

Thus *Sleeper* is set in 2173 in an authoritarian America ruled by a mysterious figure known as The Leader, revealed at the end of the film to not even be a figurehead, but a mere nose which the supporters of the status quo hope to clone into a duplicate Leader. Allen plays Miles Monroe, an unsuccessful clarinet player and part owner of the Happy Carrot Health Food Store in Greenwich Village, who had gone to St. Vincent's Hospital for a routine ulcer operation and awakens two hundred years later in a world where all his cherished assumptions have been turned upside down.

Allen playfully pokes fun at various celebrities, as Miles learns that World War III came about when Albert Shanker, president of the National Federation of Teachers, got hold of the atomic bomb. Because there is a gap in the future's knowledge of the past, he is asked to identify various figures, and so he indentifies Charles de Gaulle as a famous French chef, Norman Mailer as a man who donated his ego to the Harvard Medical School, President Richard Nixon as a politician who fell into disgrace as each time he left the White House the silverware was counted, and finally a clip of Howard Cosell (who appeared in Allen's *Bananas*), which he assents to the future's assumption that whenever someone had committed a crime against the state, they were forced to watch Cosell as punishment.

Sleeper has a plentitude of visual and physical humor, with its invention never flagging throughout its 88 minute running time. Diane Keaton, who had shown a facility for comedy in *Play It Again, Sam*, is even funnier here playing the pretentious poet Luna Schlosser, who composes horrible poems about butterflies turning into caterpillars. The film has a unique but very effective Dixieland jazz soundtrack composed and played by Allen himself along with the Preservation Hall Jazz Band and the New Orleans Funeral and Ragtime Orchestra, which is long overdue to be issued separately.

According to Allen himself, "One of the most difficult aspects of making *Sleeper* was getting futuristic locations for the budget we had. [The film was shot in Colorado and California.] It was not a big-budget picture, so it's not like Kubrick makes *2001* and spends $12 million. The budget was originally two million, but it went up to three, which is not a lot of money. For that we had to build automobiles and interior sets. The other difficulty was getting the physical jokes to work, having me able to fly in the suit, be shot through water, and hang from a ladder and from a building. The film was supposed to be shot in fifty days but it took me a hundred. Until this picture I had never gone a day over schedule."

Today *Sleeper* is remembered as one of the best early and funny Woody Allen films, albeit one which has a serious underlying message that revolutions do not change things; no matter who is in charge, life is going to be terrible, so the best thing to do is count on the people you love to help get you through it.

Noting that many young directors began as screenwriters, Schumacher then left costuming and branched out into screenwriting. He sold his first script, a TV movie about an actress-model who is found dead called *Ignorance Is Bliss*, to Barry Diller at ABC, which was never made. He then worked on a minor cult film, *Sparkle,* about three R&B singers in the 1950s before achieving genuine success with the sleeper hit *Car Wash*, which became a huge commercial success. From there, Schumacher wrote the script for *The Wiz* before moving into directing for television, making his directorial debut with *The Virginia Hill Story*.

In the late seventies, filmmaker John Landis had the idea of doing a remake of Jack Arnold's 1957 classic *The Incredible Shrinking Man*, which had been considered for sequelization in 1958 with the never made *The Fantastic Little Girl*. However, Universal Pictures, who owned the rights, considered Landis' plans to be too elaborate and so reduced the budget and assigned *The Incredible Shrinking Woman* to Joel Schumacher to direct and long-time Lily Tomlin writer Jane Wagner to write.

Wagner has taken Tomlin to both the heights (*The Search for Intelligent Life in the Universe*) and depths (*Moment by Moment*) of her varied career. Unfortunately, she proved the wrong choice to script a distaff version of the Richard Matheson classic.

For some bizarre reason, we are expected to find the idea of someone shrinking to be automatically hilarious rather than tragic. Wagner uses shrinking as a metaphor for a loss of power and authority rather than as Matheson did as a metaphor for the dwindling of life itself.

Unfortunately, Schumacher's inept direction can't save

the failings of the script, nor does he comfortably set a tone. A brief touching scene where Tomlin's husband Vance (Charles Grodin) learns that the wife he thought was dead is actually alive is crudely cut off by Tomlin's Ernestine character. Mark Blankenfield's annoying lab assistant who refuses to pay any attention to the tiny Tomlin is later revealed to be a good guy we're supposed to like.

Schumacher can't seem to find the angles which would make the special effects impressive or give them scope. There's nothing to compare with the scene in the original where Grant Williams has to dash across a football stadium sized living room to escape a now giant housecat. She is simply plopped among a few giant props or shot from overhead.

The color scheme in the film is also annoyingly wrongheaded, full of bright primary colors that suggest a coloring book approach and simply make this already unreal story more unreal. In fact, the film looks much like an overlong television commercial and plays like one which has lost its minimal appeal.

The underlying concept behind Tomlin's shrinking seemingly has to do with consumerism; the heroine Pat Kramer (Tomlin) is shrinking due to exposure to various artificial products, sprays, food coloring, additives, preservatives, etc. However, she's also rescued by this same profusion of products, hence blunting the uncertain satire of the piece which never takes off or is never effective.

There are a few brief moments of amusement with the appearance of a gorilla named Sidney (actually makeup effects artist Rick Baker in an elaborate suit). The injection of Sidney into the story is probably a holdover from John Landis' association with the project as he often inserts either gorillas or gorilla references into most of his films.

Tomlin is fine and believable as the overwhelmed Pat Kramer; however, the appearance of her Ernestine the Telephone Operator and her Judith Beasley, consumer activist, characters are both intrusive and unwelcome. Neither Ned Beatty, who plays Dan Beame, the man whose company manufactures the useless products now endangering Kramer, nor Henry Gibson, who plays Dr. Eugene Nortz, who callously tries to kidnap Kramer for study, are used to good effect as the villains of the piece.

Following the truly forgettable *D.C. Cab* about hijinks at a cab company in Washington, D.C., Schumacher had a hit in directing and cowriting *St. Elmo's Fire*, a very sappy brat pack film that follows the fortunes of seven pathetic friends from shortly after their college graduation. We are given Billy (Rob Lowe), an irresponsible rock musician who likes to use other guys' apartments and other guy's women without their permission. Despite being a freeloader and a cad with a wife and babe of his own, he attracts wealthy

Star Lily Tomlin as the shrunken Pat in Schumacher's *Incredible Shrinking Woman.*

heiress Wendy (Mare Winningham), who in the film's most unintentionally funny scene begs him to take her virginity.

We also are introduced to Alex (Judd Nelson), a social-climbing snob who hopes to make it in politics and sleeps around on his fiancée Leslie (Ally Sheedy), who sees his immaturity and beds down with Kevin (Andrew McCarthy), a struggling journalist. Then there is Kerbo (Emilio Estevez) who wants to be a lawyer and seduces old ladies. And finally, there's the group's burn-out, Jules (Demi Moore), who is addicted to cocaine and victimhood. The characters make all ex-college students out to be self-serving, sexist dolts with an innate core of inner sensitivity, but its "friends will get you through life" philosophy seems like so much hogwash when the friends are so goofily screwed up as these.

The Lost Boys began as a film project for Richard Franklin with the concept that Peter Pan and his Lost Boys stayed young forever because they were vampires. The script was rewritten by Jeffrey Boam (*The Dead Zone*) and Richard Donner was brought in to be director, but Donner decided that he would rather direct *Lethal Weapon*, so he relegated himself to a producer position and hired Schumacher, who had been trying to get a film version of Jay McInery's *Bright Lights, Big City* put together without success.

Schumacher was glad to come aboard, bringing his own sense of style to the film. He played up the film's advertising line: "Sleep all day. Party all night. It's fun to be a vampire," emphasizing that the vampires would wear trendy modern clothing and listen to hip rock and roll (from INXS, Jimmy Barnes, Lou Gramm, and Echo and the Bunnymen).

The story introduces us to all–American teenagers Sam (Corey Haim) and Michael (Jason Patric), who like comic books and girls respectively. They move with their mother Lucy Emerson (Dianne Wiest) to her father's (Barnard Hughes) place in the peaceful town of Santa Carla, California, and become involved with her mysterious video store boss (Edward Herrmann). Unbeknownst to them, the town is crawling with hoodlum vampires, and it's not long before Michael begins to fall for Star (Jami Gertz), one of the newly undead.

This movie plays with vampire lore, asserting that a person is only a partial vampire until he or she makes their first kill. The idea behind the story is that Michael falls in with the wrong crowd (Kiefer Sutherland, Brooke McCarter, Billy Wirth, Alex Winter, Chance Corbitt), and that Sam struggles to save him with the aid of teenage comic book entrepreneurs the Frog Brothers (Corey Feldman and Jason Newlander).

The entire caper is cannily crafted to appeal to the MTV generation, and on a commercial level it certainly succeeds. It may be a bit derivative, but it is slickly made, quickly paced, and features a few thrills, some funny moments ("You're a vampire ... wait till Mom finds out!") and a rousing climax. It is one of the more entertaining vampire films of the 1980s, lacking only substance (unless one wants to read vampirism as a metaphor for substance abuse, a constant concern of Schumacher's following his reckless lifestyle).

Following *The Lost Boys*, Schumacher was tapped to direct the proposed film version of Andrew Lloyd Webber's enormous stage hit *Phantom of the Opera*; however, this failed to come to fruition. Both Steven Spielberg and Michael Jackson had also expressed an interest in the project, but Webber wanted Schumacher. However, despite the promise of Michael Crawford and Sarah Brightman reprising their stage roles, no studio ended up willing to front the costs.

Schumacher ended up working on *Flatliners* instead. *Flatliners* was given $20 million based on newcomer Pete Filardi's script. The project became the topic of controversy when it was discovered that producer Scott Rudin had secretly tried to top Columbia's bid for Filardi's script despite having an exclusive deal to make films at Columbia. Filardi was paid $250,000, an amazingly high price for a first-time script.

Flatliners had one of the most terrific come-ons in cinema history. It counts as a science fiction film because it revolves around a scientific experiment to find out what happens to the soul after death. Unfortunately, the film primes the audience to discover some interesting answers, but fails to come up with a satisfactory one.

Kiefer Sutherland stars as brilliant, self-involved medical student Nelson Wright, who suffers from delusions of grandeur and is driven to discover the secrets of death itself by nearly killing himself to create his own "out of body" experiences. In semi–Faustian fashion, he flirts with immortality by utilizing modern technology to knock out his heart and brain by using injections, a heating blanket, and electric shocks, just to see what happens while he's clinically dead.

Of course, he needs his friends around to bring him out of it. "I don't wanna die," he tells them, "I wanna come back with the answers to death," and so cajoles four other med students into assisting him. Rachel (Julia Roberts) is a frigid overachiever, who attracts the attentions of both Nelson and Labraccio (Kevin Bacon), who has just been thrown out of medical school for breaking the rules in the emergency room. Joe (William Baldwin), a compulsive ladies' man who enjoys videotaping his lovemaking sessions, and Steckle (Oliver Platt), an obsessive video voyeur, round out the group.

For a studio release, *Flatliners* is fairly weird and *outré*. Schumacher does not give a damn about realism, but he can build a mood, and the out of the way location Nelson goes to to conduct his experiment is a production designer's dream, with an enormous painting of Zeus banishing Prometheus (which echoes the film's motif of punishing these seekers of knowledge for their pride and hubris). The cinematography is often dark and dreary like the subject matter, with plentiful wet streets and strange shadows. Nothing looks quite normal. Schumacher's camera is very restless as well, as it rushes and jerks from one image to another, adding a sense of nervousness that is appropriate to the enterprise.

Flatliners does create a sense of dread and disorientation, but ultimately decides that death is a descent into a private hell where the guilts of one's life return to extract their revenge, following the characters back into their real lives. The afterlife looks like an MTV video only without an appropriate rock song to accompany the flashy imagery. Thus, as each member of the team takes his turn, Rachel is haunted by her father's suicide, Nelson is stalked by a tyke he once snubbed, and Joe sees the women he's seduced mouthing his clichéd come-ons ("We can stop whenever you want," "Of course I'll still respect you," and "We don't have to do anything").

The answer to their problems ends up being as simple as "Face your fears."

Schumacher worked again with Julia Roberts on *Dying*

Young, a modern variation on *Dark Victory*, adapted by Robert Friedenberg from a novel by Marti Leimbach, only this time it's a stuffy, vain, rich young man who is dying of leukemia and decides to terminate chemotherapy after falling in love with Roberts, whom he has hired to take care of him, because he does not like the thought of her seeing him without hair. Apart from some risible dialogue, the film is a treacly, sodden mess.

Falling Down proved to be a very canny piece of agit-prop. The main character, called D-FENS through most of the film because of his license plate, is a white, middle-class defense industry worker who has seen his life and surroundings turn to *merde*. The script by Ebbe Roe Smith exploits the general disrepair of society in general and of Los Angeles in particular, all the petty annoyances that get under people's skins.

The story is exceedingly simple. Bill Foster (Michael Douglas), a defense-nerd desk jockey finds himself stuck in traffic and notices that the air is dirty, the area is hot and noisy, and traffic is totally immobile. He decides he's had enough, and simply abandons his car to walk to where he's going, his daughter's birthday party in Venice, much to the consternation of his fellow travelers who simply see another roadblock in life.

Frankly, Bill's mad and he isn't going to take it anymore. It's not just the inability of society to function smoothly, it's banal radio chit-chat, Korean markets that overcharge and don't make change, it's gangbangers who threaten people for simply walking down the street. The targets are easy, but Bill's violent responses aren't appropriate, though they are audience-pleasing.

Word of a swath of violence comes to retiring LAPD detective Martin Prendergast (Robert Duvall), who then has to track the errant protagonist down. Without much to go on, Prendergast has to figure out who and where D-FENS is. His ex-wife (Barbara Hershey) already has a restraining order that prohibits him from coming near her or their daughter, which indicates that Foster's fit of pique is not something entirely new.

Falling Down's basic strategy is to get audiences to identify with Foster and then make it clear that he's really the villain. "I'm the bad guy? How'd that happen? I did everything they told me to. They lied to me," he says with surprise when Prendergast prepares to take him in. The morality is further complicated by the fact that Foster's "victims" are often so worthy of being tormented from aggressively violent gangbangers to a militaristic racist neo–Nazi (Frederic Forrest). Schumacher even goes so far as to make Foster a modern Christ suffering for our sins, miraculously surviving a drive-by shooting, developing bleeding palms, and standing in a crucifixion pose.

While preparing *The Client*, Schumacher was contacted by Warner Bros. and offered their "largest asset," meaning the Batman franchise. Schumacher claimed he needed Burton's approval and quickly obtained it after a lunch together. He told Marc Shapiro in *Starlog*:

> I wanted to do a story where Bruce Wayne is struggling with the Batman side of himself. He wakes up one day and wonders why he became Batman. That would allow us to go back and take a mythic look at his roots. Given that set-up, Two-Face seemed the perfect villain, because nobody is more ying-yang than he is. Who better to have around to question Batman and his identity than the Riddler, the ultimate mind game player? In comes Dr. Chase Meridian, a criminal psychologist who happens to look like Nicole Kidman.... Anyway, she falls for Batman and Bruce is in love with her. Finally, you have Dick Grayson, whose parents' death fuels his desire to be a vigilante. It's a total mirror of Bruce Wayne's life and it gives Bruce something to deal with. I ended up with many characters that all feed into one idea.

Batman Forever, the sequel to the two Burton *Batman* films, is certainly informed by the look of the Burton movies (Burton served as coproducer on this one as well). Val Kilmer (*Real Genius*; *Willow*; *The Doors*) replaced Michael Keaton as Bruce Wayne/Batman and demonstrates a lighter touch without sacrificing the brooding qualities in the troubled character that Burton had emphasized.

The weak link in this entry is Wayne/Batman's love interest, Dr. Chase Meridian (Nicole Kidman), a psychiatrist, whose scenes with the hero fail to ignite any sparks of interest. She is a head-shrinker obsessed with "the wrong kind of man," who while she can hold her own (she boxes for exercise), never comes into her own as a character.

The theme this time around seems to be teaming up, as Dick Grayson/Robin (Chris O'Donnell) is added to the mix to bring out Batman's paternal qualities. Wayne recognizes in Dick his own younger self at a critical, pivotal point in his life. He knows it is important to emphasize to the younger crimefighter that killing his family's murderers won't make the pain of their deaths go away. Contrasting the dynamic duo are the villains for this go-round: Two-Face (Tommy Lee Jones), formerly district attorney Harvey Dent (played by Billy Dee Williams in the first Burton *Batman*) and Edward Nigma (James Carrey) who turns into the manic Riddler. Both bear a grudge against the Dark Knight or Bruce Wayne (Nigma having worked for Wayne Enterprises on a brain-wave-manipulator that Wayne refused to fund).

Jones gives his part the requisite brooding quality, while Carrey again demonstrates his ability to be a human cartoon, spouting a bundle of wisecracks and imparting his role with demonic neurotic energy.

There is a spare amount of satire as Nigma's "3-D television" attachment turns the populace of Gotham into media-manipulated zombies, and perhaps it is appropriate that we end up questioning the mental health of every character we see up on the screen, with the droll exception of Alfred (once more played by Michael Gough) who supplies wit and moral guidance for his masters.

Schumacher employs a sure hand with the script by Lee Batchler, Janet Scott Batchler, and Akiva Goldman, mixing his characters' mental quirks with a light, humorous touch that goes down well. His version of Batman is better adjusted, not so much driven by inner demons as choosing to accept the light and dark sides of his nature and pursue his career fighting crime, and who is complemented by Robin who provides the impetus he needs to stay Batman forever.

Schumacher has prepared a 2 hour and 40 minute version of the movie that was to premiere on the new DVD (digital video disc) format, and was expected to help kick off sales of the new players once it is released. "A lot of cultists have been asking about those extra scenes, which is basically just more back story [how Bruce Wayne became Batman, the genesis of the giant Monarch bat]," said Schumacher. "So, we'll put the scenes back in and have me talking about why they were in and why they were cut out."

Nevertheless, Schumacher has mixed feelings about the new technology, which he sees as a boon to film scholarship, but something less for filmmakers who hate to revisit old projects: "I think multiple endings are a problem," he said. "If you're really making a strong story with vision to it, it can only have one ending. Multiple endings are more suited to video games." But he feels such material is justified when it illustrates the creative process.

Forever proved that audiences would go to a Batman movie even without Tim Burton at the helm, and the film raked up enough impressive business worldwide that Schumacher was signed to direct the sequel as well.

Schumacher's *A Time to Kill* is a well-made but deeply dishonest movie. It moves novelist John Gresham's story up from an early sixties setting, where its racial politics make at least some sense, to the nineties, where they simply do not. The plot has a black man Carl Lee Hailey (Samuel L. Jackson) taking the law into his own hands by killing the Ku Klux Klanners who had raped his daughter. It pretends that segregationist feelings of the pre–Civil Rights era remain unchanged, except, mysteriously, that the Southern town has elected a black sheriff, Walls (Charles S. Dutton). Despite a sizable black population in the town, comprising some 30% of the population, we're given a highly unlikely all white jury. The film further pretends that the jury cannot sympathize with the man's situation until the hero, attorney Jake Brigance (Matthew McConaughey), tells them to imagine that the victim was a white girl.

Photograph of director Joel Schumacher taken around the time of *Batman Forever*, which featured a science fictional plot about transferring the intelligence of Gothamites into the Riddler (played by Jim Carrey).

This presumption that modern white Southerners do not feel that blacks are human beings like themselves is offensive and misleading in the extreme. Schumacher should either have kept the period setting or had the screenwriters revise the racial politics to incorporate the numerous changes in attitudes and feelings since, say, the Emmett Till case. Schumacher also goes for overkill when it comes to redneck clichés. As a consequence, this movie seems split off from reality and fails to achieve the impact it intends despite its talented cast.

Schumacher returned to the Batman saga in 1997 with the highly disappointing *Batman & Robin*, with *ER*'s George Clooney taking over the role of Batman, and Chris O'Donnell reprising the role of Robin. Together they face a bald-headed Arnold Schwarzenegger as Mr. Freeze and Uma Thurman as Poison Ivy. To stuff the film even further, the characters of Batgirl and Bane are also inserted into the narrative.

In the script by Akiva Goldsman, brilliant molecular biologist Victor Fries (Schwarzenegger) tries to save his ailing wife by cryogenically preserving her but via an accident is altered into the villain Mr. Freeze in the process, who desperately needs diamonds to power his cold suit to maintain himself and his wife. Mr. Freeze wears a freezing pack to keep himself cold and is interested in freezing the world to make it a more suitable environment for himself, and he joins forces with Poison Ivy, former botanist Dr. Pamela Isley, who is a florist parody of the PETA people, wanting to protect all plants from the ravages of plant-consuming animals. The film also introduces the comic book spin-off character of Batgirl (Alicia Silverstone), altering her origin so that she is now the alter ego of schoolgirl Barbara Wilson, a niece of Alfred Pennyworth (Michael Gough, who along with Pat Hingle's Commissioner Gordon, is the only actor to have appeared in all four films).

According to Schumacher, Clooney's is "the most human and most accessible Batman — a less dark, brooding, and damaged Batman. So that changes the tone of the film somewhat.... He has a fiancée, conflict with Robin [Chris O'Donnell], a drama between his and Alfred's [Michael Gough] friendship, and of course the villains. He's a busy billionaire, giving out money during the day and looking so good doing it; then he's out all night in a rubber suit killing people, and doing it well."

There were reports that Clooney liked to clown around on the set, once almost stopping Schumacher's heart by telling him that a very expensive day's work was shot because someone had put the Batman emblem on upside down. Clooney did not want the character becoming too dark or tragic, but the script leaves Batman and Bruce Wayne as little more than cyphers and gives Clooney little to work with.

The new film once again alters the design of the Batmobile, perhaps to generate yet more toy tie-ins. After his adding nipples to Batman's costume in the previous film, many wondered how Schumacher was going to handle Batgirl. Indeed, the opening captures a certain fetishtic quality (including once more homoerotic butt shots).

Unfortunately, *Batman & Robin* itself is sunk by Akiva Goldman's ludicrous scripting. Schumacher apparently exerted himself more on the movie's production design, so that every set looks like an elaborate dance club interior than an actual location, than on the film's narrative, which is full of implausibilities. (One of the worst occurs in the film's opening action sequence, which climaxes with Mr. Freeze abandoning a trapped Batman and Robin on a rapidly ascending rocket, only for the dynamic duo to use panels from the ship to "surf" through the atmosphere to a safe landing down a chimney.)

While the film tries to remain true to Burton's incredible production designs, no attempt is made at creating a true suspension of disbelief, hence the film lacks any sense of reality to ground it. There is a lot of busyness, but not much is really happening. Batman and Robin bicker about trusting each other and who Poison Ivy finds more attractive; in the film's most effective bit, Freeze grieves over his wife, crying iced tears; Poison Ivy is given an ersatz Catwoman origin and betrays Freeze's trust; Bane is reduced to walk-on henchman; and Alfred plants clues so that his niece can become Batgirl without any attempt to establish that she would be prepared to undertake so complex a role. (Robin, with his acrobatic background, was at least reasonably physically prepared for his attempts at derring-do.)

Comic book fans do not like to have their favorite characters treated as campy jokes and ended up abhoring the film by and large. Schumacher tried to counter that he was creating a "comic book, not a tragic book," but the problem is not with a film's having a light tone, it's with the film's flippant tone that undermines any sense of credibility. John Dykstra's effects are not so eye-catching that they can make viewers forget this fundamental flaw, and consequently, the film has had the poorest return of any of the latterday *Batman* features, though that did not stop it from grossing some $250 million worldwide.

Warner Bros. did approach him about directing his third Batman film; however, he responded, "Not for a couple of years." Schumacher has left the batcave for the time being and has been devoting himself to more mainstream projects.

RIDLEY SCOTT (1939–)

Boy on a Bicycle (short, 1960); *The Duellists* (1978); *Alien* (1979); *Blade Runner* (1982); *Legend* (1986); *Someone to Watch Over Me* (1987); *Black Rain* (1989); *Thelma & Louise* (1991); *1492: Conquest of Paradise* (1992); *White Squall* (1996); *G.I. Jane* (1997); *Gladiator* (2000)

Television: *Z Cars* (British Series, 1962–?); *The Informer* (British series); The *Apple Macintosh Commercial* (1984); *The Hunger* (cable series, 1997)

While some expected Ridley Scott to become another Kubrick, his films have consistently lacked the intellectual depth of science fiction's premier filmmaker. Nevertheless, with his obsessive attention to detail and the look of a film, Scott has fashioned two of the most influential and popular science fiction features of all time, securing his place in the pantheon. As a producer-director, he has to be a good general, a good businessman, a good artist, and a good storyteller. He has demonstrated adeptness at handling the first three talents, and in his early films, excelled at the fourth as well.

Ridley Scott was born in South Shields, Northumberland, England in 1939. He was brought up in London, Cumbria, Wales, and Germany, and returned to northeast England to live in Stockton-on-Tees. As a child, he showed little scholastic aptitude for any subject but art, so his parents encouraged him to study at the West Hartlepool College of Art, where he excelled at painting during his four years there.

While an art student at the Royal College of Art, for £100 he made a 16mm short called *Boy on a Bicycle*, starring his brother Tony Scott as a truant schoolboy and his father played a madman the boy meets. Shot on location in West Hartlepool, a depressed coal-mining and shipbuilding town, *Boy and Bicycle* is an ode to adolescent alienation. The film attracted the attention of the British Film Institute, which gave him a grant to expand and refine it. Scott's interest in painting shifted to stage design and film. He became a set designer for the BBC in the early 1960s.

Scott began his directorial career by directing episodes of the popular series *Z Cars* and later *The Informer*. *Z Cars* was a long-running cop show of the 1960s set in a lightly fictionalized Liverpool (i.e., only the names were changed). It was perhaps the first "realistic" British police show — earlier shows such as *Dixon of Dock Green* portrayed a very sentimental picture of the local bobby who would always go out of his way to help an old lady across the road. In *Z Cars*, the cops, Barlow and Watt (Stratford Johns and Frank Windsor) were under stress, would swear (mildly — this was the early 1960s), would have personal problems and rivalries, and wouldn't always get things right. This was the time that police were coming off the foot patrol and their bicycles and into patrol cars (hence the title). It was required viewing at the time and inspired later series such as *The Sweeney* and *The Bill.*

The Informer had the premise that a judge had been disbarred but was continuing to fight crime by investigating wrong-doings and passing case-solving info to the police. (There may have been a bit more to it — possibly he had been wrongly convicted and so dedicated himself to correcting miscarriages of justice.) The star of the show was Ian Hendry, a British actor (mostly TV) but who appeared in films as well, specifically in Gerry Anderson's live action film *Doppleganger* (aka *Journey to the Far Side of the Sun*).

Scott had worked three years in dramatic television before forming Ridley Scott Associates, a production company specializing in commercials. Scott soon proved himself as one of Europe's most innovative directors of commercials. He directed some 3000 television commercials in ten years which demonstrated his strong background in art direction and cinematography. A couple of his finest spots were the impressive, *1984*ish introduction of the Apple Macintosh computer unveiled at the Superbowl, intended to be shown one time only, his famous "Experience the Fantasy" spot for Chanel No. 5, which was memorably seductive, as well as work for Hovis Bread, Strongbow Cider, and Levi's jeans. Many of his commercials won awards.

Scott brought the quick-cut, striking imagery sensibility of commercials to the cinema, and as a result became one of the 1980s' most important filmmakers, whose taste for sleeky photography dripping with production design and smoky atmosphere has altered how audiences see movies, and who has, along with Alan Parker, Adrian Lyne, and Steve Spielberg, fashioned a high gloss, instantly recognizable style that has proven to be highly influential.

He finally made the move to the big screen with *The Duellists*, based on the Joseph Conrad novella "The Duel" from a script by Gerald Vaughan-Hughes, who captures the Napoleonic era's formality though not its passion. The project was originally to have been done for French television, but thanks to the director's persistence and enthusiasm, it evolved into a feature. Sumptuously photographed by Frank Tidy (with the camera operated by Scott himself), *The Duellists* is a kind of anti-swashbuckler.

The entire film revolves around notions of honor that force D'Hubert (Keith Carradine) to constantly accept the challenges of fellow French officer Feraud (Harvey Keitel), an implacable duellist who has killed the mayor's son and is incensed over D'Hubert summoning him from the salon of a "fine lady" as per his commanding officer's instructions. (Over time, both combatants seem to forget the initial reason for fighting — D'Hubert was never fully certain while Feraud cannot accept that he has persisted in challenging his enemy for such a trivial reason and so invents more

Sigourney Weaver as Ripley with director Ridley Scott (right) on the set of *Alien*.

grandiose ones. This in turn is meant to parallel the way countries perpetuate longstanding enmities even when the original disagreements that sparked them have been long forgotten.)

Rather than the rousing duels of a typical swashbuckler, though each confrontation is excitingly staged, D'Hubert comes to face each inevitable challenge with dread. Short of one of the participants dying, he can only avoid confrontation if he does not meet up with Feraud, or he is promoted over Feraud, or they are otherwise engaged in a war, which as officers in Napoleon's army is not unlikely to occur. Faroud is relentless in his pursuit of "satisfaction" over the decades in which the story transpires.

D'Hubert slowly gains a reputation as a result of the constant dueling and comes to realize that as long as he persists, he is risking his life simply to save face. Despite his involvement in wars and battles, the duel comes to dominate his life, and he comes to dread each new confrontation with Feraud. Both men prove fairly evenly matched, take turns seriously injuring one another and thereby calling a halt to the proceedings before their definitive conclusion.

In the finale, D'Hubert comes to terms with the fact that he has allowed Feraud to determine their relationship, has in a sense jumped to his tune, and so turns the tables by sparing Feraud's life and redefining their relationship by declaring him dead and insisting that Feraud conduct himself accordingly, breaking off all contact.

Scott's imagery and use of Scottish and French locations is stunningly beautiful and pictorially resplendent. The costuming and images create a well-defined sense of place despite the contrasting styles and American accents of the leads. (Keitel is appropriately fanatical and intense, while Carradine is more thoughtful and existential.) Scott also gets strong supporting performances from the rest of his fine cast including Albert Finney, Tom Conti, Diana Quick, Jenny Runacre, Robert Stephens, Edward Fox, and John McEnery.

The Duellists won a prize for best debut film at the Cannes Film Festival. Otherwise, despite its Old Master pictorial beauty with its Géricault–like compositions and its fine performances, it has been largely ignored. The film's biggest drawback is that it is largely devoid of tension, but it did establish itself as a cinematic calling card that announced to the world that here was a feature film director with a fabulous sensitivity to the effects of light and shadow.

Scott said in an interview with Danny Peary that he "had virtually *no* interest in science fiction until [he] saw *Star Wars* in 1977, other than having been tremendously impressed by *2001.*" He felt that most makers of science fiction films developed things in "nonlogical, unbelievable ways" or that they contained "silly, utopian ideas."

Following *The Duellists*, in 1977 Scott hoped to make a film of the legend of Tristan and Iseult, using *Heavy Metal* magazine as a reference for its sword and sorcery imagery. Paramount gave Scott $150,000 to develop it, writing a script and doing preliminary production designs. Scott combined four influences in his science fantasy approach to the ancient Celtic tale: Frank Herbert's *Dune*, Moebius' comic series *Arzach*, David Lean's *Lawrence of Arabia*, and George Lucas' *Star Wars*. One of his odder ideas was when Tristan finds a sword in a stone and pulls it, it turns out to be a lever which activates an ICBM that launches and explodes before Tristan's uncomprehending eyes.

However, Paramount proved equally incomprehending of Scott's offbeat approach and the project was eventually abandoned. Scott, however, was so struck by what George Lucas had accomplished in *Star Wars* that he abandoned his plans and considered that there was a great future in science fiction films after all. Coincidentally, he was sent the script for *Alien* just one month later.

Alien was conceived by Dan O'Bannon after working on Alejandro Jodorowski's aborted cinematic adaptation of Frank Herbert's *Dune* in France, where he had come in contact with design artists Jean "Moebius" Giraud, Chris Foss, and Swiss artist Hans Rudy Giger. When the film fell apart, O'Bannon was left without any money, apartment, or car, with half of his belongings in Paris and the other half in storage.

His friend Ron Shussett offered to let O'Bannon crash on his sofa and O'Bannon went rummaging through a file of his old ideas. He selected a script he worked on in 1972 called *Memory*, which was set in the year 2087 about a crew of astronauts discovering a dormant creature on an alien planet, but O'Bannon was not sure where to go with it. Shussett suggested he combine it with another tale he had written about gremlins aboard a B-17 bomber during a World War II night raid, so O'Bannon concocted a script he called *Star Beast*, which he intended to sell as a low budget, Roger Corman kind of gothic science fiction film.

After three months of writing, O'Bannon settled on the title *Alien*, which he felt would be intriguing as the word was both an adjective and a noun. He then approached artist Ron Cobb, who had designed the spaceship for *Dark Star*, which O'Bannon had cowritten, starred in, produced special effects for, and edited, and Cobb agreed to make some conceptual drawings to help sell the film.

O'Bannon was frustrated that *Dark Star* was a comedy that hadn't attracted an audience. He thought to himself, "Well, if I can't make them laugh, maybe I can make them scream." He ended up creating a demon that would terrorize audiences for decades to come.

O'Bannon and Shussett began circulating the script, according to O'Bannon, "That script, from the moment I typed 'The End,' proceeded to take on a life of its own. Everybody in town wanted it. We just couldn't believe it. Everything had fallen through for us, nothing had ever worked. It had always gone so badly, we said, 'Well, yeah, they're all yelling about it and they all want it, but it ain't gonna work 'cause it never does. It's just a lot of baloney.'"

The script attracted the attention of Brandywine Productions, a new independent company headed by Gordon Carroll, writer-director Walter Hill, and David Giler. The trio decided that *Alien* should be their first production, and bought a six-month option on the property. Walter Hill began to rewrite the script with the intention of directing it himself, and brought the project to the attention of 20th Century–Fox, who proposed that it be made into a $4.5 million film. Hill and Giler continued reworking the material and eventually tried to claim sole authorship of the screenplay, relegating O'Bannon's work to a story credit.

According to O'Bannon, "David Giler ... sat down and just kept rewriting it and rewriting it until there was very little resemblance to the original screenplay. I wasn't allowed to participate in that because he didn't want me to. He was producer.

"Then two weeks before we started shooting, he left the production for mysterious reasons.... The main producer, Gordon Carroll, and the director called me in and there were two weeks of frantic mutual work between all of us trying to put the script into shape. By the time we got done, it was maybe 80 percent of what the original draft was. What we got on the screen was actually very close to the original draft."

The matter went before the Writers Guild of America arbitration board, which was designed to protect writers from having their credits stolen by overzealous directors and producers (as well as the accompanying residuals), and they agreed. The characters in O'Bannon's script were only given last names and could have been played by men or women, they were not as fleshed out as those in the Hill-Giler script, which had added the concept of making them like truck drivers in space, but the basic sequence of events in the plot was clearly O'Bannon's, and he received sole screenplay credit.

O'Bannon's original script featured characters called Standard, Roby, Melkonis, Broussard, Hunter, and Faust who travel on a ship called the *Snark*, after the Lewis Carroll poem. Three members of the crew find the alien captain who has scratched a triangle on the panel in front of him, indicating a nearby pyramid which is filled with rows of sealed leathery urns or jars, which contain phase one of the alien lifeform, one of which attaches itself to Broussard's face.

O'Bannon came up with the concept of a monster that was constantly metamorphosing from one form to another, so that it was always surprising and visually interesting. Possibly influenced by A. E. van Vogt's story "Discord in Scarlet," the last form alters its victims into replicas of the initial spore-like form (which led to a lawsuit by and settlement with van Vogt, though others had used the same idea subsequently).

The Hill-Giler draft of the script creates the characters of Dallas, Kane, Ripley, Ash, Lambert, Parker and Brett, and specifies which were men and which were women. The ship's name is changed to the *Leviathan*, and one of the characters, Ash, is made into an android who has been planted by the evil, faceless corporation to ensure that the alien organism be preserved, even at the expense of the crew. (This started a trend in science fiction films of setting up corporations as the villains.) Ash deliberately lets the alien survive inside of Kane and get onboard and keeps a master access key for the computer from Ripley to prevent her from finding out that he is under special orders to protect the alien and not them.

O'Bannon would later rewrite the scene under Ridley Scott's guidance to indicate that Ash's main priority is to "watch for the discovery of key products," which is defined as "any substance capable of changing the course of human evolution." As the alien crosses itself with human chromosomes as part of its reproductive cycle, it is therefore a key product and must be protected, even if the crewmembers must be transformed into spores to keep it alive. (Much of this explanation ended up being cut from the film. One thing is true, however, and that is that in O'Bannon's scripts, the characters analyze and speculate in much greater detail, while in the Giler-Hill versions, most things are left a mystery.)

The script was rewritten further to indicate that the company knew about the alien ship and the hostile lifeform it contains (though just how is never clear, apparently it was able to translate the mysterious distress code), and dispatched the ship's crew, which conveniently had an android onboard, to bring it back for observation.

When because of scheduling conflicts with *The Warriors* Hill found himself unable to direct *Alien*, David Giler recommended Ridley Scott on the basis of *The Duellists*. Scott found the script to be tight, concise, very spare, he thought the characters were very defined, and the idea that the hero would be a woman he found attractively fresh at the time. He called up Brandywine right away agreeing to do it, having just seen Lucas' *Star Wars* a month before and having been impressed with that film's elaborate visual design, seeing in it possibilities for creating a commercial film of his own that would be similarly detailed.

Scott liked Cobb's preparatory drawings, finding them brilliant, and asked him and O'Bannon, who was hired as a visual consultant to the film, to come to England to continue their design work. Cobb became involved with designing every aspect of the Earth vessel and its attendant hardware, designing the detailed ship's interiors with the precision and thoughtfulness of an engineer.

Scott prepared a storyboard of the entire script, which delighted the producers and these were then shown to Fox, who in the afterglow of *Star Wars'* success, saw greater potential in the material and doubled the film's budget to $8.4 million.

Scott's main concern, as he told James Delson in *Fantastic Films* #11, was "How the hell do you make the monster? Because in every film I'd ever seen, that's always something that let everyone down. Most films you finally see it and think, 'Eh?' Then you try to go along with it, like you would in the theater. Instead of just believing it, you have to put yourself in a new state of mind, prepared to accept what you see."

Scott knew that the creature would require a totally unique concept. (O'Bannon's original conception was more like a man with an octopus on his head.) Now that *Alien* was a major studio project, O'Bannon brought a copy of Giger's book of paintings, *Necronomicon,* to Scott's attention to give him an idea of what the creature should look like. Scott immediately agreed, being particularly taken with a piece titled "Necronom IV," which became the basis of the film's adult alien.

Giger's airbrushed, surrealistic, mostly monochromatic biomechanical approach brought a totally new and heretofore alien look to the film's design. Giger's work seemed to blend past and future, and his design incorporated nightmarish textures and primitive fears (the alien has claws, tentacles, a phallus-shaped body, a mouth within a mouth, and other things humans find fear-inducing). Giger designed the facehugger alien around the idea of a crustacean-like creature that would use its large coiled tail to spring out of its leg like a Jack-in-the-box. Giger insisted on being personally involved in the construction of the creatures. Giger was also asked to design the landscape of the alien planet and the derelict ship as well.

Ivor Powell, an associate producer for Ridley Scott Associates, suggested that Michael Seymour be selected as production designer, making selections from the conceptual work and overseeing that everything was constructed on time with the aid of construction supervisor Bill Welch. Roger Christian and Leslie Dilley, both of whom had worked on *Star Wars*, were hired as art directors with Ian Whittaker being placed in charge of set decoration. Scott also insisted that the ship's name be changed from *Leviathan* to *Nostromo*, after the Joseph Conrad novel, and that it be an 800 foot spaceship towing a mile and a half refinery complex. (Unfortunately, the fairy tale castle aspect of the refinery that Scott wanted is the least convincing element in the film's wonderfully and convincingly detailed visual design. Scott wanted to get away from the futuristic look that Ron Cobb favored in favor of a more *Heavy Metal* fantasy style.)

Roger Dicken built the smaller alien forms from Giger's design while Carlo Rambaldi was brought in to design the elaborate hydraulic "head effects" for the alien, based on his excellent work for Spielberg's *Close Encounters of the Third Kind.*

John Mollo was the costume designer, giving his outfits a lived-in look. The spacesuits were based on designs by Moebius. They had the unfortunate design drawback of not allowing for actual respiration, forcing whoever was wearing them to breath his own carbon dioxide, making it necessary to remove the helmets on the completion of each take. (The jet streams out the back were just for show.)

Derek Vanlint, who had photographed commercials for Scott, was hired as director of photography, and he worked closely with Michael Seymour to determine how the claustrophobic and enclosed sets could be lit. Both Vanlint and Scott served as camera operators themselves.

Brian Johnson, who was simultaneously working on *The Empire Strikes Back,* was hired as visual effects supervisor, with his associate Nick Allder creating the various miniatures needed, as well as the necessary futuristic props.

One of *Alien*'s most unforgettable images is the discovery of the Space Jockey, an alien pilot who brought the alien predator to the planet, which was designed and created by H. R. Giger.

The cast for the film was excellent with John Hurt as Kane, Ian Holm as Ash, Veronica Cartwright (*The Birds, Invasion of the Body Snatchers, Flight of the Navigator*) as ship's navigator Lambert; Tom Skeritt as Captain Dallas; Harry Dean Stanton and Yaphet Kotto as the trouble-making Parker and Brett, and relative newcomer Sigourney Weaver as Warrant Officer Ripley. (Born Susan Weaver, Sigourney renamed herself at 14 after a character in *The Great Gatsby*. She was initially reluctant to appear in a science fiction film, which ironically led to much greater exposure for the actress and parts in several major productions.)

Principal photography for *Alien* began on July 5, 1978, at the Shepperton Studio Center in England. It was not completed until December of that year. The film was edited at Bray Studios where Johnson's special effects work was in progress. Some of the effects shots had to be redone to meet Scott's demanding specifications, and Johnson finally closed down the effects unit in February of 1979. Editor Terry Rawlings worked carefully with Scott to minimize views of the creature to allow it to retain its mystery and terror.

The most notorious and imitated scene in *Alien* is the infamous chest burster scene, whereby in an obscene parody of birth, the second phase of the alien smashes its way out of its host's chest, splattering his innards everywhere. The scene was achieved by having John Hurt stick his head, arms, and shoulders through a hole in the table while a fiberglass chest piece filled with offal and blood tubes was attached to his shoulders to give the appearance that he was lying on the table. On the first take, the chest burster failed to burst through the chest, so the actors had to change, the set be cleaned off, the T-shirt Hurt was wearing was treated with acid and slits were made with a razor blade to ensure its success. All told, four takes were made, and in the one used, Veronica Cartwright received two pints of raspberry juice (standing in for blood) right in her face. The sound editors dubbed in a combination of a viper, a pig's squeal, and a baby's cry for the chest burster's shriek.

Much of *Alien*'s sexual symbolism was quite intentional. Scott wanted the astronauts to enter the derelict spaceship through a vaginal opening. Originally, after seeing the "space jockey," the crew were to travel to a pyramid which they enter through a membrane at its bottom, as if the pyramid were a virgin. When Kane is attacked by the face-hugger alien, the alien forces its procreative organ down his throat in an obscene parody of fellatio. Scott wanted the chest burster to "be like an obscene phallic thing that was all mouth. Like a Francis Bacon image." Scott overlays a slightly distorted birth cry on the scene to underlie the horror of this perversion of natural birth. What gives away Ash's status as an android is what appears to be seminal fluid dripping down his head. Ash tries to kill Ripley by forcing a rolled up girlie magazine which he manipulates at groin level down her throat in an attempt at fatal fellatio. After Ripley knocks his head off, there appears to be ejaculate on his lips and everywhere as he equates the monster to an orgasm.

The monster's phallic head and long mouth within a mouth have already been mentioned, which the monster uses to forcibly penetrate its victims. Additionally, the monster's tail comes up between Lambert's legs, and her screams imply rape more than murder. Finally, in the finale, Ripley performs a striptease for the alien, stripping down to her underwear while nervously singing, "You Are My Lucky Star" before donning a spacesuit so that she can blast the critter out the airlock, using what appears to be a speargun (cupid's bow?) for good measure to send it out into the great beyond. (The persistent and nearly indestructible creature is apparently impervious to vacuum and still doesn't die but tries to gain re-entry through an exhaust port, but is prevented when Ripley activates the ship's rockets which finally blow him to Kingdom Come.)

The sound design was a vital element in making *Alien* the experience it is. The soundtrack is complex and filled with often unnerving sounds (amplified heartbeats, clinking chains, various machine hums and such), all of which is complemented by Jerry Goldsmith's score, although elements of Goldsmith's score were replaced by music cues from his work for *Freud* (the air duct and acid sequences) plus the finale and end titles were scored with Howard Hanson's Second Symphony.

Certain sequences were cut for budgetary reasons, including one involving a decompression where Lambert gets killed by being sucked out into space through a small hole in an airlock and Ripley saves Parker from suffering a similar fate. Scott also wanted to have small flying objects, like sensors, which would fly up and down the corridors, fixing problems wherever they would find them, but again this proved too expensive.

After previewing *Alien* with audiences, it was decided to eliminate the more graphic and explicit footage in favor of a more subtle approach, as well as eliminating scenes of the crew bickering and Ripley trying to bed Dallas in order to relieve her stress.

The most famous of the deleted scenes is the cocoon sequence in which Ripley, flamethrower in hand, discovers Dallas and Brett's bodies being transformed into cocoons that will become the alien eggs Kane found. "It's some sort of reproductivity cycle, because Brett, or what's left of Brett, is more fully absorbed in the background, slowly turning into one of the eggs. Dallas says, 'Kill me!' and she incinerates the room, killing Dallas and Brett," recalls Scott. Scott cut the sequence because he felt the audience was getting too restless at that point in the film for such a quiet, albeit horrific scene.

Alien premiered on May 25, 1979, and went on to become a sizable hit, grossing $40,300,000 domestically. The following year it won the Academy award for outstanding achievement in visual effects, beating out *Star Trek—The Motion Picture, Meteor, The Black Hole*, and *1941*. The film has gone on to be considered a classic, and rightly. It is still one of the scariest and most effective science fiction horror films ever made, and like most such successes, has led to countless imitators.

On the other hand, while not a financial success, Scott's *Blade Runner* likewise became one of the most influential SF films of all time, establishing a much imitated look and serving as one of the bases for the cyberpunk movement. This film adaptation of Philip K. Dick's classic SF novel *Do Androids Dream of Electric Sheep?* focused on the question of what it means to be human and established a comprehensive future world filled with hellish oil burn-offs, constant acid rains, and depleted animal and people populations as the better-off have resettled on the colony worlds.

Harrison Ford plays Rick Deckard, a classic shamus type, who is assigned to hunt down and kill four replicants (the film's name for artificial human beings) who mutinied on a space colony and have returned to Earth. His cold, burned-out personality contrasts with those of replicants he hunts, Roy Batty (Rutger Hauer at his most charismatic), Leon (Brion James), Pris (Daryl Hannah), and Zhora (Joanna Cassidy), who care deeply for one another and are desperately seeking their creator, Tyrell (Joe Turkel), in order to extend their limited four year lifespans.

From his opening shot, Scott sets up an eye motif. The only way to detect one of these replicants is by their lack of empathy on an emotional test that checks eye responses to various questions. He stacks the deck by having the replicants reflect back orange light from their eyes, and we discover late in the film that Deckard is also a replicant, leavening the irony of the human hunting non-humans who are more human than he. David Webb Peoples' script also revels in other ironies, such as Deckard being a hero who shoots women in the back and whose life is saved by one of the replicants he has so ruthlessly pursued. Scott also implants the theme of humanity detection with the introduction of Rachel (Sean Young), a replicant Deckard is introduced to and falls in love with who does not know she is a replicant until Deckard reveals a private programmed memory, causing Deckard to finally question his own humanity.

Originally Scott's film was released with a heavy-handed noirish voice-over narration and a "happy" ending where Rick and Rachel leave the hellish city for an uncertain future together, but this has been supplanted by the director's cut which trims the unnecessary and intrusive narration and ends the film on an ambiguous note with Deckard discovering an origami unicorn confirming that his superiors know his thoughts (a daydream he had about unicorns in a lush forest).

Blade Runner was first offered to Scott while he was filming *Alien*, and he turned it down at first because he felt that it was repeating what he had done with the android Ash. Producer Michael Deeley, however, kept in touch and got Scott involved in discussions of what the environment for such a world of the future might be like.

Instead, Scott was initially tied to the film adaptation of Frank Herbert's SF classic *Dune*, which was eventually filmed by David Lynch. Scott worked in conjunction with Rudy Werlitzer (*Walker*), who wrote the screenplay treatment for the proposed Scott version of the film.

One of the most perfectly realized future worlds in science fiction is Los Angeles in Scott's *Blade Runner*. Here Burbank's New York backlot has been retrofitted with futuristic vehicles, parking meters, and Scott's trademark smoky look.

When Scott saw that *Dune* was going to be a long time in coming to fruition, he contacted Deeley and asked to see the script again. Together they sold Filmways on making what was to become *Blade Runner*. However, in late 1980, Filmways was experiencing financial difficulties, and the projected $18–19 million cost ended up seeming like too much for them, so the project lost several months while it was picked up by Tandem, who came in as part financiers and completion guarantors, Jerry Perenchio and finally the Ladd Company, whose head Alan Ladd, Jr., knew Scott from *Alien*.

David Webb Peoples has since scripted a number of interesting films, including the Academy Award–winning documentary feature, *The Day After Trinity*, the Oscar–nominated short *Arthur and Willy*, Academy Award–winner *Unforgiven*, directed by Clint Eastwood, which ruminates on myth-making and the true meaning of murder in the old West; *Hero*, directed by Stephen Frears, a look at media expectations regarding heroism; as well as the science fiction films *Twelve Monkeys*, directed by Terry Gilliam, in which a man who might be mad or might be from the future seems to travel to the present, where as a kid he witnesses his own death; and wrote and directed *The Blood of Heroes* (aka *Salute of the Jugger*), starring Rutger Hauer and Joan Chen in a story set in a very arid environment (post–Armageddon) where a group of players of a very dangerous game (the Jugger of the film's Australian title) wanders from small town to small town challenging the local teams. The story is made more complex by the existence of a League that groups all the best players of the game, against whom the heroes must compete. The ending is relatively indifferent: the heroine gets what she wants, but she knows she has paid and will keep paying for it. As for the one-eyed hero, he doesn't get anything.

Scott's Los Angeles is a place of massive contradictions: The new is layered over the old; the street-level is crowded, while the buildings are almost empty; there is constant rain and darkness in Los Angeles, a city of desert sun; the look suggests Manhattan more than the sprawl of modern Los Angeles; pollution and dirt are everywhere, and yet sashimi (raw fish) is still available. Scott intended that there be a sense of groups that are religious, social, punk, and criminal that have hung on while others have left to the off-world colonies, a group of misfits and outsiders who help explain the underpopulated city's crowdedness.

The replicants themselves embody many contradictions. They are both benefits and hazards. They have only weeks to live, and yet they must be hunted down and terminated. They are not human, and yet they demonstrate both more passion and empathy than many of the humans around them.

When queried whether he wished to continue working in the science fiction genre, Scott responded, "Absolutely, ... [only] I don't think of it in terms of science fiction. I think of the whole scope of the future. Science fiction is a huge field, so I really don't like to be limited by the label of science fiction or fantasy anymore. It's simply another theater that one can work in to explore and expand ideas. I find there's so much more room for exotic thinking in these areas than in the more mainstream material."

Princess Lili (Mia Sara) encounters one of Scott's beloved unicorns in the forest.

Scott contacted novelist William Hjortsberg to discuss the possibility of his writing a draft screenplay based on Scott's ideas for a story about a young hermit who becomes a hero when he battles the evil Lord of Darkness, rescues a beautiful princess, and frees the world from its icy winter curse. The final result was Scott's next film, *Legend.*

"We had cocktails, and Ridley said, 'Would you be interested in writing a fairy tale?'" remembers Hjortsberg. "Coincidentally, I had begun writing fairy tales on my own during the past year, so naturally I told Ridley yes."

Their next meeting took place several months later in Los Angeles where Scott was filming *Blade Runner*. Hjortsberg recalls sitting around the kitchen table in Scott's rented house where they "batted ideas back and forth for about a week or so.... The characters really came from left field," Hjortsberg said. "We discussed the hero in many forms before deciding on Jack O' the Green.

"Then Ridley decided we should have a quest. He also wanted unicorns and thought there should be magic armor and a sword. I came up with the idea of having the world plunged into wintry darkness. So we had all these elements which had to be woven into a story." The process took some three years and fifteen script revisions before it was completed.

As is typical of a Scott production, enormous and intricately detailed elaborate sets were constructed at Pinewood from designs by Assheton Gorton. On June 27, 1984, disaster struck when the magnificent forest set was completely demolished by a fire that ripped through the legendary 007 stage at Pinewood when only two days of filming there remained. Fortunately, the cast and crew of *Legend* were at lunch at the time, and the art department was able to rebuild a section of the forest set on another sound stage.

Legend was an exercise in world-making, but you could hardly see Scott's fantasy world through all the feathers, bubbles, and pollen floating through the air in an almost desperate bid for pictorial beauty and movement.

The film's characters were so flat and uninteresting as to be hardly worthy of the name. While Tom Cruise was recruited to play Jack O' the Green, whose carefree life is interrupted by his need to undertake a heroic quest, Cruise soon became disenchanted with his underdeveloped role and refused to help publicize the film. Mia Sara made her motion picture debut as Princess Lili, but the part does not require that she do much more than be beautiful. Tim Curry takes away what little acting honors there are with his impersonation of the demonic Lord of Darkness. Despite his small stature and being buried under Rob Bottin's elaborate make-up, Curry's Lord is a very commanding and daunting presence.

The other figures in the drama are mainly characterized by their appearances. There's Honethorn Gump (David Bennent from *The Tin Drum*), leader of a band of elves who accompany Jack; Blix (Alice Playten), leader of the evil goblins; Screwball (Billy Barty); Brown Tom (Cork Hubbert), a plump, tipsy leprechaun; Pox (Peter O'Farrell), a pig-faced goblin; Blunder (Kiran Shah), another evil goblin; Tic (Mike Edmonds), the helmeted goblin; and Oona (Annabelle Lanyon), a fairy who can transform herself into human form.

Adding to the difficulties faced by the film was some post-production tampering by Universal head honcho Sidney Sheinberg, who thought the film was too long and wanted a more contemporary score for it. As a consequence, Scott's European cut was trimmed down to 89 minutes and Jerry Goldsmith's score was replaced by a synthesizer score by Tangerine Dream which did not suit the film as well. Despite being gorgeously shot and designed, *Legend* does not work well in either version, but the longer 110 minute European version is the better of the two. Bizarrely enough, the Japanese version is a third variation of the film, featuring the Goldsmith score and some material not found in the U.S. release but missing other material. Despite its inadequacies, *Legend* has become a cult film. It picked up an Academy Award nomination for best make-up, and unquestionably Bottin's work is extensive, though not as life-like as one could hope. Scott's American fans have requested that a director's cut of *Legend* be released in this country, but so far their pleas have fallen on deaf ears.

By comparison, *Someone to Watch Over Me* tells a relatively simple and straight-forward story. The film does seem to enter *Blade Runner* territory in its opening shot, a glamorous view of nighttime Manhattan with the camera circling the Chrysler Building while the Gershwins' love song tries to ease the audience into a sophisticated mood, but the shot continues by crossing the river over into Queens where a rowdy party is being held for Mike Keegan (Tom Berenger), who has just been promoted to police detective. This opening sets up the two worlds in which Keegan must operate.

At a flashy art-disco opening, Claire Gregory (Mimi Rogers), an uptown lady with a limo, arty friends, and a multimillion dollar apartment, witnesses a murder and so must be protected by the blue collar Keegan, who must "watch over" her (as Claire too often puts it, in case the audience hasn't made the connection between the title, the song, and the situation). Predictably, the two fall in love after a time, though they are worlds apart, but Howard Franklin's script imagines nothing that would make their romance convincing. The pair are not flirtatious, smoldering, or in lust.

The film centers around Keegan, who must choose between intoxicating wealth and his warm, spunky, ethnic wife Ellie (Lorraine Bracco), with both aspects (Claire and Keegan's family) being put in peril as the result of the situation and a concerned killer, who allows us to sympathize with Claire, Keegan, and Ellie, all of whom have their virtues and their foibles, unlike the similar love triangle in Lyne's *Fatal Attraction* where the Other Woman and the maniac were combined to focus on the threat of an adulterous affair to a family.

Unfortunately, Keegan, while macho, is a surprisingly passive hero who seems to prefer reacting to acting. Tom Berenger is unable to bring the character to life, partly the fault of Franklin's script which does little to characterize its protagonist in a recognizable and identifiable way. He simply moons around Claire's exquisite apartment and sweats guilt. Meanwhile, Claire is also too ill-defined, entirely lacking in any distinctive qualities which might have made her interesting. We're told she is a writer (of just what it isn't clear), but all we can tell for certain is that she is an impressive shopper.

This leaves Ellie as the only character that has any vivaciousness, with a flair for dirty-mouthed wisecracks. She easily becomes so appealing that why Keegan would be attracted to anyone else remains something of a mystery.

Scott brings little more than his visual flair to the proceedings. He certainly knows how to make the Upper East Side look attractive and alluring, with slick streets and slicker interiors. He seemingly plays around with the weather, altering a light snowy evening to a midnight thunderstorm, to create some nifty imagery on Claire's luxurious walls, but all of Scott's stylistic flourishes detailing Manhattan's lacquered veneer fail to give this bland, ordinary story the kind of pizzazz that makes for memorable moviemaking or even mythmaking. Here cinematography must substitute for show.

Director Ridley Scott, who created another elaborately detailed world in *Legend.*

While there have been many road pictures before, *Thelma & Louise* has the distinction of being the first distaff road picture. (Shirley Knight in Coppola's *The Rain People* comes close, but she is tied down with a surrogate child thereby lacking the freedom of a true road movie, while Arthur Hiller's *Outrageous Fortune* centers around Bette Midler and Shelley Long's search for a man.) Previous road pictures either involved male bonding or, when women were present, depicted couples on the run (e.g. *You Only Live Once, Gun Crazy, They Live by Night, Bonnie and Clyde, Badlands*).

The movie begins with a black-and-white shot of scrub land. As color bleeds into the image, the frame is bisected by a road that stretches seemingly endlessly to the horizon, where it runs into a mountain and vanishes, night falls, and the screen fades to black.

The shot encapsulates the movie. There is scenic beauty, the allure of wide open spaces, ending with a hint of doom. Pictorially gorgeous, the film shows Scott at his image-making best.

But the true heroine of the film is its screenwriter, an ex-waitress named Callie Khouri, who makes of her story a feminist manifesto and won an Oscar for her efforts. She mulls over women's ideas of freedom — freedom from oppressive and unsatisfying men (though men and their desires prove to be everywhere), freedom to take the law into their own hands (though this makes them outlaws), freedom from their strangled pasts (though society in the form of police is catching up with them), and the freedom to pursue self-knowledge and happiness (which they had all along but never realized it until they cut the ties to their men).

Thelma (Geena Davis) is a kooky housewife who eats frozen candy bars which cause her to burst out in pimples like an overaged teenager. Louise (Susan Sarandon), a coffee shop waitress, is her best friend who tells her, between puffs on her cigarette, "You get what you settle for." Both are seeking a sort of relief from the men in their lives — Louise's noncommittal musician boyfriend Jimmy (Michael Madsen) and Thelma's preening, philandering, self-important husband Darryl (Christopher McDonald) who wants to keep his wife at home.

What begins as an innocent fishing weekend as the women pile into a 1956 T-Bird and head out on the open road turns ugly when, due to Thelma's naiveté, she attracts a despicable creep named Harlan at a country bar who proceeds to put the moves on her. Louise can only look on in dismay as Thelma ignores her best friend in favor of Harlan's crass overtures, a not uncommon situation which many women can identify with.

Harlan persuades Thelma to go outside and almost rapes her. Louise comes out to the parking lot with a gun and puts a stop to it, but pissed off at Harlan's lack of repentance and contrition, shoots him dead. (She does not, as some have reported, shoot him to prevent him from raping Thelma, because he has backed off before he's shot. She shoots him when he makes an improper suggestion as he is leaving.)

This act instantly renders them outlaws, as Louise knows she will not get a break from the local police. (All the males in the film, with the exception of Harvey Keitel's Arkansas cop Hal, are depicted as jerks.) The pair decide to set off to Mexico, although Scott's camera heads north to Utah to the distinctive locale of Monument Valley for much of the rest of the movie.

Thelma & Louise continually makes a point of ensuring that we understand these women are not simply adjuncts to their men as so many movie women in the past have been. It carefully avoids the clichés of having the women engage in cat fights or engage in sloppy emotional sharing. Instead, we see the joy and strain of the friendship between these differing personalities, the shifts in moods, their intimacy and ease with each other.

The parts are delightfully acted by Davis and Sarandon. Davis makes for an engaging kook who chatters away with endless cheeriness while Sarandon captures both Louise's feigned bravado and her nervous unease underneath. When Thelma starts off on the trip, she acts as if she's being released from prison, and we get caught up in her effusive joy at the moment.

The women reach a turning point after Thelma picks up a handsome, vacuous cowboy named J. D. (Brad Pitt) who provides her with the great sex she's never had (the film implicitly condoning her adultery) but who then proves himself a larcenous lover by proceeding to rip her off as soon as her back is turned. At the same time, Louise makes a sad peace with Jimmy as she comes to terms with both his violent tendencies and his inner tenderness (fearing she's run off, he finally proposes). From then on, they sever all ties with men and head out on the highway. They are no longer running from the men in their lives, they are running to their own destinies.

Thelma doesn't quite seem to grasp the seriousness of their situation but instead is giddy with excitement at the prospect of an outlaw life. "Something's crossed over in me," she says delightedly, "and I can't go back." Louise simply grows more pensive, stopping to stare out at the desert which surrounds them and engulfs them in its expansive embrace of desolate destiny.

The women's feelings of liberation are clearly deceptive. They may run and discover new selves driving along the roads, but Louise's act of murder dooms them despite their likeability. (Of course, without that plot point, there would be no sense of urgency to their situation.)

But while the film is generous in its depiction of these women, the men are characterized largely as charmless yahoos. Cops pass the time reading skin magazines and jeer about women being suckers for lovey dovey talk. Darryl is depicted as a redneck businessman. The worst offender is a truck driver who waggles his tongue lewdly whenever Thelma and Louise drive by.

In one of the film's more witless bits, Thelma and Louise recognize this same truck driver by the silver nude silhouettes on his mudflaps, the same ones that appear to be on half the trucks on the road, and wreak their revenge by viciously blowing up his rig. Once more the man's only real crime is being obnoxiously ill-mannered, yet he is portrayed in such a crude, caricatured fashion that the filmmakers condone the women's act of violence against him.

Scott avoids the pitfall of having his characters overtly declaim about sisterhood is powerful or indulge in phoney *thirtysomething* hugginess. He wisely keeps the film focused on Thelma and Louise's relationship, and uses his images to set up moods. But the images are not of the real life poetry of the actual, often grungy American Southwest. Rather they are an art director's dream with oil pumps bobbing rhythmically, irrigation pipes laid out geometrically, and rock formations lit up as for a Disney extravaganza, as well as the typical Scott rain-drenched landscape shots. It's as if once Thelma and Louise's story becomes less real and more mythic, the visuals likewise throw off the shackles of reality.

Finally, Thelma and Louise run out of road and arrive at the Grand Canyon, itself a gigantic feminine symbol to counter the phallic mountain that opened the film. The sympathetic Hal does the best he can to save them, but that would mean willingly sacrificing their newfound freedom, so instead with ecstatic flourish they take the plunge into oblivion.

Scott (center) directs Gerard Depardieu (left) and Bercilio Moya during the filming of *1492: Conquest of Paradise* (photo by David Appleby).

Thelma & Louise proved extremely popular with audiences and provided for Scott a much needed hit. It won nominations for both Sarandon and Davis as Best Actress, a nomination for Scott as Best Director, a nomination for Thom Noble for Best Editing, and won the Best Original Screenplay and Best Cinematography (Adrian Biddle) awards. Ridley at last had the hit that he needed.

Roselyn Bosch, a journalist for *Le Point*, a weekly newsmagazine in Paris, convinced Scott that Christopher Columbus was someone he only thought he knew something about, and yet few people seem to know the real facts. She infected Scott with her passion for the subject and partnered with French producer Alain Goldman to raise the $45 million in presales, putting together an unprecedented French/English/Spanish coproduction deal. Because of Scott's relationship with Stanley Jaffe, producer of *Black Rain*, Paramount agreed to put up 25 percent of the budget in exchange for the North American distribution rights.

Nevertheless, there were problems as preproduction at Pinewood Studios was stalled twice for lack of funds. Scott, who in addition to being the film's director, also served as its producer and camera operator, and worked intensively on the script with Bosch, who had studied every available shred of Columbian research. They wanted to present an explorer who was an obsessive and who at the end of his life was tormented by remorse over his disastrous stewardship of the lands he discovered, while at the same time indicating that it was the Spanish nobility's savagery towards the natives that poisons this paradise.

The competition for producing a film biography for Christopher Columbus for the 500th anniversary of his landing near the Americas became rather fierce. While the main competitor, *Christopher Columbus: The Discovery* was released to theaters first, Scott's *1492: Conquest of Paradise* is, thanks to Scott's unfailing visual eye, the better film, though one which still does not fully do its subject justice.

While French actor Gerard Depardieu has shown himself to be one of the greatest actors of the 20th Century, his playing an Italian who spoke Castilian with a Portuguese accent in French-accented English is well nigh unintelligible upon occasion. Roselyne Bosch's screenplay also misrepresents the man's character, updating him into a kindly humanist who looked benevolently towards the Native Americans he wished to exploit.

And *1492* asks us to side with Columbus against the contemporary experts at the University of Salamanca when in fact it was Columbus who was wrong in his notion of geography. (All learned parties of the time accepted the spherical nature of the Earth, and the Spanish commission, like the sea-going Portuguese, had the best geographical information on the planet.) Columbus conceived the Earth as having a much smaller diameter, thus making it a much shorter distance to sail west to China than to sail east. He was, of course, grossly mistaken. He calculated the distance between the Canary Islands and Japan as being twenty-four hundred nautical miles, when it fact the actual distance is more than four times that amount.

King Ferdinand of Spain is not even shown speaking in the film, though he was the real power and had served as one of the bases for Machiavelli's *The Prince*. Despite his advisers advising against Columbus' expedition, he decided that the minuscule cost (contrary to legend, Queen Isabella had no need to pawn her jewels) was outweighed by the enormous potential benefit should Columbus be proved to be correct.

Nor do such historical characters as Alonso Pinzón (Tcheky Karyo), who is shown offering his assistance to Columbus in Seville, or Queen Isabella (Sigourney Weaver), who is constantly shown wearing coquettish, off-the-shoulder gowns even in the dead of Spanish winter, fare any better.

Strangely, *1492* does very little with Columbus' first voyage, never delving into its more dramatic elements, and then glosses over Columbus' mismanagement of the settlement from the second voyage. There is even an anachronistic hurricane which makes it seem as if God himself is chastening Columbus, with another anachronism occurring when the Spanish emissary who comes to arrest him informs him that the new land will be named for Amerigo Vespucci, which wasn't done until after Columbus' death. The film also pretends that Columbus' achievements would have been forgotten if not for his illegitimate son Hernando's biography of him, when in fact Columbus is named and praised by virtually all 16th century chroniclers.

In 1993, Ridley found himself competing with his brother Tony. Just as it was announced that Ridley had agreed to direct *Pancho's War* from a script by Marcel Montecino for Stanley Jaffe and Sherry Lansing, Tony was announced to direct another project about Villa called *Tom Mix and Pancho Villa*, a western written by Oliver Stone and Alan Sharp based on Clifford Irving's novel. Ridley compared *Pancho's War* to "a spaghetti western with crash, wallop, and bang," and loved the idea of a South of the border love story with wild-eyed gun merchants and Mexican revolutionaries. However, neither film ended up coming into existence.

Lately, Scott has been concentrating on producing films rather than directing them. He produced *The Browning Version, Monkey Trouble*, and *Pet* all in 1994. He and his brother Tony have taken over Shepperton Studios and renovated them.

Scott's next film work was *White Squall*, a sailing adventure based on a 1960 incident where 13 preppie members of the Ocean Academy set sail with captain-schoolmaster Christopher Sheldon aboard a twin-masted brigantine named the *Albatross* on a voyage from the Carribean to the South Pacific and back, an eight month, 12,000 mile trip. They not only encountered a Cuban gunboat on the eve of the Bay of Pigs invasion, but also ran into a sudden storm that sank the vessel, drowning four boys and two crewmembers, including Sheldon's wife. During a Coast Guard hearing on whether Sheldon should retain his U.S. Master Seaman's Certificate, Sheldon was accused of being a modern-day Captain Bligh whose tyranny nearly inspired a mutiny, who gave the boys too much freedom ashore and not enough instruction aboard ship.

However, *White Squall* used Sheldon as an adviser and casts him in a more heroic mode. (Jeff Bridges, who plays him, is said to have based his characterization on Mike Nelson, the character his father Lloyd played on the popular *Sea Hunt* TV series.) As scripted by Todd Robinson, the film is less "Mutiny on the *Albatross*" than "*Dead Poets Society* at Sea."

As usual, Scott demonstrates his painterly eye for dramatic composition, and the twenty minute squall sequence with a white wall of wind battering the ship and its crew is appropriately spectacular, simultaneously terrifying and exhilarating. It's also somewhat of a relief from much of the tedium that proceeds it.

Sheldon's young charges seem made up of stereotypes. There's a quick-tempered bully (Eric Michael Cole) whose temper hides his myriad insecurities; the sensitive kid (Ryan Phillipe) who must overcome his fear of heights; the browbeaten son (Jeremy Sisto) who must discover his own identity, among others.

The central character is Chuck Gieg (Scott Wolf) whose deadening narration lies at the heart of what's wrong with the film. Gieg is a high school senior who strikes out on his own by pursuing his desire to set out to sea rather than cramming for an Ivy League entrance exam as his family wants him to do. He comes across as a handsome but bland Tom Cruise type.

Jeff Bridges easily steals the show with his godlike authority, portraying Sheldon as a caring surrogate father, loving husband, and dedicated professional. Sheldon's wife Alice (Caroline Goodall) only has a couple of scenes to establish that she is a doctor and an able first mate; John Savage pops up as McCrea, a Shakespeare enthusiast, and Julio Mechoso plays a Cuban cook who helps add tension to the scenes where they confront the gunboat crew.

Scott's next genre work is Showtime's television series *The Hunger* based on his brother Tony Scott's arty vampire film. Directing chores for the series were split up between Ridley, Tony, and Ridley's son Jake, and Russel Mulcahy. Ridley Scott, as reported by Frank Barron in *Cinefantastique*, said, "Any fantasy is only powerful and only really functions well if the creator has set up parameters and within those parameters are the elements of truth for that story. Science fiction gives the director, the artists, and the writer a stage upon which anything can go — providing you stay within the bounds of the walls that you set for yourself before you set out." Scott describes the new series as psychological, sexual fantasy.

Scott's next project was *G.I. Jane* from a script by David Twohy (*Pitch Black; The Arrival*) and Danielle Alexandra. It features Demi Moore as Naval Intelligence officer Lt. Jordan O'Neil, who recruited to become the first female SEAL and must endure an intense hazing to achieve this accomplishment. (Somehow, the film makes out that nobody is interested in seeing women be successful in the armed forces and that everyone does all he can to prevent O'Neil from being successful.) O'Neil proves indomitable, however, demonstrates absolutely no sense of humor, and proves that women warriors can be just as staunch, humorless, and obsessed as their male counterparts.

Of course, the G.I.'s are army, not navy. There is no indication that O'Neil, who initially holds a staff position, is in the kind of physical shape needed to become a SEAL, and the film suggests that an admiral would risk his entire career to thwart one lowly lieutenant, and that her drill instructor Command Master Chief John Urgayle (Viggo Mortensen) would risk his by intensely physically assaulting her at one point (forcing her to respond by kicking him in the *cojones*). Even Anne Bancroft does not come across well as a Texas senator Lillian DeHaven with a variably unconvincing Southern accent, who puts O'Neil forward as a candidate while secretly expecting her to fail in order to use her as a bargaining chip for some political maneuvering.

Naturally, *G.I. Jane* had to be supplied with a rousing finish in which O'Neil proves her mettle against real ammunition, so the unseasoned SEAL candidates are thrown into combat at the end in Libya, despite the massive naval presence in that area that would suggest that more suitable and seasoned SEAL teams could have been sent except that the plot dictated that O'Neil and her now bonded compatriots need to demonstrate their competence under fire.

Scott has been praised for championing strong women in the past — Thelma and Louise, Sigourney Weaver's Ripley in *Alien*, but the truth is he just transposes stereotypical male action traits onto female heroines, rendering their femininity a moot issue as all traces of femininity are expunged. No softness nor tenderness here, but is it really liberating to assert that women can be just as much testosterone assholes as men? Ultimately, this is a superficial film, a far cry from Kubrick's *Full Metal Jacket*. It has Scott's superb sense of pictorial beauty, but the beauty is only skin deep and the story beneath lacks substance or resonance. Not surprisingly, it failed to attract audiences who responded to neither its cynicism nor its manipulation.

Scott's next project was to be a remake of Boris Segal's *Omega Man*, a loose adaptation of Richard Matheson's *I Am Legend* which starred Charlton Heston, who saw possibilities in the book after reading the paperback on a flight from London to New York and sold Walter Seltzer on the idea of making a film from it. Matheson's original story dealt with the last man on Earth who battles a plague of vampires and served as inspiration for George Romero's nightmarish horror classic *Night of the Living Dead*.

However, the filmmakers and screenwriter Bill Corrington decided to throw out the vampire idea in favor of religiously fanatical, plague-stricken albinos created when the Chinese launched a deadly bacteriological war that has infected the entire world. Heston plays U.S. Air Force Colonel Neville who has raided art museums for their treasures, is holed up in his apartment against the albino attackers who maniacally try to attack him every night, and in the daytime he attends screenings of *Woodstock*, not so much because he likes rock music, but simply to remember the crowds of people that once populated the Earth (one of the film's better touches).

The director, Boris Segal, was at odds with the cameraman Russell Metty (*Touch of Evil*), who was one of the best and speediest cinematographers in the business, because he felt threatened by the cameraman's reputation. Segal had a bad temper and his career ended tragically a few years later when he stepped into the tail rotor blade of a helicopter, making him one of the few directors ever killed in the line of duty. Despite Metty's talent, he put too much light on the albinos and failed to make them truly menacing.

Part of the premise of the film is that there are a few carriers of the plague who are young, infected, but do not have the full blown disease. At the outbreak of the war, Neville took an experimental anti-viral serum that has rendered him immune and so his blood is capable of making others immune. Heston decided to play up the Christ parallels in his death scene, assuming a crucified pose as his youthful followers obtain the blood they need to save themselves. Despite the trite ending and the perfunctory direction, *The Omega Man* was a big hit when it was released. Scott cast Arnold Schwarzenegger to play the main role in the remake, but Warner Bros. balked at the expected $100 million pricetag and canceled the project, leaving Scott awaiting a return to the genre that first brought him fame and regard.

Instead, Joaquin Phoenix (*To Die For, SpaceCamp*) and Djimon Hounsou (*Amistad, ER*) will star opposite Russell Crowe (*L.A. Confidential*) in Ridley Scott's Ancient Rome epic *Gladiator*. Nevertheless, his work on the classics *Alien* and *Blade Runner* have left an indelible mark on filmed science fiction forever and mark him as a director to watch.

FRED F. SEARS (1913–1957)

Desert Vigilante (1949); *Across the Badlands; Horsemen of the Sierras; Lightning Guns; Raiders of Tomahawk Creek* (1950); *Bonanza Town; Pecos River; Prairie Roundup; Ridin' the Outlaw Trail; Snake River Desperadoes* (1951); *Hawk of Wild River; Kid from Broken Gun; Last Train from Bombay; Smoky Canyon; Target Hong Kong* (1952); *49th Man; Ambush at Tomahawk Gap; Mission Over Korea; The Nebraskan; Sky Commando* (1953); *El Alamein; Massacre Canyon; Miami Story; Outlaw Stallion; Overland Pacific* (1954); *Apache Ambush; Cell 2455, Death Row; Chicago Syndicate; Inside Detroit; Teenage Crime Wave; Wyoming Renegades* (1955); *Cha-Cha-Cha Boom; Don't Knock the Rock; Earth vs. the Flying Saucers; Fury at Gunsight Pass; Miami Expose; Rock Around the Clock; Rumble on the Docks; Werewolf* (1956); *Calypso Heat Wave; Escape from San Quentin; The Giant Claw; The Night the World Exploded; Utah Blaine* (1957); *Badman's Country; Crash Landing; Ghost of the China Sea; Going Steady; The World Has His Jury* (1958)

A former actor who began his film acting career in *The Jolson Story* (1946), Boston-born Fred F. Sears has only one above average science fiction film to his credit, *Earth vs. the Flying Saucers*, one below average laugh riot, *The Giant Claw*, and two mediocre SF movies, yet has won a place in the hearts of rock 'n' roll fans for helping to pioneer the el cheapo rock and roll exploitation film with *Rock Around the Clock* and *Don't Knock the Rock*. Sears was never considered a stylist, but his pictures were made efficiently and most of them were entertaining.

His acting credits include *Boston Blackie's Chinese Venture; Blazing Trail; Whirlwind Raiders; Rusty Leads the Way; Phantom Valley; Gallant Blade; Adventures in Silverado; West of Dodge City; Lone Hand Texan; Law of the Canyon; It Had to Be You; Her Husband's Affairs; For the Love of Rusty; Down to Earth; Corpse Came C.O.D.; Blondie's Anniversary* and *Blondie in the Dough*.

He began his directorial career working on very low budget B westerns, and eventually branched out into other types of projects such as *Cell 2455, Death Row* and *Teenage Crime Wave*. He alternated between acting and directing for a time, continuing to appear in such films as *Rough, Tough West; Laramie Mountains; My True Story; Kid from Amarillo; Fort Savage Raiders; Cyclone Fury; Bonanza Town; Big Gusher; Bandits of El Dorado; Texas Dynamo; Hoedown; Frontier Outpost; David Harding, Counterspy; Counterspy Meets Scotland Yard; Convicted; South of Death Valley; Smoky Mountain Melody; Slightly French; Shockproof; Renegades of the Sage; Lust for Gold; Lone Wolf and His Lady; Laramie* and *Johnny Allegro* before turning his attention to directing full time. His direction was typically efficient, but usually evinced no visual flare.

Before his science fiction film work, Sears' biggest claim to fame was directing two early rock 'n' roll musicals starring Bill Haley and the Comets, which amply demonstrate why the pudgy, middle-aged Haley never reached the heights of popularity that Elvis Presley did. The first rock exploitation film, *Rock Around the Clock*, has Johnny Johnston as big band manager Steve Hollis searching out the next new thing, discovering Haley and the Comets and their attractive manager Lisa Johns (Lisa Gaye) in Strawberry Springs. Soon they are whisked to New York where Steve persuades Alan Freed to book the unknown rockers as headliners and the kids go crazy for them. Apart from showing Haley and his group performing some of their biggest hits, the film is best remembered for showing the

Platters singing their classics, "Only You" and "The Great Pretender."

This was quickly followed up with *Don't Knock the Rock*, a sanctimonious and defensive follow-up which spends an inordinate amount of time sermonizing about why rock 'n' roll should be heard. Haley shares the screen with his ace guitarist Frank Beecher, who does some nice instrumentals, fictitious teen idol Arnie Haines (Alan Dale), his favorite group, the Treniers, and in the film's best moments, Little Richard and the Upsetters play "Tutti Fruiti" and "Long Tall Sally," the mediocre movie's best argument for preservation.

To support the film, Sears churned out *Rumble on the Docks* for producer Sam Katzman, which featured James Darren as a teen gang leader who tangles with a corrupt longshoreman's union on the waterfront and finally gains maturity. At the beginning, he admires the union boss who had crippled his father, who in turn blames his son for his disability by causing him to be a longshoreman in the first place. Hostile parents became a frequent element in many subsequent juvenile crime dramas.

Sears' first science fiction project was by far his best, featuring above average script and special effects, including the most visually interesting flying saucers ever created for a science fiction film, courtesy of George Worthington Yates and master animator Ray Harryhausen respectively.

Gag shot with chalked up alien invader and Joan Taylor from Sears' *Earth vs. the Flying Saucers*.

Earth vs. the Flying Saucers began when Columbia Studios decided to combine a story by Curt Siodmak and a report by Major Donald E. Keyhoe that supposed that alien invaders might have come to Earth and that the military was covering evidence of said invasion up. Columbia Pictures picked up the rights to Keyhoe's story and combined them with a scenario "Attack of the Flying Saucers" written by Siodmak. George Worthington Yates, who had worked on *It Came from Beneath the Sea* and *Them!,* was engaged to write a script from this material, which was subsequently handed over to blacklisted writer Bernard Gordon, who wrote using Raymond T. Marcus as a front for his work.

For its time, the military is portrayed in the film in an unusually unflattering light. Belligerent, suspicious, and autocratic, the military only assesses the aliens as a threat and makes no real attempts to communicate with them. The aliens have tried to communicate with the hero, but failed to compensate for different time perceptions and so their instructions are interpreted as gobbledy-gook. Once the aliens set down near operation Skyhook, they are immediately fired upon and attacked, and naturally choose to retaliate. At that point, neither side considers exploring a more peaceful solution to the conflict, which makes both sides appear shortsighted.

The aliens are encased in unusual spacesuits, complete with opaque helmet, which the scientists discover after shooting one of the beings outside of their protective forcefield, helps the invaders by increasing the sensitivity of their senses as well as aiding their muscular strength. The suits are said to be made out of "solidified electricity," whatever that is supposed to mean apart from indicating that somehow the aliens are very advanced. Few SF films have thought to have their invaders inside spacesuits that would allow them to deal with what would be to them an alien environment, and it is to the film's credit that it does so. The aliens themselves are only briefly revealed, looking like wizened statues, though not far off from the popular images of aliens culled from the tabloid press; however, these beings dissolve on contact with Earth's atmosphere.

This increased sensitivity proves not only to be a boon, but also proves to be the alien invaders' Achilles Heel, as they find sonic waves highly disruptive to their advanced energy systems. Hence heroic scientist Russell Marvin (Hugh Marlowe), after being abducted by the aliens and given an ultimatum — Earth must capitulate in 60 days or else — learns enough about how the aliens power their ships to create an effective counterforce. After being able to test the device once, Marvin and his associates manufacture enough gizmos to wipe out the (not very numerous) invading fleet in the film's spectacular climax.

The finale of the film, where the aliens launch an assault on Washington, is particularly impressive as Harryhausen arranges to have the stop motion animated, spinning saucers affected by a sound ray that causes them to topple into almost every major landmark in sight. (Tim Burton largely recreated the look of the saucers and some of the attack in his *Mars Attacks!*) He also briefly animates the buildings flying apart, each fragment of building being suspended by a cleverly camouflaged wire as the pieces fall at subnormal speeds before an explosion is superimposed and a quick cut to another image. While impressive, the effects took such an effort that Harryhausen swore never to employ such techniques again. Shots of the film's saucer turned up subsequently in *The 27th Day*, the Three Stooges short *Flying Saucer*, *Daffy*, and Orson Welles' *F Is for Fake*.

Sears keeps the pace lively, which also aids the film's entertainment value. Hugh Marlowe comes off much better here than he did as an unsympathetic opportunist in *The Day the Earth Stood Still*, though he is still stiff and mannered. Joan Taylor makes for a fetching heroine as Carole, Marvin's bride, while Morris Ankrum is dependable as yet another military officer (and Carole's father), General Hanley. Though not as elaborate or fondly remembered as Haskin's *War of the Worlds, Earth vs. the Flying Saucers* is still one of the best alien invasion films of the fifties.

Unfortunately, the remainder of Sears' subsequent science fiction projects don't live up to it. His next such project projected the first science fictional werewolf, jettisoning the supernatural explanation for a more "scientific" one. In fact, one of Sears' best directed sequences served as the opening of *The Werewolf*, in which a drunken man (Steve Ritch) is attacked by a mugger, they struggle, with the bar patron emerging victorious, rising, back to the camera, and frightening a female spectator before running off. The material is lit and framed in such a way as to be atmospheric and interestingly mysterious.

Eventually we find out that the victor is car crash victim Duncan Marsh, who has been injected with an experimental serum by a pair of scientists who are trying to devise a way to combat the effects of radiation (though what connection there is between radiation and wolves is never made clear). When Dr. Emery Forest and Dr. Morgan Chambers (S. John Launer and George M. Lynn) learn of some mysterious wolf killings, they try to track the stranger down and kill him, and he, of course, responds in kind.

The film is somewhat erratic, but still effective for a low budget effort. There are three werewolf transformations in the film, and yet each one features a different makeup. One of these is especially impressive as the panicked Marsh tries to warn one of the scientists while in the process of transforming into a murderous, bloodthirsty werewolf. Ritch is good at conveying Marsh's confusion and fear as he discovers himself transforming into a beast over which he has no control.

The film ends with Marsh as a werewolf being shot down in a hail of bullets by a dam, one of the more conventional scenes in the film. Still, for a Sam Katzman production, *The Werewolf* looks and plays pretty well, and deserves a better reputation than its apparent present obscurity.

Sears' *The Giant Claw* is remembered, if it is remembered at all, for having the worst-looking menace to ever appear in a science fiction film, quite a feat when one considers competitors such as *The Creeping Terror*'s walking carpet monster and the titular creation of *Reptilicus*. The plot was pretty much standard issue, with mysterious occurrences in a blighted area, local natives raving about a flying monster, which later turns out to be quite "real."

The film's main debit (and source of entertainment today) is the Mexican manufactured avian marionette which represents the main menace in the film. It was so outlandishly awful looking that the studio, in advertising the film, carefully hid its visage from view in the film's poster, which proudly proclaims, "Flying Beast out of Prehistoric Skies!" The problem was not only with the lifeless wings, but especially the ludicrous head, situated atop a long, jack-in-the-boxish neck, complete with permanent sneer, enormous schnozz, Ping Pong ballish eyes, and pathetic crest that give the creature the appearance of an irate Mortimer Snerd.

Nor does it help that the film's other special effects are often of an equal caliber. The fighter jets that attack the Giant Claw look just like the plastic toys that they are. The toy train the monster picks up in its claws and flies off with keeps on putting out cute puffs of black smoke as it gets carried away.

To Sears' credit, the cast tries to deliver serious performances, and may not have seen the ridiculous results that producer Sam Katzman procured for their titular performer. Jeff Morrow performs with the same kind of earnestness which he brought to his part in *This Island*

Earth, which makes the contrast between his seriousness and the seriocomic antagonist all the more risible.

Morrow plays Mitch MacAfee, ably supported by Mara Corday as his secretary Sally Caldwell. After a number of attempts have been tried to bring the terrible turkey down have failed, MacAfee deduces that the avian terror is actually composed of anti-matter, explaining that if the monster's "mu-mesons" were to be reversed, its anti-matter shield could be broached and the monster would fall victim to "a suicidal short circuit." (Naturally, this runs counter to theories of anti-matter which would convert to pure energy if it came into contact with matter.)

In an interview in *Filmfax* magazine with Paul Parla, Mara Corday recalled, "When I first met the film's producer, Sam Katzman, he was so excited about the 'Bird' and seemed like something to look forward to. The special effects were being done in Mexico and the Mexican crew had given him the impression that 'Bird' would be very frightening, with superior special effects and production values.

"The film was near completion when Katzman finally had the chance to see the incredibly comical 'flying battleship.' Well, Katzman was shocked, but he opted to accept the thing as a joke, because it was not economical [to spend more money] to create a more realistic monster.

"I saw the film in a theater, where it played to roars of laughter from the audience. I slumped in my seat with embarrassment."

Sears also tackled *The Night the World Exploded* for Katzman which served to fill out a double bill with *The Giant Claw*. *Night* has an oddball premise concerning a scientist, David Conway (William Leslie), who discovers a new element, dubbed E-112, which when dry and exposed to the air absorbs nitrogen and then explodes, causing earthquakes. Apparently, a large supply of this earth-shattering element has been drying off and wreaking havoc, so Conway convinces the powers that be to flood all the low-lying regions of the Earth (extensive stock footage of flooding). It works everywhere, except for one volcano in Nevada, so Conway takes some E-112 and blows up a dam, flooding the remaining supply of E-112 and saving the world.

While the premise is unusual, Sears' execution and the formulaic plot are not, resulting in an ambitious film that never even makes its own title credible and never manages to generate much excitement or suspense. Sears only made a few more films before dying in 1957, little known, little mourned, but with at least some interesting genre work to his credit.

STEVEN SPIELBERG (1946–)

The Last Train Wreck (short, 1957); *The Last Gun* (short); *A Day in the Life of Thunder* (short, 1958); *Scary Hollow* (short, 1961); *Escape to Nowhere* (short, 1962); *Battle Squad* (short, 1961); *Firelight* (1964); *Senior Sneak Day* (documentary, 1965); *Slipstream* (1967); *Amblin'* (short, 1968); *The Sugarland Express* (1974); *Jaws* (1975); *Close Encounters of the Third Kind* (1977); *1941* (1979); *Raiders of the Lost Ark* (1981); *E.T. the Extra-Terrestrial* (1982); *Twilight Zone— The Movie* (codirected with John Landis, Joe Dante, and George Miller) (1983); *Indiana Jones and the Temple of Doom* (1984); *The Color Purple* (1985); *Empire of the Sun* (1987); *Indiana Jones and the Last Crusade; Always* (1989); *Hook* (1991); *Jurassic Park; Schindler's List* (1993); *The Lost World: Jurassic Park; Amistad* (1997); *Saving Private Ryan* (1998); *Memoirs of a Geisha; Minority Report* (2000)

Television: "Eyes," *Night Gallery* (codirected pilot with Boris Sagal and Barry Shear) (1969); "The Daredevil Gesture," *Marcus Welby* (1970); "Make Me Laugh," *Night Gallery*; "God Bless the Children," "Par for the Course," "The Private World of Martin Dalton," *The Psychiatrist*; "Murder by the Book," *Columbo;* "Eulogy for a Wide Receiver," *Owen Marshall Counselor at Law;* "L.A. 2017," *The Name of the Game; Duel* (1971); *Something Evil* (1972); *Savage* (aka *Watch Dog; The Savage Report*) (1973); *Strokes of Genius* (directed introductory segments with Dustin Hoffman) (1984); "Ghost Train," "The Mission," *Amazing Stories* (1985)

Other Media: *Steven Spielberg's Director's Chair* (codirector with Roger Holzberg) CD-ROM (1996)

As a filmmaker, Steven Spielberg is fascinated by the fantastic and the spiritual. His work has redefined the possibilities of science fiction cinema. As director or producer, he has created two-thirds of the most popular films of all time; he has become a modern-day Walt Disney who has dabbled in animation, television, and film production, and has the potential of overturning the Hollywood hierarchy with his DreamWorks S-K-G productions, which allow him to produce and possibly distribute his own projects entirely outside of the mainstream Hollywood system. He is also one of our most gifted filmmakers who masterfully manipulates audiences' hearts and pocketbooks though he oftimes neglects their minds. His style is one of surprise, with fast cutting that emphasizes flash rather than flow, and it often emphasizes shock over character, though that has begun to change.

Still, Spielberg's elaborate action sequences have redefined pacing in Hollywood as his films hurl pell-mell from one thrill to the next. Too often dismissed as a mere "entertainer," a man who made movies which were like theme park rides, Spielberg has shown himself to be an artist as well as a meticulous craftsman, and there are good reasons why his films linger longer in our minds than the movies of his numerous imitators.

A typical Spielberg movie depicts someone who is living a very ordinary, mundane life, and then someone comes into that life and disturbs everything, disrupts everything, makes him or her suddenly have to work at life, and really *live* it, to survive. His films are about ordinary people with ordinary problems who suddenly have to become extraordinary to overcome some new force in their lives.

Steven Spielberg was born in Cincinnati, Ohio on December 18, 1946, growing up first in New Jersey and later in Phoenix, Arizona (though he preferred to tell people he grew up in nearby Scarsdale). He was bitten by the film bug early, winning a film contest at the age of 13 with his first major production, *Escape to Nowhere*, a 40 minute war film, which was followed by some fifteen other amateur 8mm productions ending three years later with a science fiction epic called *Firelight*. *Firelight* was a two hour and twenty minute epic about scientists investigating strange lights in space from whence derive monsters who battle with the National Guard. Spielberg has referred to it as "the worst film the world has ever seen." It was shot using classmates with the sound dubbed afterwards when Spielberg rented a German projector with a magnetic sound-stripe.

However, that didn't keep *Firelight* from being a commercial success like most of Spielberg's productions. Spielberg's father rented the local Scottsdale cinema to show it and recouped the film's $500 production costs in one night. The day after the screening, Spielberg and his family left Phoenix and moved to Saratoga, California. Years later, while hunting up film work at a commercials studio, he gave what he thought were the best two reels of *Firelight* to the man running the studio, only to find a week later when he returned that the studio was now a Honda dealership and the man had completely disappeared.

He was turned down by the University of South California's film school and so ended up majoring in English at California State University Long Beach, which was ironic as Spielberg didn't like to read, attended college mostly to avoid the draft to Vietnam, and spent most of his time watching or attempting to make movies rather than paying attention to his classwork.

Spielberg enjoyed inventing his own origins, often telling an improbable story about how he sneaked into Universal Studios by pretending to be an employee there and setting himself up in an empty office. What actually happened was that Spielberg was visiting Universal during a break from school and met editor Chuck Silvers, who was assigned to reorganize the studio's extensive film library and who was asked to show Spielberg around postproduction by Arnold Shupack as a favor to Spielberg's father, Arnold. Silvers and he struck up a friendship (Silvers being one of the few willing to look at his amateur films) and Silvers allowed Spielberg to work as an unpaid clerical assistant in the Universal editorial department.

Another significant meeting for Spielberg was when he met John Cassavetes. "He met me when I was sneaking around Universal Studios watching other people shoot TV shows," remembers Spielberg. "He was doing an episode of *Chrysler Theater* that Robert Ellis Miller was directing, and he pulled me aside and he said, 'What do you want to do?' And I said, 'I want to be a director.' He said, 'Okay, after every take, you tell me what I'm doing wrong. And you give me direction.' So here I am, 18 years old, and there's a professional film company at Universal Studios doing this TV episode and after every take he walks past the other actors, walks past the director, he walks right up to me and says, 'What did you think? How can I improve it? What am I doing wrong?' And I would say, 'Gah, it's too embarrassing, right here, Mr. Cassavetes. Mr. Cassavetes, don't ask me in *front* of everybody, can't we go around the corner and talk?'

"And he made me a production assistant on *Faces* for a couple of weeks, and I hung around and watched him shoot that movie, and John was much more interested in the story and the actors than he was the camera. He loved his cast. He treated his cast like they had been part of his family for many years. And so I really got off on the right foot, learning how to deal with actors as I watched Cassavetes dealing with his repertory company."

Learning that Hollywood producers were not interested

in screening 8mm and 16mm amateur films, he resolved to make his next one in 35mm. Spielberg met an ambitious, would-be producer named Dennis Hoffman who fronted $10,000 to make the film, which was photographed by Allen Daviau, who was experienced in photographing commercials and short promotional films and whose professional feature debut would be *E.T.*

Spielberg's 25 minute, 35mm short subject *Amblin',* about two kids who fall in love while hitchhiking, and then separate without exchanging a word, won awards at both the Venice and Atlanta Film Festivals, and more importantly, it impressed Universal studio executive Sid Sheinberg and won Spielberg a seven year contract with MCA-TV at the ripe age of 20, the youngest director ever signed by a major studio (Spielberg decided to forsake graduating from college in order to start work immediately). Spielberg made *Amblin'* for about $10,000 in ten days in the Palm Desert. He shot it in 35mm because he was unable to get studio executives to look at his 16mm films, and the story was non-verbal because he could not afford sound.

Spielberg's first assignment was to direct one segment of the pilot episode of Rod Serling's *Night Gallery*, the segment starring Joan Crawford. (The other segments were directed by Boris Sagal and Barry Shear.) The story dealt with a rich blind woman who buys the eyes of a gambling debtor, despite discovering that she will be able to see only for a limited time, which ironically happens to coincide with a blackout. Spielberg's direction tries to hamfistedly emphasize the visual aspects of the story, and the pilot proved successful despite receiving lukewarm to hostile reviews.

Because of the response, Spielberg spent a good deal of time waiting in his little apartment for the phone to ring without much success. Finally, Spielberg was offered a *Marcus Welby* episode and then went through another dry spell without any offers of any kind. He attempted to write screenplays and make underground 16mm films but was unable to find any financing, so he finally returned to Sheinberg, pleading poverty and willing to take anything.

He made a foray into science fiction with a story scripted by science fiction author Philip Wylie (*When Worlds Collide* and others) entitled "L.A. 2017," an episode of *The Name of the Game* starring Barry Sullivan, Edmund O'Brien, Paul Stewart and Louise Latham, in which newspaperman Gene Barry dreams of a future where the skies of Los Angeles have become so thick with pollution that the city erects a dome over itself. The visual look of the segment imitated George Lucas' future in *THX-1138*.

Spielberg later got into trouble with a second *Night Gallery* assignment, scripted by Serling and called "Make Me Laugh" starring Godfrey Cambridge as a desperate comedian who develops the power to get people to laugh at everything he says. Spielberg employed long takes with no coverage for the editor to cut to. (In television, timing can be crucial, and Spielberg's technique left the editor with nothing to work with in order to adjust the length and pacing of certain sequences.) He was also criticized by the cameraman's union for riding a camera on a *Psychiatrist* episode.

After several undistinguished episodes of other series, Spielberg was given the first regular episode of *Columbo* to do, "Murder by the Book" written by Steve Bocho, who later became a very successful television producer in his own right. The episode helped establish Peter Falk's Columbo character and guest starred Jack Cassidy as a writer who kills his more talented partner by using the one original plot he had actually thought up.

In television, Spielberg learned how to prepare thoroughly in advance as well as how to think on his feet. His big break finally came when his secretary, Nona Tyson, discovered a Richard Matheson story in *Playboy* called "Duel" which he thought could be made into a good television movie. The story was based on a real-life episode that happened to Matheson in Colorado where a truck kept forcing him to speed up in order to get out of its way. It details a similar conflict between one David Mann and a mysterious truck which goes out of its way to endanger Mann's life. Matheson was hired to transform his tight, tension-filled little story into a teleplay.

Spielberg cut most of the dialogue from Matheson's script, wanting the film to be purely cinematic, almost like a silent movie; however, the network forced the producer, George Eckstein, and scriptwriter Matheson to keep adding narration internalizing Dennis Weaver so that the audience would understand his deepest fears.

Spielberg ordered that the truck, selected on the basis of its imposing grill, have dead bugs all over the windshield so that the driver could not be seen, and had it given a bubble bath of motor oil, clunky black, and crud-brown paint that was layered, bubbled, and pocked in the sun to make it more menacing. He carefully shot *Duel* so that the driver of the truck would remain unseen and mysterious, explaining in Judith Crist's *Take 22,* "You barely see a hand signaling Dennis Weaver to pass. Or when you see a shadow in the cockpit of the truck, this is a kind of esoteric reality. But never to identify whether the driver is human or nonhuman — that would, I think, push the film into a type of science fantasy."

To choreograph the movie, Spielberg drew a mural which detailed from an overhead view the entire chase, allowing him to plot what and where each and every event along the chase route was. He would plan three or four camera set-ups at a time in order to complete the entire film within the allotted 16 days, shooting a total of 20,000 feet of film, two and a half times the normal amount for a feature of that length.

To give a greater impression of speed, for half the film Spielberg had the camera undercranked at 18–20 frames per second, while the camera was running normally during the other half. He also used a camera car built for *Bullitt*, a made-over Corvette with the fiberglass body removed that allowed cameras to be mounted a mere three or four inches off the ground which creates a greater sense of speed and velocity. For shots from the truck's point of view, he filmed with a 9.5 fisheye lens.

Stunt man Carey Loftin came close to losing his life in the closing stunt when the truck smashes into Mann's car and goes over the cliff. Once Loftin's hand was taken off the throttle, the truck would begin to slow down, so the trick was to build enough momentum before Loftin jumped from the truck while the throttle was secured with a rope. However, at the point of no return, the cord broke, forcing Loftin to stay in the truck until a mere twenty yards from the cliff before leaping to safety.

ABC wanted the film to end with the truck exploding, but Spielberg felt that particular cliché had been overdone, and thought it would be more interesting to show the truck expiring slowly, its "life" trickling away in a cruel death. The network tried to tell him that it was in his contract to blow up the truck, but finally Eckstein talked them out of forcing Spielberg to add a truck explosion.

Duel was shot in sixteen days in Soledad Canyon, California, on a budget of $450,000. It debuted as an ABC Movie of the Week on November 13, 1971. The telemovie garnered highly favorable reviews, but there was no immediate change in Spielberg's fortunes. Years later, Universal allowed footage from the film to be used to pad an episode of *The Incredible Hulk* in 1978. As a consequence, Spielberg subsequently put a clause in his contract to prevent such cannibalization in the future.

Two years later, *Duel* was released theatrically in Europe, with its 74 minute running time increased to 90 minutes. Spielberg took out the musical crescendos that had introduced the commercial breaks and had only two days to shoot the additional materials. Having destroyed the original truck, Spielberg was able to find one almost exactly like it, except that the space between the cab and the trailer was noticeably greater. He regretted adding a scene with Jacqueline Scott, playing Mann's wife, because he felt it was too obvious, and the film does work better in the trimmer, television version than it does in the expanded theatrical one.

Nevertheless, the theatrical version of *Duel* won the Grand Prix at the Festival du Cinema Fantastique in France and the Silver Spotlight Best-Picture-of-the-Month Award in Germany. It also earned the Gariddi d'Oro Award for Best Opera Prima (First Film) at Italy's Taormina Film Festival and a special mention for direction at Monte Carlo's 11th Annual International Festival of Television. *Duel* netted $6 million in Europe alone.

Following *Duel*, Spielberg began preparing another TV movie called *Something Evil* for CBS. Darren McGavin and Sandy Dennis star as a couple who move into a creepy farmhouse in Bucks County, Pennsylvania, where something takes possession of their daughter. One of the cast members was Spielberg himself, who reportedly did not enjoy seeing himself on screen. The film was written by Robert Clouse and photographed by Bill Butler.

Spielberg's last television movie was *Savage*, written by the famed writer-producer team of Richard Levinson and William Link, creators of *Columbo*. It was a typical private eye drama, and not particularly distinguished.

Spielberg's entry into movies occurred when then 20th Century–Fox production chiefs Richard D. Zanuck and David Brown took a liking to one of Spielberg's scenarios, *Ace Eli and Rodger of the Skies*. This largely forgotten period piece, about a would-be barnstormer biplane pilot, Ace Eli (Cliff Robertson in one of his very worst performances) and his family, was directed by John Erman and garnered miserable reviews and quickly flopped upon release. Spielberg's story was rewritten by Claudia Salter, but it is interesting to note the embryonic presence of some Spielberg obsessions — namely, flying and airplanes, as well as the characters of a man-boy (Ace Eli) who is changed by his experiences with a boy-man (Eric Shea playing Rodger).

Nevertheless, the film brought Spielberg to the attention of Zanuck-Brown, who changed studios and became interested in a script called *Sugarland Express*, written by Hal Barwood and Matthew Robbins from a story by Spielberg (the pair would win the Best Screenplay Award at the 1974 Cannes Film Festival). In May of 1969, Spielberg became interested in a news story about convict Robert Samuel Dent and his young wife Illa Faye who kidnapped state trooper James Kenneth Crone while escaping from prison and led the police on a 300 mile chase.

The producing team gave Spielberg the opportunity to direct his first feature film, *The Sugarland Express*, starring Goldie Hawn. Hawn stars as Lou Jean Poplin, who springs her husband, Clovis (William Atherton), from a pre-release center in order to enlist his aid in retrieving their son, the custody of whom has been wrested from her by the state. Their irresponsible actions confirm the state's judgment, but the lengths that they go attest to their deep, abiding love for the child.

To facilitate their passage to Sugarland, home of the child's foster parents, the Poplins take policeman Maxwell Slide (Michael Sacks) hostage, which keeps the police posse at bay. The pursuit is headed by a somewhat sympathetic

Captain Tanner (Ben Johnson), who understands that the couple do not want to hurt anyone but are nonetheless defying the law. Slide comes to understand that Clovis is a similar small town type to himself, one who simply took the wrong turn in life.

Spielberg creates an auto ballet with the speeding cars moving with dance-like grace. He also plays up how the pairs actions are mythologized by the media, who turn them into instant celebrities who have people cheering them on as they wend their way towards their final destiny. Giving the film additional tension is the police preparations to put a stop to the Poplins' actions, a tragedy Tanner hopes to avert but is powerless to prevent.

Spielberg shifts the tone from light-hearted to tragic, as it finally begins to dawn on Clovis what kind of forces they have unleashed. Also disturbing is a scene where right-wing vigilantes take potshots at the pair at a used car lot, leaving an observant child in a state of shock. Finally, police marksmen shoot Clovis, having used their child as a lure, while a hysterical Lou Jean, who had pushed the anxious Clovis out of the car to claim the child, now loses control of her car.

The likable Hawn whose character initiates all the action is really the film's villain, but her charm and vitality obscure that fact. With her all-consuming mother love giving an insistent edge to her character, Lou Jean is one of Hawn's most engaging performances. Her problem is basically outlined in the story as her inability to wait for gratification, hence she must have her husband, must have sexual relations, must urinate, and especially must have her son right now, thus triggering the tragedy that follows.

Despite its many appealing aspects and Spielberg's assured direction, *The Sugarland Express* was not a financial success. The public was used to seeing the winsome Hawn in lighthearted comedies and Universal found it difficult to package and sell because its appeal could not be summed up simply. American audiences prefer their blue collar heroes to be winners, not losers, and the material was not conducive to an upbeat ending.

Having earned some money, Spielberg bought what he thought was a cool car, an orange Pontiac Trans Am, but two months later, noticing all the BMWs and Mercedes on the studio lot, he switched to a green Mercedes convertible. He fell in with the USC film crowd, but had difficulty adjusting to the counterculture. He dated Margot Kidder, but screenwriter Willard Huyck recalls Spielberg's shock when Kidder pulled up her dress to tan herself on the beach and was wearing nothing underneath.

One thing that distinguished Spielberg was that he didn't do drugs, though several of his friends were into it. As he told *McBride* magazine, "I would sit in a room and watch TV while people climbed the walls." He did, however, attach himself to Brian De Palma and Martin Scorsese, listening to their ideas about how movies could be an example of personal expression. Lacking a sense of style and wanting to be cool, Spielberg would comb the monthly magazines to discover what was considered "hip."

Richard D. Zanuck and David Brown had produced *Sugarland Express* and then tagged the 26-year-old director first to direct *MacArthur*, which he turned down, and then *Jaws*, based on Peter Benchley's best-selling novel. Zanuck and Brown had purchased the rights to the book plus an adaptation by Benchley for $175,000 for director Dick Richards, who dropped out of the project when he kept referring to the shark as a whale. Spielberg was dubious about the project at first, but became more enthusiastic. He tried to get Jon Voight to play Matt Hooper, and then considered Timothy Bottoms and Jeff Bridges, but went for Richard Dreyfuss because his energy was so kinetic. Dreyfuss turned the part down at first, becoming cast after the film had started when, seeing himself in *The Apprenticeship of Duddy Kravitz*, he panicked because he thought his performance was terrible and so called Spielberg and begged him for the job.

For Quint, Spielberg wanted Lee Marvin, but Marvin indicated that he preferred real fishing to filming. Next, he approached Sterling Hayden, who initially agreed but then changed his mind. Robert Duvall expressed an interest in the part, but Spielberg offered him Brody instead, which he turned down. Zanuck and Brown suggested Robert Shaw, based on their experiences on *The Sting*. Spielberg thought Shaw was too over the top in all his films, but decided that Quint needed a larger than life quality about him.

Spielberg's first choice for Brody was Joe Bologna, but neither Sheinberg nor Zanuck would agree. He then chanced to meet Roy Scheider at a Hollywood party and explained that he was depressed because he couldn't cast the movie, and Roy said, "Well, I can play Brody," and Spielberg realized he was right. Lorraine Gary, Mrs. Sidney Sheinberg, was cast as Brody's wife because Spielberg was impressed by her work in *The Marcus Nelson Murders*, though this upset Zanuck's wife, Linda Harrison, who hoped to get the role. (Sheinberg got her a part in an *Airport* picture as a consolation.)

After doing several drafts, Benchley left the project and scripting chores were turned over to Howard Sackler (*The Great White Hope*) and then John Milius (*Red Dawn*). Finally, Carl Gottlieb, a former member of the comedy team The Committee, was hired to streamline the script and provide some levity, which proved to be a winning combination. Even so, Spielberg improvised much of the film's final form, with much of the movie shot from the director's storyboards rather than the actual script.

Jaws was expected to be shot over a 13-week period at a cost of $2.3 million. However, shooting the film turned nightmarish as various difficulties concerning shooting at sea tripled the film's 52-day shooting schedule, sending the film grossly overbudget. To create the Great White Shark for the film, Spielberg wanted the man who created the squid for Fleischer's *20,000 Leagues Under the Sea* and hired Bob Mattey. Mattey built three separate hydraulically powered models to do all the things the script would require. Adding to Spielberg's problems, "Bruce," as the 24-foot, one-and-a-half ton mechanical shark was dubbed (after Bruce Ramer, Spielberg's lawyer), would never perform the same action twice the same way. (The fake shark also proved slightly cross-eyed and had jaws that would not shut. What's more, the saltwater would make the model's plastic skin deteriorate rapidly, requiring that it be given constant touch-up work from scuba-diving special effects men.)

Fortunately, by wisely keeping glimpses of the shark to a minimum and following the influence of Jack Arnold's *Creature of the Black Lagoon*, where a sense of menace was created by establishing an underwater viewpoint looking up at helpless humans, *Jaws* went from being an AIP monster movie into an almost Hitchcockian thriller. (According to Spielberg, every decent shot of the shark was actually used in the film, there being so few of them.) Aiding this immensely is John Williams' innovative score with its emphatic strings that suggest both menace and incredible drive.

Spielberg grabs the audience's attention from the outset by setting up a sex fantasy where a gorgeous, well-endowed young woman (Susan Backlinie) entices an equally young but not nearly so graceful paramour into a late night skinny dip only for her to be consumed by Nature's natural eating machine, an unseen Great White Shark. Remarked Spielberg to Nancy Griffin, "I guess the cliché is that when a director sees cleavage, he says, 'More!' Every time I saw cleavage, I said, 'Shit, shit.' She had to be out of the water enough so I could see her, but not too high — that would get us an R rating." Gottlieb laughingly remembers one day's dailies of Backlinie shot from the shark's point of view that consisted of twenty minutes of below the waist shots, which embarrassed everyone, though he notes that Spielberg kept his promise of using fast cuts to keep it clean.

Following the powerful opening, we are quickly introduced to the story's protagonist, Chief Martin Brody (Roy Scheider), head of a normal family including a wife (Lorraine Gary) and two kids, who is still regarded as something of an outsider by the locals because he comes from New York rather than being born on Amity Island. Adding to his difficulty in fitting in, Brody has never learned to swim and fears the water. Amity is a sleepy community, unused to serious threats, and responds negatively when Brody decides to describe the young woman's homicide as a shark attack.

Spielberg borrows a page or two from Ibsen's *An Enemy of the People* as Amity's mayor Larry Vaughn (Murray Hamilton) disputes Brody's assessment and his plans to close down the beaches, warning that "Amity is a summer town," fearing that such a report will drive off the lucrative tourist business upon which the town depends. Brody's willingness to go along with Vaughn and the coroner's insistence that the young woman was merely a drowning victim cut by a boat propeller creates within him a strong sense of guilt about his complicity, which drives his actions for the rest of the story.

He remains apprehensive about further shark attacks, which he knows he has not done enough to prevent. Even more, his actions put his own children at risk when he reluctantly gives them permission to go into the water. This is particularly brought home later when one of his own children almost becomes a victim of a subsequent shark attack (and Spielberg also deftly improvises a scene establishing that his kids mimic Brody's behavior and therefore look to him to see how to act appropriately in a given situation. Adults' responsibility towards children remains a major theme in Spielberg's work). Additionally, Brody cannot meet the gaze of the grieving woman whose child is lost, and who devastates him by informing him, "I just found out that a girl was killed weeks ago, and you knew about it. There was a shark, dangerous, but you let people go swimming anyway. My boy is dead. I wanted you to know." The slap she then gives him is nothing compared to his own awareness of his failure to act responsibly.

However, Brody's closing the beaches proves shortlived as Vaughn announces that the ban will only last 24 hours and that a $3,000 reward has been posted for the killing of the shark. This sets the scene for the introduction of Captain Peter Quint (Robert Shaw), a sub–Hemingway competent man and shark hunter who demands a $10,000 fee to get the job done. Initially, the community rejects Quint's offer and tries to kill the shark on its own, setting out to sea in a wide variety of craft with a wide variety of weapons that suggest rednecks on the rampage with often incompetent results.

This ushers in the last key player in the drama, ichthyologist Matt Hooper (a very amusing Richard Dreyfuss) from the Oceanographic Institute, whose expertise goes unheeded by the masses. In contrast to the brawny Quint, who is all Id, pursuing that which pleases him, the brainy Hooper is all Superego, with rules and procedures that ought to be followed. Each side pulls on Brody, who represents the Ego and must decide which course of action to support.

Following the attack in the supposedly safer pond adjacent to the beach which results in another death, Brody and Hooper decide to approach Quint and accept his offer, taking personal responsibility for ending this threat to the community. This triumverate takes off in Quint's ship, the *Orca*, searching for the shark in order to fire a marker into it. Brody has not properly sized up their opponent, made apparent when he catches sight of the true size of the beast and begins to insist, "We've got to get a bigger boat." They succeed in firing one bouyant yellow barrel into the beast, and Spielberg soon menaces the men with nothing more than this token of the shark's presence, saving clear glimpses of the shark for the most dramatically intense and effective scenes.

Also spellbinding is the Milius-scripted tale of the *Indianapolis*, included to provide motivation for Quint's personal antipathy toward sharks and was carefully edited by Shaw himself, where survivors of a ship sinking where surrounded and consumed by a relentless onslaught of sharks. Shaw had found the original monologue too long and effectively trimmed it down. He also persuaded Spielberg to let him play the scene while actually drunk, but when this did not work out, redid it the next day while sober. Spielberg then brings the scene to a climax with the shark battering at the sides of the ship, displaying an uncanny intelligence and further establishing itself as a very formidable adversary.

Appropriately, each man tries to battle the beast according to their personalities. Hooper relies on constraints, and faces the beast in nothing more than a metallic shark cage, but the beast breaks through the bars. Quint destroys the radio because he wants the satisfaction of finishing this fearsome fish alone, relying on his brute strength and his concentrated hatred, but is simply devoured by the huge, hungry Great White. Brody succeeds where the others failed by remembering the rules (compressed air tanks might explode) while wreaking his revenge (expertly shooting the tank in the shark's mouth).

In Benchley's book, Hooper is an adulterer who dies, but Spielberg has a more likable take on the character who now survives, having sought the safety of the ocean's bottom until the shark was dispatched. He rejoins Brody for the swim home, providing an additional sense of relief at the film's climax.

After initial filming was completed, Spielberg decided he needed an additional scare scene, so using Verna Fields' pool, he reshot the scene where Hooper examines a bite hole in a boat's frame just as a white corpse falls into view, which people assume is an oncoming shark. Few scenes have ever been as effective in making an audience jump in dread anticipation as this one, earning Spielberg accolades as a master manipulator, though Spielberg noted that it tended to diminish the effectiveness of *Jaws*' other jump scene when the shark appears while Brody is dropping chum in the water.

For Dreyfuss, working with Shaw became an ordeal. One day early on, Shaw poured himself a drink at lunch and said, "I would give anything to be able to just stop drinking," and Dreyfuss made the mistake of throwing Shaw's glass out the porthole into the ocean (as Spielberg describes it, "the shot heard round the crew"). From then on, Shaw never let up on Dreyfuss, insulting him, ragging on him, daring him to climb the *Orca*'s mast and jump off into the ocean, and turning a firehose on the hapless actor.

Spielberg too, had his fears, as the shoot approached its 60th day of overtime and word came that the studio was planning on firing him. However, Zanuck and Brown remained supportive, as did Sheinberg, who visited the set to see if the problem could be resolved. On the last day of shooting, Spielberg was convinced that the crew considered him an Ahab or a Bligh and that they wanted to put him in a boat and cast him off, so rather than sticking around for the final shot, he jumped into a boat, headed for Boston airport, and jumped on a plane for Los Angeles. For the next six pictures he made, Spielberg made a tradition out of never staying for the last shot of the movie.

Expertly marketed with a saturation television campaign, *Jaws* set off a movie-going mania unmatched until the advent of *Star Wars, E.T.,* and *Titanic*. Few thrillers or horror films provided as much involvement and excitement as *Jaws*, and soon everybody wanted to see the movie about sharks eating people. It quickly became the highest-grossing movie of all-time and permanently established Spielberg as a major director. It won an Academy Award nomination for Best Picture and won awards for Best Editing (Verna Fields), Best Score (Williams), and Best Sound (Robert L. Hoyt, Roger Heman, Earl Madery, and John Carter). It was also the first of many Best Director snubs. It succeeded in becoming an unmatched, international, cultural phenomenon, spawning endless references and parodies (a vogue for animal attack movies soon followed, including Michael Anderson's risible *Orca* and Joe Dante's semi-science fictional *Piranha*, as well as *Saturday Night Live's* "Land Shark" series of comedy skits).

While working on *Sugarland Express*, Spielberg had talked with producer Michael Phillips about their mutual love of 1950s science fiction films. Spielberg had an idea that concerned UFOs, Watergate, and a government cover-up, and they agreed to do a film initially entitled *Project Blue Book*, then *Watch the Skies*, and finally *Close Encounters of the Third Kind*. Phillips, who produced *Taxi Driver*, recommended screenwriter Paul Schrader, and Paul's brother Leonard suggesting that the encounter between the two cultures would be like Cortés and Montezuma, and would raise spiritual questions. He suggested that Spielberg make it like the life of Saint Paul, only about a UFO debunker who makes contact with a flying saucer and has his life changed.

Schrader wrote a script based on that premise called *Kingdom Come*, about an Air Force officer named Paul Van Owen who creates phony evidence that supplies alternate explanations for UFO sightings, such as sending up weather balloons or having guys dressed up in silver suits wander around the highway, who like St. Paul on his way to Damascus, suddenly has a change of heart after sighting a real saucer and is placed in charge of a secret government program to establish true contact.

The talky script had Van Owen realizing that the aliens did not exist so much in outer space but in one's own elevated consciousness. Apart from the main character's spiritual yearnings and a scene where he tries to recreate in his living room what he has seen in his mind, Schrader's *Close Encounters of the Third Kind* bears little resemblance to Spielberg's. Spielberg hated the script, and insisted that the story should be about people from the suburbs who would want to get on the spaceship at the end and not about conflicted military personnel. Schrader strongly disagreed and was dismissed from the project.

After rejecting Paul Schrader's script, Spielberg decided to write it himself and was convinced that the main character ought to be someone that all people could identify with — in other words, an Everyman who is just keeping his head above water and who has to go to work to buy the kids' clothes when school opens. At first, Spielberg thought of an older businessman about 43 years of age who does not expect a second chance. However, he admired the childlike quality that Richard Dreyfuss could project, and so rethought the character as a younger man who is more willing to take chances.

In the process of working on the script, Spielberg consulted with several other writers, including John Hill, Jerry Belson — who added humor to Neary's character and would later script *Always*— as well as Hal Barwood and Matthew Robbins, who helped him design the sequence where Barry is kidnapped and who appear in the film at the end as returned pilots. Spielberg, however, was given sole credit on both the film and the subsequent novelization of it.

Spielberg also felt that the Lacombe character would be very important, partially to show that UFOs are not an exclusively American phenomenon, but also to give the film more of an international feel, as well as explore the irony that the head of the team attempting to communicate with beings from another world could barely speak English himself. He selected French as the nationality because he felt the French have made some sober breakthroughs in UFO analysis, have been outspoken, and made no-nonsense contributions to the literature of UFOlogy. France is also the home of CNES (Centre National d'Etudes) and GEPAN (Groupe d'Etude des Phenomenes Anormaux Spatiales [Special UFO Task Force]).

Though the existence of UFOs has never been physically proven, they are indisputably psychological facts. While their actual existence is unlikely in the extreme, the belief in beings from another world who will either save us or unite us remains deep seated and almost omnipresent (and indeed, many early tales of fairies stealing humans eerily echo reports of UFO abductions). Famed psychoanalyst Carl Jung made a study of this phenomenon and in trying to explain the root cause of such sightings, reported in *Flying Saucers: A Modern Myth of Things Seen in the Skies*:

> We have a bleak, shallow rationalism that offers stones instead of bread to the emotional and spiritual hungers of the world. The logical result is an insatiable hunger for anything extraordinary. If we add to this the great defeat of human reason, daily demonstrated in the newspapers and rendered even more menacing by the incalculable dangers of the hydrogen bomb, the picture that unfolds before us is one of universal spiritual distress, comparable to the situation at the beginning of our era or to chaos that followed A.D. 1000, or the upheavals at the turn of the fifteenth century. It is therefore not surprising if, as the old chroniclers report, all sorts of signs and wonders appear in the sky, or if miraculous intervention, where human efforts have failed, is expected from heaven. Our saucer sightings can be found in many reports that go back to antiquity, though not, it would seem, with the same overwhelming frequency. But then, the possibility of destruction on a global scale, which has been given into the hands of our so-called politicians, did not exist in those days.
>
> McCarthyism and the influence it has exerted are evidence of the deep and anxious apprehensions of the American public. Therefore, most of the signs in the skies will be seen in North America.

Spielberg tapped into these spiritual longings in *Close Encounters of the Third Kind.* (Dr. J. Allen Hynek defined an encounter of the first kind as a sighting; the second kind is physical evidence; and the third kind is actual contact with an extra-terrestrial species.) It was sold to Columbia Pictures on the vague idea of being a film for anyone who had looked up at the night skies and wondered what was out there. It took four years to bring *Close Encounters of the Third Kind* to completion. Spielberg had conceived the basic story when he was eighteen, and had a handshake agreement to make the film with Michael and Julia Phillips while working on *Jaws*.

According to Spielberg, "The toughest aspect of *Close Encounters*, the thing that went through so many changes, was how much of the special forces operation did we want to show. How much of this scientific subplot did we want to do? We shot a lot more than is in the film, a lot more. For instance, the Sonora sequence was, in the original screen play, a sequence to be done forty minutes into the film in the Amazon. There were going to be a lot of bush natives in canoes taking Lacombe and his scientific explorers down the Amazon. After seeing the rough cut of the film, it seemed like the air traffic control scene was a weak way of opening *Close Encounters*. The discovery of Flight 19 served two purposes: not only was it a look into the future, but it was also a wonderful way of laying pipes. So when Flight 19 crew members come off the mother ship at the end, which was in the script from the very beginning, there would be a link from A to Z.

"We started out with Flight 19 being discovered inside an airplane hangar. Then Flight 19 was discovered on an abandoned freeway. I was looking for an atypical environment to drop the airplanes, an area where only something extraordinary could have landed these things."

In designing the look of the alien spacecraft, Spielberg noted that UFO sighters didn't describe rivets and bulkheads, or the top and bottom moving in different directions. Instead, they describe something dazzling, a bright light on some sort of a solid structure which they can't see because the lights are so bright.

Originally, Spielberg imagined the Roy Neary character as a timekeeper who would observe but not take an active part in what was happening dramatically. In his original story, the focus was on humanizing bureaucrats who are responding to an extraordinary situation. Spielberg intended to focus on a rigid military type and make him relive his childhood through a UFO encounter, the concept being of a debunker who has his whole life debunked and must now re-examine it. However, as the concept was refined, that approach was abandoned in favor of Neary as an obsessive seeker on an almost spiritual quest to learn the answers to the riddles that torment his brain.

India was selected as the site for the first major clue as to the "sky tones," partially because of money Columbia had tied up there, and also because the Hindi philosophy was open-minded and receptive, and Spielberg associated them with being "closer to the earth, sky, and each other."

According to John Williams, Spielberg was very insistent that the alien's musical signal have five notes, not four or six but five. Consequently, Williams came up with 250 variations seeking out a combination that would remind Spielberg of a signal like a doorbell. Williams intentionally ended on the fifth note of the musical scale because it is a dominant note and seemingly lacks a resolution, as if the aliens have started a conversation, but we are being invited to finish it.

While some have speculated what message the aliens and the Americans are giving each other, Spielberg has made it clear that the scientists are not saying, "Hi, how are you?" Instead, this musical morse code is indeed like the first day of school when children learn the ABCs by reciting back what the teacher has said. To Spielberg, this seemed the most logical way for two alien cultures to say hello to each other — through intervals, music, tones, and bursts of sound. The musical sequence is an attempt to bridge the cultural gap.

During the scene where Neary and Jillian are racing cross country and hurtle through a barbed wire barricade, the car ripped through the fence and sent the barbed wire snaking out around the camera crew. One of the grips got caught in about ten feet of wire and was dragged along the ground until someone screamed for the car to stop. Fortunately, he was wearing a heavy leather jacket and the wire had not penetrated his skin, so he emerged relatively unharmed.

On some level, *Close Encounters of the Third Kind* is a film that deals with fanaticism. Of course, UFOlogy, the study of possible alien encounters, is held in fanatical regard by many of its adherents. Most serious UFOlogists try very hard to present documentation of their evidence, though the "believers" don't really require it. Neary doesn't try very hard to document his experience. His main goal is to get to the Devil's Tower, no matter what other people think of his reasons.

Like most fanatics, Neary's suburban existence is basically barren and meaningless, insidiously so because he isn't even aware of this shortcoming at first because he lacked a referent to think of something better, that is, until the night he experiences his close encounter. That sighting is the catalyst that transforms him from a "mundane" into a fanatic, a true believer.

How does this happen? What is the reason for his conversion? The film does not articulate this at all. The closest we can come is to say that it was a mystical experience. Neary is completely unable to communicate the urgency or even the reality of what had happened to him. It was something so inexpressible that he doesn't really try very hard to explain it, except to his wife, whom he hoped would understand, but she doesn't. ("Don't you think I'm taking all this really well?" she asks at one point.)

Ronnie Neary doesn't have what it takes to be a true believer and fearing that her husband has gone crazy, packs up the kids and leaves as Neary attempts to recreate the Devil's Tower in his living room out of garbage, plants, and other on-hand ingredients.

Close Encounters is filled with people who are outsiders, misfits, who from this extraordinary experience are forged into a fanatical army of kindred souls. Neary's inability to articulate his experience is a theme played several times in the film. In his job — what he does for a living and is presumably good at — he is supposed to be a power-line technician, but he can't even read his own maps. As an ironic contrast, Laughlin is a cartographer, an expert in maps, who is forced to function as an interpreter. Another irony is that the head of the U.S. Army's contact team, Lacombe, can only speak French.

Even though there are a lot of people mobilized in this army (government agents surreptitiously shipped out in trucks adorned with Piggly Wiggly, Baskin-Robbins, and Coca-Cola emblems), for a long time Neary because of his relative isolation believes himself to be alone in his mission/quest. Because he is truly fanatical, this doesn't stop him. Nothing stops him — being fired, having the media ignore him, having the U.S. Air Force pressure him, having his family leave him, encountering supposed poison gas and barricades set up by the army. He is carried on the strength of his convictions which drive him on, even though even he is uncertain what his conviction is about.

Close Encounters takes a regular member of society (though a potential misfit) and provides him with a catalyst that tears him away from an unsatisfying life by substituting something worthwhile. To some extent, all of us need such a cause to motivate our lives. This driving force can be a religion, a social theory, a political stance, a familial commitment, or even just a hobby.

How well does the film handle this? Unfortunately, not too believably. Consider this: the aliens know enough about Earth to be able to broadcast 104° 44' 30"/40° 30' 10", the Earthly (Greenwich standard) longitude and latitude of Devil's Tower. (Or three other spots on the globe in the Pacific or Indian Oceans or in Inner Mongolia. Nor do these coordinates, which are close but not exact, give any indication of when the aliens would arrive; after all, it's been 30 years before some World War II planes are finally returned at the opening of the film.) This is a fairly sophisticated bit of knowledge about Earth, yet the aliens evidently don't speak any Earthly languages. How did they learn about longitude and latitude?

Also consider this: the image of the Devil's Tower projected into the mind of Neary and others depicts the natural edifice as it appears from the ground, not from the air, which is where the aliens are shown to flit about. Plus how does Neary (and the crowd we see in India) come to relate colors and hand signals to the five-note theme (D, E, C, lower C, lower G) that the aliens use as the basis for their communication?

If the aliens are interested in communication, they have a very roundabout way of going about it, sending information that does not inform and communications that do not communicate. Still, what Spielberg captures masterfully is the wonder of the moment. With his visual razzle-dazzle, Spielberg convinces us that meeting these spaceships and these aliens would be an awe-inspiring, life-changing event that would mark us forever.

At the climax, the aliens return all the kidnapped humans, including young Barry, who is reunited with his mother. Lacombe fulfills his lifelong dream of personal contact, exchanging hand signals with an alien Spielberg dubbed as Puck (created by Carlo Rambaldi). (The film features two other kinds of aliens: a large puppet alien briefly glimpsed when the saucer door first opens, and smaller aliens, played by children in masks and long finger gloves.) While a team has been selected by the government to go with the aliens and learn about them, the aliens themselves select Neary from the crowd to be their special human representative and allow Roy to fulfill what must be his destiny. The mothership/cosmic chandelier then rises to return to the mystic regions from whence it came, bringing this dazzling spiritual odyssey to a close as Neary experiences the ultimate escape from his humdrum existence.

Though it was no *Star Wars, Close Encounters of the Third Kind* did clean up at the box office, helping save the endangered Columbia Studios, and demonstrated that the appeal of a science fiction film like *Star Wars* was no fluke. The mainstream was ready and willing to embrace films of this kind, especially if they were big and dazzling.

On top of the work with two major blockbusters under his belt, Spielberg wanted to transition from making movies (i.e. entertainments) to making films (i.e. serious artistic vehicles). However, his attempts at creating a small film based on his own life called *Growing Up* were going nowhere because, according to Spielberg himself, he had not grown up enough himself. While shooting skeet at the Oak Tree Gun Club with John Milius, Milius had Robert Zemeckis and Bob Gale come by and "practice" their pitch for a project Milius had called *The Night the Japs Attacked*, much to the consternation of MGM. Desperate for a bit of humor while completing the effects for *Close Encounters* and intrigued by the project's cinematic possibilities, Spielberg agreed to attach himself to the project.

Spielberg refused to work for MGM, notorious for interfering with filmmakers, so Milius as "executive producer" brought the project to Universal, who turned it down as they figured the risky venture would likely run $20 million (the final cost was actually twice that). Milius then took the project to Columbia, who signed on, when Universal had second thoughts and offered to split expenses in exchange for releasing the film domestically (Columbia retained foreign film rights).

Regarding Robert Zemeckis and *1941*, Spielberg said, "Bob has always been amused by American history. He doesn't take it that seriously, though he is reverential about the structure of society and what makes it function. Part of Bob's values are not unlike John Wayne's, yet most of

Bob would have offended John Wayne, starting with *1941*, which did offend him. I'd sent him the script and asked him to play General Stillwell, and when he called back he spent an hour trying to persuade me not to direct it."

Filled with high concept set-pieces that required massive planning, the film did not allow for much spontaneity (often a necessity for comedy) nor did it have many good jokes or character moments to build on. The laughs in *1941* ring hollow, and for all its playfulness, sound and fury, it ultimately does not matter because it is all style and no substance. Despite Spielberg's impressive mounting, the production falls flat. Spielberg, the man who knew how to work comedy very effectively into his dramas, proves unable to work drama effectively into his comedy, leaving us with plot and characters that we can never truly connect with or care about.

Part of the problem may have been that he tried to keep too many balls up in the air at once. Perhaps the comic highlight of the film is its opening parody of *Jaws* in which Susan Backlinie returns as a member of the Polar Bear Club to swim in the cold, December waters only for the "Jaws" theme to return as a periscope plunges up between her legs and lifts her into the air. This is used to introduce us to a Japanese submarine, commanded by Commander Mitamura (Toshiro Mifune), off the coast of California with plans to shell Hollywood. The team Mitamura sends to investigate bring back lumberjack Hollis Wood (Slim Pickens) whom they interrogate for information.

In another subplot, Spielberg also brought back Lorraine Gary as Joan Douglas, a wife with a gun-nut, and Ward Douglas (Ned Beatty), for a husband who gets his sons so gung-ho about ensnaring the Japanese that they wind up trapping their own sister. Another subplot has Lt. Larry Birkhead (Tim Matheson) pretending to be an airplane pilot in order to score with Donna Stratton (Nancy Allen), General Stillwell's (Robert Stack) gorgeous secretary who only gets hot when airborne (leading to some unfortunate double entendre dialogue).

The main plot of the film has short order cook Wally Stephens (Bobby DiCicco) trying to win a dance contest with pretty Betty Douglas (Dianne Kay), who has attracted the attentions of a pushy serviceman Sitarski (Treat Williams), who in turn has attracted the attention of Betty's plump friend Maxine Dexheimer (Wendie Jo Sperber).

Add to this a lost pilot, "Wild Bill" Kelso (John Belushi) who parodies Neary's mixed-up lineman ("I'm lost!"), a crazed colonel, "Mad Man" Maddox (Warren Oates) who parodies *Dr. Strangelove's* Gen. Ripper, Gen. Stillwell spending the crisis watching *Dumbo* and not wishing to be disturbed, Sergeant Tree (Dan Aykroyd) and his tank crew, who demolish Ward Douglas' house in their efforts to safeguard it, and Claude and Herbie (Murray Hamilton and Eddie Deezen) who keep vigil atop a ferris wheel on the old Ocean Park Amusement pier that winds up rolling into the ocean.

Spielberg had the actors deliver their lines quickly in hopes of establishing a kind of slapstick pace for the film, which wound up being more frenetic than funny. It indulges in destruction derbies that are neither funny nor thrilling. Cinematographer William Fraker tried to use oil smoke and filters to give the film a nostalgic look, but which only makes the film look bleary and grainy, one of Spielberg's least attractive productions. The major irony of the film is that Wally, a lover not a fighter who doesn't wish to enlist, winds up donning a uniform and being a more effective leader in chasing away the enemy than any of the real servicemen in the film.

Speilberg's *1941* does contain some impressive bits of business, and perhaps there is a better film waiting to get out of the morass of material; however, when it came time to put out a special laserdisc edition of the film, Spielberg chose to reinstate pieces that were previously acknowledged not to work, such as Milius himself playing a gun-toting Santa Claus who shoots off his weapon and creates chaos, rather than re-editing the comedy into something more workable.

Consequently, the film expanded from 118 minutes to 146 minutes, while restoring trimmed performances by Sydney Lassick, Audrey Landers, and Dick Miller. After some disastrous previews, Spielberg himself began disowning his own movie, a comedy which never connected to the public at large, and one of the few major missteps of Spielberg's career. (Spielberg has avowed that the one kind of movie he does not wish to attempt again is an outright comedy.)

Now Spielberg decided to throw himself into making *Raiders of the Lost Ark*, a Saturday matinee–type thriller, based on George Lucas' idea for a series of archaeology-based adventure films which he initially worked on with writer-director Philip Kaufman (*Fearless Frank; Invasion of the Body Snatchers*). Spielberg suggested that elements of the Masked Marvel, Tailspin Tommy, and Spy Smasher should also be incorporated. The idea was simply to take the kind of plot of the old serials and present it as a high-quality action-thriller rather than a tacky, low-budget affair like the old serials had actually been. Here was a chance to take their favorite kind of movie as kids and do it right.

Spielberg worked closely with Lucas and scriptwriter Lawrence Kasdan in developing the final script as the initial version worked out by Lucas and Kaufman had never jelled properly. The hero, Indiana Jones, was named after Lucas' pet malamute, and was intended to be a straitlaced, square-jawed, old-fashioned hero. (Kasdan held out for giving Jones some darker edges.)

It was decided to shoot the production at EMI-Elstree

Studios, at the French coastal city of La Rochelle (where a submarine bunker was found), in the Tunisian desert, and in Hawaii. For the first time, Spielberg allowed a second unit director, Mickey Moore, to shoot a major action sequence. (Moore filmed the famous pursuit sequence of Indiana chasing after the Nazi truck, though he closely followed Spielberg's storyboard sketches.) After the excesses of *1941*, Spielberg took only $1.5 million to direct and was determined to bring the film in on time and budget, actually finishing twelve days ahead of schedule. (The film took 73 days and cost $22.8 million to make.)

Raiders of the Lost Ark audaciously begins by Indiana Jones (Harrison Ford) robbing a god. On a personal level, the opening presented the kind of climax I'd always hope to see in a film about obtaining jungle treasure where a brave hero must survive a number of ingenious booby traps designed to prevent him from obtaining his plunder. Still, the fact remains that Jones is robbing from another culture that has done him no harm, though almost no one in the audience questions his right to do so.

After the thrilling opening has introduced us to Jones, he is immediately set upon the task of recovering one of the most holy religious artifacts of all — the Ark of the Covenant, which one character describes as, "A radio transmitter for talking to God." Jones is always risking his life for religious artifacts, supposedly for the purpose of studying them and selling them, in essence, profiting from their mystery while demystifying them. Thus, a key Jewish artifact is made a mere prop in a Spielberg movie with no real regard to its place in the history and the faith of the people it came from.

While the truck driver and the shark were the implacable pursuers in *Duel* and *Jaws* respectively, and Roy Neary was equally determined in his own way in *Close Encounters*, now Indiana Jones is the implacable one who refuses to be daunted in his relentless pursuit of his chosen treasure despite the enormous obstacles placed in his path. That he must single-handedly overcome an entire Nazi military unit to do so does not deter him in the slightest, nor is he wary of the presumed metaphysical power of the ark ("I don't believe in magic, hocus-pocus," he declares), though strangely, the idea that he will encounter ex-flame Marion Ravenwood (Nancy Allen), the daughter of his mentor, the late Prof. Abner Ravenwood and shown drinking men under the table, does give him pause (women being apparently more disturbing to Indiana than God or a passel of Nazis).

"I always knew someday you'd come walking back through my door," Marion tells Indy, echoing lines from *Casablanca*. Then, borrowing from *Rio Bravo's* tough-tender Angie Dickinson, she slugs Jones. Ravenwood starts off as a Hawksian movie heroine, a woman who is respected because she is just as tough and competent as the boys, she takes Jones to task for his past treatment and betrayal of her (Jones supports causes more than people), but rather than have her be a proto-feminist, Spielberg then changes tactics, putting her in a dress and using her as a typical maiden in peril for most of the rest of the film.

A titanic popular success, there are nevertheless many troubling things about *Raiders of the Lost Ark* worth mentioning. One is its cavalier attitude towards death. Indiana is a hero who has no qualms about killing his opponents, and in one of the film's more famous sequences pulls out his revolver and shoots a sword-wielding opponent with a look of frank disgust. (Originally, an elaborate sword versus whip fight had been planned, but to save time, Spielberg had Jones killing his opponent even before he has begun an attack.)

Secondly, the film is blatantly manipulative. Spielberg has Nazis kidnapping Marion, placing her in an earthenware jar aboard a truck just before it explodes, then later shows her as a prisoner of Jones' competitor Belloq (Paul Freeman) completely unscathed. (Of course, such fake-out escapes were part and parcel of the old serials, and just as much cheats when employed there.) When the Peter Lorre–like Nazi Toht (Ron Lacey) enters, he brandishes what might be a torture device, only for him to whip it into a coathanger, a gag he had trimmed from *1941*.

Thirdly, Indiana does prove so indestructible that he never seems to be really in danger despite all his hair-breadth escapes. In one of the film's more incredible moments, he uses his whip to attach himself to a departing U-boat and survives a several thousand league pull across the ocean to the Nazi submarine base.

Lastly, according to the rules of drama, a hero should make a difference and have an impact on the outcome of the story, but such is not the case here. At the end, Jones and Marion are helpless, tied to a stake as the Nazis open up the long-sought-after Ark of the Covenant. God, apparently, gets angry and strikes them down, which would have happened if Jones had not been present. Though it is filled with spectacle, the film's ending could not have been more *deus ex machina*.

However, Spielberg keeps things moving at such a clip that audiences do not tend to stop and question what they are seeing. For film fans, Spielberg also included a number of homages and film quotes, some of them witty. He lifted footage of a DC-3 from 1973's *Lost Horizon* and borrowed a street scene from *The Hindenburg*. When a Nazi monkey dies of poisoned dates, a shot of his dead body beneath a rotating ceiling fan is borrowed from Stanley Kramer's *Inherit the Wind* about the Scopes Monkey Trials. The climax owes not a little to Cecil B. DeMille's *The Ten Commandments*, which Spielberg's DreamWorks company would remake as the animated *The Prince of Egypt*. The end, in which the U.S. government decides to hide the ark where it could not be found, is borrowed from the boxes at the end of *Citizen Kane*.

Packed with John Williams' rousing score and a veritable catalog of thrills and narrow escapes, *Raiders of the Lost Ark* proved hugely popular and racked up big box office bucks (over $200 million in the U.S. alone), securing the film fortunes of Spielberg and Lucas, and established a franchise that has thus far spawned two Spielberg-directed sequels. Despite its shortcomings as drama, *Raiders* made AFI's top 100 list and spawned numerous inferior imitators as well as establishing new expectations for modern action cinema in which spectacle mattered more than story, and sound (usually of explosions) mattered more than sense.

Spielberg served as both writer and producer on *Poltergeist*, writing his first draft in five days, averaging 20 pages a day by writing from 8 at night to 4 in the morning. He then read his work outloud to coproducers Kathleen Kennedy and Frank Marshall and director-for-hire Tobe Hooper, who hung around while he was writing the draft. (Spielberg compared the experience to "telling the story around a campfire at night to a bunch of frightened children.") This material was then rewritten by Michael Grais and Mark Victor, who turned their draft in to Spielberg, who revised it yet again.

The film took 57 days to shoot and cost $10.8 million to make. According to Spielberg, "*Poltergeist* is my way for getting back at television for what it did to me as a kid." (Television is depicted as the source through which spirits come through and kidnap young Carol Anne [Heather O'Rourke], who stares at the tube at times as if she were a zombie and makes more of an effort to communicate with it than with her family.)

Poltergeist does more than retread visuals and plot from *Close Encounters*. It places an average, suburban American family neatly between two worlds, that of consensus reality and of Other Reality. Like *Close Encounters*, its "science" is shaped by the gullible, tabloid reading public's belief of what life after death must be like, based on after-death experiences recounting participants going down a long tunnel into the light, where the spirits of their dead loved ones reside.

The family is also caught between the old-fashioned Gothic view of spirits being evil and devilish, and the psychic's New Age vision of the Other World where the spirits are merely lost, pitiful, and needy, and are doing bad things simply because they are lost and have been violated. The family experiences a wholly new (to them) view of cosmology and is forever changed in the process.

Once more, logic goes out the window as families are depicted as living so close together that their television remote controls change channels in other people's houses, but the fantastic events inside the Freelings' house are unnoticed by the rest of the neighborhood. A bit about a housing developer Teague (James Karen) moving the headstones but not the bodies, thereby creating the unquiet spirits that take their vengeance, is something right out of an old 1950s E.C. comic book story.

Poltergeist came close to being tagged with an R rating, but Spielberg's power again asserted itself. (The face-melting in *Raiders of the Lost Ark* had already pushed the envelope for what was allowed in a PG movie.) Spielberg and MGM chairman Frank Rosenfelt flew to New York to argue the MPAA into overturning their rating and giving the film a PG, pointing out that the film was devoid of sex, profanity, or much overt violence. (*Poltergeist* did disturb much of heartland America, though, with its casual depiction of Steve [Craig T. Nelson] and Diane [JoBeth Williams] as pot-smoking parents.) While *Poltergeist* would spin off two vastly inferior sequels, Spielberg was on to bigger and better things.

On the set of *Raiders*, Spielberg felt terribly lonely and isolated from family and friends. He remembered a story he had considered doing, and chatted with Melissa Mathison, the girlfriend and later wife of Harrison Ford, about doing a film called *A Boy's Life*, concerning a young boy who encounters an alien. He had admired Mathison's work on *The Black Stallion* and persuaded her to attempt to draft a script. Mathison had asked some kids what powers they would like to see in an extra-terrestrial, and was surprised when they mentioned healing, an alien that could take "owies" away.

Producer Kathleen Kennedy was an admirer of the work of John Sayles (*Alligator, Brother from Another Planet*) and had persuaded Sayles to script a film called *Night Skies*, about some hostile aliens who invade Earth, which was to feature aliens created by Rick Baker and to be directed by conceptual designer Ron Cobb. However, Spielberg came to feel that aliens who went to the great effort of crossing such vast distances would probably not be hostile and canceled the project in favor of his own more benevolent approach based on Mathison's script, which was redubbed *E.T. and Me*.

When interviewed by Michael Ventura in the *L.A. Weekly*, Spielberg said, "...*E.T.* scared me more than anything else I've ever done. It just terrified me. It was not like I'd been on the horse and had fallen off and was getting back on again, it's that I'd never been on that particular kind of horse. Except for *Close Encounters*—which I think was my most emotional movie, before *E.T.*—I had never taken off my shirt in public.... I've always been afraid to [show off my emotional inadequacies]. It's always inside of me,

E.T., America's favorite outer space vegetable (according to Spielberg, the friendly, finger-glowing alien is more plant than animal).

but it's not shown. And even though *E.T.* isn't exactly me running around the world failing at relationships — it's just the opposite, it's succeeding at a very special relationship — it took a lot of years to get around where, once I had the story, and then told it to Melissa [Mathison], who wrote the screenplay — I told her the story and then told her, 'But you know something, I may not be ready to make this movie now.'

"And she turned around and said, 'You *are* ready to make this movie. But if you don't try, nobody will know, including yourself.' So it took a while to get myself psyched up to make *E.T.*"

Spielberg changed his technique with *E.T.,* giving up his beloved storyboard preparation to make the film more instinctively because he was afraid of killing the naturalness of the kids' performances if he spent too much time premeditating the picture on paper. He came to feel that he worked best when he worked faster. While *Raiders* had taken 73 shooting days, and *1941* took far too much time, *E.T.* was filmed in only 59 shooting days and *Poltergeist* took only 57.

"*E.T.* is ... a film about winning and losing best friends," commented Spielberg. "What inspired me to do *E.T.* more than anything else was that my father was a computer expert, and he kept getting better jobs. And we would go from town to town. And it would just so happen I would find a best friend, and I would finally become an insider in school — in an elementary school, with a group of people, and usually a best friend, and at the moment of my greatest comfort and tranquillity we'd move somewhere else. And it would always be that inevitable good-bye scene, in the train station or at the carport packing up the car to drive somewhere, or at the airport, where all my friends would be there and we'd say goodbye to each other and I would leave. And this happened to me four major times in my life. And the older I got the harder it got. And *E.T.* reflects a lot of that. When Elliott finds E.T. he hangs on to E.T., he announces in no uncertain terms 'I'm keeping him,' and he means it.

"Friendship has become much more important to me than anything else. Having friends, and having good friends, is more important to me than making movies or anything else. Because when everything else is gone.... Because movies are a dream. They're a fantasy. It's a cloud over your head, a lovely blue and pink cloud, the kind of thing you see on ceilings and in children's bedrooms. But that's *all* it is."

Spielberg from the beginning saw the film as a children's movie, and began the difficult task of finding the right cast. He decided he wanted Peter Coyote, who had auditioned to play Indiana Jones, to be Keys, the major adult figure in the film apart from Dee Wallace's mom Mary. He was fortunate, after auditioning hundreds of boys, in finding newcomer Henry Thomas to play Elliott, as Thomas proved very natural and very adept at conveying emotions. He was also charmed by a young six-year-old Drew Barrymore, who at her audition astounded the director with claims of being part of a touring punk rock band. He even cast Harrison Ford in a bit part as Elliott's school principal, but later decided to cut the scene from the film (it is shown during a making-of documentary on the film available on the deluxe version of the laserdisc).

To sell the film to Sid Sheinberg, Spielberg brought in the script and some drawings of the alien by Ed Verreaux. To realize the alien, which he insisted should not look like a person in a suit, he initially approached Baker who, disappointed over the cancellation of *Night Skies* for which Baker had designed several aliens, turned him down. Spielberg then approached Carlo Rambaldi, who created the basic alien with its telescoping neck. Spielberg was also taken with the eyes of Albert Einstein and Carl Sandberg and wanted to give that "old and wise" quality to the alien, so a glass eye specialist was called in.

Because of the inherent awkwardness of mechanical hands, Spielberg hired Caprice Rothe, a mime, to play E.T.'s hands in order to give them the proper, flowing, tentative quality he wanted. The torso was placed over Pat

Bilon, a woman dwarf, or a boy born without legs. For the voice of E.T., Spielberg had initially dubbed in Debra Winger, but the bulk of E.T.'s English sounds came from a Marin County housewife and former elocution teacher Pat Welsh, with sound man Ben Burtt mixing in other noises as needed.

The merchandising of *E.T.* has unfortunately helped to trivialize the movie itself, although it certainly enriched many people's pockets and helped parlay Spielberg into one of the most powerful players in Hollywood. However, the ultimate result is that the name E.T. is more likely to conjure up images of rides at Universal Studios, endless dolls, games, candy bars, etc., than it is the image of a transcendent figure with the spiritual aura as depicted in the film. Spielberg briefly toyed with the concept of a sequel but later rejected the idea, knowing that it would cheapen the original film and the experience it represented.

Nevertheless, the character of the kindly alien struck a chord in cultures the world over. Everyone who comes in contact with the lovable alien is affected by his goodness and shares in his strength, which makes the alien akin to a spiritual teacher. Indeed, the film offers many obvious Christ parallels.

Both E.T. and Christ are extra-terrestrials in the sense of coming from outside the world. Both begin their adventures on Earth in less than auspicious circumstances — E.T. in a shed behind Elliott's home, and Christ in a manager in an animal shelter behind an inn. Neither is much to look at — E.T. looks something like a shell-less turtle while according to Isaiah's prophecy, Christ lacked any comeliness or beauty. Both have miraculous healing powers, and other powers over nature. Both are hunted down by ideological authorities. Both are resurrected from the dead, appearing at first only to their most trusted companions and being whisked from their "tombs." E.T. is even given a shroud and his "last resting place" is thrown open and revealed to be empty. E.T., like Christ, ascends to the heavens while being watched by the people who have become his figurative disciples. He tells Elliott, "I'll be right here," indicating Elliott's heart and echoing Christ's "I am with you always" (Matthew 28:20). There is also Spielberg's use of the image of the Sacred Heart.

If that were not enough, only the children with their child-like faith initially are able to relate to E.T., echoing Christ's admonition, "Unless you turn around and become like children, you will never enter the kingdom of heaven" (Matthew 18:3). Is it surprising then that the sign on Elliott's door reads, "Enter"? Both Christ and E.T. arrive at night, symbolically bringing light to a place of darkness. E.T.'s repeated notion of phoning home has a special meaning for people who consider themselves children of God and can be interpreted as representing the need for prayer. E.T.'s apparent death causes Elliott to gain strength, echoing the ideas of atonement and of God dying for man's sins.

Then there is the figure of Keys (Peter Coyote), to whom the capture of an outer space alien will unlock the secret of the universe. To him, E.T. is the key to the whole meaning of his life, the fulfillment of his fondest hopes and dreams since he was a little boy of 10 ("I've been waiting for this since I was ten years old. I don't want him to die"). He proves not to be the threatening figure which he is initially perceived as being, but Keys' truth is not so easily obtained. The key to truth is more mystical than material, more music and magic than solid matter, and so he is denied the rapport Elliott so easily and simply achieves with E.T. because of their mutual bond of love.

Melissa Mathison was educated in a Catholic school, and her internalizing aspects of Christian myth are not surprising. But Spielberg himself is Jewish and when the subject of Christian parallels was brought up to him, professed that he did not want to hear anything about it, telling the *L.A. Weekly*, "I've been too busy making movies to stop and analyze how or why I make 'em."

There is no question that *E.T.* is a love story, but the love here is one based on friendship, and is spiritual rather than sexual. It is a love that is simple, direct, and unambiguous. On a certain level, though, the film is disingenuous in the way in which it treats the supposedly wise and beneficent alien as a family pet, who takes ill and dies, only to be resurrected by Elliott's love — as if it were promising children that death can be literally defeated by love, that if you love something enough, it will come back to life, which is a horrible lie to tell any child, especially one that has lost something dear to him or her.

E.T. is largely told from Elliott's point of view. Spielberg was rather insistent that except for Elliott's mother, no adults be shown until near the end of the film. This means that the scientists who invade Elliott's home and the technology they represent appear to him to be very frightening. But Spielberg does not present these initially faceless figures of authority as evil. Instead, they desperately try to save the alien, though their invasion of Elliott's home and their scientific equipment seem dehumanizing. (What E.T. needs turns out to be the proximity of his own species, who respond to his call just in time to revive the sickly alien.) Through Keys, the scientists are revealed not as villains, but as fellow dreamers. (The true villain of the tale is the never seen captain of the ship that left without a member of his crew, stranding E.T. in a potentially hostile environment until the ship's return.)

However, as a science fiction film, E.T. does present certain problems, as it is consistently logically flawed. E.T. is depicted as being able to levitate himself and Elliott on Elliott's bicycle at the end, but if he has this power, why

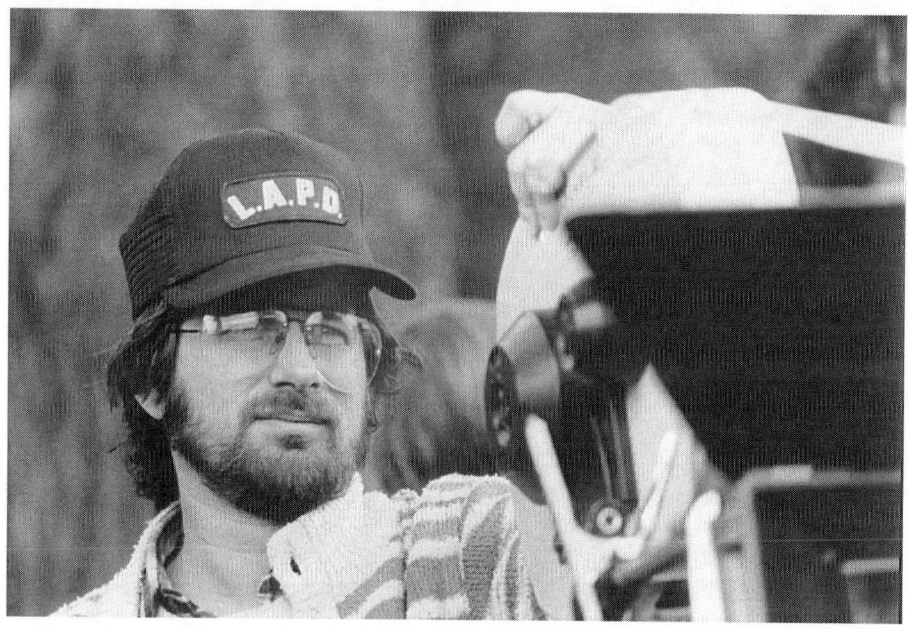

Spielberg directing the "Kick the Can" segment of *Twilight Zone — The Movie.*

doesn't he use it at the beginning of the film to save himself? Elliott's family is shown to be living in a suburban home that Elliott's mom cannot possibly afford without the support of the father, who has abandoned the family.

How is it that Elliott's mom can walk across a kitchen littered with empty beer cans and never notice? Surely, this would get a very strong reaction. E.T. rigs a phone to call home. He calls home — or at least, he calls a ship traveling at multiples of the speed of light. Now, you might think the sun would go out, supplying that kind of power; the lights in the house don't even flicker. E.T. dies. E.T. comes back to life. No explanation is ever given or hinted at.

In retrospect, what Spielberg himself objects to is the use of guns in the film, and he has declared that if the film is rereleased, he will insist that the guns be optically removed. (For example, he takes exception to his choice to have a police officer with a gun threaten kids on bicycles, which prompts E.T. to cause them to fly.)

However, while *E.T.* doesn't excel at logic, it does excel at emotion. The film is not about thoughts, but about feelings, and has reached and touched millions of people, earning Spielberg a prolonged standing ovation at the Cannes Film Festival. It garnered a Best Picture nomination from the Academy Awards, and for a time surpassed *Star Wars* as the largest-grossing picture of all time. (On its initial release, it earned almost $360 million in the U.S. and Canada alone and has been seen by more than 200 million worldwide.)

Like many artists, Spielberg had second thoughts about what he created in *Close Encounters of the Third Kind.* He asked Columbia for the opportunity to re-edit the film, which Columbia only agreed to do if he would film a sequence depicting the interior of the mothership, an additional something to use as a come-on for audiences, which Spielberg was reluctant to do, but which he agreed to prepare in order to create *Close Encounters of the Third Kind: The Special Edition.*

The Special Edition cut everything that was cute and sitcom about *Close Encounters,* emphasizing that the Neary family is entirely incapable of assimilating a spiritual experience; however, some of the film's humanity is lost in those cuts. A scrapped effects sequence involving finding a giant cargo ship, the *Cotopaxi,* in the middle of the Gobi Desert was shot and incorporated into the narrative. What is extraordinary about the new ending, which presents no new information about the alien visitors and offers little in the way of new imagery, is that it makes the final twenty minutes an audio-visual fugue to rapture. Neary is caught up in a religious experience that is beyond his and our ken, and we are caught up in his inexpressible awe.

However, the new ending does not advance the plot or our understanding one iota. While Spielberg expressed the idea that he was comfortable with two versions of *Close Encounters* being available, the *Special Edition* effectively supplanted the original cut, which only continued to be available on the Criterion laserdisc. A television version was prepared and shown which combined material from both cuts of the film, and in 1998, Spielberg released a new director's cut to both videotape and laserdisc which combined material from both cuts but eliminated the inside-the-mothership sequence.

"*The Twilight Zone* has always meant, more than anything else, those little musical notes that you hear from the other room — like a bugle call that draws you to the television set and grips you for half an hour," said Spielberg.

Spielberg met director John Landis in Martha's Vineyard while shooting *Jaws* and later invited him over to his house for dinner one evening. They discovered that they shared many interests, including a love of the old *Twilight Zone* TV series. Ted Ashley, chairman of Warner Bros., had acquired the rights to make a film version from Carol Serling, and Terry Semel mentioned the project to Spielberg, who immediately became interested and brought Landis aboard.

Landis wanted to make an original story about prejudice and bigotry in the *Twilight Zone* style while Spielberg wanted to remake "The Monsters Are Due on Maple Street." They brought in Richard Matheson, one of the original *Twilight Zone* writers, whose episode "Little Girl Lost" was remarkably similar to Spielberg's plot for *Poltergeist.*

Landis' segment was particularly ill-fated when a helicopter crashed, nearly killing the director and mincing actor Vic Morrow and the two Vietnamese children he was carrying. It turned out that not only had there not been adequate safety measures taken, but the two children were present late at night in violation of child labor laws. Landis was put on trial for manslaughter, but was found "not guilty." Spielberg did his best to distance himself from the tragedy, refusing to comment on it publicly.

His segment, shot in six days, ended up being based upon the *Twilight Zone* episode "Kick the Can" written by George Clayton Johnson, which was rewritten by Melissa Mathison under the pseudonym "Josh Rogan" and which echoes the familiar Spielberg themes of nostalgia and longing. It is a overly sentimental tale in which several discouraged rest home residents undergo a phenomenal transformation that enables them to once again rediscover the joys of life with a child's appreciation and wonder.

"There's a real symbiosis that occurs between young children from the ages of 6 to 7 and older people from the ages of 70 to 90," noted Spielberg. "They both go back to a kind of natural daring — and that's what's wonderful about working with them.... They both have trouble memorizing their dialogue, and yet they're both spontaneous beyond reason."

And yet, Spielberg's "Kick the Can" falls flat in comparison to the original version directed by Lamont Johnson. George Clayton Johnson's original story has been altered to its detriment. Originally, Charles Whitley (Ernest Truex), a desperate old man who is about to be forced to go into the isolation ward for observation, realizes that he can become young again by reverting to the games of his childhood. The episode opens with his unexpected disappointment that he cannot accompany his son home for the weekend after having told his friends goodbye, which emphasizes Charles' dashed hopes and isolation before encountering the playing children (often represented by no more than musical voices in the wind). However, he is unable to convince his doubting Thomas friend Ben Conroy (Russell Collins), who is left old and bereft at the end.

In Spielberg's version, the elderly optimist who carries the tin can and the notion is an outsider Bloom (the ever likable Scatman Crothers) who has nothing truly at stake in the outcome and simply promotes the clichéd philosophy of "You are only as young as you feel." Bloom in simple terms represents "hope," as well as a symbol of the power of belief ("If you believe, I can make you all feel like children"), promoting the idea that the only thing old people can hope for is the enjoyment of play.

The abandoned old man in Spielberg's version is his Ben character, now called Leo Conroy (Bill Quinn), who is surprised to be spurned by his children as we are told this happens every two weeks. In this version, not only the skeptical Conroy but all the other inhabitants of the old age home are won over, with the others actually being transformed into children. Only one, Mr. Agee (Murray Matheson), who explicitly evokes Peter Pan and magically flies off (an indication of the fascination which would lead Spielberg to *Hook*) at the end elects to remain a child, however. The rest ultimately reject the possibility of living a new childhood, but develop an increased zest for life from their experience.

Spielberg's heavy-handed treatment made his segment one of the least favorite in the film, which overall did not perform to box office expectations and seemed to emphasize its effects more than its people, something which was not true of the *Twilight Zone* series which had inspired it.

According to Michael Ventura, Spielberg once said that "Indiana Jones isn't like Errol Flynn, he's like Fred C. Dobbs," though that interpretation does not come through in the telling. All the two characters seem to have in common is that they often do not shave, scramble in the wilderness looking for treasure, and wear baggy pants and beaten up Panama hats. Instead, Ventura has compared Jones to Spielberg himself. "Like Spielberg, Indiana is famous in his own world, and his fame has been inflated into legend. Like Spielberg, he gets paid well to take on audacious tasks which he brings off with a technical virtuosity that is astonishing and constant....

"Both the real Steven Spielberg and the fictional Indiana Jones grapple with portentous and ancient mysteries. In fact, mystic mysteries are their stock-in-trade. It is their business to go where these mysteries are and to bring them back into the Western frame of mind — for the mysteries they seek, even when they literally occur in a suburban back yard, are decidedly unWestern in nature. For Jones, the mystery is an artifact; for Spielberg, it is a concept. But both share the same attitude toward these mysteries: they are attracted to the mystery, they grapple with it, fight for and against it, fight the mystery itself, draw others into their obsession — and then both insist that it's all just fun-and-games, the mystery doesn't really exist, it has no meaning except to sell as entertainment."

Indiana Jones and the Temple of Doom offers up a movie vision of the Hindu goddess of Kali, one based on *Gunga Din* and *Stranglers of the Swamp* more than reality. Kali is part of a living religion practiced by more people on Earth than those who believe in Judaism and Christianity's God,

Producer George Lucas and director Steven Spielberg (right) filming *Indiana Jones and the Temple of Doom.*

a goddess who does not, as the filmmakers assert, require human sacrifices and is neither good nor evil (those divisions being meaningless in the Hindu view of things) and who has a relatively positive place in Hindu worship as a whole. That the goddess is so thoughtlessly vilified speaks to the ethnocentrism of the filmmakers, and nothing in the rest of the film mitigates that arrogance, which shows respect only for white middle class reality.

The filmmakers' lack of respect for reality is thoroughly evident. For example, in the opening a map shows the hero's plane flying directly from Shanghai to Chungking as the Great Wall of China is seen below the wing. This is impossible as the Great Wall is never less than five hundred miles from the course shown on the map.

Nor is the thrilling opening remotely credible whereby Jones, Willie (Kate Capshaw) and Short Round (Ke Huy Quan) jump out of a plane with nothing more than a rubber raft and make it to safety. Willie's whining quickly becomes annoying, the violence is extreme enough to spawn the PG-13 rating, and the Indians themselves are treated with a good deal of xenophobia. The plot where children are made slaves in a mine bears little scrutiny, but the non-stop rock 'em, sock 'em action ensured the film's financial success while disappointing many Spielberg devotees.

"When I first heard what it was about, I didn't think I wanted to direct it. But once I began reading it, I couldn't put it down. It was a strong emotional read, and one of the best pieces of reading material I had picked up in years. I was particularly drawn to the heroic growth of Celie, as she goes from being a contemporary slave in the early 20th century, to being a complete — and completed — person."

The Color Purple is the story of a young girl who learns that the greatest love of all is to love and respect yourself. Through this story, and the main character, Celie (Whoopi Goldberg), we see that love, struggle, and endurance are possible even in the bleakest situations. Each individual in the story needs to share their problems with someone who cares, but Celie feels she has no one but God to talk to. Her mother died at a tender age, and Celie is raped by her stepfather, a man she believes to be her natural father, creating in her a lifelong fear of men. She bears the man two children, but he takes them away from her. Furthermore, he arranges her marriage to a man, Mister (Danny Glover), who would prefer to marry her sister, Nettie, the only person Celie truly loves.

"This movie called for more spontaneous combustion in the idea department than storyboarding and all the other technical methods I've been accustomed to using," Spielberg reported. "I had disputes with my subconscious. My conscious might say, 'hey, that's not the way to play this scene,' but my subconscious surprised me every day, telling me to just turn off my brain and go with it. It was interesting, the 'back and forth process' of it.

"I am particularly excited about the dynamic range and variety between Danny Glover and Whoopi Goldberg. Their characters are a contradiction of opposites. There's nothing team-like about Celie and Mister, yet there is something destined to be just right about the two of them being together to tell the story. For a long time, you say, 'these people shouldn't be together,' and you want her to run for her life; but you realize that in certain ways, this is a great learning experience. In certain ways, they were a match made in hell.

"Most of all, I want the audience to feel every color of Celie's rainbow, the rainbow she makes for herself, and, at the end, dives into headfirst."

Celie's life includes taking care of her husband, his rotten children, bearing her husband's physical, verbal, and mental abuse, and waiting for letters from Nettie, who has become a missionary and gone to Africa. Before she left, however, she ended up in an altercation with Mister who cruelly keeps Nettie's letters from Celie, cutting her off from the only person she loves.

"*The Color Purple* is not a general story about Mister and Celie and the struggle they endure because of circumstance, tradition and hand-me-down victimization from father to son," said Spielberg. "It indicts more the father-son relationship. From his father, Mister learns to victimize his own son Harpo. The women are simply in the path of this rapidly moving freight train. But this is about how they learn, how to become a blockade and not another victim. And, at the same time, remain human."

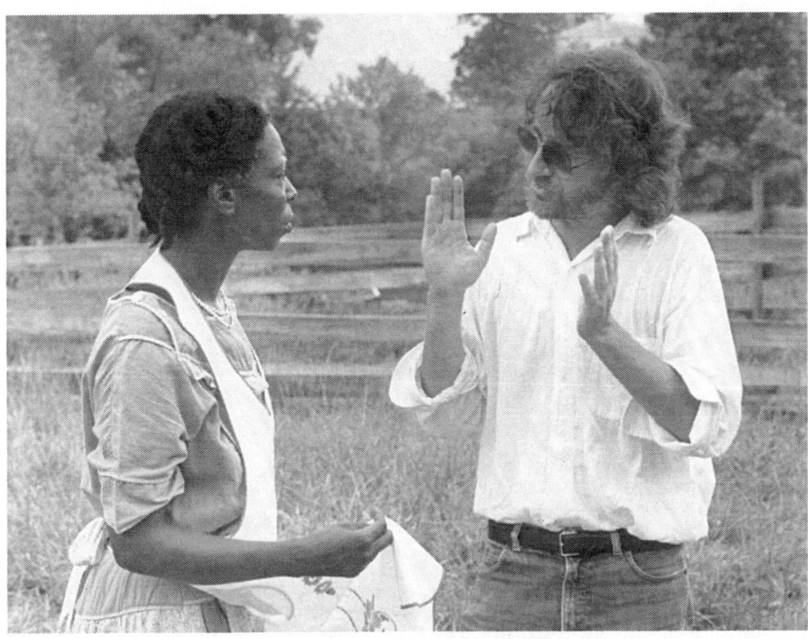

Director Spielberg guiding Whoopi Goldberg as Celie in *The Color Purple*, Goldberg's Academy Award–nominated feature debut performance.

Mister is in love with and fascinated by a singer, Shug Avery, whom he never married because of his father's sharp disapproval. Celie secretly admires Shug's ability to assert herself, and when Mister brings Shug home to help her recuperate, she falls in love with her. (Spielberg tones down the lesbian aspects of their relationship.) With Shug's help, Celie learns to assert herself, and eventually leaves her husband and makes a life for herself. She discovers that she is talented and worthy of friends, family, and love. Finally acquiring Nettie's letters with Shug's help, she learns that Nettie has been living in Africa with Celie's children and the people who adopted them, and that she has persisted writing to Celie because of her love for her, which gives Celie the courage to persevere.

Many have criticized the story for its negative depiction of black males, who are largely shown as weak, abusive, misdirected, and unloving men (with the notable exception of Celie's son). What is overlooked is that the story is also about men who suffer silently and struggle trying to find the definition of manhood. Mister is caught in a cycle of unhappiness until he learns that his life is his own and not his father's. Trying to please his father has kept him from marrying the one woman he truly loves, and anger over this fact explodes and causes him to hurt his wives. Only when Celie demands respect and leaves him, and Shug marries another man, does Mister decide that he must improve his life and grow into a man others can love and respect. He too becomes redeemed.

The Color Purple is also about how children repeat the mistakes of their parents. Harpo marries the girl of his dreams, Sofia, but still does not understand that respect of the individual is sufficient for the growth of love. Instead, he feels he has to physically abuse Sofia, like his father abuses Celie, to gain control and become the head of his house, which causes him to lose her and his children besides.

Sofia discovers that self-confidence, independence, and dignity are not enough for black women in America. Despite her strong personality, she is still subject to the indignities of the unwritten Jim Crow laws when she tries to refuse a request of a white American.

Ultimately, the story of *The Color Purple* is the story of victims who realize that they can decide not to be victims any longer. They experience emotional growth as individuals. It is also the story of a family, who because of circumstances, finally learns to behave as a strong and healthy family unit, bonded by an enduring love.

Spielberg and adapter Menlo Meyer do a marvelous job of realizing Alice Walker's Pulitzer Prize–winning novel. There are, unfortunately, a few missteps in the film however, elements which feel borrowed from Hollywood fare such as *Cabin in the Sky* (e.g., Shug's gospel reconciliation with her disapproving preacher father; Harpo's slapstick clumsiness). Additionally, Spielberg shows no feel for the rural poverty of black farmers in the South, placing them in large, middle class houses.

However, what is good about the film is very good, and it was well deserving of its numerous Academy Award nominations.

In 1985, Spielberg made television history by forcing a network to give him unprecedented creative control as well as a commitment for 44 episodes of a new anthology series called *Amazing Stories* regardless of what the Nielsen ratings were. For months before the debut, NBC proclaimed that the series was going to be revolutionary involving big money and colossal talent, with unprecedented budgets, big name actors and directors, and the golden touch of Spielberg.

Unfortunately, that proved the only amazing thing about the series, although it did attract some top flight talent (including directors Clint Eastwood and Martin Scorsese), the stories were often not really stories but rather simplistic anecdotes with hackneyed fantasy reversals. What was most disappointing was the sense of a golden opportunity blown. The network did not even require a pilot and had given Spielberg *carte blanche* to do whatever he wanted. No one was allowed to interfere with the show's development, and Spielberg was given the exact time slot he wanted, 8 o'clock on Sundays when kids are almost sure to be home and watching.

Spielberg himself directed two episodes and supplied plot notions (one hesitates to call them ideas) for much of the rest of the series (some 16 episodes have story by Spielberg credits on them). The first, the half-hour opening episode, "Ghost Train," simply features an old grandfather who believes that a ghost train is coming to collect his soul. Sure enough, the ghost train breaks into his house and spirits him on his way while the family looks on with awe, but no true thoughts or emotions.

In Spielberg's hour-long segment starring Kevin Costner, a young gunner is caught in a hole in the floor of a B-17, the landing equipment of which is inoperational. The suspense builds as the young man seems doomed, but the would-be cartoonist's life is unexpectedly spared when giant cartoon wheels appear at the last moment to safely land the plane and allow him egress before disappearing. It was amazingly trivial, baldly manipulative, and surely pointless, hardly the most auspicious debut of a promising new series.

The series seemed to indulge the worst rather than the best aspects of Spielberg's artistry. Even his vaunted feel for the bric-a-brac of suburban domesticity, which would seem to be made for the tube, was not much in evidence. Many of the other stories seemed similarly pointless (e.g., one episode told of a young boy at the battle of the Alamo who suddenly finds himself in 1985, bewildered by tour groups going through the edifice, and who ultimately decides to return in time and be slaughtered with the rest, though what motivates him to do so remains a complete mystery). The series highest point was an animated episode "Family Dog," written and designed by Tim Burton and directed by Brad Bird, which did reflect twisted suburban sensibilities and was years later spun off into a truly dreadful six-episode spin-off series sans the participation of Burton or Bird.

Amazing Stories quickly slid in the ratings, and the excuse was given out by the series first season story editor Mick Garris (later director of *Critters II* and *The Stand*) that audiences were simply expecting too much. "Steven is just too successful for the world," he said. "This is a guy who has given audiences their most enjoyable movie moments ever, and they were hoping for that every week. There's no way you can satisfy those expectations....

"We never wanted to be *The Twilight Zone* and we never wanted to be *The Outer Limits*. Our show was always intended to be, well—*amazing*. Storytelling for its own sake is great." If that is the case, then the story was amazingly unsuccessful except as a showcase for special effects that failed to dazzle because their visual flair was supplied with no emotional meanings or underpinnings. For storytelling to have meaning, it must connect somehow to the human condition. *Amazing Stories* had no more challenging theme than that of the heart of a child will win out in the end.

Science fiction writer J. G. Ballard's autobiographical novel *Empire of the Sun* attracted Spielberg as an attempt to deal with the death of innocence. The work is based on Ballard's childhood experiences in Lunghua POW camp near Japanese-occupied Shanghai. No doubt Spielberg identified with the main character, Jim, who is entranced by planes, separated from his parents, and must come to terms with an often hostile world. Scripting chores were handed over to famed playwright Tom Stoppard (*Rosencrantz and Guildenstern Are Dead; Brazil*), who keeps largely faithful to Ballard's book. (Ballard is the author of such science fiction works as *The Drowned World, Terminal Beach, The Atrocity Exhibition*, and others.)

Spielberg begins by showing us the cushy and isolated world within Shanghai that his protagonist Jim (Christian Bale) inhabits, to whom the Japanese invasion is just another exciting event. Things become more serious when hustling through the crowded streets, filled with soldiers, refugees, and panicked westerners, Jim drops his toy airplane and lets go of his mother's hand to retrieve it. She is helplessly pulled away in the thronging crowd and Jim is now forced to fend for himself.

Fortunately, he makes the acquaintance of Basie (John Malkovich), an American sailor who has learned to survive by scavenging. From Basie, Jim learns the basics of survival in this increasingly hostile world. There is also a haunting silent sequence when Jim finally returns to his former home, hoping in vain for his parents' return, which emphasizes the character's desolation and isolation.

From there Jim is taken to the Lunghua internment camp, where the boy becomes a man who is adapted to his foul environment. Jim races about the camp, filching food, running errands, cheating at marbles. He seems surprisingly happy because he has the resilience of the young, and this is the only life he now knows. Looking for heroes, he comes to admire the nearby Japanese pilots and develops a fascination with them.

Spielberg still finds time to indulge his sense of wonder, as Allen Daviau films spectacular landscapes and skyscapes, indulges in beautiful lighting, as he uses a crane to reveal a wondrous world spread out before our hero. One of the film's highlights is a B-51 bomb run on the camp (pulled off using large miniatures and pre-set explosives) that is a bravura piece of filmmaking.

Spielberg shows up a bouncing Jim going crazy with excitement at the spectacle before him. Standing atop a tall building, he sees what every young boy would love to see, a pilot in one of the Mustangs turns and waves at him, acknowledging him in this moment of triumph and tragedy. Filmed in slow motion, it has the feel of a dream, and yet we can believe this is how Jim remembers it, whether it had actually happened that way or not.

Spielberg had long wanted to remake *A Guy Named Joe*, and with *Always*, he created that rarity, a remake that was superior to the original. (The original was made during World War II and suffers from a certain amount of racism, which Spielberg bypasses by updating it to the present and making the flyers fireman rather than fighters.) Jerry Belson provided the screenplay based on Dalton Trumbo's overrated original, long a favorite film of both Spielberg and Dreyfuss, who had discussed the movie back when they were making *Jaws*.

Richard Dreyfuss stars as Pete Sandich, a hotdog forest fire fighter pilot who enjoys showing off. Pete is in love with Dorinda Durston (Holly Hunter), an air traffic controller who works for him. Spielberg communicates her love and concern for him in a classic shot where she waits on top of a makeshift control tower for Pete to return from a mission with his tanks empty of fuel. (It evokes the agony of waiting, much like similar shots in John Ford's films.)

Pete and Dorinda have a lively, wisecracking relationship, and on the night of Dorinda's birthday, they strike some romantic sparks as they dance and walk, but in an eerie shot, Spielberg shows us Pete's aircraft lit up like a distant threat in the background, an indication of where Pete's true love lies and also an omen of what will separate them. Spielberg is indicating that Pete is connected to both the plane and the girl, as Dorinda, concerned for his safety, tries to force him to choose between her and his job. (Spielberg also foreshadows Pete's fate by bathing him in the cold, blue light from the refrigerator after the pair have made love, while Dorinda remains bathed in the warm, golden glow of the fireplace.)

Pete ends up dying while saving the life of his friend Al Yackey (John Goodman, the classic good-humored best friend type) whose plane is on fire, by dumping chemicals on it and then not being able to pull up his own plane in time. After waking up in a scenic natural setting, Pete is sent by an angel, Hap (the ethereal Audrey Hepburn), to pass his essence and inspiration onto a handsome but uncoordinated young flier Ted Baker (Brad Johnson), who long to be as famously brave and competent as Pete was and who is now making time with Dorinda.

In one of the film's most effective sequences, Pete conducts an invisible courtship with Dorinda, haunting her memory by constantly speaking to her and expressing what he had failed to say in life or evoking her memories of him by recalling the times they shared. Slowly, Pete has to learn to let go and leave life to the living, but not before aiding Dorinda in a hair-raising rescue of some firemen trapped in a blazing forest fire.

Always was excoriated by the critics, who instead fawned over *Ghost*, which to me had a more unhealthful message. Part of the point *Always* makes is that while loss is a part of life, it's important to get over it and move on rather than clinging to a lost loved one forever. Pete has to learn to let go, while in *Ghost*, Patrick Swayze's character is dead and yet pledging eternal love to Demi Moore and expecting such love in return, an ultimately unhealthful obsession.

Spielberg completed the Indiana Jones trilogy with *Indiana Jones and the Last Crusade*, with the Holy Grail, the chalice that Christ drank from during the Last Supper, turning up as the sought after religious artifact in this one. It also represents another look at the Spielberg theme of the absent father, as Indiana Jones must confront his father (aptly played by Sean Connery), as well as a variation on the Fisher King myth.

Indiana Jones and the Last Crusade begins with a prologue that is supposed to establish where many elements of Jones' character came from. The late River Phoenix plays the Boy Scout Jones, who undertakes a mission to rescue a holy artifact, the Cross of Coronado, from some unscrupulous excavators because "it belongs in a museum." In the course of his confrontation, he acquires his trademark bullwhip (and gives himself Indy's scarred chin), his trademark fedora, and even the reason for his fear of snakes. (In this respect, the film plays like several recent comic book adaptations which spend much of their running time establishing why the superhero has the costume and attitude that he has.)

More importantly, when young Indy runs home to ask father Henry (Connery) for his help in protecting the artifact, the old man is too engrossed in his work to even look up, indicating perhaps that Jones picks up his obsessiveness from his father, a professor who has been fascinated with the Holy Grail all his life, who is ironically translating a passage, "May he who illuminated this, illuminate me." Despite his learning, Dr. Henry Jones lacks wisdom and fails to pay heed to his son, who is forced to surrender the cross to an Indiana Jones look-alike (Richard Young), who turns it over to a white-suited man. "You lost today, kid," the man says, giving his fedora to Indy, "doesn't mean you have to like it."

When Jones raises his head, it is now Ford aboard a storm-swept freighter in 1938 with the white suited man once more retrieving the Cross from him. (After exploring a Jewish and a Hindu artifact, Lucas apparently thought it was Christianity's turn.) Jones completes the business of bringing the artifact to a museum, however, he is still a divided man. As Professor Jones, teaching that archaeology does not feature exotic locales, lost cities, and maps where X marks the spot (though the film itself contains all these elements as part of its makeup), he is a man much like his suit-wearing father, but as Indiana Jones, he is more like the fedoraed adventurer he espied as a teenager.

As in previous Jones movies, Indiana still does not give much attention to the spiritual sphere at the beginning of the film. He has a surrogate father in Marcus Brody (Denholm Elliott), who explains that they must find the Grail Indiana's father has been searching for as the Nazis appear to be closing in on its location, so they head off for Venice. Before he departs, however, he meets with Walter Donovan (Julian Glover), a wealthy backer of the Jones' university who is both evil and a true believer in the Grail's power. From Donovan, Indiana learns his father is missing. Jones then has the twin goals of finding not only the Grail, but his father (and his father's love) as well.

While Donovan represents a typical, upper crust Hitchcockian villain, Indiana Jones discovers that his father's partner, Elsa Schneider (Alison Doody), is a Hitchcockian blonde femme fatale, with a cool surface and hot passions underneath. Elsa, Indy, and Brody use the diary that Jones Senior mailed to them to locate the burial place of Sir Richard, one of the Grail's defenders, in hopes this will lead them to the Grail. They experience a few thrilling adventures and chases, finally connecting up with fez-wearing Kazim (Kevork Malikyan) who explains that Indiana's father, whom Jones has not spoken to in twenty years, is being held prisoner in an Austrian castle. "The search for the cup of Christ is a search for the divine in all of us," Indy is told, but he is also warned that he must consider his motive as well — is he seeking the cup for Christ's glory or his own?

The chemistry between Joneses Junior and Senior is wonderful, as we see our stalwart hero being reduced into a child before his father. Separated by their lack of communication, together they have the pieces of the puzzle they need and are now able to uncover the grail's location in the lost city of Alexandretia (shot in the real-life lost city of Petra). They discover that they have both been intimate with the duplicitous Elsa, and slowly uncover other bonds between them as they make their escape from their captors.

Spielberg includes a comic scene at a book burning where Indiana Jones runs right into Adolf Hitler, who mistakes the father's diary Jones holds as a book he wants autographed (with the left-handed Hitler signing with the wrong hand). By contrast, the film's cleverest scene has Jones Senior defeating an attack from the air by using his head, or rather his umbrella to scare up a flock of birds that mess up the aircraft's intake and cause it to crash.

The Joneses find the location of the Grail, as does Donovan and their Nazi pursuers. However, the bond that has developed between them allows Indiana to make the right choices and survive. (Senior intones, "The penitent man will pass," which lets Indiana know to bow his head before a scythe-like blade lops it off). A devoted and immortal knight who has been guarding the Grail for hundreds of years takes Indy for a knight and asks seekers to choose the right Grail from among several false ones, which give death instead of life. Donovan relies on Elsa and opts for a shiny religious artifact, forgetting that Christ was himself a poor carpenter. Jones, the smarter shopper, makes the right choice, uses the Grail to heal his injured father, and unlike Elsa, is able to let it go when that is God's will.

The Last Crusade brings back many of the elements that had given *Raiders* its thrills, including snakes, vermin, hordes of Nazis, and divine intervention. It certainly returned the series to firmer footing than had *Temple of Doom*, rejecting the gore and grue that got *Temple* so criticized in favor of old-fashioned serial chases and stunts. In addition to garnering millions of box office dollars, the film won an Academy Award for Best Sound Effects Editing (Ben Burtt and Richard Hymns) as well as being nominated for Best Score (John Williams) and Best Sound (Ben Burtt, Gary Summers, Shawn Murphy and Tony Dawe). Strangely enough, although the film is clearly a fantasy, it won the Hugo award for best science fiction film of the year.

Spielberg's forays into animation have consistently been more successful than his work in television. He executive produced Don Bluth's animated dinosaur tale, *The Land Before Time*, which featured Bluth's favorite plot of an orphaned kid looking for a home, and which has since spawned five direct-to-video sequels thus far. Bluth also directed the initial installment of *An American Tail* for Spielberg, which dealt with the immigrant experience at around the turn of the century, and featured a hero, Fievel Mousecowitz, who is only separated from his loving family. Spielberg turned the reins over to another director for *An American Tale: Fievel Goes West*, which was also issued theatrically. The third film in the series, *An American Tail III: The Treasure of Manhattan Island*, will be released direct-to-video. Spielberg also produced another animated dinosaur film, *We're Back! A Dinosaur's Story* (1993), based on Hudson Talbott's book and directed by Dick and Ralph Zondag, where a scientist uses a time travel device to transport a lively set of dinosaurs into a modern-day city.

On television, Spielberg promoted an adolescent version of the classic Warner Bros. characters as *Tiny Toons*, which achieved a modicum of success and spun off one direct-to-video feature, *Tiny Toons' Summer Vacation*. One of the best episodes of *Amazing Stories* was Brad Bird's half-hour cartoon "Family Dog," which was spun off into its own long-delayed, short-lived series, also called *Family Dog*, but without the participation of Bird (who went on to *The Simpsons*) and without the wit and humor that marked the original as amusing and distinctive.

While the often amusing SF-animated comedy series *Freakazoid!* failed to catch on, featuring a computer nerd transformed into a very off-the-wall superhero, Spielberg's *Animaniacs* program proved a big hit, featuring three wild and zany characters, Wacko, Yakko, and Dot Warner, who were adept at driving authority figures insane with their anything-for-a-laugh childish antics. The supporting features on the show, however, were less successfully conceived except for the delightful and inventive *Pinky and the Brain*, in which a genetically engineered lab mouse and his dimwitted fellow rodent conspire week after week to take over the world with one off-the-wall scheme after another, resulting in the pair being spun off into their own series on the Warner Bros. network, first in prime time and then on Saturday mornings. These cartoons show that Spielberg's inclinations are more to the brash and subversive rather than the treacly and sentimental material associated with Disney.

Many people have mistakenly believed that Spielberg's films are about the difference between innocence and adulthood that follows the loss of innocence, but more often Spielberg's work is about madness, the difference between sanity and oblivion. Richard Dreyfuss must face madness in *Close Encounters* and comes away with child-like wonder. Christian Bale faces madness in *Empire of the Sun* and sacrifices his childhood to learn to survive as an adult, ultimately confronting not the wonder of towering spaceships, but the awe of Hiroshima's bombing.

Madness and the loss of childhood innocence also pop up as themes in *Hook*, which takes as its premise the idea that the boy from Neverland who was once determined never to lose his childhood has grown up and forgotten it. (In a telling bit of irony, he has become a career-obsessed "corporate" pirate.) Peter Banning (Robin Williams), who has no time for his children, has his kids kidnapped and learns that he must find his inner child again if he is to save his offspring. The Peter we see is pretty despicable, his cellular phone constantly beeping during his daughter's school play, his involvement with an environmentally destructive land deal keeping him away from his son's big baseball game — he's obviously out of touch with family values. The audience is aware of whom he is supposed to be, and so is amused by the irony of being shown a Pan who is an uptight jerk who is even afraid of flying.

However, the film's notion that at first Pan can't remember anything about his childhood and then suddenly can remember it all does not really make sense. Spielberg merely seems to be pushing emotional buttons and misjudging them in the process, so that none of Peter's feelings have any resonance. *Hook*'s script by Jim V. Hart and Malia Scotch Marmo, based on a story by Hart and Nick Castle, demonstrates a familiarity with J. M. Barrie's original, but strange to say that in this Pan story, it is the magic (i.e. sense of wonder) that flies out the window when Tinkerbell (Julia Roberts) comes in to spirit Peter off to Neverland.

J. M. Barrie, the creator of *Peter Pan*, pushed the notion that after the madness of childhood there is only aging, pain, and death, which is why Pan resists them so agonizingly. Clocks are the real enemies in the story of Peter Pan because for Barrie, growing up means forgetting childhood and who you were. Maturity is like a ticking crocodile sneaking up to steal a part of you (if not your hand, then your memory), leaving you a maimed adult.

The kids in Spielberg's films, unlike the films themselves, are never cute or slick. Their lives are not idyllic, in fact, they are often marked by feelings of alienation and abandonment (often with an absent father), which helps explain why these characters are so receptive to experiencing something wondrous (be it an extra-terrestrial or a nuclear explosion).

Hook seems retrograde for suggesting that childhood is something to be preserved in all of its confusion, crisis, and cruelty. As Williams' Peter observes, "What is this, a *Lord of the Flies* preschool?" The Lost Boys, now suddenly a racially mixed group of American children, and their fantastic treehouse never cohere into anything but an obvious artificiality with the potential to be turned into a theme park ride.

Captain Hook's rants are often funny because they seem so true and so familiar (e.g., "Your parents don't read you bedtime stories because they love you, they read you bedtime stories because they want to stupefy you to sleep! They read you bedtime stories because they want to have three measly minutes together without you!") Hoffman patterned his performance on William F. Buckley's personality, because "He's scary." (Even Buckley agreed that he was indeed scary.)

Traditionally, the part of Captain Hook had always been played by the same actor who plays the father, Mr. Darling, which might have been Hart's inspiration for having Hook steal Pan's children and insist that he is the kids' "real father." Sadly, Hoffman fails to project any sense of actual menace. Instead of being vigorously, exuberantly evil,

Hoffman seems detached, as if he were a dandy contemplating villainies instead of really relishing them. Bob Hopkins does a better job as his jovial assistant Smee.

Williams has trouble maintaining his performance in *Hook*. He keeps slipping in and out of character constantly, never fully realizing the potential of the part (which in turn is insufficiently well written) and the special zest it was expected that he would bring to it. He is quite credible as a self-absorbed businessman, but the film waits far too long for him to regain his hyperkinetic self, and the film never quite recovers from this loss. Instead, it spends far too much time, after Peter's initial confrontation with Hook, who finds him an unworthy adversary, on his training, preparing, and trying to remember his lost identity among the Lost Boys. The narrative immediately flags with a loss of tension which it never recovers.

The musical numbers are intrusive and ultimately quite unnecessary. (Most people do not even recall that *Hook* is a musical.) Also unnecessary is a subplot about Peter and the boys going to Hook's ship to steal his hook, which brings the characters into confrontation, but then is entirely forgotten about. (Why do they need or want the Captain's hook? What were they going to do with it? These and other questions are never answered.)

Everything about *Hook* promises to take flight and soar, but it never does. While a fantasy not grounded in reality, *Hook* seems firmly based on audience expectations of what a Spielberg film should be rather than what Spielberg's films actually are. It raises some potentially interesting ideas — does Peter's egocentricity lead to his becoming a corporate raider who grasps at gold without regard to the consequences to others; are the Lost Boys lovable, free souls, or aggressively irresponsible monsters — but then abandons them. Glossy and slick, it remains an utterly heartless parable about the need for assuming the responsibilities of fatherhood with no sense of the day-to-day reality of those responsibilities or how Peter's reintegration into Pan is supposed to aid in fulfilling them. (It's supposed to be enough that Peter cares about what happens to his kids and wants them back, but there is nothing that establishes that he won't be as neglectful as before.)

Spielberg made another attempt at creating a successful series with *seaQuest DSV*, which ran for two and a half seasons. Initially set in the world of 2019, the aftermath of a war had created a new world order in which international confederations have replaced nations. The world's most sophisticated submarine, the 1000 foot *seaQuest*, has been placed in the command of its designer, Captain Nathan Hale Bridger (Roy Scheider), who takes the sub through the oceans' waters on a mission of exploration.

Another important member of the crew, designed to attract a young audience, was Lucas Wolenczak (Jonathan Brandis), boy genius, who often used his computer skills to save the day. Lucas also created a device that allowed people to talk to Darwin, the ship's dolphin. Lucas became like a son to the overly paternal Bridger, who became a recluse when his own son died.

Irvin Kershner (*Empire Strikes Back; RoboCop 2*) directed the series pilot "To Be or Not to Be," which then continued on a shaky course of ever diminishing ratings. Series creator Rockne O'Bannon jumped ship early. The first season ended with Bridger destroying the ship to save the world, but a contractual guarantee meant that he would build a new ship and return for a second season. The site of production moved from California to Florida and there were some cast changes as well. The new characters were younger and were given odd or unusual abilities, including genetic engineering and ESP. The stories got even worse as the crew encountered mad scientists, monsters, giant crocodiles, man-eating plants, and even the god Neptune as the show reached the same nadir as Irwin Allen's *Voyage to the Bottom of the Sea*. The second season ended with the ship being stranded on an alien planet.

This did not prevent the production of a third season with the show, as NBC hoped to attract the small, largely male audience of the show to Wednesday nights in an effort to counterprogram the largely female-attracting shows on other networks. The series was moved ten years into the future, retitled *seaQuest 2032*, and now starred Michael Ironside (*Scanners, Starship Troopers*) as Captain Oliver Hudson, a more militaristic leader, who commanded the ship once more on Earth. Bridger would make a couple of guest appearances, but the focus of this final season was on efforts to maintain the peace between the United Earth Ocean Organization and the Macronesian Republic. The series, having lost all credibility and its audience after two bad seasons, now sank without a trace.

There were predictions that Crichton's *Jurassic Park* would cost between $80 and $120 million to make into a movie. According to producer Kathleen Kennedy, Spielberg wanted the budget kept below $60 million, and had the scope of the project whittled down so that it could be made for a relatively reasonable $59 million. He used a small device called a lipstick camera to film dinosaur models, using it to plan which camera angles would be the most cost effective.

Jeff Goldblum, who played mathematician Ian Malcolm in *Jurassic Park* and *The Lost World*, commented, "Things were run beautifully by Steven. He's very interested in acting — the people, the characters. I know he helped me with my acting a lot. He's a great general, but I felt that he liked me and trusted me. He's totally interactive....

"I have before had to play guys who are intelligent. So I've had to figure out as much as I could about chaos theory, which is Malcolm's big thing in the movie. I did actually get in touch with some of the guys who pioneered it and talked with them about it. They are a very particular breed — interesting, unusual, and lively. They sent me tapes and stuff. It was fascinating."

Two Velociraptors come looking for Tim (Joseph Mazzello) in *Jurassic Park*.

Eight Velociraptors were created for *Jurassic Park*. Some were cable-controlled, some were radio-controlled, and two were people in dinosaur costumes. They began as artists' sketches and small clay dinosaur models, one-fifth in scale. From these a full-size frame of fiberglass and clay was built. An intricate "skeleton" of wire circuits is enclosed to allow a full range of motion, with the lifelike movements controlled by computer operators. The dinosaur itself is covered with a durable, delicate latex skin, lovingly painted by a team of artists.

However, it was the computer graphics work, pushed to an unprecedented detail, that made the dinosaurs of *Jurassic Park* truly the best ever seen. The dinosaur effects were overseen by three specialists: stop motion animator Phil Tippett, who provided general advice about how the animals should move; Dennis Muren, who supervised the digital effects work of his ILM staff; and Stan Winston, who created the full-sized animatronic dinosaurs including a massive Tyrannosaurus rex that weighed 9,000 pounds and was 40 feet long. Winston's crew also supplied a Velociraptor, Brachiosaurus, Triceratops, Gallimimus, Dilophosaurus ("Spitter") and a baby Raptor that emerges from an egg.

Meanwhile, Muren's team sculpted the bones and skeletons of dinosaurs in computers and created distinctive walk cycles. Spielberg was initially wary of using computer animation, feeling that in the past it was often stilted and soulless, but he was blown away by Muren's breakthrough tests.

With computer screens as drawing pads, ILM animators created all the dinosaurs that can run, leap, and convey changes in their attitudes, which would then be transferred to film. At one time, there were not as many computer graphic effects planned for the film, but when Spielberg considered dropping a scene of the characters getting caught in a dinosaur herd because it might be too expensive to create, Muren pointed out that the computer could easily replicate the same design model numerous times, altering sizes to suggest older and younger versions, each of which was duplicated 10 times.

Two animation motions were worked out for all 30, and then the sync was shifted on them so that they did not all have their feet hitting the ground at the same time and would move at different rates of speed. The most visible of the dinosaurs were then given a custom stride, and the result became a very lifelike shot.

Each shot would take a single animator three weeks to shoot, while another animator would work on the background, ensuring that the dinosaur would always appear to have its feet on solid ground. People were especially impressed with how realistic the carefully detailed computer drawings looked in closeup.

The principal photography took some four months to complete, with production on the island of Kauai interrupted by Hurricane Iniki, which flattened all locations one day before shooting there was scheduled to wrap. However, it did not take long for production to resume back in Los Angeles as well as Red Rock Canyon State Park, which substituted for Dr. Alan Grant's (Sam Neill) Montana dinosaur dig.

The opening scenes of *Jurassic Park* are highly reminiscent of *Jaws* where an unseen, ferocious beast mangles an unfortunate person who happens to get too close, and Spielberg has lost none of his ability to generate intensity in the intervening years. We glimpse Muldoon (Bob Peck), the big game hunter who keeps the dinosaurs in check, wearing a fedora reminiscent of Indiana Jones'.

We then switch to Dr. Grant at his dig with his fiancée, paleobotantist Ellie Sattler (Laura Dern). Grant fears commitment and seems to have an antipathy towards children

("You actually want some of those?"). He delights in describing in graphic detail to a pushy kid just what a Velociraptor does to its prey with its powerful claws. His character arc involves committing to others and learning to care for children. Meanwhile, like most paleontologists, he is very dependent on outside funding, so when John Hammond (Richard Attenborough) summons him for some mysterious project, he jumps at the chance.

Spielberg knew from the outset that he wanted to alter the Hammond of Crichton's novel, who was something of a nasty, megalomaniac interested exclusively in power and making money. Instead, the film's Hammond is a well-intentioned dreamer who is overzealous in wanting to share his dream with the people of the world and pridefully presumes he has every possible problem figured out. To reassure his backers, he has assembled a team which includes Grant, Ellie, lawyer Donald Gennaro (Martin Ferrero), and chaos theorist Ian Malcolm (Goldblum) to give a report on the island. In a telling bit indicating his lack of foresight, Hammond also brings along his grandchildren, Tim (Joseph Mazzello) and Lex (Ariana Richards).

The paleontologists are blown away at seeing the animals they have been studying brought back to life, but Malcolm quickly sees the potential for disaster in the set-up despite all of Hammond's extensive precautions. Hammond shows the visitors around his theme park, which combines elements of the most modern zoos with theme park rides at Disneyland. To give the background needed to understand how dinosaurs could possibly be cloned from DNA recovered from dead mosquitoes trapped in amber, Spielberg presents an amusing cartoon that covers the basic facts. The set-up, which pays sly tribute to the world's first dinosaur film, animator Windsor McCay's *Gertie the Dinosaur*, allows Hammond to appear in both a real and a reel persona as the actual Hammond interacts with a cinematic version of himself at the beginning of the ride (as if Hammond would go from being the CEO of the mighty Ingen Corporation to being a permanent tour guide).

Crichton's idea of cloning dinosaurs out of blood samples taken by preserved mosquitoes gives the idea a nice cachet of feasibility, though in fact he greatly oversimplifies the complexity of DNA. Ellie also observes extinct species of plants which the dinosaurs feed on, but how they were created remains a mystery as plants don't leave blood samples. Gaps in the DNA sequence are filled in with frog DNA, which explains why these dinosaurs, like frogs but unlike great predators, can only see things that are moving. (Actually, animals which have this limitation overcome it by simply bobbing their heads to create motion.)

One of the things Hammond doesn't count on is industrial espionage. Disgruntled computer systems person Dennis Nedry (Wayne Knight of *Seinfeld*) arranges to steal dinosaur embryos for a rival company, partly out of pique for having to absorb cost-overruns for his work on the park's computer system, which he conveniently shuts down to achieve his theft and make his escape past the park's many security systems, leaving fellow programmer Arnold (Samuel L. Jackson) unable to untangle the mess in time. Near the end of the film, Nedry meets his demise because of his lack of understanding of the project he has been working on. He sees a small dinosaur and foolishly regards it as harmless, just before it spits acid in his face and disembowels the unpleasant fellow.

Malcolm points out the people are constantly doing unpredictable things, and Ellie illustrates his point by suddenly leaving the tour car to examine a sick Triceratops. Malcolm himself emerges as a flawed hero, one who points out that there is a difference between whether one could do something and whether one should do something. His main flaw is that he is too pushy, unable to maintain a mature relationship ("I am always on the lookout for a future ex–Mrs. Malcolm"), and despite the relationship between Grant and Sattler, he keeps trying to hit on her. His heroic side emerges, however, when after the lawyer flees to hide in a nearby toilet (a move which winds up costing the shyster his life), Malcolm risks his life to distract an escaped T. rex away from the grandchildren.

Grant likewise grows in stature as he promises the trapped children that he will not leave them, and continually risks life and limb to protect them, from all different kinds of peril. Grant holds onto the dangling Lex as they leap over a cliff to avoid the T. rex, and climbs up a tree to get Tim out of a car that is slowly but surely slipping down to disaster in one of the film's tensest scenes. He clearly becomes a surrogate father to them and by the end comes to understand that he needs them as much as they need him (Lex, a latent computer whiz, proves to be the one to get the park's security systems back on-line, a twist from the book where Tim was the one). Through his experiences, he comes to reassess what is really important to him, and discovers that people (actual life) must come before his profession (which is dedicated to the rediscovery of extinct life).

One of the more interesting comments on the film comes from Tim Lucas, who in *Video Watchdog* #26, wrote, "*Jurassic Park* is a surprising candid attack on Hollywood's merchandising mentality, a cautionary tale about the consequences of knowing how to sell something before one knows how to handle it with care. (The message is made all the more frightening by the fact that Universal, on the basis of all the logos and tie-ins glimpsed throughout this movie, obviously knew how to sell it before it was made.)"

Certainly, *Jurassic Park* was aggressively merchandized (and given the public's love of dinosaurs, there is nothing surprising about that). For a couple of years, it became the newest highest-grossing film of all time. Spielberg personally amassed a fortune from *Jurassic Park*. He is said to have received no up front cash in exchange for a bigger piece of the film's profits, making a percentage of the film's gross from the first dollar. Given the film's phenomenal success, the total could run into the nine figures or over $100 million, putting him in a profit partnership with Universal and making him the best compensated director of all time. (Michael Crichton and Kathleen Kennedy also participated in the film's substantial profits.)

Spielberg originally purchased the rights to Thomas Keneally's novel *Schindler's List* in 1982. He told *Literary Cavalcade Magazine*,

> This is the most realistic movie I've ever made. I wasn't ready to make it in 1982 because I wasn't mature enough, wasn't emotionally resolved with my life, and I hadn't had children. Yet, without knowing it, I had been preparing for it, I guess, all my life, back to the time I was a little kid in Cincinnati. My grandma would teach English to German, Polish, and Russian Jews, and I remember quite well a man who I thought was a fantastic magician because he rolled up his sleeve and there were all these numbers stamped on his arm. He taught me my numbers. Then one day, he said, "I'll show you some magic," and he pointed out a nine and then he turned his arm and said, "now it's a six." I learned what a nine and a six was on somebody's tattoo — that never left me.

Spielberg made *Schindler's List* for the millions who had never heard the word holocaust, and for the shocking numbers of Americans who had the barest knowledge of its existence, and for those who were in denial that the death of 6 million Jews ever took place. "If people don't know about the Holocaust," commented Spielberg, "how much do they really know about slavery and segregation? Wounded Knee and the Cherokee Nation, the Ku Klux Klan, and interment of the Japanese in World War II, or even the death threats to Hank Aaron when he was being considered for the Hall of Fame?

"When I made *Close Encounters of the Third Kind* in 1977, I was obsessed with the theme that we are not alone in the universe. I am still obsessed with that theme — that we are not alone with our pain. People all over the world who are oppressed share the same history. The common link between slavery and the Holocaust is the pain of racial hatred. That's why I can say to my kids, and to the audience, 'This didn't happen a long time ago. It happened as recently as yesterday in Bosnia, in Rwanda, in our own neighborhoods. You saw it on the news.'

"We cannot forget the lessons of the past. To deny and forget the hate crimes will guarantee their recurrence."

Schindler's List has been universally acclaimed and its seriousness of purpose has demonstrated to the doubting Thomases that Spielberg is indeed worthy of respect as a serious artist. More than its winning Best Picture of the Year and at last a Best Director Award for Spielberg, the film is an unrelenting spectacle of horror, a remembrance of things past that renders the rise of neo–Nazism both here and in Europe all the more terrifying.

Schindler's List is smartly adapted from Thomas Keneally's 1982 novel based on the true story of Oskar Schindler, a German industrialist and Nazi Party member who saved more than 1,100 Jews who were working in his factories. Schindler did not start life to be a do-gooder but simply worked angles to figure out the best way to turn a quick and easy profit. He initially made deals with the Nazis and hired Jewish workers because he could get government contracts, be able to pay his labor force minimal wages, and thereby maximize his profits. That over time he became so moved by the people's plight that he sacrificed his fortune to save eleven hundred of them made for a remarkable story.

Keneally himself had tried to adapt the story for an aborted MGM film version. Another script was attempted by Kurt Luedtke, but he found himself unable to bring the story into proper focus because he could not figure out how to show why Schindler did what he did. Discouraged, Spielberg considered giving the project to Martin Scorsese, who brought in writer Steven Zaillian, who had adapted Oliver Sacks' *Awakenings*, another unwieldy, potentially depressing story that became in Zaillian's hands a life-affirming work. Zaillian decided that the turning point should be when Schindler sees a beautiful little girl, blithely passing by the Nazi's nightmarish raiding of her ghetto, in essence denying the horror that is transpiring right before her eyes, just as Schindler has blinded himself to the horrors that are occurring.

Spielberg shows Schindler (Liam Neeson) as a party-giver, a man who loved women and loved to drink all sorts of spirits. He was a German, a Catholic, a war profiteer who was in the Oskar Schindler business for most of his career. But somewhere along the way, Schindler's latent humanity kicked in. He came to know his workers as people, and he was a man who enjoyed acts of kindness which made him feel good about himself, which was exceptional for people who felt as if the concept of kindness had fled from the world. While we can't really say for certain why Schindler became concerned about the very people he was helping to oppress, it is apparent that something happened that made him risk it all to rescue 1,100 human lives from the incinerators at Bergen-Belsen and Auschwitz-Birkenau.

The narrative tact is similar to film stories about South African apartheid system which centered on white people learning that racism towards blacks is wrong. Nevertheless, the film is among the most convincing denouncements of fascism ever created. Janusz Kaminski's black and white cinematography is stark and helps recall the newsreels of that era as well as the Italian neorealist cinema, but with a graphic intensity as we see murder after murder taking place that the newsreels generally failed to record.

Liam Neeson's brilliant portrayal of Schindler projects the man's coldness, ebullience and savvy. Schindler was fundamentally a businessman who primarily wanted to enjoy the good things in life, and as he repeatedly proclaims, war is good for business. The real Schindler had moved to Poland in 1939, hoping to capitalize on Hitler's conquest of the country by opening an enamelware factory and hiring Jews as cheaply exploited labor.

The film's story begins just after the invasion of Poland as Schindler comes to Cracow to take over a confiscated enamelware factory once owned by Jews. He quickly makes it lucrative by staffing it with unpaid Jewish workers and sucking up to Nazi party officials to secure contracts, though he remains very dependent on one worker, Itzhak Stern (Ben Kingsley in another brilliant performance) to be the factory's accountant. Stern, only a minor figure in Keneally's book but central to the film, begins to work as Schindler's conscience as well. Stern agrees to work for Schindler because factory work saves several Jews from being transported to the concentration camps, while Schindler begins amassing a fortune by manufacturing kitchenware and other supplies for the German army.

It is true that Schindler later uses this wealth to bribe officials and save hundreds of lives, but this was not his original intention. Schindler seems real because he is basically slick and uncaring, even after he becomes aware of the wartime atrocities which are committed around him. His main concern initially is the decimation of his very profitable labor force.

Real life Nazi Amon Goeth (Ralph Fiennes) serves as Schindler's evil doppelgänger, expressing a man who truly does not care and looks to the Jews only in terms of how he can exploit them. He keeps a Jewish mistress, Embeth Davidtz (Helen Hirsch), even though in doing so he endangers himself. As a portrait of evil, Goeth is in many ways banal, but nonetheless riveting for his pure cold-bloodedness. Schindler befriends him, partly to secure the safety of his Jews, and at one point tries to be a good influence on him, persuading him that perhaps the greatest power is the ability to pardon someone. Goeth tries it to see for himself, but his nature soon tires of pardoning those he would rather have shot.

Of course, Schindler is only half of the movie. Much of the rest of the time Spielberg shows us the Jews' collective misery through the suffering of numerous individuals. Tracing the fate of a handful of Jewish families, the film zeroes in on specific moments of terror, then pulls back to show an entire city similarly under siege to convey the scope of this inhuman outrage.

Still, fine as *Schindler's List* is, there are a few questionable choices. One is Spielberg's use of a young girl in a scarlet coat, the only colored image, wandering alone during the Nazi liquidation of the Cracow ghetto. Sentimentally, she seems to float past the horrors and shootings that surround her, which is meant to express how Schindler himself sees her. Later, the coat reappears in a pile of otherwise black and white bodies to emphasize the impression of one individual's death among hundreds like it.

There is also a highly manipulative scene where Schindler's women are sent to the showers, where the audience is prepared for them to be gassed as the stories of the gassings are passed among them, only for the showers to be showers. We are expected to feel relief that these women have been spared when thousands of others in similar circumstances were not.

Perhaps the most problematic part of the film is its ending, in which real-life survivors visit Schindler's gravesite in Jerusalem, shown in color as a mood-breaking contrast to the tones of black and grey we have been made accustomed to in the film. As an epilogue, it truly feels tacked on rather than a sincere tribute to the man who saved so many lives while the madness of the holocaust raged around them.

When *Schindler's List* debuted on television, it was given special treatment. The Ford Motor company sponsored the film to be shown without commercial interruption and it was shown uncut, with none of the nudity or language deleted. Spielberg himself appeared to introduce the film as well as warn parents that it was probably too intense for younger children.

Spielberg has expressed surprise that the film was able to attract large audiences all over the world. Additionally, the television showing attracted a U.S. audience of 65 million people, making it one of the most watched events in television history.

Another unusual success of sorts is the CD-ROM *Steven Spielberg's Director's Chair*, which Spielberg partly directed and appears in. This game is designed to help people learn and understand something of the filmmaking process as film specialists give you hints on how to make a great film. There are four levels to this game, and each level has seemingly infinite combinations of script writing and editing so you can challenge yourself with more difficult choices as your confidence builds.

The trick is to keep your project on time and on budget. (A budget screen pops up from time to time to let you know where you stand.) The P.A. (production assistant) is your guide throughout the game and also lets you know where you are in the schedule. If you need her help, you can page her. You must go step-by-step through the filmmaking process, from preproduction (i.e. writing the script), production, postproduction, sound effects, music, titles, advertising, making a print, and screening.

Writers Ted Elliott and Terry Rossio help you create a comedy or a drama. Director of photography Dean Cundey explains your choices in filming. You are taught the basics of editing, sound effects, and music cues. You can even print out tickets and posters promoting your film and make a finished copy that can be stored on disc. Spielberg himself will introduce your film, and provides assistance along the way as you encounter such realistic problems as needing makeup to finish with their actor before you can start shooting. This Knowledge Adventure Inc. effort is truly impressive.

Meanwhile, the enormous success of *Jurassic Park* (some $912 million worldwide gross) caused Universal to demand that a sequel be made. Crichton crafted a novel, *The Lost World*, which was more a sequel to Spielberg's film than his own book, resurrecting the characters of Ian Malcolm and John Hammond, who had died in his book, but not in the film. Indeed, Malcolm is the main character of the book and the subsequent film.

The basic premise of *The Lost World: Jurassic Park*, is that the island we saw in the first film was simply the showroom, and that another island existed where dinosaurs were grown to maturity, and that this island was overlooked in the wake of the disaster. Malcolm becomes driven to investigate this new island in order to rescue his girlfriend, Sarah. Crichton's original narrative also injected a pair of juveniles, though David Koepp's script alters this to include only Malcolm's stowaway daughter Kelly (Vanessa Lee Chester) as well as numerous other alterations to Crichton's story.

Goldblum returns as mathematician Ian Malcolm while Julianne Moore costars as Sarah Harding, an expert on the behavior of predators. While *Jurassic Park* has a sense of wonder about dinosaurs being genetically engineered to reenter our world, *The Lost World* is flat in comparison because it takes that as a given. Though there is a pro-environmental, anti-exploitation theme running throughout the new film, there is, in fact, virtually no plot, simply an episodic stringing along of suspense/action scenes filled with "the running and the screaming," as Malcolm puts it early on. This film is a perfect example of what Damon Knight called the idiot plot, where supposedly intelligent characters do idiotic things simply to keep things moving along.

The characterization is minimal to non-existent. Very little of Crichton's novel remains (the novel's climax occurs halfway into the film in the suspenseful trailer dangling over a precipice scene, which then proceeds to seemingly pay tribute to the remake of *King Kong* and the original version of *The Lost World*). The dinos are indeed better and more realistic than in the first film, they appear to have more musculature, move better, and are seen for longer, but in every other respect, the film is far inferior.

One of the best things about *Jurassic Park* is its sense of wonder, the idea that dinosaurs being genetically created and brought back to life was an exciting one. I appreciated the effort that went into making this idea at least appear credible and therefore an exciting and wondrous possibility. This time around, the misfit parent is Malcolm, who wisely tells his daughter, "If you want some good parental advice: don't listen to me." However, in *The Lost World* Malcolm is no longer a computer nerd who can explain chaos theory to the layman but has been transformed into an action hero who can outrun T. rexes on foot (even though he later has difficulty doing so in a red sports car). Nobody has learned from past mistakes, but everybody goes out of his or her way to create new ones. Nobody is awed or impressed by much of anything.

Hammond (Attenborough reprises his role) tries to recruit Malcolm under the guise of keeping his company, Ingen, from which he has been ousted, from exploiting the dinosaurs on Isla Sorna. Screenwriter Koepp borrows the opening of Crichton's original novel by showing some rich vacationers on a beach where a little girl gets attacked by some small, chicken-sized lizards to introduce this second island. After his previous experiences, Malcolm has no interest in going until he learns that his latest girlfriend, Sarah, is already on the island, and insists that the new expedition is now a rescue mission.

Accompanying him are Eddie Carr (Richard Schiff) and Nick Van Owen (Vince Vaughn). While Carr proves a true hero in the film, risking and losing his life attempting to save the others, the film in no way condemns the reckless actions of Van Owen throughout. Van Owen is a member of the radical environmental group Earth First!, but the film gives no sense of their guerrilla, political agenda. The guy, while cast in a heroic light, is singularly unheroic, and furthermore is responsible for most of the deaths and mayhem in the film. Van Owen is the one who sabotages the captured dinosaurs' cages so that all the equipment (including communications) is wrecked once reptiles escape to freedom, thereby trapping both expeditions in a dangerous situation and necessitating that the group walk back on foot. Van Owen also is the one who takes a baby T. rex, which is the size of a Raptor and easily as dangerous, back to the heroes' trailer, causing mama and papa to come looking for their infant, leading to the destruction of the protagonists' equipment as well as the death of Carr, whose Mercedes Benz truck incredibly seems able to keep the massive, heavy trailer from slipping over a cliff for a time. Despite his unconscionable actions,

Van Owen is never once criticized by any party in the film.

Apart from Goldblum, the only other actor who registers much is Roland Tembo (Pete Postlethwait), the film's Great "White" Hunter, who appears intense and intelligent thanks to Postlethwait's presence and performance. Tembo is an extremely experienced hunter who has shot every creature on Earth, leaving him bored and eager for a new challenge, which he expects to find in tracking and hunting a T. rex. Ultimately, he learns to opt to pursue life rather than death. For the television version, *The Lost World: Jurassic Park* inserted a new scene that introduced Tembo, showing him defending a native woman from the unwanted attentions of a boorish white hunter, whom Tembo is able to defeat with the clichéd one-hand-behind-his-back.

The television version also restored one other cut scene showing Peter Ludlow (Arliss Howard) assuming control of Ingen and promising profits from dinosaurs, but this information was already available elsewhere in the film. Ludlow, Hammond's nephew, is also depicted as an irresponsible idiot, but he is given a grisly comeuppance by the very creatures he wished to exploit at the end of the film.

However, expert zoologist Sarah Harding seems an equally dim bulb. When she tells her would-be rescuer Malcolm, "I'll be back in five or six days," he returns, "No, you'll be back in five or six pieces." She tells others to keep away, but almost loses her life to some Stegosauri because she cannot resist the urge to touch one of the babies. She's supposedly studied predators for 20 years, but doesn't know enough not to touch the unattended infants of a large animal? Or that when she takes an injured baby T. rex, the parents were likely to follow?

She does not show good sense in other ways as well. For example, why park the trailer at the top of a huge cliff? When two T. rexes split one scrawny human between them, she assumes they are full. She says at the beginning of the film to not wear cologne, deodorant, after-shave — anything that would allow a dinosaur to smell and track them, and yet later she's walking around covered in *baby T. rex blood*, she and expert hunter Tembo don't seem to have any problem with this.

Nor are the Ingen hunting experts any better. For some bizarre reason, they expect that predators would remain on the outer rim of the island instead of going after their prey who reside in the interior. Despite dozens of men from professional safari teams, none of them manages to see someone opening every cage in the place. Plus, any experienced game hunter knows to avoid going through tall grass which could conceal predators, but not only do these hunters run through tall grass, but the hunter who reminds them not to do so also runs into the grass after them where they are attacked by a swarm of Raptors (that many predators in such a small area?), who then mysteriously disappear just as our main characters come through. Meanwhile, Tembo and Ludlow also make it through without any problems.

Another thing that was unrealistic about the *Jurassic Park/Lost World* movies was the way the T. rex (who is not from the Jurassic but the Cretaceous period) ran around at high speeds through the jungle and stomped on cars without a second thought. Given the fact that the T. rex has an enormous head, a very tiny brain with which to control its motor functions, and only two useful limbs, the net result after a few thousand years of natural selection would be an animal that is constantly wary of losing its balance. For example, an elephant (whose brain/body mass ratio is much higher than that of T. rex) is very reluctant to step on an object more than a couple of feet high, and usually moves slowly, especially on uneven terrain. Yet in *Jurassic Park* and *The Lost World*, the T. rex (which could easily break its neck simply by falling over) runs at high speed all over the place, through a jungle, no less, and at one point stomps on a Jeep. And for what? To hunt down and eat a handful of humans who would hardly amount to a snack for the beast.

T. rex was also a scavenger. (In fact, dinosaur expert and the film's technical adviser, Dr. Jack Horner, continues to argue that it was *exclusively* a scavenger.) Now, what one quality does almost all dead meat have? How about: lack of motion. A scavenger either sees stuff that doesn't move, or he starves to death *very* early in life. Inferences about the diet of an extinct animal are always doubtful, so let's assume that T. rex is a scavenger is an assumption of the movie ... in which case a sense of smell will probably play an important role in the triggering of the correct brain circuitry for prey or corpse recognition.

Quite a few animals can only judge distance of objects that are in motion and so predators with eyes like this tend to attack moving prey. Cats have eyes with this limitation, so do birds, I believe, and so it is quite possible that the dinosaurs did. But these animals can see still objects and compensate for their visual limitation by moving their heads up and down to judge distance of a still object/prey before moving. Watch a bird just before it flies to another perch, or a cat pouncing on a toy that is not moving. That little head bob is very important. So you might be somewhat safer standing still if a T. rex were after you. But not safe. Better yet — you stand still and get someone else to run!

The Lost World continually alters reality for convenience. For example, the deadliest neural toxin known to man (remember the engineer's big speech — "you're dead before you know you've been shot"?) suddenly turns into a tranquilizer halfway through the movie. Perhaps most ridiculous of all, on the ship that was carrying the T. rex back to California, the dinosaur was supposed to be locked in the cargo hold. After the ship crashed into the docks at San Diego, Malcolm warns a guard not to operate the controls to open the hold and release the T. rex, but if the T. rex was locked in the cargo hold, how did it kill people all the way across the ship, including an undamaged bridge not large enough to admit its head? And if it did get out of the cargo hold, how did it manage to get locked back in?

Even the last scene in the film is a farce. Two T. rex parents and their baby are taking a walk, and about 40 yards away, two Stegosaur parents and their baby are also taking a walk, and it's as if Renoir painted a pastoral scene in the (Jurassic) park, as if Mr. T. Rex is saying to Mrs. T. Rex, "Oh, let's give them a pass. It's a beautiful Sunday afternoon. We'll hunt them down and rend their flesh and eat them tomorrow." Despite the continued danger to human beings of the dinosaurs' presence, we are supposed to be cheered at their continued, supposedly idyllic existence on the island. No one listens to Malcolm's premonitions of disaster, not even, apparently, his director.

Spielberg and screenwriter David Koepp have fun planting movie references into *The Lost World.* Crichton's title is already an hommage to Arthur Conan Doyle's acclaimed dinosaur best-seller, and Spielberg borrows an idea from Harry Hoyt's original film version, namely transporting a dinosaur to a populous area to wreak havoc in the modern-day, to serve as the film's climax. Additionally, Koepp named the ship that transports a Tyrannosaurus the *Venture* after the ship in the original *King Kong.* The extended seat Jeeps in the film are patterned after those in Howard Hawks' *Hatari!,* while the dinosaur mama-love aspects of the climax are inspired by Lourié's *Gorgo.*

Another joke in the film has several Japanese businessmen running away from the beast in a shot that deliberately echoes those of the Godzilla movies. Revealed Koepp, "That was Steven's idea. We thought it was hysterically funny. When we played the shot back on the monitor, he just dropped his head in his hands, and said, 'I'm 50 years old.... I'm 50 years old!'" Koepp admits they considered pushing the joke even further. "We briefly considered putting subtitles on the screen — the men would be shouting, 'I moved from Tokyo to get away from all this!" (In fact, Spielberg told *Variety*'s Army Archerd, such a scene will be included in the version released in Japan.)

The year 1997 proved a difficult one for Spielberg in a number of ways. He had a slight injury in a car accident that prevented him from attending the release of the first DreamWorks' effort, *The Peacemaker*, which did not live up to its box office expectations. Additionally, he was pursued by a stalker who was apparently intent on gaining access to his home, tying him up, and raping him.

In addition to *The Lost World,* in 1997 Spielberg also directed *Amistad,* the first film for his new studio, DreamWorks SKG, written by David Franzoni and Steve Zaillian, about mutinous slaves whose fate in 1839 America brings President Martin Van Buren (Nigel Hawthorne) into conflict with founding father John Quincy Adams (played by Anthony Hopkins). *Amistad* is based on a little known historical incident in which 53 Africans kidnapped from Africa to be sold into slavery slaughtered the crew of the *Amistad,* a Cuban ship, sparing only the captain and the first mate, who are instructed to take them back to Sierra Leone. Instead, the Cubans take them to New York's Long Island where the Africans are taken prisoner and put on trial.

Since kidnapping slaves had been illegal for years, the prosecutors claimed that the Africans are Cuban. The Africans in turn are led by Joseph Cinqué (played by Benin former model Djimon Hounsou), who becomes their spokesman and wins over a few allies to their cause, including a young attorney (Matthew McConaughey) and a prominent abolitionist (Morgan Freeman), despite his lack of English. Eventually, John Quincy Adams comes out of retirement to argue the Africans' case before the Supreme Court.

The project first attracted producer Debbie Allen, former star of *Fame* and producer-director of *A Different World,* who became interested in the story because of the book *Black Mutiny,* and she paid the book's author, William Owens, $250 for an option on the book with the promise of $500 if a film was made. "He was just so happy that somebody wanted to do something," Allen explains.

She tried to find a black director to tackle it, but those she approached were wary of becoming involved in a potentially risky proposition (successful black films had contemporary themes, while those with historical settings had not done as well). Meanwhile, her kids attended the same school as a couple of Spielberg's adopted kids, Theo and Mikaela, both of whom are black.

Spielberg wanted David Franzoni's original script to be rewritten by Steve Zaillian, whose revised script generated great enthusiasm and attracted the film's top three stars, though the Writers Guild awarded sole credit to the original writer. To diffuse future criticism, the production invited several black artists and intellectuals to visit the set and consult including Spike Lee, Henry Louis Gates, Jr., Maya Angelou, Cornel West, and Quincy Jones.

To find his Cinqué, Spielberg auditioned actors all over the world, and while such talents as Will Smith, Cuba Gooding, Jr., and pop singer Seal expressed interest in the role, he finally settled on newcomer Hounsou, who had projected a cloak of dignity and could be taken for a prince or a common man at first glance. Hounsou was a college drop-out who lived as a homeless man in France for over a year before Thierry Mugler, the famous fashion designer, thought that Hounsou could provide a starkly different look for a new campaign and recruited him to be a model, eventually bringing him to America in 1989, where he began working for photographer Herb Ritts, learning English, and hoping to get work in music videos and TV commercials before six years later Spielberg spotted his audition tape and became intrigued with his talent.

In the *L.A. Times* (November 9, 1997), Spielberg reported, "I shot it completely differently than my other movies. I did not want the camera to fly, as I customarily have it do, through the scenes. I wanted the camera to lock off, then tilt and pan, but not crane, not dolly, not track. I didn't want to bring modern times — which I would equate with long, slick dolly shots — into the 19th century."

Spielberg worked on the film at a rapid pace, sometimes completing more than 20 set-ups before lunch, though a strained back did slow him down somewhat. To increase the realism for the extras playing the black slaves, Spielberg had them wear genuine shackles so they would understand just what their forebears had endured. The extras frequently found themselves cold, wet, and very tired.

Before *Amistad* could be released, writer Barbara Chase-Riboud tried to get a court injunction preventing its releasing, alleging that the film infringed on her best-selling 1989 historical novel *Echo of Lions,* as well as a $10 million suit alleging that *Amistad* plagiarized the "structure and flow" as well as the "fictitious characters, incidents and relationships" from her novel. She further alleged that screenwriter David Franzoni had access to *Echo of Lions* when the book was optioned by Dustin Hoffman's Punch Prods. Additionally, she noted that she had submitted her manuscript to Amblin Entertainment for consideration as a film nine years previously, and it had been rejected and she was told the material was better suited for a miniseries than a feature film.

In a declaration, Spielberg stated that *Echo of Lions* "was rejected without being referred to me so I never saw it." DreamWorks astutely pointed out that the historical record is not copyrightable and that they had fairly purchased the rights to *Black Mutiny* by William Owens, upon which it is based. What was more, *Black Mutiny* had been published some 35 years earlier, making it more likely that Chase-Riboud had borrowed from Owens' book, and the studio cited 88 examples of similarities between the two books. (Chase-Riboud's lawyer countered that all 88 allegedly ripped-off passages appear in the original historical record of 1839–1841 that both books used for their bases.) In the end in February 1998, Chase-Riboud settled her case, belatedly announcing, "My lawyers and I have concluded that neither Steven Spielberg nor DreamWorks did anything improper."

Amistad, while in some respects the story of how white codgers with a gift for oratory aided some black slaves, earnestly endeavors to present the slaves' point of view. The Africans are allowed to speak in their native tribal languages with the words subtitled for audience understanding. With their chants and rituals, they have far more vitality than the white characters that later come to dominate the narrative, and are made to seem more spiritual and highly evolved, though fellow Africans initiated the slave trade and most were probably no more or less honorable than other men.

Spielberg, cinematographer Janusz Kaminski, and editor Michael Kahn work together superbly to create a devastating rebellion aboard the ship off the coast of Cuba led by Mende rice farmer Cinqué that risks revolting and alienating the audience as the Africans' righteous anger is unleashed, and that leads the Africans to believe that they have reasserted control of their own destinies.

However, they are tricked by the Spaniards they have trusted to guide the ship back to Africa, ending up in American coastal waters off the coast of Long Island, where they are captured and taken to a prison in New London, Connecticut, a state that, unlike New York, still considered slavery legal, where they are set for a trial to determine whether they should be considered property or as free men.

A fictional black abolitionist, Theodore Joadson (Morgan Freeman), has been added to the story, but is given precious little to do, except for one brief scene where he visits the deserted ship and sees how and where the slaves had been kept. Joadson and fellow abolitionist Lewis Tappan (Stellan Skarsgardd) want to turn the trial of the imprisoned Africans into a media event that will publicize the horrors of slavery. Meanwhile, President Martin Van Buren wants to be re-elected and fears the loss of support from the Southern states if he does not overturn the lower courts and appoint a new, more sympathetic judge. The trial embodies the nation's divided attitudes towards slavery and becomes a focal point for the debate.

The most powerful moments in the film are also the most purely cinematic ones, such as the slave rebellion and the depiction of the horrendous Middle Passage, with Africans being netted in Sierra Leone, piled onto ships, chained and sometimes thrown overboard as provisions grew low, then sold to the highest bidders in Cuba. These powerful sequences give the movie a lift above the sometimes buffoonish courtroom scenes.

"You've discovered *what* they are," Adams admonishes Roger Baldwin (Matthew McConaughey), the hustling attorney who takes the case, "now discover *who* they are, What's their story?" This telling exchange allows Baldwin to grasp a legal approach, but the key to the film is really the relationship between Cinqué and Adams, two men who cannot speak each other's language but must communicate. He learns from Cinqué, whose culture is based on the wisdom of ancestors. "Perhaps our individuality, which we so revere, is not solely our own," notes Adams. "Who we are is who we were."

Unfortunately, the depiction of Baldwin as an opportunist does the real Baldwin a grave disservice. Baldwin was a staunch, anti-slavery advocate who as early as 1831 had confronted an angry mob over his attempt to build a black training school near Yale University.

David Franzoni, in a letter to the *Los Angeles Times*, while mentioning "Steve Spielberg's clear passion guiding us all," credited producer Debbie Allen with inspiring him to write the mutiny scene so as to embody timeless black American rage, as well as with cocreating the Middle Passage scene recounting the suffering of countless African souls, and for helping shape John Quincy Adams' final speech (which in real life lasted some four-and-a-half hours of dense legalisms) before the U.S. Supreme Court.

Franzoni noted about Adams:

> At age 7, he, with his father John Adams, watched the birth of America. Educated in Paris, London, and at Harvard, he was fluent in six languages including Latin and Greek. As president, he promoted recognition of the new South American republics, scientific exploration (later created the Smithsonian Institution and sponsored unpopular ideals that got him reviled), limiting American expansion, honoring Native American rights and abolishing slavery. The gag rule in the House of Representatives was designed almost specifically to silence Adams' long anti-slavery speeches.
>
> His yearning to continue his father's invention of America and to make the philosophy of the Rights of Man (Rousseau's "man was born free, but he is everywhere in chains") alive on Earth, led to his political destruction. Like George Washington, he was terrified to see the rapid unraveling of the American Revolution. By winning the Amistad case before the Supreme Court, Adams helped set America on a course to emancipation from which black Americans would birth the civil rights movement and start on the long road to "man is born free and everywhere he is breaking his chains." I wanted to give Adams his due.
>
> I needed a speech for our Supreme Court scene that would embody every bit of my passion for Adams and I determined to hit the major points of his actual speech, yet make it accessible, something Gore Vidal suggested we might be unlikely to do. I needed to discuss the case on at least two legal levels, touch on the philosophies of Hobbes and Locke (Adams vs. the Keen Mind of the South) and get in his swipes at Van Buren. Debbie explains how the Mende summon their ancestors in times of danger, and I knew I had my key.
>
> Before the highest court in the land, I have Adams follow Cinque's example and call down the ancestors of the American Revolution.

But while Adams was a trusted adviser to the defense from the start, the film prefers to depict him as an old man past his prime puttering with his African violets rather than a man of unwavering principle, so that his entry into the case becomes much more dramatic. This makes it seem as if he is simply waiting for the cast to hit the big time before making a splashy entrance. Naturally, Adams' invocation of the founding father praises their ideals, compares their fight for freedom with the slaves' own, and glosses over the fact that many of the founding fathers owned slaves as well and that problems in racial relations have dogged this country since before its inception. Adams' speech, instead of being a highlight, becomes something of an anti-climax, mostly because it takes the form of an obvious civics lesson. (Spielberg also errs in placing nine judges on the Supreme Court bench at the time when the Supreme Court only numbered seven judges.)

Still, this does not undo the majesty of much that comes before. *Amistad* does not pretend to end with the freeing of all slaves, the Amistad slaves are freed on the technicality that being born free men in a foreign country, they could not be considered slaves in the United States, which only accepted people born into slavery as slaves, and this moving movie even ends rather bittersweetly as Cinqué returns to his home only to find that his wife and children were apparently captured by slavers. (However, the movie totally neglects Samuel Eliot Morison's contention in *The Oxford History of the American People* that the "ironic epilogue is that Cinqué, once home, set himself up as a slave trader." This would not have been unusual as, for example, the freed American slaves who founded the African country of Liberia enslaved the native population in order to raise funds.)

Despite its minor flaws, *Amistad* is the finest and most powerful film to have been released in 1997 and seems to have been unfairly overlooked by many critical groups, perhaps as part of the ongoing Spielberg backlash for his success. It is also true that the mass audience may have responded to what it considered another attempt to make whites feel guilty over historical matters which they have no control. Consequently, the film proved a disappointment at the box office.

Nevertheless, *Amistad* won the Anti-Defamation League award and was nominated for several Golden Globe Awards. The Academy Awards bypassed the film for Best Picture and Best Director, giving it nominations only for Best Supporting Actor for Anthony Hopkins and Best Costuming, neither of which won. Nevertheless, *Amistad* is alive with the possibilities of cinema, and is another glorious effort from one of our finest filmmakers.

Following *Amistad*, Spielberg seems to be concentrating more on historical productions. His next film, *Saving Private Ryan*, is based on a true story and stars Tom Hanks as a platoon leader sent behind German lines with seven other men to rescue a stranded soldier, Private James Ryan (Matt Damon) during the Allied invasion of Normandy. The men are confronted by the question of whether it is worthwhile to risk the lives of eight men to save one. However, according to *Private Ryan* producer Ian Bryce, the mission was ordered because Ryan was the only one of four brothers fighting in the war who was still alive. There had been national grief over one family's loss of five sons serving on an ill-fated cruiser earlier in the war, an event that spurred Congress to forbid siblings from serving in the same unit as well as spurring the Army to insist for morale that Ryan must be brought home safely.

Written by Robert Rodat (*Comrades of Summer*), *Saving Private Ryan* was put into development at Paramount, who decided that it would prefer to produce a pair of other World War II projects, so the script found its way into the hands of Tom Hanks, who brought it to Spielberg's attention. "Steven loved the script and wanted to do it," reported Bryce in the *L.A. Times*, "and that put it on a fast track at Paramount." The film became a Paramount-DreamWorks coproduction, with DreamWorks distributing the film in the U.S.

The story was partially inspired by the real-life case of the five Sullivan brothers, who all served on the same ship and died at the Battle of Guadalcanal in 1942 when their ship sank. Consequently, the armed forces created a policy strongly discouraging siblings from serving side-by-side. In the film, Chief of Staff Gen. George C. Marshall (Harve Presnell) orders, "We are going to send someone to find him. And we are going to get him the hell out of there."

In a nutshell, the crux of the film is the platoon must consider whether risking their lives and the lives of their comrades to save a last surviving family member is something that truly matters, and in the process of performing this task, the men have formed a family of sorts themselves. Still, while the platoon in the film grumbles about risking their necks for Private Ryan, if they were not searching for him, they would be risking their lives fighting the enemy now that the Allies had invaded Europe. They must also wrestle with the moral implications of shooting prisoners of war. Ultimately, *Saving Private Ryan* rejects the cynicism of past decades and assumes an almost 1940ish kind of outlook where ideals are things worthy of protecting at great personal risk.

The film received much praise for its harrowing depiction of the early assaults on Omaha Beach on D-Day, where a majority of the soldiers who landed were shot within seconds of their arrival. *Saving Private Ryan* is more thoroughly researched and accurate than any other war movie, though many in the audience were not used to seeing World War II depicted less than gloriously.

The Allies landed on five beaches on the Normandy coast, but Omaha tends to be singled out because it suffered the greatest casualties (more than 2,000 at Omaha alone). The Allies selected Normandy because they knew the Germans would expect them at Calais, where the English Channel is narrowest. The terrain, which included flat, broad and open beaches which would allow for landing heavy equipment, was considered ideal.

Saving Private Ryan does suffer from a few errors. The way Hanks' crew marches through the French countryside, clustered and talking loudly, goes completely against training which stipulates walking silently in single file with enough space between you and the man next to you so that if a grenade goes off, only one man goes down. The outburst by the rebellious and mouthy private (Edward Burns) would have been dealt with far more harshly. It is also unlikely that Hanks' captain of Ranger C Company would have been selected for the mission when Ryan's 101st Airborne landed behind Utah Beach, making it far more likely that an officer from Utah would have been assigned the mission, plus this type of mission is not even in his area of operation (though almost anything is possible in wartime). Also, officers sensibly avoided putting their insignia on their helmets the way Hanks does in the film because this made them targets for Axis snipers.

Saving Private Ryan quickly topped a $100 million gross and won almost universal acclaim. It reinforces the serious direction that Spielberg has now taken his career and once again makes plain his talents as a master filmmaker (as well as a master manipulator). It was awarded the Best Film award by the Los Angeles Critics Association.

Spielberg and Tom Hanks made contributions to support a D-Day museum scheduled to open in New Orleans on June 6, 2000, the 56th anniversary of the invasion. Exact figures were not given, but the museum's founder, historian Stephen Ambrose, said that Hanks and Spielberg donated hundreds of thousands of dollars each. (Ambrose also worked as a consultant on *Saving Private Ryan* and wrote a best-seller, *D-Day*.)

Spielberg participated in "The Director's Vision: Hollywood's Best Discuss Their Craft" along with fellow Oscar nominees James Cameron, Gus Van Sant, Curtis Hanson, and James L. Brooks for the Directors Guild in America's television special for the Sundance Channel. He executive produced with Tom Hanks *Band of Brothers*, a 13-hour HBO miniseries about World War II. The long term project, based on Stephen Ambrose's book about a U.S. Army unit that captured Hitler's Eagle's Nest as part of the D-Day mission, began production in early 1999.

Saving Private Ryan won Golden Globes for Best Picture and for Spielberg as Best Director. It was nominated for seven Academy Awards, losing Best Picture and Best Actor (for Hanks' performance), while winning for Best Direction, Best Cinematography (Janusz Kaminski), Best Editing (Michael Kahn), Best Sound (Gary Rydstrom, Gary Summers, Andy Nelson, and Ronald Judkins), and Best Sound Effects Editing (Gary Rydstrom and Richard Hyams).

In his Academy Award acceptance speech, where he expressed reconciliation with his once estranged father, Spielberg said, "Am I allowed to say I really wanted this? This is fantastic! Let me turn my eyes to Mr. Hanks, who from the very, very beginning said to me this is going to be extraordinary. We weren't talking about the film, we were talking about the experience of making *Saving Private Ryan*. He was right. It was one of the most extraordinary events of all of our lives, and the lives of all of our families. We're all in it together."

After thanking his wife, Kate Capshaw, and his children, Spielberg continued, "This has just been an amazing experience and I what I would like to do is just thank very, very sincerely the families who lost sons in World War II.... I want to thank all the families who incurred these tremendous losses. We tried to show a story of one such family, and it turned out that there were many such families, unfortunately.

"And Dad, you're the greatest. Thank you for showing me that there is honor in looking back and respecting the past. I love you very much. This [indicating Oscar] is for you. Thank you."

An indication of Spielberg's future direction comes with his purchase of the rights to aviator Charles Lindbergh's life story for a future film project. Spielberg is also making *Memoirs of a Geisha*, based on Arthur Golden's novel, which producer Doug Wick bought the rights to, recalling the story of an exquisite Japanese girl who managed to become an influential World War II geisha superstar after years of sexual slavery and recalls in some ways the Jennifer Jones film *Love is a Many Splendored Thing*. He has plans to one day make a small film written by his sister Anne, which he describes as a "light confection."

At the same time, Spielberg's backing such Mimi Leder films as *The Peacemaker* and *Deep Impact* (comet collides with Earth) shows that he has not given up his science fictional roots entirely, he remains a shrewd judge of what pleases audiences, but having found acclaim and respectability, seems more dedicated to the kinds of films that his detractors have chided him for not previously making, and which few filmmakers of any stripe are creating at the tail end of the nineties.

Nevertheless, Spielberg's next project is *Minority Report*, a science fiction thriller starring Tom Cruise based on Philip K. Dick's story "The Minority Report," which concerns a future police state where precogs detect "Precrime," that is they announce an awareness that someone is planning to kill someone else. These crimes are then prevented by arresting the person before he or she commits the crime. Complications arise when the head of the police state finds his own name in a report of people about to commit murder. The film will be a summer release for the year 2000 and is part of a four-picture deal with Fox.

Spielberg has recently declared that "One thing that I've achieved as a filmmaker is that I don't test my movies — and it's not because I'm so certain they're going to succeed.... I don't have to go through the anxiety of knowing that the test is on Friday — 'Oh my God, I have to go to San Jose, I've got to sit with an audience.' You don't know what that does to my giblets."

He also announced plans for privatizing Amblin and turning it into an independent entity, because "I woke up one day and realized that I really didn't work for myself and never had. I had achieved success beyond my wildest dreams, but I'd achieved that working for everybody in Hollywood." Spielberg wants DreamWorks to distribute both major and smaller, more independent films, and his plans only let him make nine live-action movies a year, though he admits, "Frankly, I have not been able to find more than six that I would really stand behind and claim pride of ownership."

Spielberg now has seven kids and has long felt the importance of family. He does not wish to compete with the output of a major studio, but rather concentrate on what he feels to be the cream of the crop. However, he is aware that all directors crave success and warns against filmmakers giving into fears of alienating their audience in a desperate search for popularity. "I've had directors asking me to change elements of their film that first attracted me to the picture, but now they've gotten cold feet based on having seen that stuff cut together. And I've found myself in situations encouraging directors, telling them it was a good idea — try not to worry so much."

When asked by Kenneth Turan of the *L.A. Times* what has remained the same for him about the film business, Spielberg responded, "What's remained the same is the passion for it, and the fact that you have to really fight your natural instincts, which is to be a father and a husband, because the movie business is such a powerful magnet.

"For me, nothing's changed from the first day when I was 12 years old and showed an 8-millimeter movie I made to the Boy Scouts. The reaction the Boy Scout troop had and the feeling that gave me inside is no different than the feeling I have today when an audience has the same reaction to something made by hundreds of people and for a lot of money.

"People don't believe me when I say this, but it's absolutely true. Whenever I have a movie coming out, I am the same nervous blob of misshapen Jell-O I was when I first began showing those little 8-millimeter films to teeny audiences. That hasn't changed, and it's a very good thing, because I think all of us do our best work when we're the most frightened."

No other modern-day director has been as masterful at inspiring awe, fright, pain, loss, and excitement as Steven Spielberg. He has an instinctive grasp of films as an emotional medium, and while some of his pictures are truly muddleheaded, no other filmmaker today can match him for pure cinematic power.

ROBERT STEVENSON (1905–1986)

Happily Ever After (codirected with Paul Martin) (1932); *Fall for You* (codirected with Jack Hulbert) (1933); *Jack of All Trades* (aka *The Two of Us*) (codirected with Jack Hulbert) (1934); *Tudor Rose* (aka *Nine Days a Queen*); *The Man Who Changed His Mind* (U.S. titles: *The Man Who Lived Again; Dr. Maniac*) (1936); *King Solomon's Mines*; *Non-Stop New York* (1937); *Owd Bob* (aka *To the Victor*) (1938); *The Ware Case; A Young Man's Fancy; Return to Yesterday* (1939); *Tom Brown's Schooldays* (aka *Adventures at Rugby*) (1940); *Back Street* (1941); *Joan of Paris* (1942); *Forever and a Day* (codirector with René Clair, Edmund Goulding, Cedric Hardwicke, Frank Lloyd, Victor Saville, Herbert Wilcox, and Kent Smith) (1943); *Jane Eyre* (1944); *Dishonored Lady* (1947); *To the Ends of the Earth* (1948); *The Woman on Pier 13* (aka *I Married a Communist*) (1949); *Walk Softly Stranger* (1950); *My Forbidden Past* (1951); *The Las Vegas Story* (1952); *Johnny Tremain; Old Yeller* (1957); *Darby O'Gill and the Little People* (1959); *Kidnapped* (1960); *The Absent Minded Professor* (1961); *In Search of the Castaways* (1962); *Son of Flubber* (1963); *The Misadventures of Merlin Jones; Mary Poppins* (1964); *The Monkey's Uncle; That Darn Cat!* (1965); *The Gnome-Mobile* (1967); *Blackbeard's Ghost* (1968); *The Love Bug* (1969); *Bedknobs and Broomsticks* (1971); *Herbie Rides Again; The Island at the Top of the World* (1974); *One of Our Dinosaurs Is Missing* (1975); *The Shaggy D.A.* (1976)

Robert Stevenson may well be the most popular "unknown" director to ever have worked in Hollywood. Mostly, that's because he devoted the latter part of his days churning out entertaining trifles for Walt Disney Pictures, where he directed such hits as *Mary Poppins, The Absent-Minded Professor, Old Yeller, The Love Bug* and others. His science fiction efforts have been consistently entertaining if usually only mildly ambitious. Incredibly, in 1997, three of his most popular efforts (*That Darn Cat!, Flubber*, and *The Love Bug*) all received large budgeted remakes.

Stevenson was born in 1905 in Buxton, Derbyshire, England, the son of a businessman. He became a science student at Cambridge, and was led to film through his graduate work in psychology. He began directing movies in 1932, and proved himself adept at a number of different genres.

He worked as a scriptwriter on the famous SF film *F.P. 1,* and would helm two important and enjoyable SF films in the 1930s: The *Man Who Changed His Mind* (U.S. Title: *The Man Who Lived Again*) and *Non-Stop New York.*

Non-Stop New York is more a Hitchcock pastiche than a science fiction film, but nevertheless, a major part of its charm is speculation about what transatlantic flight might be like, picturing a six-engine plane the size of a small ocean liner with all an ocean liner's usual amenities.

The film is set on New Year's Eve in New York City, where English chorus girl Jennie Carr (Anna Lee) has been left too poor to buy both a coffee and a ham sandwich. Bill Cooper, a kindly stranger, offers to buy her dinner, but the restaurant has run out of food, so Cooper invites her back to his apartment for dinner and she accepts.

Back at the apartment, Carr goes into a back room and runs into Henry Abel, an amiable, hungry bum who has broken in for a bite to eat. Knowing what it means to be broke and hungry, she agrees to cover for him. Meanwhile, Cooper's client, a gangster named Brant (Francis Sullivan), who has a distinctive way of lighting his matches with one hand, becomes displeased at the idea that Cooper intends to quit, so after chasing Carr from the apartment, he shoots his lawyer.

Concerned about the only witness that could possibly connect him to Cooper's apartment on the night of the murder, Brant tries to track down Carr, but Jennie has taken the ship back to England, where one of Brant's men frames her for theft so that she is arrested on arrival.

Meanwhile, Abel is found, tried, and convicted, sending out urgent pleas for the woman who could alibi him to come forward before he goes to the chair, but Jennie does not hear of his plight until she is finally released from prison and picked up by her mother. She immediately heads to Scotland Yard where many other women have already come forward, apparently hoping for publicity and a free trip to New York. She talks to Inspector Jim Grant (John Loder) who fails to believe her story.

Determined to save Abel's life before it's too late, the only way for her to reach America before the execution is to take the non-stop New York 18 hour transatlantic flight on Atlantic Airways, but lacking the funds to do so, she sneaks aboard as a stowaway after her mother creates a diversion by jumping into the water. Meanwhile, Brant is in England posing as General Costello of Paraguay whose servant (Peter Bull) comes across a missive from Brant's henchman Mortimer. Seeing a potential for it to be used for blackmail, the servant sells the letter to Sam Pryor (Frank Cellier) who boards the flight hoping to get "General Costello" to pay £1,000 to buy it back from him.

The servant also contacts Grant at Scotland Yard, who is assigned to the flight to find out what Pryor is up to. Also aboard is Arnold James (Desmond Tesher), the teen prodigy who "plays the violin like an angel," but who would prefer to practice his saxophone. Arnold proves to be a rather nosy sort, noting that Jennie does not have a ticket, telling Pryor, who poses as a policeman, about it, and continually pops up unexpectedly at the most inopportune moments.

The large, roomy plane Stevenson and his support crew imagine is a marvel. Passengers are called to dinner by bugle. There are outside observation decks (where conversation is impossible because of the noise of the engines), people have their own private cabins, and the cockpit is kept locked and off-limits to keep the captain and his copilot from becoming distracted.

The whole thing ends up with Grant falling for Jennie, Pryor confirming his suspicions about Brant, who in turn kills him in the baggage compartment, stealing James' mother's parachute, killing the pilot, and attempting to jump for safety over Newfoundland while the plane crashes. Unfortunately for him, Arnold has borrowed a significant portion of the chute to act as a muffler for his sax, while Grant saves the day by clambering over the outside of the plane into the cockpit to open the door to let the copilot in just in time.

As the film progresses, it becomes more and more enjoyable with shrewd use of Hitchcockian devices. It also becomes more and more of a self-parody with its tongue firmly in its cheek. Stevenson keeps things moving along, making use of his limited resources and the most of his talented cast. The film was based on the novel *Sky Steward* by Ken Attwill, which was adapted into a screenplay by Roland Pertwee and Jo Corton with additional dialogue by E.V.H. Emmett. While not well known, the film is delightful enough that it deserves rediscovery.

In 1939, David O. Selznick put Stevenson under contract, and made money off of him by loaning him out to various studios, including Universal, RKO and United Artists. The first of these was Stevenson's colorful adaptation of *Tom Brown's School Days* (aka *Adventures at Rugby*) starring Sir Cedric Hardwicke at his best as Dr. Arnold, Freddie Bartholomew as East, Billy Halop as the quintessential swaggering bully Flashman, and Jimmy Lydon (best known as the screen's Henry Aldrich) as the sympathetic Tom Brown. Stevenson cannily condenses Thomas Hughes' expansive novel and retains only the most interesting elements in this tale of a boy who is ostracized for telling tales. Stevenson followed this with a remake of Fannie Hurst's *Back Street* starring Charles Boyer, Richard Carlson, and Margaret Sullivan.

Stevenson really started hitting his stride with *Joan of Paris*, the U.S. debuts of Paul Henried and Michele Morgan. It tells of a Parisian barmaid (Morgan) who, inspired by Joan of Arc, sacrifices her life to aid a Free French flyer (Henreid) and his four RAF companions from the gestapo. Stevenson gives the anti–Nazi drama sensitive handling while adopting a realistic approach, and he gets notably good performances from Morgan, Thomas Mitchell (playing a French priest), and May Robson as a British agent. Also appearing in the film are Laird Cregar and in minuscule role as an RAF flyer, Alan Ladd.

One of Stevenson's very best, though not very well known, films is *Forever and a Day*, for which he directed one of eight segments (other directors included René Clair, Edmund Goulding, Cedric Hardwicke, Frank Lloyd, Victor Saville, and Herbert Wilcox). The film has an unparalleled cast of 80 British stars and was a possible inspiration for the series *Upstairs, Downstairs*. Many of its contributors donated their services for nothing as RKO agreed to distribute the film without cost so that all money raised would go to the allied war effort.

Forever and a Day tells the story of the people from two

families who live in an English house in London from the time it was built in 1804 until it is destroyed by a bomb in World War II. The story begins with the American owner of the house, Gates T. Pomfret (Kent Smith), coming to meet Lesley Trimble (Ruth Warrick) who wants to buy the house. After surviving a bombing and hearing an inspirational speech by a curate (Herbert Marshall), Pomfret goes back to the house where Trimble tells the story of its past.

The land the house was built on was sold to Admiral Eustace Trimble (C. Aubrey Smith) by Stubbs (Edmund Gwenn), and the admiral raises a young son, Bill (Ray Milland), who rescues and marries Susan (Anna Neagle), the ward of Mr. Pomfret (Claude Rains). Bill dies in a war, forcing his wife and son to sell the house to Pomfret, who finds himself miserable there.

Eventually, the Pomfret and Trimble families combine, and a young bride (Ann Lee) decides to install a bathtub, and hires Dabb (Sir Cedric Hardwicke) and his assistant (Buster Keaton) to do so, much to the consternation of her husband and their butler Bellamy (Charles Laughton); however, the bride's idea of making iron bathtubs saves her husband's company and makes the family fortune.

The Trimble-Pomfrets prosper, and one, Sir Anthony Trimble-Pomfret (Edward Everett Horton) even becomes a knight. His maid Jenny (Ida Lupino), however, is attracted to Jim (Brian Aherne), an ambitious coal man with plans for moving to America. Eventually the families separate onto two continents. In the last segment, Gladys Cooper and Roland Young particularly get to shine as bereaved parents whose son is killed in World War I, and the film ends ironically with the destruction of the house during a bomb raid, but it is clear that the spirit of its inhabitants will live on, just as Britain would survive the travails of the war. It is truly a forgotten classic that deserves immediate revival.

Another classic is Stevenson's superb production of Charlotte Brontë's *Jane Eyre*, which was overshadowed by its Rochester, Orson Welles. Indeed, the film has much of the look of a Wellesian masterpiece, leading some to speculate that Welles might have covertly directed or produced it, a notion that Selznick's records do much to dispel. Welles had played the part on the radio and did recommend Bernard Herrmann to compose the score for the film, to which Selznick agreed, and Welles was allowed to give input on the casting of the film. (*Jane Eyre* was an early credit for both Margaret O'Brien and Elizabeth Taylor.)

However, Stevenson himself was a member of the Brontë Society and had access to unpublished papers of the Brontë family, including documents which directly related to the writing of the novel. Stevenson also collaborated with Aldous Huxley and John Houseman on the screenplay.

When Selznick learned that Welles desired an associate producer credit on the film, he wrote to William Goetz of 20th Century–Fox, "If this be true, I think I would be less than conscientious in my obligations to Bob Stevenson if I did not say that in my opinion such credit would be extremely unfair to Bob, who pretty clearly took up the responsibility of producer where I left off.... [T]he unfairness to Stevenson [would be] a very severe one, robbing him of much of the credit to which he so clearly is entitled...."

Stevenson's film does a good job of condensing Charlotte Brontë's story. We watch as young Jane (Peggy Ann Garner) grows up with Mrs. Reed (Agnes Moorehead), a harsh aunt who shows her no love, and she is then sent to Lockwood, a bleak charity school run by a harsh taskmaster (Henry Daniell). There, her best friend, Helen Burns (Elizabeth Taylor), dies after being forced to stand outside in the rain as part of the school's remorseless discipline. Stevenson uses low angles and shadows to expertly emphasize Jane's childhood miseries.

However, Jane's education allows the grown up Jane (Joan Fontaine) to secure a position as a governess at Thornfield Hall, a sprawling estate located on the gloomy English moors. Lord of the estate is Edward Rochester (Welles), a moody man haunted by a mysterious past that encompasses a mad woman in his attic.

Jane becomes attracted to this simultaneously anguished and arrogant man; however, she cannot bring herself to marry him until the matter of his mad wife is resolved. A fire ends up destroying Thornfield and the wife, leaving the once brusque Rochester blinded and symbolically castrated as the formerly imperious man becomes meek and can now return Jane's love. Permeated with gloomy atmosphere and Gothic dark shadows, courtesy of George Barnes' striking cinematography, Stevenson has created a masterful movie with terrific performances from both of his leads giving what may be the best performances of their careers.

Unfortunately, Stevenson's next picture was a ponderous mystery starring Hedy Lamarr, *Dishonored Lady*, which is best forgotten. Much better, though equally forgotten, was *To the Ends of the Earth*, a superior Dick Powell thriller featuring Powell as a government agent investigating the international heroin trade.

There followed a brief downward trend in his career while at RKO, where he made the underrated *I Married a Communist* (aka *The Woman on Pier 13*) with Laraine Day, Robert Ryan, and John Agar, followed by *Walk Softly, Stranger* in which a thief (Joseph Cotten) reforms because of his love for a crippled girl (Alida Valli). Though filmed in 1948 before *The Third Man*, the film was delayed until after Reed's film was released and still lost three quarters of a million dollars. Despite Stevenson's skillful handling, the mixture of gangster thriller and soap opera fails to come off. Next was *My Forbidden Past*, a dull drama starring a typically lethargic Robert Mitchum and a very attractive

Ava Gardner with Melvyn Douglas as a seedy New Orleans aristocrat, which was followed by the embarrassing *The Las Vegas Story*. These films were followed by almost four years of inactivity. *My Forbidden Past* was made in August of 1949, but was shelved until April 1951 on orders of Howard Hughes, but whatever Hughes had in mind, the movie still lost money despite the appealing presence of Gardner and costar Janis Carter as well as Stevenson's strong visual sense that helps enliven the photography, sets, and costumes. It is the melodramatic plot, in which a young woman bribes her cousin to romance the wife of her ex-lover, and Mitchum's sleepwalking performance that conspire to sink it.

At the command of Brian Connors (right), king of the Leprechauns, Darby O'Gill (Albert Sharpe) plays a lively Irish tune in Stevenson's delightful *Darby O'Gill and the Little People.* The little people were created via ingenious use of forced perspective.

Stevenson first began his longtime association with Disney with an adaptation of Esther Forbe's popular revolutionary war novel *Johnny Tremain*. The film was originally intended to be featured on the *Disneyland* TV show, which would have split the narrative into two parts—the first set in 1773 depicting Tremain as an ambitious silversmith who is won over to the cause of the revolution and joins the Sons of Liberty, and the second in 1775 when war finally breaks out. Because of the expense, it was decided to release it as a regular theatrical feature.

While Hal Stalmaster was introduced in this film as Johnny Tremain, his career never really progressed. Stevenson's film version does feature fine supporting performances, however, from Walter Sande as Paul Revere and long-time SF stalwart Whit Bissell as Josiah Quincy.

Stevenson handles the directing chores more than competently, and achieves a look quite beyond the film's fairly meager budget. No doubt the film's popularity kept the book around in public schools for many years to come as an introductory novel and to help bring to life a lively period that is often dully depicted.

Better still was *Old Yeller*, adapted by Fred Gibson from his own novel. *Old Yeller* remains one of the all-time classic children's films, a love story about a boy and his dog. Travis Coates (Tommy Kirk) initially despises Old Yeller, a mongrel stray who has a tendency to wreak havoc on the farm once Travis' father Jim (Fess Parker) departs, but he and the family are won over by the mutt's excellence as a watch dog and family protector after he saves the life of Arliss (Kevin Corcoran) who foolishly plays around with a bear cub.

Various conflicts are thrown in, as when Burn Sanderson (Chuck Connors) arrives and claims Old Yeller as his dog, but after seeing how attached Arliss is to the canine, "trades" him for a fine frog, or when Travis foolishly listens to the shiftless Bud Searcy (Jeff York) and tries his method for capturing wild boar, only to be pulled from his tree branch and escape goring by the timely intervention of his protective pooch. Finally, and most memorable, is when Old Yeller contracts rabies and Travis must assume the responsibility for putting the hydrophobic hound out of its misery, thereby learning one of the crueler lessons of life.

Stevenson handles animals and children, both notorious scene stealers, brilliantly, aided by Yakima Canutt's able second unit direction of action sequences. Also outstanding is Charles P. Boyle's vivid Technicolor photography. The performances are very naturalistic and never venture into the overly sentimental or cloying, a constant danger with this type of material. Unfortunately, Tommy Kirk was subsequently offered few opportunities for the fine kind of playing he performs here.

Next Stevenson tackled an elaborate Irish fantasy, *Darby O'Gill and the Little People*, based on the Darby O'Gill stories of H. T. Kavanagh. Back in 1947, Disney hired Lawrence E. Watkin to work on a script for a production announced as *The Little People*. After seeing *Finian's Rainbow* on Broadway, he decided Albert Sharpe would be the perfect incarnation of inveterate storyteller and roguish layabout Darby O'Gill.

However, it wasn't until a decade later that Stevenson took over the reins of the elaborate production. Painstaking detail was expended on forced perspective shots to combine full-sized foreground players with diminutive leprechauns cavorting in the background. According to effects expert and matte painter Peter Ellenshaw in an interview conducted by Paul Sammon in *Cinefantastique*, to avoid having to make composites, Darby was placed on a foreground set:

> Then, in the background, we put the actors posing as leprechauns. We then threw the focus with a lot of light. We had slower film then, so we had to have a lot more light. And by forcing the perspective — well, not really that, but by fooling the eye, because the camera only has one eye — you couldn't tell that the people were in the background. I was involved in making sure that there was a match between the two sections, so that you couldn't see where the ground began and ended in the foreground, and that the distance matched to it. Bob Stevenson, the director, helped us tremendously. Being a mathematician and an extremely intelligent man who used to read books on quantum theories and such, it was simple for Bob to work out the differences in perspectives we were playing with. Some of those shots were counterbalanced, using a teeter-totter board. When Darby walks up to the throne he's counterbalanced right out there. He was about six or seven feet straight out in the air.

While set in Ireland, the entire film was shot in California on the Albertson and Rowland Lee ranches, as well as Disney's sound stages in Burbank.

However, *Darby O'Gill* is mostly remembered today as one of Sean Connery's earliest roles, playing Michael McBride whom King Brian (jaunty Jimmy O'Dea) persuades to make up with love interest Katie O'Gill (Janet Munro, whom Disney had just put under contract).

Stevenson brings a great deal of visual finesse to this fairy tale, especially in such sequences as the arrival of the Death Coach, seen in negative being driven by a headless coachman. Despite its charming story, imaginatively and briskly told, the film failed to perform well at the box office, so Disney decided to have it redubbed on reissue to tone down the Irish brogues of the original.

Disney decided to take another stab at a swashbuckler with *Kidnapped*, based on the famous Robert Louis Stevenson novel. Although publicity material claimed so at the time, director Stevenson was not related to the noted British writer. As an adaptation, however, the film is as faithful to the source material as the writer could have wished, improving on the earlier 1938 Fox version directed by Alfred Werker.

Stevenson does a great job of building a forlorn atmosphere at the outset, where after the death of his father amid dark, dusky skies and gusty winds, David Balfour (James MacArthur) makes his way to his uncle's penurious estate and meets two passersby who warn him away from going there.

Peter Finch makes for a very full-bodied Alan Breck Stewart, a Scottish loyalist who opposes British rule and is quick with his sword and quicker with his friendship. The supporting cast is superb, including Bernard Lee as Captain Hoseason, Niall MacGinnis as Shaun, Finlay Currie as Cluny MacPherson, Miles Malleson as Mr. Rankeillor, and John Laurie as the treacherous Uncle Ebenezer. Of particular note is a brief scene with Peter O'Toole as Rob Roy MacGregor, a rival Scottish piper, another indication of Stevenson's ability to pick out promising talent.

Stevenson finally returned to the science fiction genre with one of Disney's more fondly remembered comedies, *The Absent Minded Professor* starring the reliable Fred MacMurray as Professor Ned Brainard. Brainard is so absent-minded that he has forgotten to appear at his own wedding to his fiancée Betsy Carlisle (Nancy Olson) twice before, and at the beginning of the film, becomes so engrossed in his latest invention that he forgets for the third time. While the comic approach in the film tends toward the broad, it is nonetheless an effective crowd pleaser, filled with visual invention.

The Absent Minded Professor was scripted by associate producer Bill Walsh based on the short story "A Situation of Gravity" by Samuel W. Taylor. Walsh would work with Stevenson on his best Disney films. The film centers around Brainard's invention of "flubber," named after "flying rubber," a substance that generates its own "repulsive" energy, in effect becoming a new energy source, and the various uses to which Brainard puts the substance. "The application of an external force triggers molecular change liberating energy of a type previously unknown," he theorizes out loud. Ned is pleased when he creates a flubber ball that bounces higher with each succeeding bounce, sending dozens of the things careening through his workshop, and his joy at his discovery is infectious, thanks to Fred MacMurray's appealing performance. He rigs his Model T Ford to become a flying machine powered by flubber and radioactive isotopes which cause the substance to move in an opposite direction, including up into the air.

Betsy is understandably upset at being stood up at the altar for the third time and wants to call the relationship off, even when Brainard attempts a rather scientific explanation for his tardiness. This opens the opportunity for Shakespeare–quoting rival English professor from Rutland Shelby Ashton (Elliott Reid) to attempt to woo her away from Brainard. Her boss, Medfield College President Rufus Daggett (Leon Ames), is more concerned about meeting a half million dollar loan to banker Alonso Hawk (Keenan Wynn) of the Auld Lang Syne Loan Company who in turn in annoyed with Brainard for flunking his son Biff Hawk (Tommy Kirk), thereby preventing him from playing on the Medfield Basketball team.

Stevenson relies on stereotypes, and these same basic figures began to appear in subsequent Disney films. Films such as these celebrate the underdog and make big business and big government both the villains and the satirical targets. The main villain here is the avaricious Hawk, who is not above dirty-dealing, first using his inside information to bet on Rutland over Medfield and later stealing Professor Brainard's flying flivver and making him look a fool when representatives from the army, navy, and air force come to investigate. There are also often pompous, self-important boyfriends who create a temporary barrier between the heroine and the hero.

The Absent-Minded Professor employs plentiful, though simple, special effects supervised by Peter Ellenshaw. Brainard's car flying scenes are simply obtained by a combination of process photography, wire work, and miniatures. A stand-out sequence is the flubberized basketball game between Medfield and Rutland where Medfield is being creamed by Rutland's larger players until Brainard irons bits of flubber to the Medfield players' heels, allowing them to leap over the competition and win what would otherwise have been a hopeless game. Stevenson keeps the gags fast and lively, as the players take delight in their newfound ability to achieve hang time.

Stevenson also features a delightful up and down crane shot from Hawk's point of view when Brainard and Betsy trick him into bouncing up and down in flubberized shoes that continually cause Hawk to bounce ever higher into the stratosphere, in order to coerce him into telling them where Brainard's car has been hidden. The set-ups and pay-offs for gags are neatly achieved, showcasing Stevenson's flair for comedy, and the flubber effects are both plentiful and inventively staged.

The Absent-Minded Professor was a sensation, garnering handsome returns at the box office and largely positive reviews. It is still today one of the most successful science fiction comedies as well as one of the more entertaining of the classic live action Disney films. In 1997, the film was remade and released under the title *Flubber* starring Robin Williams in MacMurray's role of Prof. Brainard with John Hughes (*Weird Science*) rewriting Bill Walsh's script and Les Mayfield (whose first feature was the awful frozen caveman comedy *Encino Man*) directing. Unfortunately, the remake seems designed more to be a special effects showcase (flubber is now a living thing that can contort itself into all kinds of shapes; the professor's faithful dog has been replaced with a flying female robot named Weebo; a 1963 Ford Thunderbird replaces the original's Model T) than an effective comedy.

Stevenson was given a bigger budget than usual for Disney's epic adaptation of Jules Verne's *Captain Grant's Children,* which was retitled *In Search of the Castaways.* Mary and Robert Grant (Hayley Mills and Keith Hamshire) are two children who persuade Professor Paganel (Maurice Chavalier) to help them find their father, based on a note found in a bottle which gives his longitude and latitude, although they mistakenly head off to South America first, where they encounter adventures such as surviving an earthquake, bobsledding on a broken ledge, and being attacked by a giant condor. Realizing that the location is actually in the Eastern hemisphere, they head off to New Zealand to discover that their father (Jack Gwillim), while still alive, had been set adrift by Thomas Ayerton (George Sanders), who has been running guns to the Maoris.

The film is lavish but unconvincing, marred by obvious studio sets and poor miniatures and the dubious decision to have Prof. Paganel break into song in order to keep the children's spirits up.

Stevenson immediately set to work on a sequel to the highly popular *The Absent Minded Professor* entitled *Son of Flubber*. Unfortunately, the film shoots its comic wad early. It begins promisingly with Brainard (MacMurray again) first being denied an immediate pay-off by the military and then being pestered by the IRS for money he never even collected from the government because of his projected earnings. This is followed by some advertising men who show to the Brainards their ideas for various flubber products, including flubberoleum, an easy to clean surface that causes a tired commercial family to literally bounce back to life in the film's funniest and most inventive sequence.

Son of Flubber shows Brainard continuing in the same vein as before and inventing "dry rain," a raygun that causes a raincloud to appear wherever he points it. While he hopes to raise enough money to save Medfield College with the invention, it has the unfortunate side effect of shattering every window near its vicinity, causing the hapless professor to wind up in court. Alonso Hawk (Keenan Wynn) is once more trying to foreclose on the college, which desperately counted on Brainard's governmental pay-off to keep solvent. Hawk sees the potential to unscrupulously corner the glass market because of the side effect of Brainard's raygun, but Brainard refuses to cooperate and winds up being held accountable for thousands of dollars of broken glass pay-offs. But the day is saved when a county agricultural agent (Ed Wynn) announces that "dry rain" has the positive effect of creating oversized vegetables, that are considered both safe and a boon to mankind.

This sequel also does riffs on bits from the previous picture. Once Shelby Ashton (Reid again) is up to his old tricks, bringing an old flame of Brainard's by to make his wife Betsy (Olson again) get jealous, and then flirting with her after she starts suspecting the worst. Brainard gets even by using his rain-gun to fill Ashton's car with water while he is dressed as Neptune for a costume party, in turn causing Shelby to run into the same befuddled police officers he had hit previously. Instead of a wild, flubberized basketball game, we're given an equivalent football contest with a flying football player and a quarterback (Tommy Kirk) kicking a flubberized football that fails to come down to Earth.

While not as well put together as *The Absent Minded Professor, Son of Flubber* was relatively successful and is a rare, slapstick science fiction film with a few genuinely funny and inventive setpieces.

Science fiction also crops up in Stevenson's next project, *The Misadventures of Merlin Jones.* Merlin Jones lacks the gloss of most of Disney's theatrical product, looking like a pair of *Wonderful World of Color* episodes that were spliced together and given a theatrical release. Unlike Stevenson's earlier Disney efforts, this one has a low budget, flat television lighting look to it.

Merlin Jones stars Tommy Kirk as bright campus egghead and crackpot inventor Merlin Jones of Midvale College who invents a machine which helps him read minds, only to eavesdrop on Judge Holmby (Leon Ames) and discover that he seems to be plotting a robbery. Decent kid that he is, he informs the police, who fail to find his claims credible. Jones enlists the aid of his girlfriend, Jennifer (Annette Funicello). Together they finally discover that Holmby was simply plotting a murder mystery which he is secretly writing.

The mind-reading machine is then forgotten as the second half of the film concentrates on Jones experimenting with hypnotism, foolishly hypnotizing Judge Holmby into stealing the science department's experimental chimpanzee only to find himself held responsible for the ape's disappearance.

The Misadventures of Merlin Jones, despite being lightly likable as a kids' film, garnered largely negative notices, but given its low cost, easily made a tidy profit. It lead to a Stevenson helmed sequel and was even given a theatrical re-release in 1972 before being put out to video pasture.

Before then, Stevenson was given his best known and best received assignment, *Mary Poppins.* This classic children's fantasy film, loosely based on the P. L. Travers book, is filled with tuneful songs by Richard M. and Robert B. Sherman, truly eye-catching (if often unconvincing) special effects, and a delightful cast of players. The basic plot works out the redemption of a stuffy banker, Mr. Banks (David Tomlinson) as well as the reformation of his basically decent but difficult on nannies kids, Jane (Karen Dotrice) and Michael (Matthew Garber).

Mary Poppins' biggest difficulty is its 139 minute running time is a bit long for a children's feature, but it would be equally difficult deciding what could be trimmed. There are a number of stand-out scenes from the one where a gaggle of ugly nannies are blown away by a mystical wind to Poppins' singing "A Spoonful of Sugar" while the kids' nursery cleans itself to Bert (Dick Van Dyke) persuading Poppins to take him and the kids gallivanting inside a cartoon version of one of his sidewalk chalk paintings to having tea while flying through the air with laughter-loving Uncle Albert (Ed Wynn) to the elaborate chimney sweep dance sequence which serves as a partial climax to the film.

Mary Poppins garnered an amazing 13 Academy Award nominations, including Stevenson's first and only nomination as best director. It won in five categories: Best Actress, Film Editing, Original Score, Original Song, and Special Visual Effects.

While no one was really clamoring for it, *The Monkey's Uncle* does have the advantage of being a sequel that is slightly better than the film that inspired it. Once more we get Tommy Kirk as Merlin Jones aiding his campus of Midvale College. Once more we get two segments that share the same characters but with very different plots.

The first half of the film deals with Jones' experiments in sleep-learning, beginning with a chimpanzee named Stanley who is made to listen to a tape while he sleeps. Jones discovers that his system works and endeavors to help the football team by helping hopeless lunkheads Norman (Norman Grabowski) and Leon (Leon Tyler) pass an English exam. When these two big dimbulbs do too well, they are accused of cheating until Jones finally proves that his system works.

In the second half, the college is strapped for money, and the eccentric Mr. Dearborne (Frank Faylen) brings in a man who will give the school a million dollars if it will drop its football program. A desperate Judge Holmby (Ames again) meets Darius Green III (Arthur O'Connell) who will give the school ten million if they can prove his ancestor's contention that man can fly without mechanical machinery.

Jones drafts Leon to help him by pedaling his flying machine only for Leon's legs to give out. Jones takes over powering the craft himself by boosting his energy with a form of adrenaline, but just as he proves man-powered flight is possible, a pair of men in clean white coats come to take Mr. Green back to the booby hatch. All is lost until Dearborne reveals that Green was to be his source of money for Midvale as well.

Annette Funicello gets to sing the silly theme song with the Beach Boys. As the film wrapped, Tommy Kirk was caught in an embarrassing sex scandal with another boy, causing Disney to dismiss him from the studio. From there it was downhill to American International efforts such as Bert Gordon's *Village of the Giants*, Don Weis' *Ghost in the Invisible Bikini*, Stephanie Rothman's *It's a Bikini World*, to even worse films such as Larry Buchanan's *Mars Needs Women* and his *It's Alive*.

Next for Stevenson came another entertaining comedy-thriller, *That Darn Cat!*, based on the Gordon book *Undercover Cat*. Kidnapped bank teller Margaret Miller (Grayson Hall) manages to scratch the letters "HEL" on the back of her watch and put it around a scrounging Siamese cat's neck in an effort to alert the authorities to her whereabouts. The cat, D.C., belongs to Patti Randall (Hayley Mills), who guesses at its meaning and contacts the FBI. Agent Zeke Kelso (Dean Jones) is assigned to the case, despite his allergy to cats, and his task is to assign agents to track D.C.'s movements in hopes that the cat will eventually lead them to the bank robbers' (Frank Gorshin, Neville Brand) hideout.

That Darn Cat! is lively and padded out with a talented cast of eccentric supporting players, including snoopy neighbor Mrs. MacDougall (Elsa Lanchester) and her long-suffering husband (William Demerest), and Roddy McDowall as Patti's sister Ingrid's (Dorothy Provine) boyfriend Gregory. Stevenson is able to construct several amusing and cleverly staged slapstick sequences as D.C. continually gets the better of his human pursuers. (The film was badly remade in 1997 with Doug E. Doug starring as Zeke Kelso.)

Stevenson then returned to fantasy with *The Gnome-Mobile* in which lumber tycoon D. J. Mulrooney (Walter Brennan) takes his niece (Karen Dotrice) and nephew (Matthew Garber) into a redwood forest where they encounter a two-foot tall gnome named Jasper (Tom Lowell) who begs them to help find others of his kind. Mulrooney's 1930 Rolls Royce gets dubbed the Gnome-Mobile en route to their searching another part of the forest. The patriarch of the clan, 943-year-old Knobby (also Brennan), berates Mulrooney for his part in destroying the forest.

Unfortunately, Knobby raises such a ruckus that freak show owner Horatio Quaxton (Sean McClory) decides to kidnap Jasper and Knobby, causing D. J. to initiate a desperate search for them that causes members of his company to question his sanity. Naturally, the kids prove smarter than the adults and they track Jasper down and discover that Knobby has finally found Rufus (Ed Wynn), the gnome king.

While the special effects are as well handled as those in *Darby O'Gill and the Little People*, the end result is far less memorable. *The Gnome-Mobile* is a colorful and diverting kids' film, but its platitudes are obvious and its plot is unmemorable. It was the penultimate live action film that Walt Disney himself supervised.

Blackbeard's Ghost is based on the 1965 novel by Ben Stahl with Peter Ustinov, mugging more than usual, as the titular character who seemed far more charming to me as a kid than it does to me as an adult. Steve Walker (Dean Jones) inadvertently conjures up Edward Teach, better known as Blackbeard the Pirate, who is made into a lovable rogue cursed to wander the Earth until he does a good deed, helps two dotty old lady descendants keep their inn instead of it being turned into a casino by some racketeers by using his powers to help Walker win various bets. The film plays with its obvious gimmicks (Blackbeard is invisible to everyone except Walker) and tries too hard to be winsomely winning.

Even more gimmicky, and also far more popular, was *The Love Bug*, a comedy about a Volkswagen Bug called Herbie with a mind of its own that spawned a feature film series. Herbie helps his driver, Jim Douglas (Dean Jones), and his mechanic, Tennessee Steinmetz (Buddy Hackett), defeat the conniving Thorndyke (David Tomlinson), a slick driver who mistreats cars, from winning a race and a bet for Herbie himself. While the film has some ingratiating performances and is reasonable family film fare, laced with ingratiating humor thanks to Don DaGradi and Bill Walsh's script (based on a story by Gordon Buford), its greatest attraction is the wild stunts that Herbie is called upon to perform to outwit attempts at sabotage, including driving on two wheels on a winding mountain road and breaking into still working component parts which must later be reassembled.

The Love Bug led to a series of increasingly inept but still profitable sequels, the best of which is the Stevenson–directed *Herbie Rides Again*, written by producer Bill Walsh, in which Helen Hayes stars as Mrs. Steinmetz, who takes over the ownership of Herbie, who helps her overcome the machinations of villains Judson (John McIntire) and Alonzo Hawk (Keenan Wynn playing the same character as he played in *The Absent-Minded* Professor) who wish to build a skyscraper where their firehouse turned home now stands. Also aiding Mrs. Steinmetz is Hawk's nephew Willoughby Whitfield (Ken Berry) who uses his legal talents to stop construction. In the film's wildest moment, Herbie recruits Volkswagons from all over San Francisco to come to his aid, with them arriving like the cavalry to stop the bulldozers. Subsequent installments in the series, however, ran out of gas and it suffered the indignities of a badly made 1971 German imitation (*Ein Kaefer geht aufs Ganze*) and a made-for-television remake in 1997 that failed to capture any of the charm and appeal of Stevenson's original.

Disney Films had purchased the rights to Mary Norton's book *Bedknobs and Broomsticks* back in 1964, but it was decided that the material was too close to *Mary Pop-*

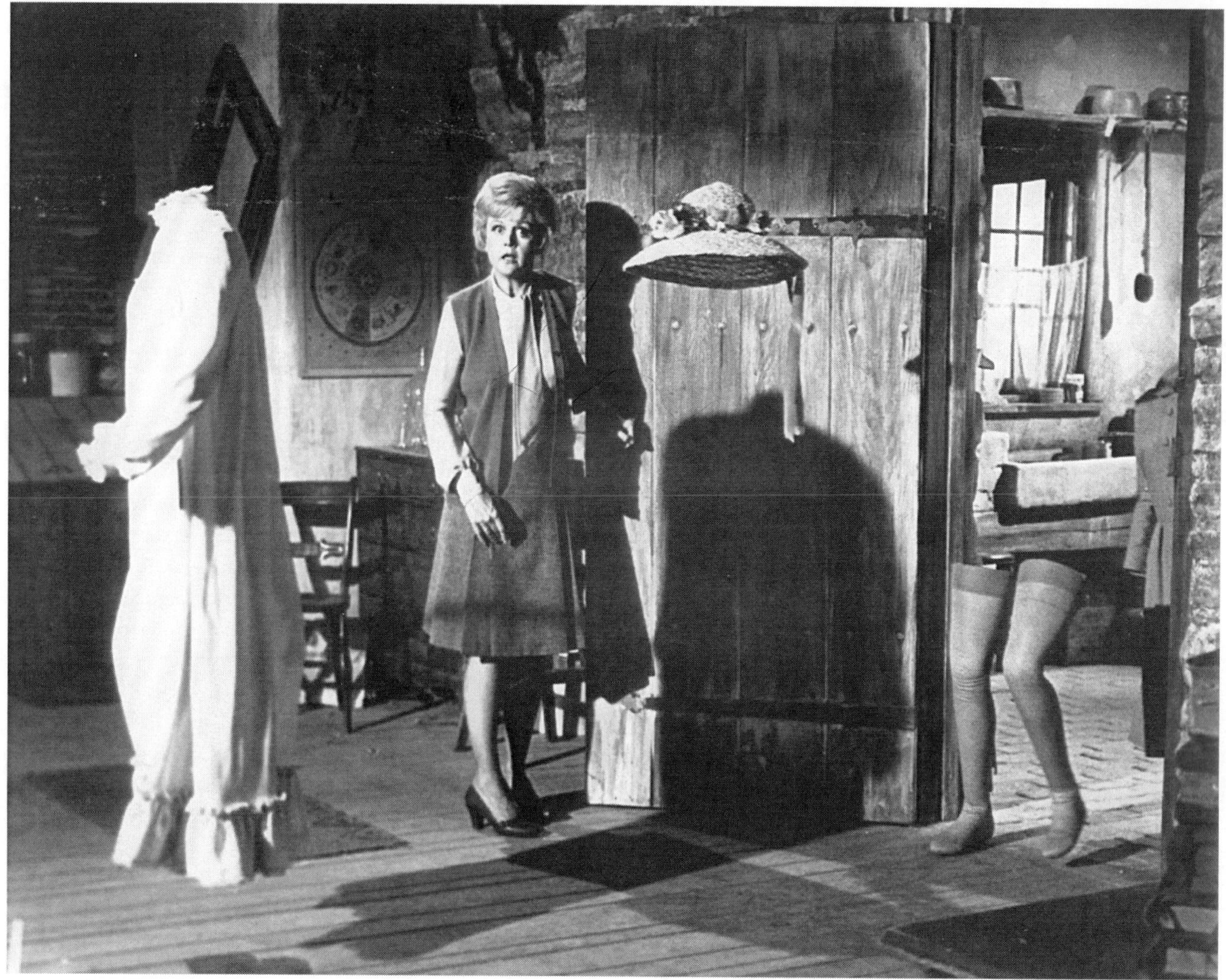

Amateur witch Elgantine Price (Angela Lansbury) brings her wardrobe to life to help fight Nazi invaders in Stevenson's recently restored *Bedknobs and Broomsticks*.

pins and the property was put on the back burner, though Richard and Robert Sherman had already written several tunes for its score. The property was dusted off in 1970, a script prepared by Bill Walsh and Don DaGradi, with the lead role of amateur witch Eglantine Price who winds up repulsing Nazi invaders to war-time England finally going to Angela Lansbury.

The plot has to do with three children being forced on Eglantine because of war-time deprivations. The children are unhappy at being relocated, but become fascinated when they learn that Eglantine has been studying witchcraft by mail and plans to make mischief if the Nazis ever land in England.

Unfortunately for her, her correspondence course is incomplete, and with the children in tow, she tracks down the head of the correspondence school, Emelius Browne (David Tomlinson) who admits the lessons he sent were copied out of a book, which it turns out is incomplete. Together, they must track down the book seller (Sam Jaffe) on Portbello Road to uncover the rest of the spells Eglantine needs.

Using a bed, Eglantine takes the kids on a wonderful ride into several fantastic worlds, the best of which is an animated segment both below and above the water climaxing in an animal soccer match, before returning. In the climax, she animates empty suits of armor and other weaponry to fend off some invading Nazis.

Back in 1971, Walt Disney Pictures booked this new feature into Radio City Music Hall, but Radio City complained that the film needed to be under two hours in length to accommodate the theater's elaborate stage show, and so some twenty-odd minutes were trimmed to bring the film to its 117 minute running length. As a result, Roddy McDowall's amorous cleric who hopes to woo Eglantine for her money was reduced to a mere one-minute cameo and two production numbers, "A Step in the Right Direction" and "Nobody's Problems for Me" were eliminated. Also, the "Portbello Road" number was reduced from ten minutes to three, and Tomlinson's "With a Flair" was likewise trimmed.

Because of its Sherman–written score, magic-filled story, elaborate effects and animal animated sequence that combined live action and animation, the film was inevitably compared to *Mary Poppins* but fell short in every category, particularly when it came to charm. *Bedknobs and Broomsticks* did win an Oscar for its special effects, and John Mansbridge and Peter Ellenshaw were nominated for their art direction. However, after its initial disappointing run, the movie was later reissued with 19 more minutes missing, which were only recently restored on a special laserdisc release and Disney Channel showing.

Scott McQueen, Disney's senior manager of library restoration, uncovered the missing footage in more than 20 erroneously marked cans of film, which was needed to replace the faded, scratchy material missing from the work prints. In some instances the audio tracks were missing, so McQueen brought in Lansbury and McDowall to redo some of their lines, while voice actors were brought in to double for the late Miles O'Shea and the three child stars. The original "Nobody's Problems for Me" had never been underscored, so McQueen consulted with composer Richard Sherman, who insisted that the song was needed to set up the last act. Even so, the footage of "Step in the Right Direction" persistently evaded detection; however, McQueen was able to restore 23 missing minutes to the film.

Stevenson followed this with *Island at the Top of the World*, based on Ian Cameron's novel *The Lost Ones*. Done in the mode of a Jules Verne adventure, Sir Anthony Ross (Donald Sinden), a wealthy Englishman, organizes a team of Arctic explorers to locate his missing son. Prof. Ivarsson (a miscast David Hartman) comes along to provide expert counsel when they venture into a mysterious valley near a massive volcano, wherein a lost Viking settlement continues the old traditions and makes life dangerous for the inquisitive explorers. Despite good intentions, the magic in this by-the-numbers adventure is sorely missing despite its being a handsomely produced production.

Stevenson's career wound up with *One of Our Dinosaurs Is Missing*, his dullest Disney effort with a soporific plot about a search for a secret formula hidden in some dinosaur bones, and *The Shaggy D.A.*, a belated, slapstick color sequel to Disney's *The Shaggy Dog* with Dean Jones playing a kind of grown-up version of the Tommy Kirk character.

While Stevenson has not been given much serious consideration by the critics, despite the excellence of his early thrillers and his sumptuous productions *Jane Eyre* and *Forever and a Day*, he will remain beloved by children for his entertaining and accessible family fare, including classics like *Mary Poppins* and *The Absent-Minded Professor* that brought a little magic into many kids' lives. Few filmmakers have provided us with such consistently entertaining and spirited work as Stevenson has.

HERBERT L. STROCK (1918–)

Storm Over Tibet (credited to Andrew Marton, 1952); *Gog* (1954); *Battle Taxi* (1955); *I Was a Teenage Frankenstein* (aka *Teenage Frankenstein*); *Blood of Dracula* (aka *Blood of My Heritage; Blood of the Demon*, 1957); *How to Make a Monster* (1958); *Devil's Messenger* (credited to Curt Siodmak, 1961); *Rider on a Dead Horse* (1962); *The Crawling Hand* (1963); *Brother on the Run* (1972); *Monsteroid* (aka *Monster*, 1975); *Witches' Brew* (codirected with Richard Shorr, 1980)

Television: *The Cases of Eddie Drake* (1952); "Beyond," "Out of Nowhere," "Conversation With an Ape," "One Hundred Years Young," "The World Below," "Dead Reckoning," "Water Maker," "Signals from the Heart," "When a Camera Fails," "The Flicker," "The Unguided Missile," "The Man Who Didn't Know," "End of Tomorrow," "The Phantom Car," "Beam of Fire," "Living Lights," "The Miracle of Dr. Dove," "Survival in Box Canyon," "The Sound That Kills," *Science Fiction Theatre* (1955–1957); *The Alaskans; Bonanza; I Led Three Lives; Favorite Story; Maverick; Meet Corliss Archer; Men Into Space; Men of Annapolis; Highway Patrol; Harbor Command; Dr. Christian; The Veil; Mann of Action (pilot); No. 13 Demon Street*

Editor-turned-director Herbert L. Strock claims to have ghost directed Curt Siodmak's *The Magnetic Monster*, about a new element that absorbs energy.

Very little is known about the background of editor-turned-director Herbert L. Strock. He was born in Boston on January 13, 1918 and came to specialize in working on low budget films and television, most prolifically for ZIV Television Productions.

Strock worked for producer Ivan Tors, who became a specialist first in science fiction television and films, and later in underwater and then animal oriented television and films (His biggest successes were *Sea Hunt* and *Flipper.*) Tors was born in Budapest on June 12, 1916 and developed an early interest in science, studying pre-medicine at the University of Budapest before shifting his attention to zoology. He tried his hand at being a playwright with some success before emigrating to the United States to escape the threat of Nazism.

Tors worked briefly as a writer for Columbia Pictures before enlisting in the Army Air Corps, where he wrote for the Glenn Miller Armed Forces radio program. After his discharge, he returned to Hollywood and began working as a low budget producer and sometime screenwriter. (He worked on the scripts of *Song of Love, In the Good Old Summertime, That Forsyte Woman*, and *Watch the Birdie.*)

In 1952, Tors formed Summit Films with fellow Hungarian emigrés Andrew Marton and Laslo Benedek. Marton tracked down a German-Austrian movie, *Demon of the Himalayas*, which he had shot in 1936, and it was decided to form a new story around the footage. Columbia released the result as *Mask of the Himalayas*, to which is added the story of a greedy scientist who steals the sacred mask of the god Sindja from a Tibetan temple, resulting in ill fortune for everyone who comes in contact with him.

Tors then had the idea of making a series of films about the Office of Scientific Investigation or OSI, a fictional government bureaucracy that looks into odd scientific phenomena. For the first film, *The Magnetic Monster*, Tors hired Curt Siodmark to direct and Richard Carlson to star, building the climax of the film around stock footage from Karl Hartl's 1934 German film *Gold.* The unusual menace in this film is the newly created, rapidly expanding radioactive element Serranium that generates a vast magnetic field while devouring any energy sources it comes into contact with.

According to Strock, he was producing the TV series *The Cases of Eddie Drake* when Tors approached him to edit *The Magnetic Monster* and work as an associate producer, and then promoted him from being an editor to being a director, after the third day of shooting, although the final credits list only Siodmak. (According to Strock, the script clerk Mary Whitlock Gibson recommended him for the job because he would best know how to incorporate the stock footage.)

He also takes credit for codirecting *Riders to the Stars* with Richard Carlson, claiming that Carlson had overextended himself by directing, acting, and rewriting the film. According to Strock, Carlson asked him to direct the scenes where Carlson had to act. He also claims to have fired cinematographer Stanley Cortez from the film when Cortez ignored his order not to take down a wall in order to light a scene. The film is one of the few fifties SF films in color.

Riders to the Stars, written by Curt Siodmak, is notable for its bad science even while making claims of accuracy. The plot has to do with the government of the United States sending up rockets in hopes of establishing an orbital satellite station, but at an altitude of 126 miles, cosmic rays turn the rockets' steel into chewing gum. However, since meteors composed mainly of nickel and iron come down in good shape, it is rationalized that there must be some sort of coating that burns off in the atmosphere that protects the meteorites. Three heroic and rigorously tested men (Richard Carlson, William Lundigan, and Robert Karnes) are sent up in a rocket to capture a meteor and discover what this substance could be. Two of the men fail, but one succeeds. It is a dull, lecturing movie which thoroughly deserves its obscurity.

Strock was also hired as an associate producer and editor on *Donovan's Brain*, the film adaptation of Curt Siodmak's most famous book, which Siodmak was slated to direct. However, according to Strock, Siodmak got into an argument with producer Tom Gries when Gries suggested altering Siodmak's story, and he was replaced with Felix Feist. Siodmak's story had been previously filmed as *The Lady and the Monster* with Erich von Stroheim, and would inspire a slew of "brain in a fish tank" movies.

This is the film where Donovan (Michael Colgan), an industrialist, crashes in the desert and gets his brain preserved by a nearby scientist, Dr. Cory (Lew Ayres), even though the rest of his body dies. Donovan's will proves so powerful that his disembodied brain takes control of Dr. Cory in order to continue his financial activities and eventually attempts to murder Cory's assistant (Gene Evans), but for the intervention of Cory's wife (Nancy Davis before her marriage to Ronald Reagan). Strock claims to have shot second unit on the film as well as creating the lightning bolt which kills the brain by scratching the negative while adding an electrical crackle to the soundtrack.

Finally, Tors formed his own production company, Ivan Tors Film Inc., and he gave Strock *Gog* to edit and to direct in 3-D, despite the fact that Strock had monocular vision, finally giving Strock a directorial credit. Unfortunately, all 3-D or even color prints of the film appear lost.

Gog was begun under the title *Space Station U.S.A.* Strock says that he worked with art director William Ferrari to use color to emphasize the moods of scenes according to some research Strock had done at UCLA about the impact of certain colors on the emotions (e.g., grays, blacks, and blues would be emphasized for scenes involving cold). He also had plates shot of the generators at Hoover Dam which were projected behind actors to create a "set."

As the story opens, David Sheppard (Richard Egan) from the Office of Scientific Investigation is sent to check out the underground installation where work on the new space station is continuing, despite some reported sabotage and now a case of murder. A good deal of screen time is devoted to little else but showing off pieces of hardware and explaining how they work. Another lengthy but dull sequence is meant to show off an antigravity chamber that features two acrobats doing routines followed by shots of them on wires.

More inventive are the deaths at the installation. A scientist and his assistant are frozen to death in a low temperature lab. (One, Dr. Hubertus [Michael Fox], falls to the floor and shatters offcamera.) The two acrobats are whirled to death in a centifuge (an idea that works much better in Byron Haskin's *The Power*, which features a far more realistic centrifuge). Another scientist dies saving Shepperd from being set on fire by an electronically controlled tuning fork.

The film's title comes from one of two robots used by Dr. Seitman (John Wengraf) and Engle (William Schallert), which are called Gog and Magog. According to the film, Gog was created to pilot rocket ships to a space station, which are being fitted with solar mirrors that could destroy a city in a fraction of a second. Gog is under the control of NOVAC, for Nuclear Operated Variable Automatic Computer, but the controlling computer suddenly seems to go berserk. (The robots in the film are given an interesting design that for a change does not make them look humanoid and were actually operated by a midget named Billy Curtis.) One clever scientist manages to outwit an attack involving the solar mirror.

It turns out that a high flying plane is overriding the controls of NOVAC, and in the climax Shepperd and others keep the robots from killing them long enough for the enemy plane to be brought down, restoring control of the computer back to the Americans. Despite a few effective moments of suspense, Strock's first science fiction credit is talky and slow.

Recalls actor and dialogue director Michael Fox,

> I think scale was then $55 a day, and Ivan Tors wouldn't pay over scale no matter what. I had a deal when I did *Gog* and *Riders to the Stars*. I was the casting director, the dialogue director, and in order to ensure that I got paid because they weren't covered by unions, I also had a part, because if I had a part, I knew I was going to get some money. Not that I discussed it with anybody. I mean, don't misunderstand me. My father didn't raise any dumb Jewish children.... We bought Herbert Marshall for two pictures [*Riders to the Stars* and *Gog*]. Back then, Marshall was a big name, of course he'd been a star at Metro for years, and we paid $25,000 for the two pictures: $15,000 upfront, and $10,000 on the release of the first film. That was a big name star for us....
>
> [So] I also played a role. We decided to experiment with this, because they wanted to see me freeze on camera. So they sprayed me with acetone and some kind of powdered alloy dissolved in the acetone. I said to Ivan, 'Don't you think you ought to try this on somebody else first?' And nobody was making less money than me, and Ivan said, 'Oh, don't worry.'
>
> I remember that we did it, and I got a slight burn on the corner of my eye, but that's how we did it. We actually did it in a series of takes, and the last one as I come up to smash the window, I had the club in my hand, and I freeze to death, and they wanted me to do a back fall out of camera.

> Now I am probably the world's lousiest stuntman, but the one thing I can do is a good fall. Somehow I learned it years ago as a baby, and I did a back fall out of camera. They put down a mattress, and the sound effect that was added was that of breaking glass, so the figure shattered to pieces.... I was really intrigued about freezing to death. Of all the ways to go, that's a helluva way to die. I died so often in so many movies, but that's the only time I ever froze to death, and I'll never forget it.

Tors then attempted to film a story about the first artificial satellite, but studio executives failed to find the notion credible and declined to provide funding (though only two years later Sputnik, the first such satellite, would be launched). Instead, Tors turned to television, where he hooked up with Ziv Television Programs Inc., a syndicator, for which he produced *Science Fiction Theater*. Strock was picked to direct the series pilot and became one of the show's main directors.

Recalled Strock in an interview with Marc Zibatkin for *Filmfax* magazine, "I felt that Ivan had a fetish for doing scientific things that an audience didn't understand. He would lose the human element — emotions that were going on — and get into technicalities. I had to constantly bandy him to try to change something that was just a bunch of technical shots into something that had meaning. He wasn't very good at dialogue; his physical dialogue had that European convolution of expressing oneself." If so, Strock did not apparently exert much influence, for Tors' science fictional films remain talky and obsessed with technicalities.

Strock takes credit for rewriting *Battle Taxi* (1955) with Richard Taylor, which he also directed. The film was made with the cooperation of the Department of Defense and makes extensive use of stock footage courtesy of the 42nd Air Rescue Squadron. The film does not have much of a true plot but rather uses its characters to jam in as many acts of rescue or heroism as could be crammed into its 82 minute running time. Sterling Hayden stars as Captain Russ Edwards, who leads a Korean War helicopter air rescue group. The film costars Arthur Franz and Marshall Thompson, who become convinced that "There are old pilots, and there are bold pilots, but there are no old bold pilots."

Strock had an active career as a television director for Ziv over a period of five years. Among the shows he directed were *I Led Three Lives, Highway Patrol, Men of Annapolis, Mr. District Attorney, Favorite Story,* and *Corliss Archer*. It was while Strock was vacationing from working at Ziv that he was contacted by producer Herman Cohen to make his next feature film. The entire film was shot during Strock's two week vacation.

I Was a Teenage Frankenstein was the rather inept follow-up to Gene Fowler, Jr.'s, superior *I Was a Teenage Werewolf.* In this one, Professor Frankenstein (Whit Bissell in an arrogant and amusing performance) is lecturing about limb transplantation at a California college as a guest of Dr. Carlton (Robert Burton), an expert in electronics, and he experiences the usual scoffing from the audience (though what he advocates here is neither that advanced nor unusual). Like his famous ancestor, Frankenstein is interested in creating an artificial man, with the added twist that he is primarily interested in breeding his "superior" creation, and when a teenager (Gerry Conway) dies in a nearby car accident, he sees a golden opportunity.

He stores the boy's body in a private morgue that he has conveniently built in his basement, later amputating the body's hands and right leg. He bullies his assistant, Dr. Carlton (Robert Burton), into aiding him in his experiments. After a plane crash in which members of a college track team die, Frankenstein has the necessary parts to complete his cadaver for re-animation. (The film never shows limbs being sawn off, though the Hays Office was squeamish about the sounds of such sawing going on.)

After Carlton administers 50,000 volts, the monster becomes conscious but is not cooperative. "Speak!" demands Frankenstein in the film's most beloved (if often misquoted line), "I know you have a civil tongue in your head because I sewed it back myself." Frankenstein sadistically administers electric shocks to keep his creation under his absolute control. When the monster begins to cry, Frankenstein rejoices, "Even the tear duct functions! The whole world will be astounded! It seems we have a sensitive teenager on our hands." (Cohen apparently felt that comic relief would given the horrific elements more impact, and Strock agreed.)

The head of the monster is initially swathed in bandages, which is a good idea because the makeup on this teenage Frankenstein's monster is hilariously awful, looking like a very fake monster eye applied to a face dabbed with too much cold cream. It nevertheless frightens Frankenstein's nurse-admirer Margaret (Phyllis Coates), who nevertheless keeps mum. (She keeps promising to be the "best watchdog you ever had.") The frustrated teen at first wants to meet other people until Frankenstein takes off the bandages and shows him his horrible visage. The teen terror escapes and breaks into a young girl's room, accidentally strangling her when he tries to stifle her screams.

Margaret threatens to blab unless Frankenstein marries her, so the manipulative mad doctor arranges for the monster to dispatch her while she gives him a vitamin shot by convincing his "wunderkind" that she is his enemy, and then he has her tossed into the convenient crocodile pit.

The monster, like many teenagers, is distraught over his looks, and so Dr. Frankenstein encourages him to go to lover's lane, select the head of his choice, and come back with it (in a birdcage which the creature takes along for that purpose). By the time Carlton returns, the teen monster is admiring his new face in a mirror.

However, things go awry when the monster overhears Dr. Frankenstein discussing with Dr. Carlton how he plans to disassemble the monster in order to ship him back home to England. Angry at the doctor's perfidy, the troubled teen throws his creator into the crocodile pit, while Carlton summons the law. In a surprise twist, the finale in which the now crazed monster stumbles into a panel and is electrocuted was filmed in color. (Cohen apparently figured that even though he couldn't shoot the entire feature in color, it would be a good shock to show the finale that way. Strock assumed that black and white and color could not be intermixed and so shot all the color scenes on the entire final reel. Later television showings often omitted the color, making its restoration on videocassette a pleasant surprise.) That the teenage monster ends up a tragic victim of adult manipulation and malfeasance is a typical plot of Cohen horror films written by Aben Kandel. Strock appears to have brought little to the project except for filming it quickly and cheaply, and the editing surely could have been tighter as many scenes seem to go on too long, losing any possible tension they might have had.

According to Strock, Cohen was continually on his back trying to get Strock to do things Cohen's way so that Strock threatened to quit and most of the crew offered to go with him. Strock, however, reconsidered, not wanting it to get around that he had walked off a film, and so decided to finish the picture.

Whit Bissell steals the day with his forceful performance as Dr. Frankenstein. His line readings suggest a lively intelligence who knows how to get his way. Typical of AIP productions, which catered to and exploited the teenage market, amoral adults are shown to be the source of the real problems in the story.

The difficulty between Strock and Cohen did not prevent them from collaborating again on a semi-science fictional double feature: *Blood of Dracula* and *How to Make a Monster*. Strock also claims to have had a hand in rewriting the scripts, though it is hard to imagine these scripts as being much worse. Most Cohen movies have a similar plot structure, which Strock accounts for by explaining Cohen would provide the basic plot and storyline, and if the screenwriter would not write the script Cohen's way, he wouldn't work with them anymore.

Blood of Dracula is simply a distaff vampire remake of *I Was a Teenage Werewolf.* The main character, Nancy Perkins (Sandra Harrison) is another troubled teen led astray after being sent to Sherwood, a girls' prep school. Nancy's father Paul (Thomas B. Henry) has remarried less than six weeks after her mother's death, and Paul has been relocated by his company to another city. Paul and her hated stepmother Doris (Jeanne Dean) are dropping her off so they can experience a delayed honeymoon.

Nancy finds herself hazed by Myra (Gail Ganley) and her sorority, the Birds of Paradise. Nancy and Myra get into a fight, but they become friends. Myra assists a teacher in the school, Miss Branding (Louise Lewis), who has an often rejected theory that every person possesses an inner power that is greater than atomic energy, and she needs a volatile person to test her theory. Myra suggests Nancy.

Together they engineer an incident in which Nancy rubs some irritating liquid on her hand. Miss Branding offers Nancy first aid and hypnotizes her instead with a cat's eye amulet. Later under the power of the amulet, Nancy transforms into a blood-crazed fiend with upswept bushy eyebrows and protruding teeth. She attacks Nola (Heather Amis), killing her.

The police compare the extreme blood loss to those of vampire tales but can find no clues. Tab (Jerry Blaine), one of the few boys in the area, attempts a pass at Nancy, transforming her once more, and is soon slain. Miss Branding uses her hypnotic amulet to help Nancy pass the investigating polices' lie detector test.

At long last, Nancy's old boyfriend Glenn (Michael Hall) arrives, having been rebuffed by Miss Branding. He reaches Nancy and tries to talk of their future together, but she finds herself beginning to transform and so runs to Miss Branding begging for release. As Branding tries to control her once more, Nancy transforms and turns on her tormentor. In the ensuing melee, Branding is choked to death while a piece of furniture impales Nancy's heart.

Strock does attempt to create atmosphere with dramatic lighting and even manages occasional bits of eerieness. The "vampire" in this film does not infect others, nor is it fearful of the light. However, the teen terror in this film never seems really powerful or frightening. (Due to the limited shooting schedule, Strock needed to avoid any long dissolves for the vampire's transformation scenes.) In fact, the most horrific thing in the flick may be Jerry Blaine crooning, "Puppy Love," which he also penned.

Strock immediately went to work on the second half of the double bill, *How to Make a Monster*, which prophetically predicted that American International Pictures would get out of the monster movie business and concentrate on musicals (little did the writers know that the Beach Party movies would soon hold sway while the black and white chillers stopped attracting the teen audience). In the film, weakly written by Kenneth Langtry and producer Cohen, makeup artist Pete Dumond (Robert H. Harris) uses a special make-up cream to hypnotize the actors playing a teenage werewolf (Gary Clarke) and a teenage Franken-

Herbert L. Strock and lead Sirry Steffen filming *The Crawling Hand.*

stein (Gary Conway) into murdering the studio execs who want to do away with monster movies in favor of musicals, as well as an increasingly suspicious security guard.

In the climax, Dumond reveals to the actors what he has done, and in a struggle, a candle is knocked over for a suitable fiery finale. Once more, Cohen wanted the climax in color because he felt that having the monsters melt in color would be more impressive.

According to Strock, he was called in by Kenneth Herts of Herts-Lion to re-do some episodes written and directed by Curt Siodmak for the Swedish produced series *No. 13 Demon Street*, which starred Lon Chaney, Jr. Three of the episodes were then strung together with a bit of additional footage directed by Strock and transformed into the feature *The Devil's Messenger*.

Herts had a plan to make a low budget horror movie from a script brought in by a producer named Joe Robertson (who had made *The Slime People*) which he showed to Strock. Strock thought the script was awful and suggested in its place *The Crawling Hand*, a script he had written with a few friends.

According to Strock in Tom Weaver's *Interviews with B Science Fiction and Horror Movie Makers*, "So Robertson looked at our script for *The Crawling Hand*, and said that the guy he had putting up the money would put up money for this. The budget would be $100,000, it would be in black-and-white, and he wanted me to direct it. I made a deal with the writers and we went into production." Strock created the titular creature in cohort with special effects man Charlie Duncan, though most of the time the hand and arm, the severed end of which was left offscreen, belonged to Strock himself.

The Crawling Hand combines the idea of a disembodied hand from *The Beast with Five Fingers* with a disembodied piece of anatomy taking possession of people à la *Donovan's Brain*. The astronaut aboard a failed moonshot whose ship has run out of oxygen suddenly re-establishes communication and insists that the red button be pushed. The men at ground control wonder why he does not push the self-destruct button himself, but something is apparently preventing him, so the button is pushed and the ship exploded at 70,000 feet.

Scientists Steve Curan (Peter Breck), Max Weitzberg (Kent Taylor), and their assistant Donna (Allison Hayes) discover that the late astronaut had been taken over by some alien organism. Meanwhile, the astronaut's severed arm turns up on a beach in Palms, California, where it is discovered by Paul Lawrence (Rod Lauren) and his girl Marta Farnstorm (Sirry Steffen, a former Miss Iceland). Paul guesses to whom the arm belongs and takes it home for further study, but the hand is alive, kills Paul's boozy landlady, and takes over Paul's mind. Paul contacts the sheriff and passes out. The ambulance drivers pick up both bodies, but when Paul wakes up, he screams in fright at the sight of the dead landlady, and leaps from the ambulance, dashing off into the night.

When Curan and Weitzberg discover that the police have found the dead astronaut's fingerprints on the dead woman's throat, they rush right down to talk to Sheriff Townsend (Alan Hale, Jr.), who has already made up his mind that Paul is the culprit. Townsend was expecting the FBI to become involved and resents these scientists involving themselves in a criminal matter. He assigns a deputy to guard the house, keeping Paul under house arrest. Paul tosses them a note to come back at night, which they do, and which allows Paul to escape while Curan and Weitzberg are detained by the police.

When Paul is taken over by the ambulatory appendage, he suddenly gets black makeup all over his eyes. He attacks his closest friend, a soda pop store owner, and later even attacks Marta, but is chased away before he does any serious damage.

The film ends happily, if bizarrely, when Paul recaptures the hand and drops it off at the city dump where he stabs it with a broken bottle and it is devoured by cats, breaking the hold it has over Paul, who lives happily ever after.

Apart from its offbeat ending, one of few enjoyable aspects of *The Crawling Hand* is the film's use of the Rivingtons' hit "Papa Oom Mow Mow" for the scenes set in the soda shop. According to Strock, Burt Reynolds tested for the part of Doc Weitzberg, which went to Kent Taylor instead, a decision that Strock was later to regret when Taylor failed to show on time, could not remember the dialogue, and took overly long lunches. Perhaps it is because the ridiculous premise is played totally straight but somehow this schlocky thriller manages to have a few moments of interest, although it is more often lethargic and dull.

Years later, Herts changed his name and formed a new company. He contacted Strock about making a monster movie in Colombia and conned him into agreeing to direct it in exchange for expenses plus a never paid $60,0000 for Strock (who would write, direct and edit), his wife (who worked as wardrobe mistress) and daughter (who was the script supervisor). However, after Herts stiffed the Colombian monster-makers for the cost of the creature they created, he became *persona non grata* in Colombia and had to relocate the shoot to New Mexico. Herts also saved costs by shooting the film in 16mm.

The film is variously called *Monsteroid* or *Monster* (the first title appears at the beginning and the other title at the end), leading to some understandable confusion. According to Strock, Herts re-edited the film, rendering it senseless. The eminently forgettable film had something to do with an alligator-like monster putting the bite on some riverside tourists. The film starred Jim Mitchum, John Carradine, Keenan Wynn, Diane McBain, and Anthony Eisley.

Strock was also brought in to reshoot some sequences and edit footage for *Witches Brew*, an unauthorized adaptation of Fritz Leiber's horror novel *Conjure Wife* (filmed previously as *Weird Woman* and *Burn, Witch, Burn* aka *Night of the Eagle*). Richard Benjamin plays a college professor whose wife (Teri Garr) has been dabbling in black magic and puts a stop to her activities. Unfortunately, this leaves him at the mercy of a full-fledged witch who is eager to unseat him from his position. The film was initially directed by Richard Shore, who had directed an unreleased science fiction film called *Once Upon a Time*, who was then replaced by executive producer Jack Bean, who called on Strock to help complete the film.

Strock is proud of having been asked to rescue several films, but as *Faster and Furiouser* writer Mark Thomas McGee noted, this is a bit like asking Stevie Wonder to drive you home after you've had a few too many. Strock consistently has shown that while he can crank material out quickly and economically, his work shows little visual acuity and not much feeling for genre material. One is struck by the flat lighting and flatter characterizations that are hallmarks of his work.

JEANNOT SZWARC (1937–)

Extreme Close-up (aka *Sex Through a Window*) (1972); *Bug* (1975); *Jaws 2* (1978); *Somewhere in Time* (1980); *Enigma* (1982); *Supergirl* (1984); *Santa Claus* (aka *Santa Claus: The Movie*) (1985); *Honor Bound* (1991); *La Vengeance d'une Blonde* (1993); *Hercule and Sherlock* (1996); *Les Soeurs soleil* (1997)

Television: "Light at the End of the Journey," *Ironside* (1967); "The Macabre Mr. Micawber," "A Matter of Love and Death," *Ironside* (1968); "The Great Chess Gambit," *It Takes a Thief*; "Dance to No Music," *Marcus Welby, M.D.* (1969); "The Girl From Wickenberg," *Alias Smith and Jones*; "Room With a View," "Little Black Bag," *Night Gallery*; "Call Me Lee," "Call Me Ellen," *Paris 7000*; "Holocaust," *The Virginian*; "Experiment at New Life," *Men from Shiloh*; "A Spanish Saying I Made Up," "A Passion for

Torches," "Aura to a New Tomorrow," *Marcus Welby, M.D.* (1970); "The Funeral," "Class of '99," "A Death in the Family," "The Merciful," "With Apologies to Mr. Hyde," "The Phantom Farmhouse," "Midnight Never Ends," "The Big Surprise," "Cool Air," "Logoda's Heads," *Night Gallery;* "Jennifer," *The Men and the City*; "A Company of Victims," *Sarge* (1971); "A Feast of Blood," "The Waiting Room," "Last Rites for a Dead Druid," "Stop Killing Me," "The Sins of the Fathers," "The Caterpillar," "Satisfaction Guaranteed," "The Return of the Sorcerer," "Rare Objects," "Spectre in Tap Shoes," "The Ring With the Red Velvet Ropes," "Whisper," *Night Gallery; Night of Terror; Weekend Nun* (1972); "Conspiracy of Fear," "Mojo," "Dead on His Feet," "Queen of the Gypsies," "Girl in the River," *Kojak*; "Lovely But Lethal," *Columbo*; "The Fortunate Painter," *Three Faces of Love*; "The Oberon Contract," *Toma*; "Population: Zero," *The Six Million Dollar Man; The Devil's Daughter; Lisa, Bright and Dark; You'll Never See Me Again; A Summer Without Boys; The Small Miracle* (1973); "The Chinatown Murders," "Acts of Desperate Men," *Kojak*; "Pound of Flesh," "The Street," "Fifty Percent of Normal," *Toma* (1974); "Two into 5.56 Won't Go," *The Rockford Files*; "The Glory Game," "On the Road," "Double Image," *Baretta*; *Crime Club* (1975); "Out of the Shadows," "Shield for Murder," "A Summer Madness," "When You Hear the Beep, Drop Dead," "Where Do You Go When You Have No Place To Go?" *Kojak*; "So Help Me God," "New Life, Old Dragons," *The Rockford Files*; "It's Hard But It's Fair," *Baretta*; "New Georgia on My Mind," *Baa Baa Black Sheep; Hazard's People* (1976); *Code Name: Diamond Head* (1977); "Last Defender of Camelot," "Red Snow," *Twilight Zone* (1985); *Murders in the Rue Morgue* (1986); *Grand Larceny* (1988); *The Burning Shore* (miniseries, 1991); *Schrecklicher Verdacht; Rockford Files: A Blessing in Disguise* (1995); *Rockford Files: If the Frame Fits…* (1996); *The Practice* (1997)

Born in Paris, France, on November 21, 1937, Jeannot Szwarc (pronounced Zhanno Shwark) and his parents fled to Portugal and Argentina when the Nazis occupied the French capital in 1942. Szwarc returned to France in 1947, and became a film buff, running a film club, while studying international politics at H.E.C., from which he earned a master's degree in International Political Science with a course of study leading to the diplomatic corps.

Bored with his studies, he began a directorial career by directing student productions of avant garde plays such as Sarte's *No Exit*, but switched his concentration to films after he landed a job as a production assistant on Stanley Donen's clever Hitchcock pastiche *Charade*, which was shooting in Paris.

He moved to TV as a second unit director and writer-director of short subjects, but work was limited and hard to find. Told by his associates that he was crazy, he nevertheless decided to try his luck in Hollywood and moved there at the age of 25.

"It was hell," Szwarc recalled. "I worked odd jobs like writing scripts for a potato chip commercial. And for three months I was the guy who put the laughs on the laugh tracks for a sitcom. After [two and a half] years of this, I realized that nobody was going to come along and say, 'hey, kid … here's a film to direct.'"

While filling a lowly position at Universal, he sent an idea memo to series producers, one of which he developed into a 70 page treatment that became the series *Ironside*, for which he was awarded jobs as writer and associate producer. He also landed a similar assignment for *Chrysler Theater*, where he worked for producer-director Gordon Hessler (*Scream and Scream Again*) and tried to interest executives in producing some science fiction, but soon discovered that no one in the executive ranks at Universal was interested in science fiction, and the concept that it could be poetic or psychological was utterly foreign to them.

His work for *Chrysler Theater* led to his working on the 1967 Raymond Burr *Ironside* series, where he was allowed to make his directorial debut directing an episode he cowrote. That led to other directing assignments, including the highly acclaimed Hallmark Hall of Fame special *Lisa Bright and Dark*.

He became a resident director on Rod Serling's *Night Gallery* series, directing such memorable segments as "Sins of the Fathers," set in 19th century Wales in which a "sin-eater" sends his son to consume the sins of a recently deceased man; "The Little Black Bag," an excellent adaptation of Cyril Kornbluth's classic science fiction story about an idiot-proof medical bag from the future that falls into the present; "The Class of '99" in which instructor Vincent Price teaches bigotry to a class of androids; and "The Caterpillar," the infamous episode where planter Laurence

Harvey plans to use an earwig to bore into his paramour's husband's brain, only for the insidious insect to fall into his own ear, and burrow through, and for him to discover that the insect was a female that has just shed its egg sack.

In 1972, Szwarc made his feature debut on *Extreme Close-up* (aka *Sex Through a Window*) from a script by Michael Crichton. According to Crichton when I interviewed him, "*Extreme Close-up* was written to be an X-rated picture. I wrote it '70 or '71.... People were beginning to make X-rated films, certain foreign films that were artsy, that had nudity, but it seemed to me that people were not taking advantage of the opportunities.

"*Deep Throat* had just come out, and a group of us were talking about the fact that these movies as movies weren't very good. I became interested in the idea of making an X-rated film that would also be a good movie. What happened to it was that it got shot as a soft R, and that just destroyed it. I mean it really had a sort of hard edge that I thought was interesting, and it was a good script, but it had to be an X. The minute it was not an X, it was just all over. I wasn't involved in the production, so I was directing my own first movie at the time it was shooting. It was a low budget picture that didn't turn out as I hoped."

The subject of *Extreme Close-up* is how technology allows for greater invasion of privacy, which is largely unregulated, and the trap of voyeurism. Presumably, the fact that the hero is named after the pseudonym used by a New York philosophy professor to write science fictional misogynist fantasies, two of which, *Gor* and *Outlaw of Gor*, have been made into movies, is purely coincidental.

After initiating a series of reports on the availability of high-tech surveillance equipment, John Norman (Jim McMullen), a successful TV newscaster, lets his imagination and fantasies run wild. He rents top of the line equipment from a salesman (Al Checco) and becomes an obsessive "Peeping Tom." At first he innocently spies on his boss at the office as he picks his nose and sniffs his underarms, but then Norman decides to take his work home, becoming more involved in the sexual lives of his neighbors, celebrities, and strangers.

Somehow, his wife Sally (Kate Woodville) doesn't ever seem terribly concerned about her husband often being away late night, apparently because he uses the techniques he picks up in bed with her. Crichton's script does tackle the issue from many angles, from industrial espionage (portrayed by Antony Carbone from *Pit and the Pendulum*) to promulgating public paranoia, from easy access of private information to the easy, unregulated use of surveillance equipment. While Norman's reports promote a public outcry, he quickly becomes the biggest offender in the film.

However, as a rumination on voyeurism, the film falls far behind such classics as Hitchcock's *Rear Window*, Tavernier's *Death Watch*, and Powell's *Peeping Tom*. The film simply ends with John and Sally becoming the subjects of voyeuristic neighbors themselves as the scoptophilic urge spreads throughout society. Made for a mere $130,000, the film suffers from compromises and ended up pleasing no one, and its distributor, National General, soon went belly up.

At the end of the year, Szwarc directed an oddball pilot, *Weekend Nun*, starring Joanna Pettet as Sister Mary Damian, a nun who doubles as a probation officer. (The unrealized series was based on the true-life story of Joyce Duco.)

Thomas Page wrote a novel called *The Hephaestus Plague* which features a series of hitherto unknown carbon-munching insects who surface from the bowels of the Earth after an earthquake and who can create fire, are superintelligent, eat meat, and kill. Famed horror producer William Castle bought the rights to the novel and collaborated on a script with Page, retitling the project *Bug*. He asked Szwarc what he thought of the script and signed him as the director. Together they assembled a cast which included Bradford Dillman, Joanna Miles, Patty McCormack, Richard Gilliland, and Jamie Smith Jackson. Szwarc was intrigued by the challenge of making a character out of cockroaches.

For the relentless and unstoppable incendiary creations, Castle went to insect specialist Ken Middleham, who worked on the infamous "beware the insect" documentary *The Hellstrom Chronicle*, and he procured some six-inch Madagascar giant cockroaches that live in bat guano that had been imported by the agricultural school at the University of California, Riverside. While Castle was pleased at procuring something that created universal repulsion, Szwarc discovered that his cast was not too pleased to have giant cockroaches crawling on them.

The subsequent generation of bugs turn into large flying insects. These scenes were achieved by photographing ordinary flies sprinkled with red phosphorescent powder. Another impressive shot where the roaches spell out "We Live" was achieved by Middleham anesthetizing the roaches and placing them in the final configuration, then shooting them in reverse as they woke up and became active.

Castle, who was famous for his gimmicks, suggested putting windshield wipers under patrons' theater seats to simulate the actions of the critters in theaters, but exhibitors declined installing anything which might inadvertently create a panic. Castle accepted, knowing that the real thing would be crawling across patrons' legs in some of America's older cinemas for free anyway. His only publicity gimmick wound up being his taking a million dollar insurance policy out on one of the giant roaches.

The result of all this effort is one very strange and

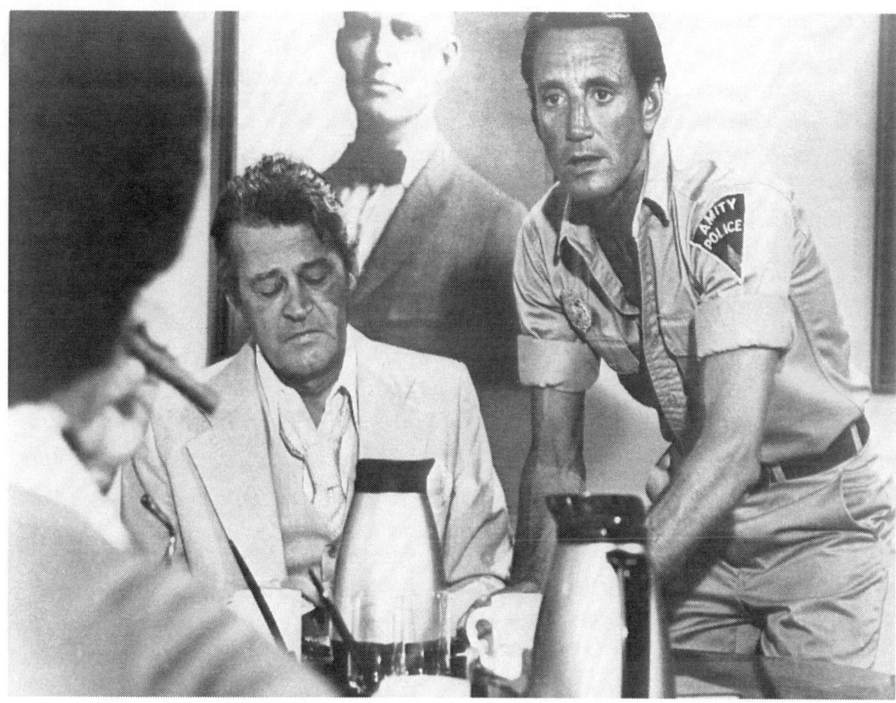

Murray Hamilton and Roy Scheider returned as Amity's mayor and chief of police in Szwarc's *Jaws 2.*

offbeat movie. *Bug* won both the Jury and Audience Prizes at the Paris Science Fiction Film Festival. The $600,000 feature had the misfortune of opening on the same day as *Jaws*, the biggest hit of the summer, and it was effectively squashed by the competition.

Ironically, *Jaws* led to Szwarc's greatest opportunity. *Jaws 2* was turned down by several other directors, including Steven Spielberg, when the original director, John Hancock, left the production after four weeks of principal photography. (Hancock saw the movie as a horror film while producers Zanuck and Brown thought they were making an adventure film.) The directors approached by the producers to take over wanted at least six months preproduction time before taking the project over, but Universal was committed to a summer release date. Editor Verna Fields recommended Szwarc on the basis of his cheaply executed earthquake scene from *Bug*, and *Jaws* production designer Joe Alves echoed her sentiments.

Szwarc leapt at the chance despite being given only three weeks to prepare. "But it was a nightmare," he said. "There were only two minutes of usable film and *Jaws 2* was three times more difficult than *Jaws* because it was almost entirely shot on water." Szwarc brought in Carl Gottlieb to rewrite Dorothy Tristan's script and knew that audiences would not be as willing to only catch a glimpse of the rubber white shark as they had in the first film.

Round the clock work on the movie to meet the deadline cost Szwarc his second marriage. He later married script supervisor Kara De Menaul in 1985. To complete the film on time, Szwarc arranged four different camera units to shoot simultaneously. Hating the script, Szwarc decided to retain the time-consuming action sequences of the last third, which he shot first, while the first portion of the script was extensively rewritten over five weeks. Complicating matters was the problem that the mechanical shark never did the same thing twice in a row, so concepts had to be constantly revamped. The production was also plagued by unseasonable cold, an invasion of jellyfish, and an invasion of butterflies in the middle of what was supposed to be the film's most horrifying scene.

In *Jaws 2*, the mayor of Amity Island (Murray Hamilton) seems to have learned nothing from the experiences of the first film. He fires Brody for causing a panic when Brody mistakes a large school of fish for a shark, draws a gun, and screams at tourists to clear the area. Brody is concerned because a photo in a dead scuba diver's camera shows what appears to him to be a shark fin.

Sure enough, two teens, Tina and Ed, (Ann Dusenberry and Gary Dubin) sail to a secluded spot when Ed is suddenly tossed out of the boat and eaten by another Great White Shark. Brody rescues Tina and learns that his suspicions have been right all along. He also learns that his two sons have elected just then to go on a boating picnic.

Panicked, he initiates a search of the area. In the film's most ludicrous scene, a helicopter pilot spots the boys adrift on their boats and lowers his chopper to tow them to safety when the Great White leaps from the sea to drag the whirlybird under. As Brody commandeers a small cruiser to investigate, the shark stalks the stranded kids. In the film's finale, Brody tricks the shark into chomping on an electrified cable, creating the world's biggest fish fry.

To explain the *Jaws* phenomenon, Szwarc came up with a theory centered around racial memory. He believes that deep in the recesses of our minds is the recollection of the prehistoric hunt. Kill or be killed. Eat or be eaten. Winning out over a mastodon must have been the ultimate catharsis, the original game-state. Szwarc believes that the need for the thrill lies right under our skin and often needs expression. We recreate it through amusements such as rollercoasters, scary movies and, most recently, electronic games.

Jaws 2 did well as expected, and Universal executives felt they owed Szwarc one. Szwarc selected as his follow-up project an adaptation of Richard Matheson's novel *Bid Time Return,* which was filmed as *Somewhere in Time.* "It is a pure romantic fantasy, and the most unusual film this town has seen in a long time," was how Szwarc described his film to *Cinefantastique.* "The way it happened was that I had just finished *Jaws 2,* and was getting a lot of offers. Ray Stark called me in for a big meeting. He had this big, big project—kind of a space opera—and he wanted to get me involved in it. I told him it was not that I wasn't interested, but that I didn't want to do another huge picture [right] after *Jaws 2.* He asked me what I was looking for, and I said a romantic fantasy—something like *Portrait of Jennie* or *The Ghost and Mrs. Muir.* Stephen Deutsch was handling business affairs for Stark's company. He practically jumped in the air, and said they had this book by Richard Matheson, but no one had clicked to it yet. I read it that night, and called back the next morning to say I wanted this to be my next project."

Christopher Reeve plays a playwright who travels back in time to find his lost love, played by Jane Seymour, in Jeannot Szwarc's *Somewhere in Time.*

Reportedly, none of the top execs understood the script, but Verna Fields was very supportive, and having Christopher Reeve agree to star proved a big break. Universal was so pleased with the way *Somewhere in Time* turned out, that they released it in 800 theaters where the $5.5 million production performed badly. Szwarc felt that the film needed a slow build-up campaign. *Somewhere in Time* has become something of a cult item and has gained in popularity from cable showings. Its John Barry score is one of Barry's very finest and has earned a cult reputation all of its own.

Richard Matheson, who based his script on his novel *Bid Time Return,* may well be the film's biggest fan. Matheson replaces Collier's terminal disease from the novel with the more identifiable gimmick of the character's vague dissatisfaction with his present life. Matheson was present on the Mackinac Island locations and even appears in the film as a man who is shocked by Collier's appearance after he attempts to shave. As a supremely sentimental romantic love story about destined but doomed lovers, the film deserves some respect, but despite a time travel story, its science fictional elements are minimal.

Szwarc and cinematographer Isadore Mankofsky decided to differentiate between the scenes set in 1980 and those taking place 70 years earlier by employing two different film stocks. Crisp-looking Kodak stock was used for the modernday scenes, while soft-focusing Fujicolor was used for the past. Szwarc also decided to use long lenses and realistic lighting for the present, and used wide angle lenses and mood lighting to distinguish the bygone era.

Christopher Reeve stars as Chicago playwright Richard Collier, who on the evening of the opening of his new play is greeted by an old woman (Susan French) who pleads, "Come back to me." Years later, suffering from writer's block, Collier stops off at the Grand Hotel and becomes enchanted with a photo of Elise McKenna (Jane Seymour), a once highly acclaimed stage actress. (To indicate love at first sight, Szwarc has light obliterate the lens momentarily so that the portrait appears out of a white haze.) Collier decides to do some research and discovers that the old woman was McKenna, who died the next day.

Consulting with Dr. Gerald Finney (George Voskovec), Collier comes to believe that it is possible to simply will himself back into the past. (The doctor's name Finney is a tribute to Jack Finney, who wrote the classic time travel novel *Time and Again,* as well as the novel basis for *Invasion of the Body Snatchers.*) For him to succeed, Dr. Finney

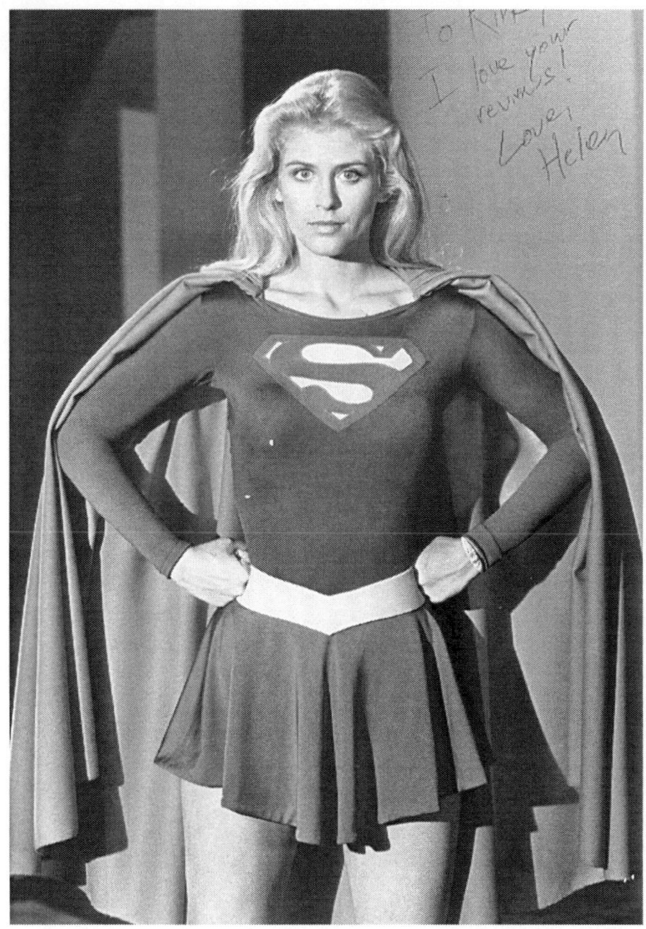

Helen Slater as Supergirl, Szwarc's super campy superhero misfire.

warns, he must remove all vestiges of the 20th century from his environment, anything that might remind him of when he really exists.

Collier purchases a period suit (actually a decade too early in design), purchases some period currency, and prepares his hotel room (although he leaves modern electric lamps over his bed and a modern electrical outlet is clearly evident on the wall). He wills himself to appear at the hour of Miss McKenna's arrival at the Grant Hotel in 1912.

Sure enough, it works. He approaches McKenna, who asks him "Are you the one?" He immediately falls in love with her, but keeps coming up against her manager, W.F. Robinson (Christopher Plummer), who does his best to isolate and protect her from interlopers, having nurtured McKenna's theatrical career from its incipient beginnings.

In a departure from the mores of the time, after Robinson has successfully separated them by arranging to have Collier beaten and bound while McKenna is in mid-performance, Collier and McKenna consummate their love relationship after a very short amount of time. However, their pledges of love prove no avail when Collier unexpectedly fishes a 1980 penny from his coat pocket, propelling him back to the present. There, having lost his one true love, he starves himself to death until he can join her in the afterlife.

In an interview with Jordan Fox, Szwarc explained:

> We wanted them reunited ... because this is a love that transcends time and lasts for eternity. Even though it's sort of a sad ending, I wanted there to be a fulfillment for the audience.
>
> What happens at the end, as the camera starts to go up to the ceiling ... is that his soul becomes the camera. When it reaches the ceiling, it turns down, and he can see himself— the doctor working on his body. Then the camera pans to the window and she's there. At the end when the camera stops, she's looking at the lens. Her eyes register some movement, and he steps in front of the lens. They are together again for all time, back as they were when they first met.

Szwarc hoped to follow the film up with another fantasy, *The Quest*, scripted by Broadway playwright Yale Yudoff (*Bad Timing*) based on a story of Szwarc's about a mythical, medieval land. Szwarc had spent a decade trying to get the project made with no success. The main character was to be a knight who is slowly being consumed by leprosy and who is on a quest to seek out the fabled unicorn to reverse a catastrophic loss. However, the project never came to fruition.

Instead, Szwarc followed *Somewhere in Time* with *Enigma*, a tale of international political intrigue written by John Briley. The head of American intelligence sends Alex Holbeck (Martin Sheen) to East Berlin to retrieve a Russian–coded microprocessor that reveals how five top KGB assassins will murder five leading Soviet dissidents who are attempting to build new lives in the West. Holbeck has been living in Paris and working for Radio Free Europe since his defection from East Germany and to achieve his mission must count on help from his ex-lover Karen (Brigitte Fossey) who lives in East Berlin.

However, he is not the only one who turns to her for help. Dimitri Vassilkov (Sam Neill), a KGB officer who has discovered the American plans to thwart the assassinations, turns to her looking for Alex. Also in the mix is wily East German police chief Limmer (Derek Jacobi), who has been kept in the dark as to what is going on. Unfortunately, Szwarc's film keeps changing its mind about the direction it is going and ends up running into numerous blind alleys. Instead of being taut and tense, it's tepid.

Anxious to recapture the box office gold of the earlier installments of the Superman saga, the Salkinds decided to hire Szwarc to bring Kara, Superman's cousin, to the screen. David Odell wrote the script based on the actual comic book character. While it contains some acceptable comic book spectacles, watered down with some very feeble fantasy,

Supergirl proved to be a disappointment on almost all fronts.

Supergirl reveals that Superman was not the only survivor of the planet Krypton when it exploded. A fragment of Krypton was hurled into inner space where Zaltar (Peter O'Toole) has created a utopian society. Kara, as Supergirl (Helen Slater) is known, lives there with her parents Zor-El (Simon Ward) and Alura (Mia Farrow). These early scenes are the most science fictional and are the best in the movie, which quickly degenerates into an unfunny madcap comedy about magical powers with ho-hum special effects.

The plot has Supergirl traveling from Argo City to Earth to recover the missing and much needed Omegahedron Stone, which powers the city of Argo and has been stolen by the sorceress Selena (a scenery-chewing Faye Dunaway). Coming to Earth gives this extra-terrestrial the same superpowers as her cousin Clark. Instead of using her powers to track down the stone, however, her first step is to enroll in an exclusive boarding school for young ladies, where she changes the color of her hair (which miraculously preserves her secret identity), adopts the name Linda Lee, and finds herself rooming with Lois Lane's kid sister Lucy (Maureen Teefy).

Supergirl comes to fall for Ethan (Hart Bochner), the school's groundsman, but keeps getting distracted by having to contend with some mischief or other that Selena has unleashed, including a violent storm which threatens the school and an invisible monster. Selena seems a low rent sorceress, holed up in a small town carnival spook house near the school, until she uses a Burundi wand of evil to tap into the power of the spinning Omegahedron stone. She then creates for herself a huge fortress atop a tall rock tower and enslaves Ethan and imprisons the people who have bugged her, including her ex-lover Nigel (Peter Cook), the school's math teacher, Jimmy Olson (Mark McClure), and Lucy.

Using her newfound powers, Selena sends Supergirl into the Phantom Zone, where Zaltar, her friend and mentor, has already been imprisoned and where poor Kara loses all her superpowers. Zaltar encourages her not to give up hope, and they climb up a wall so that she can catch a ride on a quantum vortex which transports her back to Earth just in time to save her friends and confront a demon that Selena has conjured up. Good triumphs, the Omegahedron is recovered and returned, and Supergirl swears everyone to secrecy.

Szwarc makes a fatal mistake in not playing the film's campy concept entirely seriously. Going for campy laughs, the movie misfires completely. Additionally, almost everyone delivers dialogue in an arch style that screams bad acting, except for Brenda Vaccaro who plays Selena's sidekick

Director Jeannot Szwarc, whose theatrical career was seemingly derailed after the unbearable badness of *Santa Claus: The Movie.*

Bianca, and except for Slater herself, who in her film debut is able to convey a superheroine that is plucky and highspirited and exhibits a sort of untouched freshness. Incredibly enough, in Japan the feature ran some 20 minutes longer than it did in the U.S., but rather than being a delight, the film was already something of an endurance test.

However, it was Szwarc's next movie for the Salkinds that truly proved to be a career killer. Hoping to create a seasonal perennial, the Salkinds hired David and Leslie Newman to craft *Santa Claus,* which quickly succumbed to a terminal case of the cutes. (The film was advertised as *Santa Claus: The Movie,* but the title onscreen is simply *Santa Claus.*)

Szwarc's direction is uninspired, but there is certainly nothing here that would inspire him. The film introduces Santa (David Huddleston) and Mrs. Claus (Judy Cornwell) as a kindly couple who cobble together toys for their north country neighbors which they give every Christmas. One snowy Christmas they freeze to death in the snow, only to awake and be visited by a group of elves who take them to an enchanted toy shop filled with even more elves.

There an ancient elf (Burgess Meredith) with a extra-long white beard informs them that Santa is the chosen one and that he will provide toys for all the children of the world, be able to fly, and stop time long enough to get the massive job done. The Clauses are delighted with their new vocation.

Then the film focuses on the antics of Patch (Dudley Moore mugging for all he's worth), a mischievous elf, whose fellows have names like Boog, Vout, and Honka, who is always off working on some half-baked invention or another, and is always referring to things like "elf-confidence," "elf-control," and "elf-assurance" until you want to hit the cheerful fellow with a very large mallet.

Then *Santa Claus* switches focus once again, contrasting two New York kiddies whom Santa tries to help, Joe (Christian Fitzpatrick), a street urchin who does not believe in Christmas until he gets to ride with Santa in his sleigh, and Cornelia (Carrie Kei Heim), a poor little rich girl seeking love. Both are contrived and neither is affecting or even interesting as characters.

When Santa's toys suddenly begin to break and are returned to the North Pole, Patch gets the blame and runs off to New York where he meets toy tycoon B. Z. (John Lithgow, woefully misused), currently under investigation for making unsafe toys, who could not be more delighted when the errant elf offers to create magical playthings for free.

Things get worse as Santa, discouraged that his toys have been rejected, considers calling Christmas off, while B. Z. chortles and makes plans for a sequel, "We'll call it Christmas II!" If that is not enough to make you gag, Santa is transformed into an action hero and flies to the rescue in his magic sleigh when B. Z. kidnaps Joe. Then the pair team up and save Patch while B. Z. blows himself into outer space by eating too much of Patch's magical, explosive candy. Christmas is saved from encroaching technology.

Santa Claus proved to be one of the biggest bombs ever unloaded on a highly suspicious public, and is so bad, that subjecting children to it could be considered a form of severe punishment. It is hard to encapsulate the sheer awfulness of this treacly, wrongheaded film with its hideous primary colors design, its overly sanctimonious sentiment, and its razzle-dazzle bright light effects intended to blind audiences to their shortcomings. By crafting it, Szwarc sent himself to cinematic perdition, apparently ending his once promising feature film career.

However, he continued to labor on in the television vineyards, and contributed direction to two episodes of the revived *Twilight Zone* series. One of these was George R. Martin's adaptation of Roger Zelazny's "The Last Defender of Camelot," which starred Richard Kiley as the wizard Merlin who wakes from one thousand years of sleep and seeks to install a new Arthur on the throne in order to re-establish Camelot. Szwarc also directed "Red Snow," in which a KGB colonel is sent to a Siberian gulag to investigate the death of two loyal party officials only to find a town inhabited by vampires.

Since then, Szwarc has worked overseas or on television movies-of-the-week.

ANDREI TARKOVSKY (1932–1986)

There Will Be No Leave Today (1959, short); *Katok i skripka* (aka *Steamroller and the Violin*; 1960 student film); *Ivanovo detstvo* (aka *Ivan's Childhood*; *My Name Is Ivan*) (1962); *Andrei Rublev* (1966); *Solaris* (1972); *Zerkalo* (aka *The Mirror; A White White Day*) (1974); *The Stalker* (1981); *Nostalghia* (1984); *Offret* (aka *The Sacrifice; Sacrificatio*) (1986)

Andrei Tarkovsky is relatively unknown in the United States, but his international reputation is immense. His debut film, *Ivan's Childhood*, won the Grand Prize at three major film festivals, and he's won three more awards at Cannes (including another Grand Prize, a Critics' Prize, and the Director's Jury Award) for his subsequent work. His film *Andrei Rublev* was acclaimed one of the top dozen films of all time in one critical survey.

He only managed to make a half dozen film over a two decade period and was almost consistently in disfavor with his own government, the old USSR, which shelved three of his films for up to five years each, refused all of his projects for another six, and which refused a request to submit *The Mirror* to the Cannes Film Festival despite being informed that it was likely to be a Grand Prize winner.

Nevertheless, during his lifetime, Tarkovsky insisted that he made five of his films inside the Soviet Union exactly as he wanted to with no commercial or ideological constraints ... until afterwards. He is also responsible for three of the most demanding science fiction films ever made, the

Andrei Tarkovsky, maker of three of the most demanding science fiction films of all time.

hypnotic *Solaris*, the philosophical *Stalker*, and post-apocalyptic *Sacrifice*.

Tarkovsky was the son of Arsenei Tarkovsky, a well-known poet, and was born in Laovrazhe, Ivanova district, Soviet Union, on April 4, 1932. He felt deeply indebted to his mother, Maria Ivanova Vishnyakova, who wanted him to become an artist. "We lived in terrible circumstances of poverty and hardship," he said, "but this woman brought great significance to our lives. We were very poor, during the war, and after the war — and *before* the war — I remember how my mother, after the war, would go out to the countryside and gather flowers, and take them to the city, and tie them into bouquets, and sell them at the railroad station...."

He studied at Moscow's Institute of Oriental Languages, majoring in Arabic. He then switched to the Soviet State Film School (VGIK) where he studied under Mikhail Romm. His early student films were written by Andrei Mikhalkov-Konchalovsky, who later scripted *Andrei Rublev* for him as well before becoming a famed director himself.

His work is notable for depicting a world that is slow, stately serene and eerily beautiful, a world of silences that stretch along inexorably, a still, oppressive, spiritual world that invites contemplation, that discloses landscapes of the mind, regions of the soul, regions that inspire, terrify, exalt, and mesmerize.

He felt that directors could be divided into two camps: those who attempt to realize or present the actual world, and those who are concerned with presenting their internal selves, and placed himself in the latter category along with such other poetic directors as Bergman, Buñuel, Mizoguchi, Kurosawa, Vigo and Bresson.

He also felt that art is more national than international in form. People in other cultures will perceive things differently than a creator's own contemporaries would in their own culture. "Art can have a national meaning, and an international — or 'transnational' meaning and context; they're not necessarily the same," he said. "Your spiritual values belong to you, and you alone: to your own eye, your own self. Their only assessment can be from my own point of view. I can like, I can respect, your spiritual being — but I cannot receive it, and sense it, as you can. You simply cannot translate culture adequately; it is always perceived differently. It is *never* the same."

His student film, *The Steamroller and the Violin,* won a prize at the New York Film Festival and was about the friendship that develops between the tough driver of a steamroller and a frail boy violinist who is drawn out of his claustrophobic world into the wider and more challenging one outside. The cinematographer was Vadim Yusov, who would go on to photograph all of his films, and the script was the work of future director Andrei Mikhalkov-Konchalovsky.

Tarkovsky's most accessible work remains his first, *Ivan's Childhood* (aka *My Name Is Ivan*). Ivan (Kolya Burlayev) is an 11-year-old boy surviving on the Russian front in World War II. As the Nazis have killed his mother and sister, the only family he has are the soldiers for whom he serves as a scout. The only moments of happiness he can know are memories of his "childhood" when he was five which come back to him nightly in dreams.

In one of the film's most haunting shots, Tarkovsky's camera glides in close-up along the sleeping Ivan's bare arm, which stands out as whitely as a lunar surface against the spacey blackness of the room, stopping at his fingertip, which twitches as water drips down upon it from the ceiling. The camera then pans up, and there, illuminated in the distance, we see a much younger Ivan, framed by the mouth of a well into which he's dropping pebbles. For Ivan, his present is so burnt-out by his hard life that he has nowhere to go except his past. It is a film filled with yearning and heartbreak at the world's many heedless and pitiless cruelties.

When his comrades invade Berlin at the end of the war, they learn of his capture and ultimate fate. His parents have been killed, his village destroyed, he has escaped from a Nazi concentration camp, and lived only for revenge until he was taken. Tarkovsky creates incredible tension in his tableaux of childhood and warfare, which are constantly contrasted. From the outset, the poor boy's fate is sealed, and Tarkovsky eschews any phony cheer or hysteria. The film won 15 awards at international film festivals, including Venice's Golden Lion and San Francisco's Grand Prize.

Andrei Rublev is a three hour epic about a 15th century monk who painted icons. Set roughly in Russia in 1400, superstitious Christians are engaged in a witchhunt for countless heretics, which range from scientifically minded pagans attempting flight in hot-air balloons to sexually liberated individuals indulging in free love and witches' sabbats — offenses punishable by death at the stake. Russia itself is little more than a patchwork of openly warring principalities who are constantly threatened by Mongol invasion.

In contrast to this violent landscape is the gentle artist-monk Andrei Rublev (magnificently played by Anatoli Solonitsin), whom Tarkovsky depicts as a man in vivid balance against the dynamic world around him. Given the anti-Christian sentiments of the Soviet regime, the film daringly presents Christianity in all its complexity, as an unshakable belief, a sexual barrier, a life-giving force, a defining agent of artistic vision, a vow of silence, a call for expression.

"His whole urge was toward the future," Tarkovsky once told an interviewer, "and therein lies his genius." The film was completed in 1966, was finally shown at Cannes in 1969, and was not released in Russia until 1971, by which time it had an enormous underground reputation. The film dramatizes the human responses to war, disorder and oppression, as well as meditates on the responsibility of the artist to express Man's ideas.

Tarkovsky's next film, *Solaris*, was an adaptation of a metaphysical science fiction novel by Polish writer Stanislaw Lem. ("It was very difficult to work with Stanislaw Lem on the film *Solaris*," Tarkovsky commented. "[H]e rejected everything that was done. He didn't like it very much. He insisted: 'You must follow each detail, exactly what was in the book.' He did not understand that that way, you don't get a movie.")

As Michael Ventura noted in the *L.A. Weekly*:

> Neither Tarkovsky nor his audience has been influenced by the swiftness of Western television cutting. He feels free to look at a thing for as long as it pleases him — and he liked the effect of making you look so long that you get uncomfortable and then vaguely frightened. His visual sense is almost more a painter's than a film director's. He moves his camera very slowly about the untended [space] station, with its blank walls and random rubble ... clutter, unexplained gadgets. Against this backdrop he photographs the incredible faces of these Russian players with the relish of a portrait painter — faces literally etched with their identity, or, to use a less psychological word, their souls.

While *Solaris* was compared to Kubrick's *2001: A Space Odyssey*, the comparison is more to the metaphysical subtexts of both films rather than any comparable majesty of sensuous gimmickry or comic book hardware. People in Tarkovsky's universe travel to and from their distant space station as blankly as they might ride an elevator — one is reminded of the interspace highways from Jean-Luc Godard's *Alphaville*.

The main setting is a space station above a world with an endless sea, which may or may not be alive, but which contains a vastness that people can lose themselves in. *Solaris* is suffused with a sense of alienness entirely unique to science fiction films.

According to Snouth, the oldest of three scientists hovering in the space station above the planet Solaris' great ocean, "We don't want other worlds, we want a mirror. We don't want to explore space, we want merely to extend Earth's boundaries. Science? Nonsense. In this situation genius and mediocrity are equally helpless." In exploring the universe, does man ultimately wish to seek the new or return to the familiar? Why is there the persistent myth that Paradise is a city we left long, long ago, and that if we keep searching, we can find it again?

Trapped in this isolated environment, the scientists' mental and emotional survival comes into question. The characters all experience a sense of the loss of wholeness, and their crumbling environment reflects their loss and their apparent lack of concern for where they are at present. *Solaris*' scientists are men who feel what they can't bring themselves to think, and think what they can't bear to feel.

The planet Solaris is one huge brain in the form of an ocean, which reflects like a mirror. It has the power to conjure forth, from each of the scientist's subconscious, the figure from the past with whom they most desire reconciliation. It creates that living being right there in the space station with them — alive, human, but with extraordinary powers.

It serves as a metaphor for memory; for the people of our memories who haunt us, who because they are in our heads are much more powerful, much more one-sided, much more emphatic, than the variously human beings who inspired those memories within us. These living memories prove stronger than the living men themselves. The men, whose humanity is never very pronounced, are overwhelmed and their identities obliterated.

The hero Kris Kelvin (Donatas Banionis) remains a troubled cypher who is metaphorically stuck at the top of an elevator in a psychic World Trade Center with no company apart from his memories, dreams, and the ghosts of his loved ones whom he has betrayed. At the opening of the film, he is about to leave his country homestead (a drizzly, damp, evocative landscape) on a mission, and we see that he has difficulty expressing his love for his father and is distanced from him (Tarkovsky loves using screens, glasses, windows and other visual obstructions to convey how people are cut off from one another both physically and emotionally).

Through the powers of Solaris' ocean-brain, Kelvin's late wife Hari (Natalya Bondarchuk), who committed suicide, is brought back to life. She lives with him in the space station, sometimes making idyllic love, sometimes literally ripping through a steel wall to get to him. Sadly, she is shown to be an especially vengeful spirit. She appears to him again and again with a heartbreakingly touchable, physical reality — with which she torments him by committing suicide again and again, each time by a different means. The greatest distances between the characters are therefore not spatial but psychological.

To rid himself of her painful presence, Kelvin tricks Hari into a space shuttle and fires it off to the sound of her inhuman screeching, but even this does not prevent her from materializing yet again. We understand when Snouth, watching her painful rebirth, laconically observes, "I can't get used to these resurrections." Snouth deflates Kelvin, who tries to insist that the construct really is his wife, by telling him, "Kelvin, don't turn a scientific problem into a bedroom farce."

The problem facing Kelvin is his now apparent ability to have a physical, human relationship with the embodiment of his own lost innocence. In doing so, he has traveled into a new and different kind of "space." Kelvin's worn face reveals his inner despair and only seems complete when he is looking into the fresh and sorrowful young face of Hari, faces we are meant to contemplate at great length. The unspoken emotions are enough to fill a Russian novel.

Tarkovsky believes audiences should patiently contemplate his images to unlock the mysteries of their meaning, with his slow moving camera taking in languid images of decay and despair, indicating that the station that was once a proud achievement has been untended for so long that it now lies in ruins. Or he shows us faces of the characters etched with their identity. It is very easy for audiences to become restless and impatient with his work. We expect action and resolution, but Tarkovsky seems content to simply test our patience until we seem to be inhabiting the same dislocated, fragmentary, isolated extreme of the characters who have been cut off from mortal boundaries, and even experience inexplicable momentary weightlessness.

In one sequence, Kelvin and Hari are in the station's library holding one another as they begin to float. A light candelabra floats near them, but other objects in the room do not float. The other books in the room remain in their places except for a copy of *Don Quixote* that wafts past them with the page open to that famous engraving (suggestive of the false realities of the mind) when everything takes its weight again and the film lumbers on.

To save Kelvin from further distress, Hari quaffs liquid oxygen to commit suicide yet again and she finally stops appearing. Was she sent as a message from Solaris? Kelvin does not know, and in the end, he descends to the planet's watery surface to discover a temporary island drenched by rain with an old Russian house on its surface. There Kelvin once more sees his father, only he is now a phantom himself that his father neither sees nor hears, once more expressing the poignant gulfs between people.

Kelvin in quintessentially patient, coming to the conclusion, "All that remains is to wait. For what? I don't know. Fresh miracles." Tarkovsky has explained that the point of the film is "the value of each piece of our behavior, the significance of each of our acts, even the least noticed. Nothing once completed can be changed.... The irreversibility of human experience is what gives our life, our deeds, their meaning and individuality."

The Mirror is one of Tarkovsky's most challenging and abstract if autobiographical films. A man whom we do not see sifts through memories, dreams, combinations of the two, parental memories, and bits of his unhappy present life in search of an elusive truth about his mother. In form, it is the subjective biography of Tarkovsky himself as a boy in the Stalin era.

The Mirror is the cinematic equivalent of abstract-expressionism. Isolated images and fragmentary scenes of great power are juxtaposed in conflicting, enigmatic sequences: children feed strawberries and cream to a black cat as they pour white sugar on its head; a barn on fire; newsreel footage of battle weary Soviet soldiers circa World War II; a boy enters a freshly deserted room and makes out a circle of breath-fog that the departing occupant left on a polished table top. (Many images are taken from newsreels of the Spanish Civil War and the Soviet-Chinese confrontations on the Ussuri River.)

The film forces on its viewer an act of creation — to make personal sense of the fragmentary, abstract scenes that Tarkovsky presents. For most Western audiences, this film will be a grueling ordeal that remains frustrating in its opacity. Perhaps like the famous Browning quote, when he created it, only God and Tarkovsky knew what it meant, and now that Tarkovsky is gone, only God knows. Nevertheless, the film has its adherents who consider it an achievement on a par with *8½* or *Persona*.

The film's anti–Stalinism caused it to be harshly criticized as an elitist film. It was released in Russia in 1974, but relegated to Category Three, meaning that only a few prints were made to be shown in third-rate cinemas and workers' clubs, thereby denying the filmmakers any financial return on their investment.

Tarkowsky returned to science fiction with *Stalker*, based on the story "Roadside Picnic" by the Russian science fiction writing team of the Sturgasky brothers. Compared to *The Mirror*, *Stalker*'s story is straightforward and linear, and like *Solaris*, it echoes something of the idea of a pilgrimage to a mystical, metaphorical place. It was made in 1979 after the five year impasse that followed *Mirror*.

The film seems to indiscriminately mix black and white with color footage, with the black and white primarily confined to the drab, everyday world and the color footage depicting the "Zone," a mysterious, metaphysical region created when a meteorite or a spaceship crashed. All that's known is that half a century ago, there was a massive explosion or earthquake at the center of the country.

According to an opening title, "Troops were sent into the region to investigate, but disappeared.... Others who explored the area also never returned." The government has responded by creating a huge barbed wire barrier and declaring the Zone off limits. A rumor has sprung up that somewhere in the heart of the region there's a room in the Zone that once reached will grant the traveler his or her deepest wish, and that is the real reason the government has strictly declared the region off limits.

The Stalker of the title is a modest family man who for a small fee leads people into and out of the Zone (thereby risking arrest and jail every time he does so) for the express purpose of guiding them to the fabled room, which he has never entered himself. He simply accepts his harsh life, otherwise spending his time with his daughter, who is genetically affected by the otherworldly force fields he spends his life in. When the film opens, the Stalker has just returned from spending five years in Siberia.

A Scientist and a Writer come to him to escort them through the Zone. (As in an allegory, the characters are never truly named, only described by their professions.) The Scientist wants to make some tests, take some measurements. The Writer hopes to bring back an important story. The Stalker's wife is livid when he agrees to take them. "Your daughter barely knows you," she seethes. "You just got back from prison."

"Prison is everywhere for me," he truthfully replies. Tarkovsky underlines his point by showing us the squalidness of their little flat which is constantly invaded by the sounds of coupling trains and the din of a nearby factory which is so loud that it shakes their furniture. The sooty, desolate city they live in is constantly patrolled by the military, who are more like prison guards than protectors.

The trio begin an agonizingly slow, arduous journey through a hallucinatory landscape which metaphorically depicts ideas about faith, idealism, Slavic hopelessness, art, and other deeply contemplative subjects. The Scientist considers the room he is seeking dangerous and asserts that it should be destroyed by a bomb, for example, because what if a Hitler reached it and wished for world domination?

The Writer too wrestles with his soul. "Writing comes out of suffering and self-torment," he declares. "If I go back to that God-forsaken city of ours a genius, why write?"

"The room doesn't work that way at all," the Stalker tells them. "You'll see." He explains why he can never enter the room. To be a good guide, he must keep his own intentions pure. His teacher, the previous Stalker, made the mistake of entering the room with the intention of wishing for the health of an ailing relative. Instead, the room answered his innermost, more genuine wish that he be a wealthy man, which is not what he wanted to wish for. "He killed himself three weeks later," the Stalker explains. We come to realize that the Stalker has realized his wish by never entering the room. He simply wishes to be a Stalker.

There are long stretches where literally nothing seems to be happening, apparently inserted to give viewers opportunities to simply sit and think about the ideas Tarkovsky is presenting. As a consequence, the film's long silent stretches can be exhausting, akin not so much to watching paint dry, but to watching dry paint.

Still, the cinematography is crispy, silvery, and powerfully composed. The faces of the actors (Alexander Kaidanovsky, Nikolai Grinko, Anatoli Solonitsin) are exquisitely expressive, as if one may observe an idea slowly taking form behind their weary eyes.

As critic and Tarkovsky fan F. X. Feeney has put it, "Tarkovsky, whose work always gives Soviet cultural overseers trouble, has found here a fine personal idiom — I'm thinking in particular of the scene where the trio has to cross the border to the Zone through barbed wire fences and machine gun fire — which he can freely express inner life, its demons and terrors in a fashion that can be applied to his homeland's politics, while keeping his own tread gracefully free of any tyrannical toes. *Stalker*'s very tortuousness is eloquent."

On its deepest level, *The Stalker* is more than an examination of the complex idea that one's secret desires are often the opposite of what we want to believe, it is rather an examination of the meaning of faith. Though it brings to mind Theresa of Avila's admonition, "More tears are shed in this life over answered prayers than over unanswered ones," and Stendahl's quip, "Beware your heart's desire — you'll get it," it ultimately deals with men confronting indestructible truths about themselves and having faith enough to trust that the discovery of this truth is worth knowing and worth wishing for.

Nostalghia was cowritten by Tonino Guerra, a frequent collaborator of Antonioni and Fellini, and is dedicated to the memory of Tarkovsky's mother. In it, Tarkovsky tackles a theme similar to that of Dostoyevsky's *The Idiot*, which he hoped one day to adapt, that of how pure goodness could exist in a world filled with darkness, contention, and horror as Gortchakov (Oleg Yanovsky) goes to Italy to study the life of a Russian who lived there in the 17th century. The character of Domenico (Erland Josephson) represents goodness for Tarkovsky, which he believed stemmed from sacrificing one's self. "We don't understand ourselves enough to be good to other people," he said. "We were trained to think that to love oneself is to be an egoist. But, in reality, to love oneself is to sacrifice oneself."

Nostalghia was Tarkovsky's first film to be shot outside

of the Soviet Union, and was filmed mostly near the Vigoni thermal baths in the Tuscan hills of Italy. The film does become visually redundant as we are offered shots of the same damp landscapes, marshes, hills in fog, and abandoned buildings with leaky roofs over and over again. However, this did not prevent the film from winning a special prize at the Cannes film festival.

In 1983, Tarkovsky directed a production of *Boris Gudonov* at Covent Garden in London, and then in July 1984, he defected to the West after his petition to extend his stay abroad went unanswered and he was informed that he would not be allowed to make more films upon his return. He elected to remain in Western Europe.

Tarkovsky's final film before dying of cancer was *The Sacrifice*, which demands that you give yourself over to it completely, which means enduring "dreadful, sickening, animal fear," lots of metaphysical discussion, as well as concerns about nuclear apocalypse, a birthday party, lovemaking with a witch, and a fire. The whole enterprise has a detached air, much like its protagonist, Alexander (Erland Josephson), a spiritually empty Swedish intellectual and one-time actor who lives in an elegant home by the sea.

The Sacrifice was shot by Sven Nykvist on location in Gotland in the Baltic. It was produced by Svensk Filmindustri with additional funds from Swedish and American television and from a French company. Like all of Tarkovsky's film, it is a slow, visually beautiful and intensely personal work.

The film opens with a seemingly endless take of Alexander planting a tree by the marshy shore with his silent son "Little Man," when they are interrupted by a loquacious postman (Allan Edwall) who wants to discuss Nietzsche, Alexander's birthday, and man's relationship to God.

During Alexander's subsequent birthday party, Armageddon comes with a roar of jets, a rattling of walls, and spilt milk (a Tarkovsky trademark), while the TV news intones, "No place is safe, May God protect you." Judgment Day has come and the sinners find themselves unprepared. Alexander's wife has a harrowing breakdown as she realizes that she married the wrong man.

"I've been waiting for this all my life," Alexander realizes, and offers to God a sacrifice. If God will only restore the world to its pre-war state, Alexander will give up his house, his son, and stop talking to anyone. Here, earthly loss is seen as the key to spiritual growth. (This has echoes of the Stalker's longing for the "Zone," and of Kelvin in *Solaris* who creates from his desires the family that he lost.)

Initially while filming the 10-minute take which makes up the climax, the film jammed in the camera while an essential prop burned up and had to be rebuilt before shooting could continue. The ultimate meaning of Alexander's sacrifice is not clear, with Tarkovsky unhelpfully noting, "Each episode can be interpreted differently." Alexander wakes up after spending the night with an island woman and finds the landscape returned to its former beauty, but was it just a dream or a perilous journey of the spirit?

Alexander can be seen as either another Prince Myshkin or as a deranged King Lear who thinks he has touched the infinite. The film ends with "Little Man," at last saved, asking, "In the beginning was the Word. Why is that, Papa?" But words fail and there is no answer, except the tree's barren branches against the mysterious, glistening water (another one of Tarkovsky's recurrent and potent symbols).

While as leadenly paced as other Tarkovsky works, Sven Nykvist's cinematography for *The Sacrifice* is visually rich and immaculately detailed, switching once again from color to black and white depending on the mood that Tarkovsky wishes to capture and suggesting that there are levels of reality. The soundtrack is equally meticulous in its beauty, combining Bach with lapping waves, bird cries, Japanese flute music and other melodious sounds.

Once more Tarkovsky concentrates on the basic elements of water, fire, earth and air which have always fascinated him, as well as the theme of an intellectual in search of belief, encountering along the way such stock Tarkovsky characters as an inadequate man of science, a mute or crippled child, and an exalted, nurturing woman.

Tarkovsky died on December 29, 1986, in Paris of lung cancer a few months after *The Sacrifice* opened at the New York Film Festival. He had been married twice, and had a son by his first marriage to Trina Rausch and one by his second marriage to Larissa Tegorkina. He was hailed as a major artist and world-class filmmaker.

In the final analysis, Tarkovsky often seems overly sanctimonious, but he is a true visionary who does achieve a definite artistic integrity, his films display a definite moral seriousness lacking in most other cinematic ventures, and he has, in the words of John Powers, a "luminous sense of the world beyond the screen." His films are not enjoyable in the conventional sense; they are instead tense, agonizing, at sometimes spellbinding, and very demanding. All of his films are artistically rendered and difficult to enjoy except on the most abstract, philosophical level — they have been compared to watching an oil painting to see if it moves — but because Tarkovsky thinks and feels deeply, there are rewards for those patient enough to contemplate his philosophical conundrums which make him one of the most accomplished and artistic directors of science fiction films.

DOUGLAS TRUMBULL (1942–)

Silent Running (1972); *Night of Dreams* (short, 1978); *Brainstorm* (1983); *New Magic*; *Big Ball* (shorts, 1983); *Let's Go; Tour of the Universe* (shorts, 1985); *Leonard's Dream* (short, 1989); *To Dream of Roses* (1990); *Back to the Future ... The Ride* (1991); *The Secret of the Luxor Pyramid: In Search of the Obelisk; Luxor Live? in 3-D; The Theater of Time* (codirected with Arish Fyzee; 1993)

Douglas Trumbull is known as the dean of modern special effects artists. His work on *2001: A Space Odyssey* set a new standard against which all subsequent science fiction productions would be compared. He revolutionized special effects again with his effects work on *Close Encounters of the Third Kind* and *Blade Runner*, which experimented with haze instead of sharpness to add reality to special effects images. His two mainstream features are both genre pieces and are both impressive and problematic. He has since served as a prophet regarding the possible futures of the entertainment industry, exploring new techniques for delivering new entertainment experiences.

Born in Los Angeles, California, on April 8, 1942, Douglas Trumbull became one of the film industry's top special effects artists while in his twenties, and with his development of the Showscan System and Interactive Films, he has pointed the way to possible new futures and developments for a film industry that he has, for now, abandoned.

He was educated at El Camino College in Torrance, California, for a year and a half, taking a basic architectural course which involved some design studies and some illustration. There he developed his enthusiasm for architecture before diverting his attention to drawing and painting. Trumbull then did technical illustrations for advertising firms before joining Graphic Films to work on animated promotional films about outer space for NASA, where he did pictures for the Air Force about the Apollo project as well as a public relations film called *To the Moon and Beyond*, which was exhibited at the New York World's Fair in 1964. Stanley Kubrick saw the film and hired Graphic Films to prepare artwork and preliminary concepts for *2001*.

However, once Kubrick relocated to Borehamwood, Graphic found it too awkward to continue transporting cumbersome artwork overseas and their relationship with Kubrick came to an end. However, Trumbull thought that what Kubrick was doing sounded great, so he called the director up in England and asked if he could come work on it. Kubrick assented and soon Trumbull was flying to England.

While working on the film, Trumbull began to learn the rudiments of cinematography, and in consultation with Kubrick, Wally Veevers, and Tom Howard, began to devise several complex motion control systems, which would revolutionize effects work, as well as the famous slitscan "tunnel of light" which was a centerpiece of the trip sequence near the end of the film. Initially, he was put to work making all of the HAL read-outs on the screens that surround HAL's red eye.

Trumbull had seemingly sprung out of nowhere to become at the age of 23 the co–special effects supervisor for Stanley Kubrick's *2001: A Space Odyssey*, where the hardworking Trumbull found himself involved in every aspect of the film's visual construction at some point, from painting star fields to detailing models.

"I came up with a lot of ideas and contributions that I didn't expect, and that *they* didn't expect," he says in Piers Bizony's *2001: filming the future*. "I got my finger in a lot of pies, and it was terrific. The whole crew — we were all learning as we went along. It was like a film school for me."

In *Wired* magazine, Trumbull told Jeff Greenwald, "When I worked on *2001*— which was my first feature film — I was deeply and permanently affected by the notion that a movie could be like a first person experience. That the movie could be an immersive experience. *2001* was structured in a way that doesn't grab you because of its plot construct, or its suspense, or its dramatic narrative mechanisms. It was an immersive visual experience, in 70mm, on giant Cinerama screens. And it actually became, toward the end of the film, a first-person experience. The normal editorial process just went away, and you, as an audience member, sort of became Dave Bowman and went on this trip."

Trumbull's subsequent career has been dedicated to giving the audience another equally immersive experience. However, when *2001: A Space Odyssey* did win the Academy Award for special effects, he was a bit nonplussed to see Stanley Kubrick taking the credit and the award. Unquestionably, Kubrick's insistent pushing for everyone to be realistic and do their absolute best accounts for much of *2001*'s effects' lasting quality, but that was not the same as actually designing or pulling them off himself.

Trumbull was subsequently hired to photograph the opening and closing sequences to *Candy*, the 1968 spectacular misfired adaptation of Terry Southern and Mason's pseudonymously published "novel," which reads as a series of smutty jokes.

He later crafted the effects for Robert Wise's filming of Michael Crichton's *The Andromeda Strain* before tackling his debut project as a director, *Silent Running*. Trumbull had an idea for a film about a man and three robots on a spacecraft carrying botanical specimens from Earth, and agent Michael Gruskoff encouraged him to develop it into a screen treatment.

Trumbull told Kay Anderson and Shirley Meech of *Cinefantastique*:

> I wrote the treatment for *Silent Running* about [1970]. It was based on the drones — I had the idea for them first, and started designing a story about three drones and a man on a spaceship. Then Mike Cimino, Derek Washburn and Steve Bochco wrote the screenplay, building on this idea. I had seen a movie called *Freaks* by Tod Browning. It was about a group of sideshow people, and one of them ... walked on his hands — it was absolutely incredible. He could stand on one hand and drink a cup held in the other, like a bird perched on a table. And I thought, you could make a robot that way. You could put a robot body on a guy like that and nobody would be able to figure out how it was done. And it works terrifically.

This poster for Trumbull's *Silent Running* brilliantly encapsulates the main elements of its appeal, namely the domed spaceships, the remarkable robots, an ecological message, and Bruce Dern's mesmerizing performance.

Universal became interested in the project, hiring Trumbull to direct and Gruskoff to produce. According to Trumbull, "The screenwriters didn't get what I wanted. Much of what they produced was too violent, vicious and unfeeling.... I wanted a film with compassion and feeling and intregrity. Unfortunately, this is not the industry's forte. I ended up rewriting two-thirds of the script myself. It's not the greatest writing in the world, but at least I pushed the script in the way I wanted it to go."

The final script was credited to Deric Washburn, Michael Cimino, and Steven Bochco. One of the most successful things in the film were the robot drones. The drones were played by real-life legless amputees recruited through a rehabilitation center in Long Beach. The amputees would carry plastic shells that covered up their human dimensions while walking around on their hands, giving the drones human mannerisms.

Trumbull set up an office in a warehouse in Canoga Park, which served as his workshop with an office in the back. There he worked on designing *Silent Running*, producing numerous drawings to create its spaceship setting.

Silent Running began filming on Washington's Birthday, 1971. Three weeks were shot on the U.S.S. *Valley Forge*, an aircraft carrier that was about to be scrapped, which was anchored in the Naval Harbor off Terminal Island near Long Beach. The domes that contain the last remaining forest eco-systems in the solar system were shot in an airport hangar at Van Nuys airport. The entire film, shot in

37 days with four months of optical and other effects work, cost just $1,350,000, while the special effects budget was a mere $70,000.

The story premise of *Silent Running* is that Earth has become so polluted and industrialized that the last remaining forests have been transplanted into domes mounted on giant space freighters which have been set in orbit around Saturn. As the story begins, the four man crew of the spaceship *Valley Forge* are told that the freighters have been recalled and that they are to jettison and destroy the domes, which would be potential hazards to navigation. While three of the crewmen rejoice, Freeman Lowell (an acting *tour de force* by Bruce Dern) rebels, ultimately killing his comrades and notifying the authorities that there has been an accident. The film's title derives from submarine jargon about running undetected, and this is what Lowell hopes to do.

As science, this is ludicrous. For one thing, if the freighters are capable of stably orbiting a planet, so are the domes. They could have dropped the domes where they are and left, and then come back and retrieved them years later. There are already lots of different kinds of debris in space, which is so vast that the domes could not present any kind of reasonable navigation hazard. However, apart from the visual aspect, there is no real reason for the ships to be so far away from the sun as Saturn, and the ships could just as easily have dropped the domes into an orbit around the sun on their way back to Earth.

There are indications that each dome is meant to be an enclosed ecological system, especially as the huge ships could not contain enough air, water, and fertilizer to keep the forests going indefinitely, though Trumbull undercuts this by allowing crewmen to barrel through them in electric cars through wide portals that would be disruptive to the ecosystem inside.

Yet, despite these and other failings, the film works, and not just because of the fine effects, which include impressive shots of nuclear flares thundering in the soundless void of space and brackets clanging apart, and the impressive pull-back shot that takes Lowell from his space kitchen window and pulls back to finally reveal a fleet of ships in outer space.

The story works because it has a complex character at its emotional core. Lowell is a passionate man who harangues his buddies when they prefer prepackaged junk over his homegrown vegetables, who babbles optimistically about getting the job of head forester when the domes are finally returned to Earth, who has visions of grassy meadows and balmy breezes that no longer exist back home. The other characters are simply cyphers, we get no idea why they chose to become part of this project in the first place, so when Lowell kills them to protect and preserve his forests, we do not feel as if he is a raving lunatic. (He is greatly abetted in this not only by Trumbull's surehanded direction and Dern's subtle acting, but also by Peter Shickele's sensitive score which conveys the character's emotional state very effectively.)

The full impact of what he has done does not hit Lowell immediately. Initially, he is simply scared but resourceful, then lonely and remorseful. He takes the service drones and baptizes them Huey, Dewey, and Louie after Donald Duck's three nephews. They become his only companions and he needs them to repair an injury to his knee and to keep him company.

Louie ends up lost when the ship passes through the outermost ring of Saturn. Huey and Dewey are taught how to play poker and even learn to cheat. (Like most movie robots, they are slightly anthropomorphized.) Trumbull keeps the film from falling into slapstick or maudlin sentimentality, however, and the drones do serve a useful purpose in maintaining the garden. When Huey is injured, we feel sorry for him as if he were a pet dog.

Trumbull adds plenty of nice touches that underscore Lowell's sense of loss. For example, he contrasts the sound of the drone's motorized arms with the click of an automated (and highly inefficient) pool table that conveys a sense of simply going through the motions. He has Lowell sighing in solitude as he mopes about the ship.

Most significantly, Lowell comes to realize that he is not the idealist he thought he was. He thought he was a man of principle who killed to save the forests, but when he looks through Huey's black-and-white monitor as it is tending the forest, he sees that the forest is dying. He realizes that he has forsaken his responsibility, that now that he has taught the robots to care for it, he has not been interested enough in the forest to spend time in it and has been neglecting it for weeks while he brooded in his quarters. He cared more for the idea of forests than for the forests themselves.

He works out that the last remaining forest has not been receiving enough light and resolves to die saving it. He could run away aboard his ship and never be caught (the ships searching for him are of the same model and are not likely to be able to overtake him), but he realizes that he is a murderer and he would be alone forever. He needs the humanity he once scorned. But it is not too late to save the forest, which he sends with its caretaking drone like a message in a bottle to explore the heavens while blowing up his ship and himself to cover the tracks. Perhaps some other species somewhere in the galaxy will give these plants and animals a home.

Subsequent to *Silent Running*, Trumbull was hired to provide the special effects for the ill-famed Canadian TV series *The Starlost*, created by Harlan Ellison and then so mangled that he put his pseudonym, Cordwainer Bird on it. The series was set aboard an enormous Space Ark, which houses the last remnants of mankind, with every culture given a separate dome to inhabit. In the Amish community of Cyprus Corners, Devon (Keir Dullea) becomes an outcast when he rebels over not being allowed to marry his beloved, Rachel (Gay Rowen). Complicating matters, he discovers an exit from Cypress Corners that makes him aware for the first time that he is on a spaceship (much like the characters in Heinlein's *Orphans of the Sky*), and that the ship is off course and will crash unless somebody can find the control room and change course. He returns to his community and tries to tell of what he has learned, but is accused of sacrilege.

Devon, Rachel, and Garth (Robin Ward), the man the elders want Rachel to marry, leave the community in a desperate search for the control room in order to save what is left of mankind. Each week they would enter one of the domes and encounter a new community. Shot cheaply on videotape, the series had an ugly look. Footage from Trumbull's *Silent Running* was incorporated, but Trumbull wound up having little to do with the series' subpar effects, which due to Canadian restrictions were largely farmed out to inexperienced students eager to work in television production. The series lasted 16 episodes before the plug was mercifully pulled.

A far greater accomplishment of Trumbull's was achieving a unique look to flying saucers for Steven Spielberg's *Close Encounters of the Third Kind*, for which he received an Academy Award Nomination for Best Special Effects. In discussing the project before its release with Don Shay for *Cinefantastique*, Trumbull said, "Up until recently, I've always been in a big drive to make extreme futuristic pictures — to really go *way* off and have spaceships, and cities of the future, and all this stuff. But I just decided that it creates such a barrier between what you're trying to say and the audience that's looking at it, that I'm much more apt to start from a contemporary premise now. That's the reason I've taken on *Close Encounters of the Third Kind*. I think it's one of the most fantastic scripts I've ever read. It's very contemporary, and it's understandable, and it's meaningful, and exciting. It's the kind of thing I like to have, because it takes you from a common viewpoint that everyone understands, and yet draws you into a realization that the universe is a pretty gigantic place and there are mind boggling things going on."

According to Trumbull, *Close Encounters* was "the first time in movie history that anyone has ever been able to pan and tilt and dolly a camera around a stage during a special effects shot. Ordinarily in a special effects shot — if you go through and look at every special effects movie ever made — if there's a special effect going on, either a matte painting or an optical effect of some kind, the camera is simply not allowed to pan or tilt or move around, because that creates enormous matching problems. We devised a very sophisticated electronic system that's very much like a missile tracking system that could record and accurately repeat camera moves, so that if we shot a shot on location with a camera panning 180°, changing focus, and dollying 40 feet down a track, and then we add, say, a miniature effect to that shot in postproduction, and, say, the miniature effect was 1/20th scale, we could not only accurately repeat the camera movement to shoot the miniature but modify the scale factor in the camera movement by a scale factor of 20 to 1 and match it perfectly."

During the seventies, Trumbull tried to get a project called *Pyramid* off the ground. A script was written by David Zelag Goodman, who later wrote *Logan's Run*, and he described the project in *Cinefantastique* as follows: "It was about energy, and it took place in the future. The energy suddenly began to disappear and the story involved a trek to an energy source that was on the other side of the world. And it was found to be inside an old pyramid. When they go inside the pyramid, it was very complicated and computerized."

While *Pyramid* never got made, Trumbull was involved with another project that proved to have important implications for his future. That was *Tour of the Universe*, a thrill ride which combined film and a simulator used to give the feel of a ride into outer space, which was created by Trumbull and his Future General Corporation in conjunction with Paramount Pictures. While it was well-received by the theme park industry, it failed to find a permanent home at any of the major theme parks, though the basic concept would be adopted years later by ILM and Disney for Star Tours.

He was also hired to rescue *Star Trek — The Motion Picture*, for which he received another Academy Award Best Special Effects nomination. Paramount had guaranteed to deliver the film to 750 theaters by December 7th, and taken in the highest advance guarantees from exhibitors ever. When word got around that *Star Trek — The Motion Picture* might not be delivered on time because it was having a lot of problems, that $5 million had been spent on effects and there weren't any usable effects, Paramount understandably panicked. With only seven months to go before the release date, and the possibility of a $200 million class action suit by exhibitors if the film was not delivered on time, they desperately needed Trumbull to whip up the requisite effects work. Trumbull used their desperation as a way to get out of his contract with them because he became convinced that Paramount was not going to support his Showscan concept.

In the eighties, Trumbull became upset that the motion

Special effects whiz turned director and impresario Douglas Trumbull, who revolutionized the look of special effects in science fiction.

picture industry was spending millions of dollars to create state-of-the-art product and yet exhibiting it in theaters equipped with sound and projection systems outmoded before the end of World War II. He spent eight years developing the Showscan process, which involves shooting at 60 frames per second on 70mm stock, with sound recorded on a separate 35mm magnetic tape, synchronously "interlocked" to the projector. He struck a partnership with Robert Brock of the Brock Hotel Corporation, owner of the Show Biz Pizza chain, and arranged to have Showscan theaters built inside several of them. The project started in 1976 with his Future General Corporation which was formed in conjunction with Paramount Pictures.

Trumbull first experimented with IMAX, which offered an image three times the size of a normal 70mm frame, but decided that it still was not as sharp nor as clear as he would have liked. He then tried experimenting with frame rates, hooking up individual viewers to EKG, EEG, galvanic skin response monitors and muscle sensors, and polygraphed them watching movies shot at 24, 36, 48, 60, and 72 frames per second. Trumbull received the biggest response from the 60 frames per second group.

According to Trumbull, the Showscan image is four times larger and four times brighter than any regular 35mm film in a regular motion picture theater. The seating in a Showscan theater is specially tiered so that patrons are never trying to look over the back of someone else's head. The sound equipment is actually superior to that of any professional recording studios and can transmit from 20 to 20,000 cycles per second. Trumbull expected that since the majority of top modern box office hits were special effects extravaganzas, such as *Star Wars* or *Close Encounters of the Third Kind*, that the future of movies belonged to those who could provide audiences with new thrills, spills, excitement, and dynamic events presented in a spectacular fashion. He wanted to buck the trend of ever smaller screens in crackerbox theaters with uncomfortable seating and sound spilling in from the screens next door.

To show off this process, Trumbull directed the first Showscan short, entitled "New Magic." The short begins by showing us how bad regular movie projection can be as we hear projector noises and see a scratchy print of a fireworks display that jams in the projector and burns. The film's projectionist, Jeremy (Gerrit Graham), who is of course a projected image, pops up from behind the screen and addresses the audience, promising new magic from his employer, Mr. Kellar (Christopher Lee). Showscan is then used to project images of an aerial sequence that transports the audience over snowcovered mountains, down an open road in a speeding sportscar, and other gimmicks. Jeremy then messes around with some magical paraphernalia and Mr. Kellar makes a dramatic appearance, transforms Jeremy into ShowBiz mascot Billy Bob Brokali, and ends with a display of fireworks that contrasts with that of the opening.

The short is obviously more of a demonstration reel than a dramatic entity, though it does showcase Showscan's strength of image and sound quality. The first film shot in Showscan was "Night of Dreams." Trumbull even revamped the theaters that Showscan was to be shown in, making them as deep as they are wide, with the seats steeply raked so that everyone can see over everybody's else's head, and the rows curved in such a way that every seat is a good seat. The screen is curved and the projector is absolutely square to the screen, with the image projected at the right brightness (frequently, movie theaters show films at lower light levels than optimal).

A few other shorts were shot and distributed, but Showscan shorts never really took off with the general public (the large, cumbersome reels meant that, like IMAX films, Showscan movies had to be under an hour in length, which Trumbull felt would be acceptable to audiences, pointing out how much of a film's running time typically was occupied by filler such as watching characters get places); however, the possibilities for interactive, thrill rides in simulators is present here and became the major use for Showscan.

Trumbull was taken by surprise when some of the same effects turned up in *Star Trek: The Wrath of Khan* uncredited. In the eighties he also supplied effects for Spielberg's *Close Encounters of the Third Kind: The Special Edition* and for Ridley Scott's *Blade Runner*, for which he received his last Academy Award nomination for best special effects.

After it was decided not to sell the Showscan process to amusement parks, Trumbull proposed doing a feature in the process. According to Trumbull, Charles Bludhorn had seen a Showscan film and said, "Guys! If we don't make a feature in this process, we're fools." So initially, the film *Brainstorm* was developed to showcase Showscan. Paramount ended up putting the film into turnaround, at which point Trumbull took the project to MGM, who weren't prepared to do it in Showscan, nor were Universal or Columbia or Fox or anybody else.

Trumbull went ahead and set up *Brainstorm* at MGM, which was to be shot in 35mm and 70mm Super Panavision. The basic premise behind *Brainstorm* is a basically fascinating one. What if someone invented a machine that could record your every sensation, and then play it back for someone else at the touch of a button, allowing the wearer to live any experience they could imagine? Furthermore, what happens when someone uses this device to explore the unexplored country of death?

Trumbull directs Christopher Walken and Natalie Wood on the set of *Brainstorm*.

The whole idea is a metaphor for the filmgoing experience, that of vicariously from a safe distance experiencing an emotionally wrenching or highly exciting moment in some filmed character's life. The idea of the film is to question what would happen if we had the technology to take this experience to the next level.

Trumbull worked closely with his associate and the film's cinematographer, Richard Yurcich. They interpolated the Super Panavision format using a wide angle fish-eye Omnivision lens on about half of the shots whenever anyone experiences the Brainstorm effect because they felt that the resulting image was wider and added a dimension in conjunction with the visual effects. Initially, the device is used to record experiences such as race car driving or hang gliding, but then Terson's partner abuses it to make an endless orgasm loop tape in one of the film's more inventive touches.

Other collaborators included John Vallone as production designer, Mark Stetson handled action props and miniatures, and John Walsh and Alison Yerxa did visual effects. Matte paintings in the film were handled expertly by Matthew Yuricich.

Filming on *Brainstorm* began in North Carolina in mid–1981, mostly in and around Research Triangle Park, but shooting was abruptly terminated shortly before completion due to the untimely drowning death of costar Natalie Wood. MGM, the studio backing the film, seriously considered collecting on the insurance on the film, underwritten by Lloyd's of London, as a better way of retrieving its investment rather than completing and releasing it. After two months, it was ascertained that the footage was salvageable and the film's principal photography was finally completed in Los Angeles.

The Brainstorm device is invented by Dr. Michael Brace (Christopher Walken) and Dr. Lillian Reynolds (Louise Fletcher in one of her finer performances). Overseeing the project and providing the financing is Alex Terson (Cliff Robertson, in his first film after being blacklisted for reporting that Begelman had forged his name to a check). Terson is delighted with the results, but is secretly keen on military applications that Brace and Reynolds are opposed to.

Meanwhile, Brace is having difficulties in his marriage to Karen (Wood), and to bridge the gap of estrangement, and in a very touching sequence, uses the device to record his feelings and memories of their times together to let her know how important she is to him. Events take a dramatic turn when Reynolds suffers a heart attack and records the event using the device. Terson covertly has a guinea pig try the tape, but the subject is almost given a heart attack himself. Brace becomes determined to recover the tape and play it safely in order to learn the biggest secret of them all—what happens after we die.

The screenplay by Robert Stitzel and Philip Messina from a story by the death-obsessed Bruce Joel Rubin (*Ghost; My Life*) does a good job of setting up an interesting premise, but the follow-through proves difficult. Particularly egregious is a sequence where the Braces break in to the research facility in order to acquire the tape and reprogram a robotic assembly line to pester the guards peppered with lowbrow humor worthy of an *I Love Lucy* episode.

Naturally, ultimate questions cannot be satisfactorily explained or presented. There are some fine special effects visuals (we see Reynolds' final moments becoming a globe and drifting up to intersect with thousands of other "memory bubbles," each containing a different moment in someone else's time), some obscure symbolic visuals (Lillian

Alex Terson (Cliff Robertson, right) gets his "socks knocked off" by the new technology developed by Lillian Reynolds (Louise Fletcher, left) to feed sensory experiences directly into the brain as Karen Brace (Natalie Wood) looks on.

seems to undergo a rebirth amid a mound of cow intestines) but the end result is more supermarket tabloid tripe about angels and going into white lights. One huge plus though is James Horner's memorable and effective scoring, which does give a sense of awe and of having a religious experience of some kind.

After his problems with *Brainstorm,* Trumbull vowed to leave the film industry and indeed collaborated with Robert Brock of the Brock Hotel Corporation and the Showbiz pizza chain to present Showscan, his new film process which sets speeds for 70mm projectors at 60 frames per second so that the images rely less on the eyes' persistence of vision and more closely approximate the eyes' own rate of image retention. (Average sound film is projected at 24 frames per second, with each frame projected twice to simulate 48 frames per second.)

The advantage of Showscan is that it features a slightly sharper image and improved sound. The disadvantage is that it uses a lot more expensive 65mm film stock a lot more quickly, limiting the length of the average Showscan feature to between 15 and 60 minutes, enough for an amusement park ride, but short of what would be necessary to satisfy most modern audiences.

Audiences didn't flock to Showscan in droves despite its technical improvements, but this has not left Trumbull discouraged.

For Toshiba's Expo 1985, Trumbull created a 17 minute short called *Let's Go,* described as a touching and comic tale about a boy and his robot. For the Italians, he crafted another short, *Leonardo's Dream.*

Universal Studios wanted an attraction for its California and Florida Studio Tours, and had Trumbull create *Back to the Future—the Ride,* a four-and-a-half minute filmed excursion that "transports" riders back in time 4,000 years and then forward into the future to Hill Valley in the year 2015 before returning them to the present.

Universal wanted to get away from the standard theatrical type presentation, and so spectators are placed in eight passenger DeLorean-style cars placed atop flight simulator platforms before an Omnimax screen that is 13 stories tall and at 80 feet in diameter, covering twice the area of an average Omnimax screen. (Omnimax employs 70mm film run horizontally through the camera and projected at 24 frames per second. Unlike IMAX, which is shot flat, Omnimax is shot with a fisheye lens and projected onto a hemispherical screen like that of a planetarium.)

Universal approached Trumbull and his Berkshire Ridefilm Corporation, located in Berkshire, Massachusetts. Because there was not an optical printer for the problem-ridden Omnimax format, it was decided to generate as many shots as possible in-camera. The attraction itself cost some $60 million to construct.

Viewers ride in replicas of the *Back to the Future* DeLorean, which rocks and tips like a flight simulator, and jumps when the vehicle supposedly hits an air pocket. The four-and-a-half minute film itself cost $16 million to produce. Because it is shown on a curved screen, the sets for the film had to be built specially curved so that they would appear normal to the viewer.

The plot begins with a preshow (produced by ZM Productions) while waiting in line at Doc Brown's Institute of Future Technology when Biff Tannen eludes security guards and steals one of the time-traveling DeLoreans, while Brown entreats ride-goers to catch Biff and stop him before too much inter-dimensional havoc has been wrought. The riders then board their DeLoreans and are taken on a wild ride back and forth through history, from the future Hill Valley where there are a number of near collisions with other flying vehicles to back to the Ice Age, with Biff darting in and out of icy crevasses, and the Jurassic period, where riders are almost eaten by a tyrannosaur, which spits them out. The riders then fly over some lava falls, crash into Biff's vehicles, and all cars are brought back to the present where Biff is shown being arrested.

Because of its erratic motion, children under 40 inches, pregnant women, and people with respiratory problems are prohibited from enjoying the ride, which creates a sense of motion — up, down, forwards or backwards — by incorporating movement on screen in the audience's peripheral vision. While exciting and ingeniously created given the limitations of the format, obviously such films cater strictly to sensation and are unlikely to engage viewers emotionally or intellectually. While innovative and on a level involving, it is also an artistic deadend.

For the Luxor Pryamid hotel which opened on October 14, 1993, Trumbull designed, produced, and codirected a special three-part attraction called "Secrets of the Pyramid." Commented Trumbull, "This is the opportunity of a lifetime to work on the Luxor project because it is an entertainment breakthrough.... This is the first time anybody has ever said to me you can design the whole thing. Not only the concept of the shows, the production of the shows, but the design of the theater themselves."

The Trumbull Company in Lennox, Massachusetts set to work designing and creating the attraction. Trumbull and production designer Bob Taylor were inspired by the pyramid motif of the hotel. Explains Trumbull, "We wanted to create someplace for you to go, someplace to have an adventure, someplace that we've never seen before. In designing the architectural motif and configuration of this pre–Egyptian civilization, our idea was that everything you've ever seen in Egypt is a poor facsimile of what this high technology civilization had developed. They lived in a world where gravity was no longer an issue, and they built vehicles that could levitate, so we've given this world a very spectacular and unusual look."

The first part of the attraction is designed to look like an excavation. Patrons are ushered into special theaters which house 15 passengers, who climb aboard a 5000 pound steel structure manipulated by hydraulics. The movement system is designed to put the audience into the action depicted on the 25 x 14 foot screen which curves 180 degrees around the spectators, encompassing their peripheral vision to provide a greater sense of movement.

"We created this architectural style that we called Crypto-Egypto, which was to take architectural motifs of the Egyptians and modernize them and build them out of sophisticated materials so they didn't look hand-made."

In the opening part of the attraction, audiences are led into a pseudo-elevator which will supposedly lower them 1000 feet. Actually, the "elevator" does little more than rock while a film is projected against a curved screen which suggests that the elevator has snapped its cable and has its brake engaged by a daredevil rescuer in a complementary elevator on the "other side" who clicks the brakes on just in time with a spark-spewing metal pole.

The audiences are then led to some mystical levitating craft which will supposedly carry them out of the huge underground pyramid in which they descended and away from the evil machinizations of Dr. Osiris, who is sabotaging the excavation in hopes of controlling the power of the pyramid's mystic crystal for himself.

In a "Star Tours"–like ride, the craft is piloted by the hero, Mack McFerson (Michael Corbett) who has a tendency to not pay attention to where he's going, bumping into several items or just missing them. (The display is largely formed by impressively designed, though artificial looking, computer animation.)

En route, he comes across Dr. Osiris, who has just kidnapped his girlfriend and famous archeaologist Karina Wollinsky (Marjorie Harris) and hauls the audience off in hot pursuit. A black Egyptian god materializes to destroy any weapon-bearing ships. Dr. Osiris jumps aboard the craft and the pair battle hand-to-hand before Osiris loses his balance and falls off to the side. There is a mystic explosion and the audience is suddenly at the landing zone at the top of the pyramid and led out through the side.

The second segment features a television talk show, projected in Showscan at the bottom of a stage and captured from different angles by television monitors placed around the room. A military type appears on the show to say that the government should retain control of the power of the crystal. McFerson protests. Dr. Osiris, still alive, beams a message to say that he and his followers should be the ultimate recipients of the crytal's power.

Just then an eclipse of the sun occurs (for which the audience is instructed to put on polarized 3-D glasses) and a series of computer-generated three dimensional images are projected out at the audience indicating the transformational powers of the crystal. This serves as a climax and leaves the second installment unresolved.

The last segment, "The Theater of Time," takes place in an IMAX–type theater, and indeed, it shows a film, the image of which is seventy feet high, though it is not nearly as wide as an IMAX film. It resembles a wide-screen image turned on its side and running vertical instead of horizontal. There is a design by the sides of the screen to suggest that the audience is viewing the proceedings from inside the time capsule that Osiris and our two heroes are in at the beginning of the featurette.

Osiris shows them the future, which is bleak, showing a destroyed city with burned or bombed out remnants, heavily smoggy atmosphere, and flying police cars everywhere. This is the future we are headed for if we don't change our ways. Osiris takes the crystal and makes himself the leader of the world as well as immortal. However, he doesn't retain his relative youth and looks like a ham actor in bad old age makeup. He finally decides that if he can't really live forever, then no one should succeed him and prepares to blow up the sun.

Mack heads back in time to prevent Osiris from taking possession of the crystal, stranding him outside the time capsule. Now the future suddenly becomes a rosy one with beautiful landscaping, Arco Sante–style skyscrapers, and hundreds of flying vehicles, an impressive vision of a technologically abundant fair future. Once more the heavy handed message is driven home that the shape of our own future will depend on the choices we make today.

Today, Trumbull is vice chair of IMAX as well as the president and CEO of Ridefilm Corporation, which produces motion-simulation experiences. Finding that the proliferation of multiplex theaters has resulted in smaller screens, he has abandoned traditional filmmaking in favor of exploring theme park rides and attractions which can provide him with the kind of vast, immersive canvases that he wishes to operate on. He is developing IMAX 3-D, and has an alien contact film project in the format that he is developing with Constance Congdon, which he hoped to finish in 1997.

He predicts that, like in *Brainstorm*, we are close to being able to plant images, memories, and emotional states directly into an audience's mind, with virtual reality glasses representing a transitory phase in so doing. Instead of being a great storyteller, Trumbull has dedicated himself to being a showman with his eye on the future, someone dedicated to creating new and interesting technology that will bring audiences a greater sensory experience intended to touch them forever. It's not surprising that he is still considered one of science fiction film's greatest visionaries.

SHINYA TSUKAMOTO (1960–)

The Phantom of Regular Size (short, 1986); *Tetsuo: Iron Man* (1989); *Tetsuo: Body Hammer*; *Hiruko: Yokai Hanta* (1991); *Denchu Kozo no Boken* (aka *Adventures of the Electric Rod Boy*); *Kokyo Fisuto* (aka *Tokyo Fist*; 1995); *Bullet Ballet* (1998); *Soseiji* (1999)

Tetsuo: Iron Man is a black and white slice of cyberpunk released in the U.S. in 1992 that took many critics by surprise. Shinya Tsukamoto clearly showed the influence of David Lynch (especially *Eraserhead*) and David Cronenberg (*Videodrome*), two of the masters of modern disturbing imagery. On his first film, he served as a virtual one-man film crew, and is credited with direction, writing, cinematography, lighting, art direction, editing and the special effects.

Tetsuo: Iron Man begins with Tsukamoto himself playing a man known only as a "metal fetishist," who attempts to insert a metal pipe into his leg. After unwrapping the bandages, he sees the wound infected with maggots and runs screaming into the street, where he is hit by a car driven by a drab man and his girlfriend.

Tsukamoto seems mostly concerned with textures, presenting a depressing, black and white industrial landscape. The narrative is fractured, the dialogue is minimal, and the story seems more a metaphor for how people become dehumanized in the machine age. The salaryman (Tomoroh Taguchi) later discovers a metal spike emerging from his cheek, and then slowly realizes that he is being transformed into a creature that is part flesh, part machine.

Both he and his girlfriend, who get it on after running over the metal fetishist (who remains alive inside a bit of mashed metal), discover that they have been infected. His mousy girlfriend becomes an intimidating cyborg virago who pursues him into the men's room, and later they attempt relations in the girl's apartment, only for the salaryman's penis to transform into a giant, rotating drill bit which he eventually uses to penetrate her. This spurs the fetishist to return as another menacing, metallic creature, and the pair pursue each other over the streets of the suburbs, accumulating ever more metal as they zip along.

Shinya Tsukamoto then went on to create *Tetsuo: Body Hammer*, a 35mm color follow-up, which shows an amalgam of influences. In it, Taniguchi Tomoo (Tomoroh Taguchi) is a happily married exec who cannot remember his life before the age of eight. He and his family get terrorized by body-building skinheads, led by Yatsu (Shinya Tsukamoto himself), who kidnaps and gruesomely kills Taniguchi's son. After he is shot with a rivet gun, this causes the executive to metamorph into a super cyber warrior.

Taniguchi gets kidnapped himself, though the skinheads find he is more than they bargained for. Likewise, Taniguchi slowly uncovers the connection between himself and Yatsu. The film is more linear and has a stronger narrative than its predecessor, arriving at a peaceful, if disturbing conclusion. On the down side, it is less nightmarish than the original as the mysteries do not hold up under their explanations. Still, it marks Tsukamoto as an original talent.

Few films retain the impact of this bizarre duo with their iron filing vomiting, chase scenes that go up the sides of buildings, heavy metal music from Chu Ishikawa, the three big Ms — mutilation, mutation, and merging of characters with machinery, and imagery that ranges from 100 bald men pumping iron to children being forced to watch their parents have sex at gunpoint. It's definitely not for the easily offended or faint of heart, but one can't fail to be impressed by its "magnitude of killing intention." Just watch that you don't wind up like some of the characters, "corroded to death."

Between the *Tetsuo* films, Tsukamoto directed *Hiruko*, which concerns an archaeologist who unearths evil spirits (most notably spiders with human heads) following his attempt to delve into the mystery of his friend's disappearance. Unfortunately, while very convoluted, the film lacks the impact of the *Tetsuo* films.

He followed this with *Adventures of the Electric Rod Boy*, a 50 minute featurette released on a double bill with his *Tokyo Fist*. A variation on Tim Burton's *Edward Scissorhands, Electric Rod Boy* has an electric rod growing out of his back, which makes him the butt of his friend's jokes. He escapes to another dimension, where the world is now in the thrall of a vampire (Tomoroh Taguchi). *Tokyo Fist*, like Tsukamoto's previous films, revels in physical transformations as well. Tsukamoto himself stars as Tsuda, who is transformed into a body-building martial arts killing machine after he loses Hizuru (Kaori Fujii), his body-piercing girlfriend to a former friend turned kickboxer. The three eventually all face off for a "paint the walls red" finale.

Tsukamoto is adept at wild imagery and graphic violence, but still seems to lack adeptness at storytelling and his films have more impact than thought, more style than substance. It will be interesting to see whether something truly remarkable emerges from his personal artistic obsessions.

PHIL TUCKER

Robot Monster; Dance Hall Racket (1953); *Tijuana After Midnight; Dream Follies; Bagdad After Midnight* (1954); *Broadway Jungle* (1955); *Pachuco* (1956); *The Cape Canaveral Monsters* (1960)

Television: *Space Jockey* (unaired pilot)

Phil Tucker, a lanky Westerner, is best known for *Robot Monster*, one of the most amusingly inept science fiction films of all time. After serving stints in the Marines and as a dishwasher, Tucker wrote for some of the science fiction pulps. After exhibiting low-budget burlesque films in Fairbanks, Alaska, Tucker decided to try his hand at making some quickie sexploitation pictures himself.

He made several films in the "After Midnight" series, the titles of which include *Paris After Midnight, Hollywood After Midnight, New York After Midnight, London After Midnight* (no relation to the lost Tod Browning film), and *Tijuana After Midnight*. He also made a now lost science fiction effort entitled *Space Jockey*, which he described as "a real piece of shit. In fact, [Tucker claims] it's probably the worst film ever made." (Whether it was a film or simply an unsold television pilot has still not been established.)

According to its trailer, *Robot Monster* brings you "an actual preview of the devastating forces of our future! Unsuspected revelations of incredible horrors that will terrify you with their brutal reality!" Yeah, I'll bet. Over scenes from the film, the following promises are superimposed: "See ... Prehistoric Monsters Return to Earth! See ... Sultry Beauty in the Clutches of a Half-Crazed Monster! See ... The World Battle for Survival! Overwhelming! Electrifying! Baffling!"

The only promise it fully delivers on is that last one. In many ways, this unusual film is quite baffling, but a lot of fun. It's easy to champion a quality product such as the horror thrillers of Val Lewton, but when it comes to schlock cinema, *Robot Monster* is one of the most entertaining examples ever made.

Robot Monster begins with a credit sequence superimposed on a potpourri of garish comic book covers. We may suppose that these are the inspiration for the story that follows, qualifying *Robot Monster* as one of the very first films to warn against the potentially pernicious influence of the media.

Originally Tucker wanted to star a robot in *Robot Monster*, but he could not find a robot costume that he could rent cheaply. "I originally envisioned the monster as a kind of robot," he recalls. "I talked to several guys that I knew who had robot suits, but it was just out-of-the-way, moneywise. I thought, 'Okay, I know George Barrows.' George's occupation was gorilla-suit man. When they needed a gorilla in a picture they called George, because he owned his own suit and got like forty bucks a day. I thought, 'I know George will work for me for nothing. I'll get a diving helmet, put it on him, and it'll work!"

Needless to say, it doesn't really, unless the intention was to create one of the most laughable menaces ever created. The film is rife with shots of the overweight Barrows suffering for his art by puffing up a hillside in the undoubtedly unbearably hot Ro-Man costume, which help to pad out the film but provide no palpable menace or thrills. However, a silly looking monster is not the only criterion a film should be judged by. After all, subpar acting and unintentionally hilarious dialogue should count for something.

Nevertheless, there are many larger budgeted features that have less on their minds than *Robot Monster* does. Part of what is endearing about the film is that on its meager budget, it tries to say something about global relations, about individuality and the core of humanity, and about women's roles in society while spinning a passably engaging tale.

The main characters are set up at the outset. The main characters are a charmless lad named Johnny (Gregory Moffett), his mother Martha (Selena Royle), and his sisters Carla (Pamela Paulson) and Alice (Claudia Barrett) who are on a picnic. Johnny wears a plastic space helmet and plays with a toy raygun that shoots bubbles when he sees two men in a nearby cave. (*The Fifty Worst Films of All Time* errs in asserting that the men are part of the family.) He tells the more elderly of the two, "Spaceman, you must die!"

The men are Roy (George Nader), assistant to a genial, German-accented professor (John Mylong) who responds, "Wouldn't it be nicer if we could live at peace with each other?" This is the first of many platitudinous speeches in this often all too sanctimonious movie.

Johnny responds, "OK, I'll be from a friendly planet," indicating that the choice of peace is ours. The men are archaeologists, and Johnny is excited at the prospect of their being scientists. Johnny invites the men to meet his mother and sisters. He is a lonely little boy whose father is dead and who lives in the fantasy world suggested by the lurid pulps featured under the main title. He wishes for a new father who would be a big scientist and make rocketships. The core of the film is simply his dream, much like the one in *Invaders from Mars,* where a small boy's hopes and fears are brought into play (e.g., his parents might not be his parents; army generals listen seriously to his tales of alien invasion, etc.). In this case, Johnny dreams of being one of the few heroic survivors of an alien invasion with the professor for his father and his annoying sister eventually killed by one of the invaders.

When Johnny apparently wakes up from his nap, he heads back to Bronson Caverns, the site of most of the film and one of the most frequently used film locations in Hollywood, used in virtually hundreds of films and television series. It is featured in such diverse works as *Attack of the Crab Monsters, The Cyclops, Dreamscape,* the original *Invasion of the Body Snatchers, It Conquered the World, Killers from Space, King Dinosaur, Star Trek VI: The Undiscovered Country, Unknown World, V* (mini-series) and numerous Westerns. Tucker himself returned to that location for *The Cape Canaveral Monsters.*

In the best Edward D. Wood tradition, footage of lightning, lizards dressed up as dinosaurs fighting, and animated dinosaurs are inexplicably inserted, perhaps suggesting that the world has now gone topsy turvy. (Later the aliens will release a ray to revive prehistoric reptiles, but that takes place at the end of the film, making the "dinosaurs'" initial appearance rather puzzling.)

There in the cave, which symbolizes the "pit of man's fears," is Ro-Man (apparently short for Robot-Man) and his infamous bubble machine, which adds a curious touch of surrealism to the film. Perhaps Tucker felt that bubbles drifting out towards the audience would look terrific in 3-D, but instead it simply suggests a low-budget Lawrence Welk program gone mad. Additionally, positive and negative footage have been interspersed along with crackling sounds to suggest powerful forces at work.

Ro-Man is contacted on his viewscreen by the Great Guidance, also referred to as the Great One, who looks almost identical to Ro-Man, indicating the rigid regimentation and comformity of their society which makes no allowances for individuality. Ro-Man is referred to as Extension Ro-Man XJ2, and has a round disk on his transparent faceplate (sometimes revealing the face of George Barrows with a stocking over his head) and a knob at the bottom-center portion of his helmet, while the Great Guidance has a dark, opaque faceplate and no knobs or discs.

After reporting that he was delayed because Earth's gravity is .7652 higher than on their planet, Ro-Man reports, "Hu-Mans know about atomic energy but had not mastered the cosmic ray. Wherever I directed the calcinator ray their cities crumbled. At first the fools thought it came from among their many nations and began destroying each other with hydrogen bombs. I announced myself to keep them from wiping out cities which will give our people much amusement. Too late they banded against me. Their resistance pattern showed some intelligence. All are gone now. The way is clear for our people."

Aside from the scientific ignorance of thinking there is only one "cosmic ray," this speech does reflect the concerns of many during the Cold War that paranoid leaders would begin employing hydrogen bombs against an imagined enemy, destroying much of the Earth in the process. Obviously, international conflicts make these conquerors' job easier and in its own way, the speech is a plea for people to work together and not react without thinking.

However, Guidance is upset and obsessed with details. "I want facts, not words!" he insists, pointing out that there is an error of 16 millionths, meaning that eight people are left on Earth. One of the big mysteries of the film is why the Ro-Men are concerned about a pitiful handful of survivors and delay their invasion until all are destroyed. Nevertheless, Ro-Man is instructed to find them and destroy them.

The tin-eared script for the film was written by Wyatt Ordung, who the following year directed *Monster from the Ocean Floor*, the film that has the distinction of being Roger Corman's first foray into fantastic cinema, though perhaps fantastic is a less than accurate description for this turkey which gives *Robot Monster* a run for its money in the bad movie department, lacking the humorous qualities which redeem *Robot Monster* as an entertainment experience. While the dialogue in *Robot Monster* may be risible and extremely overblown, it's not dull. A gorilla in a deep-sea helmet with antennas attached may make for a cheap monster, but at least it's amusing unlike Ordung's awful monster in *Monster*, which is merely a octopus marionette adorned with lights and an obvious light bulb sticking out of its head.

Throughout Ordung makes an attempt to suggest that the Ro-Man is part machine, hence his emphasis on calculations, and that he is unused to speaking English. Ro-Man, for example, appears before the family on a viewscreen and announces, "Hu-Mans, listen to me. Due to an error in calculation, there are still a few of you left. You escaped destruction because I did not know you existed. Now I know. I see five of you are watching that have not been destroyed. Show yourselves and I promise you a painless death." At another point he offers "a choice between a painless surrender death and the horror of resistance death." Who could resist choices like those?

Despite his presumed mechanical origin, Ro-Man proves quite fallible. Despite the Great Guidance telling him there are eight people left, Ro-Man assumes there are five because that's all he can see in his viewscreen, until Alice appears as the beauty who attracts the beast and awakens his latent lustful longings.

I wonder whether Ro-Man might not have been intended as a symbol for the Soviet Union, who was seen as swallowing up smaller countries and destroying ideologies other than its own. Russians were frequently characterized as calculating, soulless beings who worked with each other with mechanical precision, i.e., robot people. They were also seen as intent on conquest and big on oppression, whereas a subsequent mock "marriage" indicates that the surviving Americans are all good, Christian people concerned about their community.

Of course, some of the utterances by the humans prove just as strange. The Professor, who with Roy has developed an antibiotic that blocks the killing power of Ro-Man's ray, recontacts Ro-Man, who assumes they are surrendering, and bravely asserts they have fought him to a standstill. (There is no other indication of the humans fighting the alien menace as they were tricked into fighting among themselves, so this assertion proves baffling.) The Professor tells Johnny, "If Ro-Man wants us, he should calculate us," which truly makes us question the old man's sanity.

Alice says: "We want peace, Ro-Man, but peace with honor," leaving one to wonder if President Nixon ever saw this film and recalled it when he wanted to describe U.S. relations with Vietnam. When Alice accuses her boyfriend Roy of being "bossy," he counters with one of the film's funniest retorts, "I'm bossy? You're so bossy you ought to be milked before you come home at night." Nor is the mammary association in this retort accidental.

For a fifties film, *Robot Monster* is refreshingly obvious in its sexual undertones. There is a clear suggestion that Ro-Man is sexually attracted to Alice (though the voice-over on the Rhino version about dating her wasn't part of the original film and is obviously a different voice). "I will talk with the girl," promises Ro-Man to the Great One. "It is not in the Plan, but although I cannot verify it, I feel she will understand." Poor Ro-Man, denied feelings and sexual outlet by his own culture, he comes to Earth simply looking for a little understanding (and a little sex).

Consider the following sexual roles called into play: Despite the Professor insisting he is the head of the family unit and therefore should make the decisions, Alice agrees to meet with the marauding menace. "Is Alice going to have a date with Ro-Man?" asks Carla in wide-eyed wonder, one of her few lines where Johnny's pesky sister is not asking her brother to play house with her and which again emphasizes the underlying sexual element.

The sexual tension is apparent from Alice's subsequent, seemingly inspirational lines when the men object to her intentions: "You mean there are certain things nice girls don't do? Even if it means that man's millions of years of struggle up from the sea, the slime, to fight, to breathe air, to stand erect, to think, to conquer nature, you mean all this is to stop cold by a jealous father and a doting suitor?" Alice presents herself as a fearless feminist who won't be restrained by an outmoded patriarchy in her attempts to save mankind while the men try to dictate what should be her standard of virtue. (That she is virginal is pointed up when after she and Roy finally get some time alone to make out, she quickly puts a stop to their necking and insists that the Professor marry them first.)

Alice has trouble with Roy because he "wouldn't admit I was good in my field," though what that field is is never specified. Roy is consistently condescending towards her, telling her things such as "You're either too beautiful to be so smart, or too smart to be so beautiful," as if beauty and intelligence were mutually contradictory and frankly someone as good-looking as she is should stop trying to be intelligent. Strangely, Alice falls into the party line by responding, "I guess we do get along all right at that. Let's work together now — we can play later," apparently interpreting Roy's male chauvinist assertions as flirtatious.

Mention should also be made of the film's special defects, which it has in place of effects. Rather than add two more cast members and actually build an interior set (to keep the budget down, the entire film was shot outdoors), the other two surviving members of humanity are depicted as a toy rocket with a lit sparkler in the back making its way to a space platform through what appears to be dense smoke (thick clouds in the upper atmosphere?). Ro-Man destroys the ship with a mighty blast which also destroys what's left of the illusion by revealing a gloved hand rotating the ship on a stick.

Much of the effects work in the film, credited to Jack Rabin and David Commons, was lifted from other sources. There are outtakes of meteors from *Flight to Mars*, and much of the dinosaur and disaster footage, is lifted from *One Million B.C.* Shots of the destruction of civilization seem to come from *Invasion U.S.A.* Rabin could be a quite capable effects artist, supplying effects for *Rocketship X-M, Unknown World, Invaders from Mars* and *Kronos* among others, but his work could be uneven and obviously the budget here was minimal.

That human emotion is superior to alien intellect is a cliché that appears in seemingly almost every science fiction film. It's a way to assure the audience that no matter how superior some alien species may seem, humanity is still better than they are because we have feelings. (I'm not certain I buy this concept. For example, I know a man who is regularly rude to people but assuages his conscience because he feels bad about it in private afterwards. He may have feelings, but it certainly doesn't make him act any better towards other people.)

However, this seems to be the central theme of the film — that humans are sentimental idiots and that's a good thing. The drama of Alice's willingness to sacrifice her virginity to Ro-Man for the sake of what's left of humanity, however, isn't accorded serious consideration. "I don't believe that any human being should degrade himself in order to survive," says Roy.

Alice responds, "You mean you'd rather have us go out of business, is that it? Never return, no forwarding address. Can't you see you're being sentimental idiots letting your emotions run away with you?" The Professor chides her, "Perhaps that is the quality of being human — the very thing that makes us different from Ro-Man, the very thing we are trying to preserve."

If the criterion for preserving people is their being sentimental idiots who let their emotions run away, then Ro-Man certainly qualifies for preservation. The biggest shock in the film is when Ro-Man kills Johnny's sister Carla. (When her mother makes a reference to it all being over, indicating that humanity has come to an end, Carla assumes she can then go to "Janie's house and borrow her dolls," a moment meant to be poignant but which instead makes Carla come off as moronic, as do her cries of "My daddy won't let you hurt me," just before Ro-Man strangles her.) The lives of little kids were usually sacrosanct in fifties films, though in this case much of the audience is glad to see her go. However, when Ro-Man has a similar opportunity earlier with her whiny sibling Johnny, who stupidly spills the beans about the serum that protects the survivors, instead of killing the annoying tyke, Ro-Man makes a speech about humanity "getting too intelligent. We couldn't wait until you were strong enough to attack us, we had to attack you first."

Ro-Man, having fallen for Alice, succumbs to unfamiliar emotions and reports to the Great Guidance, requesting that the "plan should include one living human for reference in case of unforeseen contingencies." (The Great One is not amused and insists that all be destroyed.) Ro-Man is enraged by the sight of the now married couple necking, and attacks Roy. While Alice batters at the beast ineffectually, Ro-Man strangles him and tosses him over the edge of a precipice (Ro-Man is so distracted by

Alice that he lets Roy live long enough for him to return and tell the others what has happened). The amorous robot ape picks Alice up in his arms and carries the struggling bride away, pausing only to tell her, "I am ordered to kill you. I must do it with my hands."

"How is it you are so strong?" asks Alice, alertly searching for a weakness. "It seems impossible."

"We Ro-Mans obtain our strength from the planet Ro-Man, relayed to our individual energizers," explains the enamored alien, explaining that his is in the cave. This is clear proof that Ro-man has fallen for Alice's feminine wiles as he tells her exactly what she wants to know thereby setting something up, although this information is subsequently ignored in the rapid climax that ends the film.

Johnny, ever the hero in his dream, concocts a final plan, where the Professor tells Ro-Man that they plan to surrender to an easy death as a ruse to rescue Alice. However, Ro-Man is more intent on making moves on Alice. "Suppose I were human, would you treat me like a man?" he says while putting his hirsute arms around her as she tries to discover the whereabouts of the energizer. His intentions are clear from his removing the back of her halter top, but he is interrupted first by the Professor's surrender call ("Why do you call me at this time?" Ro-Man asks peevishly before agreeing to a delayed meeting) and then by another one from the Great Guidance.

"You wish to change the plan?" the annoyed Great One asks. "To think for yourself is to be like the Hu-Man."

"Yes," responds Ro-Man in his big, emotional moment, "to be like the Hu-Man. To *laugh, feel, want.* Why are these things not in the plan?"

Ordered to kill the girl, Ro-Man becomes an outer space Hamlet: "I cannot, yet I must. How do you calculate that? At what point on the graph do must and cannot meet? Yet I *must,* but I *cannot.*" Indeed, it is one of the most memorable speeches I've heard in any science fiction film, and one which aids *Robot Monster* in joining the screen immortals.

The Professor gives a gun to Johnny, who becomes the diversion, yelling out, "Here I am, Ro-Man!" Ro-Man ignores his leader's instruction to kill the girl first, explaining, "Great Guidance, I cannot kill the girl, but I will kill the boy (a move most of the audience can easily understand). Alice, do not hate me. I must!"

With that, the apish invader approaches and strangles the boy; however, Guidance has had enough. "You wish to be a Hu-Man. Good. You can die a Hu-Man," he intones before pointing his fingers at the screen from which emanate scratches on the celluloid suggestive of lightning shooting out and killing his Earthly representative.

The Great One then unleashes his final plan. "I shall release our cosmic Q-rays which shall release prehistoric reptiles to devour whatever remains of life," he soliloquizes as stop motion dinosaur footage and battling lizards are shown on screen. This is followed by his avowal that "Psychotronic vibrations will smash the Earth out of the Universe," which makes one wonder why he bothered unleashing those dinosaurs except that it gives the filmmakers an excuse to include the footage.

But the final twist/cheat is yet to come. As the Earth splits apart, Johnny wakes up with a bruise on his head to find himself being carried in Roy's arms. Martha invites the archaeologists to dinner. When Carla asks Johnny to play house, he reluctantly agrees, having learned to treasure his sister, but promising to watch out for Ro-Men.

"Really, Johnny," responds Alice, "you're overdoing the spaceman act. There simply aren't such things." Afterall, this is the stuff of comic books whose garish and suggestive covers were the inspiration for Johnny's obviously fevered imagination.

But Tucker has one more trick up his sleeve. They leave while out from the cave a series of Ro-Men (actually the same double-exposed shot repeated three times) come menacingly towards the camera as Bernstein's overbearing Ro-Man theme gets its last work-out. (A black curtain is clearly apparent behind Ro-Man in the double exposed footage.)

There are some odd continuity errors in the film. When Roy goes out to neck with Alice, he has blood dripping from his right ear for no apparent reason. Yet, shortly afterward when he marries Alice, the blood is gone. Later, Ro-Man will start to tie up Alice but is interrupted by a call. When he is finished, someone has finished tying Alice up, but who? Surely not Alice herself.

As noted above, the composer-conductor for the film was a neophyte Elmer Bernstein, who also scored *Cat-Women of the Moon* the same year. His work here is overemphatic and repetitive but by no means incompetent. The editor credited on the film is Merrill White A.C.E., whose credits include the classics *Love Me Tonight, The Red House* and *The Fly* (1958), though many sources award credit solely to associate editor Bruce Schoengarth. Why this should be remains another *Robot Monster* mystery.

Executive producer Al Zimbalist kept up his association with bad filmmaking and was later associated with other classic bad films such as *Cat-Women of the Moon* and its even worse remake *Missile to the Moon* (for which he is given story credit), *Monster from the Green Hell,* and Ed Bernds' *Valley of the Dragons.*

Tucker defended *Robot Monster,* saying, "I still do not believe there is a soul alive who could have done as well for as little money as I was able to do.... For the budget, and for the time, I felt I had achieved greatness." It's certainly true that with a larger budget and more time, some of the film's problems could have been fixed, though it would then lack the charm which makes it a guilty pleasure. The budget for *Robot Monster* was, according to Tucker, as little as $16,000 plus lab rentals, and the shooting schedule was a mere four days. He believes that the film collected rentals of over a million dollars, but his partners left him without a penny. "They personally made money on that picture by stealing from me. I didn't get anything from that picture. At one time, I was going to sue but I couldn't find a lawyer who would help."

Tucker was not even allowed to see his own film by his backers after it was completed, forcing him to buy a ticket to see it. Following the wretched reception which the film received, Tucker was plunged into depression and even attempted suicide, winding up in the psychopathic ward of the Veterans Administration Hospital. The film later showed up on television under the title *Monsters from the Moon.*

He struck up a friendship with Lenny Bruce and together they produced *Dance Hall Racket* (1954), which featured Bruce in what was then his natural environment, assisting strippers in strip joints. Bruce plays a murdering bouncer, and the cast included both his wife, Honey Harlowe, and his mother, Sally Marr. Tucker also made a dragstrip drama called *Pachuco* (1956), which is his favorite among his own films.

Tucker later returned to science fiction with *The Cape Canaveral Monsters* (1960), which he both wrote and directed. In it, aliens, represented by little dots sprinkled liberally on the film footage, come to Earth to sabotage our space program. The film is as bad as *Robot Monster*, but not nearly as enjoyable. It is another in a long line of films where aliens take over human bodies or corpses, so that for most of the film, the aliens are portrayed by Jason Johnson and Katherine Victor. The most clever aspect of the film is the fact that even though the corpses the aliens inhabit are decaying, it doesn't cut down on their sex drive at all.

In the book *Scream Queens*, Victor recalled the erstwhile director: "Tucker knew what he wanted and didn't hestitate to fulfill his responsibilities as a director. This, plus a two-week shooting schedule, enough money to enable him to shoot several takes per shot if something went wrong, and the added attraction of color, all made the project seem promising. The color was the first thing to go. Last minute budget cuts restricted it to black and white. Then, as film days went by, the cost of necessary special effects ate away at the money reserve. Scenes were shortened, changed, or compromised. When the film was finally screened, it proved a disappointment to everyone involved."

Abandoning his film directorial career, Tucker worked as an associate producer on several television shows and documentaries. He later found a niche as a postproduction supervisor for fellow schlockmeister Dino De Laurentiis, working on *King Kong* (1976) and the equally laughable *Orca, the Killer Whale*. He also served as editor of the notorious bombs *The Nude Bomb* and *Charlie Chan and the Curse of the Dragon Queen*, and produced the film *Death Riders* (1976).

Robot Monster, however, remains, his main claim to fame. Formed out of the sweat and toil of its ill-compensated participants, it continues to live on in the hearts and minds of those who have experienced it, a symbol of technology gone mad, or perhaps inspiration out of desperation. Perhaps the best tribute to it was paid in Ken Shapiro's one-time cult film *The Groove Tube*, a filmic series of shaggy dog sketches which featured the image of a gorilla with a television for a head prominently in ads for the film and as the climax to its *2001* parody. Anyone who had seen Tucker's film knew instantly where Shapiro had gotten the idea for it, and could not help smiling at the lucrious memory.

DAVID N. TWOHY

The Grand Tour (aka *Disaster in Time*); *The Arrival* (1996); *Pitch Black* (2000)

David N. Twohy is a screenwriter turned director. His first credit that I've been able to uncover is writing the sequel to *Critters, Critters II: The Main Course*, which was directed by Mick Garris, which brought back Charlie (Don Opper) and Brad (Scott Grimes) to fight more Krites from outer space.

Twohy's directorial debut was *The Grand Tour* (aka *Disaster in Time*), a Showtime original. It was released theatrically overseas and was the Grand Prix winner at the 1992 Festival Du Film Fantastique in Brussels. Twohy based his script on the classic science fiction novella "Vintage Season" by C. L. Moore. *The Grand Tour* alters Moore's story, but retains the basic idea of alien tourists who covertly come to Earth to witness major tragedies first hand, in this case a meteor that is about to strike a sleepy Ohio town. Jeff Daniels plays Ben Wilson, a contractor, distraught over the recent death of his wife, who has fixed up an old mansion as a hotel for visitors.

Screenwriter and director David N. Twohy directing *The Arrival.*

Soon a peculiar group of people arrive, led by Madame Iovine (Marilyn Lightshade). He uncovers his guests' secret when he learns that they carry passports with places and dates dating back to the beginning of the century, and confronts Quish (David Wells) about his findings. However, as his depression over his wife's demise has led to alcoholism, he is not considered reliable by much of the town, and Judge Caldwell (George Murdock) feels that it is appropriate to separate him from his daughter Hillary (Ariana Richards).

A meteorite falls and destroys half the town, leaving Ben distraught over the time-traveling visitors' coldness. However, he becomes even more concerned when Oscar (Jim Haynie) helps him realize that the visitors haven't left yet and are expecting another event. Many of the survivors are sheltered in the town's school, where a gas main is accidentally broken. Hillary is one of the volunteers there, and Ben rushes to get her away, but he is too late. Quish, who tries to prevent him, is killed in the resulting explosion.

Ben takes Quish's passport and figures out how to send himself back in time a few hours before the meteor hits. He tries to safeguard his daughter, who has been taken by Judge Caldwell, but his warnings are dismissed as drunken ravings and he is arrested and put in jail right where the meteor will hit. Desperate, he makes a phone call to his earlier self and insists that he come down to the jail and bring his truck. The deputy is surprised to see what is apparently his charge out of his cell, but the later Ben overpowers him so they can rescue Hillary.

Along the way, the earlier Ben argues that he cannot run away from this disaster, that he must be different than the visitors and attempt to warn people, saving as many as they can. They hit upon using the church's bells to play "Für Elise," which attracts a crowd of people from the side of town about to be hit. Not all are saved, but there are more survivors than before. An emissary from the future warns that if the future has been altered, they will undo the changes Ben has made, but Ben points out that if that were the case, they would not be having that conversation. The later Ben joins the emissary, and the film ends with Ben's resolve to use the passport one more time to go back and save his wife.

The Grand Tour is intelligent, humane, low-key science fiction, but it somehow misses the greatness of the original story. Part of the problem is that the mystery of who the visitors are does not seem very urgent at first, and the film suffers from languid pacing in its first half, but the second half does prove more emotionally affecting than most SF movies, and the entire project conveys Twohy's ability to tell a very human story in a science fiction context.

Following *The Grand Tour*, Twohy wrote the film *Warlock* for director Steve Minor and producer Arnold Kopelson. *Warlock* features Julian Sands as a warlock who is condemned to the gallows for trafficking with the Devil in the 17th century, who is able to mystically transport himself 300 years into the future. Only Giles Redferne (Richard E. Grant), a witch hunter who follows the warlock into the future, and Kassandra (Lori Singer), a contemporary resident of Los Angeles, stand in his way.

Twohy claimed to have conducted extensive research in and around Salem, Massachusetts, where the infamous Salem Witch Trials took place, and to have met with several self-proclaimed Salem witches to gather the background information needed to form his story, and that the Grand Grimoire, the object of the warlock's 20th century quest, is an actual book of occult lore, alternatively called *The Key of Solomon* or *The Book of Shadows*. Twohy also claims to have no belief in witchcraft or the occult. Two sequels to the film have been created thus far without Twohy's participation.

Twohy followed this with work on *The Fugitive*, directed by Andrew Davis (*Chain Reaction*) and based on the classic television series, also for producer Kopelson. Twohy's script was nominated for Best Screenplay Previously Produced or Published by the Writer's Guild of America in 1994.

Twohy continued to work in the thriller genre with *Terminal Velocity*, which he also executive produced and which was directed by Deran Sarafian. Charlie Sheen stars as a hotshot skydiving instructor who thinks that a student (Nastassja Kinski) has suddenly plummeted to her death. Trying to prove what happens winds up plunging him into danger and intrigue worthy of a Hitchcockian thriller. While Sheen seems miscast, the film contains some terrific action scenes.

Made for a reputed $175 million, *Waterworld* was little more than *Mad Max* on the water. Its cleverest moment comes when the Universal globe logo has its land masses slowly submerged. This is the future, a narrator tells us, "the polar ice caps have melted, covering the Earth with water. Those who survived adapted to a new world."

The division of peoples echoes that of your typical western. The majority of men are unadventurous, average citizens who dream of a mythical place called Dryland and whose towns are enormous man-made atolls cobbled together out of random pieces of junk.

Making their lives miserable are a group of outlaws called Smokers because they tool around on gas-powered Jet Skis, who live only to terrorize the decent. There are also lonely, enigmatic drifters whose relationship to good and evil is harder to pin down.

Kevin Costner plays one of these drifters called the Mariner, a kind of surly, seafaring curmudgeon who eats eyeballs without blinking and says things like "Killing is a hard thing to do well." The character is introduced urinating into a jar and drinking the recycled liquid. He travels the world on a grungy, 60 ft. Trimaran.

However, we don't learn too much about how life in such a difficult, hostile world is lived. Instead, there are some spectacular stunt setpieces, as when the Smokers make an all-out attack on one of the atolls.

Production designer Dennis Gassner provides an elaborate if rusted out future with able assistance from art director David Klassen and visual effects director Peter Chesney. Gassner won an Oscar for his work on *Bugsy* and has worked impressively with the Coen brothers on *Barton Fink* and *The Hudsucker Proxy*.

Peter Rader and David Twohy are the credited writers, though other hands also toiled on the tangled script. Director Kevin Reynolds had collaborated and tangled with Costner previously on *Fandango* and *Robin Hood—Prince of Thieves*, and ended up leaving the project after filming but before its final editing, which was supervised by coproducer Costner. (The editing is credited to Peter Boyle.)

The script relies on stock characterizations. Helen (Jeanne Tripplehorn) is the confused woman who is on-hand to ask "What's going on?" while Enola (Tina Majorino) is a mouthy girl Helen has adopted who has a strange map tattooed on her back that supposedly leads to the legendary Dryland. (The symbol tattooed there is omnipresent and far from inaccessible, though the plot pretends otherwise.) Dennis Hopper plays yet another psychotic villain, Deacon, in another over-the-top performance, who is determined to get his hands on Enola and the map.

Adding to the cost of the film is that it was primarily filmed on water, although rarely is this authenticity taken advantage of. (It could as easily have been largely filmed onshore with water in the background.)

Twohy wrote and produced *Skunkworks* for Great Oaks Entertainment.

The Arrival was marketed via heavy television saturation in a style that seemed to have gone out with the 1970s and failed to attract much of an audience. This is unfortunate, as the film was a better than average piece of science fiction.

The film follows the cliché of the man who makes an incredible discovery but cannot get anyone to listen to him. The hero is Zane Zaminski (Charlie Sheen), a radio astronomer searching for signs of intelligence from outer space, who one day picks up an unmistakable signal in the noisy FM band. He takes this information to his boss (Ron Silver) only to be told that there are cutbacks, that the entire operation is to be scaled back due to budget cuts, and he is unceremoniously dumped from his job.

Zaminski remains convinced that he has heard an intelligent signal from another planet and with the aid of a smart black kid from next door (Tony T. Johnson), he constructs his own home-made listening station up in his attic. In order to get access to satellite dishes, he gets a job as a consumer satellite dish repairman, secretly wiring each dish he works on into his own "phased array" network.

His investigation leads him to Mexico where he encounters another scientist (Leslie Crouse) who discusses with him the consequences of global warming and its connection to the strange situation they discover in a small Mexican village. They learn that global warming is actually a plot by aliens who are making the planet more comfortable for them before they invade.

The film features the requisite fights and chases of most thriller movies, but what makes it exceptional is the way it continually chases after ideas. Each piece of information Zaminski learns becomes a springboard for new surprises and ideas. Unlike many another science fiction film, this one follows through on its promise, keeping it fresh and interesting where other films go stale.

Twohy's recent credit was as scriptwriter of Ridley Scott's *G.I. Jane* (see Scott chapter for more information). He has filmed a new science fiction film, *Pitch Black*, in Australia, which is due to be released in 1999. It is said to be a very dark comedy.

PAUL VERHOEVEN (1938–)

Eén Hagedis Teveel (aka *One Lizard Too Many,* short 1960); *Niets Bijzonders (Nothing Special,* short, 1961); *De Lifters* (aka *The Hitchhikers*, short, 1962); *Feest* (aka *Let's Have a Party,* short, 1963); *Het Korps Mariniers* (aka *The Marine Corps*, short, 1965); *De Worstelaar* (aka *The Wrestler,* short, 1970); *Wat Zien Ik* (aka *Business Is Business*) (1971); *Turks Fruit* (aka *Turkish Delight*) (1973); *Keetje Tippel* (aka *Cathy Tippel*) (1975); *Soldaat van Oranje* (aka *Soldier of Orange*) (1977); *Spetters* (1980); *De Vierde Man* (aka *The Fourth Man*) (1983); *Flesh + Blood* (aka *The Rose & the Sword*) (1985); *RoboCop* (1987); *Total Recall* (1990); *Basic Instinct* (1992); *Showgirls* (1995); *Starship Troopers* (1997); *The Hollow Man* (2000)

Television: *Portret van Anton Adriaan Mussert* (aka *Portrait of Anton Andriaan Mussert*) (1968); "The Stolen Castle," "The Copper Dog," "The Black Bullets," "The Man from Ghent," "The Three Jesters," "The Hairy Devil," "The Permit," "The Mandrake," "The Burning Water," "The Miracle Worker," "The Byzantine Cup," "The Healing," *Floris* (Dutch, 1969); *Voorbij, Voorbij* (aka *Gone, Gone*) (1979); "Last Scene," *The Hitchhiker* (1986)

Paul Verhoeven showed little interest in science fiction before coming to America, but rather was a popular if critically reviled director in his own country of Holland where his films consistently shook people out of their complacent assumptions. He regularly endeavored to come up with scenes that people would talk about for some time to come. However, finding funding difficult in Holland, he resolved to emigrate to the United States where his initially uncertain grasp of American culture made the tackling of science fiction projects more appealing.

His first two SF films, *RoboCop* and *Total Recall,* both deal with protagonists who have lost their identities and must resolve how they will conduct themselves in the future given the unpleasant circumstances in which they find themselves. Both films proved to be immensely popular. After tackling an erotic thriller and a misunderstood cautionary tale that promised eroticism without delivering, Verhoeven returned to the science fiction genre with an adaptation of one of the genre's most acclaimed and controversial classics, Robert A. Heinlein's *Starship Troopers,* again creating controversy by the contradictions inherent in his material.

Paul Verhoeven was born in Amsterdam, Netherlands, on July 18, 1938, the long-sought son of a primary school headmaster and an infertile mother. His family fortunately survived the German occupation of The Hague. Verhoeven claims that his childhood memories of the Nazi takeover of his country inured him to violence at an early age. He vividly remembers walking along the street, seeing burning houses, being forced to walk on the bellies of dead people with tear gas in his eyes. However, like the child in Boorman's *Hope and Glory,* to Verhoeven the war was fun, a great big adventure. The bombing would simply mean there was no school that day. He lived right near where V-1 rockets would be launched, and the sight of rockets flying up excited him.

In George Hickenlooper's *Reel Conversations* he explains, "For me war was a wonderful presentation of seeing rockets fly up, and planes bombing, of people being killed. I mean, I was seven, yeah? It was like living in an amazing movie. I didn't know anything. You don't realize that. You see people thrown out in the street, into cars. You don't realize that they're taking away four or five million people, the children. If I'd been Jewish my experience would have been quite different."

Verhoeven had a poster of the Frankenstein monster

over his bed as a child, and was a big fan of Edgar Rice Burroughs' Mars adventures. Little did he know that years later he would create a popular variation on Frankenstein in *RoboCop*, or direct his own Martian adventure in *Total Recall*. He started going to movies during bombings of The Hague during Nazi occupation. Then in 1945 after Holland was liberated by the Americans, he reveled in American movies, which he sought out endlessly.

When he was fifteen, he remembers seeing Byron Haskin's *The War of the Worlds* ten times and thinking it was fantastic, and was an enormous fan of Robert Siodmak's vaguely science fictional swashbuckler *The Crimson Pirate*. When he was seventeen or eighteen, his uncle Arie de Groot gave him a 16mm camera, which Verhoeven started experimenting with. He practiced making three minute films of his friends.

He also became very interested in painting while studying mathematics at a university, where he also got involved with a film group. His father continued to hope that he would become a mathematics teacher. Before sending young Paul off to college, his father sent him to St. Quentin in the north of France for a year where he stayed with friends of the family while retaking his last year of high school in French and without exams.

Verhoeven was educated in the University of Leiden, the oldest university in the country, where he studied mathematics and physics. In 1959, his parents allowed Paul to register at the newly formed Nederlande Filmacademie in Amsterdam, provided he did not give up his mathematics and physics studies. Traditional Dutch filmmaking was restricted to documentaries, but the government set up a fund, the Productiefonds, which could loan filmmakers money to stimulate feature film production. Verhoeven studied under Prof. Peters and filmmaker Anton Koolhaas, but he quit the course early in his second year because he felt he was not learning anything.

However, with his circle of friends, in 1960 Verhoeven made his first student film, a three-minute short. In it, a woman stares into a pair of coffee cups, sees an image reflected in the coffee of one cup, and when she looks up, a teaspoon has unexpectedly been moved from the cup to the table. Most onlookers found the film confusing, but saw that Verhoeven was playing with visual imagery rather than simply trying to film a play. They were encouraged enough to offer him the opportunity to direct a 35-minute Buñuelean short, *Eén Hagedis Teveel* (*One Lizard Too Many*).

In it, the wife of a makeup effects artist begins an affair with a student and explains how her husband is able to sculpt anybody except her, forcing her to take on different identities while posing in a vain attempt to create a true-to-life sculpture, making her realize that he is more in love with what he wants her to be than with whom she actually is. (Verhoeven was quite enamoured of Hitchcock's *Vertigo,* with stylistic elements from Alaiun Resnais' *Hiroshima mon Amour* thrown in for good measure.) The student already has a girlfriend and the wife convinces the girl to switch places and pose for the wife's husband, thereby solving the husband's problem but not her own. Ominous lizards crawl through a couple of scenes, adding incipherable surrealistic symbolism.

Verhoeven also tried his hand at painting and was a great admirer of Salvador Dalí and Yves Tanguy, and for a long time contemplated a career as a painter. However, *Eén Hagedis Teveel* wound up winning first prize at the international student film festival Cinestud in Amsterdam, and Verhoeven committed himself to a film career by destroying several of his canvases. He went on to try his hand at several more shorts, *De Lifters* (*The Hitchhikers*, 1962), *Niets Bijzonders* (*Nothing Special*, 1961), and *Feest* (*Let's Have a Party*, 1963), the last of which won first prize at the Cork Film Festival and received commendations from other film festivals as well. However, Verhoeven was very shaken when his scriptwriting partner on all these shorts, Jan van Mastrigt, committed suicide in June of 1964.

In 1964, Verhoeven finished his studies as a mathematician, passing his doctoral examinations in mathematics and physics (main subject: theory of relativity), and went into the military service for two years, getting himself moved into the film department in the Navy. The Marines were about to celebrate their tercentenary, and Verhoeven was given the sum of 100,000 guilders to create *Het Korps Mariniers* (*The Marine Corps*) to commemorate the occasion as well as be used as a recruitment film afterwards. For the first time, Verhoeven was able to work in color and without restrictions, and the film later won first prize at a festival for propaganda films in France.

Following his two-year term of service, Verhoeven wanted to become a feature film director, but there was no Dutch film industry and the country's total output was minuscule, producing from zero to three films a year. His girlfriend Martine became unexpectedly pregnant and the pair were quickly married on April 7, 1967. Verhoeven sought guidance in a Pentecostal–type church and was informed that God wanted him to go to faraway countries to preach the gospel (an experience Verhoeven somewhat duplicated in *Spetters*).

Verhoeven considered an abortion, but while taking in a screening of *King Kong,* an advertisement urging that "In the script of your life, God plays the main role," and a perception of Kong as an avenging angel convinced Verhoeven to keep the baby while pursuing a career as an artist committed to anchoring his work in reality. Unable to get a film financed, he turned to Dutch television. He first gained attention for the children's television series *Floris*, which Verhoeven compares to Walter Scott's *Ivanhoe* and which began his association with Rutger Hauer, then an unknown 24-year-old actor.

In 1971, German-Dutch film producer Rob Houwer had seen Verhoeven's work on *Floris* and offered him the opportunity to direct his first feature film, *Wat Zien Ik* (aka *Business Is Business*), a comedy about Amsterdam's red light district, based on a popular book by Albert Mol that composited stories of various prostitutes, including some transvestites who could not satisfy their customers in the usual ways. Verhoeven and scriptwriter Gerard Soeteman turned the work into a popular sex comedy with a budget of 600,000 guilders, of which Verhoeven received 10,000 guilders. Verhoeven himself tried acting shortly after his feature debut by appearing in *Oh Jonathan, Oh Jonathan*.

However, it was *Turkish Delight*, based on a popular novel by Jan Wolkers, starring Rutger Hauer and Monique Van de Ven which first gained Verhoeven international attention. The film was nominated for an Academy Award for Best Foreign Film and was the most popular Dutch-made film of all time in Holland. It continued Verhoeven's association with screenwriter Gerard Soetemann, who would work with Verhoeven on *Cathy Tippel* and then *Soldier of Orange*.

Hauer plays Erik, a handsome young sculptor whose work is sexually oriented. He spends his free time picking up young women from all over Amsterdam for short sexual encounters. He's shown to be an insensitive male chauvinist who goes so far as to keep souvenirs of his sexual conquests.

We finally learn the source of this behavior when the film flashes back to a couple of years previously when he was deeply in love with Olga (Monique Van Der Ven). The couple is shown as sexually uninhibited, carefree, volatile, and rebellious, taking pride in affronting "respectable" society. Then it is discovered that Olga has a brain tumor, which alters her behavior, and she breaks off their relationship. The couple behave fairly obnoxiously throughout, but they have a truly passionate, sexual bond, unlike the sculptor's later conquests. When Olga inevitably dies, the film is truly tender and touching, demonstrating that Erik's lust has matured into a deeply felt love. The sculptor is depicted as a shattered man who uses sex unsuccessfully to both recapture and blot out the memory of his lost love.

"It's a very romantic film," said Verhoeven, "but the beginning of the film is extremely rough and violent, which was intended. To prepare the audience for complete nudity so that by the time you got to the second part of the film, the romantic part, the nudity in the love affair would be seen not as extreme but as normal. And from that point on you could use nudity to express *feelings*."

Turkish Delight was sexually graphic enough to earn an X rating in this country and could be considered softcore porn by some. Still, this is not a happy sex film or an erotic fantasy. It is, however, genuinely daring in depicting how these unbalanced and unstable people can relate to each other best through their sexuality.

However, despite *Turkish Delight's* financial success, Verhoeven's salary was only 20,000 guilder, and his wife was expecting a second child. Applying for unemployment, Verhoeven was anxious to begin a new project right away. Finally, after fretting over what he could do that would top *Turkish Delight* and fearing that he might get typed as a "sex film" director, Verhoeven settled on *Keetje Tippel*, based on the memoirs of Neel Doff.

Houwer convinced him that the book could be filmed on the grand, epic scale to which Verhoeven had long aspired. The costume drama was given a budget of 2 million guilders, up to that time the most expensive Dutch film ever made. However, the initial script proved too long and attempted too grand a scale, and so had to be scaled back. Monique Van De Ven was brought on to play the lead, with Hauer as one of her main costars. Cameraman Jan de Bont, who filmed Verhoeven's previous two features, fell in love with and married Van De Ven, and he began protesting her nude scenes. Houwer objected to the shipboard sex scene which opens the film in which Keetje searches for her older sister and finds her making love to a sailor in exchange for two bacon sandwiches.

Keetje's mother encourages Mina and Keetje to prostitute themselves in order to raise food to feed their family. Keetje transitions into becoming an artist's model, and she falls in love with Hugo (Hauer), a bank clerk who is friends with her painter. Hugo eventually rejects her for not being of his class, but she meets and eventually marries a rich, socialist lawyer, André (Eddy Brugman), who cares for her and completes her climb up the social ladder.

Unfortunately, rather than being a stirring saga of the emergence of socialism, *Keetje Tippel* becomes little more than an episodic Cinderella variation, lacking in verisimilitude and structure. The film, little more than a colorful collage of incidents, proved a critical and financial disappointment, and Verhoeven bristled that Houwer altered the ending after the film had been playing for seven weeks, reinserting an ending the producer had initially rejected, though the new ending made the conclusion less ambiguous.

Soldier of Orange helped make stars of Rutger Hauer and Jeroen Krabbé, though Verhoeven initially had grave doubts about having Hauer play someone with an aristocratic background. Verhoeven cowrote the screenplay with Gerard Soeteman and Kees Holierhoek, based on the autobiographical novel by Erik Hazelhoff Roelfzema. Soeteman

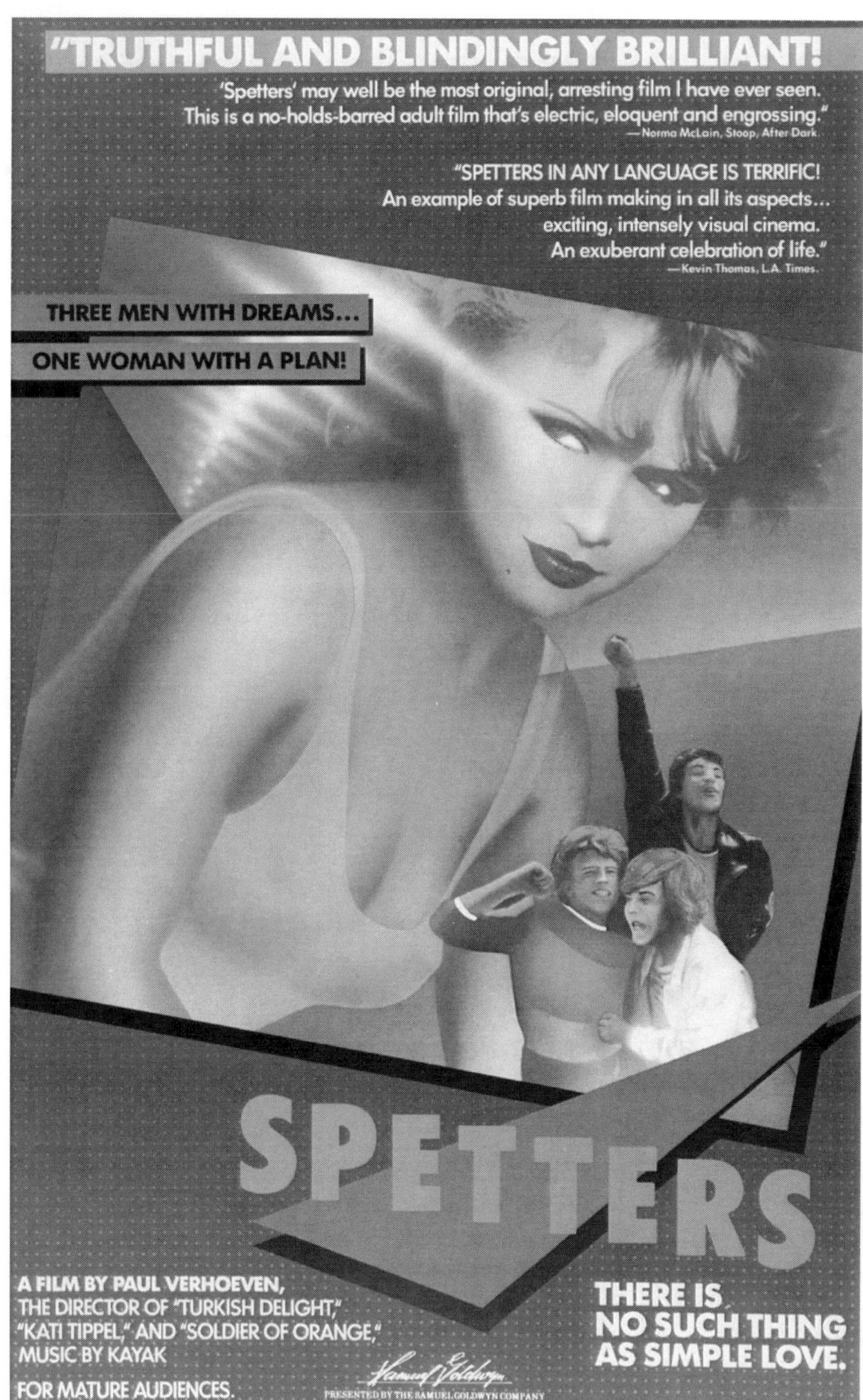

"TRUTHFUL AND BLINDINGLY BRILLIANT!
'Spetters' may well be the most original, arresting film I have ever seen. This is a no-holds-barred adult film that's electric, eloquent and engrossing."
—Norma McLain, Stoop, After Dark
"SPETTERS IN ANY LANGUAGE IS TERRIFIC! An example of superb film making in all its aspects... exciting, intensely visual cinema. An exuberant celebration of life."
—Kevin Thomas, L.A. Times
THREE MEN WITH DREAMS...
ONE WOMAN WITH A PLAN!
SPETTERS
A FILM BY PAUL VERHOEVEN, THE DIRECTOR OF "TURKISH DELIGHT," "KATI TIPPEL," AND "SOLDIER OF ORANGE," MUSIC BY KAYAK
FOR MATURE AUDIENCES.
THERE IS NO SUCH THING AS SIMPLE LOVE.
PRESENTED BY THE SAMUEL GOLDWYN COMPANY

Verhoeven was controversial back in Holland with films such as *Spetters*.

brought the book to Verhoeven's attention as the basis for a possible television series, but they couldn't manage to get the money together. Finally, Verhoeven sent the script to Prince Bernard, the prince of the Netherlands and consort to Queen Juliana, and he gave the project his honorary protection, which opened many doors in Holland, including aid from the military. Thus Rob Houwer was able to finance the film for around $2 million when it would otherwise have cost four or five million.

The attitude of *Soldier of Orange* is that war is an adventure. Erik (Hauer), the main protagonist, sums this up when he says, "There's a war? That's not bad ... that's nice, that's funny." He is not a deeply motivated anti-fascist, but simply a guy who feels the Germans shouldn't be occupying his country.

Life seems full of romance and innocent adventure for six elitist but naïve classmates at the University of Leiden as they begin their college careers in the fall of 1938. But the tide of events is not in their favor, and the German invasion of Holland interrupts whatever plans are being made. The coming of war affects each of the six differently.

Alex sympathizes with the Nazis, while Robby does whatever is necessary to protect the well-being of his Jewish fiancée. Erik and Guus (Krabbé) become freedom fighters, engineering an escape to England where they are presented to Queen Wilhelmina of Holland, now ruling her country in exile.

Under the tutelage of a daring British intelligence officer (Edward Fox), Eric and Guus return to their homeland undercover where they deliver an important message to the key members of the Dutch underground. Eventually the war ends victoriously and the two surviving classmates reunite to share their experiences and begin their lives anew.

Steven Spielberg was much impressed by the quality of *Soldier of Orange*, which his producer Kathleen Kennedy had showed him. After the film won the Golden Globe for best foreign film, Spielberg phoned Verhoeven and suggested that he come and work in America where Spielberg offered to introduce him to some of the studios. In a spirit of curiosity, Verhoeven made his first trip to the west coast of the U.S. in the spring of 1980, and he later learned that Spielberg intended to recommend to George Lucas that Verhoeven direct *Return of the Jedi* until the explicit *Spetters* dissuaded him.

Verhoeven formed a new company, VSE Film BV, with Soeteman and Joop van den Ende, and together they produced *Voorbij, Voorbij* (*Gone, Gone*) for Dutch television. The project dealt with WWII Resistence workers who bury a comrade who was shot by a Dutch SS member just days before the Liberation. Years later, Ab (André van den Heuvel) sees the former SS member and tries to get his comrades-in-arms together to extract revenge, but quickly discovers that everyone wants to leave the past alone. In a sense, it formed the flip side of *Soldier of Orange*, showing how these men would be different thirty-five years later.

Spetters is something of a Dutch *Breaking Away*, centering on the dreams of three working class young men from a village near Rotterdam, which became notorious for its unwillingness to be politically correct. The title is Dutch slang for "good-looking young men." The film was written by Gerard Soeteman and produced by Joop Van Den Ende, as Verhoeven attempted to find a new producer other than Houwer to work with. Soeteman's concept was that of a modern-day fairy tale with three knights (riding motorcycles instead of steeds) vying for the hand of a princess.

Rutger Hauer makes only a token appearance in *Spetters*, playing the idolized world class motocross champion Gerrit Witkamp (based on Dutch motocross rider Gerrit Wolsink). The story actually centers around three young men who are close friends in a small industrial town on the outskirts of Rotterdam. Rien (Hans van Tongeren) and Hans (Maarten Spanjer) are carpenters. Both are competitors on the amateur racing circuit, and Rien's special talents indicate that he will be the heir apparent to Witkamp's title. The other, Eef (Toon Agterberg) is a first-class mechanic. (Rien as the most heroic wears white leathers, while the sexually conflicted Eef is dressed in a two-toned outfit of red and black, and the timid Hans wears yellow.)

While at the races, the three men meet a young seductress named Fientje (Renee Soutendijk) who, together with her homosexual brother Jaap, runs a mobile fast food stand. Enterprising and opportunistic, Fientje will eventually entwine her life with that of each of the three comrades. (The character was condemned in some circles as a whore, though that was not Verhoeven's intention.)

First Fientje latches onto Rien, recognizing his talent on the track and the inherent potential for the wealth which follows success. After settling in his town, she does everything to gain his favor, eventually interceding on his behalf at the racetrack, convincing a well-known sportscaster (Jeroen Krabbé) that his Japanese colleagues should sponsor Rien on the circuit. Two shimmering new motorbikes and handsome royalties follow. With that, Fientje attains her own victory, edging out Rien's steady girlfriend, Maja (Marianne Boyer).

But Rien's promising future is cut short when a freak road accident leaves him an embittered paraplegic. Rien rejects his new lover — he won't allow room for another amid his self-pity. Fientje easily diverts her attentions. As she remarks to her brother when queried on her short-lived love, "Give me security and love will follow."

Next in line is Eef. The son of a bible-thumping Calvinist, he turns to mugging and blackmailing gay men. He needs to get enough money to cater to Fientje's extravagant tastes and convince her to run away with him to Canada. But his plans, too, are rechanneled after he endures a brutal rape by Fientje's brother and his cohorts. The experience forces Eef to confront his own latent homosexuality.

Last comes Hans. Inheritor of his friend's Japanese motorbikes, he hopes to one day attain champion status. Fientje decides to go along for the ride, but Witkamp makes sport of him in a practice session and Hans is soon relegated to the "also rans."

Witkamp wins the final race and is declared world champion. His victory comes in strong contrast to the shattered dreams of the three young friends with Rien's fate the most tragic as he steers his wheelchair beneath the wheels of an oncoming truck. Eef, having come out of the closet, continues his search for personal identity. Hans puts aside his boyhood dreams, sells the bikes in order to start a chip shop with Fientje — their nest egg for the secure future which all have been seeking.

Spetters was not well received in Holland, where Verhoeven was denounced as a decadent pervert and the film was decried as antigay, antifeminist, and anti-invalid. Verhoeven countered that he was simply being honest in portraying the way people act, and that some people indulge in outrageous, unethical behavior. He later admitted that he was very angry when he made the film, though he still considers it a cynical but true portrait of humanity.

The original Dutch version featured male erections and on-camera oral sex that were trimmed from the U.S. release version, where such footage would have guaranteed the film an X rating. While Holland allowed the film to be released uncut with a rating that denied admittance to anyone under sixteen, a group calling itself the National Anti-*Spetters* Committee was formed to denounce the film, telling listeners that it was a fascist movie that promoted the idea that invalids should commit suicide. Verhoeven wanted the film to be provocative, to show things that are true and real, but normally omitted. It proved an indication of the controversies to come.

Verhoeven was considered by Columbia Pictures to direct *Death Comes as the End*, based on an Agatha Christie novel as an American-Dutch coproduction. Anthony

Shaffer (*Sleuth*) had already done a draft, and another by Soeteman was ordered; however, once studio head Frank Price moved on to Universal, the project was scrapped. Verhoeven decided his next project would be based on the novella *De Vierde Man* by the celebrated Dutch writer Gerard Reve.

According to Verhoeven, *The Fourth Man* has more to do with his vision of religion. He sees Christianity as a major symptom of schizophrenia in half the world's population, an example of civilizations scrambling to rationalize their chaotic existence. He wanted audiences to ponder, "What is religion really?", to consider that Christianity is a religion grounded in a violent act of murder, that of crucifixion.

While *The Fourth Man* initially comes across as Eurotrash gloom and doom, it cunningly transforms itself into a wicked comedy. Verhoeven is obviously fond of the combination of sex, violence, and passion, and *The Fourth Man* is a cynical foray into the mysteries of human sexuality. It's a psychological mystery-thriller, an ingenious character study about a brilliant alcoholic-homosexual writer beset with premonitions of violence and death. The writer Gerard Reve (Jeroen Krabbé) fantasizes about murdering his boyfriend and then takes off to give a lecture in Flushing, Netherlands, where he keeps seeing portentous omens while romancing a blonde femme fatale because he is attracted to a photograph of her boyfriend Herman (Thom Hoffman), whom he had desperately tried to pick up in an Amsterdam train station. He is preoccupied with death, getting more misanthropic every day, and drifting into alcoholism.

The woman in the film, Christine Halslag (Renée Soutendijk), is eager to set him up in an ideal situation. She gives him money, booze, peace and comfort to write, and the promise of plenty of hot action. She is based on a real person whom the real Reve knew. She had a husband who died by an accident, and then she had a boyfriend who had died as well when Reve met her. When the writer returned to Amsterdam, he heard later that another boyfriend of hers had an accident where he lost an eye. Reve used this incident as the basis for his story. The title comes from the idea that three of the woman's previous boyfriends have died, and Reve fears that he will become the fourth.

"There can be no love between a man who is really 100 percent homosexual and a woman who is searching for a man for company," commented Verhoeven about the film to Mary Beth Crane in the *L.A. Weekly*. "Or perhaps she is a witch and wants to eat the guy — to fuck him and then crush him.... It's like a love scene in ice. Extremely cold, with this greenish moon — a really devilish atmosphere. It's something special — a horror scene in love!"

The Fourth Man is a virtual catalogue of images that make people uncomfortable: close-up of a spider in its web; male nudity; amateur violin playing; the D.T.'s; strangulation; homosexuality; premonitions; hallucination of an eyeball in a door, after which the eyeball comes out of its socket; funeral procession; public speaking; blood donation; gory auto accident; androgyny; carcasses on meathooks dripping blood; castration nightmare; broken glass; a dead bird; drowning; crucifixion and other Christian iconography; a vicious dog; free fall — parachute malfunctions during sky diving; voyeurism; masturbation; graveyard; electrical storm; entering mausoleum; men kissing; being attacked by lion; impalement through the eye; hospitals; anesthesia; loss of reason or sanity.

The result was a suspenseful, funny, and startling film that could play either to the arthouse crowd or more general audiences willing to be adventurous. Both Soutendijik and Krabbé give excellent performances, despite not being very sympathetic characters, and the finale to the film is unforgettable, outclassing everything that had gone before. Verhoeven does a high wire act throughout where we cannot really be certain whether events are real or only taking place in Reve's fevered, fertile imagination. (He even steals the dream within a dream idea from John Landis' *American Werewolf in London.*)

While Christine emerges as the ultimate femme fatale (Verhoeven even includes a lovemaking scene on a beach where she lies on some glass, but does not feel it, according to superstition, one of the ways of recognizing a witch), Verhoeven also includes a mysterious figure who can only be interpreted as the femme celeste. As in medieval imagery, this Mary wears blue, a blue raincoat. Gerard sees her for the first time when he takes the train to Vlissingen and she shares a compartment with him, complete with a little boy in her arm with an apple-peel halo above his head. In Gerard's dreams, she shows him the way to goodness, and finally manifests herself as the nurse Ria when, after Herman's fatal auto accident, the writer winds up in the hospital. He attributes his survival to protection from the Queen of Heaven, echoing the real Reve's Mariolatry.

Verhoeven found getting financing for his films in Holland increasingly difficult. There the government supplies 50–60 percent of the budget, and scripts had to go through a committee to be judged. The Dutch leftist government did not care much for either *Spetters* or *The Fourth Man*, and was reluctant to approve further financing despite Verhoeven's financial success. He resolved therefore to go to Hollywood.

Verhoeven's first Hollywood film is the largely forgotten medieval drama *Flesh + Blood*, released on video as *The Rose & the Sword.* Verhoeven and Soeteman sold Orion on producing a story of Soeteman's called "The Mercenaries," which was intended as a medieval version of *The Wild*

Bunch in which members of a gang are compelled to fight on different sides of the law. The studio wanted there to be more of a love story, so the role of Princess Agnes was greatly increased, but the story lost much of its focus in the process.

Scripted by Verhoeven and Gerard Soeteman, set in the 16th century, *Flesh + Blood* starred Rutger Hauer as Martin, a soldier of fortune whose mercenary band helps a noble, Arnolfini (Fernando Hillbeck), take a town only to be betrayed by their leader, Hawkwood (Jack Thompson), who tells the band that the noble has reneged on his deal that they could keep the loot they ransack. (Arnolfini felt compelled to stop them before they destroyed the town, and Hawkwood is suffused by guilt for having struck a nun in the head with his blade after she fired on his soldiers and hid behind a curtain.)

Martin's pregnant girlfriend Céline (Susan Tyrell) gives birth to a stillborn babe, and as the dead infant is being buried, his band of rogues uncover a statue of St. Martin, which the Cardinal (Ronald Lacey) interprets as a portent from God that Martin will lead them on to become rich men. They resolve therefore to become robbers and steal back the loot that was taken from them.

Meanwhile, the noble has arranged a marriage for his inventive son Steven (Tom Burlinson), an admirer and emulator of Leonardo da Vinci's, to a convent-raised noble virgin named Agnes (Jennifer Jason-Leigh). Agnes proves a manipulative little minx who insists that her maid make love to her boyfriend to see how it is done. She coaxes Steven into loving her by getting him to take a bite of mandrake root while she consumes the other half.

Thus when Martin's band, disguised as monks, take her away, Steven resolves not to rest until he has recovered her. Agnes is attracted to Martin, who initially is ready to let her be raped by all the male members of his band, but takes her virginity (another blood reference) and then maintains her as his concubine. Together, he and Agnes climb down the chimney of a castle, landing in a blaze of sparks and convincing the inhabitants that they have been invaded by demons before opening the doors for the rest of the band, who quickly kill the guards and take the spoils for themselves.

The lady of the castle takes her daughter in her arms and jumps from the highest tower rather than face the robbers. The child survives but carries the black plague which infects Hawkwood, who only survives because Steven instructs him to lance his boils. Steven lays siege to the castle with an ingeniously constructed (albeit unlikely) war machine; however, Martin uses one of Steven's inventions, a gunpowder barrel bomb, against him and blows it up, trapping Steven inside the castle.

Hawkwood vows revenge and hurls chunks of black plague infested dog into the castle to kill the inhabitants. At first Steven warns them, but he then chucks that last overlooked piece of disease-ridden carcass into the drinking supply, leaving it up to Agnes whether to tell them or not. She fails to mention it before some of the party who drink the water quickly come down with the plague and consequently turn against Martin, who has told them that they have nothing to fear.

Flesh + Blood ends with the decimation of everyone except the three principals, Steven, Agnes, and Martin. Ultimately, the film becomes a clash between Martin's fatalistic Christianity and Steven's progressive-thinking Renaissance man, between those guided by superstition and those who solve problems in a scientific way. It presents a thoroughly unromanticized look at the middle ages that, like much of Verhoeven's other work, ran counter to audience desires and expectations.

Verhoeven keeps the film lively and gives it a good look (along with cinematographer and future director Jan De Bont), never shying away from depicting the uglier aspects of medieval life, in fact, almost reveling in them. The title refers not only to holy communion, but also the life and concerns of a soldier, the temptations of the flesh, and the plague-infected blood of the dog. None of the characters are made to seem likable: Martin is more a steely eyed psychopath than lovable rogue (though Hauer seems to be playing his despicable character as if he were somehow heroic); Agnes is callous towards others and always uncertain of her allegiance; and even Steven is shown to be something of a hypocrite (he abhors his father's treatment of the mercenaries but delights in designing the engines of war) who cruelly coerces Hawkwood into assisting him.

The MPAA initially slapped an X rating on the film until Verhoeven removed a scene where Rutger Hauer shoots an arrow into the eye of a man and substituted a non-revealing angle on a scene where Hauer pulls Jennifer Jason-Leigh toward him by her nipples. Not surprisingly, while the basic truthfulness of much of Verhoeven's approach in *Flesh + Blood* is admirable, the detestable elements turned audiences off and prevented the film from achieving anything remotely akin to popularity or success.

Verhoeven traveled to Vancouver to shoot an episode of the HBO cable series *The Hitchhiker* as a way of easing himself into American production methods. The set of *Flesh + Blood* had proved quite chaotic, with frequent arguments between Verhoeven and Hauer, the difficulties of working on the Spanish locations, a mutinous, slow-moving Spanish crew, and American cast members more dedicated to partying than to working.

Despite these difficulties, Orion offered him another film, *RoboCop*. The project had been offered to a number of directors already who had all turned it down, but Orion

Verhoeven acts the role of the ED-209 robot for the benefit of the cast and crew.

head Mike Medavoy became convinced that Verhoeven was the right man for the job. The project appealed to Orion because of the large, unexpected grosses from James Cameron's *The Terminator*. The original script for *RoboCop* was written in 1984 by Michael Miner and Ed Neumeier, and was intended to be a live action, comic book-style film. Neumeier was inspired by *Blade Runner*, in which robots look like and become like people and decided to flip it into a cop who looked like a robot, who becomes a machine.

Neumeier and Miner decided to write it as a satire, exonerating the yuppie life style they saw around them where people dedicate themselves totally to greed and get away with it. Thus, in the Detroit of *RoboCop*, Omni Consumer Products is a corporation that runs everything and is dedicated to the idea of privatization for profit. Producer Jon Davison (*Airplane!, Twilight Zone — The Movie*) became a firm believer in the project and shepherded it along with the understanding that it would only have a 13 week shooting schedule.

"When Orion offered me *RoboCop*, I was not interested," said Verhoeven in Hickenlooper's *Reel Conversations*. "I only saw a very idiotic action movie, and I hate action and science fiction movies. But Orion asked me to take a second look at the script. They kept emphasizing that it was about the indestructibility of the human spirit, of the individual — a very American concept. So I became interested in that, and my wife also encouraged me to do it. She reminded me of how much I liked *Frankenstein*: the idea of a monster searching for himself. The same concept applied to *RoboCop*, so I did it."

Verhoeven came to realize that as a newcomer to the United States, science fiction would be a good way to go because it allowed the filmmaker a great deal of freedom and did not require specific knowledge of U.S. culture in the here and now, which a film including say racial and social comment would. Verhoeven offered several drastic suggestions for improving the script in order to make it more realistic, so the writers deleted and rewrote, with Miner falling seriously ill. Neumeier gave Verhoeven several American comics to read to help him understand the tone that the writers were after, and when Verhoeven saw the script with his changes, he pronounced it terrible and reverted back to the second draft script with a new understanding of the project.

RoboCop was produced for a mere $13.1 million, which was $4 million less than the industry average at that time. This was partially due to the efforts of producer Jon Davison, who learned how to shave costs at Roger Corman's New World and had previously produced Joe Dante's *Piranha* as well as the comedies *Airplane!* and *Top Secret*. *RoboCop* was actually budgeted for $11 million, but after Orion West Coast production chief Mike Medavoy saw Verhoeven's dailies, he allowed the film a little more time and budget.

Back in 1984, Orion gave Davison a two-year production deal. Davison's friend Jonathan Kaplan brought him the *RoboCop* script by rookie screenwriters Ed Neumeier and Michael Miner. Orion approved the project and Kaplan was set to direct, but left to helm *Project X* over at 20th Century–Fox instead. This left Davison searching for a director to replace him. When agents heard the title, Davison said, "There was immediate disinterest. Nobody wanted their client to be in it except people who hadn't worked in a long time."

Finally getting Verhoeven to agree, Davison and Verhoeven decided to shoot the second draft of the script and never considered bringing in other writers. Orion wanted a name actor for the lead, but again Davison found resistance.

"For every director who didn't want to direct *RoboCop*, there were 100 actors who didn't want to play the part," Davison said. "It was not easy to find an actor willing to spend a couple of months inside a rubber suit in Dallas in the summer with five square inches of his face showing. We needed a talented guy with good body language. Put Arnold Schwartzenegger [sic] in the RoboCop suit, and he'd look like the Pillsbury Doughboy."

It took makeup effects whiz Rob Bottin six months to sculpt the RoboCop costume, which was the single most important and most expensive item in the picture. Fights between Bottin and Verhoeven over the design became legendary (at one point, the director even took a spatula to Bottin's already existing clay sculpture), but ultimately Bottin was able to craft something that satisfied them both.

Verhoeven was influenced by the robot from Fritz Lang's *Metropolis*, one of Verhoeven's favorite films, as a starting point.

When Orion asked them to shoot outside of California, Davison and Verhoeven selected Dallas because of its modern skyline, unlike Detroit where the story is set, and because of its sophisticated production facilities. After seeing the rough cut of the film, Orion poneyed up with an additional $600,000 in extra postproduction money which allowed the filmmakers to add Basil Poledouris' symphonic score, high-tech sound effects, and Dolby stereo.

RoboCop's biggest cop-out, which reduced its overall nastiness, was transforming the head of the corporation responsible for all the mayhem into a benign father figure, making the movie seem merely glib or comic bookish and less sharply satirical. The film overall benefits from the writers' tongue-in-cheek approach, after all, the film is basically about a guy in a special supersuit walking around and should not be taken too seriously, but blunted satire becomes pointless.

Criterion laserdiscs under the guidance of Paul Sammon assembled a deluxe edition of Paul Verhoeven's *RoboCop* in a special, unrated director's cut with a few seconds of "excessive violence" that was cut from the theatrical release to avoid an X rating. (The additional violence includes some blood squibs when ED-209 blows away a hapless corporate exec and a bit of extra gore in Murphy's demise, but not enough to alter the film's 103 minute running time or its impact. According to his commentary, Verhoeven found the extra violence of the first sequence amusing and he wanted Murphy's death to be memorably powerful given that Weller has only a short amount of screen time before he dons Rob Bottin's RoboCostume.)

RoboCop shows Nancy Allen off at her most hard-hitting (her Anne Lewis is one woman who could literally blow others away) and yet human. Her ability to be both tough as nails and yet sweet was a prime asset in her roles for ex-husband Brian De Palma's films *Carrie, Home Movies, Dressed to Kill,* and *Blow Out*. She has come a long way from her sexy roles as Travolta's domineering girlfriend in *Carrie* and trading double entendres in Spielberg's *1941.*

In *RoboCop*, she's still sexy, and her ability in subduing a suspect is something to be reckoned with, but it is her partnership with Murphy and later his robotic doppelgänger that really helps the audience to care about the RoboCop character himself. She makes the connection from a characteristic move that Murphy imitated off the show *T. J. Lazer* to impress his son that RoboCop is her former partner Murphy, and so she starts addressing him like and treating him like a person, which sparks his return to humanity and his search for the thugs who killed him.

However, Allen was initially unsure about the project

Paul Verhoeven was convinced by his wife to accept the assignment to direct *RoboCop*, as she likened the project to Frankenstein.

when she first met with Verhoeven while he was filming the Bixby Snyder segments, a vapid TV show which co-opts SF writer Cyril Kornbluth's moronic catchphrase, "I'd buy that for a dollar," that plays in the background on televisions throughout the film.

Also uncertain was Peter Weller, hired to play RoboCop/Murphy. Weller had gained cult status with *The Adventures of Buckaroo Banzai Across the Eighth Dimension* and has an interesting, off-the-wall quality. He is a dedicated Method actor, and he sought the assistance of Moni Yakim, professor of movement at the New York Juilliard School to help him develop a distinctive walk for the character, but Bottin's suit arrived late and Weller found it unbearably heavy, hot, and bulky, and after twelve hours, simply refused to come out of his trailer. The $600,000 suit had been specifically tailored for him, but the filmmakers threatened to fire him as a way of bringing him around. Fortunately for the film, it did, and Weller spent the weekend practicing his movements, and let the weight of the suit work to make the character more pathetic, angular and uncertain. It is a terrific mime performance, and one notices the difference in quality when others have assumed the role.

Allen's character ends up shot, but is assured by Robo-

Makeup designer Rob Bottin poses next to Peter Weller in the RoboCop costume.

RoboCop is the work of a number of talented gentlemen, including producer Jon Davison, writers Edward Neumeier (the ED-209 is named after him) and Michael Miner, Verhoeven, whose masterful direction which keeps the film from veering too funny, too violent, too serious, or too comic book, Bottin's convincing costume and makeup, Phil Tippet's stop motion photography, the crisp cinematography of Vacano and the sharp editing of Frank J. Urioste (who received an Academy Award nomination for his work on the film), as well as a terrific cast.

As an in-joke, Urisote inserted a brief clip of Verhoeven dancing crazily in the club where RoboCop goes to look for the evil Clarence Boddicker and his stooges. Verhoeven inserted himself into the film in another way, serving as the inspiration for the bespectacled gas station attendant who is studying analytic geometry before Emil, Clarence's wheel man, threatens to blow the attendant's brains out. The attendant quickly flees before the entire gas station explodes, barely escaping a nightmare that echoes the young man's past and future.

Verhoeven's style is characterized by constant movement and energy which give the film its blistering tempo. Cameraman Volcano extensively employs prowling steadycam shots that are lit in the industrial, neon style of Cameron's *The Terminator* and Luc Besson's *Subway*.

While *RoboCop*'s view of the future is a bleak and satirical one, the film realizes that technology is not so much to be feared as coped with, and that the really dangerous powers reside in an ever coopting corporate America. In *RoboCop*, a half-naked female cop is shown next to male colleagues adjusting a protective harness without being subjected to comments or harassment, suggesting a future where gender differences have ceased being an issue.

In Murphy's memories of his previous family life, we see that life was not unpleasant for the average suburban dweller despite the highly armed miscreants that are RoboCop's duty to pursue and capture. In many ways, *RoboCop* shows our own times simply writ larger, with the transformed policeman simply the savior of his time (Verhoeven slyly inserted Christian symbolism) who undergoes death and resurrection on a technological cross, and in the end walks on water and dispatches the evils that still plague society. Murphy with his empty house and lost past, his machine body, and skin stretched onto metal face remains a supremely poignant figure. *RoboCop* has been

Cop that they can fix her, "They can fix anything." Originally, the film was to have ended with a MediaBreak ("Give Us Three Minutes and We'll Give You the World") which would have shown her recovering from her wound rather than being turned into a RoboChick, but this was excised after preview screenings when it was thought to be anti-climactic after Robo tells the Old Man (Dan O'Herlihy) to call him "Murphy," at last accepting his original identity.

Kurtwood Smith is deliberately made-up to suggest Himmler. Rob Bottin wanted the RoboSuit shot in chiaroscuro rather than the bright, reflective light d.p. Jost Vacano eventually used, adding to the director's irritation. The character is kept out of the audience's sight initially (concealed by frosty glass, shot from behind or through a cage) to give the audience time to accept it.

called a fascist fable for liberals, but it is an undeniably imaginative, engaging, and entertaining one.

The film has inspired two sequels, the over-the-top *RoboCop 2*, directed by Irvin Kershner from a script by comic book artist Frank Miller, which pits Murphy against a legion of drug dealers and finally, in the film's only interesting sequence, against an evil robot version of the ED-209 controlled by the disembodied brain of one of the villains; and *RoboCop 3*, directed by Fred Dekker, which is toned down for a PG rating, replaces Peter Weller, and features a weak story about Murphy helping Detroit's homeless who are being kicked off the streets by OCP. Neither was very successful, nor were an animated series and a short-lived live action spin-off television series that barely lasted a season.

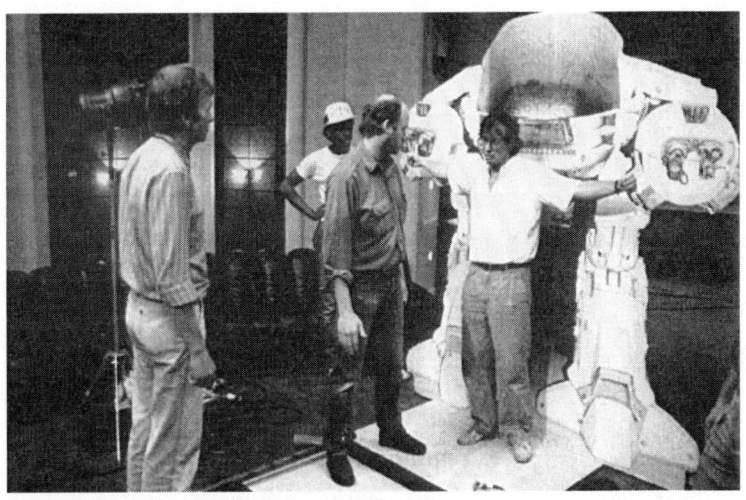

Verhoeven using a cardboard cut-out to aid in shooting a VistaVision background plate for *RoboCop* with special effects supervisor Phil Tippett.

Meanwhile, Verhoeven has long wanted to do a film which features the historical Christ rather than the mythical one. To that end, he began attending meetings of the Jesus Seminar to listen to discussions led by Professor Robert W. Funk, whose group published the revisionist *The Five Gospels* in 1993, which included the recently discovered Gospel of Thomas. Verhoeven's film is guaranteed to provoke controversy, and based on the knowledge that under Jewish law, rabbis and other spiritual teachers were forbidden to earn money from their religious teachings, assumes that Jesus made his living as a carpenter, working on everything from tables and chairs to walls and fortifications. He also thinks that Christ was possibly influenced by Greek philosophy and that most of the things attributed to Jesus were probably made up by somebody else. The proposed project has the title *Christ the Man*, and it will undoubtedly be difficult to find funding.

Verhoeven's next project began when producer Ron Shusett walked into Dan O'Bannon's apartment sporting a filthy Xerox copy of Phil Dick's "We Can Remember It For You Wholesale," and asking O'Bannon whether he thought it would make a good movie. O'Bannon thought it would make a terrific movie and, running on enthusiasm, began scripting it right away.

Recalls O'Bannon, "Phil Dick's story is a short story. It ends abruptly. You cannot take that particular story and inflate it to a full-length piece like a balloon. In my evaluation, it was a first act, which means you had to invent the other two acts. Some stories are different. *The Man Who Shot Liberty Valance*, if you look at the story it's based on, the whole movie is contained in that short story. The beginning, middle, and end is all there. The screenwriters inflated it up and did a very good job of it. But this was not three acts, it was an act, which very obviously the writer suddenly ran out and put the end. And Ronny said, 'Where do you go from here?'

"I said, 'We take him to Mars.' I kept writing and kept writing, and about that time I got an opportunity of some other work over in Europe, so I broke off and went over there for about six months, and I came back and I wrote *Alien*, and *Alien* was made, and then Ronny came back again, so we worked a little more on *Total Recall* when there was time."

In Dick's original story, the hero, Douglas Quaid, is offered a choice between death (his increasing awareness of having actually been a secret agent on Mars proves too dangerous to the powers that be) or having his memory erased again and his most secret wish fulfillment fantasy implanted in its stead. Rekal Incorporated discovers that his fantasy is that he stopped an alien invasion as a child by being kind to some aliens, who give him a powerful weapon, promise not to invade while he is alive, and erase his memory of the event. Just as this fantasy is about to be programmed into him, Rekal discovers that it is not fantasy after all, but actually occurred, setting up yet another dangerous, disorienting situation.

Right from the start, O'Bannon imagined the film as a big budget feature: "I wrote anything I wanted. I didn't think it would be worth making if it did not have this kind of detail.... I thought that part of the fun of this movie was in seeing something at that scale, because I was partly inspired by the early James Bond movies like *Goldfinger*, and I wouldn't have wanted to see *Thunderball* or *Goldfinger* done on a little, cheap basis either.... I was writing this as a science fiction James Bond movie with the additional element of imagination. As a matter of fact, one of the things I am probably most proud of about this movie is that it is something very rare: it is an actual science fiction movie.

"Far and away, the majority of science fiction movies are really something else in disguise as a science fiction movie. It could be a cowboy movie or an adventure movie or a monster movie or something else. *Alien* is a monster movie. But this is an actual science fiction movie because it depends utterly on the imaginative quality. You couldn't tell this story otherwise. It was that married to the James Bond movies that used to be, the era that I loved so much, that I wanted to see."

O'Bannon's script was declared by *American Film* magazine as one of the ten best unproduced scripts in Hollywood, and was initially going to be made by David Cronenberg for Dino De Laurentiis with Richard Dreyfuss in the Quaid role. The project then moved from director to director, going through Fred Schepsis (*Ice Man*), Richard Rush (*Stunt Man*), Russel Mulcahy (*Highlander*), Lewis Teague, and Bruce Beresford, with each taking a shot at preparing a film out of the material until De Laurentiis' DEG company finally folded due to financial difficulties.

The project then floundered until Schwarzenegger convinced Andrew Vajna of Carolco Pictures to acquire the rights for him (despite $6 million in development costs, a desperate Dino sold the rights for $3 million), and as soon as Schwarzenegger saw *RoboCop*, he knew he had found his director in Verhoeven, and convinced Carolco head Mario Kassar to hire him for it.

"Paul has a very provocative directing style," Schwarzenegger told the *L.A. Times*. "His movies have a lot of style and humor. And he knows exactly where to give scenes a light flavor to loosen up the intensity of the violence. I just showed a rough cut of *Total Recall* to my mother, who doesn't even understand much English. But she loved it. She was laughing at all the right parts!"

Total Recall was given a $55 million budget, more money than the cost of all Verhoeven's other movies combined. The director found himself yelling and screaming at people during its production as the pressures began to mount. Schwarzenegger would play peacemaker by taking offended parties back to his trailer and offering them a tumbler of schnapps.

In his original version of the story, O'Bannon notes, the hero "is, or thinks he is, a very ordinary, non-assertive kind of fella, and when they start probing deeply, I thought it would be much more of a surprise that he would turn out to be the most deadly secret agent in the universe. In my mind, the part required an actor who could have gone both ways more readily. Schwarzenegger cannot diminish himself down to be a milquetoast."

"With *Total Recall*, I found that the script reminded me of my childhood dreams and pleasures," said Verhoeven. "However, the physical making of the film had nothing to do with that. The task was so overwhelming that I felt trapped in a nightmare. I easily got frustrated and found myself yelling and screaming at people. Arnold [Schwarzenegger] was really good to me. He told me to laugh it off. So I learned to live with the fact that all movies will have their production problems. The script was wonderful. It took some work to convince Carolco to let me do it. I particularly liked the way that life on an isolated place like Mars would be more vital. There would be more antagonism and excitement, so many possibilities. Imagining myself in that kind of setting would make me feel more alive. Directing it certainly made me feel alive."

Total Recall both delights and disappoints, an inevitable problem given the casting of Arnold Schwarzenegger as Doug Quaid. Given Schwarzenegger's physique, it is not a surprise to the character or the audience that he is capable of extraordinary things, and the film slides from playing inventive mental games with the audience to a simple-minded orgy of violence at the end.

Verhoeven brought in writer Gary Goldman to write the final draft of the script and bring it into line with his vision. The film awards story credit to O'Bannon, Ronald Shusett, and Jon Povill, and screenplay credit to O'Bannon, Shusett and Goldman. The story sweeps the viewer pell mell into a paroxysm of firepower and pyrotechnical displays while parlaying enough imaginative touches and psychological twists to induce a state of giddiness.

Quaid is a construction worker on Earth in the year 2084 who is happily married to Lori (Sharon Stone), a beautiful, blonde, aerobically fit babe whose duality is suggested by the first shot of her face. However, despite this apparent paradise, Quaid is tormented by recurring dreams of himself with another woman on Mars, which is presently a mining colony being exploited by CEO-cum-proconsul Cohaagen (Ronny Cox), whom we see on TV denouncing guerrillas making trouble up there as "a bunch of lazy mutants who think they own the planet." (As is later shown, Cohaagen clearly believes that he is the one who literally owns the planet.)

Quaid decides to break out of his routine after espying an ad that promises "the memory of a lifetime." To exorcise this Martian obsession, he visits a company called Rekall Inc., which implants fantasy vacations into its customers' brains (Dick's premise was that those who could not afford real vacations could have artificial memories implanted in their brains, and for a few dollars more, an exciting scenario could be added.) However, the procedure activates an actual erased identity from Quaid's mind: in real-life he had actually been a secret agent working for Cohaagen on Mars with these facts carefully erased from his memory.

Panic-stricken, the technicians suppress both these memories and Quaid's recollections of his visit to Rekall, plopping him in a robot-driven cab (voiced by Mel Johnson, Jr.). The Agency, concerned about a security leak, sends Richter (Michael Ironside) and several operatives out to terminate Quaid, who discovers within himself great resourcefulness. (Verhoeven savagely satirizes audiences' disregard for the fates of bystanders by having Quaid hold up a human shield on an escalator who is quickly killed by the callous villains, becomes ridiculously overriddled with bullets and then is ignominiously stepped on by the pursuing villains while other bystanders ignore the unpleasant situation entirely.)

Verhoeven prepares Arnold Schwarzenegger for the memory implant scene in *Total Recall*.

Dodging bullets and laser blasts, Quaid tries to reassess what is reality for him. He discovers that Lori is really an agent sent to see that the mental rewiring worked once she tries to knife him. He learns that his memory of their years of marriage is simply another implant. He also discovers that his previous self had prepared for this eventuality by taping messages to himself, telling him that he is secretly in league with the Martian guerrillas and that he must find the rebels' leader Kuato, who has psychic powers and is engaging in terrorist activities on Mars, in order to recall from his subconscious the information that could lead to their ultimate victory.

Quaid quickly heads off to Mars where he meets up with Melina (Rachel Ticotin), the woman from his dreams, a guerrilla fighter on Mars who moonlights as a hooker in Venusville, the mining colony's red light district, and who had an affair with him in his previous life. There he meets the oppressed mutants, including a hooker with three breasts and a midget decked out in full corset regalia named Thumbelina (Debbie Lee Carrington). (Still, unexpectedly so, given Verhoeven's proclivities, none of the smuttiness on display is sexy, sinuously dirty, or even interesting.)

Total Recall cannily exploits its paranoia theme by constantly shifting our understanding of the characters and their loyalties (almost no one is who they say they are initially, so who can one trust?). It shows that Quaid, while paranoid, does indeed have real enemies. In fact, one of the boldest things about the movie is that Quaid, whose whole life is an illusion filled with duplicitous people, is such a lunkhead that he quickly exasperates everyone around him with his ignorance.

Total Recall's brightest and most interesting move is potentially pulling the rug out from under the viewer by suggesting that Quaid's incredible experiences have simply been implanted by Rekall in connection with his expressed desire to play out a secret agent scenario. There is a wonderful scene where an officious doctor (Roy Brocksmith) knocks at the door of Quaid's Martian hotel, explaining that he's been sent into Quaid's mind by Rekall to warn him that he's having paranoid delusions.

Cohaagen proves to be a thoroughly reprehensible villain, who not only rakes in mining profits, but also sells the oxygen that makes life possible on Mars, where life is lived entirely behind glass and underground. He has also helped spawn an underclass of mutants by merchandising subpar air, which they pay for by working in unsafe conditions in the mines which exposes them to greater radiation and creates additional deformities within the next generation. Cohaagen, who gloats, "I can do whatever I want," is clearly running Mars like a Nazi suzerain, an image reinforced by his underling Richter being given to wearing gestapo-like leather overcoats.

Quaid's biggest shock comes when he finds that rather than opposing Cohaagen, his original self was secretly in league with him from the beginning, and the two halves of his being, his present and former selves, must wage a quick inner battle as to where his loyalties lie. Unfortunately, by then the audience has lost all interest in Quaid's personality as he has stopped reacting emotionally to the surprising things he has learned about his past life. He has becomes transformed into another dead-behind-the-eyes man of action who battles his way to success by blowing up any potential opposition. He is forced to abandon his quest to understand the present by reconstructing his past and gives up trying to impose interpretative meanings onto his life, finding that present-day dangers are enough to occupy him full time. (Obviously, the elusive truths he learns mean more than the concrete fictions he keeps uncovering, and so his actions revolve more around saving Mars and himself by activating the latent terraforming equipment.)

Total Recall, which starts off as playfully inventive, simply goes coarse, emphasizing obvious action setpieces rather than subtle character by-play. Kuato, instead of being mystical and interesting, comes across as a crude joke of a man with a mutant baby head sprung from his stomach, a variation on O'Bannon's chestbuster from *Alien*. The film's one sympathetic non-white character, who is given a touching reason for being a guerrilla, is cheaply turned into a turncoat for the sake of an uninspired twist.

Verhoeven visually creates a world of mazes riddled with hallways and corridors, tunnels and underground chambers, indicating massive interconnection and complexity, and then delights in constantly blowing up and through the walls. Tired of being forced into one particular maze, Quaid will smash down a wall only to find himself caught in another, and has nothing really to guide him except for his own paranoia.

In perhaps *Total Recall's* subtlest and trickiest maneuver, the film sets up the possibility that the entire story is the elaborate adventure that Quaid wanted Rekall to program into him. This is indicated first by dialogue as he is going under and about to be programmed about a two-headed monster (Kuato) and a surprised technician commenting on "blue skies on Mars." It is further reinforced at the end after the atmosphere factory has indeed turned the red skies of Mars blue by ending the movie with an unusual fade to white rather than the traditional black titles, as if a dream or reverie has just come to an end.

O'Bannon has strong reservations about Gary Goldman's ending in which Mars is terraformed in two minutes flat. "The end that they filmed in my estimation is lame," said O'Bannon. "It lacks impact. It has no meaning. I mean the fact that it's spectacular doesn't mean anything — so what? Who cares? Is this movie called *Air*? Is this movie called *Pressure*? No, this movie is called *Total Recall*. The end of this movie should have been the final, stunning revelation about his identity as recalled by him. Instead, it's air!"

Quaid's dream of Mars that opens the film was supposed to take place in an ancient Martian settlement inside a pyramid. (Strangely enough, while the pyramid was cut out of the film, it still appeared on the film's poster.) In the film, Quaid regards this as a dream, but originally he eventually realized that it was part of a memory of his original trip to the Martian compound, indicating that he had been there before.

"When he goes there that second time," explained O'Bannon:

> You recall that three-fingered Martian print? Well, that wasn't supposed to have been a three-fingered Martian print, that was supposed to have been a print of his hand which matched only his hand. So what happened was as follows: at the end of the movie, there were a lot of complexities — which I don't want to give a repeat or we'll be here all night — what he recalls is that he is not Quaid at all. Quaid, who is supposed to have been Earth's top secret agent, went to Mars and entered this compound. The machine killed him and created a synthetic duplicate of Quaid. He is that synthetic duplicate.
>
> That synthetic duplicate has some curious qualities, one of which is he cannot be killed because he can anticipate danger before it happens, and several other interesting properties. He also is omnipotent, and because he is omnipotent and because he cannot be killed, Earth wants to kill him but cannot kill him. That's why they go to all this trouble to erase his brain to make him think he's nobody and forget because it's the only way they can control him.
>
> And when he cuts loose, [that's] the reason nobody kills him throughout the entire movie. Audiences don't question it because movie heroes always go through stuff and don't get killed, but I thought it was clever to actually have a reason for it.
>
> Now at the end of the picture, he puts his hand on the thing, and it all comes back to him who he really is. His total recall of his identity is that he is a creation of a Martian machine. He is, in effect, a resurrection of the Martian race in this synthetic body that's been created, and as he turns and says to all the other characters, "It's going to be fun to play God."
>
> But they thought that a giant pimple was much more exciting. Squeeze that mound. I didn't even know about the ending until I saw the movie. I wouldn't have minded if they changed my ending, but I just don't think what they arrived at had any emotional impact at all, because it wasn't really where the audience's concerns had been led to be.

O'Bannon was also disturbed by the amount of extreme violence in the film. He says he would have "scraped away all of Verhoeven's squibs, cut down the volume of the soundtrack mix by half or two-thirds, so you don't get hearing loss, cast somebody else as Quaid, done a proper ending, then I think you would have had a pretty decent picture. What Verhoeven said when they've been nailing him on [the violence], ... when they asked him about it, he said, 'Well, as a child in Holland I saw Nazi atrocities, so I don't take these things seriously on screen.'

"But Paul, it doesn't matter whether *you* take them seriously, it's what the audience thinks. If all you think about is what *I*, as the director, take seriously, [then you've made a $60 million home movie]. His judgment is obviously way off of norm. Because of the horrors he had to experience as a child, he's now reached a point of psychic numbing to where this doesn't mean anything to him, but it still means something to an audience."

Nevertheless, *Total Recall* proved a huge hit with audiences, quickly grossing over $100 million domestically. Its dream-within-a-dream science fiction nightmare offered audiences something spectacular that they had not seen before. It also kept Mario Kassar's independent Carolco company afloat for a few more years until it finally sank with the mega-flop of Rene Harlin's *CutThroat Island*.

In mid–1990, Joe Eszterhas made Hollywood history by becoming the first writer to earn $3 million for a screenplay (including his executive producer's fee) for his original script *Basic Instinct*. Eszterhas was fortunate in creating a property that was considered highly desirable as former partners Mario Kassar of Carolco and Andy Vajna of Cinergi Productions tried to outbid each other for the rights. The winner was Kassar. Kassar also paid $10 million for star Michael Douglas to play the lead.

Bootleg copies of the script made their way to Eszterhas' home town of San Francisco. Almost immediately, gay activist groups Queer Nation and GLAAD discovered that the story's main killer was a bisexual lesbian and, concerned over negative stereotyping, began a call to have the film altered.

After his big success with *Total Recall*, Verhoeven was hired to direct *Basic Instinct* for $5 million, and he and Eszterhas met with the complainants. While Eszterhas pretended to come away enlightened, promising to rectify his gross insensitivity, Verhoeven denied the charges of homophobia and was just as adamant about sticking to the original script, especially as the film was just about to start production. Eszterhas did produce a more "politically correct" version of the script in which he emphasized Gus' homophobia and had Nick constantly calling him on his prejudices, but Verhoeven thought that the changes were terrible and refused to make them. Consequently, protesters blew whistles and honked horns during the production to disrupt filming.

In an interview with Alex Demyanenko in *Village View*, Verhoeven explained that when he came to America, he wanted to avoid normal movies. "I was afraid I didn't know enough about the United States to do normal situations. I thought *RoboCop* and *Total Recall* would have so much to the side, so much action and special effects, that my lack of knowledge of English and the nuances of the language wouldn't hurt me too much. And since it's science fiction and in the future, if it was wrong culturally, it would be accepted because it's a different world.

"Then I got this script and I had the feeling that I could do this. I really liked the script. I felt it would give me the opportunity to, for once in my life, do my own Hitchcock movie. I'm really an admirer of Hitchcock, and *Vertigo* is one of the movies I really studied when I was 20 or so. And it also felt a little bit like the Americanization of *The Fourth Man*, a more middle-of-the-road version."

Basic Instinct caused a big stink all right, but despite its stupidities (e.g., a psychiatrist is flown down to attend an interrogation and the only observation he makes is the incredibly obvious, "Whoever did this was a sociopathic maniac"), the film is very entertaining thanks to Eszterhas' ripe dialogue.

Detective Nick Curran (Michael Douglas) is a troubled police detective being investigated by Internal Affairs after shooting some tourists. While investigating the murder of a rock star who was killed during sex, he becomes attracted to Catherine Tramell (Sharon Stone), the rock star's girlfriend and possible suspect, especially as she has written a novel in which a rock star was murdered in precisely the same way. (Eszterhas has a thing for writing love stories where one person is emotionally involved with someone he or she suspects is a killer, using the same plot on *The Jagged Edge*, *Betrayed*, *The Music Box*, and *Sliver*.)

When the police try to interrogate her, Catherine flirts shamelessly and uses their male libidos to manipulate them, partially by revealing that beneath her skirt, she is not wearing underwear. Her dangerousness excites Nick and entrances him further, and so he plunges further into the investigation, discovering Catherine's lesbian past and her association with a female killer.

Nick keeps getting warned by the film's most amusing character Gus (George Dzundza), not to lose his head over her. Catherine's girlfriend Roxy (Leilani Sarelle) seems to follow him around acting suspiciously. Everything is filmed in such a way to keep up the ambiguity, but for Verhoeven, Catherine represents a feminine incarnation of the devil, and at the end of the film, Nick is given only a temporary reprieve.

After the film was released, it also drew protest from the National Organization for Women on the grounds that it was sexist. Verhoeven felt that all the characters in the movie have problems, not just the women in the film. It is known from the outset that the killer is a woman, so all women in the film are presented as potential suspects in order for there to be a mystery. Nevertheless, they are all strong-willed individuals or strong women characters. Catherine Tramell is coolly in control and certainly not the victim of anybody.

Conversely, the men do not come off any better. For example, Nick indulges in unforgivable behavior. He shoots at tourists while high on cocaine, and at the end of the film has killed Beth (Jeanne Tripplehorn), the woman who loves him. If Catherine is the murderer, which Verhoeven intended to indicate with his last shot, then Nick has murdered an innocent woman.

Some complaints centered around the scene where Nick rips Beth's clothes off and has sex with her, which some took as rape. However, Verhoeven and actress Tripplehorn explained that this just represented rough sex between consenting adults. (Beth does not put up much of a protest.) Even so, it does not cast Nick in a good light.

There was also a bogus protest by Sharon Stone that she was "tricked" into displaying her pubic hair for the camera, though she clearly must have understood what was required. (Stone apparently thought the image registered clearer on film than she expected, but came to terms with it.) It also made her one of the most talked about actresses in Hollywood and created more demand for her acting services in future films.

Basic Instinct became a huge, worldwide hit, and created a demand for more erotic thrillers, most of which lack its luster. The European version of the film was 45 seconds longer and was later released on disc and tape as the unrated director's cut.

Showgirls, scripted by Joe Eszterhas, borrows not only from Eszterhas' own *Flashdance*, but also classics such as *All About Eve* and *Stage Door*, and grafts the clichés onto the story of would-be dancer Nomi Malone (Elizabeth Berkley) who dreams of becoming a dancer in Vegas but gets ripped off, befriends a friendly black wardrobe mistress named Molly, and ends up shaking her booty at a tacky lap-dancing club where she demonstrates enough flair as a dancer that she's asked to audition for *Goddess*, a nude stage show that stars a cantankerous Cristal Connors (Gina Gershon) and that steals its moves from Bob Fosse's "Air-Rotica" number from *All That Jazz* and its tacky glitz from the worst Vegas has to offer. (The show is so bad it has to be seen to be disbelieved.)

According to Eszterhas, who was paid $3.7 million for his script, "The lap-dancing scene, on its most obvious level, is a very sordid scene. I remember watching a young woman who couldn't be over 16, although they claimed she was over 18, who had track marks on her legs and ankles." By 30, he asserted, "essentially it's all over because the body can't handle the wear and tear of two shows a day. There's ligament damage, knee damage and you see girls in braces."

Nomi must confront the question of what she would be willing to do to achieve fame and success (prostitute herself, hurt others, look the other way, etc.), or as Verhoeven put it, "Everybody that wants a thing desperately has to pay a price. The question of the whole movie is, 'Are you willing to pay the full price, the full price being sacrificing your soul?"

Connors develops a love-hate relationship with the ambitious dancer because Nomi reminds her of herself when she was younger and lesbian undertones underlie their scenes together. Jake (Kyle Maclachan), the Stardust's Entertainment Manager, is attracted to her after Connors pays for Nomi to do a lap dance with him, but he proves to be as scheming and manipulative as everyone else.

Unfortunately, the scheming heroine basically proves herself to be as unsympathetic and manipulative as everyone else. A former hooker who tries to hide her past, she seems far too naïve at first, falling too readily for a cowboy's line of blarney. She demonstrates an unappealing habit of blowing her stack and immediately jumping down the throat of anyone who she thinks has crossed her before she has even had time to consider the situation. She pulls a despicable stunt to secure the lead in the show, and only takes stock of her situation when her only true friend Molly is gang-raped at the instigation of a celebrity Nomi introduces her to. It takes Nomi far too long to realize that her values aren't what they should have been.

The plot is needlessly trashy, the characters unbelievable, and much of the dialogue is execrable, a far cry from the sharper and funnier work Esterzhas came up with for *Basic Instinct*. The film garnered notoriety because it was a major studio production daringly filmed as an NC-17 project (the rating created when Universal released *Henry and June*, which flopped and had not been employed by any major studio since then). It was a risky move because many newspapers won't advertise and many theaters won't play NC-17 movies, but despite the allure of more bare flesh than had previously been presented in a major studio release, the public stayed away in droves and the critics were merciless.

To Verhoeven's credit at least, nude dancing is not treated as a disgrace or as something the heroine is forced to do, but rather as something she has chosen to do. While there are those who try to victimize her, Nomi is not a victim nor is she depicted as an amoral slut. She is always someone who is in control of her life, and it is she who makes the sometimes difficult choices.

Suddenly, the highly risible result was remarketed as a camp classic, as if all the film's rottenness were intentional rather than simply misjudged. And indeed, this hooter filled hootfest does have its (admittedly few) pleasures as its haridans deliver horribly hackneyed dialogue that is hilariously unreal. Instead of taking things to the edge, Verhoeven seems to have sailed right past it into ridiculousness.

Showgirls attempted to break past the NC-17 barrier, but the film's ample notoriety and female flesh on display were not enough to attract a large audience. It swept, however, the derogatory Raspberry Awards, and Verhoeven broke tradition by personally appearing to pick up his trophy, claiming that it was more enjoyable to do so than reading the reviews when the film first opened.

Nevertheless, Verhoeven's career has refused to stall. Despite *Showgirls'* flop at the public box office, Verhoeven was entrusted with his film adaptation of Robert Heinlein's science fiction classic *Starship Troopers*, an over $100 million screen spectacular that continued to secure his place in the pantheon of important science fiction directors.

Johnny Rico (Casper Van Dien) warns the Mobile Infantry of an approaching Tanker Bug in *Starship Troopers*.

Scriptwriter and coproducer Ed Neumeier reported to the *L.A. Times* that he "wanted to do a big, silly, jingoistic, xenophobic, let's-go-out-and-kill-the-enemy movie, and I had settled on the idea that it should be against insects.... I wanted to make a war movie, but I also wanted to make a teenage romance movie." The movie Verhoeven has made is more Neumeier's teenage romance movie than it is Heinlein's SF classic *Starship Troopers*, but Neumeier's script was turned down until producer Jon Davison suggested they get the rights to *Starship Troopers*. TriStar then agreed to make a film of that.

Heinlein's still controversial novel proposed a society where citizenship (i.e. voting privileges) was denied unless you enlisted for a period of public service, most often military. Heinlein's idea was that citizens should come from people who have learned to put the concerns of others above themselves. Such service was not mandatory unless you desired citizenship.

The plot of the novel recounts the career of Johnny Rico during a war against inhuman alien insects and what he learns in the process of becoming an officer. Unlike the film, there are only two battle scenes in the book, which is more concerned with depicting Rico's development into a responsible officer. Because of its pro-military, admittedly jingoistic attitude, the work has often been accused of being fascistic, though the society depicted is never explicitly labeled as such.

According to Verhoeven in *Cinefantastique*, "The book was attacked when it came out for its kind of fascistic attitude. We didn't go away from that; basically, we created a society which has this kind of Heinleinian set-up, and we're not saying to the audience that it's wrong. There's a certain ambiguity in seeing this society. The people inside this society are not fascistic, but the society itself is, so you have to make up your mind, if a society can be fascistic while its citizens are people that you like. The ambiguity is on another level than it was with *Basic Instinct* or *Total Recall*. Basically, it's a society that's really cleaned up, like everybody would like it to be if you listened to the politicians. It's that type of society, where criminality is reigned in, where there's no drugs, where people in high school are back in uniform, where everybody thinks that mathematics are important to achieve something in life."

Verhoeven alters the theme of the story to "War makes fascists of us all," which was never Heinlein's intent. One element of Heinlein's future, though, is quick and swift capital punishment, which Neumeier retains, appearing in a bit part in the film as one of the victims of such a policy as an indication that his sympathies lay elsewhere. The only part

A somewhat weary Verhoeven directing *Starship Troopers*' Planet P fort sequence.

of Heinlein's book largely unaltered is Rasczak's (Michael Ironside) speech to his class about violence being "The supreme authority from which all other authority is derived."

Starship Troopers began principal photography on April 29, 1996 at Wyoming's Hell's Half Acre County Park, where Verhoeven staged two of the film's most spectacular sequences: the bug attack against the infantry on Planet P, and the massive night-time invasion of Klendathu, where reportedly extras were worked long hours and were underpaid. The company then moved to a private ranch in Badlands, South Dakota, where the battle on Tango Urilla was shot. A portion of the film was shot in Fountain Valley's Mile Square Park, Orange County, where a sprawling, futuristic military base was created with conical cabins and mylar pup tents. Other shooting was done at Malibu, a Delta Airlines hangar, and Sony Pictures' Culver City studio. Principal photography took six months to complete.

In order to get the greenlight to make the project, Verhoeven had to show that the computer generated alien arachnids could be both menacing and convincing enough, and with the help of Phil Tippett, he created a 40 second clip that convinced backers. However, developments in CGI technology continued so rapidly that this test footage was soon outdated by superior, revised versions which appeared in the actual film. Tippett developed a "digital input device" that allowed stop motion animators to get their hands onto and manipulate computer-linked armature, creating a new level of reality for computer-generated figures. The filmmakers consciously departed from Heinlein's descriptions in his novel, finding the notion of gun-wielding insects too farfetched.

Verhoeven describes his film as being like *The Battle of the Bulge* or *A Bridge Too Far* "if the Germans were insects," and praises his collaboration with Tippett, saying, "I never would have thought of making this movie if not for the cooperation of Phil Tippett. He's a genius at this kind of fantasy." Tippett decided to base his creation on an amalgam of every revolting insect he could find, filling his Bay Area studio with living examples.

Most of the alien arachnids measure seven feet tall with 15-foot leg spans and enormous jaws, though Tippett has also created 30 foot long "tanker" bugs and 80 foot long "plasma" bugs. "They're like insects as sharks — all they do is come up to you and kill you," Neumeier said. "They have a ground speed of 35 mph. Their mode of attack is overwhelming force. My science teacher in seventh grade said, 'The Chinese, they'll march at you like zombies, with wooden sticks in their hands, and even if you had a machine gun in your hand they'd overwhelm you!' That's what I think about the bugs."

In an interview with the *Daily News*, Verhoeven declared, "We're taking the genre a step further in a certain direction, into realism, in fact. It's definitely sci-fi, but it's grounded in a very timely, realistic world. Although it's also romantic and adventurous, even funny and light sometimes, it's realistic in its depiction of war and of people dealing with fear.... It's a war movie, like the ones you saw in the 1940s. It's gung-ho kids thinking they'll have fun, then learning that war is very violent, very ugly. Some of them will survive, and as you'll see, some won't."

Starship Troopers introduces us to Johnny Rico (Casper Van Dien), Carmen Ibanez (Denise Richards), Dizzy Flores (Dina Meyer), Carl Jenkins (Neil Patrick Harris), and Zander Barcalow (Patrick Muldoon) as they are graduating high school. Carmen is determined to become a star pilot, and Johnny, desperately in love with her, enlists in Federal Service not out of any passion for or commit to military ideals or desire to become a citizen rather than simply a civilian, but in hopes of being near her. However, his math scores are too low to become a fellow pilot and he is sent to Marine basic training.

The most inventive aspect of the film is the clever and satirical way it dispenses exposition in a series of "Federal Network Reports," clearly propagandistic pieces designed to look like computer hypertext scenes. The tone of these one-sided reports is meant to evoke the George Stevens "Why We Fight" series. There are hints that Earth might have initiated the war by settling a colony of Mormons on one of the bugs' planets, but of course the report on it simply concentrates on the massacre of innocents.

Career Sergeant Zim (Clancy Brown) is an over-the-top rendering of the tough drill sergeant who trains his raw recruits into fighting machines. He takes on all comers and is not above breaking an arm or jabbing a dagger through someone's hand to make a point. Rico learns the terrible responsibilities of command when leading his platoon, he allows a member to remove his helmet during a training exercise only for the man to get his head blasted off. Rico is then sentenced to a flogging and considers leaving the force.

One thing which surprised the filmmakers is that audiences hated the character of Carmen, who writes Johnny a "Dear John" letter and is torn between her love of Johnny and her interest in fellow pilot Zander. They resented the woman for rejecting the hero and being unable to make up her mind, while they had no problem with Johnny being torn between his love of Carmen and his attraction to Dizzy. Consequently, a few short scenes with Denise Richards were trimmed after previews of the film.

Carmen's life, contrasted with Rico's flogging, is a very comfortable one as she sips coffee on the bridge of the *Roger Young*. She has found her place in the universe, and proves herself adept as a hotshot pilot. Some of the scenes of her piloting the spaceship are truly spectacular, eliciting the beauty, glory, and excitement of spaceflight.

Suddenly peace is shattered as an asteroid the Bugs have launched destroys Buenos Aires and Rico's parents along with it. Despite the flogging and receiving a "Dear John" letter from his girl, Rico decides to commit himself to the Mobile Infantry as *Starship Troopers* becomes a real war movie, though the weapons employed by the heroes are surprisingly non-futuristic and conventional ones. Despite the gung ho tone, the film demonstrates that the military is capable of making horrible mistakes, such as the misguided and disastrous attack on Klendathu that leaves much of the force dead or crippled.

The military forces regroup at the *Ticonderoga* space station, where a recovered Rico (whose bug-speared leg is repaired in a healing tank) joins Rasczak's Roughnecks, who are ordered to do clean-up duty on Tango Urilla, encountering one frightening Bug menace after another. Johnny loses Rascazk and Dizzy and is forced to take command, rescuing the remnants of his company from being overwhelmed by the masses of oncoming Bugs. The various Bugs themselves all seem rather unlikely, particularly the Bombardier Beetles that send enormous amounts of deadly "bug plasma" out into space, but the wealth of detail is diverting as well as discovering what each Bug type is capable of. (Despite its confident stance, the military remains largely in the dark about its enemy until the very end.)

Starship Troopers ends with the carefully planned capture of one of the leaders of the Bugs, the horrific Brain Bug, which is a blobby pink mass with multiple spidery eyes and a rather vaginal opening in the front, plus feelers capable of puncturing a man's cranium and sucking out the brains. Carmen falls into the clutches of one, but Johnny comes to the rescue, saving her, while a demoted Zim (who left training to join in combat) captures a brain bug in a piece of giant netting, allowing Jenkins to study it and probe the enemy's weaknesses.

The film is one continuous satire on militarism and all associated, especially the jingoism inherent in militaristic films. There is nothing in the film that is to be taken straight — every aspect ridicules hawkish attitudes, jingoist ferver, pro-colonialist thinking. Just consider the myriad ways in which aggression against the Bugs is justified, in which violence against the Bugs is justified (and portrayed), and in which the bugs themselves are turned from a space voyaging (and presumably civilized) race to monstrous, animalistic "bugs." The climactic scene where the SS-costumed intelligence officer Carl Jenkins declares the brain bug to be "afraid" and the troops ecstatically cheer is a brutal jab at the propagandistic aspects of militarism and on the de-humanization of the enemy essential for war to be heroic in the way films make wars heroic.

As is classic Verhoeven, the violence is over the top. Here, also, the characters are over the top as well. (Comic-booky is about right, exploded versions of stock military characters. The jawlines couldn't be sharper cut.) The blurring of the lines between the wonderful newsreels and the action proper puts the entire film within the framework of propaganda, and opens the door for the situation where the extremes and absurdities of the film work as satiric humor.

Unlike previous Verhoeven projects, *Starship Troopers* did not suffer much at the hands of the MPAA, which awarded the film an R rating after a mere two seconds of footage had been cut, which greatly pleased the director. The first shot in the film is taken directly from Leni Riefenstahl's *Triumph of the Will*, with soldiers looking at the camera and saying, "I'm doing my part!" The fascistic future is underscored by having the characters wear gestapo-like uniforms, live amidst Albert Speer–style architecture, and spout Goebbelsque dialogue. Neumeier told *Entertainment Weekly*, "The reason for all the German uniforms and everything is because the Germans made the best looking stuff. Art directors love it."

Verhoeven added in the same piece, "I just wanted to play with these [Nazi images] in an artistic way.... I wanted to do something more than just a movie about giant bugs. What I tried to do is use subversive imagery to make a point about society. I tried to seduce the audience to join [*Troopers'*] society, but then ask, 'What are you really joining up for?'"

Verhoeven's next project will be *Houdini*, a biography of the escape artist-magician, which he describes as an intimate period piece. However, Verhoeven has no intention of abandoning science fiction. "I'd like to do another science-fiction film at some point, but not right away," he said. "The next sci-fi film I'd like to do would be a *Troopers* sequel, but let's see how this one does first."

Verhoeven has been lined up to direct another big-budget genre effort, *The Hollow Man*, and his work on *Starship Troopers* was clearly an influence on Paul Anderson's *Wing Commander*, a movie based on a video game. Meanwhile, Verhoeven's work has become fodder for others. *RoboCop* lived on as both a live action and an animated series, *RoboCop*, *Alpha Commando*, and Showtime transformed his thriller *Total Recall* into a new series, *Total Recall 2070*, which premiered in 1999. The pilot, "Machine Dreams," introduced police detective David Hume (Michael Eston) and his android partner Ian Farve (Karl Pruner), whose mission is to defend innocent parties from unchecked societal powers. Even *Troopers* has an animated spin-off. With his extreme action and satirical jabs, Verhoeven has provided several potent additions to the genre.

JERRY WARREN (1925–1988)

Man Beast (1956); *Teenage Zombies; The Incredible Petrified World* (1960); *Invasion of the Animal People* (codirector with Virgel Vogel); *Terror of the Blood Hunters; The Violent and the Damned* (1962); *Attack of the Mayan Mummy* (aka *The Aztec Mummy*); *Bullet for Billy the Kid; No Time to Kill* (1963); *Curse of the Stone Hand* (1964); *Face of the Screaming Werewolf; Creature of the Walking Dead; House of the Black Death* (uncredited codirector) (1965); *The Wild World of Batwoman* (aka *She Was a Hippie Vampire*, 1966); *Frankenstein's Island* (1982)

Jerry Warren's films are notorious as some of the very worst ever made, known for their ridiculously low budgets, stagnant direction, and lengthy and excruciatingly dull dialogue scenes. While he told Tom Weaver that his "directing is what is adequate for the type of film [he] wanted to put together," he is alone in his opinion of adequacy. Lacking the racy elements of gore and nudity that have elevated equally incompetent filmmakers such as Jesus Franco to cult status, Warren is known as one of the all-time worst directors of all time whose incompetent movies lack even the earnest and antic spirit that make Ed Wood movies enjoyable hoots for the crowd that specializes in derision.

Jerry Warren grew up with the ambition of making it in movies. After high school, he formed a small music combo for which he played piano and bass, but it was his talents as a jitterbug dancer that got him noticed by some talent scouts. (He did release a record of "Monkey Walk" b/w "Street of Love" by Jerry Warren and the Pets from Arwin Records.) He played bit parts in such films as *The Canterville Ghost, Ghost Catchers, Anchors Aweigh*, and *Unconquered.* He is perhaps best known for taking footage from old Mexican movies, re-editing them, inserting deadly dull dialogue, and thereby creating some of the worst science fiction films of all time.

When not making movies, he supported himself by running "police shows," variety shows that supposedly benefitted the local police, which would get a small fraction of the overall take. He died of lung cancer on August 21, 1988 in Escondido, California.

Warren's first film was the dreadful *Man Beast*, one of the worst films ever to deal with the subject of the abominable snowman of the Himalayas. Warren had purchased from the Allied Artists' film library some stock footage of men mountain climbing and decided to build a short feature around it. He cast his actors based on their resemblance to people in the stock footage. His Yeti suit was actually *White Pongo's* gorilla outfit.

Being of limited resources, he hired a woman named Bri Murphy to handle props, makeup, hair, wardrobe, script and take stills for the princely sum of $50 a week. She later married and then divorced Warren, then became a director (*Blood Sabbath; Virgins from Venus*) and an Emmy–winning cinematographer. Most of the shooting on *Man Beast* was done in Lone Pine, California.

Murphy told Tom Weaver in *Monsters, Mutants, and Heavenly Creatures*,

> Jerry had a very interesting technique of shooting closeups against the sky. His theory was, you *walk, stop* and *talk*, and then somebody says, 'Let's get out of here,' and you *walk* and *stop* and *talk* some more.... Now, closeups against the sky was a very interesting technique: You take each actor and film them against the sky. 'Okay, now look surprised. *Tha-a-at's* it. Turn to the right and look *down* and look surprised. Look *up* and look surprised. Turn quickly to the right and — oh, *horror! You're* horrified! Now you're happy to see somebody. That's very good....' He would put actors through this, each and every one of them, so that we would have a 400 foot roll of each one of them reacting to *anything* that could possibly go on, and we could always cut them in!

In *Man Beast*, Connie Hayward (Virginia Maynor aka Asa Maynor, later an executive at NBC) and Trevor Hudson (Lloyd Nelson) assemble an expedition to find Hayward's missing brother. Their guide, Steve Cameron (Tom Maruzzi), takes them to Dr. Erickson's (George Wells Lewis, one of the film's backers) camp. Erickson has a theory that the Yeti is the presumed missing link between humans and apes. The group sets off to find the lost sibling.

Reaching the correct site, they discover it deserted except for his sherpa guide Varga (George Skaff). While there, they are attacked by the Yeti (Jack Haffner most of the time, though credit is given to "Rock Madison"). (The snowmen have been kidnapping and mating with human women.) Varga is in cohoots with the Yeti and arranges for the deaths of most of the expedition, but falls to his death while slithering down a rope trying to eliminate Steve, whom Connie has fallen in love with.

Man Beast was largely shot at the tiny Larchmont stage,

with editing done at Keywest Studio on Santa Monica Boulevard. Warren claims the Tibetan village material was acquired by climbing over the fence at the Paramount Ranch and shooting on their set. Warren decided to distribute the film himself by driving all over the country and making deals with independent distributors in every state, claiming that the picture had cost $100,000 to make and cobilling it with *Prehistoric Women.*

Man Beast contains Warren's hallmark deadly pacing, and would be considered possibly the most tedious SF film of all time had Warren not continued his career and manufactured ones that were even worse.

Teenage Zombies and *Incredible Petrified World* came about because when Warren was negotiating with backer Maurice Bernard to get $30,000 for the budget for one, Murphy thought that two pictures could be made for the same price, provided they were shot back to back using the same locations and the same resources. Bernard went on to play a cave-dwelling hermit in *Petrified World* who keeps warning of a monster that never shows up.

Katherine Victor, who starred in Warren's *Teenage Zombies* and four other Warren pictures, recalled for Paul and Donna Parla in *Filmfax,* "Warren just threw everyone into the picture with virtually no time to rehearse. Cameras rolled and that was it. This was basically the way Jerry Warren did his films — rushed and with little desire to upgrade their quality with time....

"[A]s time went on, I became disappointed with the way Warren was doing things. He would yell a lot or just wanted to get the job over with; he didn't have a polished approach. To Jerry, everything was just a short cut to the next project and it showed. If Jerry had not paid me what he did — around $300 — I would not have done the film because, at the time, the Screen Actor's Guild ... was paying just *under* $300."

In *Teenage Zombies,* six teenagers visit a mysterious island, where Dr. Myra (a hammy Victor) has created nerve gas capsules that revive dead teenagers and transform them into obedient zombie slaves. She plans to drop this insidious material into reservoirs all over the United States. So far her efforts have created one, and only one, zombie, but she has hopes for her hapless visitors. Incredibly, for the finale her loyal servant Ivan (Chuck Niles) suddenly turns on Myra, allowing the teens to escape, and then blows everything sky high. According to Warren, when he showed the film to Frank King and told him how much it cost, the experienced lowbudget filmmaker could not stop laughing. Too bad there is nothing about the film as amusing for the rest of us.

In *The Incredible Petrified World,* Craig Randall (Robert Clarke) and several companions go down in a diving bell developed by Dr. Wyman (John Carradine) to the bottom of the ocean and discover a frozen cave (actually the Colossal Cave in Arizona) that has a pocket of breathable air. A lot of running time is taken up with nothing more than Dr. Wyman speculating that another bell will be lowered to rescue them while the group wander about staring at the cavern walls. (There was supposed to be a monster in the film that would menace the party, but the suit created ended being unusable.) Finally a nearby volcano creates a landslide that kills one scientist, but the long sought bell arrives just in time for the others to be rescued. As a movie, this sinks to the lowest depths and never recovers. It and its *Teenage Zombie* cofeature are two of the most tremendously tedious movies ever made.

Invasion of the Animal People (aka *Terror in the Midnight Sun; Space Invasion from Lapland*) was initially a Swedish drama set and filmed in Lapland called *Rrymdinvasion i Lappland* (Space Invasion of Lappland). The original version was directed by Virgil Vogel, who had directed such lackluster science fiction fare as *The Mole People* and *The Land Unknown* for Universal, both of which were meanderingly mediocre, but look scintillating in comparison. There is some good material in this footage, which was shot for $40,000, including a nice spaceship landing, some decent forced perspectives and miniatures, but the work is undone by Warren's later tampering. (Vogel had better luck directing TV movies.)

Warren oddly alters geography by setting the film in Switzerland while retaining references to nearby Lappland, while another Warren-added scene has actors poring over a map of Greenland. The additional footage featured John Carradine (who begins the film spouting nonsensical gobbledy-gook) and there is a long discussion about women and flying saucers. In the main story, Dr. Frederick Wilson (Robert Burton) investigates a saucer crash and is surprised to encounter his niece, Diane (Barbara Wilson), who is attracted to Wilson's womanizing assistant Erik (Stan Gester). Eventually, Diane is kidnapped by a huge furry beast who turns her over to some very human looking aliens, who then disappear from the narrative, apparently leaving in their ship later via some reversed crash footage.

For the climax, some torch-bearing villagers arrive and set the Kong–like beast on fire, who obligingly puts Diane down before his flaming form falls from a high precipice. The whole thing ends with Carradine telling us that "without a future, there would be no present." This is Warren's best film, but it also features the same horrible editing that is the hallmark of his work.

My initial exposure to Jerry Warren came through *The Aztec Mummy* (aka *Attack of the Mayan Mummy*), which was Warren's infamous recutting of Rafael Lopez Portillo's Mexican monster movie *La Momia Azteca,* with Warren adding additional footage of Richard Webb, Nina Knight, John

Burton, and Bruno Ve Sota, who are mostly there to explain the plot and save Warren on dubbing costs.

The plot involves an archaeological expedition uncovering an Aztec pyramid containing a mummy guarding an ancient ceremonial mask, which is coveted by an underworld criminal known as the Bat (Ramon Gay). A psychiatrist and his wife unleash the curse of Popoca, the Aztec mummy with the silly name. The film is incredibly talky and dull with long discussions going nowhere before the titular creature finally puts in a token appearance, only to get run down by a car at the end. Nevertheless, the Mexican version went on to sprout three livelier sequels, Portillo's *Momia contra el robot humano* (aka *The Robot vs. the Aztec Mummy*) and *La maldición de la momia* (aka *The Curse of the Aztec Mummy*), and René Calderón's *Las luchadoras contra la momia* (aka *The Wrestling Women vs. the Aztec Mummy*).

Warren admitted to Weaver that he does not like to travel, so he made a deal with L.A. based Azteca Pictures to create American versions of south of the border films. He recut the Brazilian *The Violent and the Damned*, the Mexican film *A Bullet for Billy the Kid*, and an international coproduction, *No Time to Kill*, none of which I have seen, and given Warren's track record, have no interest in catching up with. However, there were two more Mexican movies that I did catch which have genre elements.

Face of the Screaming Werewolf was crafted, if that is the word, out of the Mexican film *La Casa del Terror*, a comedy-horror film directed by Gilbert Solar, with additional footage from *La Momia* thrown in to help pad out the pretty thin proceedings.

In Warren's version, which trims most of the original's comedic material in favor of making this a "serious" sci-fi thriller, a mad scientist (Raymond Gaylord) revives dead bodies with blood. Because of his graverobbing activities, the police have put a guard on the local cemetery, forcing the scientist to try his hand at re-animating an Egyptian mummy which legend has it was once a werewolf. The serum fails, but a fortuitous lightning bolt brings the mummy back to life, and the moonlight transforms it into the familiar figure of the Wolf Man (Lon Chaney, Jr., playing his most famous role for the last time).

The Wolf Man is caged by the scientist, but ends up killing one of the mad doctor's assistants. The scientist transplants the assistant's brain into the Wolf Man, which then escapes and abducts Paquita (Yolanda Varela), the girlfriend of the janitor Casamiro (Tin Tan) whose blood serum the doctor was using in the first place. The Wolf Man takes the girl up the side of a skyscraper where in a decided anti-climax, he slips and accidentally falls to his death.

Creature of the Walking Dead was carved out of another Mexican horror film, *La Marca del Muerto*, directed by Fernando Cortés, to which Warren added new footage starring Tom Maruzzi (acting under the name Rock Madison), Katherine Victor as a medium, and Bruno Ve Sota as a police inspector. Basic plot has to do with a scientist resurrecting a corpse that feeds on blood to stay alive. Warren wrote the revised screenplay under the pseudonym Joseph Unsain.

John Carradine, Katherine Victor, and Lon Chaney were also involved in *House of the Black Death* (aka *Night of the Beast*), which was produced by Bill White until there were financing problems. Warren took over the production and attempted to cut it together and pad it out to a releasable length, mostly done by stopping the action to depict dance after dance on a cemetery set à la *Orgy of the Dead.* (Entertainment value has never seemed to be one of Warren's concerns.)

The resulting film was credited to Harold Daniels, and has something to do with dueling de Sades, one of which (Chaney) seems to be the devil (complete with cloven feet and silly looking horns on his head), but ends up being turned into a skull by his brother. There is also a werewolf who wears what appears to be a gorilla mask and Victor obligingly undulates as a sexy witch. Like other Warren productions, it is largely incoherent, but not amusingly so.

Warren hoped to cash in on the *Batman* craze with *The Wild World of the Batwoman*, but a lawsuit delayed its release by several years, so it went out under the title *She Was a Hippy Vampire*. The film was shot in a week, and had Katherine Victor as the Batwoman (decked out in a black strapless party dress with a mask on, a rubber bat spirit-gummed across her breasts, and teased out hair) pitted against Dr. Neon (George Andre) and Ratfink (shades of Ray Dennis Steckler) who want to obtain an atomic bomb to extort money for his nefarious schemes (that's right, they both turn out to be the same guy). Much of the film is dull scenes of people talking, girls dancing in bikinis, and stock footage from Virgil Vogel's *The Mole People*. Though Warren won his suit, there was not much interest on the part of others in releasing the film and Warren apparently retired from filmmaking to work on his avocado ranch.

Years later, Robert Christopher put up nearly $90,000 to make *Frankenstein Island* (1982), and even at that Warren's awful film proved unable to turn a profit, though it was the only one of Warren's ultralow-budgeted efforts to fail to do so. Warren himself wrote the screenplay, a retread of his earlier *Teenage Zombies*, and the score for the film under the names Jaques LaCatier and Erich Bromberg respectively.

Frankenstein Island starred Steve Brodie and Robert Clarke as its heroes. It features four balloonists who land on an island of grade Z movie clichés, with John Carradine popping up as the Ghost of Dr. Frankenstein chanting "The power!" over and over, while Warren regular Katherine Victor in a fright wig is a mad doctor married to Dr. Frankenstein's 200-year-old bedridden assistant, Dr. Van Helsing. The film also features a group of women in leopard skins who are actually aliens, a group of zombies in sweatshirts and sunglasses, Cameron Mitchell as a sea captain who is being drained of his blood and has fathered a child with one of the aliens, and even a brief appearance by the Frankenstein Monster. Despite his years of experience, Warren's work is once more a desperately assembled awful mess. (Warren claimed to have extensively revised and improved a television version of the film, but the videocassette contains the theatrical version.)

Warren had a life-long aversion to doctors, so he ignored a pain in his side for many months before going to a physician in 1988. He was diagnosed as having a form of asbestos-related cancer, and six weeks later in August of 1988, he died in his home in Escondido. Despite the consistent awfulness of his films and the ennui they inspire, or perhaps more likely because of them, he has become a cult figure.

NORMAN J. WARREN (1942–)

Fragments (short, 1965); *Her Private Hell* (1967); *Loving Feeling* (1968); *Satan's Slaves* (1976); *Terror* (1977); *Alien Prey* (aka *Prey*) (1978); *Outer Touch* (aka *Spaced Out*) (1979); *Inseminoid* (aka *Horror Planet*) (1982); *Gunpowder*; *Bloody New Year* (aka *Time Warp Terror*, 1987)

Norman J. Warren was born in London, June 25, 1942. Some of his earliest memories were of seeing *The Beast with Five Fingers* and Robert Wise's *The Day the Earth Stood Still.* He entered the film industry in 1959, working for Screenspace Ltd.'s production office on such films as *The Millionairess* and *Mr. Topaze*. He later became an editing assistant with the same company. He studied drama with the English Stanislavsky School of Drama, and joined James Hill's *The Dock Brief* as an assistant director in 1962.

At the age of 21, he became manager of the Holland Park Film Studios and assisted on a number of commercials for Valley Films, then worked as an assistant editor on various documentaries and television commercials. His first directorial effort was creating three promotional films for a dance group called the Zonies, which Warren also edited. He tried his hand at a short, *Fragments.*

Warren describes *Fragments* as a love story — "It's basically girl meets boy, they fall in love, and then girl loses boy," he told Paul Higson in *Bleeder's Digest.* "At the end of the film you are left with a choice of thinking did the girl in fact dream the whole thing and did she or did she not commit suicide. There's no dialogue in the film. It's purely told with pictures and sound effects on music."

Warren made the mini-movie in an effort to show potential backers that he could get something up on screen. Photographing the interiors for the film was Peter Bizou, who would later film *Bugsy Malone, Midnight Express*, and *Time Bandits*. *Fragments* was briefly seen in England, and later sold to Holland and Germany.

After directing his first two features, Warren concentrated for a time on importing and distributing vintage films in England. He tackled a $50,000 horror film, *Satan's Slaves*, written by David McGillivray, which has been described as a "confused mess." The plot has Candace Glendenning running across English satanists including her uncle (Michael Gough) and cousin (Martin Potter), who want to use her body to resurrect a two-century-old ancestor once burned as a witch. The heroine's boyfriend (Michael Craze) is unexpectedly killed off early in the proceedings.

Warren followed this up with *Prey*, in which an alien (Barry Stokes) invades the home of a pair of lesbians and later eats them. Jessica (Glory Annen) awakens when an alien spacecraft lands nearby. After dispatching a young couple, the alien assumes the identity of the recently dispatched young man, Anders (Barry Stokes). Jessica and her possessive lover Josephine (Sally Faulkner) invite "Anders" in when it appears he's hurt. Soon Jessica becomes suspicious of Josephine's overbearing ways, and relies more on the alien for support, but the alien ends up calling home to inform his superiors that humans are not only rich in protein, but also are easy prey. The basic story is patterned after D. H. Lawrence's novel *The Fox.* In 1984, *Prey* was used as the basis by Italian filmmaker Ferruccio Casacci to create *Terror at Amityville Park.*

Then came *Terror*, also scripted by David McGillivray, which has another incoherent narrative, this one about a witch's curse bringing about the deaths of the last surviving members of an afflicted family, one of whom, John Nolan, is a director of horror movies. This allows Warren to play with audience expectations by indulging in some reversals — blood proves to be red paint dripping; a monster is then revealed to be an old man in rain-soaked clothes.

Warren's 1979 British sci-fi sex comedy *Outer Touch* was re-edited and released in America as *Spaced Out* in 1981. A trio of beautiful women from a planet circling Betelgeuse decide to take four Earthlings prisoner, and decide to check the men out, having never encountered any before.

For the American release, comedian Bob Saget from the annoying *Television's Funniest Home Videos* wrote and voiced over some insipid jokes poking fun at the gay and drug subcultures, and providing advice from a computerized psychiatrist to one member of the group who has been hopelessly trying to bed his fiancée.

Inseminoid arrived on these shores as *Horror Planet* at the tail end of 1982, and played just like it was, as a low budget *Alien* rip-off. This $2 million production was scripted in four days by makeup artist Nick Maley and his wife, actress Gloria Maley, after Warren informed them that he had backers but needed a screenplay. The film was shot largely in the Chiselhurst Caves in Kent, England, on a tight four week schedule. The cave saved on set construction costs, but proved to be a cold, damp place to work.

Explorers from Earth including Sandy (Judy Geeson), Mark (Robin Clark), Holly (Jennifer Ashley), and Kate (Stephanie Beacham) investigate a catacomb-like maze of caves on a distant planet that orbits twin suns, when one of the crew is inexplicably killed after handling some crystals. If this were not bad enough, a bug-eyed monster attacks Sandy, rapes her and successfully impregnates her.

Naturally, Sandy undergoes a few changes, such as being able to breathe the planet's atmosphere and desiring human blood, and goes crazy, becoming convinced that the only way to save her babies is to murder all her fellow crewmembers. She is soon holding the rest of the crew under siege, killing them one by one, and feeding off their corpses. No wonder she's so hungry as she gives birth to twin monsters. Soon only Mark is left as he must save himself from Sandy and her ravenous offspring.

Warren leaves the characters as complete cyphers, having apparently no clue as to how to construct characterization. Most of the film is simply cat-and-mouse searches punctuated with occasional fight scenes. Nick Maley, who cowrote the screenplay with Gloria Maley, also supplies the gory makeup, along with the puppety monsters. Horror veteran Stephanie Beacham is wasted in her small role, with her most memorable line being, "We've got to try something — we've got chainsaws."

As a director, Warren does make the most of the claustrophobic settings, and his alluring female crew are easy on the eyes.

Bloody New Year tells the story of six young people (Lesley [Suzi Aitchison], Janet [Nikki Brooks], Spud [Colin Heywood], Rick [Mark Powley], Carol [Catherine Roman], and Tom [Julian Ronnie]) brought together on a coastal holiday who venture out in a small boat that becomes wrecked. They find themselves on an island complete with its own Grand Hotel and are followed by three greasers with whom they had an earlier scuffle. Inside the hotel, the group finds a far greater terror.

The entire film was shot on locations in and around Barry Island, with the Friars Point House standing in for the hotel. The film came about when Maxine Julius approached Warren and asked him if he would do a horror film for her. When time became available, Warren locked himself in a room with line producer Hayden Pearce and hashed out some ideas over a period of several days.

According to Warren in an interview in *Bleeder's Digest #2*, he saw the film as a "horror adventure and a very affectionate reminder of the 1950s B Movies. I certainly had this in mind when making the film, and I hope to have created that feel about it. There is a certain amount of blood-letting and a number of shock moments. In addition to this, there are a few crazy monster scenes. One in particular, a table monster, which was for me very reminiscent of earlier 'man in a rubber suit' films such as *The Monster of Piedros Blancas, The Hideous Sun Demon*, and *The Mole People*."

Part of the premise of the film is that the whole island is trapped in a time warp where it is always New Year's Eve of 1959.

According to Warren, "We thought that during the fifties, science fiction writers in particular were very keen on — and at times obsessed with — theories of relevant time. And also there was at the time a great belief that if you could decompose somebody and break them down into minute particles and then bring all these particles together again, there was a good chance that the form they came back in would not necessarily be the same as their previous form, an idea that was used in the original *The Fly*."

The guests at the hotel were part of an experiment that went wrong, with everybody at the hotel broken into minute particles and then reformed, but not in their original shapes. The table monster referred to is one of the guests who has come back in the shape of a table which has come to life.

The film was not an easy one on the performers. In one

sequence, Julian Ronnie grabs onto Nikki Brooks' leg as she closes the door to an elevator and starts it going up. Ronnie was required to hold onto her leg until the last possible minute to set up a shot where his arm is supposedly severed off. If he had waited any longer before letting go, his own arm would have been severed for real. Also, stunt coordinator Steve Emerson, who plays a greaser named Dad in the film, was rigged 60 feet in the air above a cliff, had the door handle he was supposed to hold onto break off and managed to grab the top of the door before falling over himself.

Unfortunately, despite John Shann's reasonably good cinematography, *Time Warp Terror* ranks with Warren's worst, with clichéd and uninteresting characters mouthing deadly dull dialogue. People are murdered simply to "attract" their attention, as if the screenwriters Frazer Pearce and Hayden Pearce could think of no better way for the "furniture people" to get someone's attention. But then such blatant, exploitative grue is commonly how Warren has gotten attention for his mostly miserable movies, and the results have discouraged further financing.

W. LEE WILDER (1904–)

Glass Alibi (1946); *Pretender; Yankee Fakir* (1947); *Vicious Circle; Woman in Brown* (1948); *Once a Thief* (1950); *Three Steps North* (1951); *Phantom from Space* (1953); *Killers from Space; Snow Creature* (1954); *Big Bluff* (1955); *Fright; Manfish; Spell of the Hypnotist* (1956); *Man Without a Body* (codirected with Charles Saunders 1957); *Spy in the Sky* (1958); *Bluebeard's Ten Honeymoons* (1960); *The Omegans* (1968)

The older brother of Billy Wilder, Austrian-born W. Lee Wilder has eked out a far less reputable career. He left his native Vienna and pursued an industrial career in Europe for twenty years before abandoning it to come to New York as the head of William Wilder Productions, and producing his first film in 1945, *The Great Flamarion*, which was made at the Charlie Chaplin Studio and later sold to Republic for its 1944–1945 program. The film, tautly directed by Anthony Mann with Erich von Stroheim in a splendid performance playing the world's greatest sharpshooter who falls for a married woman (Mary Beth Hughes) who persuades him to murder her alcoholic husband (Dan Duryea), was unfortunately Wilder's best. While a low budget B film, it features a serviceable script, some fine acting by Hughes and Duryea, and atmospheric noirish photography from James S. Brown, Jr.

Wilder made his directorial debut the following year helming Republic's *The Glass Alibi*, concerning a grifter who marries a terminally ill heiress only to discover that she is unexpectedly recovering. It is a grubby, low budget, undistinguished film that proved to be typical of Wilder's work.

Still, while most of Wilder's works were cheaply made at independent studios and are now largely forgotten or even lost, his first attempt at science fiction, *Phantom from Space*, is at least oddball enough to be somewhat interesting. Its story centers around an invisible spaceman who walks around in a spacesuit and killing, perhaps accidentally, two men.

The main characters are Lt. Bowers (Harry Landers), a detective with the L.A. homicide department, and Lt. Hazen (Ted Cooper) from the Federal Communications Commission, who have been assigned to track the invader down. There is a report about a man in a "diving suit," with no head visible inside the helmet.

The invader, dubbed the Phantom (Dick Sands), when cornered by a scientist, simply takes his clothes off and slips away unseen. Meanwhile, his clothes are taken to a lab (recognizable as the Griffith Observatory's Planetarium) to be studied. Dr. Wyatt (Rudolph Anders), a scientist, learns that Phantom's suit is highly radioactive (though the only protection he uses in handling the material is some rubber gloves), and that it has been creating disruptions in local broadcasts. Wyatt combines with Bowers, Hazen, and a military man to make tests on the suit and discovers that the alien is silicon-based rather than carbon-based (like life on Earth), though nothing much is done with this idea, which is simply used to try to account for the alien's invisibility. Somehow the fact that the Phantom is an alien still comes as a surprise to Bowers.

The Phantom cannot exist comfortably on Earth without his suit and airtanks, and is forced to replenish his air supply periodically, which he does despite the protagonists' attempts to capture him. Everyone chases after each other until an infrared beam is turned on the Phantom, rendering him visible. He has a very human appearance, with a high forehead, lacking only ear lobes. Caught by surprise, the alien falls off a ladder and dies, for some reason his suit as well as his body disintegrating when he does so.

The effect of an ambulatory "empty" spacesuit is fairly creepy, but most of the movie is consumed with stock footage, and endless talk and banter that leads nowhere. The movie takes itself very seriously, and does have a moody look to it, as does Wilder's subsequent SF feature, the infamous *Killers from Space*.

Killers from Space will probably be the film W. Lee Wilder is best remembered for. Not because it is any good, but simply because the device of having the film's aliens put cut-out ice cube tray bits as eyeballs (not Ping Pong balls as has often been erroneously reported) to create bug-eyed alien looks so ludicrous that the end result is unforgettable. Like a lot of low budget efforts, the film is heavily padded with stock footage, including atomic bomb tests, military and police scenes, nature documentaries, and even shots from William Cameron Menzies' *Things to Come*.

Future *Mission: Impossible* specialist Peter Graves stars as Dr. Doug Martin, a nuclear physicist, who disappears in a plane crash after an atom bomb test. He later reappears with amnesia, but when he tries to steal some atomic secrets, the military and the FBI get suspicious. Fearing that he has become a communist agent, they inject him with truth serum and learn that he was kidnapped and hypnotized by bug-eyed aliens from the planet Astron Delta who are currently holing up in some caverns beneath the test site at Soledad Flats, where they have been accumulating energy from atomic bomb tests to create giant creatures (spiders, cockroaches, lizards, grasshoppers) which they plan to unleash on Earth's population.

Martin figures out how to thwart them by turning off some of the power they have been stealing from a local power plant, which creates an overload that blasts the aliens from their subterranean lair. Apart from make-up artist Harry Thomas' bad design for the jump-suited aliens, this recklessly assembled feature offers little in the way of entertainment value.

Next Wilder tackled *The Snow Creature*, a low budget Abominable Snowman movie. Unfortunately, the minuscule budget did not stretch enough to allow the production to produce a decent yeti costume, so Wilder elected to have cinematographer Floyd Crosby keep all the lighting as dark and shadowy as possible to obscure the inadequacy of the suit, which does add to the atmospheric moodiness of the movie.

The plot has a woman kidnapped by a yeti, and yet the head of an expedition, Frank Parrish (Paul Langton), refuses to look for her because he will not even entertain the notion of the existence of a yeti. The woman's sherpa husband (Teru Shimada) heads off to search for her but finds instead a different yeti, which they capture.

In an unusual twist, Parrish sends the captive yeti to the United States where it runs afoul of U.S. immigration officials who refuse to allow it into the country. The frustrated yeti breaks out of his box prison and kills several people before escaping into the sewers of Los Angeles. There he is finally cornered and killed. Exactly whatever happened to the kidnapped woman is ultimately forgotten.

Wilder's work here is hampered by a lack of imagination. The yeti often does not do more than take a few steps forward or back. Like all of W. Lee Wilder's movies, and quite unlike his far more talented brother Billy, this movie singularly lacks a sense of humor.

Edgar Allan Poe's story "The Gold Bug" was made the basis for *Manfish* starring John Bromfield, Lon Chaney, and Victor Jory.

Wilder's final foray into science fiction was his most offbeat and entertaining genre film, *The Man Without a Body*, which for some reason has never received the attention that such equally bad but offbeat films such as *The Brain That Wouldn't Die* and *Plan 9 from Outer Space* have, despite having famed seer and prognosticator Nostradamus as one of its central characters.

George Coulouris stars as egotistical industrial Karl Brussard, a brusque and unpleasant man who discovers that he has a brain tumor. He insistently demands that Dr. Phil Merritt (Robert Hutton) replace his faulty brain with a new one, bizarrely convinced that the new brain will take on his personality and identity once it is transplanted into his body. Dr. Merritt has been decapitating monkeys and keeping their brains alive. He has also had some success in restoring decayed brain tissue.

But what brain to pick? Brussard settles on the brain of notorious psychic Nostradamus, apparently in hopes that Nostradamus' predictive powers will lead him to greater wealth. He hires Dr. Brandon (Tony Quinn) to steal Nostradamus' head from its crypt and bring it to Dr. Merritt, who then manages to revive it, even though Nostradamus died in 1566.

Of course, the Nostradamus' head requires no lungs and speaks perfect English, but unfortunately for Brussard, he can't convince the now living head that it is Brussard and not Nostradamus, and so they argue back and forth in the film's most sublimely humorous and absurd moments.

Convinced of Nostradamus' powers of prophecy, Bussard makes a number of major investments, which end up ruining him instead. Brussard's mistress, Odette (Nadja Regin in an hammy and awful performance), has been cheating on him with Dr. Merritt's assistant Lew , and the now angry and broke Brussard decides to kill them both, strangling Odette with her own jewels and then pursuing Lew through some London fog before shooting him. Miffed at the French prognosticator as well, Brussard puts a bullet in the decapitated head's life support equipment.

When Lew's body is delivered to Dr. Merritt with the "cranial nerves" severed, Dr. Merritt jumps at the opportunity to transplant Nostradamus' head onto Lew's body and rendering him into a Frankensteinian monster that looks like a man with a large white wastepaper basket over his head.

The Monster and Brussard pursue each other until Brussard chases it up the stairs of an old tower and falls to his death after a struggle. The Monster with the transplanted head topples into a convenient noose which yanks the head off the body which plummets to the ground, leaving the man without a body yet again and the audience with the image of a white container hanging from a noose to supposedly chill their bones.

If it weren't for the lugubrious pacing, *The Man Without a Body* would surely have a cult following for being so unintentionally humorous and bizarre. Wilder's credited codirector, former editor turned crime director Charles Saunders, directed the oddball science fiction effort *The Womaneater*, about a carnivorous tree which also starred George Coulouris as a mad scientist, that same year, but may have been added to satisfy British union or other regulations that stipulate that a certain amount of British talent be used on all British-made productions.

Wilder's directorial career was almost at an end. His last films were *Bluebeard's 10 Honeymoons* starring George Sanders as Landru, a wastrel who marries and murders a succession of women on his way to success, and *The Omegans*, where a jealous artist convinces his wife and her lover to stand in a radioactive river.

IRVIN S. YEAWORTH, JR. (1926–)

Born to Live (documentary, 1950); *Twice Convicted* (1952); *The Flaming Teen-Age* (1956); *The Blob* (1958); *4-D Man* (aka *Master of Terror; The Evil Force*, 1959); *Dinosaurus!* (1960); *The Gospel Blimp* (1961); *Way Out* (1966)

Irvin Yeaworth, Jr., director of *The Blob, Dinosaurus!*, and *4-D Man*.

Irvin S. Yeaworth, Jr., will always be best remembered as the man who brought us *The Blob*, which for years had been treated as if it were a terrible little movie instead of a nifty science fiction thriller. However, the worm has turned and *The Blob* now earns respectful comments more often than derisive ones, as well it should.

Yeaworth got his start in show business singing on the radio at the age of 10, assisting his father, a minister, with his gospel radio program. By the time he was 17, Yeaworth was producing *Good News*, his own radio program. By 1949, he entered the field of television, producing ABC's *Youth on the March* from Philadelphia. He entered film by taking over a documentary, *Born to Live*, which had been abandoned. From there, he started working on filming commercials and religious films in 16mm.

Eventually, he created a small filmmaking community which worked out of Valley Forge, Pennsylvania, which mainly subsisted on filming religious shorts shown at various churches. His first feature has shown up on tape in much altered form as *The Flaming Teen-Age* with additional material shot by Charles Edwards, but it was originally released under the title *Twice Convicted*. The primary plot deals with the problem of teen drinking, with Noel Rayburn as a young man who moves to New York and is immediately able to produce a play before boozing and gambling catch up with him. After going to jail, he finds God and tries to get others to see the error of his way.

Yeaworth wanted to finally shoot a film in 35mm, and partnered with Lou Kellman, developed a Bridey Murphy story. However, distributor Jack H. Harris let the filmmakers know that Bridey Murphy films weren't selling and suggested that they make a science fiction instead. He gave them a story idea called "The Molten Meteor" by Irvin H. Millgate, and after agreeing to make it, Yeaworth, Harris, and Mike Friedman pooled their limited resources to fund the resulting film, better known as *The Blob*.

The Blob was not a Hollywood film, but was shot independently on stages in Valley Forge, Pennsylvania, and on location in nearby Phoenixsville in three weeks for about $120,000 and was later sold to Paramount at a substantial profit for $500,000. The script by Theodore Simonson and

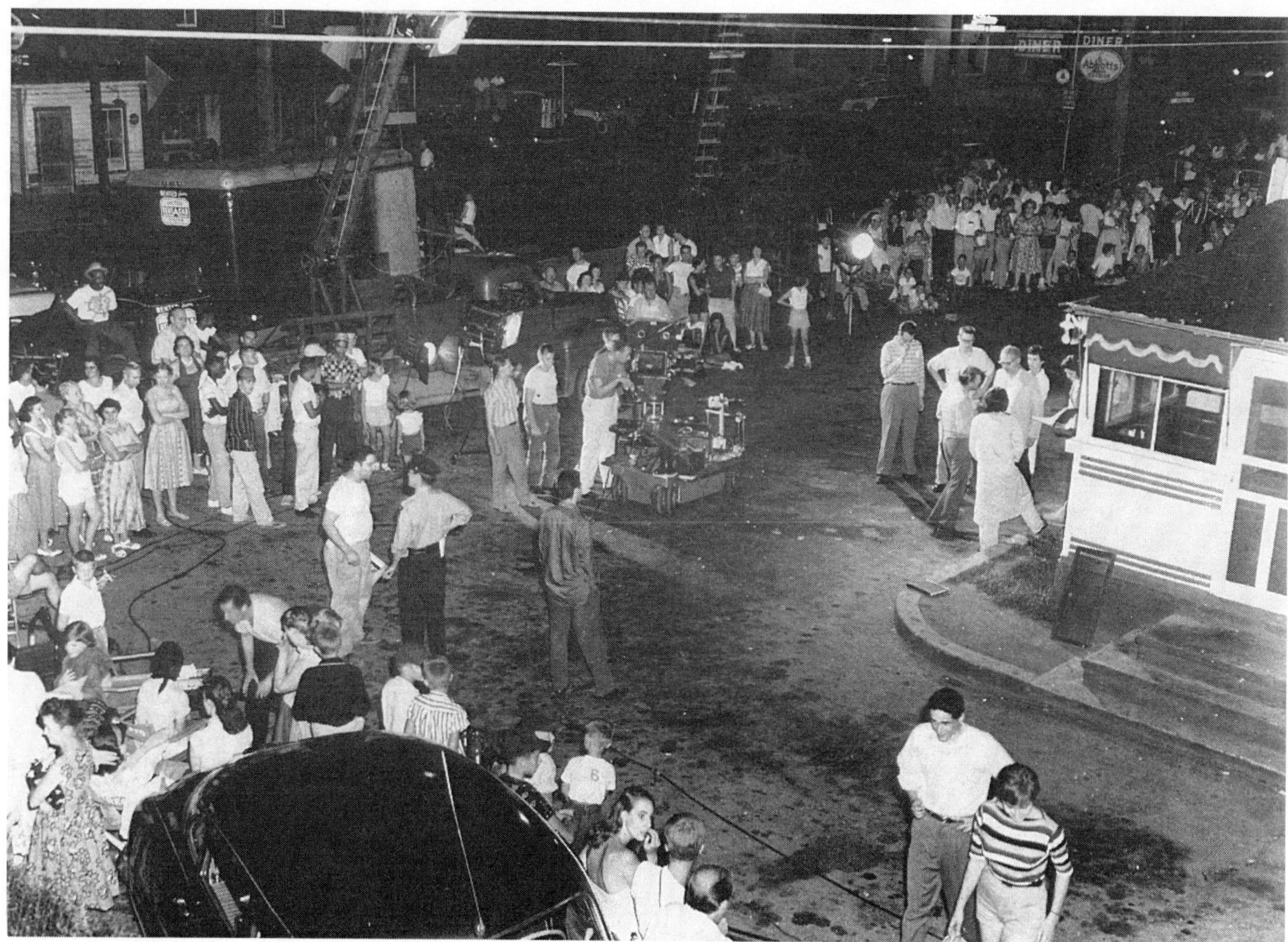

Behind the scenes of *The Blob*, Yeaworth (far right in glasses) provides direction to Steve McQueen and Aneta Corseaut as director of photography Thomas Spalding lines up the shot.

Kate Phillips, from Millgate's story, is above average for its time and makes some real attempts at characterization and provides motivation, while eschewing some standard Hollywood clichés along the way.

Yeaworth met Steve McQueen after seeing him perform on *Studio One* and he agreed to star in the film as the lead. Yeaworth only had a few difficulties with McQueen wanting things done his way, though McQueen did tend to let his dog on the lot where its barks spoiled takes, and after Yeaworth lent McQueen his station wagon, McQueen brought it back with a dent on its roof. Nevertheless, McQueen already had a commanding quality which is quite evident in this film (which is often erroneously reported to be his first, though it was the only one on which he took the billing "Steven McQueen").

The Blob benefits from a number of things, not the least of which is that it has a catchy theme song solicited by Paramount and written by a young Burt Bacharach and Mack David, which became a minor hit single for the 5 Blobs (actually singer Bernie Knee double-tracked several times), and its star performance by a young Steve McQueen (who came to resent being needled about the film for years afterward, but who in this film has not yet picked up any of his scene-stealing mannerisms — McQueen loved to fiddle with the scenery to attract attention from other actors). It also has an elegantly simple monster, amorphous goo that swallowed people up, with oft-times decent effects created by Bob Sloane.

The story begins when Steve (McQueen) and Jane (Aneta Corseaut, later Andy's girl on the *Andy Griffith Show*) are necking in Lover's Lane as a meteor falls. The meteor lands nearby, and an old wino (Olin Howlin) approaches it and pokes it with a stick, only to have it break open and reveal a mass of goo which he picks up on his stick. It's a bit that was chilling when I was a kid: the man points the stick down, but the goo comes rushing up and turns pink as it starts to ingest his hand.

Steve and Jane come up and see that the old fellow is in trouble, and so rush him to a doctor (Steven Case). When Steve and Jane go outside, some other teens challenge them to a drag race, except that he insists that the race must be in reverse. Officer Dave (Earl Rowe) catches Steve and gives him a stern lecture instead of a ticket. Steve heads off to try and find the old man's relatives.

Meanwhile, the doctor examines his patient. Under the blanket, something is moving in ways that do not resemble an arm, and the doctor informs his nurse that a parasite is "assimilating his flesh at fantastic speed." It's not long before the old geezer is completely swallowed up and the blob searches for a fresh meal. The nurse tries to stop it by throwing acid on it, which changes its color for a moment, but it then comes after her. The doctor shoots his shotgun at it, but the heaving and rapidly growing blob simply assimilates the bullets. Yeaworth creates some surprisingly chilly and tense scenes here.

Unfortunately, much of the rest of the film is more slackly paced and not all of the effects are as convincing as these early ones. Typically, Steve heads back to the physician's and discovers that the doctor has been consumed. Immediately, he alerts the police, his old pal officer Dave, who naturally has difficulty believing him, while his partner Jim has hated teens ever since one killed his wife in a car accident. Heading back to the doctor's office, there is no sign of him or the blob, while a housekeeper announces that the doctor has undoubtedly headed off to his medical convention. Meanwhile, the Blob gobbles up a mechanic just as he looks up from working on a car.

It then becomes Steve and Jane's thankless task to spread news of the danger to disbelieving adults all over town. (Jane's father, the school principal, ends up forbidding her to see Steve ever again.) The pair are only able to convince some other teens attending a horror double-bill at the theater.

There are some tense scenes such as when the Blob corners them in an empty supermarket, but by hiding in the freezer, they discover the thing's dislike of cold. However, the earlier eerieness of the picture completely dissipates. Frustrated by their attempts to warn a disbelieving populace, the town's teens honk their horns and set off every alarm they can to attract attention, much to the annoyance of the adults. However, just before the adults can give them a good scolding, there is the infamous theater scene where the Blob oozes through the projection holes in the nearby theater onto the crowd below, causing all the patrons to run screaming from the cinema in a panic, thereby giving credence to Steve's tale.

Steve, Jane and her annoying, pajama'ed kid brother hole up in a diner, which the Blob quickly surrounds. (It becomes obvious during this section that some of the effects were achieved by placing small blobs on photographs of the sets and locations.) Jim tries to kill it by shooting some high tension wires so that they fall on it, but electricity has no effect (some nice animation effects, though). The electricity starts a fire, which the diner's owner (Vince Barbi) puts out using a CO_2 extinguisher. Steve notes that the Blob once again shrinks from the cold and urges everyone to get their CO_2 extinguishers to freeze the thing solid. At the end, the Blob is airlifted to the Arctic, followed up by a "The End" title that transforms into a question mark. (Yeaworth's other SF films use the same cornball device.)

Alan Roberts and Gregg Martell as the boy and Neanderthal who bond in *Dinosaurus!* while riding on a brontosaurus.

The Blob inspired a Japanese imitation, *H-Man*, one of the best films directed by Inoshiro Honda, about a drug dealer who becomes a blob after being exposed to radiation and proceeds to turn other people into blobs as well; a comedy sequel years later, *Beware! The Blob* (aka *Son of the Blob*), which was very insipid and was directed by Larry Hagman, and an 1980s remake (see section on Chuck Russell). When the *Dallas* "Who Shot J.R.?" campaign was heating up, Harris rereleased the sequel under the slogan, "The Film J.R. Shot."

Pleased with their success, Harris and Yeaworth teamed up again on *4-D Man*, the rights to which they sold domestically to Universal while Warner Bros. took the foreign rights. Though it is not as effective, the film is even more ambitious than *The Blob*. Once more, Bob Sloane handled the effects and there is an above average script by Theodore Simonson and Cy Chermak which emphasizes characterization more than thrills.

The basic concept of *4-D Man* had to do with a man who develops the ability to move his body through solid matter; however, each time he does this, it costs him years off his life that he can only replace by draining the life-force off of another person. Future TV star Robert Lansing stars as Scott Nelson, a research scientist working for Dr. Theodore W. Carson (Edgar Stehli) at the Fairview Research Center. Carson has the unfortunate habit of taking credit for work done by the people in his employ, including Nelson's development of an impenetrable metal, which at a press conference he named Cargonite.

Nelson's brilliant brother Tony (Jame Conglon), also a physicist, shows Scott something that has fired his imagination: a pencil that has passed partially through a piece of metal, leaving the atoms of the pencil and the metal commingled. Tony had been attempting to amplify atomic fields, but apparently his device was able to amplify his brain waves so that he could literally will it to happen. Scott arranges to get Tony hired at the lab, and he soon begins to fall in love with Scott's attractive assistant Linda (Lee Meriwether).

Worried that he is losing Linda, Scott rushes to her house to propose, only to find that he's too late, Tony has beaten him to it. Scott returns to the lab and tries Tony's equipment, willing a metal dowling through a steel block. Suddenly it works, but his hand goes with it and gets stuck. Roy Parker (Robert Strauss), an unscrupulous colleague, approaches, forcing Scott to hire him while Parker purloins Tony's notes.

Soon, Scott is able to draw and withdraw his hand at will, and alerts Tony, who is surprised to find that Scott can do so even without his equipment. Scott gets Tony to promise not to tell anyone about his new ability, and spends an amusing jaunt practicing his newfound skill, by taking mail, an apple in a store window, handling some jewelry, and finally robbing a bank as a prank (he never uses the money, he simply hides it).

This latter feat succeeds in adding decades to his appearance (some not very convincing makeup). Scott hurries to Dr. Schwartz's house to see if he can help, but by touching him accidentally drains the life out of him so he withers and dies instantly of old age while some of Scott's youth is restored. This drives Scott on a downward spiral of killing, revenge, and madness. It is not long before his employer has his life taken, and at one point, Scott even drains a little girl (Patty Duke). Despite the cost to him, he uses his power at an alarming rate, and therefore, has to keep seeking new victims.

In one of the neatest of the film's effects, he passes through an electric fence, which allows us to see briefly his skeleton outlined in the electricity. Eventually, Linda uses her attractiveness to lure Scott into becoming solid enough for her to shoot while his brother Tony lures him into a vault made out of his "impenetrable" Cargonite, and Scott requires so much energy to pass through the thick material that he expires inside a Cargonite wall, his life-drained hand drooping a final farewell in the process.

Producer Jack H. Harris offered a million dollars to anyone who could duplicate the effect of the *4-D Man* in real life. Considering that the film centers around the ability of a man to walk through walls, Harris made a pretty safe bet, not to mention that if someone could perform such feats, he or she would not need Harris' million dollar offer as there would be far more lucrative avenues available.

Harris saw an opportunity to relocate to Hollywood and wanted to make another picture with Yeaworth. This time they received money up front from Universal to make their independent production, filming first in the Virgin Islands and then at a local studio in Hollywood. This time Yeaworth cowrote the script with his wife Jean, and they intended to make a kid-oriented dinosaur film called *Dinosaurus!* (Yeaworth credits his wife with having created the film's amusing comedy scenes, most of which involve the caveman [Gregg Martell] in the picture reacting to a modern day household.)

Dinosaurus! is a pleasant little family film set in the West Indies where lightning revives a Neanderthal, an Apotosaurus, and a Tyrannosaurus rex. (The dinosaur models were taken out of Marcel Delgado's hands before he had finished putting the final skin coverings on, giving them a somewhat awkward appearance. They were then animated by Tim Barr, Wah Chang, and Gene Warren, George Pal's regular effects men.)

It follows the adventures of Julio (Alan Roberts) who befriends the frightened Neanderthal (Gregg Martell) and later gets to ride the tame Apotosaurus, who gets frightened by some police and winds up sinking in some quicksand. The Neanderthal sacrifices himself to save Julio and in the imaginative climax, the Tyrannosaurus battles a steam shovel before being destroyed by being pushed over a cliff into the ocean. While not as clever as Yeaworth's other SF films, it is an enjoyable diversion that succeeds in its purpose of entertaining young children. Yeaworth has since left the film business to work in World's Fair and theme park pavilion design and production.

NORIAKI YUASA (1933–)

Shiawase Nara Te O Tataki (1964); *Daikaiju Gamera* (aka *Gammera, the Invincible; Gamera*) (1965); *Gamera Tai Gaos* (aka *The Return of the Giant Monsters*; *Gamera vs. Gaos* (1967); *Gamera Tai Uchi Kaijo Bairusa* (aka *Destroy All Planets; Gamera Tai Viras; Gamera vs. Outer Space Monster Viras*) (1968); *Anata sukimi no*; *Hebi—Musume to Hakuhatsuma*; *Attack of the Monsters* (aka *Gamera vs. Guiron*) (1969); *Gamera Tai Daimaju Jaiga* (aka *Gamera vs. Monster X)* (1970); *Gamera Tai Shinkai Kaiju Jigura* (aka *Gamera vs. Zigra*); *Ju hyo eveji*; *Seijuky* (1971); *Uchu Kaiji Gamera* (aka *Space Monster Gamera*) (1980)

Television: *Ultraman 80* (1980); *Electroid Zaborger* (1974)

Born Sept. 28, 1933, in Tokyo, Japan, Noriaki Yuasa is the main auteur behind the childish *Gamera* series, in which a giant flying space turtle befriends small boys and battles other oversized monsters. The series was clearly Japanese studio Daiei's attempt to cash in on the box office success of Toho's *Gojira* or *Godzilla* series.

The son of a stage actor, Noriaki Yuasa himself became a child actor for some years before attending university. Upon graduation, realizing that he disliked the actor's life, he sought work on the other side of the camera, joining Daiei Studios in 1955. There he studied under such accomplished directors as Yuzo Kawashima, Koji Shima, and Umeji Inoue. In 1964 Daiei promoted him to director with the musical comedy *Shiawasa nara te o tatake* (*If You're Happy, Clap Your Hands*, 1964). He was tapped next to make *Dai gunju Nezura* (*The Great Rat Swarm*), which was to be made with real rats crawling over miniatures of cities. But the rats brought with them fleas, and the resulting epidemic rendered the product impractical. Since the miniatures were already built, however, Daiei had to think of something else to destroy them. Studio chief Masaichi Nagata had had a whimsical idea about a giant flying turtle; screenwriter Nisan Takahashi and director Yuasa fashioned it into *Daikaiju Gamera* (1965), a surprise smash hit which became the first real challenger to the primacy of Toho's Gojira or Godzilla character.

Yuasa went on to direct all but one of the seven Gamera sequels through 1980 (he directed only the special effects for *Gamera tai Barugon* [1966]). As the series grew more juvenile, Yuasa actually enjoyed it more, as making entertainments for children appealed to him more than making more "serious" monster pictures. His favorite of his own movies was the first most obviously childish of all the sequels, *Gamera tai uchi kaijo bairusa* (1968). Except for *Uchu Kaiju Gamera* (1980), Yuasa has directed only television work since Daiei's financial collapse in 1971.

The first film in the series was *Daikaiju Gamera* (American title: *Gamera the Invincible*) and was marketed specifically for children. It was also the only episode shot in black and white. Dr. Hidaka (Eiji Funakoshi) heads a scientific expedition to the Arctic, when an American pilot shoots down some enemy planes carrying atomic weapons which explode. Gamera, a two hundred foot turtle, is awakened by an atomic blast. Hidaka learns about Gamera from an Eskimo, while Gamera smashes into Hidaka's ship, crushing it. Hidaka assumes the beast will soon die of radiation poisoning.

The film also introduces a young boy named Kenny who is obsessed with turtles. When Kenny goes to the beach, he happens to see Gamera appearing over a ridge and runs towards a lighthouse to see him better. The clumsy reptile knocks the lighthouse over, but saves Kenny by catching him, establishing Gamera's fondness for young boys which would continue throughout the series. However, considering how Gamera is constantly incinerating extras, the boy's fondness for him seems pathological and unhealthy.

Instead, the titanic turtle heads for a geothermal power plant, seeking out energy sources to consume (he enjoys the electricity from the power lines), and blows fire from his mouth at any opposition. Hidaka suggests that since heat oriented weapons don't work, perhaps they should use cold. The army drops a cold bomb, but the turtle unexpectedly pulls its head and feet in, flames sprout from its leg openings, and it spins off into the air.

Gamera attacks Tokyo and the army initiates Plan Z, which turns out to involve luring the turtle into a rocketship and blasting him safely off into space. Most of the Gamera movies are slow-moving and silly, but despite its schizophrenic approach, this is the most serious and best of the lot until the series was revived in the 1990s.

The American version of the film featured extra footage starring Brian Donlevy, Albert Dekker, and Diane Findlay, and makes the Americans the heroes by having them discover a way of getting rid of the marauding terrapin. The America version has better dubbing and better pacing, but has largely withdrawn from circulation in favor of a Japanese English–dubbed version.

The second film in the series, *War of the Monsters* (aka *Gamera vs. Barugon)*, was directed by Shigeo Tanaka, but Yuasa handled the film's special effects. *War of the Monsters* was the first of the series to be shot in color, but the participation of Gamera proves surprisingly minimal as the great turtle only appears in three scenes, and overall the film is talky, dull, and over long. It does pick up where the last one left off, with Gamera breaking free after the meteor he is trapped in is hit by a rocket. He immediately gravitates to Earth and hurls himself at a large dam. Barugon, a cross among a gila monster, a rhinoceros, and an apartment complex, is unearthed by some inept gangsters and eventually comes to blows with Gamera.

Yuasa returned to the director's chair with *Gamera vs. the Gaos* (aka *The Return of the Giant Monsters*). Gamera is now fully on the side of children and good and battles a giant flying pterodactyl called Gaos who fires laser beams out of its mouth. The most interesting things in the film are scenes of various model cars, helicopters, and planes getting sliced in half by Gaos' beams.

Next came *Destroy All Monsters* (aka *Gamera vs. Viras*), which follows two Boy Scouts as they sneak aboard a submarine and submerge it only to be taken prisoner by some aliens. The aliens have hypnotized the giant turtle and sent him off on a rampage, and it is up to the two young heroes to break the aliens' hold over Gamera and have the titanic terrapin chase them out of our skies.

One of the more disturbing films in the series is *Attack of the Monsters* (aka *Gamera vs. Guiron*), in which its two young heroes are a Japanese and an American boy who are captured by female aliens who take them back to their planet where they lock them in cages and announce, "While they are sleeping, we'll eat their brains raw." Gamera comes to rescue them, but the aliens are protected by the hatchet-headed monster Guiron, who damages the flying tortoise. However, Gamera quickly recovers from his wounds to return and save the day once more.

The dubbing and dialogue in *Attack of the Monsters* is spectacularly bad. ("Come in please. This is Oshima. You can start Z-Plan.") The little boys in the film sound as if 20-year-old women speaking with high pitched voices while imitating a bored Roseanne Barr-Arnold dubbed them. Still, the film does provide an imaginative setting, gruesome scenes of blood spurting from giant monster limbs, and makes for one of the better features in this increasingly jejune series.

This was followed by *Gamera vs. Monster X* set at the 1970 World's Fair, where Gamera fights a giant lizard named Jaiga who is determined to trash the fair because it dared locate atop its sacred resting place. The oddest touch in the film is that Jaiga plants an egg inside an open wound it creates on Gamera's chest, and the hatchling emerges and begins sucking the life's blood out of the heroic turtle. In a variation on Fleischer's *Fantastic Voyage*, the two heroic kids are sent inside a submarine which is shot into Gamera's artery in order to search out and destroy the invading organism.

Yuasa directed one more film for the series, *Gamera vs. Zigra*, which once more features nasty female aliens who attempt to take control of the Earth. While the film has a strong anti-pollution theme, it is largely inept. Gamera is actually killed off early on, but the heroic children bring it back to life by pumping electricity into the water. Zigra is a large crown-like spaceship in the first half of the film, and turns into a nasty metallic monster fish in the second half.

Yuasa returned to the series after a long absence with *Space Monster Gamera*, which cheesily adds stock footage from earlier films in the series to tell the tale of space pirates from the planet Zanon who send a fleet of monsters to destroy the Earth. Luckily, spacemen from Planet M38 know enough to send for Gamera to meet the threat.

Subsequent films in the series are produced by one-time rival Toho and have been directed by Shusuke Kaneko. They are said to be of much higher quality with more contemporary looking special effects. Thus far Kaneko has fashioned *Gamera, Guardian of the Universe* (1995) and *Gamera 2: Coming of Legion* (1996).

BRIAN YUZNA (1949–)

Bride of Re-Animator (1988); *Society* (1989); *Initiation: Silent Night, Deadly Night 4* (1990); *Return of the Living Dead III* (1993); *Necronomicon* (codirected with Christophe Gans and Shusuke Kaneko) (1994); *The Dentist* (1996); *Zen, Intergalactic Ninja; The Progeny; The Dentist II* (1998); *Faust* (forthcoming)

Television: *Tarzan: The Epic Adventures* (1996)

Brian Yuzna is still perhaps better known as a producer than a director, though he has done both. He has specialized in making horror films that often succeed in making audiences squirm, and some of his films have a definite science fictional twist. He has produced *Re-Animator*, in which Herbert West creates a serum to bring the newly dead back to life; *The Guyver* (aka *Mutronics*) in which a college student dons an alien suit to gain powers to fight bad guys who turn into monsters; as well as directing *Society*, in which a teenager discovers a secret, flesh-altering society that feeds off the skin of others; the *Re-Animator* sequel, in which West performs some rather surreal experiments, and *Return of the Living Dead Part III*, where the military molds zombies for their own uses.

Brian Yuzna was born in Manila in the Philippines and was raised in there and in Nicaragua, Panama, and Puerto Rico as well before his family settled in Atlanta, Georgia.

He is best known as the producer of Stuart Gordon's best-known films, *Re-Animator, From Beyond* and *Dolls*. Since then he has continued working in the horror genre, both as a producer and as a director, as well as cowriting *From Beyond* with Dennis Paoli and coming up with the idea for *Honey, I Shrunk the Kids*, which was originally to have been directed by Gordon.

Yuzna went to high school in Atlanta, Georgia, then went to college at Western Michigan University in Michigan and also University of North Carolina. At the age of 35, he decided to go into movies, having acquired the rights to a obscure series of early Lovecraft stories, known as "Herbert West — Reanimator," and attracted the interest of Chicago theater director Stuart Gordon, who wanted to make his film debut.

"I was a big movie fan like anybody," said Yuzna. "The ones that influenced me greatly were the ones that gave me my first nightmares such as *Creature with the Atom Brain, The Seventh Voyage of Sinbad* and *House On Haunted Hill*, and those things that came out when I was a kid. I think I've always been trying to recapture those feelings.

"I just borrowed a bunch of movies and decided to make a movie. So I looked for a director. A guy named Bob Greenberg met me in Chicago and introduced me to Stuart. Originally we were going to do it in Chicago."

Re-Animator was the result of their collaboration, winning critical notices and a cult following, and giving fledgling distribution company Empire Pictures a boost. The original film was released to theaters unrated, one of the last horror films to do so, but due to censorship problems, was also offered in an R-rated version on videocassette. Additionally, a third version featuring cut scenes was prepared for television syndication.

Said Yuzna, "I only made one version frankly because I paid for it; I never took it to the MPAA. When I began working with Stuart on it, one of the first decisions I made was to not hold back because I'd seen too many horror movies that tried to pretend to be something else, and they undermined the basic audience which will like even a lousy movie if it delivers. I thought, hey, what if it turns out lousy? At least we're going to deliver the goods.

"We're lucky that it turned out real good and delivered the goods also. I had made a deal with Charlie Band because he was the first guy I met when I came to town to release it for no money. I just gave it to him. And he released it and sold it, but I had no problem with the idea of making other versions. When I was in Italy with Stuart making *From Beyond*, Charlie had it recut and delivered these other versions [R-rated and TV versions]. I think I saw the TV version on TV once, or most of it, and I saw the R-rated version once with Stuart, and to be honest with you, I hated it.

"The original version of *Re-Animator* was two and a half hours long, and when we had an 87 minute movie it was because that's what it seemed like it took to make that movie work. That's another thing that I don't think people understand and that is that rarely do movies just turn out the way they're planned. It's usually a really complicated journey making something out of whatever you have.

"The rough cut of *Re-Animator* was two and a half hours and I thought I'd lost all my money. I thought oh my God, this is a disaster. It was obviously a rough cut, and I didn't know about rough cuts, but it's like you start tweaking things and sometimes it really works and sometimes it doesn't. There were lots of scenes that were lost. What really made it work I think is that there was a relationship at the center of it which played, it was about Dan and Meg. Finally it was about Herbert, because we took out all their scenes, but it didn't change the fact that there was an emotional core — I mean the ending of that was the greatest scene.

"Whereas in *Bride of Re-Animator*, there was no ending. When it got up to them, we just got out of it, but you didn't care about these people, so you had nobody to win and nobody to lose. Now if we had been with those characters and really cared for them, then anything else that happened would have been a lot of fun and insanity. We would have felt secure at the end that we had been entertained. But when you just sort of run away from them, when you don't buy what's going on with them, you sort of feel like you've been left adrift. With *Re-Animator*, you really felt that there was an emotional thing happening there. Originally, in *Re-Animator* Dr. Hill's eyes lit up and he kind of controlled people and mesmerized them and all this other stuff which just was sort of lost."

The pair continued to make films, creating *From Beyond* and *Dolls*. Yuzna thought up the concept for *Teeny Weenies*, about some children who are shrunk down to the size of mites and have adventures in their own backyard. Gordon agreed to make the movie and Disney agreed to finance it; however, Gordon became too ill to complete the production and Disney turned the project, now called *Honey, I Shrunk the Kids*, over to former ILM effects man Joe Johnston (*The Rocketeer*) who took Yuzna off the project.

Said Yuzna, "After he [Gordon] got sick on that, I tried to hang in and once Joe Johnston came on, he got rid of me and brought in another producer. I was pretty well crushed by losing *Honey, I Shrunk the Kids* because it was my original idea, and I didn't realize they could take it away like that. I just thought they couldn't get rid of me because I thought it up and I was involved and I had gotten the effects boards done and built the sets, and it just seemed like it was a devastating feeling.

"Then we tried to do the *Shadow Over Innsmouth* thing and it got bogged down in some politics between the executive producers. It was just a complicated story, and what it meant to me is that I did a couple months work on it and it just wasn't panning out. At the same time I was working with Dan O'Bannon. I had been working with him for over a year on *The Men*, which is an idea that he had about a woman who discovers that all men are aliens. [Sort of a distaff version of Fritz Leiber's *Conjure Wife* which has been filmed as *Weird Woman* and *Burn, Witch Burn*.] I used to go to his house once or twice a week at night and sit with him, and we worked up this story."

Yuzna arranged for *The Men* to be financed by Cinecom, but on the eve of having everything set, O'Bannon, who was to direct, pulled out. Dan Jakoby (*Blue Thunder, Arachnophobia*) was initially going to write it, but Jakoby didn't want to write it as a genre piece. Then O'Bannon planned to get another writer to write it for him. "We had a treatment and everything, it was a great project," said Yuzna. "Dan's going to do it at New Line. I got it totally financed, I had $5 million to do it from Cinecom, and at the eleventh hour we got together with Dan and his manager and his lawyer and we're doing the deal, and the next day he pulled out and then wouldn't answer my calls. I think that what happened is that his manager didn't like the deal. I don't know what happened. I was working with him without anything on paper."

Naturally this devastated Yuzna once more, who resolved to become a director. "It's a natural thing to want to do if you work with movies anyway," said Yuzna, "but I just felt like I wasn't in control of my destiny, because I had all these deals and *I* was always there, you know what I mean? But the deals were falling apart because of the director. And I'm sure if you get involved in bigger pictures, it's the actor, because you need the actor and the director. If I could build myself up as being a credible director, not only would I like it a lot, but also I could then make a deal and if the director wasn't going to work out, then I could direct. I just felt like I would have more pieces of the puzzle."

As a producer, Yuzna feels he is more of a filmmaker than what is normally thought of as a producer, which is a dealmaker. He says he has never been comfortable just leaving it at the deal level, which has been bad for him financially because most of the money is made at the deal level. Yuzna prefers to be creatively involved "with the actual scheming and movie-making," as he refers to it.

He teamed up with Keith Walley, whom he had known at Empire, and who came to him when he was getting ready to do the *Unnamable*. Walley had started up a new production company called Wild Street and they made *Society* and *The Bride of Re-Animator* with Yuzna learning how to direct by doing it.

Bride of Re-Animator, as the sequel to a cult favorite, was considered something of a disappointment by horror fans, and Yuzna acknowledges that the screenplay, which was quickly cobbled together in six weeks, and the film have aspects that simply don't work. Gordon was originally considered as the project's director.

"Originally Dennis Paoli worked on it, Phil Norris and Stuart, and then as it came down the pike, Stuart was doing *The Pit and the Pendulum* and I had a window of opportunity to shoot it," said Yuzna. "I had to start it in June of 1989 because the money was all there, and to be honest with you, I'm pretty driven by having to pay the rent and the bottom line is I had to make the movie then and it didn't fit into what Stuart's schedule was.

"As it turned out, *The Pit and the Pendulum* got pushed, so I would have run into it again — we ended up shooting about the same time. He's gracious enough to speak well about it. I feel the same way about *Honey, I Blew Up the Kid*. I wasn't involved in that, because I felt God, that was my baby, and I wasn't apart of it. I wasn't asked or consulted, but I accepted the business reality that when you go in and do some work and get paid for it, you don't own it anymore, so you have to go forward.

"I think the first problem was that the script was rushed, so part of it is the script, part of it may be some ineffectual direction. I think that the main relationship in it was a disaster and the ending was just getting out of there. What was happening between Dan and the girl was just a disaster in terms of how that played out, it didn't work, and it probably started with the writing, which I take responsibility, because I basically shepherded it very closely.

"There's another issue that made it a little difficult and that was carrying forward the characters was really tough because the story of Dan Cane and Herbert had already been told, and I think that was a problem that was never really solved. Also there was a lot of false beginnings to that movie. Maybe in a way I tried to do too much with it. We could have stayed in Peru and told the whole story there. I think the thing [where] that fell apart for me, the areas that are uncomfortable for me, are the zombies in the hospital somehow getting them into the story, getting them out of there, calling them from the distance, the Doctor Hill stuff.

"I like the scene in the tent in the beginning, but it doesn't have anything to do with the story. Originally there was much more of it, and we introduced the girl and everything, but ultimately we just cut it all out. All it did was say they got something from there that is going to be able to make goop. Maybe one of the problems was that I tried to use everything that was left from the [original] stories in the book into the movie. We actually did shoot a scene which picked up where the last movie left off, and we cut that out. We shot a scene where the cop finds the Hill head in the carnival. We had like three or four beginnings.

"The part of it that I really like personally is the area where Dan Cane comes home and we introduce the whole situation, the heart and all that stuff. I love the little hand-eyeball creature. To me I love that kind of stuff. If you don't like that...." For *Bride*, unfortunately, more creativity was given over to Screaming Mad George's surreal makeup designs than to inventing an interesting or gripping narrative.

"I always reach too far anyways," said Yuzna. "I always try to put much more into the stories than they can support because I'm an idea person and I'm just learning dramatization. A lot of scenes didn't work very well, it was quite ambitious, but the major relationship in the movie was never very clear and we weren't with it. In *Return of the Living Dead 3*, it sticks right with the major relationship and never really gets afield from that, so I think as an emotional experience is very tight whereas *Bride of Re-Animator* kind of meanders. It's about this, and then it's about that. I feel it should have just been about the *Bride* and she probably should have come earlier in the story."

Yuzna has tried to work with Gordon since then, trying to revive the abandoned *Shadow Over Innsmouth* project and coming up with the possibility of a *Re-Animator 3*. "The problem we have about working together is Stuart is on a much faster track than I am. After *Honey, I Shrunk the Kids*, I went back down to the low-budget end and Stuart got an office at the studio. *Fortress* is a $10 million movie and I'm still making a million and a half dollar movies. Also Stuart has really topnotch representation, which he certainly deserves, because when we first started, he had been doing plays his whole life, and I was brand new to movies. I had been a carpenter and an artist and when I was 35 I decided to make movies whereas Stuart had been working on staging and story and directing, and I think that was recognized. He had serious successes, and *Re-Animator* just fit in with what he was doing. He's just on a different level than I am.

"I have to make a lot more movies just to survive. He's in the league where he gets paid a lot to develop stuff. He wrote that *Body Snatchers* thing with Dennis Paoli [Abel Ferrera remake], but he gets paid a lot more than I do. I don't make much on these things. In terms of working in a factory, I get paid a lot, but in terms of Hollywood, I'm sort of Triple-A; I'm not with the Dodgers, I'm back in Albuquerque or something. I'm thrilled just to be able to make a living doing what I do."

While Yuzna recognizes the difficulty of the limited time and budgets of low-budget production, he is also aware that such filmmaking has its benefits as well. "The upside is when I go into the editing room, and we scheme out what to do, the few guys that you see there we're going to decide what to do today and that's what we'll do," said Yuzna. "There's not a lot of money involved so that people come in and second guess it, whereas when you get up to that *Honey, I Shrunk the Kids* level or higher, there's a lot of people that have a lot of say. Everything is a political issue, much more complicated than what we deal with. The upside is that we get to invent things. I can call up J. K. Potter [noted surrealist artist whose designs inspired the opening sequence for Yuzna's *Necromicon*] and ask for some pictures and by God we'll try to make those pictures in the movie, whereas if I was working on a bigger budget, I would have to go through a lot of approvals just to get Potter be accepted and a lot of people would say, 'Isn't that just too weird?' You go through this process, and that's what Stuart has to deal with. I think Stuart's best when he can just let it all hang out, but the bigger the budgets get....

"The downside of what I do is that we have to struggle without the money, so we don't get to deliver the effects that if we could deliver, we could really compete with it. If we could deliver the production values, we could compete in a major way. And secondly, we just don't get enough money to survive long enough to be able to work long enough on these movies. I've got to keep churning them out. But then, if you don't do it, how do you get any better at it? I think it's a lot of fun to do these and to develop what you know about doing it."

Yuzna tackled directing again with the direct to video *The Initiation: Silent Night, Deadly Night 4*, in which Maud Adams leads a coven of witches who decide to initiate a young reporter and turn her into some kind of mutant cockroach. Said Yuzna, "It doesn't have anything to do with the others. I like a lot of scenes in it. I have to admit that the last half hour is sort of a cheat and not very satisfying. It suffers from having this rushed job to get to shooting which was based on Live [Entertainment]'s needing to get it out to stores at a certain time, but it also had a script that was never finished. What I was doing there was fooling around with the myth of Lilith and with simulacra. Between those two things I evolved all these wild ideas and tried to use them in the movie.

"To be honest with you, you might think that it just doesn't make any sense, and it may not. I don't know if we ever got it to the point where it made sense, but actually there are a number of scenes in there that I think are great and worth seeing. Unfortunately, there is only one

Producer-director Brian Yuzna with model for self-mutilating zombie for *Return of the Living Dead III* (photo by author).

what they wanted with it — that was part of the deal."

Next Yuzna worked on *Silent Night, Deadly Night 5: The Toymaker* which he cowrote with director Martin Kitrosser, who had been script supervisor on *Guyver*.

"I suggested we do a killer toys thing at Christmas," explained Yuzna about the film, which features a bloated Mickey Rooney creating a surrogate son who goes berserk. "It suffered a lot from the minuscule budget that the Live (Entertainment) things have. They are like Corman budgets. The difference is Corman owns his own equipment and we had to rent it, but it's the same routine. They got one actor who can be on the video box, the money's real low, and they pay something for the serial rights. Once again I liked the story a lot, and what hurt it a lot is we just didn't have enough money to do the toys properly.... The story to that is very clear whereas with *Initiation* the story is a complete mess."

Part of Yuzna's philosophy of making horror movies is that when the budget is low, you can get by with wild and interesting designs if you don't have the money for major mainstream type effects. "With less money," he said, "if you can depend on design a lot and concept, that stuff doesn't cost, but if you have to depend on real good execution, you're in trouble if it has to do something."

Yuzna is very pleased with his subsequent projects. He was an executive producer on Tony Randel's *Ticks*, which he describes as being "like *The Mod Squad* out in the woods. It's aimed at a teenage audience. Every time you make a movie, you try to make it real good, you just never know when it's going to click. *Re-Animator* worked. *Honey, I Shrunk the Kids* worked. *From Beyond* didn't work as well. Each movie you make you hope is going to be magic — you put just as much into it. For whatever reasons, some click and some don't. *Ticks* is one that clicked. It's not like it was this great script and great cast and great this and great that. It was no different than any other movie. And it was a movie that had great troubles when it was finished."

Ticks involves some teens who go up into the mountains and encounter some chemically altered ticks who have become large and menacing after falling into a marijuana farmer's secret grow mixture. Yuzna felt that the film needed to get to action sequences more quickly and wanted to push up the squeamish aspects as well to make a more effective, creepy horror film. He explains, "It wasn't working very well. We had to think up new scenes. New scenes were

version — the R version. The MPAA really gave us a hard time on this, but even though I think there are some classic scenes in it."

Next Yuzna tackled producing a live action version of *The Guyver*, a six volume Japanese graphic novel by Yoshika Takaya, which had already been adapted in an adult-oriented animated version. *Guyver* was a $3 million film financed by a consortium of companies in Japan. Codirected by Screaming Mad George and Steve Wang, the film features a college student (Jack Armstrong) who finds "the Guyver," an alien device that transforms him into an invincible armored fighting machine. Mark Hammill appears as a CIA agent who tries to keep the device from falling into the wrong hands. Jeffrey Combs and David Gale from *Re-Animator* appear respectively as Dr. East and as the Zoanoid leader, whose huge, eight-legged Zoanoid mutation supplies the film with its climax.

In America, *Guyver* was recut to eliminate some of the humor and briefly released as *Transmutations* with a poster parodying that of *Teenage Mutant Ninja Turtles*. When the film was acquired by New Line, New Line used the revised cut but retained the original title. Explains Yuzna, "The Japanese version is Steve Wang and (Screaming Mad) George's cut, and I think it's better to see the whole thing. I think they cut it to be a more commercial movie. It's shorter and they cut it to get to the action more, it doesn't spend as much time with the characters.... Some of the things they did I felt were kind of odd, like cut the slash cuts out — there were these cartoony slash cuts and stuff. I didn't see the point of cutting that stuff out. But ultimately, Imperial cut the movie for foreign. They bought it and did written and new scenes were shot with a new d.p. [director of photography] and new effects guys, KNB came in, and these were intercut with what was there because there was no real action upfront, and so it was intercut with scenes where there was action, and the editing pulled it all together."

Necronomicon, named after H. P. Lovecraft's *Book of the Dead*, was an anthology film with three directors, Yuzna being one as well as a creative producer on the project. In Yuzna's wrap-around story, Lovecraft (Jeffrey Combs) visits a monastic library and steals the key to the restricted room that harbors the fabled *Necronomicon*. As he reads from its pages, we see the stories it relates.

The first and best, "The Drowned," directed by Christophe Gans, a French genre journalist, is about a man (Bruce Payne) who inherits a cursed house, the ancestor (Richard Lynch) of which had burned his Bible and banished God from the home when his wife and son were drowned. This reminds the man of his own fiancée (Maria Ford) who had drowned and whose figure suddenly beckons to him from the sea caves beneath the house.

The second tale, "The Cold," was directed by Susuke Kaneko and is based on the Lovecraft story "Cold Air." In it, an abused runaway hides at her upstairs neighbor's (David Warner) heavily refrigerated apartment, only to discover that he is in league with the landlady (Millie Perkins) to extend his life by murdering people and draining them of their spinal fluid.

The last story is "Whispers," directed by Yuzna, in which a pregnant auto accident victim (Signy Coleman) tracks the blood of her injured husband into a building, where a peculiar couple (Dan Calfa and Judith Drake) offer her up to be sacrificed to an alien being with a taste for bone marrow.

In the final wrap-around story, Lovecraft drives off in a cab driven by Yuzna himself, whose voice is mysteriously dubbed. The film does deliver some nice atmosphere and some good performances, but some of its effects are repulsive and it failed to get a theatrical release domestically, with New Line releasing it direct-to-video.

Along with *Necronomicon*, Yuzna worked on the disturbing *Return of the Living Dead 3,* which has already been branded as too disturbing and sick for distribution in South Africa and about which he says, "I think it's the best moviemaking I've done in terms of the planning out and the mechanics of making a movie, but it's only because I've been practicing."

Return of the Living Dead 3, scripted by John Perry, speculates about what might be done with a chemical that induces the people who are exposed to it to turn into zombies. The military sees the possibility of virtually unkillable soldiers, provided that the zombies can be controlled, and Yuzna presents some clever ideas about how this might be attempted.

However, things get messy when the teenage son (J. Trevor Edmond) of one of the men (Kent McCord) involved in the project tries to use the chemical to revive his girlfriend (Mindy Clarke) after a motorcycle accident. She is fortunately able to retain her personality, but can only control her urges to eat human brains by distracting herself with pain, which she achieves through continual body piercing.

Adding to the squirm-inducing outrageousness, a multi-racial street gang all get the zombie juice as well and infiltrate the Los Angeles sewer system. There are a lot of inventive ideas here, taking the series in entirely new directions, but the result is far from pleasant for anyone who can't abide S&M imagery.

Yuzna then went on to *The Dentist*, a variation on Joseph Ruben and Donald Westlake's *The Stepfather* in which a dentist who is a pill-popping control freak begins to viciously assault his patients. Corbin Bernsen stars as Dr. Feinman who suspects his wife Brooke (Linda Hoffman) of two-timing him with the pool boy (Michael Stadvec) and who is being hounded by an IRS agent (Earl Boen from *Terminator 2*) who expects free dental work in exchange for looking the other way at the doctor's financial practices.

The Dentist was written by Stuart Gordon and Dennis Paoli, and then revised by David Finch, and mostly consists of patients putting themselves into vulnerable positions while Dr. Feinman goes quietly mad and does things like sexually assault a beauty queen after knocking her out with nitrous oxide, forcibly extracting another patient's teeth, breaking the IRS man's jaw, and injecting air into a patient's brain. It ultimately seems mean-spirited and unpleasant rather than enjoyably gruesome. Yuzna has not lost his knack for creating sequences that are truly disturbing, but that does not automatically make them worthwhile.

Still, the film was successful enough to spawn a Yuzna-directed sequel, *The Dentist II*, and in addition to producing *Crying Freeman* and directing Joe Lara as Tarzan for television's *Tarzan: The Epic Adventures*, Yuzna has recently directed the features *Zen, Intergalactic Ninja* and *The Progeny*. Working on lower budgeted projects has meant that Yuzna must replace quality with quantity in order to make his living, but his enthusiasm for the field does shine through in all he does.

Yuzna, after completing the sci-fi comedy *Zen Intergalactic Ninja*, has been signed to direct an adaptation of David Quinn and Tim Vigil's horror comic *Faust*.

ROBERT ZEMECKIS (1952–)

The Lift (short, 1972); *A Field of Honor* (student short, 1973); *I Wanna Hold Your Hand* (1977); *Used Cars* (1980); *Romancing the Stone* (1984); *Back to the Future* (1985); *Who Framed Roger Rabbit* (1988); *Back to the Future Part II* (1989); *Back to the Future Part III* (1990); *Death Becomes Her* (1992); *Forrest Gump* (1994); *Contact* (1997); *Fireflies* (1999); *The Castaways; What Lies Beneath* (2000)

Television: "Head of the Class," *Amazing Stories* (1985); "And All Through the House," *Tales from the Crypt* (1989); "Yellow," *Tales from the Crypt* (1991); *Johnny Bago* (1993); "You, Murderer," *Tales from the Crypt* (1995); Untitled Showtime Project (1999)

Robert Zemeckis, born in 1952, grew up in Mayor Daley's Chicago, which may partially account for his cynicism. The son of a construction worker on Chicago's South Side, he describes his childhood as "one of those kids who sat in front of the television all the time."

He was impressed by the first film he ever saw, *The Blob* with Steve McQueen, and gained early film experience while working as an editor for NBC News in Chicago. At film school, he dismayed more pretentious classmates by voicing a preference for the films of Jules White, who directed Three Stooges shorts, James Bond films, and Jerry Lewis movies.

Zemeckis directed a 15 minute student film called *A Field of Honor*, in which a newly discharged mental patient is driven to a murderous rampage by the everyday violence of American life and shoots up the town, while his equally deranged, wheelchair-bound father sits at the window waiting for Commies to invade (all scored to music from Elmer Bernstein's score for *The Great Escape*). The film shows many of Zemeckis' trademarks already in place, including black humor and sudden bursts of random violence as well as a breakneck pace. The film served as a calling card, winning him an internship with Steven Spielberg, who executive produced his first film.

Zemeckis met his long-time writing partner Bob Gale at USC film school where they discovered that they shared an interest in Disney films and action films rather than the more pretentious foreign films favored by most film school enthusiasts. Zemeckis began to sneak onto various studio lots, parking in George Lucas' spot at Universal, for example, because he knew Lucas to be away in San Francisco. While there he would eat meals off companies shooting on the lot and get to know the assistant directors who could inform him about opportunities.

Zemeckis quickly learned that the lowest rated shows were often more open to newcomers, and found that *Kolshak the Nightstalker* was at the bottom of the ratings. He and Gale walked into the producer's office and sold him on the idea of a headless motorcycle phantom who comes back from the fifties, which was made into the episode "Chopper." After a few more screenplays, Universal offered the team a writing contract, which they turned down.

The offer of such a contract was enough to interest an agent, who advised them to forget television and concentrate on films. Together they concocted a couple of screenplays, *Bordello of Blood* and *Tank*. *Bordello of Blood* was eventually produced years later as *Tales from the Crypt: Bordello of Blood* starring Dennis Miller, which Zemeckis executive produced and with the script heavily rewritten by other hands. *Tank* was about some dissidents who steal a Sherman tank from the National Guard Armory and threaten to blow up a Chicago building in an effort to protest the actions of the oil companies. The script got the attention of writer-director John Milius, who found the story's underlying social *irresponsibility* appealing. (The project has no relation to the 1984 movie directed by Marvin Chimsky and starring James Garner.)

Milius hired the pair to write a World War II movie called *The Night the Japs Attacked* for his A-Team Productions unit at MGM based on a news story they found about how people in Los Angeles responded one night when they felt that the Japanese had attacked them shortly after the start of World War II. The project, an anarchic comedy intended to have something to offend everyone, was quickly objected to by members of the Japanese-American community and the title eventually changed by Steven Spielberg to *Rising Sun* and finally *1941*. (For more on *1941*, please turn to the chapter on Spielberg.)

After working for several weeks on the script of what came to be *1941*, Zemeckis and Gale turned their attention to Beatlemania. The result was *I Want to Hold Your Hand*, a charming, energetic evocation of the early days of Beatlemania in the United States which was the first film Spielberg executive produced without directing.

Zemeckis was able to interest two female producers in the project, Alex Rose and Tamara Asseyev, because he did not have enough clout to make a deal on it. Warner Bros. had the deal, but did not care for the script and was unwilling to let Zemeckis as a first-time director handle it. Spielberg took it to Universal, which made a deal within 24 hours.

As a director, Zemeckis does a wonderful job recreating the hysteria of Beatlemania, centering the entire film around the Beatles staying at the Plaza Hotel in New York before their appearance on *The Ed Sullivan Show*. The focus is entirely on the frantic fans rather than the Beatles themselves, and both Nancy Allen, who becomes a suddenly obsessed Beatles convert, and Eddie Deezen as the geeky would-be exploiter who hopes to make a mint selling souvenirs of the Beatles' stay, are wonderful.

Zemeckis was told that he could not use real footage of the Beatles on the *Sullivan Show* in the film, but after showing a rough cut to Ned Tanen, he agreed that the film needed the footage and would not work without it. If the Beatles decided to sue, that would just mean more publicity for the picture. Zemeckis was able to go back and cleverly presented the actual Beatles footage on monitors in the studio while look-alikes were filmed out of focus imitating their actions onstage. As an exercise in nostalgia, the film was a success, but in the future, Zemeckis would be far less respectful of the facts and feelings of the past.

The production was extremely rushed. Zemeckis told *Take One*:

> [W]e had eight months, and it was an incredible experience, but we won't do it again. In editing you have to go through phases. When you first assemble the movie you're practically catatonic 'cause it's so awful. Then for a couple of weeks you like the movie, then you hate everything in the movie. You need to go through all of that, and there wasn't time.
>
> The movie played well in previews. We never had any negative response to the movie. Reviews were favorable, and we thought we had a smash. We had heard the sneak audience in New York bursting into applause five, six times during the movie. Then it opened, and dropped dead. It can't be bad word of mouth: Not enough people have seen the movie to kill it by word of mouth. There is simply no audience. It's the worst thing that can happen to you: dropping dead.

Next Zemeckis and Gale worked on *After School*, a low budget ($1.5 million) comedy that was meant to show what kids were really like, which was intended to serve as the next Steven Spielberg film. In Joseph McBride's book *Steven Spielberg*, he quotes Bob Gale as explaining, "Zemeckis and I being the renegades that we are — certainly we were more so then — we thought that to make it really interesting, it should be rated R, and we wrote it that way.... We swore like truck drivers when we were twelve. A lot of kids do that, and we thought that would be the way to go. It was the classic nerds-against-jocks story. The nerds had a dogshit bomb on a radio-controlled car." Spielberg considered making it and gave the script to cinematographer Caleb Deschanel who declared that he detested it, and Spielberg was being pressured to make big films rather than little ones, and so lost interest and the project foundered.

Only slightly more successful was Zemeckis' next film, the effervescent comedy *Used Cars*, one of the most hilarious comedies of the 1980s which suffered the misfortune of coming out at the same time as *Airplane!*, the Zucker brothers and Jim Abraham's smash hit comedy which brought *Hellzapoppin'*-style, anything for a laugh comedy back into vogue for a short time.

Used Cars features Kurt Russell and Gerrit Graham as fast-talking used car salesmen who unscrupulously unload lemon after lemon onto the largely unsuspecting American public. When their boss (Jack Warden) dies from a heart attack, they are forced to cover up his death so that his even more ruthless and unscrupulous brother (also Warden) with the car lot across the street won't take over the operation. Meanwhile, the boss's daughter (Deborah Harmon) shows up and Russell begins making time with her.

What makes the film so amusing and memorable are the off-the-wall scams that the dealers pull to outshine the competition and sell the cars. It runs the gamut from telling one customer that her black hair matches the color of the car's tires to hiring strippers and in the film's funniest moment, interrupting *Monday Night Football* to present an outrageous car commercial and blaming it on Iranian dissidents.

It was, in fact, this scene which got Zemeckis in trouble with Columbia. When he originally shot it, Zemeckis had Graham disguise himself by wearing a pair of glasses with a plastic penis nosepiece. Frank Price told him it was the most disgusting thing he had ever seen, so the footage was reshot with Graham wearing Groucho glasses, but one shot of the dicknose glasses does remain in the film and was even used in the film's trailer.

Surprisingly, *Used Cars* was turned into an unsuccessful pilot in 1984 by director Victor Lobl, which was written and produced by Bob Gale. (Zemeckis was granted a creator credit.) The pilot had Barbara Fuchs (Deborah Harmon) inheriting a struggling Las Vegas used car lot run by Rudy Russo (Fred McCarren) who will use any underhanded scheme to beat out Fuchs' unscrupulous Uncle Roy (Pat Corley), the competitive owner of every used car lot in town.

In 1980 Zemeckis and Gale immediately began writing *Back to the Future* for Columbia pictures, but after two drafts nobody wanted to make it as the humor was perceived as being too innocent at a time when the top grossing comedies were in the *Animal House* mold and time

Rudy Russo (Kurt Russell), the unscrupulous, wheedling used car salesman of Robert Zemeckis' antic comedy *Used Cars* in a typical pose.

travel films had traditionally not made money. Zemeckis didn't work for three years as a director afterward due to the failure of *Used Cars*. Despite the quality of his first two features, both had been financial flops, and he did not want to work with Spielberg again until after he had had a hit, because otherwise Zemeckis knew that his directing career would be sunk.

Zemeckis and Bob Gale were writing a gangster movie for ABC Cirlce Films when Michael Douglas needed a director for a movie he wanted to produce called *Romancing the Stone*. "The project was originally at Columbia," reported Douglas in *Playboy*, "and Bob had an office near us on the lot, so we got together and talked. I'd seen *Used Cars* and loved it. I thought he had a wicked sense of humor and a wonderful gift for telling a story."

Romancing the Stone was created by the late Diane Thomas, a frustrated, unpublished novelist at the time. She created a romp where a timid lady writer of Harlequin romance type novels centered around a heroic character named Angelina becomes trapped in the jungles of Colombia, meets a roguish soldier-of-fortune type who surpasses the fictional heroes in the books she has been writing, and discovers that she herself can be the woman she has always wanted to be. The script immediately appealed to Douglas, who decided to both produce and star in the eventual film.

The film was largely shot in five months in Mexico, with the production making the mistake of going down in the rainy season. Since the production was largely shooting in sequence, Douglas felt that Zemeckis should shoot the toughest stuff first, and it almost ended up burying them. At one point, a boulder the size of a room slid by a wet mountain road where the camera crew had been standing only moments before.

Kathleen Turner at one point was buried in mud up to her waist, and later sued the production for the cost of plastic surgery on her leg after her leg was severely scraped in the mud slide. Turner also had to have some stitches to her head from a fall and some stitches on her arm from some jagged metal she caught herself on. Douglas selected Turner based on her work in the offbeat SF comedy *The Man with Two Brains*, which showcased a shy, gentle side as well as comic ability.

The comedy adventure was eventually made by 20th Century–Fox and helped make a star out of Turner, who plays Joan Wilder, a romance novelist who gets caught up in a wild, real-life adventure, a sort of lower budgeted *Raiders of the Lost Ark*, but with more humor and more human characters.

Romancing the Stone proved a punishing shoot, involving as it did high speed chases and exotic tropical locations, but Zemeckis handled the logistics well. "Even then," comments Douglas, "you saw how Bob could hang on to all the facets of his vision, and you saw his stamina. He has such energy and humor, but he doesn't dwell on shots or great moments. He makes it look easy."

There are few characters as morally bankrupt as Danny DeVito's greedy looter in *Romancing the Stone*, who seems a kindred to the small minded used car salesman Kurt Russell played in *Used Cars*. Both, however, remain likable, retaining some recognizable good qualities, and both are victims of their appetites. They were an indication that Zemeckis' main characters all tend to be compulsives of one type or another.

Romancing the Stone went on to gross some $70 million. Despite being seen by some as a *Raiders of the Lost Ark* rip-off, the film has more heart and humanity in it than Spielberg's mechanical thrill ride approach which made characterization secondary to spectacle. We end up liking Joan Wilder, a bad romance novelist who yearns for a good man and an exciting adventure that lives up to her romantic daydreams (depicted in the film's deliberately artificial opening sequence), and come to respect Douglas' Jack Colton, who finds months of work flying off at Wilder's appearance (he has been collecting rare and exotic birds) and whose initial intentions are purely mercenary, but who we see come to care for and then fall in love with her.

Zemeckis playfully tweaks the genre, incorporating staples (a pit of snarling alligators), but also often indicating that things are not always what they seem. One of my favorite bits in the movie is Alfonso Arau's Juan, a local drug lord whom Jack fears, who in a surprising twist is an enormous Joan Wilder fan, has read all of her romances, and offers to help her with his "little mule," which turns out to be a souped up, four-wheeling Jeep.

Originally, Zemeckis was to have followed up *Romancing the Stone* with *Cocoon*, which was eventually directed by Ron Howard. Zemeckis had given a lot of input into the project but had not been able to solve its fundamental difficulty — its complete lack of conflict. The story had no villains, no antagonists to play off of, and suggested that the solution to the problem of old age was simply to be carted off in a flying saucer to another planet. Howard was able to direct a fine cast of old character actors to great acclaim, but never did fix the problems that Zemeckis noted in the story.

Then Zemeckis and Gale went to Universal where they started to prepare a film version of *The Shadow*, based on the old pulp and radio character (the film was eventually made years later by Russell Mulcahy, director of the *Highlander* films), when Universal expressed an interest in doing *Back to the Future*. Zemeckis and Gale decided that they would rather work on their own characters rather than bring to life somebody else's.

Zemeckis began shooting *Back to the Future* finally with Eric Stoltz in the lead, but after six weeks' work, Stoltz (a fine actor who shined in *Mask, Some Kind of Wonderful*, and other films) was fired when, after consultation with producers Steven Spielberg, Kathleen Kennedy, Frank Marshall, and Neil Canton, it was decided that he did not have the requisite light touch Zemeckis was after. Stoltz, it was agreed, was a fine actor, but he brought more maturity than energy to the role of an eighties kid encountering the fifties, and that was not what Zemeckis had envisioned for the character.

(Additionally, the filmmakers had wanted John Lithgow to play Doc Brown, but Lithgow was unavailable, and Christopher Lloyd proved the perfect substitute. A similar situation occurred on *The Purple Rose of Cairo* where the film was largely shot before Woody Allen decided he needed to replace Michael Keaton with Jeff Daniels.)

Enter television star Michael J. Fox of *Family Ties* whose smirking Alex Keaton character had become a comedy hit. Zemeckis decided he would be perfect, and arranged for Spielberg to give a copy of *Back to the Future*'s script to *Family Ties* producer Gary David Goldberg, who was busily scripting the unmade *Reel to Real* for Spielberg based on Spielberg's life. Fox took over the role of Marty McFly with a frenetic style all his own.

Director Robert Zemeckis while working on *Back to the Future.*

The script for the film went through several rewrites before the final draft. In an earlier version, the time machine was not mobile but had been built in the fifties, and McFly happens to get back to when it was actually built. In another draft, the film ended with McFly driving the DeLorean through a nuclear explosion at a New Mexico testing site to get the power to return to the future, but it was decided that it would be both too expensive to shoot and too high tech an ending to engage the audience.

"This movie is jammed with all the great stuff you loved in the *Twilight Zones*," Zemeckis told Lee Goldberg in *Starlog*, "like the great Cliff Robertson *Zone* or the one when the plane goes into time warp. For me, that's what is most fun about time travel. I don't particularly find it fun when a character goes to a future that is alien to us because you can't identify anything.... *Time After Time* was a clever time travel movie and *The Time Machine* was the greatest time travel movie ever done. What was the most fun about it was that, he went into the future we didn't know and it became a monster movie."

The opening of *Back to the Future* pans past numerous chronological devices (obviously indicative of the time theme) to depict a crazy professor's Rube Goldbergesque device for feeding his dog while he is away. It clearly seems a variation on Terry Gilliam's "breakfast" scene at Sam Lowry's apartment in *Brazil*. The hero, Marty McFly (Michael J. Fox), comes in on skateboard looking for Doc Brown (Christopher Lloyd) and in a visual gag, overamplifies his guitar with disastrous consequences that blow out the speakers and the room.

Zemeckis and Bob Gale's script is undeniably cleverly constructed, with small details recurring and becoming telling such as news clippings, a ruined clock tower, etc. Everything is designed to neatly contrast and fall into place at the appropriate point in the plot. The movie also sets up several motifs which would be slavishly followed in the subsequent sequels.

"[W]e thought we were presenting the 1950s through

the eyes of somebody in the 1980s who didn't want to be there. We never presented the 1950s as a great time in American history. But a lot of people saw it as a nostalgic romp," said Zemeckis. Indeed, the film only captures the surface of the 1950s—fifties products, movies, songs, and clothes are featured, but not 1950s Cold War fears and other concerns. Zemeckis' film makes the decade seem almost interchangeable with the 1930s and 1940s. Marty, on the other hand, represents a product of 1980s malaise, of an American dream gone mysteriously wrong.

One of the biggest challenges for Zemeckis was how to deal with the Oedipal romance between the young Marty McFly and the oversexed teen who was to become his mother. Zemeckis struggled for months trying to figure out how to keep this aspect from becoming grotesque. "All these events were coming together, but we didn't know how to get out of them," said Zemeckis. "We were locked in because we felt it was Marty who had to end the oedipal story, because he knew she was his mother. But he kept looking very perverse. Then came the great inspiration—it was his mother who would end it. Some cosmic thing happens when she kisses her own son and it doesn't feel right. That was the perfect solution. I remember being so exhilarated when we came up with the idea that she doesn't want to do it, and she says, 'This is like kissing my brother.' That's my favorite line in the movie."

Something *Back to the Future* does not do is offer an insightful look at how the past shapes the present, how teenagers turn into adults (with all the gains and losses that process entails), and how living in the past might change one in the future. Nor does it seem to consider that by altering the past, Marty has in effect killed his admittedly flawed parents and replaced them with alternate ones, who have gained in social status but lack the unique personalities of his originals.

At the end of *Back to the Future*, turning the parents into successful Yuppie types was supposed to be a satirical jab. "Yeah, that is a joke," said Zemeckis. "I was amazed at the way the nation *embraced* that. We weren't saying that wealth and success lead to happiness. But, somehow, everyone accepted that as the American way."

Back to the Future humanized its time travel concept with an Oedipal complication—Marty has to romance his own mother in order to be born. Besides saving his life, and teaching Chuck Berry how to "duck walk," Marty also saves his father from wimphood and an insufficient future income by showing him how to seduce women and stand up to bullies. Some have complained that the ending puts forth the proposition that violence solves problems, but McFly's punch is more emblematic of his ability to stand up for himself, an indication of his increased confidence, which makes a significant difference in his life. Ignored is the question that however bad he was, Marty's father is no longer the same man, that metaphorically speaking, Marty has killed his father whom he presumably loved and cared for and replaced him with a new one.

Following *Back to the Future*, Zemeckis hoped to create a film about the Shadow, the famous pulp and radio hero, which he saw as a combination of Indiana Jones and Dracula. However, the project would not reach fruition until years later when Russell Mulcahy (*Razorback; Highlander*) brought his good-looking but ultimately disappointing interpretation to the screen.

Back to the Future Part II returns to the theme of Marty frantically rushing across space and time to repair the consequences of a blighted paternal legacy, albeit in this case his own. Picking up where the last film left off, Doc takes Marty and his girlfriend to the year 2015 A.D. where something bad is about to happen to Marty's loser son (Fox again), Marty, Jr.

Zemeckis depicts this future as much like our present, only more so. Pepsi is $50 a can, and the strong are still beating up on the weak, with Biff's grandson Griff terrorizing Marty, Jr., the way Biff used to beat on George McFly. Marty, Jr., like his counterpart in the first one, suffers from an unfulfilled life.

As Marty covertly observes, he is fired from his job, his son is a multi-screened couch potato ("librium mode, please") and near-criminal, and that he himself had to give up his career as a guitarist because he injured his hand slugging a Rolls Royce driver. Additionally, the police bring Jennifer home, assuming she is a refugee from suburbia's nest of alcoholics, pill-poppers and tranquilizer addicts. Marty's daughter Marlene (also Fox in drag) ditzes aimlessly. Despite the glittering gadgets designed to delight and make life easier, these folk are far from joyful in their suburban malaise. Unfortunately for this episode, these important problems are left undealt with until the sequel, which manages to solve them quite perfunctorily after Marty learns a lesson about name-calling and supposed cowardice.

Instead, Zemeckis then further complicates the plot by having Griff, now a crotchety, embittered old man, steal a sports almanac and take it back to the past so that his grandfather can make a killing by making sure-thing sports bets and vastly improving his wealth and social position. Consequently, Marty returns to an alternate and even more depressing 1985 than the one he left.

Just as George Bailey's present becomes blighted in his nightmare vision of Bedford Falls grown fetid and foul under Potter's malign influence, so McFly finds his comfortable neighborhood in decay and disarray, indicated by streets strewn with garbage, trashed automobiles, chalk outlines of murder victims, and a black family now living where his once dwelt (an idea which has disturbingly racist undertones).

One change was made in *Part II* before it was released. Originally, when Biff returns to the future after altering his past, the elderly Biff staggers out of the DeLorean, falls down in the street, and fades out of existence because he has altered his past and the future that he returns to is a future where that particular Biff does not exist and so he was erased from existence. However, this confused audiences, so the shot was trimmed with Biff simply falling out of frame presumably from his frailty.

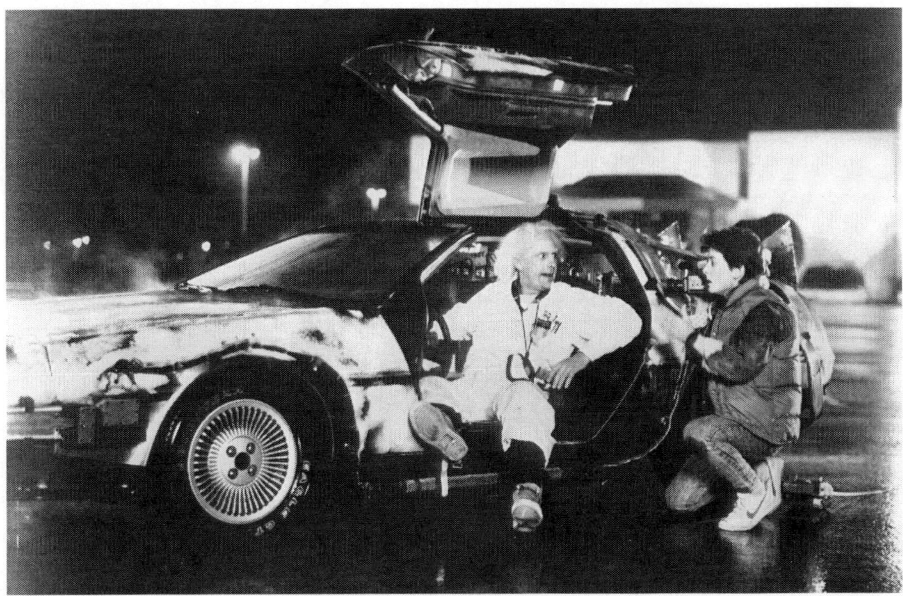

Doc Brown (Christopher Lloyd) explains how he transformed his DeLorean into a time machine to Marty McFly (Michael J. Fox) in *Back to the Future.*

Back to the Future Part II cannot help but disappoint, given that it is a very incomplete story utterly dependent on its sequel for resolution and following the upbeat, breezy original, turns comedy into one long scream of despair and desolation. It presents a series of complications and problems which only make life worse and more depressing for the likable main characters. It depicts a universe where whatever changes and alterations are wrought, the characters are continually thrown into violent conflicts, with a recurring nightmare of chases, confrontations, and last-minute getaways, where the weak are bullied and women are helpless, and the successful are those who can exploit others the best. That these are unchanging, immutable laws of nature is rather a frightening concept if you think about it. Not surprisingly, the film suffered a 50 percent drop in attendance in its second week of release.

When presenting *Back to the Future Part III*, Zemeckis made it clear that he was not trying to make a personal tribute to nor revive the mostly moribund western genre. In contrast to the amphetamine rush of the second film in the trilogy, *Part III* starts off at a gallop and slows down to a canter, taking more time to develop the characters further and reflecting the less hectic pace of the past. (Few people really understand how modern technology has speeded up both expectations and the pace of life itself.)

Zemeckis picks up the story just where he left off in 1955 with Dr. Emmett Brown surprised to see Marty, whom he has just sent off into the future, coming running down the main street of Hill Valley. Marty reveals that Brown's future self was riding in their time machine when he was hit by an electrical storm and sent back to 1885 instead of returning Marty back to 1985.

The older Brown discovers that he loves 1885 and stashes the DeLorean in a cave with instructions for the 1955 Brown to repair it so that Marty can make it home; however, the pair quickly discover a tombstone that indicates that Brown died a few days after composing the note, which diverts Marty back to the wild west in order to save Doc Brown.

One of Zemeckis' visual gags is that in order for Marty to appear in an isolated area, he must drive the DeLorean to a drive-in theater (in Ford's Monument Valley no less) and drive directly at the movie screen so that he will be launched back in time when he hits the magic number of 88 miles per hour (an indication that Marty is driving in the movie old west rather than the real article). This is further underscored when the mural depicting Indians along the drive-in's walls are suddenly transformed by Marty's time trip into real Indians who whoop in old-fashioned western movie style (lifting the basic gag from countless old comedies where Hollywood Indians and real Indians are confused). The Indians, pursued by blue-shirted cavalry, pay no attention to the automobile, but rather abruptly ride out of the movie forever.

Zemeckis also invokes other western clichés, from men boarding trains in motion and holding up passengers at gunpoint to barroom brawls, from gunfights on the street to a lone woman who must wait patiently while a train pulls into the station. These are not inflated operatically, as Sergio Leone would do, but merely seem a passing nod to cinematic predecessors.

Once more McFly's nemesis is a relative of the Tannen family, this time an ancestor of Biff's called "Mad Dog" Tannen (Thomas F. Wilson again), the local badman who bullies Marty and winds up in manure once more. Marty discovers himself in an environment where his penchant for fighting whenever he is called chicken can have fatal consequences, and in the process of the story finally learns that the assessment of his courage depends on himself and not on the opinions of others, thereby allowing him to escape the awful fate for himself prognosticated in *Part II.*

To aid him in learning his lesson, Marty meets up with his ancestor Sean (Fox with a mustache in a dual role) and his wife (Lea Thompson), and comes to see that the moral code about avoiding starting trouble and never backing away from it originated in the old West, and had awful consequences even back then. Sean, who takes a strangely paternal interest in Marty, advises him to just ignore Mad Dog's challenges and stand down from a scheduled gunfight even if it tags him a coward.

As if Zemeckis has not loaded the western lore thick enough, he has Marty adopting the moniker Clint Eastwood, be a crack quickdraw thanks to time spent at a video arcade, and peoples his bar with familiar western character actors (Harry Carey, Jr., Pat Buttram, Dub Taylor) as well as a cameo by ZZ Top as a western bar band. Marty is thus neatly locked into a choice of living up (and possibly dying because of) the role of Clint Eastwood or being himself.

Another important aspect of the film is the growing romance between Jules Verne–loving country school teacher Clara Clayton (Mary Steenburgen) and the ever inventive Doc Brown. Their sometimes troubled romance does become touching as Brown gets torn between his attraction to the woman he loves and his love of problem-solving and his desire to help Marty power the DeLorean up to speed in order to return him to his proper time.

Zemeckis became part of a group of filmmakers who purchased the rights to the *Tales from the Crypt* comic books to create the well-known HBO cable series. His partners in this effort were fellow horror comic enthusiasts Richard Donner, Joel Silver, and Walter Hill. Zemeckis was too young to have read the comics in the 1950s, but caught them during the 1960s and when Silver suggested he also be involved, he readily agreed.

Zemeckis had long harbored the hope of directing a horror film, but given the scope and quality of his pictures, it was unlikely that it would help his career to take on something of a reduced stature. "It would have been loftier for me to invest time in a feature," he told Sheldon Teitelbaum of *Cinefantastique.* "Which is too bad, because directing horror is really directing. I would have hated to go through my life as a director without having done it."

Silver allowed him to pick any story from the comic to do on the series's pilot, and Zemeckis chose "And All Through the House," which was adapted by Fred Dekker (*Night of the Creeps; RoboCop 3*), despite it having already been done by Freddie Francis for the Amicus produced *Tales from the Crypt* feature. The story has to do with a woman (Mary Ellen Trainor, Zemeckis' wife) who kills her husband who is then visited by an insane asylum escapee dressed as Santa (Larry Drake). Zemeckis restricted himself to one set, a small cast, and a one week shooting schedule for his half hour segment. It allowed him to experiment a little stylistically, but did not end up one of the better episodes on the long-lived series.

Much better was Zemeckis' other *Tales from the Crypt* episode, "Yellow," partially a tribute to Stanley Kubrick's *Paths of Glory,* with Kirk Douglas now playing a World War I French general who persuades his cowardly son (Keifer Sutherland) to act bravely in front of the firing squad, to which the son has become sentenced, by telling him that the bullets will be replaced with blanks. The opening montage gets across the horrors of trench warfare very succinctly, and Zemeckis smartly references our memory of Kubrick's classic in many ways.

Pynchon described a miracle as "the intrusion of one world into another." By that definition, *Who Framed Roger Rabbit* is little short of miraculous. Starting with a Tex Avery–style cartoon pumped up on amphetamines and then given the hotfoot, the movie begins with a classic recreation of the cartoon styles of the past, and then dazzles by going behind the scenes to show cartoon characters existing in real-life and rubbing shoulders with those who exist in three dimensional space. This colossal "what if" is the science fictional premise of the movie, based on Gary K. Wolf's amusing mystery novel *Who Censored Roger Rabbit?,* which focused on newspaper 'toons rather than movie cartoon figures.

In 1982, Disney purchased the rights to *Who Censored Roger Rabbit?,* a private eye pastiche with the novel idea of cartoon strip characters being real-life people whose posed antics are "photographed" and published in the funny papers. The studio commissioned two young writers, Jeffrey Price and Peter Seaman, whose only credit was an original script called *Trenchcoat,* to turn the book into an animated feature. Zemeckis expressed an interest in the project after having made *Used Cars,* but Disney did not go ahead with it until several years later and after offering it to other directors.

Spielberg's Ambin Productions got hold of the project, which went through other drafts and other writers. After the success of *Back to the Future,* Spielberg approached Zemeckis with the idea of doing *Roger,* who asked for and got the project's original writers back. While earlier drafts had largely kept the animation separate from the live action, Zemeckis insisted that they be more integrated into the real world, and the storyline was spiced up with a subplot about the systematic dismantling of the Red Line, Los Angeles' public transport system of the 1940s. Further, the concept of a cartoon ghetto, underscoring the subtext of racial segregation, was developed.

Zemeckis shot a 30-second test to see if the process would work, and it did. *Who Framed Roger Rabbit* took two years to complete and ended up costing 10 to 15 percent more than its original budget. The animation was handed over to Richard Williams (Academy Award winner for his short version of *A Christmas Carol*) and a crew of 320 full-time animators. He and Zemeckis agreed that the cartoon characters reflect the style and appearance of their 1940s counterparts, but with greater camera movement and perspective. (Almost every great cartoon character of the era was included in the film, except for Popeye and Felix the Cat. Even so, Warner Bros. insisted that Bugs Bunny and Daffy Duck receive equal screen time as Mickey Mouse and Donald Duck.)

Zemeckis cast Bob Hoskins because Hoskins reminded him of Humphrey Bogart, and similarly chose Joanna Cassidy because he felt that she was a modern day Ann Sheridan. "They had to be good actors, too, because they'd often be playing to empty spaces on the screen which would later be filled in with animation," Zemeckis said.

Zemeckis cast veteran stand-up comedian Charles Fleischer, who acted in such films as *Bad Dreams, Night Shift*, and *A Nightmare on Elm Street*, as Roger Rabbit after seeing Fleischer's act at the Comedy Store. To get into the part, he wore a Roger Rabbit costume, including red overalls, a bow tie, and floppy ears. If a scene called for Roger to carry a gun, Fleischer carried a gun. He had to be able to react on the spot to what Bob Hoskins was doing to his character. "I looked at the space and created Roger and projected myself at the place where Hoskins was looking," Fleischer said.

Fleischer also played Benny the Cab and two weasels. Flesicher felt that cartoons should talk differently than people: "Toons talk fast. Most of them have a Brooklyn accent. It's similar to the way kids talk. They lack certain vowels." After Richard Williams, Roger's head animator asked Flesicher to come up with a speech affectation for Roger, Flesicher responded. "All the great Toons have some identifiable speech hook. Roger's is 'p-p-please!'" Williams then photographed Fleischer's face in order to see how to draw his lip movements.

To play Jessica Rabbit, Roger's sexy wife ("I'm not bad, I'm just drawn that way") Zemeckis contacted his *Romancing the Stone* cohort Kathleen Turner, who agreed to appear sans screen credit. However, Jessica's singing voice was supplied by Amy Irving, who was Spielberg's wife at the time.

Zemeckis, in an interview in the *L.A. Weekly* with John Powers, described directing *Who Framed Roger Rabbit* as "backbreaking, tedious work. From a creative standpoint, there was no difference. I directed everything and everybody, including the animators, the way I would actors. The difference is that you don't see the final shot till it's finished."

Roger walks a thin line between too soppy and too obnoxious. He is unlike any of the traditional animated characters, although his kinship with them is all too clear. However, a lot of thought went into Roger's psychological motivation, unlike the traditional pop characters such as Mickey Mouse, Bugs Bunny or Daffy Duck, who evolved over a series of films.

Who Framed Roger Rabbit itself opens with a cartoon, as all films used to, which features Roger being his usually overconfident self. Set to the simple task of watching a baby, Roger encounters one over-the-top mishap after the other, all in the style of a Tex Avery MGM cartoon (although the Maroon Cartoon logo is clearly meant to evoke Warner Bros. cartoons). Richard Williams brilliantly captures the glossy look and style of early 1940s cartoons while adding a detailed sheen all his own. (Williams' solo work includes the animated features *Adventures of Raggedy Ann and Andy* and *Thief and the Cobbler*, both noted for their sumptuous animation and their gooey, treacly stories. His outfit has also produced several brilliant animated commercials, practically each one in a different, detailed style.)

This opening short not only moves from the standard back and forth, up-and-down camera movements of traditional cartooning to spatial moves around corners (thereby animating the entire background and adding to the shot's complexity), but then has the camera pull back to reveal that the action is taking place on a painted set in front of real cameras, a real crew, and a furious director who berates Roger for using the wrong cartoon cliché after being hit on the head. The "baby" then saunters off the set, looking more three-dimensional than flat, naughtily poking a finger up a woman's skirt he passes under.

With such devices, Zemeckis quickly establishes that 'toons inhabit the same world as regular people, that they perform like movie stars, and that we are about to enter a wondrous new world. (Not that this premise was an entirely new one — it served as the basis of the Warner Bros. cartoon "You Ought to Be in Pictures," for example.) *Who Framed Roger Rabbit* is more fantasy than science fiction, but it does speculate on what it would be like if cartoon characters with their anarchic personalities inhabited the same world as the rest of us.

Roger Rabbit takes place in 1947 Hollywood during the heyday of cartoons and film noir, the two genres the movie cleverly combines. Its protagonist, a gumshoe named Eddie Valiant (Bob Hoskins), bears an especial grudge against Toons because one killed his brother. Nevertheless, the down on his luck private detective heads for Maroon

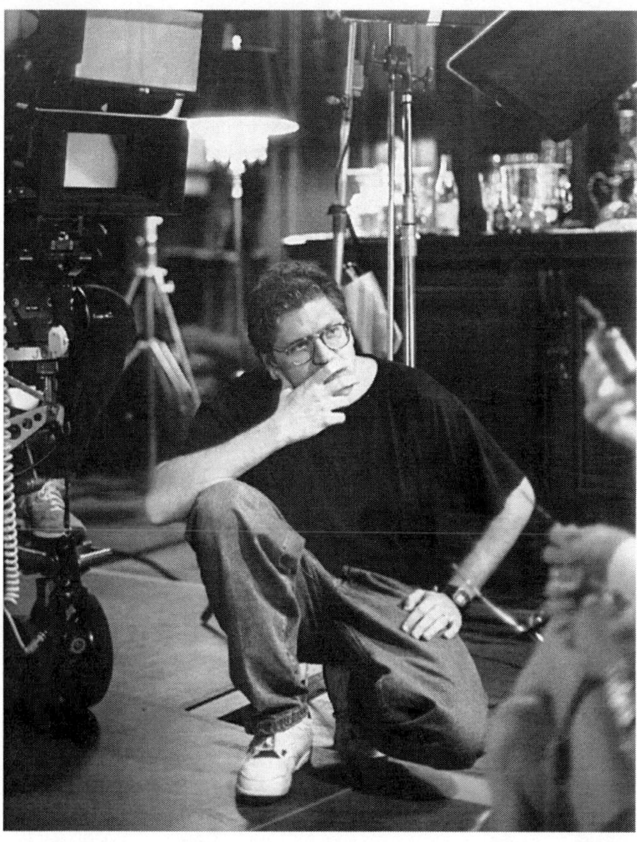

Director-producer Robert Zemeckis contemplating changes on *Death Becomes Her.*

Studios at the behest of its boss who is worried about one of his Toon stars, a sweet, fun-loving rabbit named Roger. Roger's concentration and work are going to pieces because he fears that his femme fatale wife Jessica (Kathleen Turner), a Toon in human form, has been fooling around on him, playing paddy-cake (literally) with Marvin Acme (Stubby Kaye), a supplier of cartoons and cartoon gags.

When Eddie's investigation leads to murder, Roger becomes the prime suspect and has to plead with Eddie to save his bacon from the nefarious Judge Doom (a typically cartoonish Christopher Lloyd). Doom wants to "rein in the insanity" of Toons, who are virtually indestructible until plunged into Dip, a turpentine mixture that dissolves the lovable creations.

Zemeckis' compulsive theme surfaces here with a vengeance. Roger can't resist doing outrageous comedy bits, even though by doing so he can give away his presence and endanger his life. Eddie is not only a compulsive alcoholic, but is also compulsively running away from his past which only results in his having to come to terms with it and with 'toons after his dealings with Roger.

Deftly employing noir conventions, *Who Framed Roger Rabbit* has a cohesion that other cartoony films lack. Although the script by Jeffrey Price and Peter Seaman never reaches the inspired nonsense of the best Warner Bros. cartoons, it knows the conventions of each form and how to have fun with them. You can almost hear at the end when Eddie has to confront his brother's murderer, "Forget it, Eddie, it's Chinatoon."

For there is a big subtext to the film, like Polanski's, which is based on L.A. history. The film pulls into its world the real world conspiracy by four companies (including Firestone, a tire company; Standard Oil, an oil company, and General Motors, a car company) to eliminate Los Angeles' Red Line trolley system as an efficient mode of public transportation in order to sell more cars to anxious Angelenos trying to navigate one of the largest and most sprawling cities in the world.

Zemeckis keeps up his standard, relentless, pell-mell pace throughout, throwing gags, good and cornball, at you with equal zest. Still, the movie finds its center in its relationship between the bitter, boozing Eddie and the ever-cheery Roger, who finally succeeds in restoring to Valiant his long missing sense of humor.

Hoskins' work in the film is nothing short of amazing. He gives his character an expressive, over-the-top quality without ever repeating himself. You actually begin to believe that he is interacting before your eyes with cartoon figures that actually are optically added later. You identify with his emotions, his frustration at Roger's constant blithering, his delight in defeating a dimwitted Toon antagonist, or his sympathy for poor black and white Betty Boop who has been reduced to selling cigarettes at the Ink and Paint Club, one of the film's better touches, where Toons perform live for human audiences seeking something different.

The frantic film often comes up more impressive than funny, which is not to discount its many pleasures and achievements. It succeeded in being unlike any other feature that combined animation and live action and proved to be a sure audience pleaser.

Zemeckis and Gale supplied the script and were co-executive producers for *Trespass*, Walter Hill's failed update of *Treasure of the Sierra Madre,* which has some white men seeking a fortune in the inner city, and which was originally titled *Looters* until the Los Angeles riots occurred just two months ahead of the film's release. *Trespass* previewed badly because Ice Cube's character died in the film, and Zemeckis and Gale were ordered to alter the ending, which took several attempts to perfect, though the film still only attained lackluster results.

Zemeckis tried to make a full-fledged live action cartoon with his next film, *Death Becomes Her*, complete with characters whose bodies are abused in very cartoony ways. While *Roger Rabbit* dealt with treating cartoons (somewhat) like real people, *Death Becomes Her* faced the challenge of treating people like cartoons.

Death Becomes Her, written by Martin Donovan and David Koepp, was outrageous and has some witty lines, but proved more ugly than amusing, more frantic than funny. Meryl Streep starred as narcissistic showbiz personality Madeline Ashton whose beauty is fading as rapidly as her career. Her worst enemy is her former friend Helen Sharp (Goldie Hawn), a mousy, nebbishy editor. Madeline steals Helen's fiancé, plastic surgeon Ernest Menville (Bruce Willis, surprisingly effective as a wimp), marries him and makes him miserable (though why such women would want to fight over such a pathetic specimen remains questionable).

When Madeline steals Menville away from Helen, humiliating her, it proves to be the final straw. Dumped and depressed, she goes into a major decline, becoming a hugely overweight recluse who is nevertheless pathologically obsessed with Madeline. After another seven years, however, Helen has bounced back, looking mysteriously youthful and sexy and acting surprisingly well-adjusted. Actually, she secretly seeks to eliminate her old rival now that Madeline has aged badly, her marriage has gone on the skids, and her career has crashed.

Helen manages to convince Menville, who now specializes in making up corpses, that murder is the simplest solution to the problem of his continuing emasculation by Madeline. (The obvious choice of divorce is unconvincingly dispensed with.) Unfortunately for them, that very night Madeline stumbles across the secret of eternal life and youth from a weirdly behaving enchantress Lisle von Rhuman (Isabella Rossellini). As a consequence, no matter what damage is inflicted on her body, she will continue to live and foil Helen's plans.

Thus, when Ernest tries to kill his wife, he finds himself married to a living corpse. Madeline in turns tries to murder Helen, only to discover that she too has taken a drink from the same bottle. Eventually, the enemies decide to join forces and entice Ernest to use his skills to maintain their beauty indefinitely, but for him to do that, they need him to take the potion as well, which he resists doing.

Originally, Ernest befriended Toni (Tracy Ullman), a kindly and understanding bartender at Dominick's. After a brief initial meeting, Ernest reencountered Toni while trying to escape from Madeline and Helen with the potion in hand. Toni encourages him to go to the police, and when a drunk patron dies in the bar, convinces Madeline and Helen that the covered body is Ernest's. Then 27 years later in Switzerland, the beautiful but bored pair encounter a very elderly Ernest and Toni happily enjoying a picnic and each other's company.

Director Zemeckis told *Cinefex* magazine:

> The original ending was soft and didn't keep with the tone of the picture. Even though Bruce did a wonderful job acting the part of this gentle old man, and the make-up was really terrific, the problem was you still knew it was the same Bruce up there that you'd seen for the whole rest of the picture. And we were asking the audience to accept all this right at the end, which is tough, whereas you ask the audience to suspend their disbelief early on — Goldie's getting fat is a good example of that — because you are still in the process of telling them what the rules of the movie are. By ending the movie at his funeral as he is eulogized, the audience could use its own imagination to envision how Bruce had turned out, which seemed to give the sequence more power.

David Koepp was asked to go back and make clear to the audience what the drawbacks of being young and beautiful forever might be. In the new ending, Madeline and Helen attend Ernest's funeral at which a priest refers to the fact that Ernest had found the secret to eternal life in the hearts and minds of his friends, and eternal youth in the hearts of his children and grandchildren. (The still of Willis as an old man at the funeral was taken from the earlier version.) Meanwhile, the pair remain constantly at each other's throats, continue to deteriorate without Menville's ministrations, and in leaving break into still living pieces.

In the process, Ullman's Toni character was eliminated entirely because it was felt that her scenes slowed down the film and did not fit in with the tone of black comedy already established. Also cut were scenes with Jonathan Silverman as Madeline's long-suffering agent, Adam Storke as Madeline's equally narcissistic boyfriend, and a sequence where the maid finds Madeline inside the household fridge leading to Menville letting all the help go.

Zemeckis fills the screen with elaborate cartoony effects as the two actresses try to stretch or blow away parts of each other into non-existence. (Hence you have scenes where Streep's head is all twisted around or Hawn appears with a cannon ball hole clean through her.) Unfortunately, these effects are more ingeniously created than actually funny.

When it comes to comedy, Streep has shown herself to be far from surefooted despite her notable accomplishments in perfecting foreign accents (which is especially notable in *Sophie's Choice* and *Out of Africa*, where her ability to capture difficult Polish and Danish accents respectively were nothing short of phenomenal). However, she is fiendishly cutting as Madeline, a faded movie star who sings and hoofs it on the Broadway stage to great acclaim with a chorus of beefcake to back her up. Streep, with her pale white skin and affected manner, seems perfectly cast as someone who has been embalmed.

Hawn, too, gets a good character moment when after Madeline has stolen her man, Helen Sharp obsessively

Eddie Valiant (Bob Hoskins) attempts to remove handcuffs connecting him and Roger Rabbit (voiced by Charles Fleischer) with a hacksaw in *Who Framed Roger Rabbit*, an Academy Award winner for Best Visual Effects, Best Editing, and Best Sound Effects Editing.

watches her in a death scene over and over again on her VCR. Hawn seems to relish taking apart the 1960s cute girl image that almost entombed her career. Rarely do you see a movie where the women are this catty, prepared to be perfect bitches to each other and the hell with audience sympathy for either of them.

The film's satirical edge centers around the "youth obsession" of our culture. It even postulates a secret society of immortals, among whose members can be glimpsed Elvis Presley and Jim Morrison of the Doors. Unfortunately, after playfully introducing this notion, it doesn't take it anywhere except for providing a few unexpected cameos from look-alikes.

Zemeckis does all he can to give the film life, but the characters are either loathsome or insipid, which makes for a less than pleasing experience whatever Zemeckis' knack for visual outrageousness. As a comedy, there is a surprising dearth of amusing lines, so the film is forced to rely on its broad visual humor.

Producer Wendy Finerman came across an obscure novel by Winston Groom called *Forrest Gump* about a mentally retarded man whose life is inseparable from the events of the fifties to the seventies, and decided that it would make an interesting basis for a motion picture. However, everywhere she took the project, she was met by indifference until she met fellow converts Steve Tisch and Steve Sharkey, who persuaded Warner Bros. to develop the project. Groom was hired to write a screenplay, which was rejected and Warners decided to pass on the project, putting it in turnaround.

Finerman then took it to Paramount and writer Eric Roth was hired to write the final episodic screenplay, which broke all the rules of moviemaking (a dim-witted hero, no villain, rambling plot, no sexy stuff). Finerman interested Tom Hanks in taking the unusual role, and Hanks and the producers agreed that the ideal director for the project would be Zemeckis, especially considering that the story would require unique effects that would allow Gump to interact with figures of history much in the same way that Hoskin's detective interacted with Toons in *Who Framed Roger Rabbit*.

In *The Films of Tom Hanks*, Zemeckis reported, "I read the screenplay and couldn't put it down. It was compelling in a strange way because it didn't have any typical plot devices, and all I wanted to do was find out what was going to happen to this guy." Zemeckis told *Playboy*, "One of my first reactions when I read the screenplay was that it was very emotional and compelling.... At first I was mystified by how compelling the story was, because it had none of the conventions of a dramatic screenplay. I learned in the course of breaking it down that the true suspense comes from Jenny and Forrest — that's the dramatic glue that holds the movie together."

Concerning having a moron for a hero, Zemeckis commented, "I always assumed that Forrest's intellect being below average was a device that enabled me to take this journey, because it freed me up. I don't have to worry what Forrest's agenda is since he's an innocent. He's like a six year old. Who wants to see a story about a normal guy going through the Sixties and Seventies? You knew what he was going to say was the truth, and that allowed you to make these comments on historical events that I thought were ironic and dark and poignant."

Zemeckis suggested Sally Field play Mama Gump and cast the other roles in the film as well, including Robin Wright as Gump's girl Jenny, Gary Sinise as Lieutenant Dan, and Mykelti Williamson as Bubba, Forrest's slow-witted friend who inspires him to enter the shrimp business.

Shot for $40 million in 1993 on locations all over the country, *Forrest Gump* was an elaborate production. Ken Ralston of ILM helped supply the film's numerous effects, from its $100,000 opening shot of a feather floating on the breeze and connecting with Gump's shoe to inserting palm trees to represent Vietnam on the Fripp Island, South Carolina location, to making 1500 extras look like thousands in Washington, D.C., to inserting the Ping Pong ball as Gump demonstrates his table tennis prowess, to inserting Gump and making celebrities' mouths match the revised dialogue given them in the famous meeting scenes.

Reports Zemeckis in *The Films of Tom Hanks*, "The hardest thing about this movie is the overall scope and the epic size of it, the logistics we had to handle. We built 150 sets, shot in eleven states, costumed twenty thousand people. But part of me subscribes to the George Lucas binary theory: Movies are either ones or zeroes — they either work or they don't. When you say, 'I'm going to make this movie,' that's it. That's the decision, and everything you do after that isn't going to matter if you've signed on to a concept that's faulty. So that's the big fear. You go through all the complication and the suffering, and you wonder, 'What if nobody wants to see a movie about this guy?'"

Everyone remembers the movie's opening, with Forrest sitting on a park bench, explaining to anyone who would listen that "Life is like a box of chocolates, you never know what you'll get," and telling his life story to whomever is nearby as the day wears on. Forrest explains that he grew up with his mother in an Alabama boarding house (Michael Humphreys plays the young Forrest) and learned from his mama that "Stupid is as stupid does."

Zemeckis revels to smartass humor, showing how the eternally receptive Gump subtly influences things around him. Thus, his dancing in leg braces inspires Elvis in his dancing style. His comments about China having no religion and no possessions inspires fellow Dick Cavett guest John Lennon to write the song "Imagine." What bothers me about the film is that Forrest becomes a winner by always doing what he is told. Told to run, he becomes a football hero. Told to help his fellow G.I.s, he rescues them in Vietnam and becomes a Medal of Honor winner. Told to play Ping Pong, he tours China and becomes a national hero. Told to go into the shrimp business, he becomes a millionaire. (He even invests in the newly formed Apple Computers because he thinks it is a fruit company.)

At the same time, he is always at pivotal negative moments in history. He stands next to George Wallace when Wallace tries to block the entrance of blacks into college. He meets Kennedy before the assassination, shows LBJ his buttocks, and reports the Watergate burglars while staying at the Watergate hotel in Washington on the recommendation of President Nixon. Great moments of history get trivialized and used nostalgically to evoke our memories of them.

Meanwhile, his friend Jenny takes all the wrong turns. She becomes a stripper, gets an abusive boyfriend, joins a bunch of phony peace protesters in the counterculture, takes drugs, and eventually catches AIDS. Here the rebellion of the sixties gets trivialized and is made to seem unwise, rather than as a necessary reaction to the horrors of the Vietnam War and the oppressive conformist mentality that had been building in the country that was finally challenged by the women's movement, the peace movement, and the civil rights movement, all of which promoted positive and significant change.

Jonathan Rosenbaum in the *Chicago Reader* called *Forrest Gump* "the most pernicious movie of the year," one in which "obliviousness parading as purity, stupidity parading as honesty and xenophobia and narcissism parading as patriotism triumph over gross misrepresentation of the countercultural values of the Sixties and Seventies."

Historical images for Zemeckis are not sacrosanct, but simply a part of shared popular culture, things that everyone in the culture should be able to relate to. He is a cheerful ironist who touches on dark things with a light tone marked by moments of darkness, irreverence, and sweetness.

Unquestionably, *Gump* is a cynical and clever movie that promotes the idea of a beguiling innocence and purity. Friendly and sweet-natured Gump is made to seem preferable to the scheming, unhappy masses around him. He is basically decent and always appealing because even though he does not understand everything that is going on, he is unswervingly loyal to his mama, his beloved Jenny, and his friends. (He saves Lt. Dan despite Dan's pleas to die on the battlefield like his forebears, and later provides the legless vet with a job on his fishing boat out of the goodness of his heart. He also takes care of his dead friend Bubba's black kinfolks, making them millionaires along with himself.)

Forrest Gump's faultiest misstep is a prolonged sequence parodying Flo-jo where Gump jogs across the country, running without stopping, inspiring a legion of followers, and growing a beard in the process. (Hanks himself argued against it, but it was retained to represent Gump's grieving process which then abruptly comes to an end.) Although it could have been intended as irony, the film also seems to possess the message of always single-mindedly pursue what your superiors tell you and you will be a success.

Still, *Forrest Gump* is relentlessly entertaining, featured an interesting and unusual hero and story, and was moving for millions of people as it made its wry skips down memory lane. It quickly became one of the most talked about movies of the year, winning mass critical acclaim and charming audiences the world over. Straight arrow Forrest seemed to show that it was sincerity, not smarts, that made for success, and many bought into the dream.

Forrest Gump swept the next year's Academy Awards, winning Best Picture, Best Actor, Best Director, Best Adapted Screenplay, Best Film Editing, and Best Visual Effects. It grossed over $100 million in the first 18 days of its U.S. release alone and has earned over $600 million at the box office, making it for a time the fifth most successful film of all time, parked just behind *Jurassic Park, The Lion King*, and *E.T.*

"Bob's main love," said Spielberg, "is to tell a really great, kicky story, with more twists and turns than the audience can ever imagine. When the lights go down I defy anyone to guess where he's going. His strategy as a storyteller is to be unfathomable. You can never outguess Bob Zemeckis."

Zemeckis and Bob Gale's very first script, *Bordello of Blood*, was dusted off and given a rewrite in 1996 to become the second *Tales from the Crypt* film. Zemeckis, as one of the coproducers of the *Tales from the Crypt* TV series, was given executive producer credit on the film as well as a writing credit. Zemeckis also served as executive producer on Peter Jackson's *The Frighteners* the same year, and in 1995 served as producer for the television production *W.E.I.R.D. World*.

Zemeckis told John Powers, "I have only two criteria when I choose a movie. First, the script is everything. I literally wouldn't know how to make a movie without a good script. I actually go on the set and make my first decision about where to put the camera based on the script. I would never record an image that was just beautiful without advancing the story. The second thing is, I gravitate toward something filmic. I wouldn't want to record on film anything that could be better presented on stage or in a novel or in a circus. This medium has a lot to do with *time*—movies are constantly shortening and expanding it. I just love to manipulate time."

Zemeckis seals his position in the SF film pantheon with his adaptation of Carl Sagan's novel *Contact* for Warner Bros., released in the summer of 1997. The film, scripted by Michael Goldberg and James V. Hart, is based on the late Carl Sagan's novel as well as a story by Sagan and his widow Ann Druyan, who is also credited as a producer on the film. It was originally optioned by George Miller, who offered the lead to Jodie Foster.

Contact actually began its existence as a screenplay around 1980. The concept had trouble finding backers, so Sagan turned *Contact* into a very successful novel. Ten years later, the efforts finally paid off and *Contact* was turned into a major film. The general success of the motion picture also put the novel back on the best-seller book lists.

Sagan's strongest contention was always that finding intelligent life beyond Earth will be the most important and significant event in human history and will change us forever, hopefully for the better. To quote the man: "In a very real sense this search for extraterrestrial intelligence is a search for a cosmic context for mankind, a search for who we are, where we have come from, and what possibilities there are for our future — in a universe vaster both in extent and duration than our forefathers ever dreamed of."

The project ended up being directed by Zemeckis, who told Douglas Eby in *Cinefantastique* that what drew him to *Contact* was that "It's true science speculation. In other words, it's not so fantastic that it's pure entertainment. It really does go back to the roots of classic science fiction in the works of, say, Jules Verne or H. G. Wells, and it poses the classic 'what if' question: *What if this really could happen?* And we put it in a form of reality that we hope is so real that if you are a science fiction fan, you can't help but come away from this in a serious way thinking, 'My God, what would we do if this really happened?...' That's why I think it's different from most movies that fall into the sci-fi category — because they're usually so fantastic that they're never based in any real reality. They are wonderful, and they're entertaining on that level, but this transcends your classic science fiction definition."

Foster plays Dr. Eleanor "Ellie" Arroway, a talented CETI radio astronomer who receives some coded instructions from the Vega star system to build a machine designed to do no one knows what, as its components are combined in a radically new way. The film establishes that Arroway's mother died at childbirth and that she lost her loving, indulgent father at a young age (Jena Malone plays Ellie as a child), and in a sense, has been searching for him ever since. In an obvious manner, this background is supposed to explain why she has become a questing atheist.

She finds a contrasting counterpart in religious scholar and White House spiritual adviser Palmer Joss (Matthew McConaughey in a highly unconvincing performance), whom she meets while listening for extra-terrestrial messages in Puerto Rico and whom she immediately falls for before hastily abandoning. Their kinship is established when years later, Joss has written a book entitled *Losing Faith: A Search for Meaning in Modern Life* and he also identifies himself as a fellow seeker of truth. He seems, however, perpetually on the make as he keeps seeking to relieve Arroway's loneliness, and ironically ends up on the committee to select the first person to make contact with the newly discovered alien life. (Later Ellie seems far too forgiving of Joss for blackballing her, supposedly because he feared that she wouldn't return from the mission.)

Because the new National Science Adviser David Drumblin (Tom Skerrit) shuts down her funding, Ellie is forced to seek out private funding and winds up at the VLA (Very Large Array) in New Mexico. Although it is unlikely and inefficient that Ellie would personally listen in on headphones to the random noises from space rather than relying on a computer to sort through the noise, it does make her seem more personally involved. While it may not be realistic (radio astronomers don't work like that) it does feel right.

As do some other bits. There is a scene just before the Message (as the transmission from Vega is called in the novel) is first detected where two of Ellie's assistants, Fisher and Willie, are on duty monitoring the galactic frequencies. They are also busy carving pumpkins (indicating the reception of the Message from Vega takes place either on or around Halloween, October 31). Willie, with his face behind a pumpkin, asks Fisher what kind of person he thinks would have the best kind of lifestyle and career to be an astronomer. When Fisher says he doesn't know, Willie ducks out from behind the round orange vegetable and shouts "Vampires!" while flashing a set of plastic fangs.

It does make sense that the ETI (Extra-Terrestrial Intelligences) in *Contact* caught Earth's attention with the use of prime numbers (numbers divisible only by themselves and one), which cannot be generated by any natural means that we know of. This sets up the scene of the visiting Senator asking why the aliens didn't just speak English and making a blank stare when Ellie told him that prime numbers were an easy way to let the radio astronomers know that the signal was not a natural one. In the space of one minute, this scene deftly exposes two flaws among the less educated masses. The first is the view of most United States citizens that English either is or should be the first language of every culture. The second are the lacking levels of scientific knowledge with many politicians, who are the ones who make decisions which profoundly impact scientific programs such as SETI, space development, and others without really understanding them. These people are literally deciding the future of humanity, thus their actions should not be taken lightly, especially in a democracy where everyone has a voice and a vote.

Another good move was the sending back of the television broadcast of the 1936 Summer Olympic Games in Berlin, Germany. Nazi leader Adolph Hitler as one of our first representatives into the Milky Way galaxy? Unthinkable but true. It is very effective but sensible, surprising many theater audience members when they and the film's characters realized that the initially fuzzy black shape was a swastika grasped in an eagle's talons.

Sagan used this fact to increase awareness of those who produce and transmit our television and radio entertainment that their audience is possibly far wider and larger than they can imagine, thanks to the microwave leakage displayed at the very beginning of *Contact.* Perhaps a few of them (besides PBS) will try to show the Universe at large that not everything about the human race is relentless advertising, lame sitcoms, and cheesy movies of the week — but don't hold your breath waiting for that day to come from the mainstream media. Money is a far greater concern to most of them than impressing our galactic neighbors (or humanity) with the good traits mankind possesses.

Naturally, any ETI encountering our technological leakage will not completely understand what they have picked up from distant Earth. There is, however, conjecture that the reason we have not heard from anyone out there yet is that they already know of the human race through our radio and television leakage and want nothing to do with us because of what it contains.

Going back to the Olympics scene in *Contact,* why would the ETI want to use that television broadcast among their first transmissions to Earth? (They certainly understood the conquering and oppressive nature of the Nazi regime in the novel.) They comprehended humanity's good and bad natures in the film as evidenced during Ellie's meeting with the ETI on the "beach." As "Ted," her father, said: "You're capable of such beautiful dreams and such horrible nightmares." Why, then, would they want to present us with such a threatening image as Hitler if they knew what horrific evil he represented to most of Earth? Despite Ellie's protests that the ETI probably did not fully understand the leakage they were receiving from us, one could also empathize with those in *Contact* who were paranoid about the ETI finding the Nazis to be an "appealing" culture to them. If the ETI were trying to send us a "warning" against such behaviors as conducted by the Nazis, then perhaps they should have done so later in the "discussion."

Still, if the ETI in *Contact* knew what the Nazis meant to humanity, then they should have left it out of the Message and gone with the next strong television transmission as stated in the novel, the Coronation of Great Britain's King George the Sixth in 1936, or even more appropriately, the broadcasts from the 1939 World's Fair in New York City. Not only would the Fair have been preferable in terms of its more global significance, but Sagan himself attended it at the age of five.

Meanwhile, once it is received, Arroway has a hard time convincing the male-dominated world that the rhythmic sounds she has picked up are alien messages. She comes into conflict with National Security Adviser Michael Kitz (James Wood) who feels that contact is not advisable because it poses uncertain security risks. Then there is Arroway's superior, David Drumlin, who attempts to take credit for her work and vies with her to be the first person to try the now-decoded alien transport device and meet with these mysterious Vegans.

Contact's story is a fairly realistic portrayal of how humanity would deal with a message from alien beings as seen through the scientific, religious, political, cultural, and social realms. Ellie comes into conflict with the powers that be and initially is rejected as a representative of humanity because, unlike most of mankind, she does not believe in God (though the 90 percent figure bandied about in the film seems rather dubious to me).

Still *Contact* stretches credulity a number of times, as when it suggests that a physics team with a supercomputer couldn't figure out the panels were cubes. Just imagine: they have three sheets in their hands. A guy connects two on the board, puts the third one up and says, "Which one does it connect to? This side matches this one, this side this one." The solution is a little too simple for everyone but the mysterious Haddon to have missed.

A fanatical saboteur blows up the initial model, killing Drumlin, though the apparent ease with which he infiltrates a highly secured areas is rather dubious. How the hell does a fanatic with a bomb get on a launch tower without being recognized? The crews in such operations are crews — they've been together for some time. They are not minimum wage labor that has a 50 percent turnover every week. Everyone would know everyone they normally come in contact with, and there would be no strangers on the launch tower minutes before launch.

Fortunately for Ellie's hopes, multinational corporate tycoon and baldheaded weirdo S. R. Haddon (John Hurt) had learned the governmental bureaucratic rule of why build one when you can make twice as much building two, and he has covertly financed a Japanese version of the transportation device which can carry Arroway. Haddon, who lives his life in an airplane, and later aboard a Soviet space station, is a figure above earthly concerns and acts as a kind of both literal and figurative angel.

Contact consistently shows government agents as evil or misguided (except for President Bill Clinton, who objected to having his press conferences shown out of context so that he seemed to be commenting on events in the movie), and so Haddon's visionary billionaire becomes one of the few sympathetic characters in the movie. Eventually, Arroway enters the machine and it transports her on an odyssey that has, in the words of Zemeckis, a "profound metaphysical dimension." Her journey is not only a trip to the stars, but also a spiritual journey into her own soul.

Arroway's spacesuit is meant to suggest the armor of a Joan d'Arc, and her entering the pod is symbolic of her isolation. Commented Zemeckis, "I love Jody's [sic] performance because of what she doesn't do ... the typical science fiction movie heroine situation. She knows she could possibly die, and that's what she plays in this walk.

"The machine had to be big. It had to be dangerous, it had to look like it was incredibly complicated, but it had to look like we could build it here on Earth. In other words it couldn't be made out an alien organic material that we didn't know what it was, because that would prove that the aliens exist, and of course the point of the movie is to always have there be a certain amount of doubt.

"The breakthrough on the machine came through this idea of dropping the pod into this mass of energy, and that allowed the audience to understand it, and resonated to pollination and things that we know about here on Earth."

Zemeckis had almost finished filming on the pod set with only a half day of filming left when a fire actually erupted and everybody had to scatter. Several brave electricians, grips, and special effects guys ran to save the set, some of whom got minor asphyxiation, but they succeeded. Only a small bit of reconstructing was required, but they had to go for one more half a day to finish our filming.

The lighting inside the pod was very tricky. The sources of light were three little lights in addition to the little video screen, so everything that you see comes from those sources. It was very difficult for Foster to film as she had to be continually shaken in a chair all day long, so that she felt her brain moving inside her head, but she hung in there.

"We wanted to be able to have the audience experience the danger of the ride," commented Zemeckis, "and the question was where does the portal come from, and that [the translucence] was the idea that helped us believe it....

"The idea here was that the spinning rings create some kind of core of energy which no one knows what it is, and, of course, the energy that emits from the rings causes the translucence in the bottom of her pod, so the light from below is coming up on her face. Of course, it is like the core of an atomic bomb, [which] is what we tried to describe to the artist when we were conceiving this. We thought we would throw a shockwave or two in there. What we wanted to do is make it as suspenseful as we possibly could and build up to what we call the section of the ride, but make it somewhat believable they would send her into this thing. So we had to have them thinking responsibly that maybe they would abort this whole thing, and then getting the confirmation that the weather inside the core is fine — you believe it, I think."

Arroway's trip conjured up many different conceptual ideas. Zemeckis decided to take the human energy chakra and change the color palette of what Arroway sees based on that. One great difficulty for this sequence was in order to create the illusion of speed and movement, there would have to be some effect of light on her face, but where would that light come from? It was decided it should come from the TV monitor in front of her, so video was projected on her face until each stop.

Finally, Ellie reaches the planet Vega, or the way Ellie might have imagined the planet Vega in her mind's eye, which is based on her conception of a beach which she drew at the beginning of the film when she was a little girl, which allows for the possibility that she could have imagined her entire experience. The point of the movie becomes that there is a limitation to science when some things have to be accepted on faith.

One of the more controversial aspects of the movie is that when Ellie makes contact with an alien, he has downloaded her subconscious and takes the form of her father (David Morse), explaining, "This is easier for you to understand." This is meant to indicate that the alien could be an incomprehensible higher power of some sort, so they have to take a form like this or it could also be a hallucination or dream. Arroway could have had a near death experience. What matters is that for her it is a powerful emotional experience that changes her life and her outlook.

Near the end of both the novel and film version of *Contact*, we learn that the Universe is not empty of life beyond Earth. Indeed, the aliens Ellie encounters tell her how they are restructuring major portions of the Cosmos to keep it from succumbing to entropy. For example, the radiation spewing from the center of the Milky Way galaxy is due to one of their current projects. Apparently ETI of equally high capabilities are conducting similar "save the neighborhood" activities in their own galaxies. And let us not forget the mysterious super aliens who built the wormhole transit system and perhaps the entire Universe and left messages of conscious intent in various mathematics.

To top it all off, the aliens declare to Ellie that the one thing they have found in all the Cosmos that keeps them alive and together is the bond of love to fight against the overwhelming emptiness and cold indifference of the inanimate existence at large. William Hurt's character came to a similar conclusion in Ken Russell's 1981 film, *Altered States*, after taking a mind-altering trip back to the very beginnings of space and time and finding nothing but "atoms and the void," to quote the ancient Greek scientist Democritus of Abdera. Humans are social creatures. What other reaction could be expected by our species to being alone with the unfamiliar?

Said Zemeckis, "This was always in Carl's book that she was on a beach at the center of the universe, but if you look very closely here, the waves are moving in reverse, the shadows are moving in time lapse speed, although the wind is moving through the palm fronds in slow motion. It's very surreal. The thing that Ken [Ralston] and the Sony guys did that was really beautiful here is this really cool color, and if you look closely here there is that palm tree that she drew in her imagined Pensacola, so this is also something, this beachscape could have been imagined in her mind's eye or her subconscious.

"My feeling about the point of *Contact* always was that it was a metaphor for belief of any type, which seems to be part of the human experience. All through every civilization and all through time, man has never been able to answer all the questions and has always pondered his place in the universe. To me the idea of not knowing everything, being OK, is what the movie is about in the simplest terms. Ideologies become ideals. We have to live our life as humans connected to other humans because we won't ever know everything."

When Arroway returns to be questioned about what has happened, she acknowledges that her statements should be skeptically treated, but she feels the truth of her experiences just as she has felt the love of her father, which is something else that she cannot scientifically prove. She comes to understand you can believe in something without having some sort of definitive mathematical proof for it. *Contact* expresses the feeling that science and spiritual belief are compatible, they don't have to be independent of each other, and they should be tolerated by each other as both involve a search for truth.

Foster is well cast for her ability to project intelligence while at the same time conveying Arroway's passionate desire for discovery. Unfortunately, while sympathetic and driven, the character is also abrasive, unyielding, and sometimes not very appealing. (Foster has always excelled at characters who fight past their anguish with their intelligence.) Like the pacifist who becomes aware of the error of his ways, she is set up as the atheist who relents on her beliefs. She never really relaxes or becomes romantic, she is so tightly controlled that she almost never really opens up to the wonder of it all.

Ellie is a very repressed character, and it becomes an emotional moment when she explains that she has been given "a vision of the universe that tells us undeniably how tiny and insignificant, and how rare and precious we all are. A vision that tells us that we belong to something greater than ourselves, that we are not, none of us, are alone." She's cast perfectly in this role, brings it a wonderful intelligence, but never falls into any cliché as far as playing a female scientist. She brings a grace, an elegance, a warmth and a humanity to the part.

Zemeckis tries to indicate a change in her by subtly altering Ellie's body language. He did not want to end *Contact* with Ellie looking up at the stars, which would have been cliché, so he thought it would be really interesting if she just looked at the universe in a grain of sand. If you look very closely, there are glints on these pebbles that are in exactly the same shape as what happened with her father out in space.

However, the film still has its shortcomings. It is disconcerting that *Contact*, like *Forrest Gump*, implies that intelligence keeps people from truly feeling, and that the truly important thing is to be sweet-souled. With all its pretensions to being profound, it ultimately tells others to seek their own answers and confidently assures us that everything is going to be all right. Such feel-good, find your bliss philosophizing can make for potent box office, but it does not make for potent motion pictures.

Zemeckis, unduly praised for featuring an unbeliever as his protagonist, ends up letting his smart movie go softheaded. It is by turns provocative and monotonous, ambitious and dumb. Many previous SF films have confronted the concepts of God and aliens, from the lamebrained *Red Mars* and *The 27th Day*, to the ingenious little films like Roger Corman's *Attack of the Crab Monsters,* to Kubrick's deeply spiritual *2001: A Space Odyssey*. Zemeckis may push the concepts more into the foreground, but in the process, reveals that he does not have anything really new or interesting to say about the questions of alien contact and its spiritual implications.

Zemeckis' next film project was to be *Fireflies*, starring Richard Gere as a one-night-stand Lothario who falls in love with a woman (Renée Zellweger) only to discover that she is dying from a terminal disease. He also committed to direct a feature-length documentary on drugs and alcohol for cable's Showtime network, exploring their influence in shaping society over the past 100 years. (Other directors involved in similar projects for Showtime are Norman Jewison [humor], Barry Levinson [visions of the future], Garry Marshall [marriage], Gregory Nava [the melting pot], and Robert Townsend [sex].)

For some time, Zemeckis has long been interested in making a movie version of Mike Royko's book *Boss*, about the late Democratic mayor of Chicago, Richard J. Daley. However, he has had a hard time convincing studios that the public at large will find Daley and the world of Chicago politics from 1902 to 1976 interesting. Zemeckis would like to cast Bruce Willis in the title role should he ever find funding for the film.

Zemeckis has a multi-picture deal which includes a Tom Hanks film called *Castaway*, and a supernatural thriller starring Harrison Ford and Michelle Pfeiffer to be titled *What Lies Beneath*.

Helen Hunt (*Mad About You*) costars opposite Tom Hanks in Robert Zemeckis' *Castaway*. Hanks added on a few extra pounds for the early scenes in the film, which has him playing a workaholic stranded on a deserted island for four years. Hunt plays his girlfriend. We will undoubtedly be hearing from this talented filmmaker for a long time to come.

A Guide to the Directors Covered in Appendix A

Appendix A: Classic Science Fiction Films from Non-Genre Directors

While most of the great science fiction classics have been directed by people who have specialized in the genre, nevertheless, a good number of the genre's classics have been created by inspired directors who made a single (or sometimes double) excursion into the genre. Any respectable survey of the science fiction genre should not leave out the following classics, some well-known and some obscure, that have earned their place in the pantheon of the greatest science fiction films of all-time.

H. G. Wells followed *Things to Come* with another Korda-produced film, *The Man Who Could Work Miracles* (1936), directed by Lothar Mendes and based on Wells' story "The Man Who Had to Sing." While Wells receives the screenplay credit, there was an uncredited polish done by Lajos Biro, and after Korda's experience with Wells on Menzies' *Things to Come*, the author was kept far away from the sound stages where the film was being made. Undeservedly obscure, this delightful science fantasy examines what might happen if a celestial being, the Power-Giver, who considers mankind weak and pitiful, were to give an unimaginative Essex shop clerk, George McWhiter Fotheringay (Roland Young, who specialized in milquetoast heroes such as Topper), nearly ultimate power.

While Fotheringay cannot read minds or make Ada Price (Joan Gardner) fall in love with him, almost anything else he requests instantly happens. (The numerous special effects are ingeniously created by Ned Mann with assistance by Laurence Butler and Edward Cohen.) Having assured himself of his ability, Fotheringay remains at a loss what to do with it and seeks advice. Maggie Hooper (Sophie Stewart), the girl at Grisby and Blott's that he is attracted to, suggests that he use his power to cure people, and he responds by curing her sprained arm.

Ada's boyfriend Bill Stoker (Robert Cochran) suggests that he use his power to benefit himself. Businessman Grigsby (Edward Chapman) suggests that he become a partner and use his power exclusively to benefit the firm. When George demonstrates that he can make money through a miracle, Grigsby and his banker are appalled, explaining that want is what drives mankind.

Still seeking answers, Fotheringay consults with the philosopher Maydig (Ernest Thesiger), who thinks on a grander scale and whose grandiose ideas include eliminating all disease everywhere and ushering in an era as peace and plenty. As a symbolic gesture, he asks George to transform his conservative neighbor, a blustering, crotchety Colonel Winstanley's whiskey into water and his weapon collection into farming implements. (Ralph Richardson is delightful as he examines a sickle and comments that it looks rather "bolshie" to him, as is George Zucco as his butler Moody who comments that he would rather poison a baby than tamper with the colonel's whiskey.) The conservative has the police bring Fotheringay to him the next day.

He is appalled at Maydig's concept that after people's wants are met, they could occupy themselves with loving one another, as those are to him very private feelings. As a beneficiary of the status quo, he has no interest in seeing it changed, and feeling himself threatened, attempts to shoot Fotheringay, who decides to make himself invulnerable.

George decides to rule the world and summons all the world's leaders to an enormous palace he instantly erects

Among those contemplating the Thing in the block of ice in Chris Nyby and Howard Hawks' *The Thing* are (left to right) Scotty (Douglas Spencer), Carrington (Robert Cornthwaite), Dr. Chapman (John Dierkes), Hendry (Kenneth Tobey), and Dr. Vorrhees (Paul Frees).

on the spot, and tells them all to run the world better. Maydig explains that it will take time and that he does not understand inertia. George scoffs and orders the world to stop turning, but inertia causes all things including the building and the vast crowd of world leaders to start flying into the air. Realizing his error, Fotheringay orders everything to return to the way it was before he discovered his power and then wishes his power to make miracles away.

The Power Giver notes that mankind has a long way to grow, but sees in the species a special inspiring spark that demonstrates that men can see beyond their petty concerns. Hungarian director Lothar Mendes, whose best film this is, gives the story a light touch (at one point George tells an English bobby to go to blazes, which he does until George revises his wish by sending him to San Francisco) and fills the screen with visual delights. Wells takes his simple concept and uses it to present his theories about why the world is run as it is while holding forth the possibility that things could be run much better. It is the playful exploration of ideas and concepts that renders this a classic piece of science fiction.

The origin of 1951's *The Thing from Another World* (so-titled to distinguish it from Phil Harris' popular novelty song, "The Thing") is a memorable SF story by famed SF editor John W. Campbell, Jr., called "Who Goes There?" Campbell grew up in a household shared by his mother and her twin sister, and was frequently unnerved when the woman he approached was not the loving mother he expected. He translated these fears into the story of a shape-changing creature from outer space that terrorizes some men in an isolated location.

Most of Campbell's story was discarded for this initial feature film version, which simply retained the idea of an alien monster attacking men in a very isolated situation. Artist Harper Goff did design an actual prosthetic-mechanical creature that had three eyes and four tentacles to be the Thing, matching somewhat the description in the original story. The suit was designed to be worn by a paraplegic who could fit into the suit and give it movement, but studio execs felt the result would have been too horrifying for contemporary audiences, and so the Thing ended up being played by James Arness in a Frankenstein–style makeup. (Greenway tried out a number of different designs, most of which included a large, rounded head both with and without large, bushy eyebrows.)

While writing partner Charles Lederer usually gets credit for *The Thing's* witty script, it was actually the work of Hollywood legend Ben Hecht. Hecht's draft of July 31, 1950, describes the creature as having "a bulbous head, a tiny suck-hole for a mouth, multiple eyes, no ears. Its arms are extra-long, ending in thorny clusters, rather than hands. It stares malevolently through the ice."

The Thing was the feature directorial debut of Chris Nyby under the close supervision of Howard Hawks, whose Winchester Pictures made the movie. Unquestionably, *The Thing* shows many of Hawks' trademarks, from a group of men who are individuals but function together as a group, stressful situations undercut by verbal humor, a strong female character who is accepted as "one of the boys," to overlapping dialogue carefully arranged so that all pertinent information comes through to the audience.

The characters in the film are engaging, from Air Force Captain Pat Hendry (Kenneth Tobey, who made a career out of similar roles including *The Beast from 20,000 Fathoms, It Came from Beneath the Sea* and *The Vampire*), to the reporter Scotty (Ned Scott), and Hendry's love interest and Prof. Carrington's secretary Nikki Nicholson

(Margaret Sheridan). Like many women in fifties SF films, Nikki has a masculine name and is for the most part treated as one of the boys. Hendry's men tease him for going up to the North Pole every three weeks to see his girlfriend, and when they arrive at the beginning of the film, he makes a beeline for her. However, Nikki confronts Hendry and explains that during their last date, Hendry got drunk and she tells him, "You had moments of making like an octopus. I've never seen so many hands," in other words equating him with a rampaging thing.

Later, there is a bizarre scene that was later cut out of matinee showings of *The Thing* (and is also missing from some video versions) where Hendry suggests she tie his hands, and in a playful bondage scene, she does just that—in essence emasculating and infantilizing him to make him a suitable suitor—while she pours him drinks and kisses him on the lips. But the joke ends up on her as he demonstrates that he was not tied at all by holding his glass for her to pour another drink for him. (Nyby then cuts to the Thing bound in its block of ice tied with rope which is shortly to get loose, suggesting a powerful force about to break loose once the ice breaks.) However, this sexual subtext is largely ignored in the rest of the film.

The military men are depicted as sensible, resourceful, and courageous, and band together, rather than squabbling as in Campbell's story (indicative of the post World War II can-do spirit), and they are opposed by the scientists, headed up by Dr. Carrington (Robert Cornthwaite) whose neatly trimmed goatee and fur cap are meant to suggest a Soviet influence.

Carrington became an archtype for mad scientists of future SF films with his concerns for science ahead of humanity and his belief that the alien's lack of emotion rendered it superior because its emotions would not hinder its intellectual development. (Not surprisingly, after the invention of the atomic bomb, in the fifties scientists were more feared and distrusted because of the horrors progress might unleash.) He epouses a kind of value-free pragmatism that was widely distrusted. ("There are no enemies in science, only phenomena to be studied," he intones at one point. "Knowledge is more important than life" at another.) He has contempt for the average and can't be trusted because "he doesn't think like we do." He seems to think man is the servant of science rather than the other way around. At the same time, he is intelligent, professional, dedicated, courageous, and even willing to die for his beliefs.

Hendry arrives at a remote Arctic outpost of scientists to help them investigate a strange item buried in the ice and finds an enormous, circular object. Following procedure, he uses thermite bombs which inexplicably turn the flying saucer into a *frying* saucer, making one wonder how the ship could have survived entry into the Earth's atmosphere.

Hendry's main concern, however, is the ship's occupant, the titular Thing from Another World that comes to life when it thaws out, and they soon learn that it lives on blood. As an enemy, the Thing proves remorseless and cruel, so that Carrington's attempts at negotiation (read appeasement) prove futile. The Thing is more plant than animal ("An intellectual carrot? The mind boggles!" exclaims Scotty), and as such feels no pain, has no emotions, and feels no moral scruples (thereby fitting a stereotype of the Red Menace as remorseless reason run amok). As the situation becomes desperate, Hendry's job becomes to seize control of the base, assert the authority of soldiers over scientists, and eliminate the threat posed by the Thing.

However, in the division between soldiers and scientists, things are not all black and white. Some of the scientists prove reasonable and some of the soldiers, unreasonable. Hendry must defer certain decisions to his superior, General Fogarty in Anchorage, who must consult the brass in Washington ("That's what I like about the Air Force," quips Scotty, "smart all the way to the top"). When the orders do come, they are worthless. Fogarty instructs Hendry to "avoid harming the alien at all costs." Hendry must disobey these orders, but his actions are exonerated.

The question of how to destroy a vegetable menace is simple enough, as Hawks' wife pointed out to him, "you boil them." With Carrington confined to quarters, the conflicts in the film become resolved as the soldiers and scientists are finally able to work together to combat the menace, devising a way of using electricity to fry the fiend. Newspaperman Scotty has been anxious to report on a big story, but has to submit to military authority. ("The whole world wants to know," Scotty points out, to which Hendry responds, "I work for the Air Force, not the world.") He cannot tell his story until he gets permission from the authorities to release it. At the end of the film, Scotty is allowed to give his story and speak for everyone, both soldiers and scientists. He even goes out of his way to pay special tribute to Carrington (originally the Thing was to have killed Carrington and then died, Scotty was to have said, "Both monsters are dead," but in the final film this is softened to emphasize plurality), papering over differences so that the center can hold together and face the possible (Soviet-like) threat from the skies. "Keep watching the skies," Scotty warns, focusing attention away from the differences that divide people down on Earth.

Differences that divide people was also the inspiration for producer Julian Blaustein to make a science fiction film addressing some of the serious issues that confronted the world in the early 1950s. He read dozens of stories before

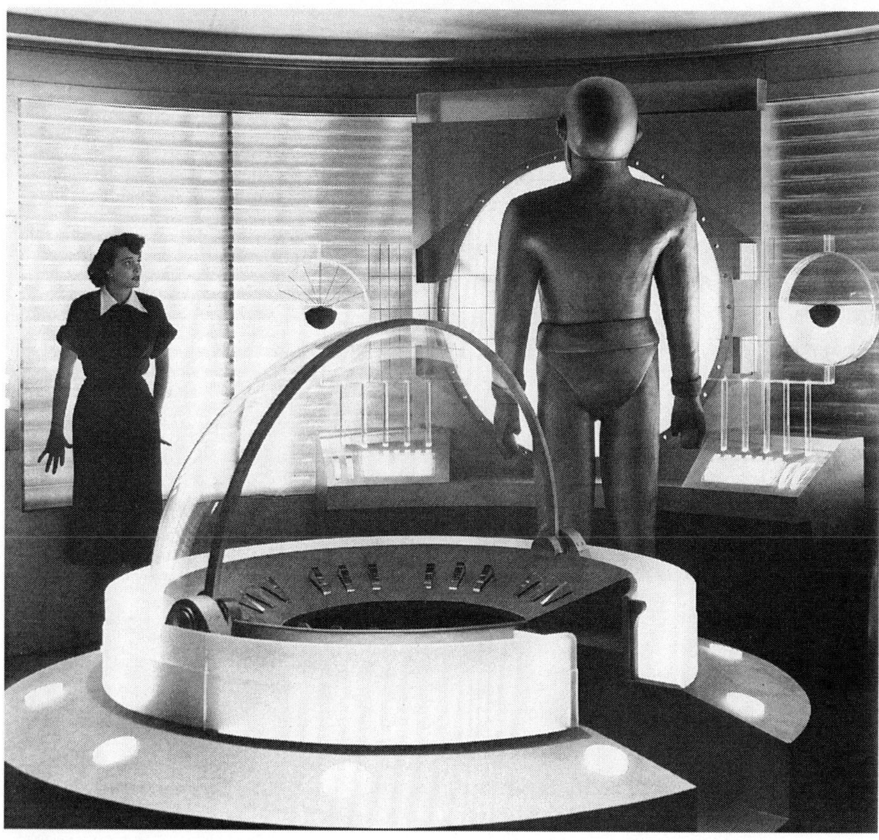

Patricia Neal confronts the robot Gort (Lock Martin) aboard Klaatu's modern spaceship in Robert Wise's classic *The Day the Earth Stood Still.*

With studio head Darryl Zanuck's approval, Blaustein hired Robert Wise to direct the project. Wise read the script quickly and liked it quite a bit. Zanuck insisted that the opening scene set aboard a spaceship be cut, and that the film begin with the script's second sequence where radio programs are interrupted by a newsflash concerning a flying saucer. He disliked the idea of the visitor, Klaatu, being able to see through walls because if Klaatu had too much supernatural power, he would never seem to be in any danger (and this was dutifully eliminated). He objected to Klaatu being able to cure himself with a mysterious salve and suggested that after Klaatu is shot and killed that Helen be given something that would serve as a password to Gnut (as the robot was called in the original story and screenplay, later changed to Gort). He also objected to a scene showing the destruction of the Rock of Gibraltar, deeming it unnecessary, and lastly suggested changing the title to *The Man from Mars.* Apart from the final suggestion, Zanuck's suggestions were incorporated. The title was changed from *Farewell to the Master* to *The Day the World Stopped* and then finally to *The Day the Earth Stood Still.*

he saw something he liked in Harry Bates' story "Farewell to the Master." While he did not care for the entire story, he liked the set-up where a visitor from another place and time comes to Earth with a robot and a peace offering only to be shot by a nervous soldier who does not understand his action, and this became the inspiration for *The Day the Earth Stood Still* (1951). (The final twist of the original story is that the robot isn't the visitor's servant, but his master, that the world he comes from is ruled by machines. Though this is not stated explicitly in the film as it is in the story, there is still an echo of this idea present in the movie at its end.)

Blaustein used the basic idea and a simple outline to take to screenwriter and old army pal Edmund H. North (*In a Lonely Place; Patton*) who fleshed out the idea into a screenplay. It was North who incorporated suggestions of Christ into the script, assuming that no one would pick up on them. (Klaatu comes from the heavens with a message of peace. He takes on the name Carpenter and goes among the people. He is killed, then resurrected and delivers a final message.) The only problem the script had from the Breen office was an objection to the resurrection, so Klaatu's resurrection was made only temporary and a line added that the power of life over death "is reserved for the Almighty Spirit."

As to who would play Klaatu, Zanuck initially suggested Spencer Tracy, but Blaustein felt that would be a big mistake, as when the spaceship opened and a movie star stepped out, all credibility would be lost. Wise initially favored Claude Rains, but Rains was tied up elsewhere. Blaustein felt the lead needed to be someone that audiences had never seen before, and Zanuck suggested a new contract player he had just signed to Fox after seeing him in a play in England, Michael Rennie, who proved to be the perfect choice.

Rennie projected a sense of seriousness softened by humor as well as sharp intelligence that was ideal for the role of an alien ambassador. Rennie had been acting in films in England since the 1930s, but was still not well known to U.S. audiences. He tended to appear in epics, became known as the star of the TV series *The Third Man,* and also appeared in the science fiction films *The Lost World, Cyborg 2087,* and *The Power.*

One major problem the production faced was when an underling approached Blaustein with the information that

Sam Jaffe, whom Blaustein had signed to play the Einstein-like Prof. Barnhardt, was on the blacklist and that he should get someone else to play the part. Blaustein insisted on Jaffe and Zanuck supported him. (Jaffe would not work on another U.S. film for seven years, though he later returned to the limelight by playing Dr. Zorba on the *Ben Casey* TV series.)

Another difficulty was finding someone to fill the shoes of the eight foot robot Gort, which Wise did when he remembered Lock Martin, the seven foot seven inch doorman at Grauman's Chinese Theater, who was placed on platform shoes and given a periscope set-up inside the helmet in order to see out the front. (The helmet itself rose above his head.) To cover the laces, two different robot suits were used, one with laces up the front and the other with laces up the back, plus a lightweight mock-up for when Gort is simply standing. (Unfortunately for Martin, the stand-up could not be used for scenes where the robot is standing on an inclined plane as on the edge of the saucer, requiring that Martin stand motionless for hours. If you look closely in the film, you can sometimes see his arms twitching.)

Another difficulty came when the Department of Defense refused to give an OK to use army equipment because it did not like the theme of the picture. Wise was able to substitute with equipment from the Washington National Guard, who were filmed by a second unit director according to Wise's instructions.

While Zanuck was very supportive of the project in general, he did circulate memos around the studio suggesting that directors reduce the number of angles they employed to reduce the time it took to set up each angle and thereby save the studio money. (He loved to point to *Twelve O'Clock High* and *Father of the Bride* as examples of what he meant, both of which rely more on medium shots than close-ups.) He criticized Wise for shooting too many angles for the sequence around the boarding house breakfast table, but Wise responded with a memo of his own explaining what coverage he had and why he felt it was necessary, and Zanuck ceased to trouble him.

The film's verisimilitude is aided both by its location shooting in Washington, D.C., and by the use of actual news commentators Elmer Davis, H. V. Kaltenborn, and Drew Pearson, who deliver news of the approaching saucer, each in his own style. Greatly adding to the atmosphere is Bernard Herrmann's superb score, which added two theremins to an unconventional orchestra and added a sense of outer space eerieness.

The spaceship lands next to a baseball diamond, a ramp extends from the seemingly seamless skin of the ship, and Klaatu (Rennie) emerges in a shiny suit with a bubble helmet and proffers a mysterious device in his hand. "We have come to visit you in peace, and with goodwill," he offers reassuringly in excellent English. A trigger-happy soldier fires a round, wounding the emissary and causing his companion, a tall, almost featureless silver robot, to emerge. The army fires at the mechanical man, but the bullets simply bounce away. A laserbeam shoots out from behind the raised visor, reducing weapons to sludge while leaving soldiers unharmed.

Klaatu recuperates quickly after being taken to Walter Reed Army Hospital, where the President's aide comes in to discuss a meeting. "I want to meet with representatives of all the nations on Earth," Klaatu demands. "That's impractical," protests the aide. "Our world is full of tensions and suspicions, and in the present international situation, such a meeting is impossible. I'm sure you know the evil forces on our planet which have caused trouble."

"I'm not concerned with your petty squabbles," replies Klaatu testily. Such a political attitude was quite striking for the fifties, especially as the Korean War had just begun and the Cold War was in full swing. To much of Western Civilization, there was no bigger issue than thwarting the Communists, and yet here is an intergalactic visitor (though screenwriter North screws up on the distances involved) who considers the whole thing a minor local squabble. What's more, he states, "I will not speak to the representative of one nation and increase your petty jealousies."

The government attempts to keep him prisoner, but Klaatu sneaks out, borrowing a suit from a man called Carpenter and adopting that as his name. He wishes to go among the people to learn what they think. However, when the authorities learn he has escaped, they incite panic. As Klaatu walks down the street, he hears the hysterical voices of TV and radio commentators saying, in essence, that a monster is loose. (Gabriel Heatter, another real-life newscaster, reports, "This creature must be tracked down like a wild animal. He must be destroyed!")

Going inside a boarding house, Klaatu receives a cross-section of opinion about the space man. One woman insists that he must be a Red from Russia, but Helen Benson (Patricia Neal) springs to his defense, pointing out that it should not be assumed that he is an enemy, that it was he who was shot, and not the Americans. Klaatu rents a room and soon befriends Benson's son Bobby (William Gray) and they see Washington together. At one point, the media wants to exploit the fears of the people, asking passers-by what they fear. To one of these, Klaatu responds, "I'm fearful when I see people substituting fear for reason," which only gets the microphone pulled away from him.

The film points out that many people do not take the time to think things through calmly and rationally, and that others are eager and anxious to exploit those fears for their own purposes. Klaatu realizes that he needs another approach and queries Bobby as to who is the greatest man on Earth. Bobby does not understand what he means by "greatest" at first, then volunteers Professor Barnhardt, the greatest scientist.

When the pair get to Barnhardt's home, the professor is not there, but Klaatu decides to correct some of the professor's equations in celestial mechanics as a kind of calling card, though he has to prevent the professor's housekeeper from erasing it first. The professor is indeed curious, and Klaatu explains, "Soon one of your nations will apply atomic energy to spaceships — that will threaten the peace and security of other planets." He asks the professor to convene a meeting of the world's scientists (à la the Cultural and Scientific Conference for World Peace held at the Waldorf-Astoria Hotel in 1949), and to ensure their attendance, promises a demonstration of his power, as that's "the only thing your people understand."

This is perhaps the great SF "meet cute" scene of all time. To establish Klaatu's authority and brilliance, he corrects the mistakes of the world's brightest scientist and asserts the correctness by noting that the equation worked well enough for him to use it to reach other planets. (A variation of this scene has been employed elsewhere, including the *Galactica: 1980* TV series.) While not hostile, Klaatu has shown himself to be confident and quite capable, despite his lack of knowledge of Earth's customs. He responds to kindred spirits, such as Abraham Lincoln, whose memorial he visits with Bobby. It is his demonstration that inspires the film's title.

At precisely noon, he sees that all electrical items come to a halt, with a few significant exceptions. (Planes flying and medical equipment are allowed to continue operating, showing that Klaatu is not without his humanitarian side, though how he manages to be so selective in his global targets is not even broached.) Barnhardt is impressed with this display (as the apparent inventor of the atomic bomb, he knows power when he sees it), and is also happy to see that the demonstration makes his housekeeper fearful, that it causes her to stop and think. He immediately begins setting up the meeting Klaatu asks for.

Unlike many science fiction films (but not SF literature), *The Day the Earth Stood Still* respects intellect. Scientists are not seen as the sowers of the seeds of our destruction or as mad, evil, or foolish. Instead, they are sensible, clear-sighted, rational, and above petty politics that beset so many segments of society.

The villain becomes Tom Stevens (Hugh Marlowe, giving the worst performance in the film), Helen's beau and an insurance salesman, who becomes suspicious after Klaatu gives Bobby some diamonds. Stevens has them appraised and learns that there are no stones like them on Earth. This is enough to convince him of Mr. Carpenter's true origin, and he ignores Helen's pleas not to inform the authorities. "I can write my own ticket," he speculates excitedly. "I can be the biggest man in the country. You'll feel different when you see my picture in the papers." He, in effect, becomes the story's Judas, and although he may be doing what he thinks is right, we are against this seeming betrayal.

The authorities are in total panic after Klaatu's demonstration. They have encased the robot Gort in a block of KL9T, a new plastic "stronger than steel." (Gort is able to dissolve it easily.) The city of Washington gets quarantined. Orders have been issued to shoot on sight, and sure enough Klaatu is soon spotted and killed, but before expiring he supplies Helen with the famous password for Gort, "Gort ... Klaatu Barada Nikto," which apparently means something like "Klaatu's dead, go to plan B."

The robot recovers Klaatu's body and brings it back to temporary life so that he can address the assembled group of scientists who meet at his flying saucer. "The Universe grows smaller every day," he begins. "Threats of aggression cannot be tolerated. There must be security for all." The other planets are concerned about Earth's aggressive tendency, but they have a solution. "We have created a race of robots as policemen. They have absolute power over us. At the first sign of violence, your Earth will be reduced to a burned-out cinder. Your choice — join us and live in peace or face obliteration. The decision rests with you."

Having delivered this ultimatum, Klaatu returns to his ship and the stars. There is a naïve belief that technology could create perfect and infallible policemen, and the fascistic undertones of such a notion seem to have escaped the filmmakers, who basically saw their film as supporting a United Nations–like coming together to solve our mutual difficulties while putting aside unimportant nationalistic differences. The essential concern of many was that with the Cold War heating up and with the power of the H-bomb at man's disposal, we did not end up obliterating ourselves, that it was far preferable to seek peaceful means of resolution, so here an outside force comes to foist such a resolution on us because the alternative would be unthinkable.

Wise keeps the film realistic and moving at a good pace, getting excellent performances from most of the leads. (What we see is basically a rough cut — after Zanuck saw the initial assemblage, he ordered it shipped out.) The ending is a bit preachy, but it does work well in the context (even if its politics can and have been questioned). *The Day The Earth Stood Still* won the Golden Globe Award for the Best Film Promoting International Understanding. It was one of the first science fiction films to be treated as an A production, and set a standard for craftsmanship and intelligence that few subsequent science fiction features would meet. It has been hailed as a science fiction classic ever since.

British director Alex Mackendrick created one of the wittiest and most amusing science fiction satires in *The Man in the White Suit* (1951), the script for which he wrote with Roger Macdougall, and John Dighton from Macdougall's play. It is one of the few science fiction films to truly come to terms with the consequences of a technological innovation. It depicts a society that discourages innovation and is a network of vested interests unconcerned with the welfare of the common good. The main characters are Birnley (Cecil Parker), a paternalistic textile mill-owner and captain of industry who narrates the film, and Sidney Stratton (Alec Guinness), a young scientist with an idea about how to make an indestructible cloth who is at first oblivious but eventually becomes aware of this human truth.

Sidney Stratton (Alec Guinness) conducts covert clothing experiments in Alexander Mackendrick's brilliant SF satire *The Man in the White Suit*.

As the film begins, Birnley is shown around his son-in-law Michael Corland's (Michael Gough) neighboring mill when their carefully ordered world is disturbed by a strange sound which proves to be emanating from an experiment of Sidney's. Mackendrick depicts a system that is obstructive to research and innovation. Since Stratton is unable to get approval through official channels, he has become a pirate, slipping in unnoticed to acquire materials, but his initially explosive results gets him thrown out of Corland's factory.

Undiscouraged, he sets up shop at Birnley's laboratory, where he finally achieves a breakthrough of potentially great value to the firm. The head of research, hearing Sidney's sounds of triumph, sends for the medical department. The buxom and bossy Nurse Gamage appears, slaps Sidney's face, and immediately administers a sedative, while the uninquisitive research man pours Sidney's solution down the sink.

Undaunted, Stratton lays siege to Birnley's house in order to bring his innovation to his attention, but all kinds of obstacles (a Japanese butler, a vase, bells, stairs, doors) are placed in his way. Birnley meanwhile is confounded by the financial discrepancy caused by Stratton's experiments, is informed about them by his head of research, and simultaneously orders Sidney to be brought to him and sent away at the same time. (Mackendrick shows industry at cross purposes with itself, with the left hand constantly not knowing what the right hand is doing.)

Fortunately for Sidney, Daphne (sultry Joan Greenwood), Birnley's daughter, has been taken with the way Sidney put one over on both Corland and her father, and she actually listens to Sidney and intervenes on his behalf. (When he says to her, "You know the problem of polymerizing amino-acid resolutes," she spends half the night up with the *Encyclopaedia Britannica* to figure it out.) Sidney has devised a miracle fabric that actually repels dirt and never wears out. Birnley sees an opportunity to dominate the market and achieve a financial coup, and in a montage we see the work that goes into developing the fabric and creating a dazzlingly white prototype suit (a symbol of its bright promise and Sidney's purity). Daphne looks on Stratton as a knight in shining armor and proclaims that people will praise Sidney for his invention.

However, she proves to be quite wrong because she has failed to take into consideration the implications of Sidney's invention. Both labor and management will be affected because everlasting suits mean that people will buy fewer suits resulting in less work for the factories. That it repels dirt will also mean less work for washerwomen like his former landlady Mrs. Watson (Edie Martin), who plaintively tells him, "Why can't you scientists leave things alone? What's to become of my bit of washing when there's no washing to do?"

Summoned by Corland, the belligerent black-suited and black-hearted textile owners, led by Sir John Kierlaw (Ernest Thesiger, terrific as the grotesque grandfather of the industry), band together quickly to suppress this dangerous innovation and they attempt to bribe and then, failing that, abduct Stratton, who has no vision of the social implications of his work and no interest in them either. (In one of the film's more amusing moments, the extremely frail Kierlaw ineffectively swipes at Stratton with his silver-topped walking stick, belying Birnley's statement that he "will not resort to violence.")

Bribery having failed, Corland suggests that Sidney might be bought off by a woman, agreeing that Daphne, his own fiancée, should be asked to use her charms on Sidney for the sake of the industry. Certainly this proposal allows her to see Corland in a new light, responding to his proposal archly with, "I'm not experienced in these matters, but I've always understood this work was very well paid." While her father is shocked, this is the kind of business transaction Kierlaw understands and they agree on the sum of £5,000. (Capitalism, it is metaphorically implied, is a form of prostitution.)

Daphne, however, has simply made her offer to expose their venality and humiliate them and uses her privacy to free Stratton. She is a dynamic character who can meet cunning with cunning, and she respects Stratton's integrity and shares his delight in his discovery. More receptive to the implication of things, she cleverly suggests that since his material is unbreakable, Sidney can let himself down from the upstairs window by using a single strand.

Sidney dashes off, his white suit making him an easy target for the united bosses and workers who pursue him. The problem hastily resolves itself when Stratton's "indestructible" cloth suddenly pulls apart easily because the compound used to make it was unstable (it also serves as a symbol of Sidney's lost innocence). The crisis has been averted for now, but a clever sound cue (the theme music associated with Sidney's bubbling apparatus) alerts us that Sydney may one day solve this problem and throw a spanner in the works once again.

Though unsuccessful financially, this is the finest film made by the English Ealing Studios. While the plot relies on caricatures rather than characters, the performers are all aptly cast and bring an accomplished professionalism to their roles. Mackendrick's sense of timing is particularly fine, bringing out the nuances of the comedy and carefully building to his climactic scenes. It is unquestionably one of the smartest SF comedies ever made.

Kiss Me, Deadly (1955), directed by Robert Aldrich, is *film noir* at its darkest. It combines expressionistic shadows with both realism (most of the film was shot on location in Los Angeles) and the fantastic. It begins in the darkest night with the opening image that of a woman (Cloris Leachman) running down a dark highway. Instead of the customary establishing shot, Aldrich alternates between a series of medium and long shots, showing her first from the waist down, then in full view as she runs towards the camera, and finally in medium shot from the waist up, suggesting a split character, but something is definitely off-kilter. In the initial close-up, she is clearly running down the center of the highway, while in the approaching POV, she is running along the side of the road, and the film continues to alternate between these mismatched shots that help to disorient our point of view.

Detective Mike Hammer (Ralph Meeker in his finest characterization) is surly and hostile to this damsel in distress, not the action of a typical hero. The woman, naked beneath her coat, identifies herself as Christina, an escaped mental patient. The credits scroll in the reverse direction so that we have to read from the bottom up rather than the top down while Nat "King" Cole croons the haunting "I'd Rather Have the Blues (Than What I Got)." Right away, Aldrich establishes that all is not right in the world of Hammer.

In some ways, Hammer is depicted as a typical private eye. He keeps getting hit on the head and knocked out, and Christina, the woman he sought to protect, is cruelly killed by torture. (The villain behind this, Dr. Soberin [Albert Dekker], is only identified by his voice and his shoes, offering up another incomplete person of uncertain identity; in fact, the film often disorients by allowing us to hear human voices without identifying their source.) Hammer has Velma (Maxine Cooper), a secretary who loves him and does his bidding. He has contacts at the police station. He is committed to avenge the death of a friend.

But unlike other screen detectives of the time and before, Hammer is a "bedroom dick," specializing in divorce cases, usually by having Velma make a play for an erring husband and then filming the results. He is a user whom the police regard with contempt and scorn, and it does not bother him one bit. He is a sadist who enjoys inflicting pain, humiliating his victims. In one sequence, reality is broken as a prominent neon clock moves minutes for what should take seconds in a scene that ends with Hammer pushing a man down a long flight of stairs, shot so that the man appears to fall up into the camera. In pursuit of the great "whatsit," Hammer smashes the hand of a doctor at the morgue for taking a bribe, and then slaps around an attendant at a club for not taking one.

Clearly, Aldrich detests his hero, who is portrayed as an uncultured, unsympathetic lout whose constant refrain is "What's in it for me?" He uses people with no regard for the consequences, not only Velma but also his mechanic pal Nick (an overly ethnic Nick Dennis), who gets crushed by a car. Velma sarcastically disputes Hammer's claim that he is simply motivated to get those who killed Nick: "You want to avenge the death of your dear friend Nick ... how nicely it justifies your quest for the great whatsit."

His friend from the police, Pat Murphy (Wesley Addy), tries to warn him also in a speech which gives away the science fiction orientation of the film. Murphy tries to get

Hammer to drop the case, alluding to complexities which the dick does not understand: "Now listen, Mike. Listen carefully. I'm going to pronounce a few words. They're harmless words, just a bunch of letters scrambled together, but their meaning is very important. Try to understand what they mean: Manhattan Project. Los Alamos. Trinity."

The tragedy is that Hammer does not understand. Like the hawks in the Cold War, he is playing with incredible forces that he does not understand and cannot control. The missing material that the crooks are searching for has been altered by screenwriter A. I. "Izzy" Bezzerides from drugs in the Mickey Spillane novel into a stolen suitcase of fissionable material, a suitcase that glows inside and burns those who would open it. (The film's *Repo Man* and *Pulp Fiction* both borrow this suitcase concept.)

Kiss Me, Deadly is filled with surreal touches and stylistic finesse. Aldirch uses a prize-fight on the radio to comment on the action in the scene where Evello and Sugar Smallhouse are killed. When Hammer tracks down Christina's former roommate Lily Carver (Gaby Rogers), her bed is shown against a blank wall, and the next shot through the head railings is from an unreal space, the point of view of the wall. When Nick is killed, the camera takes the point of view of the car crushing him. There is even a reel-to-reel phone answering machine, a seemingly science fictional device in the fifties.

Aldrich originally intended his film to end with Mike and Velma escaping into the sea while Soberin's precariously perched beach house explodes almost apocalyptically. He wanted his hero to survive at least momentarily to contemplate his mistakes and perhaps gain wisdom. When the picture was released in 1955, Aldrich found that most American critics passed it over as no more than "a Spillane movie done with a little more energy.... So they didn't understand at all the political implications," the director lamented, the implicit indictment of the assumption that the defense of America justified any means (including McCarthyism) and any weapons (including atomic ones). The film was better received critically in Europe.

For years most prints of the film have thwarted narrative expectations by simply showing the house exploding as Mike and Velma attempt their escape, no survivors in sight as the world seemingly comes to an abrupt end. Only recently has MGM/UA spliced the original 80 seconds of footage back into the film (obtained from Aldrich's own print of the film) for its video re-release, and has now followed Aldrich's wishes in designating this restored edition as the definitive one.

Producer Walter Wanger discovered Jack Finney's story "The Body Snatchers" in *Collier's* magazine, and gave a copy to director Don Siegel, who was excited by the idea and suggested that Daniel Mainwaring (*Out of the Past; The Big Steal; The Phoenix City Story; Space Master X-7; Atlantis the Lost Continent*) write the screenplay for the science fiction classic known as *Invasion of the Body Snatchers* (1956). Mainwaring worked closely with Siegel, taking out sequences, writing them, and then showing them for approval.

Commented Siegel in his autobiography, *A Siegel Film*:

> The story concerns alien beings taking over the bodies of humans. The aliens assume the exact likeness of real people while gestating in pods. But these "pods" possess no soul, emotion or culture. They exist like cows munching grass, without a care plaguing them. They are incapable of love; passion is unknown. They simply live—breathing, eating, sleeping. Danny [Mainwaring] and I knew that many of our associates, acquaintances and family were already pods. How many of them woke up in the morning, ate breakfast (but never read the newspaper), went to work, returned home to eat again and went to sleep?

Invasion of the Body Snatchers was shot in 19 days for a budget of about $250,000. The town of Santa Madre stood in for the town of Santa Mira, and additional locations included Bronson Canyon and the Hollywood Hills. The film was shot in SuperScope, a non-anamorphic process which took a normal 35mm frame, cropped the top and bottom, and squeezed it into a 2:1 proportion in the laboratory after photography was finished. For proper framing and composition, the film needs to be viewed in this widescreen format.

Apart from a studio-imposed prologue, which seemingly exposes the hero as a wild-eyed madman, the story of *Invasion of the Body Snatchers* begins with Dr. Miles Bennell (whose name suggests "banal"; he is superbly played by Kevin McCarthy in his most famous role), a general practitioner in Santa Mira (a name which means "holy look," introducing the theme of appearances), a small, average California town, returning from a trip and noting, "At first glance, everything looked the same. It wasn't. Something had taken over the town."

Bennell's first clue comes appropriately enough after he has been picked up by his nurse Sally (Jean Wiles) while by a closed vegetable stand (foreshadowing the alien's plant origins) a small boy, Jimmy Grimaldi (Bobby Clark), insists that his mother isn't his mother and dashes out in front of his car. Back at his office, Bennell finds several similar patients, most of whom cancel a short time later. (Disturbingly, Bennell gives Jimmy a pill which instead of curing him will speed his transformation into podhood.)

Even his sweetheart, Becky Driscoll (Dana Wynter) is afflicted, and something is peculiar about her father. Both Bennell and Becky are divorced, which is unusual for a fifties film and introduces the idea of crumbling families as

Director Don Siegel (above) prepares Kevin McCarthy and Dana Wynter for this climactic scene from *Invasion of the Body Snatchers.*

well as explaining why they hesitate to commit to one another. I'm just a general practitioner, Bennell tells Becky, love is for the specialists. But of course, the movie's point is that the average people should not dispense with their feelings or they will simply be "vegetating." Becky's warmth is underscored by her being introduced wearing a sexy strapless gown, hardly typical daywear but indicative of her open sexuality.

One woman, Wilma (Virginia Christine), notes that when she looks at her Uncle Ira (Tom Fadden), "There's something missing. Always when he talked to me there was a certain look in his eyes. Now it's gone." She worries that she is crazy. But when Bennell checks on Uncle Ira, he looks and acts perfectly normally.

In some ways, this is a reflection of fifties' fears that the people one knew could be transformed into subversive communist agents working to undermine the community. Others have read the film as an attack on McCarthyism, where people were expected to get into line and attack those who thought differently. Both readings are too narrow, as from interviews with Siegel, it is quite clear that he intends an attack on stifling conformity, on people who appear to go through life without really partaking of its pleasures or passions.

Miles and Becky meet psychiatrist Dan Kaufman (Larry Gates) at an underpopulated night spot (pods do not care for partying), who offers his own explanation: it's an "epidemic of mass hysteria." Becky playfully asks how Miles can know she is Becky, and he responds by kissing her and telling her, "You're Becky all right." Seeing her isn't enough, as the film shows over and over again that appearances can be deceiving, and this kiss is neatly mirrored at the end of the film.

However, Kaufman's explanation cannot explain why Bennell's writer friend Jack (King Donovan) has a body that resembles an unfinished impression of Jack himself laid out on his pool table. In an eerie moment, moments after Jack has cut his hand, the double starts bleeding from the exact same place, causing his wife Theodore (Carolyn Jones) to scream in horror. (There is a perverse inversion of Christian mythology here, with the pod double displaying stigmata and representing a being come from the heavens to take away people's pains.) Yet when Kaufman is summoned to look at the body, it has disappeared and the characters at first cannot believe what has happened and try to carry on normally.

Bennell takes Becky home and suggests that he tuck her in, but she initially refuses, indicating that "that way lies madness." "What's wrong with madness," Bennell responds with a smile, but graciously prepares to depart as Becky's father Mr. Driscoll (Kenneth Patterson) emerges from the basement. Later, when Bennell sees Charlie the gas man (future director Sam Peckinpah, who assisted Siegel on the film) in Jack's basement, he becomes concerned what Driscoll might have been up to and takes Becky to the safety of his own house.

Following a fade-out, there is a domestic kitchen scene that makes it clear that the couple have spent the night together. They try to return to normal life, even having a barbecue with Jack and Theodora, but their complacency is shattered with the discovery of pods with bodies in Jack's greenhouse that bear resemblance to each of them. (Significantly, Miles cannot bring himself to stab Becky's simulacrum with a pitchfork and stabs his own instead.)

Siegel's art director, Ted Haworth, figured out a way to create pods that was simple and inexpensive. (The special effects budget for the film was a mere $15,000.) The greatest difficulty was creating likenesses of the leading actors when their doubles emerge from the pods. Impressions of the naked actors were made out of thin, skin-tight latex and then combined with soap bubbles that would gradually disappear but still be numerous enough for modesty's sake. Haworth was worried how the executives at Allied Artists would react to nudity, but Siegel reassured him that the top executives were all pods, that they couldn't care less about nudity, sex, or dirty words, because they have no real feel for anything.

Siegel related that one of the executives hadn't changed to a pod yet and insisted that there be no nudity in an Allied Artists picture, though Siegel observed that he "looked sleepy" and so ordered the impressions made secretly, fully convinced that the exec would be a pod before the film was completed.

The insidiousness of Miles and Becky's plight is underscored when they try to contact the proper authorities and are thwarted at every turn. They try to call the FBI, but the operator tells them there is no answer. They phone the governor in Sacramento, but the Sacramento circuits are dead. They try Los Angeles, but the lines are down. They urge Jack and Theodora to flee to another town, and when they try to leave themselves, discover that a gas station attendant (Dabbs Greer) has placed pods in their trunk, which they take out and burn. (The pods burn quite well and do resemble huge rolls of tobacco.)

Seeking somebody they can trust, Dr. Bennell goes to his nurse's house only to see Driscoll taking a pod to lower into a baby's playpen. (No more tears for this tyke, but no more personality either.) The police put out an all points bulletin for the pair. The enemy is seen to be everywhere, forcing them to take refuge in Bennell's office. They spend another night together, but this time after the fade-out, instead of the former domesticity, all we see is an ashtray of stubbed out cigarettes and the couple's ongoing anxiety.

They then get cornered by Kaufman and the now transformed Jack, who try to use reason to convert them. "People are nothing but problems," observes Kaufman, but once they become pod people, "there's no pain. You'll be born again into an untroubled world." Bennell asks about love; Kaufman responds, "There's no room left for love. You've been in love before. It doesn't last. Life is simpler without it." The use of a psychiatrist, a man dedicated to helping others adjust to society's norms, to deliver these sentiments is very deliberate and slyly satirical. The pods are not violent, they know that they simply have to wait and their opponents will be assimilated, so they patiently guard outside the door.

"I don't want a world without love or faith or beauty," responds Becky when they are alone. Miles uses the pods' own methods of infiltration against them, sneaking around with hypodermics to knock the men out from behind, with Becky bravely doing to same to the chief of police who pops up to intervene, and then the fleeing pair make their escape, but they must remain eternally vigilant, only to be given away by the sensitivity they are forced to repress when Becky calls out as a truck is about to run over a small dog.

Siegel was a chronic insomniac, and he added the emphasis on falling asleep that was not so present in Finney's novel. In the film, falling asleep is dangerous, for when people doze off, the pods absorb their thoughts and memories and implant them in duplicates. (What exactly happens to the original bodies is never made clear, though in Phil Kaufman's semi-sequel/remake of the film, this was given major emphasis.) Another addition not in the book is Miles' speech about how people tend to lose their humanity, bit by bit, and reminder that we must be ever vigilant against encroaching podism.

One night, as a practical joke, Siegel broke into Dana Wynter's house and slipped one of the pods under her bed. The threat of the pods had become real enough to the actress that the next morning when she found the pod, she went into a state of near hysteria. A few subsequent comedies have played explicit tribute to the pods, including the space shuttle disaster comedy *Airplane II: The Sequel.*

The film's most dramatic sequence occurs when a crowd pursues the couple into the hills, and they are forced to hide under the ground (a reminder of the grave) in a mine, as the crowd speeds over them. Later, they hear music and see in it a sign of hope, but in checking it out, Bennell discovers that pod workers are simply listening to the radio awaiting the weather report.

He returns to the terribly tired Becky and pulls her away. She falls and he gives her a tender kiss. In close-up we see her black eyes that have lost the soul behind them, followed by a close-up of Miles horrified expression. His beloved is now one of them. "A moment's sleep, and the girl I loved was an inhuman enemy bent on my destruction," declares Bennell after Becky has succumbed to the pods. Of course, previously the pods produced replicas which replaced the original human beings, but for dramatic purposes in this instance, Becky herself becomes an unfeeling pod person, delivering the film's biggest and most memorable shock.

We have seen the pod people work as activists who spread their malign influence far and wide. In turn, Siegel's film seeks not to reassure but alarm, not to tranquilize and restore the status quo, but to mobilize the audience watching the film to be on our guard against the soulless automaton conformists who seek to control our thoughts, our feelings, and our world. Siegel wanted to end the film at the moment when Miles hops aboard the back of a truck heading into Los Angeles, only to discover that it is full of pods, turn to the camera in horror and chant, "You're next!" as a final disturbing warning.

According to Siegel:

> Allied Artists, bursting at the same seams with pods, took Wanger's and my final cut and edited out all the humour. In their hallowed words, "Horror films are horror films and there's no room for humour." I translated it to mean that in their pod brains there was no room for humor. The studio also insisted on a prologue and epilogue. Wanger was very much against this, as was I. However, he begged me to shoot it to protect the film, and I reluctantly consented.

The epilogue starts with Miles being taken back to the town's hospital, trying to convince the incredulous psychiatrist (Whit Bissel) and the hospital doctor (Richard Deacon) of the pods taking over the world. An emergency case is brought in whom the ambulance driver says was injured when a truck full of pods turned over. The psychiatrist looks at Miles, picks up the phone and asks for the FBI. This is certainly a less hysterical ending with a promise that normalcy can be restored. The main problem with the framing story is that it does not allow the story to build gradually, with the audience slowly picking up on clues that things are not what they seem. However, it does what Allied Artists execs wanted it to do, that is establish from the start that the audience is watching a horror film, though one would think that the title they gave the film would be a dead giveaway.

Siegel himself never cared for the title, preferring Kevin McCarthy's suggestion *Sleep No More*. Nevertheless, it was always one of the films he was most proud of, and with good reason. Siegel specialized in action films, and only returned to science fiction in directing a couple episodes of *The Twilight Zone*, but made the concept of pod people a permanent part of his vocabulary. *Invasion of the Body Snatchers* is one of the most thought-provoking, finely crafted, and intelligent science fiction films ever made, and its message remains as timely as ever — a true classic.

Forbidden Planet (1956) was the most lavish science fiction film of the 1950s, and in its influence on the subsequent *Star Trek* series, which echoes several of its elements, perhaps one of the most influential. The film initially germinated inside the mind of Irving Block, a special effects artist who provided the effects for a number of low budget efforts such as *Destination Moon*, *Atomic Submarine*, *War of the Satellites* and *Kronos*, who cowrote a treatment called *Fatal Planet* with Alan Adler. Block had intended to sell the treatment to Allied Artists, but at the suggestion of his agent, he brought the treatment, a science fictional variation on Shakespeare's *The Tempest*, to MGM's Nicholas Nayfack in the spring of 1954.

In Adler and Block's story, Prospero becomes philologist Morbius, Miranda becomes Altaira, the enchanted island becomes the planet Altair 4, the group of Italian nobles become the crew of the United Planets Cruiser *C-57D*, while Caliban and Ariel are combined as Robby the Robot. Block also had the idea of using Freudian psychology to create "monsters from the Id." (The Id is that part of a personality only concerned with gratifying one's basest needs.)

As Block told Steve Rubin, "The idea of bug-eyed monsters is a pretty childish illusion. But there are real monsters and demons that exist within us that we know nothing about. We're capable of doing the most horrendous things and we're often shocked at this truism. The monster from the Id is nothing more than the invisible demonic spirit of Morbius. In the very end MGM couldn't accept the fact of total invisibility so they got the Disney people [special effects animator Josh Meador] to create an example of the Id. It was quite poor."

Block acted out portions of the plot for Nayfack, who was intrigued by the idea of a scary, invisible monster, bought the story and put it on the production schedule immediately, though production head Dory Schary remained unenthusiastic about the film. Nayfack hired his friend Fred McLeod Wilcox (*Lassie Come Home*) to direct and set Arthur Lonergan to create some pre-production drawings. He then hired Cyril Hume to write the screenplay, who increased the role of the advanced alien race the Krel in Block and Adler's story and changed the title to *Forbidden Planet* (as Fatal was thought to be too negative). A. Arnold Gillespie was hired to attend to the film's elaborate and impressive special effects.

Gillespie and Lonergan began working with Warren Newcombe and set designer Hugh Hunt experimenting with new ideas. The art department under the direction of George Gibson created a huge 350 foot cyclorama depicting the arid Altairian surface complete with pebbly rock and brush, one of the finest alien planet sets ever made. Gillespie gave the job of designing Robby the Robot to Bob Kinoshita, a brilliant draftsman who also designed the flying saucer-shaped *C57D*'s interior and the dazzling underground complex of the Krel. Adding another unique element to the film was its electronically derived musical score by Lou and Bebe Barron which greatly aided in establishing an otherworldly atmosphere.

While many have criticized Fred McLeod Wilcox's direction as slow paced and uninspired, and it is true that many of the performances are bland and the editing rough in spots, but to me it has the essential "sense of wonder" that makes for great science fiction. Though aspects of the film were inspired by its Universal predecessor, *This Island Earth*, MGM went all out to take viewers on a trip to another planet and invite us to speculate about the civilization of the Krel which once existed there. (It is, I believe, the first science fiction film to be set entirely on another planet, and with a $1.9 million budget, was the most expensive science fiction film of the 1950s.) To me, it is this element of speculation and wonder that truly makes *Forbidden Planet* one of the greatest science fiction films of all time.

A narrator sets the story in the 23rd century where the men on the ship the *C57D* are on their way to Altair via hyperdrive to see if there are any survivors from the *Bellerophon* mission sent there twenty years previously. The ship is commanded by Commander J. J. Adams (Leslie Nielsen), who uses the ship's doctor, Doc Ostrow (Warren

Stevens), as a sounding board for his ideas. While many have criticized the film's "booze and broads" humor in which the enlisted men, especially the comic relief Cook (Earl Holliman), are only after a good time, this immediately creates in the audience's minds an association with military movies, where commanding and noble leaders look after the affairs of their hedonistic enlisted men. However far this is set in the future, these are people such as we.

Onboard the spaceship C57D with Commander J. J. Adams (Leslie Nielsen with mike) and Chief Quinn (Richard Anderson, right) in *Forbidden Planet*, the fifties science fiction classic that helped inspire *Star Trek*.

One of the things that makes *Forbidden Planet* so effective is the way it piles wonder on wonder, each time elevating the film to a new level. While the ship and its crew are pretty amazing and far-out, the people aboard are comfortably familiar types. They are warned away from the planet by Morbius (Walter Pidgeon), but insist on landing anyway. They are greeted by a technological marvel, Robby the Robot (voice by Marvin Miller), who greets them in English and via transport escorts them to a futuristic house filled with even more marvels, not the least of which is Morbius' beautiful daughter Altaira (Anne Francis in a delightfully coy performance).

Morbius explains that the reason for his warning was that all the fellow members of his expedition were torn limb from limb by a monstrous, unseen force, which mysteriously never bothered Morbius nor his family, except in "nightmares of those times. And yet, always in my mind I seem to feel the creature lurking somewhere close at hand, sly and irresistible, and only waiting to be reinvoked for murder." (Amusingly, Morbius speaks more truthfully than he knows.) Adams wants to take Morbius and his daughter back home, but Morbius resists and Adams decides to radio back to Earth for instructions.

That night the ship is attacked by the mysterious entity, which leaves enormous pawprints in the sand. Adams heads back to Morbius' house to get more information and encounters Altaira swimming in the nude (though a white dress is clearly visible on Francis as she leaves the water). The virginal Alta is very intelligent, but she lacks any experience with men other than her father. She is attracted to Adams, flirting with him and making a coy reference to her knowledge of biology, and apparently does not understand why he is so upset about the influence she has on his crew and himself.

Altaira is initially shown cavorting with her pets, which include a deer and a tiger. In the film's rough cut, Ostrow likens her relationship with these wild animals to the myth of the unicorn. Now that she has fraternized with the spacemen, her former pet tiger attempts to jump her and has to be vaporized by Adams' blaster.

Wanting answers to the mysteries of Morbius, like how a philologist could build a robot beyond the future Earth's science, Adams and Ostrow invade the privacy of Morbius' study. There they are greeted by even more amazing revelations. The planet was once home to an extremely advanced alien race known as the Krel, and Morbius takes the men on a tour of the technology that once powered their civilization. By utilizing a "brain booster," Morbius has been able to translate some of their knowledge and shows that he has the power to create a three-dimensional image of his daughter on a table.

The film constantly invites the audience to awe and wonder. One of my favorite aspects of the film is that we are never shown what the Krel looked like, but are given hints in the form of their oddly shaped doorways and a stairway with a smooth middle apparently designed to accommodate a dragging tail, something never explicitly commented on. *Forbidden Planet* sketches out interesting possibilities and lets the audience's imagination fill in some of the blanks, unlike some pedantic pictures that fear audiences will be bored or confused if everything is not thoroughly spelled out.

Morbius reveals that the Krel were working on power without instrumentality, and that at the pinnacle of their civilization, they were mysteriously wiped out in a single night, but he has no idea how or why.

The monster resumes its homicidal attacks on the ship, and in the outline of the blaster beams, we get an outline

George (Rod Taylor), the time traveler of George Pal's *The Time Machine*, sits in his Victorian barber chair temporal vehicle and prepares to witness the wonders of the future.

of its shrieking form (it resembles the Leo the Lion logo standing on two legs and roaring). Suddenly, it simply disappears as Morbius awakens with the power gauges glowing brightly behind him.

Adams and Ostrow decide that one of them will have to get back to the lab and try the Krels' brain booster. While Adams talks with Altaira, Ostrow sneaks off and is carried back by Robby. Ostrow has boosted his I.Q. beyond Morbius', but has fatally wounded himself in the process, though not before he can divulge his flash of insight. Finally the pieces of the puzzle begin to fit together. The Krel had forgotten about the powerful desires of the subconscious, and their new technology created anything they gave thought to, so all their hidden murderous desires were suddenly given actual form.

Morbius' only companion for the past twenty years has been his daughter, and now that visiting Earthmen are proposing to take her away, he refuses to relinquish her and his subconscious has been taking the form of a monster that attacks the crew. Altaira suddenly chooses Adams over her father, which prompts the monster from the Id to attack Morbius' house, burning through its protective shields by drawing on the energy of the Krel. Morbius orders Robby to stop the beast, but the robot has a prohibition against harming human beings, and understanding that it must hurt Morbius to do so, short-circuits instead.

The trio flee to the Krel laboratory where the monster starts melting the massive doors at the entrance in an effort to punish Morbius' errant daughter for aligning herself with Adams. Finally, Morbius recognizes the truth and confronts the invisible beast, rejecting it and giving it up. Fatally wounded by the confrontation, Morbius gives Adams his blessing to take his daughter with him and asks Adams to throw a self-destruct switch which will destroy the Krels' machinery forever. In the coda, Adams and Altaira watch the destruction of the planet as Adams notes, "A million years from now, the human race will have crawled up to where the Krel stood in their great moment of triumph and tragedy. And your father's name will shine again like a beacon in the galaxy. It's true, it will remind us that we are, after all, not God."

Forbidden Planet is an unforgettable piece of eye candy with plentiful action, excitement, and speculation. When a preview was shown of a rough cut of the film, the audience responded so well that it was ordered shipped as is, leaving a few rough edges. (The few scenes that had been trimmed are available on the Criterion laserdisc version.) While one of the most enjoyable science fiction epics ever made, *Forbidden Planet* was not a financial success, though less than a decade later *Star Trek* would follow its formula of a gallant captain and his crew of contemporary people aboard a spaceship exploring the cosmos.

The film did spawn a semi-sequel of sorts, a cutely crafted kids' film directed by Herbert Hoffman called *The Invisible Boy*, also written by Hume and produced by Nayfack, in which Robby the Robot (once again voiced by Miller) has apparently been sent back in time and disassembled by the military. A brilliant scientist's (Philip Abbott) ordinary son (Richard Eyer) is hypnotized by his father's computer and given the knowledge to get Robby working again. Robby proves an ideal playmate except that the evil computer has other intentions. However, Robby's basic decency overcomes the computer's counterprogramming and saves the day.

Despite numerous discussions, there has yet to be a remake of *Forbidden Planet*, though most of the other famous science fiction films of the fifties have now been remade in one form or another. Perhaps it is just as well that people's memories of this glorious fifties gem have not been tampered with. It remains a delight, particularly on the widescreen.

When asked by writer Steve Wiater in *SF Movieland* why Pal chose to keep *The Time Machine's* (1960) Victorian setting rather than updating it as he had with *War of the Worlds,* producer-director George Pal responded, "In *Time Machine,* the main character didn't work because he was such a Victorian thinker. The main reason was, you would have to prove the time machine really works. But if you start the film at the turn of the century, and show this machine working up to the present, then you believe it. And I liked the style of that Victorian type of machine, instead of the streamlined, computerized model."

H. G. Wells' son Frank offered Pal an inexpensive option on *The Time Machine* after the release of Haskin's *War of the Worlds.* It was Pal's intention to make the movie at Paramount, which professed itself to be uninterested in the idea. Nevertheless, Pal secretly commissioned David Duncan to write the screenplay.

After Pal made *tom thumb* for MGM, Matthew Raymond, head of MGM's British studio, asked Pal what other projects he might be interested in, and Pal offered up *The Time Machine.* Pal even approached Paul Scofield about playing the part of the unnamed time traveler. (Pal also considered Michael Rennie and James Mason for the role.)

However, Sol Siegel insisted that the film be made in Hollywood where Pal was able to both produce and direct the film for slightly under its $850,000 budget. Director of photography Paul C. Vogel gives the film a rich and colorful look, while art directors George W. Davis and William Ferrari provided the film's memorable designs.

Ferrari created the memorable time machine itself around the concept of a Victorian barber's chair, which he attached to a sled-like design. The look suggests a potentate's sedan chair. A big, spinning, radarlike wheel was affixed to the back to indicate movement. The machine's controls are personalized as being manufactured by H. George Wells (Herbert George Wells never cared for his first name, and this suggests that the story's George is actually Wells himself). The actual prop has subsequently appeared in Joe Dante's *Gremlins* and in one of filmmaker Mike Jitlov's inventive shorts.

The story begins with four companions, David Filby (Alan Young), Dr. Hillyer (Sebastian Cabot), Anthony Bridewell (Tom Helmore), and Walter Kemp (Whit Bissell), waiting at the clock-filled home of their belated friend George (Rod Taylor) who suddenly staggers in dirty and bruised. It then flashes back to the week before, New Year's Eve, 1899, when the same men had gathered together at the same house. George announces that he has invented a time machine, and demonstrates using a miniature model. His friends think it is a joke except for Filby, who lags behind for a time to talk and attempts to persuade him to destroy his mechanism before it destroys him. George truthfully promises he won't walk out the door that night and Filby heads for home.

His friends' skepticism and belief that he should apply his talents to help fight the Boer War only increases George's resolve to try out his machine. He is disgusted by the constant war and killing of his own time and hopes to find a better world in the future. He experimentally inches ever further forward in time. (George's progress is measured by the sun streaking across the sky and changes in fashion on the dressmaker's dummy in the shop window across the street.)

However the future does not display the peace he seeks. George stops in 1917 to discover his house in disrepair and through Filby's son James (also Young) learns that the world is once again at war. He pauses in 1940 to find himself in the middle of a London blitz. Next stop is 1966 where he encounters a very elderly James Filby who recognizes him just before the civil defense sirens sound and an atomic blast buries the quickly retreating George and his machine in lava (created out of oatmeal dyed red, which really began to stink after a time in the studio).

As the centuries swiftly pass, the rock is eventually eroded away, and George finally and abruptly stops in the year A.D. 802,701. George's inertia causes him to fall head over heels, and he looks up to see a great sphinx-like statue above him. The world is lush and green, a veritable Garden of Eden, populated by the young blond-haired Eloi, none of whom look older than their twenties. "So this is man's future," George marvels, "to bask in the sunlight, bathe in the clear streams and eat the fruits of Earth with all knowledge of work and hardship forgotten." However, his idyll is shattered when the Eloi ignore the screams of Weena (Yvette Mimieux), a pretty drowning damsel who has swum out too far.

George is bewildered at the Elois' indifference and dashes off into the water to save the girl. Grateful, Weena comes to him and starts to fill him in on the Eloi's stagnant and decaying culture. George is dismayed to discover that the library is full of unread books which crumble in his hands, tacitly telling the tale. "What have you done?" demands an outraged George. "Thousands of years of building and rebuilding, creating and recreating, so that you can let it crumble to dust. A million yesterdays of sensitive men dying for their dreams. For what? So you can swim and dance and play."

As evening comes, George returns to his craft only to find it has been dragged away inside the sphinx. Weena tries to warn him that it is not safe to be out after dark when she is attacked by a loathsome creature she calls a Morlock (a goofy-looking greenish blue-skinned yeti in makeup by William Tuttle).

Weena takes him to a museum where a set of talking

The sinister, half-alien children of Wolf Rilla's chilling *Village of the Damned* with leader David (Martin Stephens in light sweater) in front.

rings fills him in on the Elois' missing history, explaining that an atomic war had almost wiped out the human race. George surmises that the Eloi represent what is left of the surface dwellers while those who descended into their bomb shelters became the Morlocks.

Weena takes him outside where from openings in the ground he hears the throbbing of machinery underground. Suddenly a siren sounds, and the Eloi obediently head towards the shelters where their numbers are culled by the cannibalistic Morlocks who secretly keep their tables supplied with food. Weena is taken inside the sphinx before George can prevent her, so he discovers an alternate means to invade the Morlocks' underground home. There he uses a torch to drive off the Elois' captors and inspires the timid Eloi to fight their way back to the surface.

Discovering his time machine inside the sphinx, George hops aboard and escapes through time, watching a downed Morlock rapidly decay (built by Wah Chang and animated by David Pal, George's son) before returning to the year 1900. This is the adventure that he relates to his friends, who except for Filby remain skeptical. George resolves to rebuild civilization by teaching the Eloi, and removing three books from his library, returns once more to his machine and disappears. Filby leaves the audience pondering what three books they would take if they had to restart a world, giving the audience something to think about as they leave the theater thoroughly entertained.

The tone of the ending is certainly radically different from Wells' pessimistic view of the future. The film also eschews Wells' conception of the Eloi as the pathetic, frail descendents of the pampered elite upper classes with the Morlocks representing the base descendents of the laboring classes. Instead, Pal offers the exciting challenge of building a better future.

Pal intended to film a sequel to *The Time Machine*, and even co-wrote a novel based on his ideas for the film, but it was not to be. The film won an Academy Award for best special effects and proved to be quite successful and popular at the box office. Pal is well beloved for producing many fine science fiction and fantasy films, and it is appropriate that one of his very best was one he directed himself as well. Though some of his productions are flawed by flashes of crudeness, *The Time Machine* remains tasteful and charming throughout, a splendid achievement from a dedicated filmmaker who managed to make some very memorable and miraculous imaginative movies on very tight and limited budgets.

Village of the Damned (1960), directed by Wolf Rilla, based on the novel *The Midwich Cuckoos* by John Wyndham, and featuring an intelligent screenplay by Rilla, Sterling Silliphant, and producer Ronald Kinnock who uses the name George Barclay, is another very successful adaptation of a science fiction novel. Wyndham's book explores the idea of unseen aliens knocking out the inhabitants of a small town and impregnating all the women with rapidly growing, superintelligent offspring which are raised by humans, much like cuckoos leave their eggs in other birds' nests so that other birds will hatch them and raise the offspring as their own.

Here children, normally a symbol of innocence, take on a malign significance that is only slowly realized. Rilla does a brilliant job of creating a mood of mystery and foreboding as physicist Gordon Zellaby (George Sanders, who appeared briefly as Indifference in *The Man Who Could Work Miracles*) learns that the English town of Midwich has been suddenly cut off from the outside world and that anybody who approaches the town's outskirts mysteriously passes out. The army cordons off the area and soon discovers that gas masks fail to prevent the effect. Even pilots in planes flying over the town are affected.

Then as strangely as it began, everyone wakes up, only to learn later that every woman of child-bearing age is pregnant, even the virginal ones. Many of the cuckolded men gather in the pub, exchange sullen looks, and hope that the unborn children will not survive. Others are simply suspicious given the circumstances.

At first Zellaby is overjoyed at the news his wife Anthea (Barbara Shelley) is expecting, but his joy turns to consternation as their son David (Martin Stephens), as well as the other children, prove to possess unusual powers. In one chilling moment, Anthea finds herself forced to put her hand in boiling water after offering David a bottle that was too hot. Although Anthea senses a lack of warmth in her son, she continues to react to him as a mother with love and affection.

The children all possess telepathic powers, and what one masters (such as an intricate puzzle box containing a treat), they all immediately learn, indicating that they have a gestalt mind. They all have strikingly blond hair, high foreheads, and dark eyes, which disturbingly glow white when they unleash their power (achieved by Rilla by simply overlaying a negative image of their irises). They are also extraordinarily self-possessed and mature for their age. (Rilla expertly guides their performances so that they truly seem unearthly, making them move in a stifled, controlled, and unchildlike manner.)

Gordon gets together with his brother-in-law, Major Alan Bernard (Michael Gwynne), and learns that similar children have been born elsewhere around the world. An Eskimo group killed the inexplicably golden-haired kids while they were young, and later an entire Russian village containing alien children is atom bombed out of existence. While others are fearful of what the children might do, Gordon defends the children, sees them as a potential source of knowledge, and asks for time to study them. He becomes their tutor.

However, he is the one who learns that the children will destroy anyone who threatens their survival, using their mental powers to cause others to injure or kill themselves. At last, he decides that they are too dangerous to live and brings a time bomb into the schoolroom. He concentrates his mental energies on the image of a brick wall, which the children work to break down, but they are too late. The bomb explodes killing Zellaby and his twelve charges.

Rilla carefully builds excitement and unease, and keeps the film moving at a spritely pace. Much of the photography has a *cinéma vérité* feel about it, adding to the picture's realism. The movie was made for a mere £82,000 (roughly $225,000 at the time) and the entire project was wrapped in six weeks. *Village of the Damned* is engrossing, intelligent science fiction that relies on a fascinating story rather than elaborate effects.

The success of the film inspired two loosely similar follow-ups. In the first, *Children of the Damned*, directed by Anton M. Leader, the six alien children are no longer uniformly similar in features but represent a kind of outer space United Nations intent on doing good, but are threatened by the military and encounter prejudice. Despite being well-meaning, it is not nearly as effective as the original. Connected only by title and children is Joseph Losey's *The Damned* (aka *These Are the Damned*), based on H. L. Lawrence's novel *Children of the Light*, in which normal Earth children are revealed to have been altered and exposed to lethal amounts of radiation as part of a scientist's experiment to create human beings immune to the effects of atomic radiation.

A pair of uninformed but well-meaning adults (MacDonald Carey and Shirley Ann Field) attempt to free the children from the cave they live in only to be poisoned by exposure to their radioactivity. *The Damned* is decidedly downbeat film that somehow falls short of the emotionally powerful connection it seeks. John Carpenter made a remake of the Rilla original that, while it featured superior special effects, contained trite dialogue and characters that fell far short of Rilla's definitive version.

A guilty pleasure that has two excellent versions is *Little Shop of Horrors* (directed by Roger Corman in 1960 and by Frank Oz in 1986). Though both films are at the opposite ends of the budget extreme, they have basically the same characters and tell basically the same story, though the Oz version does have the added benefit of slick photography, elaborate mechanical effects, and several highly tuneful Howard Ashman and Alan Mencken songs (winners of the Academy Award for their work on Disney's *Little Mermaid, Beauty and the Beast*, and *Aladdin*).

The story comes from beatnik artist and Corman scribe Charles B. Griffith, who decided to write a science fictional farce with elements of Yiddish theater. The basic story becomes a variation on the Faust legend, as an amazing talking plant (created by radiation in the Corman version and from falling from outer space in the Oz version), packs customers into Mushnik's flower shops and promises a lifetime of success for Seymour Krelboin (Jonathan Haze or Rick Moranis) provided he murder people to sate the vegetable's voracious appetite.

For the Corman version, the majority of the film was shot television style in two days on simple sets, with screenwriter Griffith shooting location second-unit material on Los Angeles' skid row. Its protagonist is a schlemiel stuck with living on skid row, which the *Dragnet*-like narration informs us, "The tragedies are deeper, the ecstasies are wilder, and the crime rate is consistently higher than anywhere else." When Seymour nurtures the plant by dripping blood

Lule Conway's elaborate, cable-controlled Audrey II for Frank Oz's multi-million dollar remake of *Little Shop of Horrors*. Oz's original downbeat ending was briefly released on a rare, pulled from circulation DVD.

on it from his own fingers, it grows into something unusual which attracts customers to Gravis Mushnik's (Mel Welles) usually empty shop. (Mushnik claims the plant has a scientific name, "but who can denounce it?")

Two girls from Cucamonga High have been given the task of buying flowers for their float in the Rose Parade, and because of Audrey, Jr. (voice by Charles Griffith), as Seymour names the plant after his colleague Audrey (Jackie Joseph) whom he hopes to date, the girls take their order to Mushnik's. Griffith decided to include a plant-eating man, Byrson Fouch (Dick Miller), in his story of a man-eating plant, who promises to give the small, out-of-the-way shop his recommendation (this comic character is dropped from the Oz version).

In the Oz version, Audrey (Ellen Greene) sings a song expressing her longing for a tacky, little tract house right out of *Better Homes and Gardens* magazine complete with a chain link fence and TV dinners. However, Audrey does not see much hope and so settles for Orin Scrivello (Steve Martin), a sadistic dentist who abuses her. Seymour, who stands by and does nothing when Scrivello accidentally gases himself to death, is the savior she turns to. In turn, her paen to him, "Suddenly Seymour," resurrects his flagging spirit in the end, as he realizes that he has something valuable to offer Audrey besides the plant, his friendship and sweet understanding.

In both versions, the plant's victims are mostly overly masculinized figures who employ phallic objects to take advantage of more passive characters. There is a sadistic dentist who enjoys inflicting pain on his patients with a drill in both versions (he's Dr. Farb in Corman's). The 1960 version features a burglar (Griffith) with a gun who comes to rob the now successful store but is fooled by Seymour into reaching into the plant's maw. In the 1986 version, it is Mushnik (Vincent Gardenia) who threatens Seymour with a gun before being devoured by the plant, here dubbed Audrey II, easier to rhyme than junior would have been. The 1960 version also adds a prostitute who dubs herself Lenora Clyde, who, though not masculine, uses her sexuality as a weapon (she also uses a banana to slip Seymour up only to be killed by Seymour's casually tossed rock).

By contrast, the plant, despite its masculine voice, suggests an engulfing femininity, suggestive of *vagina dentata* if you will. As a plant, it is connected to Mother Earth and is the receiver of masculine attention. Devouring females also appear in the Corman version in the form of Seymour's hypochondriac mother, Mrs. Winifred Krelboin, who is obsessed with health and yet stays in bed all day and demands "soothing" syrup. (She insists that Seymour not get married until he buys her an iron lung.) Women are also associated with death in the form of Mrs. Shiva (named for the Jewish practice of sitting for the dead), who constantly comes into the shop to buy flowers for the many funerals that she attends.

One of the funniest characters in the plot is that of the overly feminized masochistic dental patient Wilbur Force (Jack Nicholson in 1960) or Arthur Denton (Bill Murray in 1986). They solve the problem of pain by trying to get off on it, sending out orgasmic screams as the non-anesthetized drilling begins. (Denton pleads lustily for a long, slow root canal.)

Despite the killings, Seymour remains the perpetual innocent and is a sympathetic figure. He is clumsy and inept, but good-hearted. His demise is foreshadowed in the Corman version with a visual pun (several times in the story, he keeps kicking a bucket). He looks for guidance from people who only tend to look out for themselves. With realization finally dawning on him, in the Corman version he crawls inside the plant in an attempt to kill it.

The next day, the plant is healthy, but Seymour is nowhere to be found until the last bloom opens, revealing Seymour's face along with the other victims, then dramatically and pathetically, Seymour's bloom drops, indicating his defeat and death.

The Oz version originally was to have ended with the deaths of both Seymour and Audrey capped by shots of the plants taking over the world and with a warning that "whatever they offer you / Don't feed the plants!" However, preview audiences hated seeing the protagonists die, and so a new ending was filmed in which Audrey is almost eaten but then rescued by Seymour, who kills the plant, marries the girl, and moves into a suburban home "somewhere that's green" (with an Audrey-like plant growing in the garden). (Oz still hopes that audiences will see his original ending on a future special edition release of the film.) Both versions warn viewers to consider the Faustian price of fame and fortune.

One of the most unusual science fiction films ever made, partially because its visual style suggests book engravings come to life, is Czech filmmaker Karel Zeman's *The Fabulous World of Jules Verne* (1961), released in Europe in 1958, where it won the Grand Prix at the Brussels Film Festival. Zeman's film is based on Verne's story *Face au Drapeau* (aka *Face the Flag; An Invention of Destruction*), with elements of *20,000 Leagues Under the Sea* thrown in for good measure. (The Czech title for the film is *Vynález Zkázy*.)

Zeman's heavily stylized film tries to present the world as a member of Verne's original audience would have found it. The hero, Simon Hart (Lubor Tokos) notes the marvels of his age: steamships, balloons propelled by bicycles that turn propellers, submarines, airplanes, airships, steam automobile, even motion pictures. Hart is a great believer in man, the rational animal, taming his world, and has been assisting Prof. Roche (Arnost Navratil) in discovering a new explosive.

Hart and Roche wind up kidnapped by pirates intent on having their explosive for themselves. They are taken aboard a submarine and introduced to Count Artigas (Miloslav Holub), who has grown rich by plundering the treasures of sunken vessels. The Count orders the ship to wreck a passing merchantman by ramming it. The pirates then raid the sinking ship, using a conveyor belt to transport their swag back to the submarine, as well as rescue a fair damsel, Jana (Jana Zatloukalova).

The Count brings his prisoners to his secret castle hidden inside an island volcano and puts the professor to work developing this new weapon while Hart spends his time in an isolated shack. The Count tries to persuade Hart to assist, but Hart only uses the Count's materials to send up balloons containing messages revealing their whereabouts. (Fortunately for the hero, the message is received.)

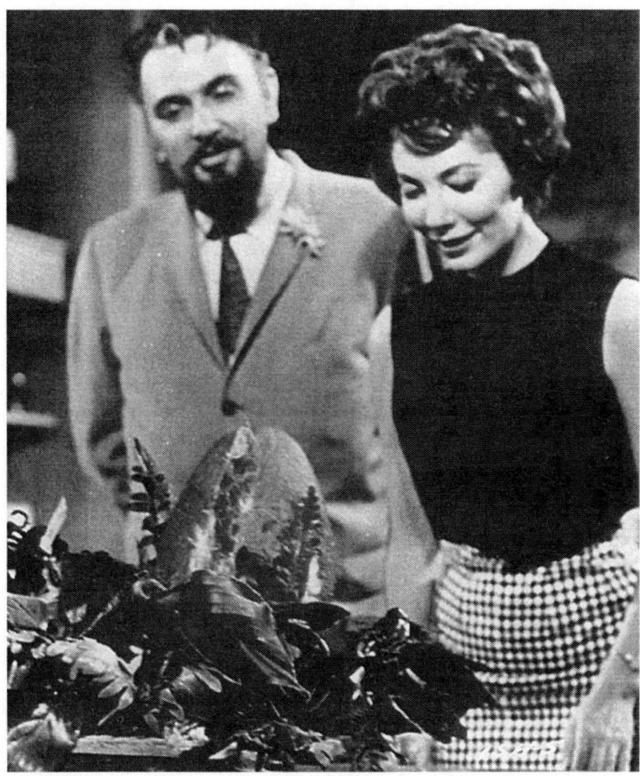

Mel Welles and Jackie Joseph admire the people-eating plant Audrey Jr. in Corman's $27,000 production *Little Shop of Horrors*.

Hart asks to assist repairing an undersea cable, and this request is granted. While under the water with two other men, Hart is attacked by a giant squid who kills his compatriots but Hart wounds it and it retreats in a cloud of ink. Hart hides from a search party and tries to reach the undersea entrance before his air gives out. A funky little submarine that paddles through the water with four flipper-like fins (the most charming of the film's many devices) arrives just in time to rescue Hart.

Artigas' submarine spots the minisub and ruthlessly rams it, leaving Hart to swim ashore and climb to Jana's window in the castle where she makes him wait dangling by his fingertips as she finishes dressing. (Jana is presented very whimsically throughout.)

Roche has finished his explosive, and the Count hopes to load it into his cannon to destroy the approaching fleet of ships. Roche is horrified to learn that his new invention is being used as a weapon of war, so he sabotages the Count's plans by pulling the bomb free from the cannon and letting it tumble down an incline right into the midst of Artigas and his piratical crew, blowing them to Kingdom Come. The film carries a not-so-veiled message about the dangers of allowing scientists absolute freedom to invent

Karel Zeman creates a look like moving steel engravings for the often overlooked gem *The Fabulous World of Jules Verne.*

without considering the consequences, though it is by no means anti-science or anti-technology.

While the basic plot is nothing special, the fabulous and surreal style that Zeman employs to tell this tale combining live action and animation is. Once seen, it is never forgotten. His approach comes closest to reproducing the wonder and enchantment of the short films of George Méliès and encompasses a wide array of filmmaking techniques. *The Fabulous World of Jules Verne* is the best of the Zeman fantasies that I have been able to see (which include Zeman's versions of *Baron Munchausen, On the Comet,* and *Sinbad the Sailor*) and is a cinematic treasure trove of wonders and marvels.

An often overlooked science fiction film is Frank Tashlin's comedy *The Glass Bottom Boat* (1966), perhaps because the science fictional aspect is fairly incidental to the rest of the film. The film is an above-average Doris Day comedy with Day playing Jennifer Nelson, an attractive widow and public relations specialist moonlighting as a mermaid on Catalina Island for Axel Nordstrom (Arthur Godfrey) and his glass bottom boat, who gets her suit reeled in by Bruce Templeton (Rod Taylor), a handsome fisherman. (Naturally, he is the one who becomes hooked.) It is hate at first sight for her, however, until she learns that Templeton is a top-notch scientist at the space center where she has been hired. Templeton has developed an anti-gravity room and a breakthrough device known only as G.I.S.M.O.

Templeton tries to woo the catch of his life, and soon becomes more interested in the demure Miss Day. However, just when she falls hook, line, and sinker for him, her activities soon create suspicion that she might be a Russian spy intent on leaking G.I.S.M.O.'s secrets. (Nelson has a habit of calling her own phone in order to exercise her shut-in dog, which rouses concern within the CIA.) Dom DeLuise plays Julius Pritter, the inept spy hired to keep her under surveillance, though he more often than not puts the wrong foot forward.

An agent plants incriminating documents in Nelson's purse and then tries to retrieve them. She resourcefully escapes through a window and leads her pursuer on a merry chase that brings the film to a successful climax including a romantic clinch with Templeton.

Among the other science fictional gadgets that Tashlin, a former cartoon director who turned to writing and directing cartoony live action comedies such as *Will Success Spoil Rock Hunter, The Girl Can't Help It,* and some of the better Martin and Lewis features, works into his story include a remote control speedboat, little robotic vacuums that clean up around Taylor's futuristic house, and a minuscule microphone in a cocktail olive. Other cast members include Paul Lynde, John McGiver, Dick Martin, Edward Andrews and Ellen Corby. The feature is slapstick, but avoids the stigma of being too silly.

François Truffaut elected to adapt Ray Bradbury's science fiction classic *Fahrenheit 451* (1967) as early as 1962 when he purchased the rights, only to sell them to American producer Lewis Allen in expectation of making the movie in America. Because of contractual requirements, it became Truffaut's first color film (photographed by Nicolas Roeg) as well as his only English language film shot in England. (Truffaut's command of English was and would remain quite limited. Nevertheless, he accepted the challenge and co-wrote the script with Jean-Louis Richard.)

Truffaut evokes a future where print is forbidden from the very opening of the title, where the credits are spoken over a montage of television aerials. Set in a fascistic future where black-suited firemen set fire to books in a feeble attempt to stamp out unhappiness, the main character, Montag (Oskar Werner) is asked by a neighbor, Clarisse (Julie Christie), if he ever reads the books he burns, and he becomes obsessed with doing so.

The title refers to the temperature at which paper begins to burn and that number itself is imprinted on the firemen's arm patches. Clarisse asks if firemen have always burned books, but the banning of books must have been relatively recent, otherwise why would the firemen be able to find so many to burn and why would some members of the society, Montag included, still have the residual ability to read? Clarisse is a new schoolteacher, but we never get a glimpse inside her classroom and her teaching techniques, attempting to make education enjoyable, meet with disapproval from the rest of the staff so that she is soon fired from her job and alienated from her charges who seem to flee at the sight of her.

Montag's wife Linda (also Christie) has a closer relationship with their wall-sized television set than she does with him, living her life on pills while waiting for her programs. When she talks to him, she usually keeps her eyes on the television set which almost continually blares in the background, bringing in the typical Truffaut theme of difficulties in communication. When Montag asks her how they met, she cannot remember, her viewing habits have sapped her memory.

Montag is potentially up for a promotion, and his Captain (Cyril Cusack) understands the temptations that Montag is going through, giving the disagreements contained within the various books' pages as a rationale for the burning. He knows too much about the books not to have read them himself when he was younger and condemns them passionately (which makes him almost the only passionate figure in this society who is not a rebel). He notes truthfully that literature can "make people want to be something else," and that those who read will naturally feel superior to those who have not, subverting his society's sense of equality. He constantly addresses Montag in third person, keeping an emotional distance at all times, though Cusack's performance hints at an underlying fondness for Montag. (We also learn later that the Captain's wife was also a book lover.)

The society shown is narcissistic and self-involved, conveyed by images of a girl kissing her reflection in a train window, an older woman caressing the fur around her neck, and Linda stroking her own body rather than Montag's. When the firemen check for hidden books in a park, one taps a man who is revealed to be embracing himself. Linda only reaches out to Montag after she has passed out from pills and Montag has called an ambulance, whose attendants handle 50 similar cases a day. They simply pump her stomach, leaving her hungry in more ways than one when she awakens the next morning.

Truffaut cannily uses copies of books that have created controversy or been the subject of attacks, from *Don Quixote* to Henry Miller. He also keeps the dialogue to a minimum, letting his visuals tell the tale. Also contributing to the film's sense of excitement is Bernard Herrmann's frenetic scoring that conveys the urgency of the firemen's mission.

Montag is morbidly fascinated when his team comes across a woman who would rather burn with her books than live. He soon finds books stimulating companions, and is caught up in the idea that behind each book is a man (similar to the way that Truffaut learned that behind each film was a man). He undergoes an almost religious conversion, underscored by his being dressed in a white bathrobe that suggests a monk's robe. He abandons the company of his wife for the company of books, causing her to betray him. When the Captain takes him to his own house to burn his books, Montag sets fire to the bed, indicating his immolation of his old identity and his ties to Linda. He also coldbloodly burns his enemy, the Captain, to a cinder, demonstrating none of the Captain's compassion.

Montag follows Clarissa's instructions and discovers the "Book People," who have committed the texts of various works of literature to memory (emphasizing the importance of text as the repository for memory), while emphasizing their role as outsiders who may one day make a valued contribution to a new and better society. This community is not seen as a cohesive whole, but as a group of eccentric characters who recite to themselves (and to others when asked), each lost in their own little world.

Truffaut's images of them in a snowfall in the woods are both very beautiful and underscore the sense of something still and trapped that could emerge once the repressive society has thawed in its attitudes and experiences a re-birth or renaissance, while at the same time echoing the lines a young boy commits to memory regarding the death of his father in a snowfall (echoing the importance of passing knowledge from one generation to another). In another sense, these Book People are clockwork oranges who are mechanically involved in storing knowledge through the future's dark ages and are as bereft of life as the television watching drones.

As a cute in-joke, one of the teens announces that he is the *Martian Chronicles*, Bradbury's most famous and most poetic science fiction book. Significantly, the difference between Clarissa and Linda is underscored by Clarissa becoming *Les Mémoires de St.-Simon*. Montag elects to become Poe's *Tales of Mystery and the Imagination,* whose stories are often about men trapped in the throes of an idea. When Montag escapes, he does not find freedom but rather enslaves himself to the task of committing Poe to memory to preserve him.

According to his journals, Truffaut's plan of action in *Fahrenheit 451* was "a question of treating a fantastic story in an offhand way, making the fantastic seem banal and the banal seem odd." He also credits Hitchcock for inspiring his approach to the story, and that is evident as Montag becomes a typical Hitchcockian hero who assumes a new identity and becomes both hunter and hunted.

Fahrenheit 451 does have a few problems, however. Truffaut and Werner quarreled over their interpretations of Montag, with Werner preferring to emphasize the character's fascistic qualities while Truffaut wanted to stress his vulnerability and receptivity to language. Also, Montag learns to read much too quickly in a society where the newspapers are comics without words and file folders contain nothing but pictures and numbers. Despite the grand-

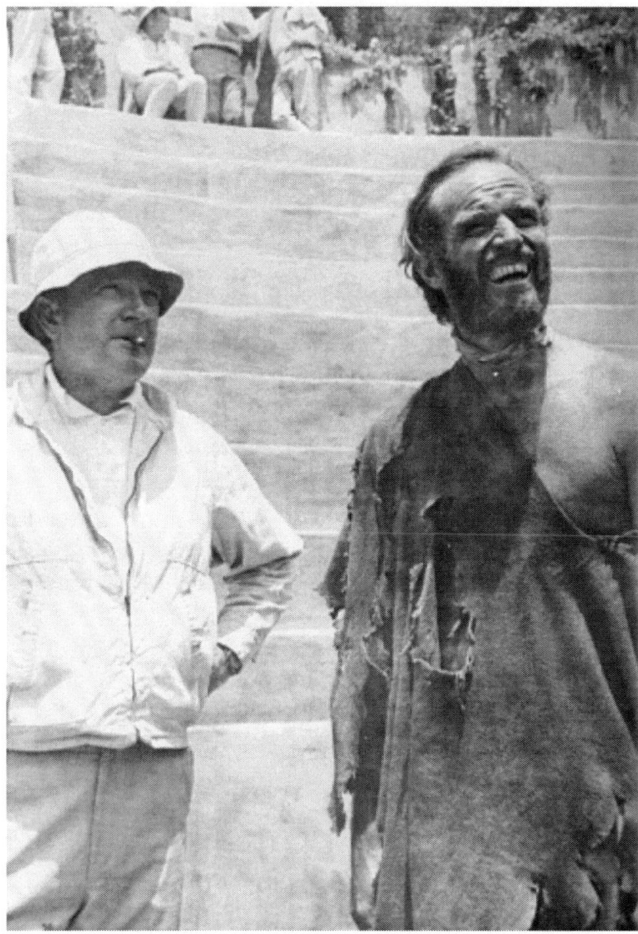

Director Franklin J. Schaffner confers with Charlton Heston in *Planet of the Apes*.

standing of having Christie play two different characters, both parts are shallowly written and Christie does not find much she can do with them.

Nevertheless, it is a beautifully expressive film that finds a visual poetry at the end to match the verbal poetics of Bradbury's prose. Actor-director Mel Gibson has expressed an interest for some time in remaking the film. One hopes that he will be able to do at least as fine a job as Truffaut has done.

Another classic SF film is Hammer's version of Kneale's *Quatermass and the Pit* (U.S. title: *Five Million Years to Earth*; 1967), one of the greatest science fiction epics of all time. This time Andrew Keir, the studio's sometime Cushing substitute, assayed the role of Quatermass, caught between the stiffbacked officiousness of Col. Breen (Julian Glover) and warm intelligence of Dr. Matthew Roney (James Donald), who is ably assisted by the ever attractive Barbara Shelley.

Kneale provided his own condensation of his own story, quite satisfactorily, and production designer Bernard Robinson once more demonstrates his flair for getting the most out of minimal budget. The spaceship uncovered is far more attractive and sleek than the bell-like design from the teleseries, the Hobbs End Underground station is very convincing, and the wrecked up London street of the finale maintains its believability on limited resources. (The only thing that fails to come off are the videos of mental images of the Martian "locusts" in action which clearly look like the stick puppet figures they are.)

Director Roy Ward Baker does a brilliant job of generating ever increasing mystery and tension while getting effective performances from all the principals that help to quickly characterize each one.

The Bowie Films effects are also quite impressive and effective from objects flying around a telekinetic man, shaking tiles off the walls, to the ground undulating alarmingly under an affected individual. The spaceship gives off an unearthly glow with suggestions of capillaries to convey the idea that the ship itself is a living presence, something which Quatermass himself hints at when he notes the apparent lack of instrumentality. The arthropod aliens suggest both locusts and the "horned one" (aka the devil), especially in the giant energy image that Roney helps to destroy by simply grounding it.

What really fascinates is how Kneale builds his seemingly simple mystery into an elaborate line of speculation that ties in the origins of man, evil, and prejudice in the world, coming up with the idea that the Earth might have been colonized by proxy a few years before von Däniken helped to popularize the notion. By genetically altering man's simian ancestors to have greater intelligence, these aliens set the course for man's evolution. Unfortunately, these insect-like beings have regular purges of those beings who do not conform to the norm and so inculcate mankind with a hereditary fear and hatred of all who are "different" in some way.

Kneale's script also suggests that telekinesis and other psi powers are latent potentials in all human beings, instilled for the purpose of purging nonconformists from the hive, and that images of evil beings common to cultures all over the world are racial memories of these beings, and that ghosts and poltergeists are simply phenomena that have been improperly observed and are in fact vestiges of clairvoyant faculties "gifted" to us by alien ancestors.

Interestingly, the true hero of the piece turns out not to be Quatermass but Dr. Roney, the excited archaeologist who also represents restrained intelligence. Even the brilliant Prof. Quatermass succumbs to the power of the mob at one point, is pulled out and brought back to normal by Roney, who reminds him that it is an act of will not to give into hysteria and that intelligence can defeat conditioned programming, and he ultimately sacrifices his life to save mankind.

Kneale has brilliantly provided explanations and rationalizations for things considered unexplainable; however, under all the intellectual play, he has a serious point to make: that it is only through knowledge of ourselves that we can destroy the ancient, destructive urges within us, which grow more deadly with the expansion of our knowledge and technology. War crises, witch hunts, race riots and purges are all things we must guard against, our heritage of hatred, and if such things cannot be controlled, then the "Martians" will have created a second dead planet — Earth.

Naturally, this Baker-Kneale collaboration has proven influential, and its influence is particularly noticeable in Dan O'Bannon and Don Jakoby's adaptation of Colin Wilson's *Space Vampires—Lifeforce*, where aliens prove to be the source of all vampire legends, and Stephen King's novel *Tommyknockers*, directed by John Power, which was turned into a TV miniseries and provided readers with a big dose of *déjà vu* with its story of someone unearthing a spaceship and falling under its malign influence.

One of the smartest spy satires with a science fiction overlay is *The President's Analyst* (1967) directed by Theodore J. Flicker. Flicker mercilessly spoofs the rivalry between intelligence agencies, Cold War tensions, the rising dominance of corporations, gun rights and other forms of social paranoia, the counterculture's feelgood ineffectiveness, and other ripe targets. The main plot concerns how analyst Dr. Sidney Schaefer (James Coburn) has been privy to the President's deepest secrets and therefore becomes the target of competing intelligence agencies (the Central Enquiries Agency and the Federal Board of Regulations as well as several foreign agents) who hope to undercover the President's secrets and weaknesses from him.

Schaefer is forced to spend his time fleeing from one uncomfortable situation after another, never knowing whom to trust. For example, Schaefer joins an acid rock band (fronted by Barry McGuire, whose original music has unfortunately been replaced on the film's video release), but soon discovers that "dropping out" is no solution. Along the way, aspects of American society are satirized, culminating in one of the cleverest denouements in American films, whereby a vast conspiracy to implant a communications device into every person's brain at birth is revealed to be the machination of the phone company (and eerily predicts the growth of cellular phone technology). Flicker adds a brilliant final twist that undercuts the ostensibly happy ending, in which he reveals that the film we have been watching is being shown to a group of individuals — all of whom have phone cords extending from their heels as the corporate man is shown to be little more than an automaton himself. Unfortunately, Flicker's career stalled and this genuinely inventive spoof has become largely forgotten.

Bernard Quatermass (Andrew Keir, left) and Roney (James Donald) recover one of the locust-like Martians from their capsule in Roy Ward Baker's *Quatermass and the Pit.*

It took five years for producer Arthur P. Jacobs to find a studio willing to produce an adaptation of Pierre Boulle's *Planet of the Apes* (1968), in which a vacationing, spacegoing couple retrieve a bottle containing a message from Ulysse Merou, a journalist, who traveled to Betelgeuse where he lands on a planet run by apes. The book satirizes elements of western life. In a final twist, it is revealed that the couple who find the message are chimpanzees.

Jacobs acquired the property and hired *Twilight Zone's* Rod Serling to draft a screenplay. Serling felt himself written out and so his script was polished and revised by Michael Wilson (*A Place in the Sun, Bridge on the River Kwai*), who also wrote to reduce the budget. (A final polish was done by John T. Kelley.) Serling's draft was quite different with Serling envisioning a detailed simian society with "an altogether 20th century technology, a New York city in which the doors were lower and wider. All living was adjusted to the size of the anthropoid." Serling's apes lived in a modern civilization, operated flying machines rather than traveling on horseback, and transformed the

The moment when George Taylor (Heston) discovers his fellow crewmember has been lobotomized at the orders of Dr. Zaius (Maurice Evans, right). Note the otherworldly ape architecture that helps give *The Planet of the Apes* a unique look and feel.

talking human, Thomas, into a media superstar. The concept of finding the Statue of Liberty that provided the film with its memorable ending was Serling's.

To help sell the film, Jacobs hired a team of conceptual artists to create sketches of key images in the film. Warner Bros. expressed some interest in the project with Blake Edwards directing until they estimated that Serling's script would cost over $10 million to produce, an astronomical sum in the 1960s.

Jacobs got the script to Charlton Heston, who was looking for something different, and Heston suggested Franklin J. Schaffner, who had directed him in *The War Lord*, as a possible director. Schaffner agreed to become involved, but Richard Zanuck at 20th Century–Fox was skeptical about the filmmakers coming up with a credible makeup that would not leave audiences laughing.

Edward G. Robinson agreed to play Zaius, the simian Minister of Science, and played the character in a makeup test opposite Heston. Former *Outer Limits* makeup man John Chambers was hired to create the ape makeup, eventually winning a special Academy Award for his work. Only $5,000 was allocated to film the test, and Robinson wore only a very simplified version of Chambers' final makeup. (Also appearing in the scene as apes are James Brolin and Linda Harrison, the latter, actually Zanuck's mistress at the time, would eventually be cast as Nova, Taylor's love interest.) The test was shown to the Board of Directors and proved that no one laughed at the concept, but the aging Robinson found the makeup ordeal exhausting and dropped out of the project.

Because of the success of Richard Fleischer's *Fantastic Voyage*, 20th Century–Fox decided to approve the film provided that the budget was no more than $5 million. A full 20% of the budget went to provide the large number of makeups needed. Make-up artists, wigmakers, and sculptors all worked together to design the apes. Three basic styles were created by Chambers: gorillas, orangutans, and chimpanzees. The ape society is depicted as highly stratified with gorillas being hunters and guards, orangutans as leaders and lawgivers, and chimpanzees as intellectuals and scientists. (Heston noted wryly that during lunch breaks, the apes segregated themselves by species, showing some habits are hard to break.)

The first make-up attempts took as much as six hours to apply and stiffened the actors' faces so that it was hard for them to register emotions. The make-up was redesigned to allow full facial movement, took three or four hours to apply, and one to two hours to remove. For scenes that called for hundreds of apes, a huge make-up staff was recruited.

Maurice Evans stepped into the role of Zaius with James Whitmore and James Daly recruited to play the President of the Assembly and Deputy Minister of Justice respectively. More importantly, Roddy McDowall and Kim Hunter were hired to play the sympathetic chimpanzees, Cornelius and Zira. They quickly learned that to keep the ape make-ups from looking like masks, they would have to move their facial muscles and mug constantly. With their affectionate glances and evident senses of humor, the pair quickly steal the movie by being by far the most appealing characters.

The make-ups posed other problems as well. Though they could take lunch breaks while fully made up, they had to use mirrors to direct their forks past their false mandibles and into their mouths. The film was shot in late spring and early summer, and several of the performers including Kim Hunter ended up suffering from heat exhaustion several times.

Planet of the Apes was filmed on locations from George Stevens' *The Greatest Story Ever Told*— Page, Arizona, and Lake Powell, Utah. It took a full week to film the astronauts' trek across the desert Forbidden Zone to the lush lands of the apes, shooting mostly in remote and almost inaccessible locations with the crew carrying equipment in by foot or by mule team. (Cameraman Leon Shamroy called it the roughest filming experience he'd ever had.) Schaffner uses this material to establish an eerie mood and a desolate location that seems utterly barren and forboding. Jerry Goldsmith's unusual and atonal score helps make the lifeless landscape seem even more daunting.

To reduce costs, the exterior of the astronauts' spaceship is never seen in flight. The captain of the group, Taylor (Heston), is established as a misanthrope who seeks to escape the 20th century, while Dodge (Jeff Burton) is a seeker of knowledge and Landon (Robert Gunner) a gloryhound who wants to be considered a hero back home even though everyone he knows will be dead before he lands at their distant destination. The mission is to travel 320 light years while in suspended animation, and the group arrives in the year A.D. 3978, losing their female companion because of a leak in her suspended animation container.

Art director William J. Creber created the primitive and otherworldly ape city, based on sites in Turkey and Tunisia as well as Spanish architect Antonio Gaudi's undulating forms, out of polyurethane foam and cement at the Fox Ranch. The result created an impression of something fresh, innovative, and new, an alien approach to architecture, though the structures did pose some lighting problems and so Schaffner and Shamroy were forced to employ a flat lighting style.

Planet of the Apes skirts a number of issues, including the fact that the apes all conveniently speak English, how it is possible for Taylor to have traveled so far and yet end up back where he started, what exactly is the nature of his mission, etc. There are also a few cornball touches that mar the movie, from lines like "human see, human do" to the infamous "hear no evil, see no evil, speak no evil" grouping of orangutans on the ape council. (Heston reveals that this was a last minute inspiration that was expected to be cut after the preview process, but the audience responded so positively that it ended up being retained.) Still Schaffner has created an engaging adventure film that makes good use of widescreen compositions.

Taylor is often overbearing and arrogant, certainly not the most likable of protagonists, but this makes his humiliation at the hands of the apes all the more powerful as he is deprived of speech (by a shot in the throat), his clothes, his status as he is variously caged, stoned, beaten and put on trial. Once he does communicate, the apes do not believe his tale of being an astronaut from another planet and consider him a mutant.

Even worse, Dr. Zaius considers him highly inconvenient. Head of both the scientific and religious communities, Zaius rejects the search for truth in favor of supporting his scriptures. His religious teachings warn him to beware of the beast man, and he sees in Taylor all the aggressive tendencies of mankind, and so conspires to castrate him to prevent his breeding, followed by "experimental brain surgery" (i.e., a lobotomy, the fate of Landon). When Cornelius uncovers evidence of a pre-simian civilization that includes talking human dolls, Zaius simply orders the evidence destroyed and orders Cornelius and his mate to be tried for heresy. His loyalty is to the established order rather than scientific truth.

And yet some of Zaius' criticisms hold water, as he notes of man that he "alone among God's primates ... kills for sport, or lust, or greed. Yes, he will murder his brother to possess his brother's land." This is followed by the scene echoing Shelley's "Ozymandias" where Taylor looks upon the Statue of Liberty (a matte painting added to the scenery at Point Dume, California) and despairs. A new freedom of expression allows Taylor to rage, "We finally did it. You maniacs! Damn you. Goddamn you all to hell." Mankind's aggression and nuclear foolhardiness are revealed as the causes of the race's secondary status in this topsy-turvy world of mute, beastial humans and civilized simians.

Planet of the Apes became one of the first science fiction films to be extensively marketed with a plethora of tie-in merchandise. It finished $800,000 over budget, but that was forgotten when it raked in a very healthy profit at the box office. It also garnered Academy Award nominations for Jerry Goldsmith's score and for Morton Haack's costume design.

Heston agreed to appear in the sequel if he would be killed off in the first scene. Instead, Zanuck got him to agree to appear at the very beginning and very end of *Beneath the Planet of the Apes*, directed by Ted Post, which follows a fellow astronaut played by James Franciscus only to have Heston's Taylor reappear at the end and set off a doomsday device that destroys the planet. A clever sequel followed, Don Taylor's amusing *Escape From the Planet of the Apes*, with Cornelius and Zira using Taylor's retrieved ship just before the explosion to travel back to 1971. Two less interesting Apes films followed, *Conquest of the Planet of the Apes* and *Battle for the Planet of the Apes*, followed in turn by both a live action and an animated television series.

In 1993, 20th Century–Fox decided to remake *Planet of the Apes*, giving a go-ahead to producers Don Murphy, Jane Hamsler, and Oliver Stone, who hired Terry Hayes (*The Road Warrior*) to write the script. Hayes came up with the story of a geneticist who time-travels back to an ape-dominant society. Stone chose Arnold Schwarzenegger to star, but Fox expected a comedy and Hayes wrote a very *Terminator*-type script. Schwarzenegger approved Philip Noyce (*Patriot Games*) to be the director, and the film was greenlighted with a $100 million budget, but Fox was still unhappy with the script. Noyce committed to do *The Saint*, which featured a science fiction subplot dealing with cold fusion, instead. Fox brought in Chris Columbus (writer of *Gremlins*) who rewrote the script with Sam Hamm (*Batman*). Meanwhile, Schwarzenegger left to make *Eraser* with Chuck Russell. James Cameron was offered the chance to produce, but he ended up passing. Columbus ended up leaving to do the disastrous *Jingle All the Way* with Schwarzenegger. Fox offered the film to new golden boy Roland Emmerich, who declined, and then Fox tried to offer it to Peter Jackson (*Bad Taste*) who was tied up with a planned *King Kong* remake for Universal, leaving the project in limbo.

Charly (1968) became the first science fiction film to have its lead win the Best Actor Oscar since Fredric March's performance in *Dr. Jekyll and Mr. Hyde*. The movie originated in Daniel Keyes' classic science fiction short story "Flowers for Algernon," which Keyes later expanded into a novel. Rights to the story were purchased for adaptation by The Theatre Guild, who adapted it for their show *The U.S. Steel Hour*, calling it "The Two Worlds of Charly Gordon." The lead was actor Cliff Robertson, who had been the lead of the John Frankenheimer television version of "Days of Wine and Roses," and who had lost the chance to play the lead in the film version made with Jack Lemmon in the role.

Not wanting another great opportunity to pass him by, Robertson purchased the film rights to Keyes' story and tried to interest a studio, which found stories involving mental retardation an anathema. Recalls Robertson, "I argued, of course, that any movie's success depends on the ingredients that go into it. I felt the public needed something like this, to come out of the closet, if you will, as far as recognizing that mental retardation was an illness, it was something that respected no economic, social or ethnic groups of people, it struck everywhere....

"I continued to hang in there. And I finally got a call from the late Selig Seligsman, God rest his soul, who was a big honcho with ABC Paramount — which is not to be confused with ABC Television. He said, 'Cliff, I may be crazy and I know you've been getting a lot of turndowns on this for a long time. But you know, my wife, Muriel, has been kind of telling me I really ought to do that film with Cliff Robertson. So I'm going on a hunch, but you're going to have to give up a lot.' And I said, 'Listen, I'll give up anything except my relatives — or maybe even a few of those.'"

Robertson approached director Ralph Nelson a couple of years before, and Nelson expressed a definite interest in the project. They decided to hire Sterling Silliphant to do the adaptation, with Robertson writing a few of his own scenes. Originally, Anne Heywood was to have been the lead, but during rehearsals before the start of filming, it was apparent that she was not quite right, and Claire Bloom was called up in London and substituted at the last minute.

Robertson dominates as Charly Gordon, a 30-year-old bakery assistant with an IQ of 68 who is recruited by doctors Nemur (Leon Janey) and Straus (Lilia Skala) to undergo an experimental procedure to enhance his intelligence. The experiment was previously tried out on a white mouse named Algernon, and Charly is impressed with how Algernon is able to run a maze faster than he can solve it. Robertson's initial performance relies a bit too much on eye-rolling and lip-smacking to convey idiocy, but gains in power and subtlety as the story progresses and ends up being quite affecting.

After undergoing the procedure, Charly's intelligence develops beyond all expectation. Once the butt of his co-workers' jokes, Charly's new mental abilities scare and alienate his associates, leaving him more alone. He gravitates towards his teacher, Alice Kinian (Bloom), though their affair ends up being romanticized by Nelson rather than psychologically explored. (Another misstep of Nelson's involves Charly going through a rebellious phase, complete with motorcycle gang and Lester-like fragmented images.) Gordon also gives glib responses to the ills of the age, spouting clichés about dehumanization, alienation, computerization, and bad TV programs.

Charly (Academy Award–winner Cliff Robertson) and his teacher (Claire Bloom) in Ralph Nelson's *Charly*. Robertson has recently been trying to finance a sequel.

However, the film achieves its full emotional power once the now genius Gordon learns that the effect is only temporary and that he will soon return to retardation. He works desperately to stave off the inevitable, but to no avail. *Charly* raises a number of interesting philosophical issues that regrettably are not more fully explored in the film. Like Forrest Gump, Charly's goodheartedness is seen as more important than intelligence, and the bright Charly observes that society is more interested in controlling individuals than letting them grow. The ending is both tragic and moving, one of the most powerful in any science fiction film.

Director Ralph Nelson later returned to the science fiction genre with the inferior *Embryo* (aka *Created to Kill*) in which Dr. Paul Holliston (Rock Hudson) is a scientist who uses a growth hormone to rapidly develop first a dog and then a woman, Victoria (Barbara Carrera), outside the womb with tragic results. Victoria's fetus was rescued from the womb of her teen mother who committed suicide, and while the hormone gives her rapid growth and intelligence, it also gives her homicidal tendencies.

Loosely based on the novel by Charles Eric Maine and directed by Alan Cooke, *The Mind of Mr. Soames* (1970) explores a similar concept to *Charly*'s and is one of the most overlooked science fiction films of all time. It is a character study that explores the interesting concept of what would happen if an unformed man woke to find himself in an adult body. What does adulthood mean? Of what does education consist? How would he have to adjust?

The main character, John Soames (Terence Stamp) has been in a coma since his birth thirty years before, his body maintained at a low temperature, fed intravenously, and massaged to prevent muscular atrophy, when Dr. Maitland (Nigel Davenport) figures out how to revive him. Surgeon Dr. Michael Bergen (Robert Vaughn) is flown in to perform the operation that will awaken him, though he notes that in his slumber, Soames looks "happier than most conscious people."

The revival of Soames has attracted media interest, leading to a circus-like atmosphere surrounding the event. Thomas Fleming (Christian Roberts) plans to film a documentary about Soames, and Bergen decides to check on his patient's progress. He foresees problems in Maitland's proposed training program for Soames, calling it too inflexible. Not "inflexible," counters Maitland, but "controlled."

Actually, we know that children who do not develop their visual acuity at an early age are never able to comprehend visual input, and there are similar difficulties with language, as per the famous Kaspar Hauser case of a child raised by animals. Soames finds the input his newly awakened self receives confusing and bewildering, and is soon terrified by the entourage of media people. "Welcome to the human race, John Soames," whispers Bergen. "Go ahead and let it out. It was never easy being born."

Initially, Soames is little more than a young child in a man's body, playing with his educational toys. Dr. Maitland works at encouraging and even forcing him to take his first steps and walk. Cooke makes the sequence more effective by the use of a subjective camera that puts the audience in Soames' place, allowing us to sense his uncertainty. However, Soames frustrates Maitland in his attempts to recover a brightly colored ball, with Bergen being far more effective by gently asking for the ball rather than trying to take it.

At first Soames is receptive to Maitland's educational

techniques, but he grows increasingly restive and frustrated. In one scene, we can see that Maitland is beginning to be bored by teaching, and yet he scolds John when he likewise loses interest. Maitland asserts that Soames cannot have his own way in everything, while ironically insisting on having his own way himself. Soames becomes aware that he is little more than a prisoner and grows listless. Bergen warns that Maitland is going "to teach Mr. Soames to death." He sees a need for Soames to play and learn at his own pace.

As an experiment, Bergen lets Soames wander freely about the grounds, and John delights in his newfound freedom, exulting in the sights of flowers, fresh water, and a frog. Maitland is appalled, thinking that Bergen has taken an unnecessary risk and bans further contact between them.

When Maitland tells Soames that he must wait six months before he will be allowed on his own, Soames appears to understand but quickly uses his first opportunity to escape. Soames is a fish out of water, unable to understand that he cannot take sandwiches without paying for them, that though he wants to play ball with smaller boys, he will not be accepted.

Stealing a coat because he is cold, Soames heedlessly runs into the road and is struck by a car. The Bannermans (Scott Forbes and Judy Parfitt) decide to take care of him themselves, not wishing to involve the police or take him to a hospital. Jenny Bannerman reads a newspaper account of Soames and resolves to take him back to the institute, but John steals some money from her coat, buys a train ticket, and runs away on board a train. There he encounters a nervous young woman who mistakes his friendly overtures for an attack, screams, and pulls the emergency cord. Soames jumps the train, hurting his ankle in the act.

Soames finds himself trapped in a barn with police surrounding it. Bergen volunteers to go in and talk with him, persuading him to come out but telling him that he must make the decision himself. Bergen leaves and John follows, pitchfork in hand, when he is panicked by the lights of the TV cameras, causing him to throw the pitchfork which embeds itself in Bergen's arm. Overcome by emotion, John collapses in tears and in desperate need, reaches out to Allen (Donal Donnelly), who at last understands and comforts him by taking his hand.

Cooke achieves some subtle and sensitive performances from his actors. Davenport portrays Dr. Maitland as cold, rational, and ambitious. He is more interested in the attention the experiment will net him than in the subject of his experiment. He always addresses Soames by his last name, unlike Bergen or Allen, who call him John. This is contrasted by Vaughn's Bergen, who is warm and easygoing, perceives that John is a person and not just a publicity opportunity and seems genuinely concerned for his welfare.

Slaughterhouse Five (1972) is one of the most perfectly realized novel into film adaptations, thanks to Stephen Geller's brilliant and faithful script from Kurt Vonnegut's novel and to George Roy Hill's sensitive direction. Hill initially turned down the project because he felt it would be too difficult to do successfully until he read Geller's script.

The main character, Billy Pilgrim (Michael Sacks), was a chaplin's assistant in World War II who, like Vonnegut himself, survived the bombing of Dresden, a non-military attack that cost the lives of 130,000 people (more than Hiroshima), mostly civilians, for the sole purpose of further discouraging the Germans, who were already losing the war.

At the start of the narrative, Pilgrim has become unstuck in time, and we follow his progress along three different time lines as sounds or images from one time period remind him of something that occurred in another. The three timelines are Billy's war experiences where he is befriended by father-figure Edgar Derby (Eugene Roche) and earns the undying enmity of the sadistic and paranoid Paul Lazzaro (Ron Leibman); Billy's present in 1965 Ilium, Illinois, where he is a successful optometrist who undergoes shock therapy after surviving a plane crash; and finally the future where Billy is able to live out a male sexual fantasy living with sexy film star Montana Wildhack (Valerie Perrine) as the guest of an invisible alien race known as the Tralfamadorians (voice by director Hill). Cinematographer Mirislov Ondricek gives each of these timelines a different look: dark and rich hues from Dresden, bright and sunny for the scenes set in the present, and artificial lighting for the future.

Vonnegut's Tralfamadorians have discovered that the universe's timeline is fixed and predetermined, and so counsel Billy to accept his fate and concentrate on the good times. Billy even becomes aware of his own death one day at the hands of the vengeful Lazzaro, who blamed Billy for the death of his friend Roland Weary after the Germans confiscated Weary's boots. Sacks does an incredible job of conveying Pilgrim's unfailing sweetness along with his indestructible innocence and passivity. Billy doesn't make things happen, but rather constantly falls into situations: yanked into a snowbank at the beginning, pushed into the snow by the Nazis, falling face-first into his soup, sinking to the bottom of the pool his father has thrown him into as a child, falling out of the sky when his plane crashes, collapsing after giving the Tralfamadorian greeting, "Hello, farewell," at the end of his lecture on time when Lazzaro shoots him.

Billy's single self-initiated act comes when a German officer (Friedrich Ledebur) asks the American prisoners to elect their own leader and Lazzaro nominates himself. Billy, fearing the worst, nominated Edgar and patterns himself after Derby, as indicated by his giving the exact same speech when Billy is chosen president of the Lion's Club back home. However, Derby is a nice guy, but not a leader, and in one of the film's most heavily ironic scenes, is shot for placing a small china dancer like one he had back home that has miraculously survived the bombing of Dresden into his pocket. One of the German soldiers who orders the sudden shooting looks at the doll and simply tosses it away, so that Derby dies for an object that those who killed him consider worthless.

The devastation caused by Dresden and Derby's death leaves Billy alienated and isolated in his suburban life back home. He regresses into an infantile state, expressing most of his love and devotion to his dog rather than his overweight but highly affectionate wife Valencia (Sharon Gans), the boss's daughter. In another of the film's most blackly comic scenes, the wife destroys her prized brand-new Cadillac and unwittingly kills herself with carbon monoxide poisoning by her frantic effort to reach Billy at the hospital, plowing past all obstacles in her path. (She shows far more passion for him than he ever does for her.)

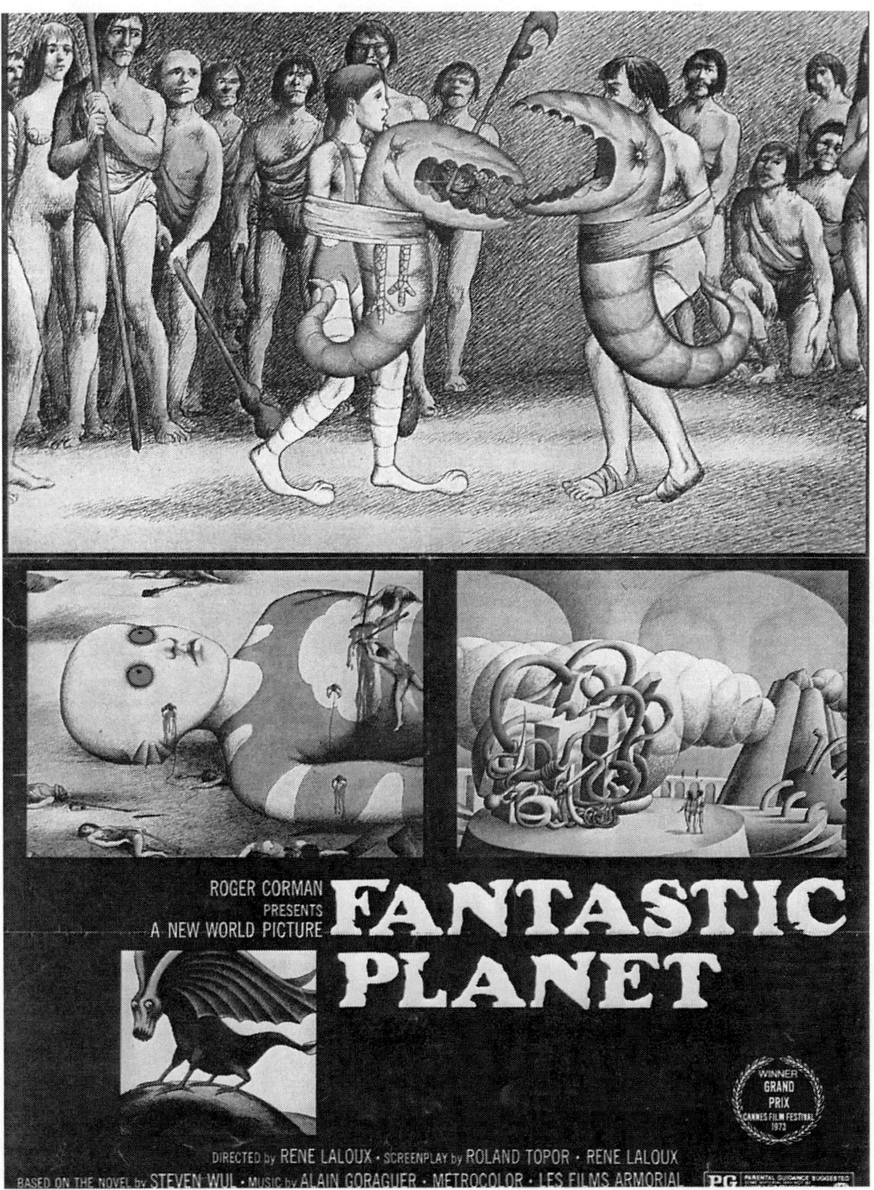

Poster for René Laloux's *Fantastic Planet*, filmed in an arresting paper cut-out technique and featuring a fully realized alien world.

The film features exquisite editing from Dede Allen, who cuts scenes to echo Billy's feeling of incompleteness, and it also has a truly ethereal score comprising Bach piano pieces sensitively performed by Glenn Gould. Comic and tragic, cartoony and highly realistic, *Slaughterhouse Five* deserves to be considered among the best science fiction films ever made, and even pleased Vonnegut himself, who was to have appeared in it as Colonel Rumsford, a historical revisionist who poo-poos the importance of Dresden, only to have his scenes reshot with another actor (John Dehner). Few science fiction films are as dramatic and as deeply humanistic as this one.

French animator René Laloux created the film *La Planète Sauvage*, better known in this country as *Fantastic Planet* (1973). Based on the novel *Oms en Serie* by Stefan Wul, designed and scripted by Roland Topor (*The Tenant*), Laloux's film creates one of the most alien and imaginative environments ever committed to celluloid, a science fictional feast for the eyes. Laloux's film combines two different animation techniques, cell animation and moving hinged paper drawings, that give the film an especially detailed look.

Set on the planet Ygam, a race of humans, the Oms (based on the French word *l'homme* for man) are puny compared to the blue giants who rule the planet, the Draags, who play with the wild Oms for sport and even keep them as pets. Especially jarring is the opening scene where a woman is fleeing and a huge blue hand drops into frame to block her progress. The story follows the adventure of a baby Om whose mother is killed and who is adopted by a young female

Draag, Tiwa. While Tiwa is absorbing her lessons, the knowledge is passed on to the Om she pets in her lap.

The Om grows up, flees Tiwa, and syncs up with other Oms, though not before being tested in a bizarre ritual where fierce toothsome creatures are strapped onto him and become his opponent for a fight. With his knowledge of the Draags, the Om leads a revolt and discovers the secrets of Draag reproduction.

Adding to the alien atmosphere are a plethora of odd alien creatures of imaginative design that we glimpse in the background of the story, including ball-like animals that spin clothes for the Oms and an anteater type creature that sucks them up into its snout. Also exquisitely detailed are the bizarre and desolate landscapes of this alien world with appropriate flora. Like the best science fiction films, it takes us to a fully realized alternate world. Adding to its strangeness is the unusual musical score by Alain Gorageur, which is unconventionally orchestrated.

Fantastic Planet provides an atmospheric and menacing setting for a science fictional adventure. Unfortunately, the story ends rather abruptly, with the narration promising a peaceful future for the Oms and the Draags. Laloux strangely described the film as "an epic, surrealistic Western." Laloux made two earlier films with Topor, *Les Temps Morts* (1964) and *Les Escargots* (1965) as well as a subsequent science fictional effort with an English-language script by Isaac Asimov called *Light Years* (1988) that proves tedious, lacking the fascination of *Fantastic Planet.*

What can one say about *Flesh Gordon* (1974)? Bill Warren in *Cinefantastique* called it the "best mounted turd" he'd ever seen. Indeed, much of the acting seems quite bad, except that it so accurately reflects the terrible thesping in the original Buster Crabbe serials. What started out as a softcore science fiction spoof gradually became more and more elaborate as an incipient group of talented special effects men (including David Allen, Jim Danforth, Greg Jein, Doug Beswick, Rick Baker, Dennis Muren, and others) kept adding to the film's beauty and look, far eclipsing the awkward work by the film's live action directors, Howard Ziehm and Michael Benveniste.

The film begins with Professor Gordon (Hollywood veteran John Hoyt) explaining how the world came to be plunged into carnal chaos. A sex beam directed at Earth inflames human libidos so that people everywhere are shedding their clothes and having sex with the closest partners at hand. A sex beam hits the Ford Tri-Motor plane containing Flesh Gordon (Jason Williams) and Dale Ardor (Suzanne Fields), who both parachute to safety and come into contact with Dr. Flexi Jerkoff (Joseph Hudgins), who while boasting that he was unaffected by the sex ray has built a very phallic rocketship.

Together, the trio blast off from Earth into the Moronisphere and head for the ray's origin, the planet Porno. There they encounter various menaces, including a Penisaurus (animated by Bill Hedge), meet the Emperor Wang (Bill Hunt, who also cowrote the screenplay with Mike Light), the Impotentate of the Planet Porno; raping robots with drill-like penises (created by Tom Scherman cleverly imitating the designs of Republic serials); Chief Nellie, hook-handed head of the militant Amazons, as well as the effeminate Prince Precious and his Merry Men.

Flesh Gordon features one of the most fluid stop-motion battles committed to film when Flesh fights the Beetle Man (animated by Danforth), and the climax of the film features the first talking stop motion animated monster, the great god Porno (animated by Robert Maine), who does a Kong imitation after picking Dale up in his paw. Some of the film's designs by Mike Minor are exquisite, especially the beautiful Swan ship of the evil queen, while other effects are deliberately done ineptly to ape the style of the serials.

Made for $700,000, of which $500,000 went to make the effects, *Flesh Gordon* quickly became a cult item, eventually turning a tidy profit. Two decades later a belated and badly made satirical sequel arrived, also directed by Ziehm, called *Flesh Gordon Meets the Cosmic Cheerleaders.* Its idea of satire is having Jerkoff think he can solve the world's problems by making women's breasts bigger, and its crude, scatalogical humor only serves to demonstrate how much better the admittedly sophomoric original was.

Harlan Ellison's Nebula Award-winning novella "A Boy and His Dog" provided the basis for actor L. Q. Jones' cult classic *A Boy and His Dog* (1975), which demonstrated how post-apocalyptic science fiction could be filmed on a limited budget. (It seems to me very likely that the film influenced George Miller's *Mad Max* movies.) Ellison wrote the story partially to parody the "boy and his dog" books of Albert Payson Terhune (the source of Blood nicknaming Vic "Albert") and partly as a screed against the mindless conformity of conservative middle America.

According to Ellison, he was offered a large amount of money by a major studio who wanted to make the tale into a feature, but Ellison rejected the offer when the man making it asked how they were going to animate the dog's mouth. (In Ellison's story, Blood is a telepathic dog who has befriended Vic, a rover who finds him food in return for which Blood sniffs out danger and women.)

L. Q. Jones was born Justice E. McQueen, but adopted the name of the first film role he played in *Battle Cry.* Best known for playing rednecks in the movies, he formed a partnership with Alvy Moore and the pair had begun making low budget films such as *The Devil's Bedroom, The Witchmaker*, and *The Brotherhood of Satan.* He convinced

Ellison to sell him the film rights to the story and write the screenplay. However, when it came to writing the script, Ellison developed writer's block about 14 pages into it, causing Jones to take up where he left off and finish the script, keeping close to the book for the most part.

In creating the setting, Jones seized upon that idea that a nuclear war could alter the rotation of the Earth on its axis, causing mountains of mud to engulf land masses. He decided to set the opening of the film on the ruins of what was once Phoenix, Arizona, which was shot on a dry lake bed 20 miles outside of Barstow, California where various kinds of industrial detritus was strewn about to create the post-holocaust environment. When the original director got cold feet, Jones took over that function as well.

A Boy and His Dog was shot in 27 days from April to May, 1973. A young Don Johnson was selected to play Vic with Susanne Benton cast as the manipulative Quilla June while Jason Robards, Alvy Moore, and Helene Winston were set to portray the Committee, leaders of the Downunder community of Topeka who select Vic as a potential breeder. All are good in the film, however, the best performance is turned in by Tiger, the *Brady Bunch* dog selected to play Blood (voiced by Tim McIntire, who also supplied the film's musical score) who was trained by Joe Hornak. Originally Ellison had hoped to do Blood's voice himself, but Jones vetoed his interpretation. Jones wanted Blood to be the most normal and likable character in the picture, smart-mouthed and funny, but not as cynical or bitter as Ellison's conception.

Jones makes the ugliness of this world apparent from the outset. Vic and Blood watch as a pack leaves a female victim behind. Seeing their chance, they go into a hole and find her bloody corpse. "Hell, they didn't have to cut her," Vic complains. "She could have been used two or three more times." Clearly, this is a vicious world which does not value women except as sex objects to be exploited and discarded. The group we see, Fellini (Ron Feinberg) and his gang, are scavengers, picking through the ruins of civilization to literally eke out a very meager existence. Vic simply steals from them.

The crux of the film is the relationship between Vic and Blood. They constantly threaten and harangue each other, which only serves to cover up their deep, underlying affection. Blood can read and teaches an ignorant Vic history; he supplies the brains while Vic supplies the brawn. Vic wants Blood to find women for him, and Blood wants Vic to satisfy his gnawing hunger. They each supply what the other needs and have meshed into a good team, with Blood's sometimes snide remarks goading Vic into doing what is right. Despite all that Blood has to offer (knowledge, companionship, wisdom, experience), he knows he needs Vic to survive.

That night they watch a stag reel at a makeshift movie theater when Blood smells a female dressed as a solo. Vic and Blood follow the scent to a bombed out YMCA where Vic espies Quilla June undressing. The discovery of Quilla June helps satisfy Vic's sexual urges, but it also alters his and Blood's relationship. At first Vic tells her, "You make one move off there and I'll shoot your leg out from under you. And you'll still get it, except you'll be without a leg." Vic is then surprised when she turns around and seduces him. He has never met a woman who actually wanted to have sex with him, and he is delighted by this new experience. (Blood's tired expression as they go at it again and the mattress starts shaking is hilarious.)

However, Quilla June proves a mean-spirited, manipulative little minx who is after power. She is later revealed to have been set out as bait for Vic and she lures him back to the underground city of Topeka, abandoning the now injured Blood. A lack of sunlight has caused the people of Topeka to become pale, which they obscure by adopting clown makeup as a fashion (and in turn it emphasizes that their façades are phony). This agrarian community is run by the repressive Committee, who executes people (euphemistically called sending them to the farm) for displaying "a lack of respect, wrong attitude, failure to obey authority." Vic at first is overjoyed to learn that living underground has rendered the society sterile and they need him to impregnate their women.

Quilla June can't wait to be a member of the Committee, but having carried out her part of the bargain, discovers that the Committee plans to artificially inseminate her with Vic's sperm and marry her off to a local farmboy. Jones' notion of Vic strapped to an artificial insemination machine while a preacher performs wedding ceremonies for the prospective mothers is an improvement over Ellison's original where the misogynistic Vic is allowed to have intercourse with the farmers' precious daughters, and it makes for a much funnier scene. Quilla retaliates by convincing some of her friends, including a boyfriend named Gary (Mike Rupert) to revolt against the tyranny of the Committee and by hiding a tire iron in a wedding bouquet, she is able to free Vic.

However, Quilla's plans go awry when most of her group are killed by Michael (Hal Baylor), an android with a smiling face dressed in farmer overalls who breaks the necks of transgressors. Having recovered his gun, Vic destroys the pursuing Michael as Lew sardonically comments, "Let's get another Michael out of the warehouse — (no smile this time")."

While Ellison praises Jones' adaptation overall, he objected to the misogyny that Jones added to the story (his Quilla June is far more innocent) and particularly objected to Jones giving Blood misogynistic comments to make since

The title creation of the science fiction/disaster film comedy *The Big Bus*, featuring an atomic powered superbus being sabotaged during its cross-country maiden voyage.

Blood is the one who knows better and is the true hero of the story. Supposedly, several of these comments were removed prior to the film's release by redubbing some lines, but Ellison still objects to the film's final line in which Blood treats Quilla June's death as a joke. (Vic returns to the surface with Quilla June and finds he has to choose between the survival of his dog or his girlfriend. The film ends with the boy and his dog walking off into the sunset with Blood remarking, "She had marvelous judgment — if not particularly good taste," and then laughing at his own horrendous pun.)

The film itself won a Hugo Award for Best Dramatic Presentation at the 1976 World Science Fiction Convention and has developed a small cult following. Ellison wrote another story about Vic and Blood called "Eggsucker," and was asked to write a pilot script for a possible television series that was never produced. He planned to combine the stories to create an *A Boy and His Dog* novel. Jones re-released the film theatrically with a slightly different prologue and a new ad campaign in 1982, and recorded a commentary track to accompany the Lumivision laserdisc release of the film. Not for the easily offended, it truly lives up to its promise to be a decidedly different tale of survival, as well as in terms of Blood and Vic's relationship a credible albeit unusual love story.

The Big Bus (1976), a gloriously silly send-up of disaster movies directed by James Frawley with an all-star cast, concerns the adventure of Cyclops, the world's first nuclear-powered bus. Iron Man (José Ferrer), an oil tycoon forced to spend his life in an iron lung, orders his brother (Stuart Margolin) to sabotage Cyclops, which is about to embark on its maiden non-stop voyage from New York to Denver. The resulting explosion cripples Cyclops' trained drivers and embeds a Saint Christopher medal into the heart of the bus' creator (Harold Gould), with his doctor (Larry Hagman) insisting that he not be moved because the slightest jar might kill him and attending to him and administering various tests on the spot through all kinds of weather.

The designer's daughter, Kitty (Stockard Channing), is forced to recruit her ex-beau and now blackballed bus driver Dan Torrance (Joseph Bologna) who in turn recruits the assistance of codriver "Shoulders" (John Beck), so-called because he has a medical problem that constantly results in his driving on the shoulders of the road when he is not suffering from a sudden blackout. (Sample gag: Beck backs Bologna in a barroom fight over Bologna's supposed cannibalism by breaking a carton of milk on the bar and threatening other patrons with the carton's jagged edge.)

All the clichés of the disaster genre are made to seem more ridiculous when applied to this atomic powered, two-tiered bus with its usual assortment of colorful stock characters including a priest (Rene Auberjonois) who doubts his faith, an old woman (Ruth Gordon) running away from home, a bickering but passionate couple (Richard Mulligan and Sally Kellerman) about to get a divorce, a man (Richard Schull) with six months to live, a disbarred veterinarian, a flamboyant Swansonesque fashion designer (Lynn Redgrave), an annoying lounge pianist (Michael Murphy), etc. Further conflict is generated at control where engineer Scotty (Ned Beatty) is more concerned with his frequently criticized and quitting first assistant Jack (Howard Hesseman) than with the safety of the bus's passengers.

The bus itself is a prize monstrosity, 106 feet long, 75 tons, 32 wheels, with a number of unusual features, including the ability to break the wind (resistance) at 90 miles per hour (portrayed as creating a hurricane-style gale in its wake), an automatic tire changer that jettisons and replaces a tire without slowing down, a self-cleaning mechanism, an indoor bowling alley and swimming pool, a Bicentennial dining room, and an Oriental piano lounge. In addition to the efforts of the mad bomber, the bus's brakes fail, an out-of-control pick-up smashes into it (à la *Airport 1975*), and it winds up teetering on the edge of a precipice.

Produced by Julia and Michael Phillips (*Close Encounters of the Third Kind*), this buoyant parody failed to attract much of an audience but quickly became a cult item for its sometimes inspired silliness. Today it is mostly overlooked and forgotten, but lovers of Irwin Allen and *Airport* movies are sure to get some guffaws from it.

In Walter Tevis' original novel of *The Man Who Fell to Earth* (1976), an alien comes to Earth for the purpose of saving the planet from reducing itself to an atomic rubble heap. However, in Nicolas Roeg's film of the book, from a screenplay by Paul Mayersberg, the alien is depicted as ever the outsider, coming from a planet dying from a lack of water, who loses sight of his goal and descends into alcoholism, self-pity, and loneliness by the story's end.

The alien (David Bowie) names himself Thomas Jerome Newton after being ejected from his spacecraft and landing in a lake, an abundance of water that mocks his planet's scarcity. He raises funds by selling rings that he brought with him to various jewelers and pawnshops and uses a British accent to make his alienness seem more readily understandable to the Americans he encounters. (In one of the odder moments of the film, he imagines an early American pioneer family can suddenly see his limousine driving down the road.)

The film keeps citing echoes of the tale of Icarus, showing both Breughel's painting and the Auden poem. The film creates a sense of a fall from grace for this otherworldly character, who could also be interpreted as an erratic if brilliant millionaire who hallucinates that he comes from a waterless world.

Newton then raises vast sums by exploiting his knowledge of alien technology to create nine innovations (including a very Polaroid-like camera) which he markets with the assistance of Oliver Farnsworth (Buck Henry), a patents lawyer. Together, they transform the entire communications industry and form a powerful and innovative conglomerate known as World Division Enterprises. He also recruits philandering chemistry professor Nathan Bryce (Rip Torn) to help create a fuel for a rocketship that could return him home.

He meets hotel clerk Mary Lou (Candy Clark) when she takes him up too fast in an elevator, which causes him to pass out (not your typical space traveler). Mary Lou's looks remind him of the wife he left back on his planet (also played by Clark), and following her tender care of him, the pair develop a relationship. Initially clearheaded, he drinks nothing but water until Mary Lou introduces him to alcohol. He then becomes depressed by the beauty and the

David Bowie's alien and his wife mysteriously cavorting in foam in this flashback from Nicolas Roeg's spellbinding *The Man Who Fell to Earth.*

violence he observes on Earth, losing himself in alcohol, sex, and television. Mary Lou becomes increasingly estranged from her lover, whom she can no longer get to communicate with her in any meaningful way.

One of the film's many ironies is that in commenting upon Newton's impact on him, Farnsworth says, "When Mr. Newton came to my apartment, my life went straight out the window." Later, Farnsworth is assassinated by some thugs who literally throw him out the window, as he too becomes a man who falls to Earth. Farnsworth serves as Newton's buffer to the world, running World Division Enterprises for enormous profit. However, the company's success endangers the livelihood of competitors, and although Farnsworth is aware of the dangers involved, he does nothing to prevent secret government operatives from killing him and his male lover.

The Man Who Fell to Earth also knowingly evokes the theme of voyeurism. Newton obsessively watches a multitude of television screens simultaneously as a way of picking up knowledge of Earth behavior. The images evoke other themes in the film: *Billy Budd* (innocence destroyed), *The Third Man* (a friendship betrayed), *The Sound Barrier* (difficulties of starflight), *Love in the Afternoon* (flirtations between ill-matched couples, people crossing paths across great distances). However, as Newton aptly notes, the "strange thing about television is that it doesn't tell you anything."

John Phillips also cannily arranges the film's musical

score to comment on the action, from *Afternoon*'s "Fascination" to Eddy Arnold singing, "Make the World Go Away (and Take It Off My Shoulders)" to "Blue Bayou," the Roy Orbison song emanating from an orb, one of WDE's improved sound systems. We also see Newton as feminized as he watches passively from a gynecological examination chair, and Mary Lou freaks out when in making love, Newton's body seems to melt onto hers and he finally reveals his alien nature.

Perception is important. Farnsworth has his glasses removed right before his death, screaming, "Those are my eyes." Newton has his contact lenses fused to his eyeballs by X-rays, becoming semi-blinded by government experimentation that renders him merely human. Bryce realizes that Newton is an alien when he covertly takes an X-ray picture of him that reveals no skeletal structure inside. Mary Lou bonds with Newton when they share sights (she glimpses through his microscope; Newton buys her a telescope), but comes to see that she has lost her Tommy as he finds himself adrift in a seemingly meaningless universe in which his closest associates can provide him with no stimulation or comfort.

Roeg quotes the cookie scene from Richard Lester's *Petulia* (which Roeg photographed), when Newton knocks a tray of cookies that Mary Lou bakes for him into the air, symbolizing his rejection of their now dull, stifling relationship. Newton has been corrupted by the hedonistic culture around him and winds up joining the liars, chauvinists and fools that he once decried. He remains a loner and cuts an album called *The Visitor* as a tribute to his wife, it ends up in the bargain bin, and he lives out his life a desolute drunkard.

When it came time to release the film in America, Roeg's 139 minute cut was trimmed to 117 minutes by American distributor Cinema 5 to avoid an X rating and to fit into a more profitable two-hour theatrical slot. Nearly half of the material in the last 20 minutes of the film was cut, obscuring the resolution and neutering Newton and Mary Lou's relationship.

Said producer Si Litvinoff:

> Nic likes to tell a story his way — you're talking about a man who used to carry around a copy of Voltaire and quote him all the time saying, "I am not interested in the triumph of the immediate." All these people are in a movie that is so different in every way from beginning to end. It's not the kind of movie you can judge by the same standards as other kinds of movies, and have it cut by somebody who's in a whole other world. That is the brutality of the way it was cut.

In the American version, three scenes were entirely deleted (two for sexual content) and numerous others were altered. When Auden's poem is shown, a voice-over reads the poem in the American version because it was believed that an audience would not take the time to read it. A scene where Bryce has sex with two young coeds who tell him, "You're not at all like my father" was dropped, though it helps establish the psychic link between Bryce and Newton. Also omitted were Bryce's narration about his professional and sexual obsessions, Mary Lou questioning Newton about why he called himself Sussex (the name change becomes unremarked upon in the American version), 20 seconds of the TV montage were trimmed, Newton's line about not being interested in photography, that his "interest is energy — the transference of energy," establishing what he hopes Bryce will help him accomplish for himself and his planet, is gone; Mary Lou losing all control and urinating in her underpants when she learns Newton as an alien is gone; Newton's betrayal is truncated, making his kidnapping seem arbitrary; his captors cutting off his nipple was deleted; 40 seconds were lost from Mary Lou wandering through Newton's holding area, losing the sense of a cultural labyrinth; a scene where Newton threatens Mary Lou with a gun, indicating that his wishes are still catered to, that his captivity is somewhat self-imposed, and demonstrating what he has learned about being human are gone along with a gunplay (with blanks) and sex romp set to the tune "Hello, Mary Lou," with the violent edge contrasting with their earlier tenderness was excised; Newton's escape was shorted by 25 seconds, losing its suggestion of self-captivity and the sense that Newton, now human, has been rendered harmless; and a scene in a liquor store showing Mary Lou changing brands and now married to Bryce is also gone.

The film had a profound impact on science fiction writer Philip K. Dick, who thought the film was speaking directly to him. Oddly enough, in 1987 it was remade as the pilot for a prospective series by director Robert J. Roth and starring Lewis Smith, Beverly D'Angelo, Wil Wheaton, Annie Potts, and Robert Picardo. Not surprisingly, the television version lacked the imagination and intelligence of Roeg's original and the pilot did not sell but was simply aired as yet another made-for-television movie.

Roeg's film is long, detailed, and complex as well as deliberately ambiguous. It is a science fiction that deliberately avoids the clichés of science fiction, and yet in Bowie's character captures a true sense of alienness. When I first saw the American cut as a teenager, I did not much care for the film, but later seeing Roeg's full cut in widescreen (a necessity for its carefully crafted compositions), I thought it a brilliant and mature work.

Back in the domain of the guilty pleasure is Jimmy T. Murakami's science fictional remake of Kurasawa's *The*

Seven Samurai, Battle Beyond the Stars (1980), with a tongue-in-cheek script by John Sayles (who also scripted such low-budget, SF related gems as *Piranha, Alligator*, and *Brother From Another Planet*).

John Saxon chews the scenery as Sador, an evil conqueror whose next project is the planet Akir. Akir's elders send young Shad (Richard Thomas of *The Waltons*) to find mercenaries who can defend their homeworld. Shad goes to seek the advice of Dr. Hephaestus (Sam Jaffe), a bodyless head who runs a space station of androids. Hephaestus is more intent on getting Shad to breed with his daughter Nanelia (Darlanne Fluegel) than helping out, so Shad leaves with Nanelia in tow.

Shad finds Cowboy (a corny George Peppard), a space-going trucker type from Earth, and is then able to recruit a number of other mercenaries, including Gelt, a bored assassin who merely works for food and a bed, played by Robert Vaughan as a reprise of his character from *The Magnificent Seven*, and most amusing of all, St. Exmin (Sybil Danning), a busty Valkyrie who lives by the motto of live fast, fight well, and expose as much flesh as the censors will allow in a PG-rated film.

Sayles peppers the script with numerous humorous touches (including the *double entendre* laden-line, "You haven't seen anything until you see a Valkyrie go down!"), and the then newly created New World special effects department headed by George Dodge and Dennis Skotak provides a wide variety of interesting ship designs and colorful laser battles. The best realized character in the film is Shad's computer Nell (Lynne Carlin), who derides Shad for his inexperience as compared to her last pilot, Zed the Corsair. It is Nell who saves the day at the end by plummeting Shad's ship into Sador and self-destructing, and given her liveliness, we are sorry to see the old girl go.

Derivative and unpretentious with paper-thin characterization, *Battle Beyond the Stars* is not an example of a great science fiction film, but it remains nonetheless a fun one, and isn't that what guilty pleasures are all about.

One of the best realizations of a science fiction novel as well as one of the finest science fiction films of all time is the undeservedly obscure *Lathe of Heaven* (1980), based on Ursula K. LeGuin's novel and directed by David Loxton and Fred Barzyk, the same team who did the marvelous Vonnegut tribute *Between Time and Timbuktu*. LeGuin was fascinated by the shifting realities in the works of Philip K. Dick and wrote *Lathe* as a tribute to him. (She told me herself that she was very pleased with the film version and wishes that it were more widely available.)

Lathe of Heaven was a production of the Television Laboratory at WNET, made for a mere $800,000, and received its premiere on PBS on January 9, 1980. It has rarely been rebroadcast since. The story, centering around the character of George Orr (Bruce Davison), plays with concepts of objective and subjective realities, blending dreams and realities in an interesting fashion. The film opens with Orr crawling his way through a desolate landscape, or is it only a nightmare?

Suddenly we are in a slightly futuristic Portland, Oregon, where Orr has been ordered to take therapy from Dr. William Haber (Kevin Conway), who is skeptical about Orr's claims that his dreams, which he calls "effective dreams," can alter reality until he realizes that Orr has altered the entire climate of soggy Oregon. Then a not well-hidden tendency towards megalomania comes out in Haber, who wishes to exploit Orr's gift to improve his circumstances while benefiting the rest of humanity.

Using hypnosis to dictate Orr's dreams, he has Orr create the William Haver Institute of Oneirology (the study of dreams), which gives him a power base; however, Haber's other requests do not prove so fortunate. Wanting Orr to do something about overpopulation, Orr dreams up a plague that wipes out six billion people. Orr goes to an attorney, Heather Lelache (Margaret Avery of *The Color Purple*), in a futile attempt to try to prevent Haber's experimenting with his mind and reality further.

Haber asks that humanity be united, so Orr dreams up an alien invasion that unites the people of Earth against a common foe. Lelache tries to help by suggesting that Orr dream the invading aliens off the moon, so they come to Earth instead. (The aliens in this intelligent but very low budget effort look like a cross between a turtle and an asparagus tip.) The aliens are now friendly and have insinuated themselves into life on Earth, running stores and so on.

Meanwhile, Haber uses the influence and power of his institute to create a machine he calls the Augmentor in hopes of transferring Orr's power to himself. He asks Orr to eliminate the racial problem, with the resulting solution turning all human beings a pale grey. Haber's schemes, however, eventually shatter reality in the clever finale sequence.

Wonderfully imaginative and engrossing, Roger E. Swaybill and Diane English's script intelligently adapts LeGuin's original novel. The film creates its sense of the future by shooting in and around futuristic buildings in Dallas, Texas. The performances are both fine and exquisitely detailed, with the protagonists conveying subtle changes in their characters as a result of their experiences. Rarely has visual science fiction been so thought-provoking and fresh.

Another obscure but highly intelligent 1980 science fiction film began with the premise, "What if Jesus Christ came back today as a woman from the San Fernando

Valley?" The premise, posed by producers Renee Missel and Howard Rosenman, intrigued star Ellen Burstyn, who nevertheless felt that Stephen Geler's script needed to be completely rewritten. It was turned over to scriptwriter Lewis John Carlino, who wrote the script for *Resurrection.*

Carlino made Burstyn's character, Edna McCauley, an ordinary woman who "dies" on the operating table after an auto accident. When she revives, she discovers that she suddenly has the power to heal. Universal head Ned Tanen selected Daniel Petrie (*Sybil*) to direct the film.

McCauley uses her newfound power first to cure her damaged legs and later hosts weekly healing sessions. However, when her Grandma Pearl (Eva Le Gallienne) suggests that these powers are God's work, she responds, "I don't know very much about God."

Edna is a humanist rather than a Bible-spouting Christian. She prefers to offer her services in the name of love rather than in the name of some unseen Holy Spirit. The film notes that faith healers have a limited success rate, and there is a reference to Edna "missing 30 percent of the time." One of the most emotionally wrenching moments in the film occurs when Edna cures Louise (Sylvia Walden) of torsion dystonia, a crippling muscle disease. The people around her are familiar with faith healers, and it is highly disturbing to them that Edna did not call on the Lord while using her powers. Especially unnerved is her lover Cal (Sam Shepard), a preacher's son who begins to think that something satanic might be involved.

Petrie elicits some powerful performances in the film, concentrating on the people rather than the seeming miracles performed. Unlike most science fiction films, there is no explanation offered as to why Edna McCauley gains this power; it simply and poignantly examines the effects of her using it. There is a sense that this is a project that has been passionately and earnestly made, though the film was greeted by poor box office and little attention despite its many fine qualities as an unusual rumination on death and healing.

Death Watch (aka *La Mort en Direct*) (1980) is critic-turned-filmmaker Bertrand Tavernier's brilliant adaptation of D. G. Compton's science fiction novel *The Unsleeping Eye* (aka *The Continuous Katherine Mortenhoe*), co-scripted by Tavernier and David Rayfiel. Oddly, there are major differences in the American and French versions of the film, though they tell roughly the same story.

Katherine Mortenhoe, a young woman who writes computer-generated best-sellers for a living in a near future where disease has been almost abolished, is told by her doctor that she is soon going to die (ironically played by Romy Schneider who herself died a short time afterwards). Shot in the gloomy banality of Glasgow, Scotland, it depicts a future where death of the young is almost unheard of, and in which a cunning television producer, Vincent Ferriman (Harry Dean Stanton), decides that the woman's unusual trauma will garner him enormous ratings from the morbid society at large.

Ferriman convinces Katherine to sign a lucrative contract, but she takes the money and runs, an eventuality that Ferriman has prepared for by putting Roddy (Harvey Keitel) on her trail. Roddy's eyes have been replaced by television cameras that can both broadcast and allow him to see; however, this ability has imposed on Roddy a terrible price in that he must continuously have light shining in his lenses or he will be rendered blind, and because of this, he can never go to sleep again, so is constantly in need of both light and drugs to keep him awake. Roddy is a personality who does not like to sleep for fear of missing anything, and he is enthralled at the idea of whatever beauty and drama he views will be recorded forever, so he proves an eager volunteer for the procedure, little realizing the eventual cost and toll it will take on him. (He cannot even make love to his wife without unwillingly "sharing" the experience with untold others.)

The main difference between the U.S. domestic and the uncut foreign version of the film is that in the original, her disease is fictitious and her "doctor" has been giving her poison that is slowly killing her, in order to effect an intervention that would allow for a "miraculous" recovery for the finale. However, in the U.S. version of the film which is six minutes shorter, she is actually dying of a mysterious illness and just wishes to be left alone to die in privacy away from the prying eyes of the public. But she can never escape from the watchful, covert camera eye of her companion.

The feel of the film changes because of the cuts — what little suspense the uncut version generates is dissipated as the urgency for locating her is reduced; however, as a film of ideas, the shortened version curiously enough allows for more contemplation. In it, we stoically accept the heroine's eventual demise as she does herself. This allows us to vicariously experience her coming to grips with death, and yet, in watching her die, we the audience become implicated in the detestable act of voyeurism, violating the woman's privacy during one of her most personal and intimate moments just as the television viewers are that view the broadcasts from Roddy's eyes.

At the climax of the film, Roddy is so overcome with remorse at his exploitation of Katherine, with whom he has fallen in love, that he throws away the flashlight that keeps his photo-receptors working and renders himself blind. He confesses his remorse to her, and she takes him to Gerald's house where she downs enough sleeping pills to permanently and quietly end her misery before the arrival of the anxious television executives who either want to save her life or capture her last moments on Earth, the climax of their program.

Death Watch is extremely thoughtful and subtle. Cinema as a voyeuristic experience has been explored in the past in such classic films as Hitchcock's *Rear Window* and Powell's *Peeping Tom*, and like them, *Death Watch* inspires feelings of excitement, guilt, and justification for peering into the personal life of another. In essence, the film is a stern warning about media abuse and manipulation, about duplicity and privacy, about beauty and betrayal.

Roddy (Harvey Keitel) and Katherine Mortonhoe (Romy Schneider) in Bertrand Tavernier's brilliant meditation on the lure of technology and voyeurism in *Death Watch*.

This is not a typical science fiction action film, but a genuine drama of thoughts and feelings. The film contains an oblique commentary on such current aspects of society as the lure of television, the fascination with death and celebrityhood, the makings of a public figure and the lack of privacy that ensues. One need only recall the deaths of John Lennon, Grace Kelly, and Princess Diana to observe the need of many people to feel the death, to experience it, become fascinated by it, and to finally achieve release through anguish and grief to understand just how closely our society has come to the death-obsessed, thanatolistic culture depicted in the film. (David Cronenberg's *Crash* has a similar theme.) Death, rendered rare, becomes the new pornography.

Director Michael Radford (right) with Burton during filming of *1984*.

As a movie, *Death Watch* is both disturbing and beautiful, much like the haunting modern musical piece by Antoine Duhamel that Moretenhoe's ex-husband Gerald (Max von Sydow) plays near the end of the film. (He is the person that Katherine runs to see before she departs from the planet.) Pierre-William Glenn's Fujicolor photography is rich and subtle, exquisitely setting the despairing mood required while capturing the nuances of the actors' performances. This is an exemplary production that treats its science fictional premises with an intelligence rarely evident in most science fiction films, and contains a true level of human tragedy that has rarely been equaled in other SF films. While it is atypical of Tavernier's work (e.g. *Coup De Torchon, 'Round Midnight, A Sunday in the Country*), it is nonetheless one of the French filmmaker's most splendidly realized films.

Talented British director Michael Radford (*Another Time, Another Place; Il Postino*) successfully adapted George Orwell's portentous science fiction classic *1984*, producing what is possibly the bleakest English language film of all time. Orwell created what may be the ultimate in anti-wish fulfillment narratives, as the State's torture chamber, Room 101, contains whatever one thing the torturee fears most, crushing the reader's last hope that something of value can survive the dull victory of the inhuman, all-controlling totalitarian state. The reader is left rattled with no chance for political complacency and no romantic beliefs that heroic resistance or private humanity can give meaning to life under tyranny.

Radford's England of 1984, renamed Airstrip One and

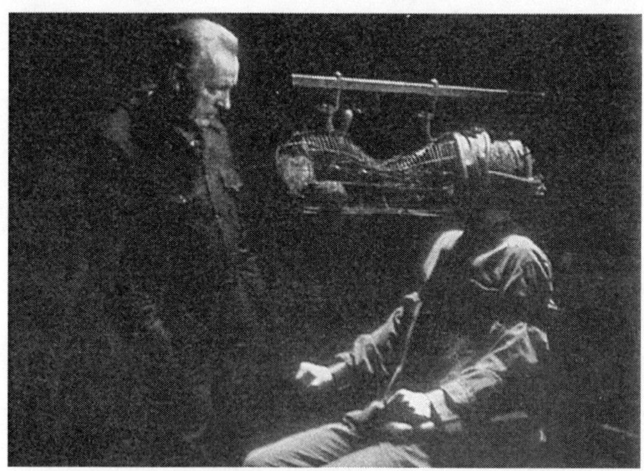

O'Brien (Richard Burton, left) tortures Smith (John Hurt) with a rat cage on his head in *1984*.

assimilated into the giant State of Oceania, is gray, dusty, and labyrinthine, and is in an unspectacular state of slow decay. Radford meticulously builds his depressing atmosphere, lingering on broken, smoky light in cavernous halls, and giving prominence to realistic sound effects. His dramatic approach becomes clear in the striking first scene, a mass meeting in which a propaganda film rouses the crowd to an impassioned expression of their hatred for the enemies of the state. Rather than showing something that would make this hysteria comprehensible, Radford's standoffish camera tracks slowly through the hall, observing the varied, strangely anguished reactions of the crowd.

John Hurt gives a brilliant performance as Winston Smith, the obscure Outer Party worker who revises history for the state by day and nurtures his private rebellion on the side. Hurt expertly and subtly limns Smith's innate sensitivity and vulnerability, as well as more importantly his impassivity, letting only the lines of worry around his eyes betray his anxiety.

Richard Burton provides one of the finest performances of his checkered film career as O'Brien, providing a performance of surprising restraint and effective ambiguity. Suzanna Hamilton is properly mysterious as Julia, Smith's clandestine lover whose rebellion against society takes the form of a partial identification with evil. As a consequence of these fine performances, these characters seem more alive than the cardboard cut-outs inhabiting Orwell's novel as the characters try to make sense of each other and of the brutalities of the world which they are in the process of discovering. This gives the project a thoughtful, life-sized perspective to which the viewer can easily relate.

Still, as strong as the performances are, what is most effective about Radford's film is his willingness *not* to exploit the nightmarish aspects of the story (we see very little of Big Brother's oppressive tactics; there are no rousing scenes of fascist police beating up on the proles). Julia and Winston observe this hellish society, captured most effectively in its chilling peripheral details, from a detached perspective. Radford is more concerned with minute shifts in mood instead of huge social upheavals, establishing a quiet, melancholy rhythm to his film. The film's attack is cerebral rather than emotional.

Another powerful science fiction film released in 1984 was Lynne Littman's *Testament*, which was made for $750,000 for public television and then given a brief theatrical release by Paramount. Littman, the wife of director Taylor Hackford, had been doing documentaries for 20 years, winning an Oscar in 1977 for *Number Our Days*, before doing *Testament*, a powerful look at the possibilities of a catastrophic nuclear war based on Carol Amen's story "The Last Testament" from *Ms.* magazine. It focuses on the tragedy of one "average" American family trying to cope with the impossible and face the unthinkable. Because its easily identifiable characters are very realistic, the audience is forced to come to grips with the bleakness, futility, and heartbreaking reality of such a situation. Dealing with the consequences of radiation sickness, rationing, and disposal of the dead, the film packs a wallop.

The primary location is significantly named Hamlin and it learns of nuclear disaster when the television set loses its signal from the networks — New York has been nuked and West Coast cities are hit a few seconds later, though Hamlin itself receives no direct damage. Carol Wetherly (Jane Alexander) has lost her husband Tom (William Devane) and must take care of their three children (Roxana Zal, Ross Harris, and Lukas Haas) by herself, and it soon becomes apparent that society has collapsed and everyone will die slowly of radiation.

Testament won an Oscar nomination for its star, Jane Alexander, who in her finest scene tries to convey to her daughter what making love is all about while realizing that her daughter will never live to experience it herself. The moment is heartbreaking and the film one of the most powerfully realized pieces of science fiction ever made, as well as one of the simplest.

An SF film that would be easy to overlook because it is unconventional is Jean-Jacques Annaud's *Quest for Fire*. Instead of being set in the future, it speculates on what life was like for humans 80,000 years ago when fire was primitive man's most prized possession. The film's story involves four tribes, the Ulam, primitive Homo sapiens whose very existence depends on fire preserved within their caves; the Wagabou, plundering Neanderthals who prey on weaker tribes; the Kzamm, cannibals who capture members of rival tribes and eat them; and the Ivaka, Homo sapiens more advanced than the Ulam who possess the knowledge of how to create fire. Special prosthetics were created to emphasize the tribes' primitiveness, unlike most cavemen epics.

While author Anthony Burgess was hired to create special languages, Annaud's film conveys its story (scripted by Gerard Brach from J. H. Rosny's novel) purely cinematically. The actors largely communicated using body language and gestures created by behavioral theorist Desmond Morris.

Quest for Fire follows the fortunes of the Ulam, who are attacked by the Wagabou and are almost entirely wiped out, their fire lost. The tribe's three bravest warriors, Naoh (Everett McGill), Amoukar (Ron Perlman), and Gaw (Nameer El-Kadi) are sent on a quest to find fire for the preservation of the tribe.

The trio's stamina is tested by treacherous terrain, rival warriors from other tribes, and predatory mammals including bears, mammoths, and sabre-toothed tibers. They rescue Ika (Rae Dawn Chong) from the Kzamm, and Naoh and Ika fall in love and discover the missionary position. They learn to share emotions such as laughter, sorrow, compassion and concern.

Ika then shows them to the Ivaka, who teach them the secret of making fire, and the group return to save their tribe by not only bringing fire, but also by demonstrating a new commitment among human beings.

Annaud took three years to prepare and research the film, and a fourth year to actually film it. A strike by Screen Actors Guild shut down production in Iceland, and months later resumed filming in the highlands of Scotland, with other sequences shot in Kenya and the Badlands of the U.S. and Canada, with temperatures ranging from freezing to 120°. Locations had to have a grand scale and an unspoiled appearance as well as resembling the proper period in prehistory. One can believe this is how it might have been.

D.A.R.Y.L., directed by Australian director Simon Wincer, is a family oriented science fiction film written by David Ambrose, Allan Scott, and Jeffrey Ellis, in which a boy android, nicknamed Daryl (Barret Oliver), is helped to escape from the Defense Department by some caring scientists. Daryl is given a foster home and tries hard to adapt to human ways, but betrays that he is unusual when he can suddenly play sonatas by sight and hit home runs with unerring accuracy, earning admiration from his foster dad (Michael McKean) who wants to have his losing baseball team get a shot at winning. He is by all appearances a perfect child — he is well-behaved, always polite, and picks up after himself perfectly so that he seems too good to be true, too much so to suit his foster mother (Mary Beth Hurt), so Daryl learns to mess up once in a while.

Eventually, the military succeeds in tracking Daryl down and his foster parents learn the truth, that however life-like he may appear, Daryl is really a machine, but one with human thoughts and feelings. Another kindly scientist (Josef Sommers) helps Daryl escape a second time, and Daryl arranges an elaborate ruse whereby he steals a jet and flies it, forcing it to be shot down, which leads the Defense Department to assume his demise. However, he cleverly ejects beforehand and returns to the loving arms of his foster family in the heart-warming finish.

An often overlooked science fiction film is Joe Dante's *Explorers* (1985), which played with the conventions of the science fiction film. The script was by Eric Luke, who based the characters on kids he knew from his childhood. The main characters are three junior high school boys, daydreamer Ben Crandall (Ethan Hawke), genius kid Wolfgang Mueller (River Phoenix in one of his earliest roles), and grease monkey Darren Woods (Jason Presson), who represent the heart, the head, and the hands à la *Metropolis*. They dream up the idea to create their own homemade spaceship out of a Tilt-a-Whirl with washing machine doors, TV set portholes, and a tire for a bumper. The ship, which they dub the *Thunder Road* after the Bruce Springsteen song, is powered by a force field bubble which Mueller creates.

In one playful scene, they take the ship out for a test drive and buzz a local drive-in, where an Antonio Margheriti-style low budget, badly dubbed, internationally cast sci-fi flick is playing with a special effects camera disguised as a spaceship. Dante packs the scene with numerous in-joke references to 1950s science fiction films.

What hurts the film is that these kids create an awe-inspiring piece of technology, but there is no sense of wonder regarding their achievement. Additionally, Dante enjoyed tweaking the expectations of those raised on *Close Encounters* that meeting aliens will solve all the problems of the world. In the last part of the film, the boys meet up with two aliens on a spaceship, Wak (Robert Picardo buried under a ton of makeup giving a delightfully wacked out performance) and Neek (Leslie Rickert), who are the goofiest looking aliens ever put to film, looking like caricatures from a bubblegum card (and are neatly realized by make-up effects expert Rob Bottin). They enjoy parroting catch-phrases from television and turn out to be a couple of kids joyriding in their father's spaceship. In the right frame of mind, this material is very funny, but it went against the grain of what audiences had come to expect from science fiction films.

The end of *Explorers* holds a subtle message about holding onto one's dreams as Ben experiences a new dream and a new idea. *Explorers* was rushed into the cinemas before Dante had time to fine-tune the editing, leaving a few threads dangling. When it came time for the film to appear on video, he recut the material for a special video version, trimming about two minutes, and that version is the only one commercially available. Not quite fish nor fowl and given a bad advertising campaign, despite the fact that *Explorers* is one of the few science fiction films to feature real characters, it failed to find an audience and seems to be largely forgotten. Likewise, Dante's semi-science fictional cable movie, *The Second Civil War*, is well worth seeking out as an SF satire that ruminates intelligently on how the media have increased divisiveness in this country, and speculates on how it could lead to another civil war.

John Binder's *UFOria* was shot in 1981, but sat on the shelf at Universal until achieving a limited release in 1985. This is a quirky little comedy about the eccentricities of small town America with a science fictional twist that unfortunately failed to find an appreciative audience. It follows a happy-go-lucky drifter named Sheldon (Fred Ward) who falls for a dippy and somewhat neurotic grocery store cashier named Arlene (Cindy Williams), whose life is dedicated to the notion that UFOs are the chariots of God, and are coming back soon to pick up the faithful. Sheldon simply wants to get into her pants and sweet-talks his way into her tiny trailer home.

Also in town is Sheldon's seedy con artist cousin Brother Bud (Harry Dean Stanton), who sees in Arlene's scattershot religion with its combined elements of Christianity and flying saucer cult a potentially lucrative new market for his brand of phony evangelical fervor, which mainly entails luring folks into a tent for a little preaching and faith healing in exchange for donations. Binder's kooky characterizations keep up interest in this offbeat comedy and eccentric character study which has a genuinely science fictional climax.

The Wings of Honneamise (aka *Oneamisu No Tsubasa Oritsu Ochu Gun; Starquest*) (1987), written and directed by Hiroyuki Yamaga when he was only 23, is a truly unusual animated science fiction epic. It had an ¥8 million budget, the biggest ever for an *animé* film, and was the first film from Gainax, who wanted to make an elaborate showcase out of it.

It records the development of a space flight program on a distant planet, patterned after Japan. The protagonist, Cadet Shirotsugh "Shiro" Lhadatt (whose character is based on Treat Williams), wants to distinguish himself, but his test scores are mediocre and he winds up in the Royal Space Force, a branch of the service that is not taken very seriously, but rather is regarded mostly with ridicule and apathy by the military leaders. He earns condemnation when he almost sleeps through a dead colleague's funeral and arrives without his uniform.

One night, the pleasure-seeking Shiro has a chance encounter with Riquinni Nonderaiko, an attractive but impoverished young evangalist, and he decides to attend one of her religious meetings. She is thrilled that he is prospective astronaut, and he basks in the glow of her admiration. She inspires him to try harder and achieve, despite the fact that most of his colleagues seem to have the wrong stuff and many of the test rockets have blown up upon launching.

Lhadatt's country is competing against an English-speaking foe and is on the verge of war. The military leaders decide to militarize the space program in order to capitalize on the possible conflict. A now-reformed Shiro transforms from head loafer to dedicated astronaut-volunteer. Tensions mount as he and a team of aging scientists must then race against time to complete the first launch before the enemy reaches the launch site and before all efforts are diverted towards the country's military program.

The Wings of Honneamise depicts a fully realized and detailed world that is similar, but not quite the same, as our own. Many of the images are inspired by the actual space program, as well as Philip Kaufman's *The Right Stuff*. Complex and slow, Lhadatt genuinely develops as a character, losing some of his naïveté but not his increasing idealism, as he becomes inspired to be his country's first man into space. An attempted rape scene was censored in the British film version, and does seem out of place. The film suggests that man's faith and devotion are faithful friends that should guide him in his quest for conquering space, and is a fascinatingly alternate look at a space program, well worth the time of any science fiction fan.

Killer Klowns from Outer Space (1987), directed by Stephen Chiodo of the Chiodo Brothers, who supplied special effects for *Critters*, *Pee-wee's Big Adventure*, and *UHF* among other features, is a twisted evocation of 1950s alien invaders films, particularly *The Blob* and *Invasion of the Saucer Men*. One of the most delightful aspects of this inventive low budget gem is the way Charles Chiodo's production designs carry the offbeat circus motif throughout (including the terrific Killer Klown makeup). Perhaps inspired by Robert Bloch's observation that a clown in a circus is funny, but a clown in the moonlight would be scary, the alien invaders look like grotesque clowns with bulging heads and four-fingered hands.

Mike Tobacco (Grant Cramer) and Debbie Stone (Suzanne Snyder from *The Last Starfighter*) are out at lovers' lane when they see a meteorite fly over head. Also investigating the crash site is an old coot, Farmer Gene Green (Royal Dano) and his dog, who is surprised to see a glowing big top circus tent. Mike and Debbie also find the tent and discover Green inside suspended from a cotton candy cocoon. They are soon pursued by the Killer Klowns, who fire a popcorn gun at them and use a balloon dog to help track them down.

Veteran actor John Vernon plays the stereotypical teen-hating cop, Officer Curtis Mooney, while his partner is the more reasonable Dave Hansen (John Allen Nelson), Debbie's former boyfriend who orders her to go home. The center of the film is a variety of setpieces whereby the Klowns puzzle, perplex, and destroy the townspeople. For example, a biker gang gets approached by a small Klown on a tiny bike with training wheels. A bully smashes the bike, the Klown returns with boxing gloves, the bully asks, "What are you going to do? Knock my block off?" which the Klown does in one punch. Another amusing sequence has a Klown entertaining some elderly people at a bus stop by creating unlikely shadows (elephant with wagging trunk, Washington crossing the Delaware, a Hula girl) before the shadow turns into a red-eyed dinosaur that devours them.

No clown cliché is left untouched, from puppet shows to the small car with the large amount of clowns inside to clown firemen holding out a safety net. The Klowns are practically invulnerable unless one shoots their bulbous noses, in which case they explode and scatter confetti. The popcorn they leave behind turns into vicious clown heads that spring at Debbie from long stalks.

Officer Mooney ignores the calls for help because he thinks they are a college prank being done by the Terenzi brothers (Michael Siegel and Peter Licassi), who drive a Jojo (the Clown) ice cream truck in hopes of picking up women. (The overly juvenile and nerdish Terenzi brothers are the least amusing and least successful element in the film.) The Klowns fill up their ship with people they have changed into cotton candy cocoons and prepare to head on their way, wiping out a local guard with killer cream pies. Using a crazy straw, one of the Klowns makes a sanguinary drink from the contents. However, all ends well as Officer Dave gets close enough to destroy the nose of the head Klown, who destroys the ship when he explodes. TransWorld Entertainment never supplied the Chiodos with enough funds to properly fix the soundtrack, but for the patient and receptive, this is a visually inventive and blackly comic science fiction effort you will not soon forget.

Bad Taste (1988) was the ultra-low budget first feature by New Zealand horror director extraordinaire Pete Jackson, who also wrote, acted, and worked on the effects and music for the film. He also gives the film's best performance as an ill-fated moronic alien hunter who gets knocked off a cliff, has his brains fall out, and yet bandages his skull with a tie and continues on in this blackly humorous story. While in many ways a crude and amatuerish effort and reveling in the titular bad taste, it remains a lively and in many ways inventive, though little known, SF comedy.

In their search for a new culinary sensation, a gang of extraterrestrial gourmands representing Crumb's Crunchy Delights Ltd., an intergalactic fast-food chain, find just what they're looking for in New Zealand — human flesh. The day before they plan to leave, however, their nefarious scheme is uncovered by the government's new Alien Investigation and Defense Service — four basically inept yahoos in a funky car, who decide to squelch the alien plans on their own. This is gross-out humor of the first rank, with witty stagings of spurting blood, severed limbs, and a chainsaw rebirth. Gory and definitely not for the squeamish, *Bad Taste* truly lives up to its title.

Jackson is best known for *Heavenly Creatures* and for the ultimate gore comedy *Brain Dead* (aka *Dead Alive*). He has also codirected with Costa Botes an obscure, alternate world pseudo-documentary called *Forgotten Silver* (1995) for New Zealand television. *Forgotten Silver* purports to tell the true story of Colin McKenzie, whom the film credits with making the first feature length motion picture, making the first talkie, inventing color film (as well as inadvertently inventing pornography when local bare-breasted Tahiti women walk into the shot), shooting the first close-up, inventing the tracking shot, photographing the first plane flight (by real-life aviator Richard Pearse) and inadvertently causing it to crash, and creating a three-hour epic film, *Salome*, that rivals Griffith's *Intolerance* in scope. To give credence to this hoax, actor Sam Neill, film critic Leonard Maltin, and Miramax cochair Harvey Weinstein all appear on camera extolling McKenzie's virtues and accomplishments. Jackson also shot the supposedly long lost footage that represents clips from McKenzie's fictional career, using various techniques to give them an appropriately dated look. (The film provoked some outrage when some New Zealanders discovered it was only a hoax.) Jackson is currently devoting his life to filming J. R. R. Tolkien's *Lord of the Rings* trilogy as a series of three films.

Tremors (1990), directed by Ron Underwood, who collaborated with S. S. Wilson and Brent Maddock on the story, is a deliberate tribute to the desert-set science fiction films of the fifties, particularly Jack Arnold's work. According to genre conventions, it is set in an isolated small town (Perfection, Nevada), stocked with colorful characters, a visiting scientist, blocked roads and communications, and a terrifying monster. The trio had met each other at USC's film school and created the project on speculation before selling it to Universal with the aid of executive producer Gale Anne Hurd.

Tremors largely works thanks to its knack for characterization, particularly its engaging two main characters, Earl Basset (Fred Ward) and Valentine McKee (Kevin Bacon), dimbulb handymen who discover a previously unknown burrowing species of monster-sized mutant maggots under the minuscule town of Perfection, which they dub the "graboids."

Underwood's film builds up mystery and suspense as the local population become decimated by the initially unseen monsters. He tweaks various genre conventions, having the local visiting scientist, shapely student seismologist Rhonda LeBeck (Finn Carter) contribute little to understanding the problem, and having the day saved by the dumb handymen, who are really more interested in finding a way out of this dead-end town than saving it. Peppered with colorful supporting characters, including Burt Gummer (a cast-against-type Michael Gross) and his wife Heather (singer Reba McEntire) as a pair of gun-nuts who see the graboid invasion as a golden opportunity to test their survivalist skills, and Victor Wong as the store owner who hopes to figure out a way to financially exploit this discovery.

The special effects, created by Alec Gillis and Tom Woodruff with miniatures by Robert and Dennis Skotak, are nifty and used sparingly to good effect. The film even risks looking stupid while being smart as survivors pole vault from one rock outcropping to the next in an effort to avoid being eaten by the swiftly tunneling graboids. *Tremors* proved popular enough on videotape to spawn a direct-to-video sequel, *Tremors 2: Aftershocks*, directed by S. S. Wilson, which physically alters the graboids and makes a joke about replacing Bacon with a new guy (Christopher Gartin, who gets dubbed "the new guy"), but it lacks the eerie atmosphere and inventiveness of the original, turning into just another special effects showcase (with Phil Tippet adding some CGI to the effects work of the returning Gillis and Woodruff).

Until the End of the World (Original title: *Bis Ende die Welt*; 1991) was originally a five-hour epic that was whittled down to 158 minutes for its 1994 U.S. release (the Japanese version runs 181 minutes), and is said to work much better in its extended version. Even so, Wim Wenders' condensed version is a challenging, often fascinating science fiction "road" movie concerning the effect technology has on people and how they look at the world.

Technology is simultaneously central to the end of the world scenario, used to produce hypnotically beautiful dream images, crucial to forming and maintaining human relationships, and responsible for the devastation and transformation of those relationships. The immediate threat of nuclear annihilation underlies the film's chase-conspiracy-romance plot which takes place across ten different countries. The "end of the world" scenario is significant because it is the backdrop against which the actions of the characters occurs and is interpreted. It signifies the destructive power of the technology we have created which may ultimately overwhelm us. *Until the End of the World* shows both the beneficial and destructive capabilities of technology. It ultimately privileges the centrality of human relationships which are nonetheless inseparable from their technological context. In addition, the film plays on the idea of romance that can last for all time, or "until the end of the world." This promise of timeless romance between individuals is not kept, but human relationships do endure, sometimes through technological means.

The threat posed by technology is immediately a primary concern of the film. Novelist Eugene Fitzpatrick (Sam Neill) tells us, "1999. The year the Indian nuclear satellite went out of control. It soared over the ozone layer like a lethal bird of prey. No one knew where it would land. The whole world was alarmed." Here, nuclear disaster develops in a political void. It is the uncontrollable accident which most people fear more than full scale nuclear war.

Claire Tourneur (Solveig Dommartin), bored with her relationship with Gene and with the "satellite emergency" threatening a nuclear holocaust, sending hordes away from some of the larger cities, heads off the crowded highways and becomes involved in a car accident caused when Chico (Chick Ortega) carelessly throws his beer bottle out the window. Chico and his partner Raymond (Eddy Mitchell) are bank robbers fleeing from Nice, and with their car out of commission, they persuade Claire to transport their loot to Paris in exchange for a cut of the proceeds.

En route she encounters Sam Farber (William Hurt), who explains that people are trying to kill him because he borrowed a lot of money that he can't pay back. She tries to help him, but he only ends up stealing the loot. She tries to reunite with Eugene, but catching a glimpse of an associate of Sam's who has called a missing persons bureau in Berlin, she heads off to Berlin and discovers that Farber is wanted for stealing some opals and has relocated to Lisbon. A missing persons detective (Rudiger Vogler) offers to find Sam for her for $3,000, provided that she assist him.

From there, the pair head off to Lisbon, Moscow, the Transiberian Express, China, Tokyo, and San Francisco. Claire discovers that the purpose behind all of Farber's traveling is that he has a device for recording images and he is storing up images that can be directly transmitted into the brain of a blind mother Edith (Jeanne Moreau). The U.S. government has hired bounty hunters to chase Sam in order to retrieve his special camera, which has the side effect of damaging his vision. Claire offers an herbal cure.

Finally, the film makes a sudden turn as the main characters wind up in the Australian outback just as the "end of the world" occurs — an electromagnetic pulse that shuts down all electrical equipment, including the plane that they are flying. Able to land safely, they make their way to Farber's father, Henry Farber (Max von Sydow), who has a place hidden in some ancient caves, so that his equipment has been protected from the effects of the pulse. Henry Farber is engaged in dream research and is using his equipment to record the dreams of others. With Claire's help, Farber's work bears fruit, allowing the blind to "see"; however, depressed at the way the world has changed, Edith dies. The others become addicted to using the technology to videotape and watch their own dreams.

Wenders, who co-wrote the script with Peter Carey from an idea by him and Solveig Dommartin, explores his typical themes, the difficulty of communication, the urge for wanderlust, urban alienation, in highly unusual fashion in this *fin de siècle* film. The soundtrack is superb, featuring some of the top pop artists of the 1980s (REM, U2, Talking Heads, Lou Reed, Peter Gabriel, Nick Cave, etc.), and the film itself is rather hypnotic, though the ending in which real life is extolled over "reel" life seems rather banal.

Spirit of 76 (1991) is less a science fiction film than a time capsule of all that was wretched about the 1970s. Written and directed by Lucas Reiner with spot-on production design by Daniel Talpers and seventies fashions from Sofia Coppola, the movie is a trip down a nightmarish seventies avenue. It's all here: mood rings, platform shoes, striped bell-bottom trousers, polyester suits, 8-tracks ("Don't they have those in the future?"), "What sign are you?" queries, streakers, head shops, Pacers and Pintos, EST seminars, bean bag chairs, Tang, Pop Rocks, Sno-Balls, kung fu, disco, Twister games, dune buggies, gas lines, Iron Eyes Cody crying at pollution, and of course smiley faces.

The film begins in America of 2176 where pollution-filled skies cover up white gleaming buildings and there is no vegetation in sight. A magnetic storm has wiped out all recorded history. Concepts such as liberty, freedom, and the 4th of July have all been lost. The Ministry of Science (played by members of the rock group Devo) ask Dr. Van Mobil (Carl Reiner) about what has been lost, but all he can give them are incoherent ramblings, including something about the Constitution and the Spirit of 76, when it all began.

The Ministry decides to approve fuel for Adam (1970s icon David Cassidy) and his time machine (Adam hopes one day to find the scene depicted on a damaged postcard he calls "ikiki Beach") provided he take Chanel No. 6 (Olivia d'Abo) and Heinz 57 (Geoff Hoyle) back to 1776. However, the machine has a slight malfunction and the trio end up in 1976 instead, where they are amazed at the growing plants.

Two local teens, Chris (Jeff McDonald) and Tommy (Steve McDonald), ride up on bikes equipped with banana seats and assume that the travelers must be fried on acid. Obnoxious science geek Rodney Snodgrass (Liam O'Brien) also appears and assumes their ship must be a UFO, so Chris and Tommy take the trio into hiding along with their vehicle. In order to be less conspicuous, the group decides to outfit themselves in hideous seventies fashions, while the CIA (the Kipper Kids) attempt to track down the reported aliens from their van and have summoned a bevy of patrol cars to assist them.

Chanel hides out in a head shop patronized by Tommy Chong, where she throws herself at Eddie Trojan (1970s icon Leif Garrett) to avoid being captured. Eddie, a self-described "Bone Master," takes her back to his pad and shows her how to do the Hustle. Meanwhile, Heinz 57 flees from the police into a strip club where the Spirit of Liberty (Julie Brown of *Earth Girls Are Easy*) lectures him about Watergate, and then into the Be-Inc. seminar run by Dr. Cash (Rob Reiner) who talks about freedom and choice, and calls everybody an asshole.

Meanwhile, Adam samples 1970s food with Chris and Tommy, discovers that Snodgrass has broken in and stolen the ship's battery (powered by tetrahydroziline, eye drops that the 1970s teens use to keep the parents from seeing that they are stoned), and help the pair win the science fair while they help him repower the ship to take the group back to save the future. Upon their return, the future is transformed into a rainbow of day-glo colors and happy smiling faces, remaking itself in the images of the 1970s.

Reiner keeps the tone light and allows a kind of anti-nostalgia to provide most of the laughs, though O'Brien's Snodgrass is less a comic foil than a badly performed, obnoxious intrusion. The soundtrack is peppered with appropriate 1970s hits to remind us that yes, indeed, the music really was that bad. The ultimate message of the film is that if we don't learn from the mistakes of the past, we might have to repeat it (as a resurgence in seventies fashions recently proved).

Tim Burton's *Mars Attacks!* (1996) is one of the greatest sci-fi, as opposed to science fiction, features ever made. Adapted from a notorious bubblegum card series that was ultimately banned in the U.S., the film takes delight in resurrecting the gory and gaudy imagery of the cards, as well as the best aspects of low budget fifties science fiction films, while at the same time presenting them with state of the art computer effects, and in the process wasting (in both senses of the word) a wonderful all-star cast.

As is typical for a Burton film, the main people are mostly caricatures, and the sympathetic characters are lonely outsiders such as Lucas Haas' donut shop server or the daughter of the President. While the humor is slow to get started and never reaches the Strangelovian heights some might have imagined, there are some terrific character bits, such as Sylvia Sydney cackling with glee as she notes that the Martians have killed Congress, while Jack Nicholson as President (a funny idea in and of itself) makes a speech about how they still had two out of three branches of government, and "two out of three ain't bad!"

Mars Attacks! works and must be approached and embraced on a very adolescent level, reveling as it does in bright, gaudy, trash sci-fi imagery presented in all its destructive gleefulness (it is definitely not a film for all tastes and left the mass audience cold and unamused). The Martians themselves are simply bad boys who delight in destruction while ironically proclaiming friendship, indicative of many mixed messages we receive today where what is expected is often made to seem more important than what is real. *Mars Attacks!* after its careful build-up becomes a twisted orgy of destruction and delightful effects. Among the more perverse aspects are the Martians' pointless experiments to attach the head of a reporter to the body of a Chihuahua while Pierce Brosnan's Fred MacMurrayesque scientist becomes a living disembodied head. Burton designs shots to frequently pay tribute to the SF B movies of the fifties for fans of the genre to catch. The feature is speckled with satirical jibes, but mostly serves as attractive eye candy that despite its high cost and promotion failed to attract a large audience. Nevertheless, *Mars Attacks!* is sci-fi on a grand order, never to be taken seriously, but also never to be forgotten either.

Nirvana (1997) is basically an ironic, unofficial version of William Gibson's story "Burning Chrome." There is a popular and quite rich simulation game designer (Christophe Lambert), who has just finished programming a new VR game called Nirvana (hence the title). But soon after he discovers that one of the characters in the VR game, Solo (Diego Abatantuono), has self-consciousness and is aware of living in a VR set. Solo asks his creator to be destroyed, but the designer can only destroy his copies of the program: the source files are well protected in the databanks of the entertainment zaibatsu he's working for.

So the designer has to ask for the help of two hackers: a rather inefficient and penniless console jockey (Sergio Rubini) with a remarkable and incredibly funny Pugliese accent, and a nice girl who has lost all her memories due to some cyberspace accident.

The rest is much like "Burning Chrome," but the ending is less happy. Add the fact that the designer's woman (Emmanuelle Seigneur) has practically self-destroyed her mind to achieve a Buddhist annihilation of the self (Nirvana, indeed), but has recorded all her memories in a nanochip that can be read by a socket engrafted in the head of the hacker girl.

The soundtrack is by the classic rock group Traffic. In the film, Nirvana is a VR simulational game (Doom style). The director's name is Salvatores. Basically the plot is 30 percent *Blade Runner*, and 60 percent *Neuromancer* (there is 10 percent which is Salvatores, but if you haven't seen his earlier films that won't tell you anything). It could be labeled the Italian answer to *Strange Days*, without the idiotic ending. Not very original, but not bad.

Barry Sonnenfeld's *Men in Black* is a science fiction action-comedy based on the late 1980s Malibu comic book series *The Men in Black* created by Lowell Cunningham from a script by Ed Solomon (co-screenwriter of the *Bill & Ted* series as well as the execrable sci-fi comedy *Mom & Dad Save the World*). Sonnenfeld asked that the story be set in modern-day New York.

Men in Black stars Tommy Lee Jones and Will Smith, both of whom give expert comic performances. The film's premise is that The Men in Black is an organization established in the early 1960s after the first alien sighting on Earth. Initially, it was a government agency established to cover up the fact that aliens had landed on Earth, but later it became so powerful that it functions as an independent agency to keep the peace. Aliens are allowed to stay here as long as they keep the peace. If they break the law, the Men in Black, who constantly monitor the aliens, will deport them from the Earth.

Edgar (Vincent D'Onofrio), an intergalactic insectoid terrorist, arrives to claim a miniaturized galaxy belonging to one of the visiting alien species, but if he achieves his aims, it will mean war and the destruction of Earth. The Men in Black's mission is the stop this terrorist. Smith plays an NYPD officer (later designated as J) who demonstrates that he has the ability to become one of the Men in Black to K (Tommy Lee Jones), the agency's world weary, ultra-cynical top agent who is currently seeking a new partner and recruits him into the agency (which is covertly financed by licensing alien inventions to mankind).

Rick Baker handled the makeup effects for the film's various aliens in the film, while visual effects including a few CGI aliens were supplied by ILM.

Bo Welch is the film's production designer and has created a retro–1960s future look, based in part on the '64 World's Fair in Flushing Meadows, New York, which according to the film was created as a cover-up for one of the first true alien sightings. The main set for the Men in Black Immigration Headquarters is reminiscent of sets from *The Man from U.N.C.L.E.* and the *UFO* TV series crossed with the look of famous Finnish architect Saarinen, who designed many U.S. airports in the 1960s. Welch places circles all over his design, suggestive of saucers, and he suggested the Guggenheim Museum for an early sequence where J tracks down a swift-footed alien trying to escape.

"I think it's mainly a comedy," commented Sonnenfeld to me about the film, "but the comedy plays out because of the reality of the situation. It takes place in New York with aliens, but the way I like the comedy to play is that you have people talking to aliens and yet never acknowledging that they're an alien.

"[For example,] Tommy [Lee Jones] is interrogating this alien and the alien has all these excuses and is talking in this alien tongue, and Tommy just sort of says, 'Oh yeah, that's enough. Put up your hands and all your flippers right now,' but without going, 'Put up your hands [punchline emphasis] *and all your flippers.*' The more you play it straight, the funnier it is. It's not like a broad comedy, it's a sophisticated alien adventure action-comedy."

Regarding why he tackled this particular project, Sonnenfeld explained, "I just have a feeling we don't really have a clue about what's going on. I don't know if there are aliens or that there aren't aliens, but I do believe that everything that any expert has ever told us in our life has been proven wrong.

"I mean 500 years ago, everyone on the planet believed that the Earth was flat and according to Copernicus the Earth was the center of the universe. When I was growing up, there were no black holes and no.... To think that we actually have a clue about what's actually out there is amusing to me, so that's why I did this."

Sonnenfeld found Solomon's script amusing and felt he could be a good director for it. While the project is much larger than Sonnenfeld's previous directorial efforts, he said, "This has been the most relaxed shoot I've been on. Rick Baker is incredibly professional; ILM is. Will Smith and Tommy have been great to work with, so it's actually been the easiest shoot. "There is a great deal of pressure, because it's a lot of money and there's a lot of effects, and you got to really think about what you want in the cutting room nine months from now, so that's sort of annoying, but it's been fun actually."

Sonnenfeld has high praise for his actors, especially Jones, whom he feels is funnier the flatter he plays it. "When I sense that Tommy thinks he's being funny, I say, 'Let's do one flatter, Tommy, even straighter." Sonnenfeld also praises Smith as also being funny and full of energy.

"Although the comic book is very dark and very good, and totally different," said Sonnenfeld, "the script I read was very funny, and I read it well over three years ago. We changed it a lot. It was a very different script. It took place in Neveda, Philly, Washington — all over the country, and it was broader in nature. I felt that if aliens exist, they would live in New York because they could blend in without actually having to hide the fact that they are aliens. In fact, I feel sure I've been driven by a few alien cab drivers. So I had it rewritten for New York and made it less broad."

Sonnenfeld described a very harmonious relationship working with executive producer Steven Spielberg, who lived not far from him on the East Coast for a time and who helped him persuade Smith to do the film. (Spielberg had wanted Sonnenfeld to direct *Casper*, but the director had just adopted a daughter and turned the assignment down.) "[Spielberg's] been great! He's been unbelievably smart and funny and supportive. Sometimes he makes suggestions and we do them, and sometimes he makes suggestions and I say, 'You know what, I don't see it that way,' and he says, 'Fine.' He's been really supportive and really fun." Spielberg helped to greenlight one of the film's best gags which Sonnenfeld came up with during filming, in which J assists with the birth of a powerful baby whose tentacles lift and bang him on the roof of a station wagon while his partner is calmly interrogating the father on the New Jersey turnpike.

The cast also includes Rip Torn, who plays Zed, the head of the MiB agency, and Linda Fiorentino, who plays Dr. Laurel Weaver, who's the deputy medical examiner for the city of New York.

Sonnenfeld put a rough cut of his film together before he was able to convince TriStar to finance the opening and closing sequences of the film, which added another $4 million to the budget. The opening features a computer-generated dragonfly that soars over a desert (and at one point parodies production partner Amblin's logo) before being splattered on a truck windshield, and the finale pulls back from the Earth to reveal it trapped inside a marble that encompasses the Milky Way Galaxy that is being played with by some inconceivably large alien being (what Sonnenfeld calls his "powers of ten" shot, after the famous school short).

Mimic (1997) is a superior SF horror thriller by Mexican director Guillermo Del Toro (*Cronos*). It succeeds in being genuinely scary at a time when truly scary films have become quite rare. Dr. Susan Tyler (Mira Sorvino) and her epidemiologist husband Dr. Peter Mann (Jeremy Northam) are geneticists who created the "Judas breed," a band of winged insects created from the DNA of termites and praying mantises who can alter or mimic their shape and composition to overcome any enemy. (*Mimic* is based on a story by SF author-editor Donald Wollheim.)

This film is about fighting a child-killing epidemic spread by cockroaches, but when the "Judas breed" start imitating humans, the human race is the one likely to wind up on the endangered species list.

However, these bright scientists decide to largely go it alone to combat this menace, never thinking to summon up outside help. They instead rely on an autistic boy who can imitate the insects' clicking sounds and who calls the sole virile male insect "Mr. Funny Shoes." At least Charles

S. Dutton adds a derisive air as an amusingly surly transit cop and F. Murray Abraham provides some able assistance as Dr. Tyler's menacing mentor.

Mimic effectively creates a creepy atmosphere and cannily exploits communal fears about disease, technology, and the sewer system. Del Toro knows how to build apprehension and demonstrates his visual flair. The film is not the classic Gordon Douglas' *Them!* is, but it is ably assembled, though it does not demonstrate much progression from the insectoid sci-fi horrors of the past except in terms of the film's sophisticated effects.

The brightest science fiction film of 1998 was Peter Weir's *The Truman Show*, written by Andrew Niccol (*Gattaca*) about Truman Burbank (Jim Carrey in a brilliantly apt perky performance), a man owned by a corporation that has decided to manipulate and exploit his life for profit. Truman is the unwitting star of an elaborate, nonstop television show, and everyone around him is in on it except him. He has an open, sunny, gee-whiz cheerful personality.

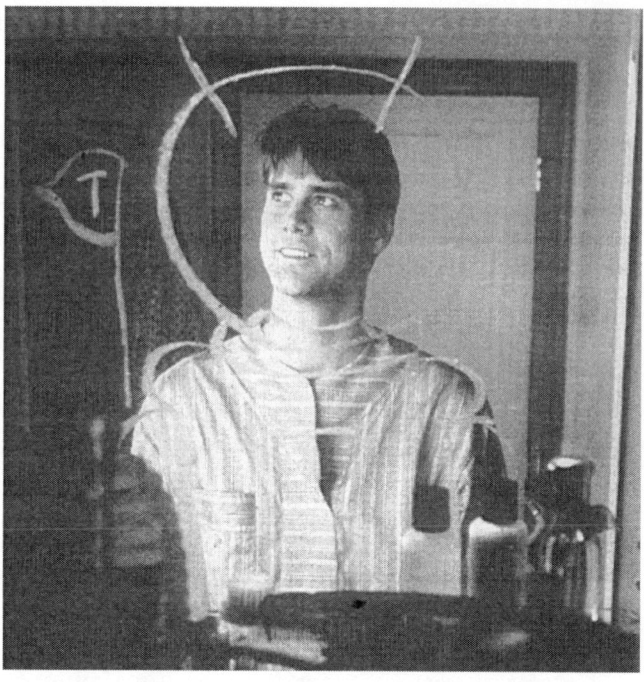

Truman (Jim Carrey) contemplates being an astronaut in a not-so-private moment in Peter Weir's brilliant *The Truman Show* (photo by Melinda Sue Gordon).

The film opens with televisionary Christof (Ed Harris), the show's creator and director, informing us, "We've become bored with watching actors giving us phony emotions. We're tired of pyrotechnics and special effects. While the world he inhabits is to some respects counterfeit, there is nothing faked about Truman. No script, no cue cards. It isn't always Shakespeare, but it's genuine. It's a life." In essence, for many people, closely watched celebrities become reality entertainment.

We experience the life of a man who is never allowed to have a private moment, who is constantly barraged with product placement commercials by those closest to him, and who manipulate him according to Christof's wishes for the show. Slowly, Truman catches on that something is not quite right, as when a "star" falls from the sky and smashes on the street, only for Truman to discover a kleig light.

Truman lives in a community called Seahaven, which has been dubbed "a nice place to live." The eeriely ordered world has echoes of the Village from Patrick McGoohan's classic SF TV series *The Prisoner*. He has been provided with a psychological trauma (the memory of his father drowning before his eyes) that prevents him from taking a boat and leaving the island. He trades pleasantries with his wife Meryl (Laura Linney) and splits six-packs with his always available buddy Marlon (Noah Emmerich). In many respects, it seems a typical life in a beautiful community.

Even though his world revolves around him, Truman is unhappy with it. He yearns to break out of his rut and explore, but first he must overcome his uncertainty and fear. He is unsatisfied for reasons that he can't put his finger on. He remembers things like a girl (Natascha McElhone) who was attracted to him and then was mysteriously taken away by her father for no apparent reason. As the façade is peeled away, he becomes increasingly desperate.

The Truman Show is by turns funny, touching, inventive, and inspired. It is barbed with satiric points about the influence of media on our lives, about conformity, about commercialism, about manipulation and the desire to play God, to build a perfect world, to overcome one's limitations, and about distinguishing between what's real and what's artificial, about the search for the truth. There are also some marvelously surreal images, as when the (artificial) moon turns into a searchlight to help locate the missing Truman. Perhaps what's freshest is that you have never seen another film quite like it (though Gary Ross' *Pleasantville* is a brilliant fantasy inversion of it).

For Weir, the film presented tremendous challenges, and he was uncertain whether he could pull it off. He decided that in order to make it believable, it needed to be set in the near future, and that while the story bristled with metaphors, it would be best to leave them alone and let them take care of themselves.

Christof, despite the "Christ" in his name, is not God, but rather a malign satanic influence who thinks that he knows what's best for Truman. He sincerely believes that he has created a better world, and that his show is an attempt to educate people to a certain way of seeing things.

The Truman Show is filled with emotions that people can recognize and identify with. Everybody has felt unrequited love for a person they could not have. Everybody gets to a point where they have to separate themselves from what people want for them and what they want for themselves. Everybody at some point goes into an unknown territory and knows that you sometimes have to risk losing everything. *The Truman Show* brilliantly touches on these feelings, and is quite thought-provoking besides. Unfortunately, truly thought-provoking science fiction has become a rarity, which makes a success like this one all the more to be treasured.

The biggest SF picture of 1999 was Andy and Larry Wachowski's *The Matrix*, which mixed Hong Kong style kung fu action with a virtual reality movie underlaid with subtle philosophical and religious messages. The plot centers around a young man named Neo (Keanu Reeves), a computer hacker who seeks the legendary hacker Morpheus (Laurence Fishburne), who is seeking the "One," a savior who will rescue imprisoned, sleeping humanity. Like Alice falling down the rabbit hole, Neo discovers that what he thought was reality has been artificially created by a vast computer known as the Matrix, which somehow lives off the energy of the human population kept docile by living out their entire existences in a computer generated artificial reality. The story also includes a beneficial love interest, Trinity (Carrie-Ann Moss), and a Judas figure, Cypher (Joe Pantoliano).

According to the Wachowski brothers, "All of our stories tend to be set in an alternative world.... We've always enjoyed fiction that relates to other dimensional realities, in particular science fiction writers such as J. G. Ballard. A few years ago, a friend of ours called to say that his publisher wanted an idea for a new comic book series and did we have anything? We said no, but after we'd hung up we came up with some crazy ideas and within a 48 hour period we had a complete story that eventually became *The Matrix*.

"This was at a time when the whole cyberpunk thing had just begun. We first thought that it wouldn't translate very well into a movie because in a visual sense cyberspace is not particularly interesting. Our challenge then was to make it interesting. We began with the premise that every single thing we believe in today and every single physical item, is actually a total fabrication created by an electronic universe. Once you start dealing with an electronic reality, you can really push the boundaries of what might be humanly possible. So if *The Matrix*'s characters can have instantaneous information downloaded into their heads, they should, for example, be able to be as good as a kung fu master as Jackie Chan."

While the action scenes and special effects are spectacular, the computers used in the film seem primitive (the hero doesn't use a mouse and the computer types out one letter at a time) and the science is unrealistic. (In this future world, pollution has virtually destroyed the world and the evil Satanic computer is using the human populace as batteries, though the energy output needed to maintain them would exceed the potential gain.)

The Matrix is rife with Christian allusions. The scene where Trinity is delivering food and is questioned by Cypher is right out of the Gospel. There is a "last supper" scene, a death and resurrection with a final scene where Neo gives his final sermon, then ascends into heavens. The entire premise seems to draw from Revelation. Satan (the AI program) rules the world for a brief time, then a savior comes leading the forces of Heaven and defeats Satan. Admittedly there is a nod toward other religions with the Oracle and the Dali Lama styled child (the one doing the Uri Geller impression in the Oracle's living room).

There are also philosophical overtones, as Neo stores his VR discs in a hollowed out copy of French sociologist Jean Baudrillard's *Simulation and Simulacra*. A further reference is the page of the book, *On Nihilism*, invoking Nietzsche and his concept of the Übermensch. These concepts allow one to read the film as a philosophical tract on the absence of a profound reality. However, the ending of the film still does not resolve the basic problem of how to take care of an entirely dependent humanity yet to be woken from its fitfull dreams.

The success of the film (over $100 million at the domestic box office and over 1 million copies sold on DVD alone) means that the Wachowskis have been hired to create two sequels which will carry the saga further. Meanwhile, at the Academy Awards, *The Matrix* was honored with awards for best sound, best sound editing, best special effects, and best editing.

Appendix B: The 100 Most Popular Science Fiction Films

(According to the Internet Movie Database Team)

Each movie has received at least 500 votes and was rated on a scale of 1 to 10. The ratings were then averaged to determine the results. Titles skew towards the present-day, reflecting current audience tastes, and omit some excellent if obscure SF films. The list also includes a few fantasies.

1. *Star Wars* (1977)
2. *Blade Runner* (1982)
3. *Dr. Strangelove, or How I Learned to Stop Worrying and Love the Bomb* (1963)
4. *La Cité des enfants perdus* (1995) aka *The City of Lost Children* (1995)
5. *Contact* (1997)
6. *The Empire Strikes Back* (1980)
7. *Stalker* (1979)
8. *2001: A Space Odyssey* (1968)
9. *A Clockwork Orange* (1971)
10. *Metropolis* (1926)
11. *Aliens* (1986)
12. *Bis ans Ende der Welt* (1991) aka *Until the End of the World* (1994)
13. *Brazil* (1985)
14. *The Day the Earth Stood Still* (1951)
15. *Return of the Jedi* (1983)
16. *Alien* (1979)
17. *Delicatessen* (1991)
18. *The Fifth Element* (1997)
19. *Star Trek: First Contact* (1996)
20. *The Transformers: The Movie* (1986)
21. *Akira* (1988)
22. *Army of Darkness* (1993)
23. *Babylon 5: The Gathering* (1993) (TV)
24. *Dawn of the Dead* (1978)
25. *Forbidden Planet* (1956)
26. *Twelve Monkeys* (1995)
27. *Mystery Science Theater 3000: The Movie* (1996)
28. *Terminator 2: Judgment Day* (1991)
29. *Dark Star* (1973)
30. *Back to the Future* (1985)
31. *Strange Days* (1995)
32. *Terminator* (1984)
33. *The Thing* (1982)
34. *The Abyss* (1989)
35. *Men in Black* (1997)
36. *The Rocky Horror Picture Show* (1975)
37. *Silent Running* (1971)
38. *Heavy Metal* (1981)
39. *King Kong* (1933)
40. *Mad Max II* (1981) aka *The Road Warrior* (1981) (US title)
41. *Repo Man* (1984)
42. *Close Encounters of the Third Kind* (1977)
43. *Sleeper* (1973)
44. *Star Trek: The Wrath of Khan* (1982)
45. *The Dark Crystal* (1982)
46. *Dune* (1984)
47. *E.T. the Extra-Terrestrial* (1982)
48. *Jurassic Park* (1993)
49. *Planet of the Apes* (1968)
50. *Star Trek IV: The Voyage Home* (1986)

51. *Tank Girl* (1995)
52. *The Adventures of Buckaroo Banzai: Across the Eighth Dimension* (1984)
53. *The Andromeda Strain* (1971)
54. *The Lord of the Rings* (1978)
55. *Naked Lunch* (1991)
56. *Star Trek VI: The Undiscovered Country* (1991)
57. *Jumanji* (1995)
58. *Predator* (1987)
59. *Escape from New York* (1981)
60. *Mad Max* (1979)
61. *Spaceballs* (1987)
62. *Starship Troopers* (1997)
63. *Total Recall* (1990)
64. *Independence Day* (1996)
65. *Mars Attacks!* (1996)
66. *Poltergeist* (1982)
67. *Star Trek: Generations* (1994)
68. *Tron* (1982)
69. *The Fly* (1986)
70. *Space Jam* (1996)
71. *StarGate* (1994)
72. *Starman* (1984)
73. *2010* (1984)
74. *Alien: Resurrection* (1997)
75. *The Arrival* (1996)
76. *RoboCop* (1987)
77. *Demolition Man* (1993)
78. *The Last Starfighter* (1984)
79. *Logan's Run* (1976)
80. *The Nutty Professor* (1996)
81. *Superman* (1978)
82. *Back to the Future Part II* (1989)
83. *Back to the Future Part III* (1990)
84. *Diamonds Are Forever* (1971)
85. *Cocoon* (1985)
86. *Enemy Mine* (1985)
87. *Innerspace* (1987)
88. *The Rocketeer* (1991)
89. *Flash Gordon* (1980)
90. *Gremlins* (1984)
91. *The Running Man* (1987)
92. *Barbarella* (1968)
93. *Star Trek III: The Search for Spock* (1984)
94. *Superman II* (1980)
95. *The Lost World: Jurassic Park* (1997)
96. *Alien 3* (1992)
97. *Arachnophobia* (1990)
98. *Darkman* (1990)
99. *Moonraker* (1979)
100. *Short Circuit* (1986)

Bibliography

Those books that were the most helpful in researching this book are marked with an asterisk (*).

Aberly, Rachel and Volker Engel. *The Making of Independence Day*. New York: Harper Paperbacks, 1996.

*Adamson, Joe. *Byron Haskin*. Metuchen, New Jersey: Scarecrow Press, 1984.

*Agel, Jerome (ed.). *The Making of Kubrick's 2001*. New York: The New American Library Inc., 1970.

Altman, Mark A., Ron Magid, and Edward Gross. *Charting the Undiscovered Country: The Making of Star Trek VI*. Massapequa Park, New York: Cinemaker Press, 1992.

Amelio, Ralph J. (ed.). *Hal in the Classroom: Science Fiction Films*. New York: Monarch Press, 1976.

Anderson, Craig. *Science Fiction Films of the Seventies*. Jefferson, North Carolina: McFarland & Company, 1985.

Arnold, Alan. *Once Upon a Galaxy: A Journal of the Making of The Empire Strikes Back*. New York: Ballantine Books, 1980.

Asherman, Allan. *The Making of Star Trek II: The Wrath of Khan*. New York: Pocket Books, 1982.

Atkins, Thomas R. *Science Fiction Films*. New York: Monarch Press, 1976.

*Barsacq, Léon. *Caligari's Cabinet and Other Grand Illusions: A History of Film Design*; revised and edited by Elliott Stein. Boston: New York Graphic Society, 1976.

*Baxter, John. *Science Fiction in the Cinema*. New York: A. S. Barnes, 1970.

*_____. *Stanley Kubrick: A Biography*. New York: Carroll & Graf Publishers, 1997.

*_____. *The Unauthorized Biography: Steven Spielberg*. London: HarperCollins, 1996.

Benson, Michael. *Vintage Science Fiction Films, 1896–1949*. Jefferson, North Carolina: McFarland & Company, 1985.

*Biskind, Peter. *Easy Riders, Raging Bulls: How the Sex-Drugs-and-Rock 'n' Roll Generation Saved Hollywood*. New York: Simon & Schuster, 1998.

*_____. *Seeing Is Believing: How Hollywood Taught Us to Stop Worrying and Love the Fifties*. New York: Pantheon Books, 1983.

Bizony, Piers. *2001: Filming the Future*. London: Aurum Press, 1994.

*Boorman, John, and Walter Donohue, editors. *Projections 2: A Forum for Film-makers*. London: Faber and Faber, 1993.

_____ and _____. *Projections 5: Film-makers on Film-making*. London: Faber and Faber, 1996.

Bouzereau, Laurent. *The Cutting Room Floor*. New York: Citadel Press Book, 1994.

*Brode, Douglas. *The Films of Steven Spielberg*. New York: Carol Publishing Group, 1995.

*Brosnan, John. *Future Tense: The Cinema of Science Fiction*. New York: A.S. Barnes, 1970.

_____. *Movie Magic: The Story of Special Effects in the Cinema*. New York: New American Library, 1976.

_____. *The Primal Screen: A History of Science Fiction Film*. London: Orbit Books, 1991.

Champlin, Charles. *George Lucas: The Creative Impulse: Lucasfilm's First Twenty Years*. New York: Harry N. Abrams, 1992.

*Ciment, Michel. *Kubrick*. (translated by Gilber Adair) New York: Holt, Rinehart and Winston, 1980.

Clarke, Arthur C. *The Lost Worlds of 2001*. London: Sidgwick & Jackson, 1972.

_____. *Report on Planet Three*. London: Victor Gollancz, 1973.

Crawley, Tony. *The Steven Spielberg Story*. New York: Quill Press, 1983.

*Crist, Judith. *Take 22: Moviemakers on Moviemaking*. New York: Viking, 1984.

Derry, Charles. *Dark Dreams: A Psychological History of the Modern Horror Film*. South Brunswick, New Jersey: A.S. Barnes, 1977.

Dohler, Don (ed.). *Science Fiction Invasions*. Baltimore: Movie Club, 1998.

Durwood, Thomas (ed.). *Close Encounters of the Third Kind: A Document of the Film*. New York: Ariel Books, 1978.

Ebert, Roger. *Roger Ebert's Video Companion* (1996 Edition). Kansas City: Andrews and McMeel, 1996.

_____, and Gene Siskel. *The Future of the Movies: Interviews with Martin Scorsese, Steven Spielberg, and George Lucas*. Kansas City: Andrews and McMeel, 1991.

Edelson, Edward. *Visions of Tomorrow*. New York: Doubleday, 1975.

Ellison, Harlan. *Harlan Ellison's Watching*. Los Angeles: Underwood-Miller, 1989.

Evans, I. O. *Jules Verne and His Work*. London: Arco, 1965.

Everman, Welch. *Cult Science Fiction Films: From The Amazing Colossal Man to Yog—Monster from Space*. Secaucus, New Jersey: Citadel Press, 1995.

*Fischer, Dennis. *Horror Film Directors: 1931–1990*. Jefferson, North Carolina: McFarland & Company, 1991.

*Fleischer, Richard. *Just Tell Me When to Cry*. New York: Carroll & Graf Publishers, 1993.

Flynn, John L. *The Films of Arnold Schwarzenegger*. New York: Citadel Press, 1993.

Frank, Alan. *Sci-Fi Now*. London: Octopus, 1978.

*_____. *The Science Fiction and Fantasy Film Handbook*. Totowa, New Jersey: Barnes and Noble Books, 1982.

*Galbraith, Stuart, IV. *Japanese Science Fiction, Fantasy and Horror Films*. Jefferson, North Carolina: McFarland & Company, 1994.

Gallagher, John Andrew. *Film Directors on Directing*. New York: Praeger, 1989.

Gelmis, Joseph. *The Film Director as Superstar*. Garden City, New York: Anchor Press, 1970.

Gifford, Denis. *Science Fiction Film*. London: Studio Vista, 1971.

*Goldberg, Lee, Randy L'Officier, Jean-Marc L'Officier, and William Rabkin. *Science Fiction Filmmaking in the 1980s: Interviews with Actors, Directors, Producers and Writers*. Jefferson, North Carolina: McFarland & Company, 1995.

Harry, Bill. *Heroes of the Spaceways*. London: Omnibus Press, 1981.

Harryhausen, Ray. *Film Fantasy Scrapbook*. Cranbury, New Jersey: A.S. Barnes, 1972.

*Heard, Christopher. *Dreaming Aloud: The Life and Films of James Cameron*. Toronto: Doubleday Canada, 1997.

Heisner, Beverly. *Hollywood Art: Art Direction in the Days of the Great Studios*. Jefferson, North Carolina: McFarland & Company, 1990.

*Hickman, Gail Morgan. *The Films of George Pal*. Cranbury, New Jersey: A.S. Barnes, 1977.

Hill, Geoffrey. *Illuminating Shadows: The Mythic Power of Film*. Boston: Shambhala, 1992.

Hogan, David J. *Dark Romance: Sexuality in the Horror Film*. Jefferson, North Carolina: McFarland & Company, 1986.

*Jancovich, Mark. *Rational Fears: American Horror in the 1950s*. New York: Manchester University Press, 1996.

*Jenkins, Garry. *Empire Building: The Remarkable Real Life Story of Star Wars*. Secaucus, New Jersey: Citadel Press, 1997.

*Jensen, Paul M. *The Men Who Made the Monsters*. New York: Twayne, 1996.

Johnson, Barbara Pearce, Sam L. Grogg, Jr., and Annette Bagley. *Steven Spielberg Study Guide*. American Film Institute, 1979.

Johnson, John "J. J." *Cheap Tricks and Class Acts: Special Effects, Makeup and Stunts from the Films of the Fantastic Fifties*. Jefferson, North Carolina: McFarland & Company, 1996.

Johnson, Kim "Howard." *Life Before and After Monty Python: The Solo Flights of the Flying Circus*. New York: St. Martin's Press, 1993.

Johnson, William (ed.). *Focus on the Science Fiction Film*. Englewood Cliffs, New Jersey: Prentice-Hall, 1972.

Kagan, Norman. *The Cinema of Stanley Kubrick*. New York: Grove Press, 1972.

*Katz, Ephraim. *The Film Encyclopedia* (second edition). New York: HarperPerennial, 1994.

*Kerman, Judith B. (ed.). *Retrofitting Blade Runner: Issues in Ridley Scott's Blade Runner and Philip K. Dick's Do Androids Dream of Electric Sheep?* Bowling Green, Ohio: Bowling Green State University Popular Press, 1991.

Kolker, Robert Philip. *A Cinema of Loneliness: Penn, Kubrick, Scorsese, Spielberg, Altman* (revised edition). Oxford University Press, 1988.

Koszarski, Richard (ed.). *Hollywood Directors 1941–1976*. New York: Oxford University Press, 1977.

Kuhn, Annette (ed.). *Alien Zone: Cultural Theory and*

Contemporary Science Fiction Cinema. New York: Verso, 1990.

*Lee, Walt. *Reference Guide to Fantastic Films: Science Fiction, Fantasy & Horror*. Los Angeles: Chelsea-Lee Books, 1972–1974. Three volumes.

Leeman, Sergio. *Robert Wise On His Films: From Editing Room to Director's Chair*. Los Angeles: Silman-James Press, 1995.

Lloyd, Ann (ed.). *There's Something Going On Out There*. London: Orbis Publishing, 1982.

*LoBrutto, Vincent. *Stanley Kubrick: A Biography*. New York: Donald I. Fine Books, 1997.

*Lourié, Eugène. *My Work in Films*. Orlando, Florida: Harcourt Brace Jovanovich, 1985.

*Lucas, Tim. "Margheriti: The Third Man of Italian Fantasy." *Video Watchdog* #28, 1995.

_____, and the contributing editors of *Video Times* magazine. *Your Movie Guide to Science Fiction/Fantasy Video Tapes and Discs*. Canada: Publications International, Ltd., 1985.

Lyon, Christopher and Susan Doll (eds.). *The International Dictionary of Films and Filmmakers: Volume II—Directors/Filmmakers*. Chicago: St. James Press, 1984.

Mabery, D. L. *Steven Spielberg*. Lerner, 1986.

Madsen, Axel. *The New Hollywood*. Cromwell, 1975.

*Maltin, Leonard. *The Disney Films*. New York: Crown, 1973.

Manchel, Frank. *An Album of Great Science Fiction Films* (revised edition) New York: Franklin Watts, 1982.

*Mandell, Paul. "Of Beasts and Behemoths: The Fantastic Films of Eugène Lourié," *Fantastic Films* #14–17, Feb.–July, 1980.

Marrero, Robert. *Godzilla: King of Movie Monsters*. Key West, Florida: Fantasma Books, 1996.

*McBride, Joseph. *Steven Spielberg: A Biography*. New York: Simon & Schuster, 1997.

*McDonagh, Maitland. *Filmmaking on the Fringe: The Good, The Bad, and the Deviant Directors*. New York: Citadel Press, 1995.

McDonnell, David (ed.). *Starlog's Science Fiction Heroes and Heroines*. New York: Crescent Books, 1995.

McGee, Mark Thomas. *Faster and Furiouser: The Revised and Fattened Fable of American International Pictures*. Jefferson, North Carolina: McFarland & Company, 1996.

McGilligan, Patrick. *Backstory 3: Interviews with Screenwriters of the 1960s*. Berkeley: University of California Press, 1997.

Medved, Harry, with Randy Dreyfuss. *The Fifty Worst Films of All Time (and How They Got That Way)*. New York: Popular Library, 1978.

Menville, Douglas. *A Historical and Critical Survey of the Science Fiction Film*. New York: Arno Press, 1975.

Meyers, Richard. *The Great Science Fiction Films: From Rollerball to Return of the Jedi* (aka *S-F 2: A Pictorial History of Science Fiction From 1975 to Present*). New York: Citadel Press Book, 1990.

Morse, L.A. *Video Trash & Treasures*. Toronto: Harper & Collins, 1989.

_____. *Video Trash & Treasures II*. Toronto: Harper & Collins, 1990.

Morton, Alan. *The Complete Directory to Science Fiction, Fantasy and Horror Television Series: A Comprehensive Guide to the First 50 Years 1946 to 1996*. Peoria, Illinois: Other Worlds Books, 1997.

Mott, Donald R., and Cheryl McAllister Saunders. *Steven Spielberg*. Boston: Twayne Publishers, 1986.

Naha, Ed. *The Science Fictionary: An A–Z Guide to the World of SF Authors, Films & TV Shows*. New York: Seaview Books, 1980.

*Nelson, Thomas Allen. *Kubrick: Inside a Film Artist's Maze*. Bloomington: Indiana University Press, 1982.

*Nichols, Peter (ed.). *The Science Fiction Encyclopedia*. Garden City, New York: Doubleday, 1979.

_____. *The World of Fantastic Films: An Illustrated Survey*. New York: Dodd, Mead, 1984.

Nimoy, Leonard. *I Am Not Spock*. New York: Ballantine Books, 1977.

*_____. *I Am Spock*. New York: Hyperion, 1995.

O'Neill, James. *Sci-Fi on Tape*. New York: Billboard Books, 1997.

Parish, James Robert, and Michael R. Pitts. *The Great Science Fiction Pictures*. Metuchen, New Jersey: Scarecrow Press, 1977.

_____ and _____. *The Great Science Fiction Pictures II*. Metuchen, New Jersey: Scarecrow Press, Inc., 1990.

*Peary, Danny (ed.). *Omni's Screen Flights/Screen Fantasies: The Future According to Science Fiction Cinema*. Garden City, New York: Doubleday, 1984.

Perry, George. *Life of Python*. Boston: Little, Brown, 1983.

Pfeiffer, Lee, and Michael Lewis. *The Films of Tom Hanks*. New York: Citadel Press, 1996.

Pickard, Roy. *Science Fiction in the Movies, an A–Z*. London: Frederick Muller, 1978.

Pirie, David. *A Heritage of Horror: The English Gothic Cinema 1946–72*. New York: Avon Books, 1973.

Pohl, Frederik, and Frederik Pohl IV. *Science Fiction Studies in Film*. New York: Ace Books, 1981.

*Pollock, Dale. *Skywalking: The Life and Films of George Lucas*. New York: Harmony Books, 1983.

*Pratley, Gerald. *The Cinema of John Frankenheimer*. New York: A.S. Barnes, 1969.

Pye, Michael, and Lynda Myles. *The Movie Brats: How the Film Generation Took Over Hollywood.* New York: Holt, Rinehart & Winston, 1979.

*Reemes, Dana M. *Directed by Jack Arnold.* Jefferson, North Carolina: McFarland & Company, 1988.

Richards, Gregory B. *Science Fiction Movies.* Greenwich, Connecticut: Bison Books Corp., 1984.

Rovin, Jeff. *A Pictorial History of Science Fiction Films.* Secaucus, New Jersey, 1975.

*Sadoul, Georges. *Dictionary of Film Makers* (translated by Peter Morris). Berkeley: University of California Press, 1972.

Saleh, Dennis. *Science Fiction Gold: Film Classics of the 1950s.* New York: McGraw-Hill, 1979.

Sammon, Paul M. *Future Noir: The Making of Blade Runner.* New York: HarperPrism, 1996.

Sanello, Frank. *Spielberg: The Man, the Movies, the Mythology.* Taylor, 1996.

Sauter, Michael. *The Worst Movies of All Time.* New York: Citadel Press, 1995.

Scanlon, Paul, and Michael Gross, edited by Charles Lippincott. *The Book of Alien.* New York: Heavy Metal Books, 1979.

Schanzer, Karl, and Thomas Lee Wright. *American Screenwriters.* New York: Avon Books, 1993.

Schneider, Wolf (ed.). *Steven Spielberg.* (American Film Institute Life Achievement Award program booklet.) AFI, 1995.

Schow, David J., and Jeffrey Frentzen. *The Outer Limits: The Official Companion.* New York: Ace Science Fiction Books, 1986.

Searles, Baird. *Films of Science Fiction and Fantasy.* New York: Harry N. Abrams, 1988.

Seymour, Simon. *Mad Scientists, Weird Doctors and Time Travellers in Movies, TV and Books.* New York: Lippincott, 1981.

*Shatner, William, with Chris Kreski. *Star Trek Movie Memories.* New York: HarperCollins, 1994.

Shay, Don, and Jody Duncan. *The Making of Jurassic Park.* New York: Ballantine Books, 1993.

_____ and _____. *The Making of T2: Terminator 2 Judgment Day.* New York: Bantam Books, 1991.

Short, Robert. *The Gospel from Outer Space.* San Francisco: Harper & Row, 1983.

Siegel, Don. *A Siegel Film.* London: Faber and Faber, 1993.

Siegel, Richard, and J. C. Saurès. *Alien Creatures.* Los Angeles: Reed Books, 1978.

Singer, Michael. *A Cut Above: 50 Film Directors Talk About Their Craft.* Los Angeles: Lone Eagle, 1998.

*Sinyard, Neil. *The Films of Richard Lester.* London: Croom Helm Ltd., 1985.

_____. *The Films of Steven Spielberg.* London: Bison Books Ltd., 1986.

Skal, David J. *Screams of Reason: Mad Science and Modern Culture.* New York: W. W. Norton, 1998.

Smith, Dian G. *American Filmmakers Today.* Poole, Dorset: Blanford Press, 1983.

*Sobchak, Vivian Carol. *The Limits of Infinity: American Science Fiction Films 1950–1975.* South Brunswick, New Jersey: A.S. Barnes, 1980.

Somazzi, Claudio. *Steven Spielberg: Dreaming the Movies.* Santa Cruz: E/K/S Group, Inc., 1994.

*Stanley, John. *Creature Features Movie Guide Strikes Again.* Pacifica, California: Creatures At Large Press, 1994.

Steinbrunner, Chris, and Burt Goldblatt. *The Cinema of the Fantastic.* New York: Galahad Books, 1972.

Stevens, Jon. *Actors Turned Directors: On Eliciting the Best Performance from an Actor and Other Secrets of Successful Directing.* Los Angeles: Silman-James Press, 1997.

*Stover, Leon. *The Prophetic Soul: A Reading of H. G. Wells's Things to Come.* Jefferson, North Carolina: McFarland & Company, 1987.

Strick, Philip. *Science Fiction Movies.* London: Octopus Books, 1976.

*Strickland, A. W., and Forrest J Ackerman. *A Reference Guide to American Science Fiction Films Volume 1.* Bloomington, Indiana: T.I.S. Publications, 1981.

*Svehla, Gary, and Susan Svehla (eds.). *Bela Lugosi.* Baltimore: Midnight Marquee Press, 1996.

_____. *Guilty Pleasures of the Horror Film.* Baltimore: Midnight Marquee Press, 1996.

_____. *Son of Guilty Pleasures.* Baltimore: Midnight Marquee Press, 1998.

_____. *We Belong Dead: Frankenstein in the Cinema.* Midnight Marquee Press, 1997.

Taylor, Philip M. *Steven Spielberg: The Man, His Movies, and Their Meaning* (expanded edition). New York: Continuum, 1994.

Telotte, J. P. *Replications: A Robotic History of the Science Fiction Film.* Urbana: University of Illinois Press, 1995.

Tombs, Pete. *Mondo Macabro: Weird and Wonderful Cinema Around the World.* London: Titan Books, 1997.

Tudor, Andrew. *Monsters and Mad Scientists: A Cultural History of the Horror Movie.* Cambridge, Massachusetts: Basil Blackwell, 1989.

Van Hise, James (ed). *The Aliens Story.* Las Vegas: Pop Cult Inc., 1988.

_____. *Hot Blooded Dinosaur Movies.* Las Vegas: Pioneer Books, 1993.

*Van Scheers, Rob. *Paul Verhoeven.* London: Faber and Faber, 1997.

VideoHound's Complete Guide to Cult Flicks and Trash Pics. Detroit: Visible Ink Press, 1996.

VideoHound's Sci-Fi Experience. Detroit: Visible Ink Press, 1997.

Von Gunden, Kenneth. *Postmodern Auteurs.* Jefferson, North Carolina: McFarland & Company, 1991.

*_____, and Stuart H. Stock. *Twenty All-Time Great Science Fiction Films.* New York: Arlington House, 1982.

*Wakeman, John (ed.). *World Film Directors: Volume 2 1945–1985.* New York: H. W. Wilson, 1988.

Walker, Alexander. *"It's Only a Movie, Ingrid": Encounters On and Off Screen.* London: Headline, 1988.

_____. *Stanley Kubrick Directs.* New York: Harcourt, 1972.

*Warren, Bill. *Keep Watching the Skies!* Jefferson, North Carolina: McFarland & Company, 1982, 1986. Two volumes.

*Weaver, Tom. *Attack of the Monster Movie Makers: Interviews with 20 Genre Giants.* Jefferson, North Carolina: McFarland & Company, 1994.

*_____. *Interviews with B Science Fiction and Horror Movie Makers: Writers, Producers, Directors, Actors, Mogols and Makeup.* Jefferson, North Carolina: McFarland & Company, 1988.

_____. *It Came from Weaver Five.* Jefferson, North Carolina: McFarland & Company, 1996.

*_____. *Monsters, Mutants, and Heavenly Creatures.* Baltimore, Maryland: Midnight Marquee Press, 1996.

*_____. *Science Fiction Stars and Horror Heroes: Interviews with Actors, Directors, Producers and Writers of the 1940s through 1960s.* Jefferson, North Carolina: McFarland & Company, 1991.

*_____. *They Fought in the Creature Features: Interviews with 23 Classic Horror, Science Fiction and Serial Stars.* Jefferson: North Carolina: McFarland & Company, 1995.

Weisser, Thomas, and Yuko Mihara Weisser. *Japanese Cinema Encyclopedia: Horror, Fantasy and Science Fiction Films.* Miami: Vital Books, 1997.

*Weldon, Michael. *The Psychotronic Encyclopedia of Film.* New York: Ballantine Books, 1983.

*_____. *The Psychotronic Video Guide.* New York: St. Martin's Griffin, 1996.

Williams, Lucy Chase. *The Films of Vincent Price.* New York: Citadel Press, 1995.

Willis, Don. *Horror and Science Fiction Films: A Checklist.* Metuchen, New Jersey: Scarecrow Press, 1972.

_____. *Horror and Science Fiction Films II.* Metuchen, New Jersey: Scarecrow Press, 1982.

_____. *Horror and Science Fiction Films III.* Metuchen, New Jersey: Scarecrow Press, 1984.

*_____. *Variety's Complete Science Fiction Reviews.* New York: Garland Publishing Inc., 1985.

Wingrove, David (ed.). *Science Fiction Film Source Book.* Essex, England: Longman Group Limited, 1985.

Worrell, Denise. *Icons: Intimate Portraits.* New York: Atlantic Monthly Press, 1989.

Worth, D(avid) Earl. *Sleaze Creatures.* Key West, Florida: Fantasma Books, 1995.

Wright, Bruce Lanier. *Yesterday's Tomorrows: The Golden Age of Science Fiction Movie Posters, 1950–1964.* Dallas: Taylor Publishing Company, 1993.

Wright, Gene. *The Science Fiction Image.* New York: Columbus Books, 1983.

*Yule, Andrew. *Losing the Light: Terry Gilliam & the Munchausen Saga.* New York: Applause Books, 1991.

*_____. *Richard Lester and the Beatles* (aka *The Man Who "Framed" the Beatles*). New York: Primus, 1994.

Periodicals

American Cinematographer
American Classic Screen
The Bewilderbeast
Cine Fan
Cinefantastique
Cinefex
Daily Variety
Enterprise Incidents
European Trash Cinema
Fantastic Films
Fatal Visions
Femme Fatales
Film Comment
Filmfax
The Hollywood Reporter
Horror Fan
Imagi-Movies
L.A. Reader
L.A. Weekly
The Little Shoppe of Horrors
Los Angeles Times
Midnight Marquee
New Times
Outré
The Perfect Vision
Playboy
Psychotronic Video
Retro-Vision
Samhain
Sci-Fi Universe
SF Movieland
Starburst
Starlog
Take One
Video Watchdog
Videoscope
Wet Paint

Index